UNCTAD/DTCI/30(Vol. II)

United Nations Conference on Trade and Development
Division on Transnational Corporations and Investment

International Investment Instruments: A Compendium

Volume II
Regional Instruments

United Nations
New York and Geneva, 1996

NOTE

The UNCTAD Division on Transnational Corporations and Investment serves as the focal point within the United Nations Secretariat for all matters related to foreign direct investment and transnational corporations. In the past, the Programme on Transnational Corporations was carried out by the United Nations Centre on Transnational Corporations (1975-1992) and the Transnational Corporations and Management Division of the United Nations Department of Economic and Social Development (1992-1993). In 1993, the Programme was transferred to the United Nations Conference on Trade and Development and became the Division on Transnational Corporations and Investment. The Division on Transnational Corporations and Investment seeks to further the understanding of the nature of transnational corporations and their contribution to development and to create an enabling environment for international investment and enterprise development. The work of the Division is carried out through intergovernmental deliberations, policy analysis and research, technical assistance activities, seminars, workshops and conferences.

The term "country", as used in the boxes added by the UNCTAD Secretariat at the beginning of the instruments reproduced in this volume, also refers, as appropriate, to territories or areas; the designations employed and the presentation of the material do not imply the expression of any opinion whatsoever on the part of the Secretariat of the United Nations concerning the legal status of any country, territory, city or area or of its authorities, or concerning the delimitation of its frontiers or boundaries. Moreover, the country or geographical terminology used in these boxes may occasionally depart from standard United Nations practice when this is made necessary by the nomenclature used at the time of negotiation, signature, ratification or accession of a given international instrument.

To preserve the integrity of the texts of the instruments reproduced in this volume, references to the sources of the instruments that are not contained in their original text are identified as "note added by the editor".

The texts of the instruments included in this volume are reproduced as they were written in one of their original languages or an official translation thereof. When an obvious linguistic mistake has been found, the word "sic" has been added in brackets.

The materials contained in this volume have been reprinted with special permission of the relevant institutions. For those materials under copyright protection, all rights are reserved by the copyright holders.

It should be further noted that this collection of instruments has been prepared for documentation purposes only, and their contents do not engage the responsibility of UNCTAD.

UNCTAD/DTCI/30. Vol. II

UNITED NATIONS PUBLICATION
Sales No. E.96.II.A.10
ISBN 92-1-104464-2
Complete set of three volumes: ISBN 92-1-104466-9

PREFACE

This selection of international instruments relating to foreign direct investment (FDI) and the activities of transnational corporations (TNCs), presented in three volumes, is intended to fill a gap in existing publications on the topic. In spite of the proliferation in recent years of multilateral and regional instruments dealing with various aspects of FDI, there has been no collection of texts that would make them conveniently available to interested policy-makers, scholars and business executives. Lately, this *lacuna* has become particularly apparent as new initiatives are underway to negotiate a multilateral agreement on investment. In response to this need, and in pursuance of its analytical and consensus-building function, UNCTAD has designed and prepared the present *International Investment Instruments: A Compendium (I.I.I. Compendium)*.

While by necessity selective, the present collection seeks to provide a faithful record of the evolution and present status of intergovernmental cooperation concerning FDI and TNCs. While the emphasis is on relatively recent documents (more than half of the instruments reproduced date from after 1980), it was deemed useful to include important early instruments as well, with a view towards providing some indications of the historical development of international concerns over FDI in the decades since the end of the Second World War.

The core of this collection consists of legally-binding international instruments, mainly multilateral conventions and regional agreements that have entered into force. In addition, a number of "soft law" documents, such as guidelines, declarations and resolutions adopted by intergovernmental bodies, have been included since these instruments also play a role in the elaboration of an international framework for FDI. In an effort to enhance the understanding of the efforts behind the elaboration of this framework, certain draft instruments that never entered into force, or texts of instruments the negotiations of which were not concluded, are also included; and, in an annex, several prototypes of bilateral investment treaties are reproduced. Included also are a number of influential documents prepared by professional associations, business, consumer and labour organizations. It is clear from the foregoing that no implications concerning the legal status or the legal effect of an instrument can be drawn from its inclusion in this collection.

In view of the great diversity of instruments -- in terms of subject matter, approach, legal form and extent of participation of States -- the simplest possible method of presentation was deemed the most appropriate. Thus, within each subdivision, instruments are reproduced in chronological order:

- Volume I is devoted to multilateral instruments, that is to say, multilateral conventions as well as resolutions and other documents issued by multilateral organizations.

- Volume II covers interregional and regional instruments, including agreements, resolutions and other texts from regional organisations within an inclusive geographical context.

Both volumes cover international instruments widely differing in scope and coverage. A few are designed to provide an overall, general framework for FDI and cover many, although rarely all, aspects of investment operations. Most instruments deal with particular aspects and issues concerning FDI. A significant number address core FDI issues, such as investment liberalization, the promotion and protection of investment, dispute settlement and insurance and guarantees. Others cover specific issues, of direct but not exclusive relevance to FDI and TNCs, such as international trade, transfer of technology, intellectual property, avoidance of double taxation, competition and the protection of consumers and the environment. A relatively small number of instruments of this last category has been reproduced, since each of these specific issues often involves an entire system of legal regulation of its own, whose proper coverage would require an extended exposition of many kinds of instruments and arrangements.

The three annexes in volume III cover three types of instruments that differ in their context or their origin from those included in the two main parts:

• Annex A reproduces investment-related provisions in regional free trade and integration agreements. The specific function and, therefore, the effect of such provisions is largely determined by the economic integration process which they are intended to promote and in the context of which they operate.

• Annex B (the only section that departs from the chronological pattern) offers the texts of prototype bilateral treaties for the promotion and protection of foreign investments of several developed and developing countries, and a list of these treaties concluded up to July 1995. The bilateral character of these treaties differentiates them from the bulk of the instruments included in the *I.I.I. Compendium*. Over 900 such treaties had been adopted by July 1995.

• Annex C supplies the texts of documents prepared by non-governmental organizations; these give an indication of the broader environment in which the instruments collected here are prepared.

The *I.I.I. Compendium* is meant to be a collection of instruments, not an anthology of relevant provisions. Indeed, to understand a particular instrument, it is normally necessary to take into consideration its entire text. An effort has been made, therefore, to reproduce complete instruments, even though, in a number of cases, reasons of space and relevance have dictated the inclusion of excerpts.

The texts collected are not offered as models. On the contrary, an effort has been made to select instruments that reflect a broad variety of political backgrounds, forms, attitudes towards FDI, preferred approaches and policies, and effectiveness of their provisions. The collection is intended as a record of international action, not as a codification of legal prescriptions.

For the same reason, the UNCTAD Secretariat has deliberately refrained from adding its own commentaries to the texts reproduced. The only exception to this rule are the boxes added at the beginning of each instrument which provide information on some basic facts, such as its date of adoption, date of entering into force, status as of 1995 and, where appropriate, signatory countries. Moreover, to facilitate the identification of each instrument in the table of contents, additional information has been added, in brackets, next to each title, on the year of its signature and the name of the institution involved.

UNCTAD hopes that the *I.I.I. Compendium* will help policy makers, business executives and researchers to understand better past developments and the current state of the regulatory framework relating to FDI.

Rubens Ricupero
Secretary-General of UNCTAD

Geneva, March 1996

ACKNOWLEDGEMENTS

The *I.I.I. Compendium* was prepared by Victoria Aranda and Michael Gestrin, with inputs from Anna Joubin-Bret, Vincent Casim, Mohamed Fayache and Letizia Salvini, and assisted by Mario Ardiri, Eric Gill, Per Kall, Christine Jeannet, and Liane Wolly, under the direction of Karl P. Sauvant. Arghyrios A. Fatouros prepared the Introduction and provided overall guidance and advice. Secretarial support was provided by Medarde Almario, Nayana Hein, Elisabeth Mahiga and Jenifer Tacardon.

CONTENTS

VOLUME II
REGIONAL INSTRUMENTS

REGIONAL INSTRUMENTS

VOLUME III
REGIONAL INTEGRATION, BILATERAL AND NON-GOVERNMENTAL INSTRUMENTS

**ANNEX B. PROTOTYPE BILATERAL INVESTMENT
TREATIES AND LIST OF BILATERAL
INVESTMENT TREATIES (1959-1995)**

ANNEX C. NON-GOVERNMENTAL INSTRUMENTS

REGIONAL INSTRUMENTS

CODE OF LIBERALISATION OF CAPITAL MOVEMENTS[*]

> The Code of Liberalisation of Capital Movements was adopted by the Council of the Organisation for Economic Co-operation and Development on 12 December 1961. The Code has been amended on several occasions. The text of the Code reproduced in this volume incorporates the most recent amendments. Annexes B, C, D and E to the Code have not been reproduced in this volume.

Contents

Preamble

Part I
Undertakings with regard to capital movements

Part II
Procedure

[*] Source: Organisation for Economic Co-operation and Development (1995). *Code of Liberalisation of Capital Movements*, (Paris: OECD) [Note added by the editor].

List of Council Acts Included in the Present Edition of the Code of Liberalisation of Capital Movements

PREAMBLE

THE COUNCIL,

Having regard to Articles 2 (d) and 5 (a) of the Convention on the Organisation for Economic Co-operation and Development of 14th December 1960;

Having regard to the Code of Liberalisation of Current Invisible Operations;

Having regard to the Articles of Agreement of the International Monetary Fund of 27th December 1945;

Having regard to the European Monetary Agreement of 5th August 1955, and the Protocol of Provisional Application of that Agreement of the same date;

Having regard to the Report of the Committee for Invisible Transactions on the Codes of Liberalisation of Current Invisibles and of Capital Movements of 28th October 1961, and the Comments by the Executive Committee on that Report of 8th December 1961 [OECD/C(61)37; OECD/C(61)73];

DECIDES:

CODE OF LIBERALISATION
OF CAPITAL MOVEMENTS

Articles

PART I
UNDERTAKINGS WITH REGARD TO CAPITAL MOVEMENTS

Article 1
GENERAL UNDERTAKINGS

a.   Members shall progressively abolish between one another, in accordance with the provisions of Article 2, restrictions on movements of capital to the extent necessary for effective economic co-operation. Measures designed to eliminate such restrictions are hereinafter called "measures of liberalisation".

b.   Members shall, in particular, endeavour:

i)   to treat all non-resident-owned assets in the same way irrespective of the date of their formation, and

ii)   to permit the liquidation of all non-resident-owned assets and the transfer of such assets or of their liquidation proceeds.

c.   Members should use their best offices to ensure that the measures of liberalisation are applied within their overseas territories.

d.   Members shall endeavour to extend the measures of liberalisation to all members of the International Monetary Fund.

e.   Members shall endeavour to avoid introducing any new exchange restrictions on the movements of capital or the use of non-resident-owned funds and shall endeavour to avoid making existing regulations more restrictive.

Article 2
MEASURES OF LIBERALISATION

a.   Subject to the provisions of paragraph (b)(iv), Members shall grant any authorisation required for the conclusion or execution of transactions and for transfers specified in an item set out in List A or List B of Annex A to this Code.

b.   A Member may lodge reservations relating to the obligations resulting from paragraph (a) when:

i)   an item is added to List A of Annex A to this Code;

ii)   obligations relating to an item in that List are extended;

iii)   obligations relating to any such item begin to apply to that Member; or

iv)   at any time, in respect of an item in List B.

Reservations shall be set out in Annex B to the Code.

c.   Whenever the liquidation proceeds of non-resident-owned assets may be transferred, the right of transfer shall include any appreciation of the original assets.

d.   Whenever existing regulations or international agreements permit loans between residents of different Members otherwise than by issuing marketable domestic securities or by using, in the country in which the borrower resides, funds the transfer of which is restricted, the repayment obligation may be expressed or guaranteed in the currency of either of the two Members concerned.

Article 3
PUBLIC ORDER AND SECURITY

The provisions of this Code shall not prevent a Member from taking action which it considers necessary for:

  i)   the maintenance of public order or the protection of public health, morals and safety;

  ii)   the protection of its essential security interests;

  iii)   the fulfilment of its obligations relating to international peace and security.

Article 4
OBLIGATIONS IN EXISTING MULTILATERAL
INTERNATIONAL AGREEMENTS

Nothing in this Code shall be regarded as altering the obligations undertaken by a Member as a Signatory of the Articles of Agreement of the International Monetary Fund or other existing multilateral international agreements.

Article 5
CONTROLS AND FORMALITIES

a.   The measures of liberalisation provided for in this Code shall not limit the powers of Members to verify the authenticity of transactions or transfers nor to take any measures required to prevent evasion of their laws or regulations.

b.   Members shall simplify as much as possible all formalities connected with the authorisation or verification of transactions or transfers and shall co-operate, if necessary, to attain such simplification.

Article 6
EXECUTION OF TRANSFERS

A Member shall be deemed to have complied with its obligations as regards transfers whenever a transfer may be made:

  i)   between persons entitled, by the exchange regulations of the State from which and of the State to which the transfer is to be made, respectively, to make and/or to receive the said transfer;

  ii)   in accordance with international agreements in force at the time the transfer is to be made; and

iii)   in accordance with the monetary arrangements in force between the State from which and the State to which the transfer is to be made.

Article 7
CLAUSES OF DEROGATION

a.   If its economic and financial situation justifies such a course, a Member need not take the whole of the measures of liberalisation provided for in Article 2(a).

b.   If any measures of liberalisation taken or maintained in accordance with the provisions of Article 2(a) result in serious economic and financial disturbance in the Member State concerned, that Member may withdraw those measures.

c.   If the overall balance of payments of a Member develops adversely at a rate and in circumstances, including the state of its monetary reserves, which it considers serious, that member may temporarily suspend the application of measures of liberalisation taken or maintained in accordance with the provisions of Article 2(a).

d.   However, a Member invoking paragraph (c) shall endeavour to ensure that its measures of liberalisation:

i)   cover, twelve months after it has invoked that paragraph, to a reasonable extent, having regard to the need for advancing towards the objective defined in sub-paragraph (ii), transactions and transfers which the Member must authorise in accordance with Article 2(a) and the authorisation of which it has suspended, since it invoked paragraph (c); and

ii)   comply, eighteen months after it has invoked that paragraph, with its obligations under Article 2(a).

e.   Any Member invoking the provisions of this Article shall do so in such a way as to avoid unnecessary damage which bears especially on the financial or economic interests of another Member and, in particular, shall avoid any discrimination between other Members.

Article 8
RIGHT TO BENEFIT FROM MEASURES OF LIBERALISATION

Any Member lodging a reservation under Article 2(b) or invoking the provisions of Article 7 shall, nevertheless, benefit from the measures of liberalisation taken by other Members, provided it has complied with the procedure laid down in Article 12 or Article 13 as the case may be.

Article 9
NON-DISCRIMINATION

A Member shall not discriminate as between other Members in authorising the conclusion and execution of transactions and transfers which are listed in Annex A and which are subject to any degree of liberalisation.

Article 10
EXCEPTIONS TO THE PRINCIPLE OF NON-DISCRIMINATION
SPECIAL CUSTOMS OR MONETARY SYSTEMS

Members forming part of a special customs or monetary system may apply to one another, in addition to measures of liberalisation taken in accordance with the provisions of Article 2(a), other measures of liberalisation without extending them to other Members. Members forming part of such a system shall inform the Organisation of its membership and those of its provisions which have a bearing on this Code.

PART II
PROCEDURE

Article 11
NOTIFICATION AND INFORMATION FROM MEMBERS

a.   Members shall notify the Organisation, within the periods which the latter may determine, of the measures of liberalisation which they have taken and of any other measures which have a bearing on this Code, as well as of any modifications of such measures.

b.   Members shall notify the Organisation forthwith of any cases in which they have by virtue of remark (ii) against Section I of List A of Annex A to this Code imposed restrictions on specific transactions or transfers relating to direct investments and shall state their reasons for doing so.

c.   Members shall submit to the Organisation, at intervals determined by the Organisation, but of no more than eighteen months, information concerning:

   i)   any channels, other than official channels, through which transfers are made, and any rates of exchange applying to such transfers, if they are different from the official rates of exchange;

   ii)   any security money markets and any premiums or discounts in relation to official rates of exchange prevailing therein.

d.   The Organisation shall consider the notifications submitted to it in accordance with the provisions of paragraphs (a), (b) and (c) with a view to determining whether each Member is complying with its obligations under this Code.

Article 12
NOTIFICATION AND EXAMINATION OF RESERVATIONS LODGED UNDER
ARTICLE 2(b)

a.   Each Member lodging a reservation in respect of an item specified in List B of Annex A to the Code shall forthwith notify the Organisation of its reasons therefor.

b.   Each Member shall notify the Organisation within a period to be determined by the Organisation, whether it desires to maintain any reservation lodged by it in respect of an item specified in List A or List B of Annex A to this Code, and if so, state its reasons therefor.

c.   The Organisation shall examine each reservation lodged by a Member in respect of an item specified in:

   i)   List A at intervals of not more than eighteen months;

   ii)   List B within six months of notification, and at intervals of not more than eighteen months thereafter; unless the Council decides otherwise.

d.   The examinations provided for in paragraph (c) shall be directed to making suitable proposals designed to assist Members to withdraw their reservations.

Article 13
NOTIFICATION AND EXAMINATION OF DEROGATIONS MADE
UNDER ARTICLE 7

a.   Any Member invoking the provisions of Article 7 shall notify the Organisation forthwith of its action, together with its reasons therefor.

b.   The Organisation shall consider the notification and reasons submitted to it in accordance with the provisions of paragraph (a) with a view to determining whether the Member concerned is justified in invoking the provisions of Article 7 and, in particular, whether it is complying with the provisions of paragraph (e) of that Article.

c.   If the action taken by a Member in accordance with the provisions of Article 7 is not disapproved by the Organisation, that action shall be reconsidered by the Organisation every six months or, subject to the provisions of Article 15, on any other date which the latter may deem appropriate.

d.   If, however, in the opinion of a Member other than the one which has invoked Article 7, the circumstances justifying the action taken by the latter in accordance with the provisions of that Article have changed, that other Member may at any time refer to the Organisation for reconsideration of the case at issue.

e.   If the action taken by a Member in accordance with the provisions of paragraph (a), (b) or (c) of Article 7 has not been disapproved by the Organisation, then if that Member subsequently invokes paragraph (a), (b) or (c) of Article 7 of the Code of Liberalisation of Current Invisible Operations, or, having invoked one paragraph of Article 7 of this Code, invokes another paragraph of that Article, its case shall be reconsidered by the Organisation after six months have elapsed since the date of the previous consideration, or on any other date which the latter may deem appropriate. If another Member claims that the Member in question is failing to carry out its obligations under paragraph (e) of Article 7 of this Code or paragraph (e) of Article 7 of the Code of Liberalisation of Current Invisible Operations, the Organisation shall consider the case without delay.

f.   i)   If the Organisation, following its consideration in accordance with paragraph (b), determines that a Member is not justified in invoking the provisions of Article 7 or is not complying with the provisions of that Article, it shall remain in consultation with the Member concerned, with a view to restoring compliance with the Code.

    ii)   If, after a reasonable period of time, that Member continues to invoke the provisions of Article 7, the Organisation shall reconsider the matter. If the Organisation is then unable to determine that the Member concerned is justified in invoking the provisions of Article 7 or is complying with the provisions of that Article, the situation of that Member shall be examined at a session of the Council convened by its Chairman for this purpose unless the Organisation decides on some other procedure.

Article 14
EXAMINATION OF DEROGATIONS MADE UNDER ARTICLE 7
MEMBERS IN PROCESS OF ECONOMIC DEVELOPMENT

a.   In examining the case of any Member which it considers to be in the process of economic development and which has invoked the provisions of Article 7 the Organisation shall have special regard to the effect that the economic development of the Member has upon its ability to carry out its obligations under paragraph (a) of Articles 1 and 2.

b.   In order to reconcile the obligations of the Member concerned under paragraph (a) of Article 2 with the requirements of its economic development, the Organisation may grant that Member a special dispensation from those obligations.

Article 15
SPECIAL REPORT AND EXAMINATION CONCERNING DEROGATIONS MADE
UNDER ARTICLE 7

a.   A Member invoking the provisions of paragraph (c) of Article 7 shall report to the Organisation, within ten months after such invocation, on the measures of liberalisation it has restored or proposes to restore in order to attain the objective determined in sub-paragraph (d)(i) of Article 7. The Member shall, if it continues to invoke these provisions, report to the Organisation again on the same subject -- but with reference to the objective determined in sub-paragraph (d)(ii) of Article 7 -- within sixteen months after such invocation.

b.   If the Member considers that it will not be able to attain the objective, it shall indicate its reasons in its report and, in addition, shall state:

   i)   what internal measures it has taken to restore its economic equilibrium and what results have already been attained, and

   ii)   what further internal measures it proposes to take and what additional period it considers it will need in order to attain the objective determined in sub-paragraph (d)(i) or (d)(ii) of Article 7.

c.   In cases referred to in paragraph (b), the Organisation shall consider within a period of twelve months, and, if required, of eighteen months from the date on which the Member invoked the provisions of paragraph (c) of Article 7, whether the situation of that Member appears to justify its failure to attain the objective determined in sub-paragraph (d)(i) or (d)(ii) of Article 7 and whether the measures taken or envisaged and the period considered by it as necessary for attaining the objective determined, appear acceptable in the light of the objectives of the Organisation in the commercial and financial fields.

d.   If a Member invokes the provisions of both paragraph (c) of Article 7 of this Code and paragraph (c) of Article 7 of the Code of Liberalisation of Current Invisible Operations, the periods of twelve and eighteen months referred to in paragraph (c) shall run from the date of the earlier invocation.

e.   If following any of the examinations provided for in paragraph (c) the Organisation is unable to approve the arguments advanced by the Member concerned in accordance with the provisions of paragraph (b), the situation of that Member shall be examined at a session of the Council convened by its Chairman for this purpose unless the Organisation decides on some other procedure.

Article 16
REFERENCE TO THE ORGANISATION INTERNAL ARRANGEMENTS

a.   If a Member considers that the measures of liberalisation taken or maintained by another Member, in accordance with Article 2(a), are frustrated by internal arrangements likely to restrict the possibility of effecting transactions or transfers, and if it considers itself prejudiced by such arrangements, for instance because of their discriminatory effect, it may refer to the Organisation.

b.   If, following the consideration of a matter referred to it under paragraph (a) the Organisation determines that internal arrangements introduced or maintained by the Member concerned have the effect of frustrating its measures of liberalisation, the Organisation may make suitable suggestions with regard to the removal or modification of such arrangements.

Article 17
REFERENCE TO THE ORGANISATION
RETENTION, INTRODUCTION OR REINTRODUCTION OF RESTRICTIONS

a.   If a Member considers that another Member which has not invoked the provisions of Article 7 has retained, introduced or reintroduced restrictions on capital movements or the use of non-resident-owned funds contrary to the provisions of Articles 1, 2, 9 or 10, and if it considers itself to be prejudiced thereby, it may refer to the Organisation.

b.   The fact that the case is under consideration by the Organisation shall not preclude the Member which has referred to the Organisation from entering into bilateral conversations on the matter with the other Member concerned.

PART III
TERMS OF REFERENCE

Article 18
COMMITTEE ON CAPITAL MOVEMENTS AND INVISIBLE TRANSACTIONS
GENERAL TASKS

a.   The Committee on Capital Movements and Invisible Transactions shall consider all questions concerning the interpretation or implementation of the provisions of this Code or other Acts of the Council relating to the liberalisation of capital movements and the use of non-residents-owned funds and shall report its conclusions thereon to the Council as appropriate.

b.   The Committee on Capital Movements and Invisible Transactions shall submit to the Council any appropriate proposals in connection with its tasks as defined in paragraph (a) and, in particular, with the extension of measures of liberalisation as provided in Article 1 of this Code.

Article 19
COMMITTEE ON CAPITAL MOVEMENTS AND INVISIBLE TRANSACTIONS
SPECIAL TASKS

a.   The Committee on Capital Movements and Invisible Transactions shall:

i)   determine the periods within which the information provided for in paragraphs (a) and (c) of Article 11 and the reasons provided for in paragraph (b) of Article 12 should be notified to the Organisation by the Members concerned;

ii)   subject to paragraph (c) of this Article, consider, in conformity with paragraphs (c) and (d) of Article 12, each reservation notified to the Organisation in accordance with paragraphs (a) and (b) of that Article and make, where appropriate, suitable proposals designed to assist Members to withdraw their reservations;

iii) determine, in accordance with the provisions of Article 12, the date on which any reservation should be re-examined, if the reservation has not been withdrawn in the meantime;

iv) consider, in accordance with the provisions of paragraph (d) of Article 11, the notifications submitted to the Organisation;

v) consider reports and references submitted to the Organisation in accordance with the provisions of Article 13 or paragraphs (a) and (b) of Article 15 where a Member has invoked the provisions of Article 7, or submitted in accordance with the provisions of Article 16 or Article 17;

vi) determine the date on which the case of a Member which has invoked Article 7 should be reconsidered in accordance with the provisions of paragraph (c), paragraph (e) or paragraph (f)(ii) of Article 13;

vii) transmit to the United States Government, with any comments it considers appropriate, notifications received from Members in accordance with paragraph 2(a) of the Decision in Annex C to the Code; and

viii) consider information received from the United States Government in accordance with paragraph 2(b) of the Decision in Annex C to the Code.

b. When examining the reservations notified in accordance with paragraph (b) of Article 12, the Committee may, at its discretion, consider together either all reservations made by the same Member or all reservations made in respect of the same item specified in Annex A to this Code.

c. The Committee shall, however, not consider any reservations notified to the Organisation in accordance with paragraph (b) of Article 12 by a Member which, at the time of the examination in respect of the item subject to that reservation, is invoking the provisions of Article 7 or is enjoying a dispensation in accordance with paragraph (b) of Article 14.

d. In the cases provided for in sub-paragraphs (ii), (iv), (v) and (viii) of paragraph (a), the Committee shall report to the Council, except in cases of notifications under Article 11 (b) on which the Committee shall report only if it considers this appropriate.

e. The Committee shall, whenever it considers it necessary:

i) consult other Committees of the Organisation on any questions relating to the liberalisation of capital movements; and, in particular,

ii) request other Committees of the Organisation to give their views on any questions relating to the balance of payments and the state of the monetary reserves of a Member.

Article 20
PAYMENTS COMMITTEE

Before they are considered by the Council, the Payments Committee shall:

i) review the reports and proposals by the Committee on Capital Movements and Invisible Transactions made in accordance with the provisions of this Code; and

ii) forward to the Council any comments thereon which it considers necessary.

PART IV
MISCELLANEOUS

Article 21
DEFINITIONS

In this Code:

i) "Member" shall mean a Member of the Organisation which adheres to this Code;

ii) "Domestic securities" shall mean securities issued or to be issued by a resident;

iii) "Foreign securities" shall mean securities issued or to be issued by a non-resident;

iv) "Recognised security market" shall mean a stock exchange or security market in a Member country (including an over-the-counter market organised by a recognised association of security dealers),

-- which is officially recognised in the country where it operates,

-- on which the public can buy and sell securities, and

-- on which dealings take place in accordance with fixed rules;

v) "Securities quoted on a recognised security market" shall mean securities which have been granted an official quotation or are officially listed on such a market or for which dealing prices on such a market are published not less frequently than once a week;

vi) Security dealing on a "spot basis" shall mean dealing with payment and delivery to be made immediately the transaction is concluded or on the next periodic settlement date of the stock exchange where the transaction takes place;

vii) "Money market securities" shall mean securities with an original maturity of less than one year;

viii) "Collective investment securities" shall mean the share certificates, registry entries or other evidence of investor interest in an institution for collective investment which, irrespective of legal form, is organised for the purpose of managing investments in securities or in other assets, applies the principle of risk-spreading, issues its own securities to the public on demand either continuously or at frequent intervals and is required on the request of the holder to redeem such securities, directly or indirectly, within a specified period and at their net asset value;

ix) "Financial institutions" shall mean banks, savings banks, bodies which specialise in the granting of credits, insurance companies, building societies, investment companies, and other establishments of a similar nature;

x) "Deposit" shall mean a sum of money paid on terms: a) under which it will be repaid, with or without interest or premium, and either on demand or at a time or in circumstances agreed by the person making it or receiving it or by his order, and b) which are not referable to the provision of property or services or to the giving of security;

xi) "Official channels" shall mean foreign exchange markets in which an officially established rate or officially established rates apply and in which spot transactions take place at rates which are free to fluctuate within the official margins;

xii) "Blocked funds" shall mean funds owned by residents of other Member States in accordance with the laws and regulations of the Member where the funds are held and blocked for balance-of-payments reasons;

xiii) "Unit of account" shall mean the sum in the national currency of a Member which is equal to a unit of value of special drawing rights as valued by the International Monetary Fund.

Article 22
TITLE OF DECISION

This Decision, referred to in the present text as the "Code", shall be known as the "Code of Liberalisation of Capital Movements".

Article 23
WITHDRAWAL

Any Member may withdraw from the Code by transmitting a notice in writing to the Secretary-General of the Organisation. The withdrawal shall become effective twelve months from the date on which such notice is received.

Annex A
LIBERALISATION LISTS OF CAPITAL MOVEMENTS[1]

LIST A
I. DIRECT INVESTMENT

Investment for the purpose of establishing lasting economic relations with an undertaking such as, in particular, investments which give the possibility of exercising an effective influence on the management thereof:

A.   In the country concerned by non-residents by means of:

    1.   Creation or extension of a wholly-owned enterprise, subsidiary or branch, acquisition of full ownership of an existing enterprise;

    2.   Participation in a new or existing enterprise;

    3.   A loan of five years or longer.

B.   Abroad by residents by means of:

    1.   Creation or extension of a wholly-owned enterprise, subsidiary or branch, acquisition of full ownership of an existing enterprise;

    2.   Participation in a new or existing enterprise;

    3.   A loan of five years or longer.

Remarks: Transactions and transfers under A and B shall be free unless:

i)   an investment is of a purely financial character designed only to gain for the investor indirect access to the money or financial market of another country; or

ii)   in view of the amount involved or of other factors a specific transaction or transfer would have an exceptionally detrimental effect on the interests of the Member concerned.

The authorities of Members shall not maintain or introduce:

Regulations or practices applying to the granting of licences, concessions, or similar authorisations, including conditions or requirements attaching to such authorisations and affecting the operations of enterprises, that raise special barriers or limitations with

---

[1]All items in the General List of International Capital Movements and Certain Related Operations (see Annex D to the Code) appear on either List A or List B in this Annex A.

---

respect to non-resident (as compared to resident) investors, and that have the intent or the effect of preventing or significantly impeding inward direct investment by non-residents.

II. LIQUIDATION OF DIRECT INVESTMENT

A.   Abroad by residents.

B.   In the country concerned by non-residents.

III. OPERATIONS IN REAL ESTATE[2]

A.   Operations in the country concerned by non-residents:

    1.   (See List B)

    2.   Sale.

B.   Operations abroad by residents:

    1.   (See List B)

    2.   Sale.

IV. OPERATIONS IN SECURITIES ON CAPITAL MARKETS[3]

A.   Admission of domestic securities on a foreign capital market:

    1. Issue through placing or public sale of

        a) shares or other securities of a participating nature;
        b) bonds or other debt securities (original maturity of one year or more).

    2. Introduction on a recognised foreign security market of

        a) shares or other securities of a participating nature;
        b) bonds or other debt securities (original maturity of one year or more).

B.   Admission of foreign securities on the domestic capital market:

---

[2]Other than operations falling under Sections I or II of the General List.

[3]Other than operations falling under Sections I, II, III or V of the General List.

1. Issue through placing or public sale of

    a) shares or other securities of a participating nature;

    b) bonds or other debt securities (original maturity of one year or more).

2. Introduction on a recognised foreign security market of

    a) shares or other securities of a participating nature;

    b) bonds or other debt securities (original maturity of one year or more).

C.   Operations in the country concerned by non-residents:

    1. Purchase

        a) shares or other securities of a participating nature;

        b) bonds or other debt securities (original maturity of one year or more).

    2. Sale

        a) shares or other securities of a participating nature;

        b) bonds or other debt securities (original maturity of one year or more).

D.   Operations abroad by residents:

    1. Purchase

        a) shares or other securities of a participating nature;

        b) bonds or other debt securities (original maturity of one year or more).

    2. Sale

        a) shares or other securities of a participating nature;

        b) bonds or other debt securities (original maturity of one year or more).

Remarks: The liberalisation obligations under B1 and B2 are subject to the regulations of the security markets concerned. The authorities of Members shall not maintain or introduce restrictions which discriminate against foreign securities.

Members may:

a) With regard to transactions and transfers under A, B, C and D require that:

    i)   Such transactions and transfers must be carried out through authorised resident agents;

ii)   *In connection with such transactions and transfers residents may hold funds and securities only through the intermediary of such agents; and*

iii)   *Purchases and sales may be contracted only on a spot basis;*

b) With regard to transactions and transfers under C2, take measures for the protection of investors, including the regulation of promotional activities, provided such measures do not discriminate against the residents of any other Member;

c) With regard to transactions and transfers under D1, regulate on their territory any promotional activities by, or on behalf of, the residents of other Members.

V. OPERATIONS ON MONEY MARKETS[4]

(See List B)

VI. OTHER OPERATIONS IN NEGOTIABLE INSTRUMENTS AND NON-SECURITISED CLAIMS[5]

(See List B)

VII. OPERATIONS IN COLLECTIVE INVESTMENT SECURITIES

A.   Admission of domestic collective investment securities on a foreign securities market:

1. Issue through placing or public sale.

2. Introduction on a recognised foreign securities market.

B.   Admission of foreign collective investment securities on the domestic securities market:

1. Issue through placing or public sale.

2. Introduction on a recognised domestic securities market.

C.   Operations in the country concerned by non-residents:

1. Purchase.

2. Sale

---

[4]Other than operations falling under Section IV of the General List.

[5]Other than operations falling under Sections IV, V or VII of the General List.

D.   Operations abroad by residents:

1. Purchase.

2. Sale

Remarks: The liberalisation obligations under B1 and B2 are subject to the regulations of the security markets concerned.

The authorities of Members shall not maintain or introduce restrictions which discriminate against foreign collective investment securities.

Members may:

a)   *With regard to transactions and transfers under A, B, C and D require that:*

      i)   *Such transactions and transfers must be carried out through authorised resident agents;*

      ii)   *In connection with such transactions and transfers residents may hold funds and securities only through the intermediary of such agents; and*

      iii)   *Purchases and sales may be contracted only on a spot basis;*

b)   *With regard to transactions and transfers under C2, take measures for the protection of investors, including the regulation of promotional activities, provided such measures do not discriminate against institutions for collective investment organised under the laws of any other Member;*

c)   *With regard to transactions and transfers under D1, regulate on their territory any promotional activities of foreign institution for collective investment.*

VIII. CREDITS DIRECTLY LINKED WITH INTERNATIONALCOMMERCIAL TRANSACTIONS OR WITH THE RENDERING OF INTERNATIONAL SERVICES

      i)   In cases where a resident participates in the underlying commercial or service transaction.

A.   Credits granted by non-residents to residents.

B.   Credits granted by residents to non-residents.

      ii)   In cases where no resident participates in the underlying commercial or service transaction.
      (See List B)

21

IX. FINANCIAL CREDITS AND LOANS[6]

(See List B)

X. SURETIES, GUARANTEES AND FINANCIAL BACK-UP FACILITIES

i) In cases directly related to international trade or international current invisible operations, or in cases related to international capital movement operations in which a resident participates.

A. Sureties and guarantees:

1. By non-residents in favour of residents.

2. By residents in favour of non-residents.

B. Financial back-up facilities:

1. By non-residents in favour of residents.

2. By residents in favour of non-residents.

Remark: Transactions and transfers under X(i)A and B shall be free if they are directly related to international trade, international current invisible operations or international capital movement operations in which a resident participates and which do not require authorisation or have been authorised by the Member concerned.

ii) In cases not directly related to international trade, international current invisible operations or international capital movement operations, or where no resident participates in the underlying international operation concerned.

A. Sureties and guarantees:

1. By non-residents in favour of residents.

2. By residents in favour of non-residents.

B. Financial back-up facilities:

(See List B)

---

[6]Other than credits and loans falling under Sections I, II, VIII or XIV of the General List.

XI. OPERATION OF DEPOSIT ACCOUNTS[7]

A. Operation by non-residents of accounts with resident institution:

    1.   In domestic currency.

    2.   In foreign currency.

B. Operation by residents of accounts with non-resident institutions:

    (See List B)

Remark: Transactions and transfers under XI/A shall be free provided the deposit accounts are operated with financial institutions authorised to accept deposits.

XII. OPERATIONS IN FOREIGN EXCHANGE[8]

(See List B)

XIII. LIFE ASSURANCE

Capital transfers arising under life assurance contracts[9]:

A.   Transfers of capital and annuities certain due to resident beneficiaries from non-resident insurers.

B.   Transfers of capital and annuities certain due to non-resident beneficiaries from resident insurers.

Remark: Transfers under A and B shall be free also in the case of contracts under which the persons from whom premiums are due or the beneficiaries to whom disbursements are due were residents of the same country as the insurer at the time of the conclusion of the contract but have changed their residence since.

---

[7]Other than operations falling under Section V of the General List.

[8]Other than operations falling under any other Section of the General List.

[9]Transfers of premiums and pensions and annuities, other than annuities certain, in connection with life assurance contracts are governed by the Code of Liberalisation of Current Invisible Operations (Item D/3). Transfers of whatever kind or size under other than life assurance contracts are always considered to be of a current nature and are consequently governed by the Current Invisibles Code.

XIV. PERSONAL CAPITAL MOVEMENTS

A.   Loans.

B.   Gifts and endowments.

C.   Dowries.

D.   Inheritances and legacies.

Remark: Transfers under D shall be free provided that the deceased was resident and the beneficiary non-resident at the time of the deceased's death.

E.   Settlement of debts in their country of origin by immigrants.

F.   Emigrants' assets.

Remark: Transfers under F shall be free upon emigration irrespective of the nationality of the emigrant.

G.   Gaming.

    (See List B.)

H.   Savings of non-resident workers.

XV. PHYSICAL MOVEMENT OF CAPITAL ASSETS

A.   Securities and other documents of title to capital assets:

    1.   Import.
    2.   Export.

B.   Means of payment:

    1.   Import.
    2.   Export.

Remark: In the case of residents the obligation to permit an export applies only to the export of foreign securities and then only on a temporary basis for administrative purposes.

XVI. DISPOSAL OF NON-RESIDENT-OWNED BLOCKED FUNDS

A.   Transfer of blocked funds.

B.   Use of blocked funds in the country concerned:

1.   For operations of a capital nature.
2.   For current operations.

C.   Cession of blocked funds between non-residents.

LIST B[1]
III. OPERATIONS IN REAL ESTATE[2]

A.   Operations in the country concerned by non-residents:

1.   Building or purchase.
2.   (See List A)

B.   Operations abroad by residents:

1.   Building or purchase.
2.   (See List A)

V. OPERATIONS ON MONEY MARKETS[3]

A.   Admission of domestic securities and other instruments on a foreign money market:

1.   Issue through placing or public sale.
2.   Introduction on a recognised foreign money market.

B.   Admission of foreign securities and other instruments on the domestic money market:

1.   Issue through placing or public sale.
2.   Introduction on a recognised domestic money market.

C.   Operations in the country concerned by non-residents:

---

[1]All items in the General List of International Capital Movements and Certain Related Operations (see Annex D to the Code) appear on either List A or List B in this Annex A.

[2]Other than operations falling under Sections I or II of the General List.

[3]Other than operations falling under Section V of the General List.

1. Purchase of money market securities.
2. Sale of money market securities.
3. Lending through other money market instruments.
4. Borrowing through other money market instruments.

D. Operations abroad by residents:

1. Purchase of money market securities.
2. Sale of money market securities.
3. Lending through other money market instruments.
4. Borrowing through other money market instruments.

Remarks: The liberalisation obligations under B1 and B2 are subject to the regulations of the security markets concerned.

The authorities of Members shall not maintain or introduce restrictions which discriminate against foreign money market securities or other money market instruments.

Members may:

a) *With regard to transactions and transfers under A, B, C and D require that:*

   i) *Such transactions and transfers must be carried out through authorised resident agents;*

   ii) *In connection with such transactions and transfers residents may hold funds, securities and other instruments only through the intermediary of such agents; and*

   iii) *Purchases and sales may be contracted only on a spot basis;*

b) *With regard to transactions and transfers under C2, take measures for the protection of investors, including the regulation of promotional activities, provided such measures do not discriminate against the residents of any other Member;*

c) *With regard to transactions and transfers under D1, regulate on their territory any promotional activities, by or on behalf of, the residents of other Members.*

VI. OTHER OPERATIONS IN NEGOTIABLE INSTRUMENTS AND NON-SECURITISED CLAIMS[4]

A.   Admission of domestic instruments and claims on a foreign financial market:

    1.   Issue through placing or public sale.
    2.   Introduction on a recognised foreign financial market.

B.   Admission of foreign instruments and claims on a domestic financial market;

    1.   Issue through placing or public sale.
    2.   Introduction on a recognised domestic financial market.

C.   Operations in the country concerned by non-residents;

    1.   Purchase.
    2.   Sale.
    3.   Exchange for other assets.

D.   Operations abroad by residents;

    1.   Purchase.
    2.   Sale.
    3.   Exchange for other assets.

Remarks: The liberalisation obligations under B1 and B2 are subject to the regulations of the financial market concerned.

The authorities of Members shall not maintain or introduce restrictions which discriminate against foreign negotiable instruments or non-securitised claims.

Members may:

a)   *With regard to transactions and transfers under A, B, C and D require that:*

    i)   *Such transactions and transfers must be carried out through authorised resident agents; and*

    ii)   *In connection with such transactions and transfers residents may hold funds, negotiable instruments and non-securitised claims only through the intermediary of such agents;*

---

[4]Other than operations falling under Sections IV, V or VII of the General List.

b) *With regard to transactions and transfers under C2 and C3, take measures for the protection of investors, including the regulation of promotional activities, provided such measures do not discriminate against the residents of any other Member;*

c) *With regard to transactions and transfers under D1 and D3, regulate on their territory any promotional activities by, or on behalf of, the residents of other Members.*

VIII. CREDITS DIRECTLY LINKED WITH INTERNATIONAL COMMERCIAL TRANSACTIONS OR WITH THE RENDERING OF INTERNATIONAL SERVICES

i) In cases where a resident participates in the underlying commercial or service transaction.

(See List A)

ii) In cases where no resident participates in the underlying commercial or service transaction.

A. --

B. Credits granted by residents to non-residents.

Remark: Transactions and transfers under VIII(ii)/B shall be free if the creditor is an enterprise permitted to extend credits and loans on its national market.

IX. FINANCIAL CREDITS AND LOANS[5]

A. Credits and loans granted by non-residents to residents.

B. Credits and loans granted by residents to non-residents.

Remarks: Transactions and transfers under IX/A shall be free if the debtor is an enterprise.

Transactions and transfers under IX/B shall be free if the creditor is an enterprise permitted to extend credits and loans on its national market.

---

[5]Other than credits and loans falling under Sections I, II, VIII or XIV of the General List.

X. SURETIES, GUARANTEES AND FINANCIAL BACK-UP FACILITIES

i) In cases directly related to international trade or international current invisible operations, or in cases related to international capital movement operations in which a resident participates.

(See List A)

ii) In cases not directly related to international trade, international current invisible operations, or international capital movement operations, or where no resident participates in the underlying international operations concerned.

A. Sureties and guarantees:

(See List A)

B. Financial back-up facilities:

1. By non-residents in favour of residents.
2. By residents in favour of non-residents.

XI. OPERATION OF DEPOSIT ACCOUNTS[6]

A. Operation by non-residents of accounts with resident institutions:

(See List A)

B. Operation by residents of accounts with non-resident institutions:

1. In domestic currency.

2. In foreign currency.

XII. OPERATIONS IN FOREIGN EXCHANGE[7]

A. In the country concerned by non-residents:

1. Purchase of domestic currency with foreign currency.
2. Sale of domestic currency for foreign currency.
3. Exchange of foreign currencies.

---

[6]Other than operations falling under Section V of the General List.

[7]Other than operations falling under any other Section of the General List.

B.   Abroad by residents:

      1.   Purchase of foreign currency with domestic currency.

      2.   Sale of foreign currency for domestic currency.

      3.   Exchange of foreign currencies.

Remark: Transactions and transfers under XII/A and B shall be free provided the operations are carried out through authorised resident agents.

XIV. PERSONAL CAPITAL MOVEMENTS

A. to F.   (See List A.)

G.   Gaming

Remark: Transfers under G shall be free only in respect of winnings. The provision does not cover the stakes wagered.

H.   (See List A).

*   *   *

CODE OF LIBERALISATION OF CURRENT INVISIBLE OPERATIONS*

> The Code of Liberalisation of Current Invisible Operations was adopted by the Council of the Organisation for Economic Co-operation and Development on 12 December 1961. The Code has been amended on several occasions. The text of the Code reproduced in this volume incorporates the most recent amendments. Annexes B, C, D and E to the Code have not been reproduced in this volume.

Contents

---

*Source: Organisation for Economic Co-operation and Development (1995). *Code of Liberalisation of Current Invisible Operations* (Paris: OECD). The numbering of footnotes in this reproduction do not necessarily correspond to their numbering in the original source document [Note added by the editor].

Annex V to Annex A

Films

Annex B

Reservations to the Code of Liberalisation of Current Invisible Operations

Annex C

Decision of the Council regarding the Application of the Provisions of the Code of Liberalisation of Current Invisible Operations to Action taken by States of the United States

Annex D

Decision of the Council regarding the Application of the Provisions of the Code of Liberalisation of Current Invisible Operations to Action taken by Provinces of Canada

*****

List of Council Acts included in the present edition of the Code of Current Invisible Operations

PREAMBLE

The Council,

Having regard to Articles 2 d) and 5 a) of the Convention on the Organisation for Economic Co-operation and Development of 14th December, 1960;

Having regard to the Code of Liberalisation of Capital Movements;

Having regard to the Articles of Agreement of the International Monetary Fund of 27th December, 1945;

Having regard to the European Monetary Agreement of 5th August, 1955, and the Protocol of Provisional Application of that Agreement of the same date;

Having regard to the Report of the Committee for Invisible Transactions on the Codes of Liberalisation of Current Invisibles and of Capital Movements of 28th October, 1961, and the Comments by the Executive Committee on that Report of 8th December, 1961 [OECD/C(61)37; OECD/C(61)73];

Decides:

CODE OF LIBERALISATION OF CURRENT INVISIBLE OPERATIONS

Articles

PART I
UNDERTAKINGS WITH REGARD
TO CURRENT INVISIBLE OPERATIONS

Article 1
GENERAL UNDERTAKINGS

a.   Members shall eliminate between one another, in accordance with the provisions of Article 2, restrictions on current invisible transactions and transfers, hereinafter called "current invisible operations". Measures designed for this purpose are hereinafter called "measures of liberalisation".

b.   Where Members are not bound, by virtue of the provisions of this Code, to grant authorizations in respect of current invisible operations, they shall deal with applications in as liberal a manner as possible.

c.   Members shall use their best offices to ensure that the measures of liberalisation are applied within their overseas territories.

d.   Members shall endeavour to extend the measures of liberalisation to all members of the International Monetary Fund.

e.   "Member" shall mean a Member of the Organisation which adheres to this Code.

Article 2
MEASURES OF LIBERALISATION

a.   Members shall grant any authorization required for a current invisible operation specified in an item set out in Annex A to this Code.

b.   A Member may lodge reservations relating to the obligations resulting from paragraph a) when:

    i)   an item is added to Annex A to this Code;

    ii)   obligations relating to an item in that Annex are extended; or

    iii)   obligations relating to any such item begin to apply to that Member.

Reservations shall be set out in Annex B to this Code.

Article 3
PUBLIC ORDER AND SECURITY

The provisions of this Code shall not prevent a Member from taking action which it considers necessary for:

i) the maintenance of public order or the protection of public health, morals and safety;

ii) the protection of its essential security interests; or

iii) the fulfillment of its obligations relating to international peace and security.

Article 4
OBLIGATIONS IN EXISTING
MULTILATERAL INTERNATIONAL AGREEMENTS

Nothing in this Code shall be regarded as altering the obligations undertaken by a Member as a Signatory of the Articles of Agreement of the International Monetary Fund or other existing multilateral international agreements.

Article 5
CONTROLS AND FORMALITIES

a. The measures of liberalisation provided for in this Code shall not limit the powers of Members to verify the authenticity of current invisible operations nor to take any measures required to prevent evasion of their laws or regulations.

b. Members shall simplify as much as possible all formalities connected with the authorization or verification of current invisible operations and shall co-operate, if necessary, to attain such simplification.

Article 6
EXECUTION OF TRANSFERS

a. A Member shall be deemed to have complied with its obligations as regards transfers whenever a transfer may be made:

i) between persons entitled, by the exchange regulations of the State from which and of the State to which the transfer is to be made, respectively, to make and/or to receive the said transfer;

ii) in accordance with international agreements in force at the time the transfer is to be made: and *iii)* in accordance with the monetary arrangements in force between the State from which and the State to which the transfer is to be made.

b.   The provisions of paragraph a) do not preclude Members from demanding payment of maritime freights in the currency of a third State, provided that such a demand is in conformity with established maritime practice.

Article 7
CLAUSES OF DEROGATION

a.   If its economic and financial situation justifies such a course, a Member need not take the whole of the measures of liberalisation provided for in Article 2 a).

b.   If any measures of liberalisation taken or maintained in accordance with the provisions of Article 2 a) result in serious economic disturbance in the Member State concerned, that Member may withdraw those measures.

c.   If the overall balance of payments of a Member develops adversely at a rate and in circumstances, including the state of its monetary reserves, which it considers serious that Member may temporarily suspend the application of measures of liberalisation taken or maintained in accordance with the provisions of Article 2 a).

d.   However, a Member invoking paragraph c) shall endeavour to ensure that its measures of liberalisation:

   i) cover, twelve months after it has invoked that paragraph, to a reasonable extent, having regard to the need for advancing towards the objective defined in sub-paragraph ii), current invisible operations which the Member must authorise in accordance with Article 2 a) and the authorization of which it has suspended since it invoked paragraph c), and, in particular current invisible operations relating to tourism if, in whole or in part, their authorization has been suspended; and

   ii) comply, eighteen months after it has invoked that paragraph, with its obligations under Article 2 a).

e.   Any Member invoking the provisions of this Article shall do so in such a way as to avoid unnecessary damage which bears especially on the commercial or economic interests of another Member and, in particular, shall avoid any discrimination between other Members.

Article 8
RIGHT TO BENEFIT FROM MEASURES OF LIBERALISATION

Any Member lodging a reservation under Article 2 b) or invoking the provisions of Article 7 shall, nevertheless, benefit from the measures of liberalisation taken by other Members provided it has complied with the procedure laid down in Article 12 or Article 13 as the case may be.

Article 9
NON-DISCRIMINATION

A Member shall not discriminate as between other Members in authorising current invisible operations which are listed in Annex A and which are subject to any degree of liberalisation.

Article 10
EXCEPTIONS TO THE PRINCIPLE OF NON-DISCRIMINATION
SPECIAL CUSTOMS OR MONETARY SYSTEMS

Members forming part of a special customs or monetary system may apply to one another in addition to measures of liberalisation taken in accordance with the provisions of Article 2 a) other measures of liberalisation without extending them to other Members. Members forming part of such a system shall inform the Organisation of its membership and those of its provisions which have a bearing on this Code.

PART II
PROCEDURE

Article 11
NOTIFICATION AND INFORMATION FROM MEMBERS

a.   Members shall notify the Organisation, within the periods which the latter may determine, of the measures of liberalisation which they have taken and of any other measures which have a bearing on this Code, as well as of any modification of such measures.

b.   The Organisation shall consider the notifications submitted to it in accordance with the provisions of paragraph a) with a view to determining whether each Member is complying with its obligations under this Code.

Article 12
NOTIFICATION AND EXAMINATION OF RESERVATIONS LODGED UNDER
ARTICLE 2 b)

a.   Each Member shall notify the Organisation within a period to be determined by the Organisation, whether it desires to maintain any reservation lodged by it in respect of an item specified in Annex A to this Code, and, if so, state its reasons therefor.

b.   The Organisation shall examine each reservation lodged by a Member in respect of an item specified in Annex A to this Code at intervals of not more than eighteen months, unless the Council decides otherwise.

c.   The examination provided for in paragraph b) shall be directed to making suitable proposals designed to assist Members to withdraw their reservations.

Article 13
NOTIFICATION AND EXAMINATION OF DEROGATIONS MADE UNDER ARTICLE 7

a.   Any Member invoking the provisions of Article 7 shall notify the Organisation forthwith of its action, together with its reasons therefor.

b.   The Organisation shall consider the notifications and reasons submitted to it in accordance with the provisions of paragraph a) with a view to determining whether the Member concerned is justified in invoking the provisions of Article 7 and, in particular, whether it is complying with the provisions of paragraph e) of that Article.

c.   If the action taken by a Member in accordance with the provisions of Article 7 is not disapproved by the Organisation, that action shall be reconsidered by the Organisation every six months or, subject to the provisions of Article 15, on any other date which the latter may deem appropriate.

d.   If, however, in the opinion of a Member other than the one which has invoked Article 7, the circumstances justifying the action taken by the latter in accordance with the provisions of that Article have changed, that other Member may at any time refer to the Organisation for reconsideration of the case at issue.

e.   If the action taken by a Member in accordance with the provisions of paragraphs a), b) or c) of Article 7 has not been disapproved by the Organisation, then, if that Member subsequently invokes paragraphs a), b) or c) of Article 7 of the Code of Liberalisation of Capital Movements, or, having invoked one paragraph of Article 7 of this Code, invokes another paragraph of that Article, its case shall be reconsidered by the Organisation after six months have elapsed since the date of the previous consideration, or on any other date which the latter may deem appropriate. If another Member claims that the Member in question is failing to carry out its obligations under paragraph e) of Article 7 of this Code or paragraph e) of Article 7 of the Code of Liberalisation of Capital Movements, the Organisation shall consider the case without delay.

f.   *i)*   If the Organisation, following its consideration in accordance with paragraph b), determines that a Member is not justified in invoking the provisions of Article 7 or is not complying with the provisions of that Article, it shall remain in consultation with the Member concerned, with a view to restoring compliance with the Code.

       ii)   If, after a reasonable period of time, that Member continues to invoke the provisions of Article 7, the Organisation shall reconsider the matter. If the Organisation is then unable to determine that the Member concerned is justified in invoking the provisions of Article 7 or is complying with the provisions of that Article, the situation of that Member shall be examined at a session of the Council convened by its Chairman for this purpose, unless the Organisation decides on some other procedure.

Article 14
EXAMINATION OF DEROGATIONS
MADE IN ACCORDANCE WITH ARTICLE 7

MEMBERS IN PROCESS OF ECONOMIC DEVELOPMENT

a.   In examining the case of a Member which it considers to be in process of economic development and which has invoked the provisions of Article 7, the Organisation shall have special regard to the effect that the economic development of that Member has upon its ability to carry out its obligations under paragraph a) of Articles 1 and 2.

b.   In order to reconcile the obligations of the Member concerned under paragraph a) of Article 2 with the requirements of its economic development, the Organisation may grant that Member a special dispensation from those obligations.

Article 15
SPECIAL REPORT AND EXAMINATION
CONCERNING DEROGATIONS MADE UNDER ARTICLE 7

a.   A Member invoking the provisions of paragraph c) of Article 7 shall report to the Organisation, within ten months after such invocation, on the measures of liberalisation it has restored or proposes to restore in order to attain the objective determined in sub-paragraph d) i) of Article 7. The Member shall, if it continues to invoke these provisions, report to the Organisation again on the same subject -- but with reference to the objective determined in sub-paragraph d) ii) of Article 7 -within sixteen months after such invocation.

b.   If the Member considers that it will not be able to attain the objective, it shall indicate its reasons in its report and, in addition, shall state:

   i)   What internal measures it has taken to restore its economic equilibrium and what results have already been attained; and

   ii)   What further internal measures it proposes to take and what additional period it considers it will need in order to attain the objectives determined in sub-paragraphs d) i) or d) ii) of Article 7.

c.   In cases referred to in paragraph b), the Organisation shall consider within a period of twelve months, and, if required, of eighteen months from the date on which the Member invoked the provisions of paragraph c) of Article 7, whether the situation of that Member appears to justify its failure to attain the objective determined in sub-paragraph d) i) or d) ii) of Article 7, and whether the measures taken or envisaged and the period considered by it as necessary for attaining the objective determined, appear acceptable in the light of the objectives of the Organisation in the commercial and financial fields.

d.   If a Member invokes the provisions of both paragraph c) of Article 7 of this Code and paragraph c) of Article 7 of the Code of Liberalisation of Capital Movements, the periods of twelve and eighteen months referred to in paragraph c) shall run from the date of the earlier invocation.

e.   If, following any of the examinations provided for in paragraph c), the Organisation is unable to approve the arguments advanced by the Member concerned in accordance with the provisions of paragraph b), the situation of that Member shall be examined at a session of the Council convened by its Chairman for this purpose, unless the Organisation decides on some other procedure.

Article 16
REFERENCE TO THE ORGANISATION

INTERNAL ARRANGEMENTS

a.   If a Member considers that the measures of liberalisation taken or maintained by another Member in accordance with Article 2 a) are frustrated by internal arrangements likely to restrict the possibility of effecting current invisible operations, and if it considers itself to be prejudiced thereby, it may refer to the Organisation.

b.   If, following the consideration of a matter referred to it under paragraph a), the Organisation determines that internal arrangements introduced or maintained by the Member concerned have the effect of frustrating its measures of liberalisation, the Organisation may make suitable suggestions with regard to the removal or modification of such arrangements.

Article 17
REFERENCE TO THE ORGANISATION

RETENTION, INTRODUCTION OR REINTRODUCTION
OF RESTRICTIONS

a.   If a Member considers that another Member which has not invoked the provisions of Article 7 has retained, introduced or re-introduced restrictions on current invisible operations, contrary to the provisions of Article 1, paragraph a) of Article 2, or Article 9, and if it considers itself to be prejudiced thereby, it may refer to the Organisation.

b.   The fact that the case is under consideration by the Organisation shall not preclude the Member which has referred to the Organisation from entering into bilateral conversations on the matter with the other Member concerned.

PART III
TERMS OF REFERENCE

Article 18
**COMMITTEE ON CAPITAL MOVEMENTS
AND INVISIBLE TRANSACTIONS**

a.   The Committee on Capital Movements and Invisible Transactions shall consist of members chosen by reason of the knowledge they have of problems relating to capital movements and invisible transactions and of the personal standing which they enjoy within the Organisation or in their respective countries. They shall be appointed by the Council from persons nominated by the Member States. The Council shall ensure that no more than one nominee of each Member State shall serve on the Committee at any given time. Unless the Council decides otherwise, the term of office of members of the Committee shall be one year; they may be reappointed.

b.   Each member of the Committee shall designate an alternate. Alternates may attend the meetings of the Committee. They shall exercise the functions of members if the latter are unable to attend.

c.   The Council shall designate each year from among the members of the Committee a Chairman and a Vice-Chairman.

d.   A delegate of any Member State, a nominee of which is not serving on the Committee, may attend its meetings as an observer.

e.   The Chairman or the Vice-Chairman of the Payments Committee may attend the meetings of the Committee with the right to participate in its discussions.

f.   A representative of the Commission of the European Communities may attend the meetings of the Committee and take part in its work in accordance with Supplementary Protocol No 1 to the OECD Convention.

g.   The Committee may invite other persons to attend its meetings.

h.   The proposals of the Committee shall be adopted by a majority of its members. A member who is in disagreement with the majority may request that his views should be recorded in the report of the Committee.

i.   The Committee shall adopt its own rules of procedure.

Article 19
COMMITTEE ON CAPITAL MOVEMENTS
AND INVISIBLE TRANSACTIONS

GENERAL TASKS

The Committee on Capital Movements and Invisible Transactions shall consider all questions concerning the interpretation or implementation of the provisions of this Code or other acts of the Council relating to the liberalisation of current invisible operations and shall report its conclusions thereon to the Council as appropriate.

Article 20
COMMITTEE ON CAPITAL MOVEMENTS
AND INVISIBLE TRANSACTIONS

SPECIAL TASKS

a.   The Committee on Capital Movements and Invisible Transactions shall:

   i)   Determine the periods within which the information provided for in paragraph a) of Article 11 and the reasons provided for in paragraph a) of Article 12 should be notified to the Organisation by the Members concerned;

   ii)   Subject to paragraph c) of this Article, consider, in conformity with paragraphs b) and c) of Article 12, each reservation notified to the Organisation in accordance with paragraph a) of that Article and make, where appropriate, suitable proposals designed to assist Members to withdraw their reservations;

   iii)   Determine, in accordance with the provisions of Article 12, the date on which any reservations should be re-examined, if the reservation has not been withdrawn in the meantime;

   iv)   Consider, in accordance with the provisions of paragraph b) of Article 11, the notifications submitted to the Organisations;

   v)   Consider reports and references submitted to the Organisation in accordance with the provisions of Article 13 or paragraphs a) and b) of Article 15 where a Member has invoked the provisions of Article 7, or submitted in accordance with the provisions of Article 16 or 17;

   vi)   Determine the date on which the case of a Member which has invoked Article 7 should be reconsidered in accordance with the provisions of paragraph c), paragraph e) or paragraph f) ii) of Article 13;

vii) Transmit to the United States Government, with any comments it considers appropriate, notifications received from Members in accordance with paragraph 2 a) of the Decision in Annex C to the Code; and

viii) Consider information received from the United States Government in accordance with paragraph 2 b) of the Decision in Annex C to the Code.

b.   When examining the reservations notified in accordance with the provisions of paragraph a) of Article 12 the Committee may, as it deems fit, consider together either all reservations made by the same Member or all reservations made in respect of the same item specified in Annex A to this Code.

c.   The Committee shall, however, not consider any reservations notified to the Organisation in accordance with the provisions of paragraph a) of Article 12 by a Member which, at the time of the examination in respect of the item subject to that reservation, is invoking the provisions of Article 7 or is enjoying a dispensation in accordance with paragraph b) of Article 14.

d.   In the cases provided for in sub-paragraphs ii), iv), v) and viii) of paragraph a) the Committee shall report to the Council.

e.   The Committee shall, whenever it considers it necessary:

i) consult other Committees of the Organisation on any questions relating to the liberalisation of current invisible operations; and, in particular,

ii) request other Committees of the Organisation to give their views on any questions relating to the balance of payments and the state of the monetary reserves of a Member.

Article 21
PAYMENTS COMMITTEE

Before they are considered by the Council, the Payments Committee shall:

i) review the reports and proposals by the Committee on Capital Movements and Invisible Transactions made in accordance with the provisions of this Code; and

ii) forward to the Council any comments thereon which it considers necessary.

PART IV
MISCELLANEOUS

Article 22
TITLE OF DECISION

This Decision, referred to in the present text as the "Code", shall be known as the "Code of Liberalisation of Current Invisible Operations".

Article 23
WITHDRAWAL

Any Member may withdraw from the Code by transmitting a notice in writing to the Secretary-General of the Organisation. The withdrawal shall become effective twelve months from the date on which such a notice is received.

Article 24
DEFINITION OF THE UNIT OF ACCOUNT

"Unit of account" shall mean the sum in the national currency of a Member which is equal to a unit of value of special drawing rights as valued by the International Monetary Fund.

*   *   *

CODE OF LIBERALISATION OF CURRENT INVISIBLE OPERATIONS

Annex A
LIST OF CURRENT INVISIBLE OPERATIONS

A.   **Business and Industry**

A/1.   Repair and assembly.

A/2.   Processing. finishing, processing of work under contract and other services of the same nature.

Remark: In cases where goods are involved, liberalisation applies only if the importation of the goods concerned is liberalised by the Member ordering such processing, finishing, etc.

A/3.   Technical assistance (assistance relating to the production and distribution of goods and services at all stages, given over a period limited according to the specific purpose of such assistance, and including e.g. advice or visits by experts, preparation of plans and blueprints, supervision of manufacture, market research, training of personnel). See also Note 3 of the Notes following Annex A.

A/4.   Contracting (construction and maintenance of buildings, roads, bridges, ports, etc., carried out by specialised firms, and, generally, at fixed prices after open tender).

A/5.   Authors' royalties. Patents, designs, trade marks and inventions (the assignment and licensing of patent rights, designs, trade marks and inventions, whether or not legally protected, and transfers arising out of such assignment or licensing). See also Note 3 of the Notes following Annex A.

A/6.   Salaries and wages (of frontier or seasonal workers and of other non-residents).

Remark: Free transfer to the country of residence of the recipient. The amounts to be transferred shall be the net salaries and wages, i.e. after deduction of living expenses, taxes, social insurance contributions or premiums, if any.

A/7.   Participation by subsidiary companies and branches in overhead expenses of parent companies situated abroad and vice versa (i.e. overhead expenses other than those included under A/3 and A/5). See also Note 3 of the Notes following Annex A.

B.   Foreign Trade

B/1.   Commission and brokerage.
Profit arising out of transit operations or sale of transhipment.
Representation expenses.

B/2.   Differences, margins and deposits due in respect of operations on commodity terminal markets in conformity with normal commercial practice.

B/3.   Charges for documentation of all kinds incurred on their own account by authorised dealers in foreign exchange.

B/4.   Warehousing and storage, customs clearance.

B/5.   Transit charges.

B/6.   Customs duties and fees.

C.   Transport

C/1.   Maritime freights (including chartering, harbour expenses, disbursements for fishing vessels, etc.).[1]

Remark: See Note I of the Notes following Annex A.

C/2.   Inland waterway freights, including chartering.

C/3.   Road transport: passengers and freights, including chartering.

C/4.   Air transport: passengers and freights, including chartering.
Payment by passengers of international air tickets and excess luggage charges; payment of international air freight charges and chartered flights.

Remark: Without prejudice to the provisions of Annex III.

Receipts from the sale of international air tickets, excess luggage charges, international air freight charges, and chartered flights.

Remark: The transfer of these receipts to the head office of the air transport company concerned shall be free.

C/5.   For all means of maritime transport: harbour services (including bunkering and provisioning, maintenance, repairs, expenses for crews, etc.).

Remark: In the case of repairs, current maintenance, voyage and emergency, repairs (see also C/6).[2] (See Note 1 of the Notes following Annex A.)

For all means of inland waterway transport: harbour services (including bunkering and provisioning, maintenance and minor repairs of equipment, expenses for crews, etc.)

Remark: In the case of repairs, current maintenance repairs only (see also C/6.)

For all means of commercial road transport: road services (including fuel, oil, minor repairs, garaging, expenses for drivers and crews, etc.).

For all means of air transport: operating costs and general overheads, including repairs to aircraft and to air transport equipment.

Remark: Including all charges in connection with the delivery of oil and petrol to air

---

[1]This item does not cover transport between two ports of the same State. Where such transport is open to foreign flags, transfers shall be free.

[2]For definition of terms employed here and in the Remarks against C/6, see Note 2 of the Notes following Annex A.

> *transport companies which are incurred in the currency of the*
> *State where the delivery takes place.*

C/6.   Repair of ships.

Remark: Transactions other than those covered by C/5 (i.e. classification, conversion and other major repairs)[3] to the extent to which they do not constitute visible trade.

Repairs of means of transport other than ships and aircraft.

Remark: Transactions other than those covered by C/5 to the extent to which they do not constitute visible trade.

D.   Insurance

D/1.   Social security and social insurance.

Remarks:

1.   *Free transfer of:*

a)   *contributions of premiums in respect of social security or social insurance payable in another Member State;*

b)   *social security, and social insurance benefits payable to an insured person or beneficiary residing in another Member State or, for their account, to a social security or social insurance authority in that other State.*

2.   *If the transfer relates to an insurance considered as social insurance by only one of the Members concerned the provisions according the more liberal treatment shall apply.*

3.   *Social insurance transactions carried out by private insurers shall also be subject to the provisions of Parts III and IV of Annex I.*

Transactions[4] and transfers   )   *Remark: Direct insurance transactions between insurers*
in connection with direct   )   *in one Member State and insured in other Member*
insurance (other than social)   *State and transfers of premiums and contributions*

---

[3]For definition of terms employed here and in the Remarks against C/5, see Note 2 of the Notes following Annex A.

[4]Transaction shall be deemed to mean the conclusion of a direct insurance contract by a person in one Member State with an insurer in another Member State.

security and social insurance).	)))	*between insured insurers in two different Member States. Transfers by insurers in one Member State of settlements and benefits paid or to be paid in another*
D/2. insurance relating to goods in international trade.	)))	*Member States and transfers of sums necessary for the enforcement of claims arising under an insurance contract. Within the limits specified in Part I of Annex*
D/3. Life assurance.	))	*I.*
D/4. All other insurance.	)	

D/5.   Transactions and transfers in connection with reinsurance and retrocession.

   Remark: The provisions of Part II of Annex I shall also apply.

D/6.   Conditions for establishment and operation of branches and agencies of foreign insurers.

   Remarks:

   1.   Authorization within the limits specified by Part III of Annex I for insurers of other Member States to establish themselves and to transact business.

   2.   Transfers between branches and agents of such authorised insurers and their head offices: within the limits specified in Part IV of Annex I.

E.   Banking and Financial Services

General Remarks:

   1.   Regarding operations in the country concerned, Members may take measures for the maintenance of fair and orderly markets and sound institutions and for the protection of investors or other users banking or financial services, provided those measures do not discriminate against non-resident providers of such services.

   2.   Regarding operations abroad, Members may regulate on their territory the promotional activities of non-resident providers of such services.

   3.   Transactions and transfers concerning capital movements in connection with operations covered by Section E of this Code are governed by the Code of Liberalisation of Capital Movements.

E/1. Payment services.

    Payment instruments (including the issuance and use of cheques, travellers' cheques, cash cards and credit cards, other than for credit).

    Fund transfer services [including transfer of funds by mail, telephone, telex, telegraph, telefax, electronic connection or money transfer (giro)].

    Remark: Transactions and transfers for travel and tourism are governed by item G of this Code.

E/2. Banking and investment services (for securities, collective investment securities, other negotiable instruments and non-securitised claims, credits and loans, sureties, guarantees and financial back-up facilities, liquid funds and foreign exchange).

    Underwriting (syndication and distribution of new financial assets).

    Broker/dealer services (intermediation and market-making in the purchase, sale or exchange of financial assets, including liquid funds and foreign exchange).

    Financial market information, communications and execution systems.

E/3. Settlement, clearing and custodial and depository services (for securities, collective investment securities, other negotiable instruments and non-securitised claims, liquid funds and foreign exchange).

    Settlement and clearing systems.

    Custodial and depository services.

    Remark: Members may require that non-residents participate in a domestic settlement and clearing system only through a branch or subsidiary established in the territory of the Member concerned.

E/4. Asset management.

    Cash management.

    Portfolio management.

    Pension fund management.

    Safekeeping of assets.

    Trust services.

E/5.   Advisory and agency services.

Credit reference and analysis.

Investment research and advice (including securities rating agencies).

Mergers, acquisitions, restructurings, management buy-outs, venture capital.

E/6.   Fees, commissions and other charges.

Remark: Transfers under item E/6 shall be free provided the underlying transaction is not subject to authorisation or has been authorised by the authorities of the Member concerned.

E/7.   Conditions for establishment and operation of branches, agencies, etc. of non-resident investors in the banking and financial services sector.

See Annex II to Annex A.

F.   Income from Capital

F/1.	Profits from business activity.	)
		)
F/2.	Dividends and shares in profits.	)
		)
F/3.	Interest (including interest on debenture, mortgages, etc.)	)
		)
		)
F/4.	Rent.	)

Remark: Does not apply to income deriving from capital acquired otherwise than in conformity with the laws covering the acquisition of capital.

G.   Travel and Tourism

Remark: This section covers all international travel as well as stays abroad for purposes other than immigration, such as pleasure, recreation, holiday, sport, business, visits to relatives or friends, missions, meetings, conferences or for reasons of health, education or religion.

No restrictions shall be imposed by Member countries on expenditure by residents for purposes of international tourism or other international travel. For the settlement of such expenditure, no restrictions shall be placed on transfers abroad by or on behalf of travellers or on the use abroad of cash cards or credit cards, in accordance with the provisions of Annex IV. Travellers shall, moreover, be automatically permitted to acquire, export and import domestic and foreign bank-notes and to use travellers' cheques abroad in accordance with the provisions of Annex IV; additional amounts in travellers' cheques and/or foreign bank-notes shall be allowed on presentation of justification. Lastly, travellers shall be permitted to undertake foreign exchange transactions according to the provisions of Annex IV.

H.   Films

H/1.   Exportation, importation, distribution and use of printed films and other recordings -- whatever the means of reproduction -- for private or cinema exhibition, or for television broadcasts.[5]

   Remark: The provisions of Annex IV shall also apply. Members shall grant any authorisation required for transactions which they had authorised on 1st January, 1959, in virtue of regulations or international agreements in force on that date.

J.   Personal Income and Expenditure

J/1.   Pensions and other income of a similar nature.

   Remark: In favour of persons who, after having spent their life in a Member State other than their State of origin, establish themselves in any other member State including their own.

J/2.   Maintenance payments resulting from a legal obligation or from a decision of a court and financial assistance in cases of hardship.

J/3.   Immigrants' remittances.

   Remarks: Free periodic transfer to the Member State of which the person demanding the transfer is a national, of salaries, fees, wages, and other current remuneration, after deduction of living expenses, taxes, and social insurance.

   No less favourable treatment shall be accorded to demands for the transfer of earnings of self-employed persons or members of the liberal professions.

J/4.   Current maintenance and repair of private property abroad.

J/5.   Transfer of minor amounts abroad.

J/6.   Subscriptions to newspapers,   )
       periodicals, books, musical   )   *Remark: To the extent to which*
       publications.   )   *transactions in connection with*
)   *these items do not constitute*
)

---

[5]The provisions of this item do not apply to Canada which accordingly has neither obligation nor rights thereunder [OECD/C(61)89 of 12th December, 1961 and C(63)154/FINAL of 3rd March, 1964].

Newspapers, periodicals, books,)   *visible trade.*
musical publications and records.)

J/7.   Sports prizes and racing earnings.

Remark: In accordance with the laws of the Members concerned.

K.   Public Income and Expenditure[6]

K/1.   Taxes.

K/2.   Government expenditure (transfer of amounts due by governments to non-residents and in connection with official representation abroad and contributions to international organisations).

K/3.   Settlements in connection with public transport and postal, telegraphic and telephone services.

K/4.   Consular receipts.

L.   General

L/1.   Advertising by all media.

L/2.   Court expenses.

L/3.   Damages.

L/4.   Fines.

L/5.   Membership of associations, clubs and other organisations.

L/6.   Professional services (including services of accountants, artists, consultants, doctors, engineers, experts, lawyers, etc.).

L/7.   Refunds in the case of cancellation of contracts and refunds of uncalled-for payments.

L/8.   Registration of patents and trade-marks.

---

[6]The items in this section apply to transfers only.

NOTES

Note 1. The provisions of C/1 "Maritime freights, including chartering, harbour expenses, disbursements for fishing vessels, etc.", of C/5, first subparagraph "For all means of maritime transport: harbour services (including bunkering and provisioning, maintenance, repairs, expenses for crews, etc.)", and of the other items that have a direct or indirect bearing on international maritime transport, are intended to give residents of one Member State the unrestricted opportunity to avail themselves of, and pay for, all services in connection with international maritime transport which are offered by residents of any other Member State. As the shipping policy of the governments of the Members is based on the principle of free circulation of shipping in international trade in free and fair competition, it follows that the freedom of transactions and transfers in connection with maritime transport should not be hampered by measures in the field of exchange control, by legislative provisions in favour of the national flag, by arrangements made by governmental or semi-governmental organisations giving preferential treatment to national flag ships, by preferential shipping clauses in trade agreements, by the operation of import and export licensing systems so as to influence the flag of the carrying ship, or by discriminatory port regulations or taxation measures -- the aim always being that liberal and competitive commercial and shipping practices and procedures should be followed in international trade and normal commercial considerations should alone determine the method and flag of shipment.

The second sentence of this Note does not apply to the United States.

Note 2. The following are the definitions of the terms employed in the Remarks against C/5 (Maritime transport) and C/6 (Repair of ships) which have been adopted by the Council:

Current maintenance: work which may conveniently be undertaken during a vessel's stay in port, which will contribute towards her general upkeep and efficiency, without being immediately necessary for her continued operation.

Voyage repairs: work which is required during a voyage, due to the normal risks of the sea (e.g. weather damage) to enable the vessel to complete the voyage.

Emergency repairs: similar to voyage repairs, but due to less normal causes, such as sudden machinery breakdown or collisions.

Classification: the special works required to pass the survey which the Classification Society holds on each ship every four years.

Conversion: the major operation of altering the size of a ship or the type, e.g. from steamer to motorship, from passenger/cargo to cargo ship, or from coal-burner to oil burner.

Note 3.   According to the type of knowledge and/or the nature of the contract, "know-how" and manufacturing processes fall under any of the three headings of A/3, A/5 and A/7.

Annex I to Annex A

INSURANCE

Part I

D/2.   Insurance relating to goods in international trade.

1.   The conclusion of insurance contracts relating to goods in international trade:

a)   Between a proposer in a Member State and a foreign insurer not established in the country of residence of the proposer;

b)   Between a proposer in a Member State and a foreign insurer established in the country of residence of the proposer, such contract being entered into:

i)   *From the head office of the foreign insurer;*

ii)   *From a place of business of such insurer situated in a Member State other than the country of residence of the proposer;*

shall be free, subject to the right of Member States to regulate the activities of the insurer himself or of a third party in seeking insurance business.

The transfers required for the execution of such contracts or for the exercise of rights arising therefrom shall be free.

D/3.   Life assurance.

2.   Transactions and transfers relating to life assurance, except group assurance, between a proposer in a Member State and a foreign insurer not established in the country of residence of the proposer shall be free, subject to the right of Member States to regulate the activities of the insurer himself or of a third party in seeking insurance business.

3.   Under existing contracts:

a) Transfers of premiums[7])   *Such transfers shall be free also in*
   due to non-resident)   *the case of contracts under which*
   insurers from residents)   *the persons from whom premiums*
   shall be free;)   *are due or the beneficiaries to*
)   *whom disbursements are due were*

b) Transfers of pensions)   *residents of the same country as*
   and annuities other than)   *the insurer at the time of the*
   annuities certain[7] due to)   *conclusion of the contract but have*
   non-resident beneficiaries)   *changed their residence since.*
   from resident insurers)
   shall be free.)

4. Member States in which premiums paid are allowed, totally or partially, as a deduction for tax purposes shall grant the same benefits whether the contract has been concluded with an insurer established on their territory or abroad.

D/4. All other insurance.

5. Transactions and transfers between a proposer in a Member State and a foreign insurer not established in the country of residence of the proposer, relating to insurance other than that covered under items D/2 and D/3, except group insurance and insurance which is compulsory in the country of residence of the proposer shall be free, subject to the right of Member States to regulate the activities of the insurer himself or of a third party in seeking insurance business.

6. Transactions and transfers shall be free whenever it is not possible to cover a risk in the Member country in which it exists.

7. Member States in which premiums paid are allowed, totally or partially, as a deduction for tax purposes shall grant the same benefits whether the contract has been concluded with an insurer established on their territory or abroad.

8. a) Transfers of amounts due in respect of indemnities to be settled abroad and paid or payable in execution of in insurance contract by an insurer acting on his own behalf or on behalf of his client shall be free[8]

---

[7]Transfers of capital and annuities certain in connection with life assurance contracts are governed by the Code of Liberalisation of Capital Movements (List A, items XIII).

[8]The following transfers in particular are included under this item (the list is not exhaustive, but includes the most frequent cases of transfer of insurance indemnities):
- Transfers of indemnities payable by reason of the insured's liability;
- Transfers of indemnities to cover physical damage to a ship, aircraft, motor vehicle or any other means of transport;
- Transfers of indemnities under baggage insurance;

b) Transfers of costs, subsidiary expenses or sums necessary for the exercise of any rights arising out of an insurance contract shall be free;

c) Without prejudice to cases which are settled individually, each Member shall authorise insurers or their agents who are established in its territory and who settle claims under reciprocal arrangements to offset the payments made on each side and to transfer the balance thereof.

Part II

D/5. Reinsurance and retrocession.

1. Accounts relating to reinsurance operations, including the constitution and adjustment of guarantee deposits held by the ceding insurers, as well as accounts relating to cash losses, may be drawn up on the currency of the direct insurance contract, in the national currency of the ceding insurer or in the national currency of the acceptor, according to the provisions of the reinsurance treaty or agreement.

2. The settlement of balances resulting from the account referred to in paragraph 1 shall be authorised. Settlement may be made either by a set-off of any reciprocal credits of the ceding insurer and the reinsurer or (as agreed between the parties):

a) By transfer to the country of residence of the creditor; or

b) By payment through a bank account opened in accordance with the provisions of paragraph 3 below; or

c) By transfer to another Member State to the credit of a bank account opened in accordance with the provisions of paragraph 3 below if the contract stipulates that payment should be made in that Member's currency.

3. Reinsurers shall be authorised to open accounts in banks established in Member States. These accounts may be credited with the amounts due to their holders arising out of reinsurance operations which are to be settled in accordance with the provisions of paragraph 2 b) and c). They may be debited, at the choice of

---

- Transfers in payment of benefits covered by accident insurance (including individual insurances) or sickness insurance;
- Transfers to fulfil commitments arising from marine insurance not covered by the above paragraphs (provisional or final contributions in respect of general average, paid by the insurer on behalf of the ship's owner or the consignee of the goods or his agent, the transfer of interest on any bank security substituted for a provisional contribution, transfer of interest in respect of provisional contributions, the transfer of remuneration of assistance and salvage, etc.).

their holders, with the amounts due under any settlement in connection with reinsurance operations if it is made in accordance with the provisions of paragraph 2 b) and c) and complies with normal practice. The balances of such accounts may also be transferred to the country of residence of the reinsurer holding the account in question.

4.   The provisions of paragraphs 1 to 3 shall apply also to retrocession operations.

Part III

D/6.   Conditions for establishment and operation of branches and agencies of foreign insurers.

General

1.   All statutory and administrative controls of insurance shall ensure equivalent treatment for national insurers and insurers from other Member States so that the latter shall not be liable to heavier burdens than those imposed on national insurers.

Authorisations

2.   Where the establishment of insurers in a Member State is made subject to authorisation:

a)   That Member shall accord insurers from other Member States treatment equivalent to that applied to national insurers;

b)   The competent authorities shall make available to each insurer from another Member State applying for authorisation a written statement setting out fully and precisely the documents and information that the applicant insurer must supply for the purpose of obtaining authorisation, and shall endeavour to simplify and accelerate as appropriate the procedures to be followed prior to the lodging of an application;

c)   Where in addition to legal, financial, accounting and technical requirements (e.g. requirements concerning the form of the undertaking, qualification of directors or managers, reinsurance arrangements, etc.) the grant of authorization is also subject to other criteria and in particular is also subject to economic criteria such as the needs of the national insurance market, the competent authorities shall inform applicant insurers of such criteria at the time of their application, and shall apply these criteria in the same way to national insurers as to insurers from other Member States;

d)   The competent authorities shall decide on each application for authorization by an insurer from another Member State not later than six months from the date on which that application has been completed in all particulars and shall without further delay notify their decision to that insurer;

e) Where the competent authorities ask an insurer from another Member State for modifications to a completed application for authorisation, they shall inform that insurer of the reasons for seeking such modifications and shall do so under the same conditions as for the national insurer;

f) Where an application for authorisation by an insurer from another Member State is refused, the competent authorities shall advise that insurer of the reasons for their decisions, and shall do so under the same conditions as for a national insurer;

g) Where authorisation is refused, or where the competent authorities have not dealt with an application upon the expiry of the period of six months provided for under paragraph d) above, insurers from other Member States shall have the same right of appeal as national insurers.

Representatives

3. An insurer from one Member State operating in another Member State may appoint on his representative any person who is domiciled and actually resident in that other State, irrespective of his nationality.

Financial guarantees[9]

Common provisions

4. Present and future statutory and administrative controls of insurance in each Member State shall keep to as low a figure as possible the amounts required from

---

[9]For the purposes of this Code, the term "financial guarantee" includes the assets constituting respectively the fixed or initial deposit, the adjustable deposit and the variable deposit, and also the technical reserves and any reserve of another description required under the respective national laws, insofar as the assets constituting such reserves are required to be kept in the country in which the insurer is carrying on business:

- the fixed or initial deposit is the amount which an insurer must constitute and lodge with a prescribed institution in the country in which he is operating, prior to any operation in one or more branches of insurance;
- the adjustable deposit is a deposit which is adjusted according to the amount of business written by the insurer and is not allowed to count towards his technical reserves;
- the variable deposit is a deposit which is adjusted according to the amount of business written by the insurer but is allowed to count towards his technical reserves;
- the technical reserves are the amounts which the insurer sets aside to cover his liabilities under contracts of insurance.

insurers from other Member States as financial guarantees in order to prevent the dispersal of the insurers' assets, insofar as this is compatible with the protection of policy holders and other claimants. Guarantee deposits shall have no other aim than such protection.

Provisions concerning fixed or initial deposits and adjustable deposits

5. A Member which requires fixed or initial deposits and/or adjustable deposits both from national insurers and from insurers from other Member States operating in its territory shall:

    a) Accord to insurers from other Member States the same treatment as that applied to national insurers with respect to the amount and the calculation of such deposits as well as to the eligibility of fixed or initial deposits to count towards the covering of technical reserves;

    b) Allow, at its discretion, any such deposit to be constituted by one or more of the following means, viz.;

        i) Up to the amount of the required deposit:

            -   A guarantee by an approved bank whose head office is situated in that Member State; or

            -   A guarantee by an approved insurer whose head office is situated in that Member State, established by the lodging of a policy; or

            -   The lodging of securities by an approved bank or approved insurer whose head office is situated in that Member State and who has declared that the securities are lodged in the name and for the account of the insurer concerned;

        ii) Up to at least 50 per cent of the required deposit:

            -   The lodging of currency of the State in which the insurer's head office is situated and/or of securities expressed in the currency of that State, provided either that such securities are negotiable in the State in which the insurer is operating or that the authorities of the State in which the head office of the insurer is situated undertake to authorise the transfer of the proceeds of the sale of such securities if the latter should have to be sold in that State. Securities and currency which are to be used to constitute such guarantees shall first be approved by the insurance supervisory authorities of the State in which the insurer is operating; they shall remain under the control of those authorities, according to the rules governing the constitution and utilisation of similar national assets.

6.　　A Member which requires from insurers from other Member States operating in its territory fixed or initial deposits and/or adjustable deposits which are not required from national insurers shall allow, at its discretion, such deposits to be replaced as to not less than 50 per cent by:

　　　a)　　A guarantee by an approved bank whose head office is situated in that Member State; or

　　　b)　　A guarantee by an approved insurer whose head office is situated in that country, established by the lodging of a policy unless it allows fixed or initial deposits to count subsequently towards the covering of technical reserves or of any other guarantee required from insurers from other Member States operating in its territory.

Provisions concerning variable deposits and technical reserves

7.　　A Member which requires variable deposits both from national insurers and from insurers from other Member States operating in its territory shall apply to the latter the same treatment as to national insurers with respect to the calculation of such deposits and their eligibility to count towards the covering of technical reserves.

8.　　Where a Member requires from insurers from other member States operating in its territory variable deposits or the deposit of technical reserves which it does not require from national insurers, such requirements shall not have the effect of making the mode of calculating such reserves and/or deposits more burdensome than the customary rules for calculating the reserves of national insurers.

Controlled investments and deposits

General provisions

9.　　Each member State shall subject national insurers and insurers from other Member States operating in its territory to identical rules for the choice and valuation of their investments and for the adjustment of any depreciation in the value thereof, subject, where appropriate, to the provisions of paragraph 5 b) ii) above.

10.　　Where a Member requires the same deposit of investment both from national insurers and from insurers from other Member States operating in its territory, it shall subject both kinds of insurers to identical rules with respect to the manner in which the deposit is to be lodged.

11. Where a Member requires a deposit of investments from insurers from other Member States only, the requirements as to the choice and the valuation of the investments deposited shall not be more burdensome for such insurers than those applicable to national insurers.

12. Where a Member requires insurers from other Member States operating in its territory to deposit investments to cover the technical reserves and does not impose the same obligation on national insurers, in calculating such deposits the following shall be deducted:

a) In the case of classes of business other than life assurance, marriage and birth assurance, and capital redemption business, cash in hand or at banks and premiums or subscriptions (net of taxes, duties and commissions) which have been outstanding for not more than three months, up to an amount equal to 30 per cent of the unearned premiums reserve;

b) In the case of life assurance, marriage and birth assurance, and capital redemption business:

   i) Cash in hand or at banks, up to an amount equal to one-twelfth of the premium income in the last financial year; and

   ii) Up to 90 per cent of premiums or subscriptions (net of taxes, duties and commissions) which have been outstanding for not more than three months.

Acceptable investments

13. Each Member shall endeavour to allow insurers from other Member States operating in its territory the greatest possible choice for their investments.

14. In addition to investments expressly designated therein, the national laws and regulations of each Member for the supervision of insurance should provide that technical reserves and deposits may be constituted by insurers from other Member States by means of any other investment which are admitted by the competent authorities of the Member concerned on such conditions as the latter may determine.

15. Each Member shall allow insurers from other Member States operating in its territory to use immovable property situated therein or mortgages on such property, up to an amount equal to not less than 25 per cent of the technical reserves and variable deposits after excluding, where appropriate, any part thereof which may be constituted by means of fixed or initial deposits.

Change of investments

16.   If at any time between prescribed periodic adjustments an insurer from one Member State operating in another Member State which requires the deposit of technical reserves can prove to the insurance supervisory authorities of the latter that the sum deposited exceed those required to constitute such technical reserves, the supervisory authorities shall authorise without delay the release of any sums deposited in excess.

17.   Each member shall allow insurers from other Member States operating in its territory to change their investments with a minimum of formalities.

   a)   In particular, the prior replacement by other investments shall not be required where;

   i)   With the prior authorisation of the insurance supervisory authorities, deposited securities are withdrawn from deposit and replaced within one and the same duly authorised institution; and

   ii)   Securities are replaced by immovable property which the insurers wish to acquire, or by mortgages on immovable property, provided that the replacement takes place within a short time.

   b)   In all other cases where the prior replacement cannot be dispensed with, the insurance supervisory authorities shall allow such replacement of investments to take place with the least delay, and shall keep all charges incumbent on the insurers to the minimum, without, however, in any way diminishing the protection afforded to the policy holders and other claimants.

Part IV

D/6.   Conditions for establishment and operation of branches and agencies of foreign insurers (transfers).

1.   The transfer of all amounts which the statutory or administrative controls governing insurance do not require to be kept in the country shall be free.

2.   The insurers from a Member State who execute direct insurance transactions in another Member State through one or more branches or through agents shall be authorised, insofar as such insurers, their branches or agents have no adequate funds available in that country, to transfer to that country such amounts as they require to continue to meet the legal liabilities and/or contractual obligations arising from such transactions.

3.   In accordance with item F/1 of the List of Current Invisible Operations, the transfer of profits arising out of direct insurance operations shall be free. Profits shall be understood to mean the surplus available after providing for liabilities in respect of all legal and/or contractual obligations.

Annex II to Annex A

CONDITIONS FOR THE ESTABLISHMENT AND OPERATION OF BRANCHES, AGENCIES, ETC. OF NON-RESIDENT INVESTORS IN THE BANKING AND FINANCIAL SERVICES SECTOR

General

1.   Laws, regulations and administrative practices shall ensure equivalent treatment of domestic enterprises and of branches or agencies of non-resident enterprises operating in the field of banking or financial services (including securities dealing) so that the establishment of branches and agencies of nonresident enterprises shall not be subject to more burdensome requirements than those applying to domestic enterprises.

Authorizations

2.   Where the establishment of banks, credit institutions, securities firms, or other financial enterprises is made subject to authorizations:

a)   The competent authorities shall make available to each non-resident enterprise applying for authorization a written statement setting out fully and precisely the documents and information that the applicant must supply for the purpose of obtaining authorization, and shall ensure that any procedures to be followed prior to the lodging of an application are straightforward and expeditious;

b)   Where in addition to legal, financial, accounting and technical requirements (e.g. requirements concerning the form of the undertaking, qualifications of directors or managers, etc) authorization is also subject to other criteria, the competent authorities shall inform applicant enterprises of such criteria at the time of their application and shall apply these criteria in the same way to both domestic and non-resident enterprises;

c)   The competent authorities shall decide on each application for authorization from a non-resident enterprise not later than six months from the date of which the application has been completed in all particulars and shall without further delay notify the enterprise of their decisions;

d)   Where the competent authorities ask a non-resident enterprise for modifications to a completed application for authorisation, they shall inform the enterprise of the reasons for seeking such modifications and shall do so under the same conditions as for a domestic enterprise;

e) Where an application for authorisation by a non-resident enterprise is refused, the competent authorities shall advise the enterprise of the reasons for their decision and shall do so under the same conditions as for a domestic enterprise;

f) Where authorisation is refused, or where the competent authorities have not dealt with an application upon the expiry of the period of six months provided for under sub-paragraph c) above, non-resident enterprises shall have the same right of appeal as domestic enterprises.

Representation

3. An enterprise from one Member country operating in another Member country may appoint as its representative any competent person who is domiciled and actually resident in that other country, irrespective of his nationality.

Representative Offices

4. a) An enterprise from one Member country may establish a representative office in another Member country, subject to advance notification to the other Member country;

b) A representative office shall be permitted to promote business on behalf of its parent enterprise.

Self-Employed Intermediaries

5. Members shall impose no restrictions upon the nationality of persons authorised to act as intermediaries in banking and financial services activities, to operate in any segment of the markets relating to those activities or to become members of institutions such as professional associations, securities or other exchanges or markets, self-regulatory bodies of securities or other market intermediaries.

Membership of Associations or Regulatory Bodies

6. Members shall be responsible for assuring that discrimination by nationality is not practised in their jurisdiction as to conditions for membership in any private professional association, self-regulatory body, securities exchange or market, or other private association, membership in which it is necessary to engage in banking or financial services on an equal basis with domestic enterprises or natural persons, or which confers particular privileges or advantages in providing such services.

Prudential Considerations

7. Domestic laws, regulations and administrative practices needed to assure the soundness of the financial system or to protect depositors, savers and other claimants shall not prevent the establishment of branches or agencies of non-resident enterprises on terms and conditions equivalent to those applying to domestic enterprises operating in the field of banking or financial services.

Financial Requirements for Establishment

8.   a) Where financial requirements of any kind are imposed for the establishment of a branch or agency of a non-resident enterprise to engage in banking or financial services, the total amount of such financial requirements shall be no more than that required of a domestic enterprise to engage in similar activities.

   b) Any financial requirement may be met by payment in the currency of the host country.

   c) Any financial requirement may be applied to more than one branch or agency of a non-resident enterprise, but the total of the financial requirements to be furnished by all the branches and agencies of the same non-resident enterprise shall be no more than that required of a domestic enterprise to engage in similar activities.

   d) Whenever a ratio or other measure is used for prudential or other purposes, for example, for assessing the liquidity, solvency or foreign exchange position of a branch or agency of a non-resident enterprise, full account shall be taken of the total amount of any financial requirements that have been met in the establishment of such branches or agencies and of any financial contribution of the same nature that has been provided in excess of such requirements.

   e) Whenever a ratio measure is used for prudential or other purposes, the ratio applied to the branches or agencies of non-resident enterprises shall be no less favourable than that applied to domestic enterprises, and shall not differ in any way other than in the replacement of paid-up capital for domestic enterprises by the total amount of any financial requirements that have been met in the establishment of branches or agencies of non-resident enterprises and of any financial contribution of the same nature that has been provided in excess of such requirements.

   f) Any other measures used for prudential or other purposes shall be no less favourable to the branches and agencies of non-resident enterprises than to domestic enterprises.

Annex III to Annex A

AIR TRANSPORT

C/4.   Air transport, passengers and freights, including chartering.

Payment by passengers of international air tickets and excess luggage charges; payment of international air freight charges and chartered flights.

Remark: Each Member shall authorise residents of other Member States and its own residents to use its national currency to make the necessary payments on their own account within its own territory in respect of this item.

Annex IV to Annex A

INTERNATIONAL MOVEMENT OF BANK-NOTES AND TRAVELLERS' CHEQUES, EXCHANGE OF MEANS OF PAYMENT BY TRAVELLERS AND USE OF CASH CARDS AND CREDIT CARDS ABROAD

1.   Import of domestic bank-notes

When entering a Member State, non-resident travellers shall be automatically permitted to import at least the equivalent of 1250 units of account in that Member's bank-notes. Resident travellers returning to their country of residence shall be automatically permitted to import bank-notes of that State up to the total amount exported on their departure therefrom, or lawfully acquired during their stay abroad.

2.   Export of domestic bank-notes

When leaving a Member State, resident and non-resident travellers shall be automatically permitted to export at least the equivalent of 150 units of account per person per journey in that Member's bank-notes. No justification shall be required concerning such export.

3.   Import of travellers' cheques and foreign bank-notes

When entering a Member State, resident and non-resident travellers shall be automatically permitted to import foreign bank-notes and travellers' cheques regardless of the currency in which they are denominated. This provision does not imply an obligation for the authorities of Member States to provide for the purchase or exchange of travellers' cheques and foreign bank-notes so imported beyond that in paragraph 5 below.

4.   Export of travellers' cheques and foreign bank-notes

a)   Residents

When leaving a Member State, resident travellers shall be automatically permitted to acquire and to export in a proportion left to the traveller the equivalent of at least 1250 units of account per person per journey in travellers' cheques, regardless of the currency in which they are denominated, and in foreign banknotes. No request for justification shall be made concerning such acquisition and export. Under this provision, foreign exchange dealers shall be free, within the limits of their national regulations, to obtain foreign bank-notes and to sell them to travellers. The present provision does not imply any obligation for the authorities themselves to provide such travellers' cheques or foreign bank-notes either directly to the travellers or to foreign exchange dealers.

b)   Non-residents

When leaving a Member State, non-resident travellers shall he automatically permitted to export travellers' cheques, regardless of the currency in which they are denominated, and foreign bank-notes up to the equivalent of the total previously imported or lawfully acquired during their stay.

5.   Exchange of means of payment: non-residents

Exchange into Member States' currencies.

Non-resident travellers shall be permitted to exchange into means of payment in the currency of any foreign Member State:

   i)   Means of payment in the currency of another foreign Member State which can be shown to have been lawfully imported; and

   ii)   Domestic bank-notes which can be shown to have been acquired against such means of payment in the currency of another foreign Member State during their stay.

Under this provision foreign exchange dealers shall be free, within the limits of their national regulations, to exchange the means of payment in question. The provision does not imply any obligation for the authorities themselves to provide such means of payment either directly to the travellers or to foreign exchange dealers.

6.   Use of cash cards and credit cards abroad

The principle of the free use of cash cards and credit cards abroad provided for under Section G of the Code does not imply any obligation for the agencies issuing cash cards or credit cards to amend the rules governing the use of such cards for the settlement of expenditure relating to travel or stays abroad or for obtaining cash abroad.

Annex V to Annex A

FILMS

Aid to production

1.   For cultural reasons, systems of aid to the production of printed films for cinema exhibition may be maintained provided that they do not significantly distort international competition in export markets.

Screen quotas for printed films for cinema exhibition

2.   For full-length films made or dubbed in the language of the importing country, internal quantitative regulations may be maintained in the form of screen quotas requiring the exhibition of films of domestic origin during a specific minimum proportion of the total screen time actually utilised over a specified period of not less than one year.[10]

3.   Original versions of feature films produced in other Member States in a language foreign to that of the importing country shall be:

   i)   *Excluded from the calculation of the screen quota for domestic films; or*

   ii)   *Admitted for exhibition in specialised cinemas which, as a general rule, are not obliged to observe the screen quotas; or*

   iii)   *Admitted for exhibition in cinemas other than those mentioned in ii) under a global screen quota instead of a screen quota applying to individual cinemas.*

4.   Short information or documentary films produced in other Member States shall gradually be excluded from the calculation of the screen quota for domestic films.

Freedom from duties, deposits or taxes

5.   Printed films shall not be subject to any duties, deposits, or taxes which against imported films.

6.   Short information or documentary films produced in other Member States

---

[10]Any screen quotas as defined in this provision shall be calculated on the basis of screen time per cinema per year or the equivalent thereof. With the exception of screen time reserved for films of domestic origin, screen times shall not be allocated formally or in effect among sources of supply.

shall enjoy certain of the benefits if any, granted to domestic films in this category (e.g. substantial prize awards according to merit, or tax relief on showing).

7.   Provided they are intended solely for non-commercial exhibition and are imported by organisations approved by the competent authorities of the country concerned for the purpose of importing such films free from import duties and import taxes, the following categories of films produced in other Member States shall be free from those duties and taxes:

a)   Newsreels, at least for two copies of each subject;

b)   Educational, scientific or cultural film recognised as such by:

   i)   *the importing and the exporting country;*

   ii)   *or the Fédération Internationale des Archives du Film (FIAF);*

c)   Tourist publicity films, provided they comply with the conditions laid down in Articles 13 c) and 14 of the Annex to the Decision of the Council dated 20th February, 1968, concerning administrative facilities in favour of international tourism [C(68)32]. (See Note over page).

Co-production

8.   The regulations defining domestically produced films shall be such that any film produced under an international co-production arrangement shall automatically enjoy, in all the Member States that are parties thereto, treatment as favourable as that given to domestically produced films.

NOTES

Tourist publicity films. Conditions for import free of import duties and import taxes, laid down in Council Decision C(68)32. [See paragraph 7 c) of Annex V.]

1.   Article 13 c) of the annex to the Decision of the Council of 20th February, 1968, concerning the importation of tourist publicity documents and articles [C(68)32], lays down that, subject to the conditions laid down in Article 14 of the Annex to the Decision, the following articles (inter alia) shall be admitted temporarily free of import duties and import taxes, without entering into a bond in respect of those duties and taxes, or depositing those duties and taxes, when imported from one of the States chiefly for the purpose of encouraging the public to visit that State, *inter alia* to attend cultural, touristic, sporting, religious or professional meetings or demonstrations held in that State:

Documentary films, records, tape recordings and other sound recordings intended for use in performances at which no charge is made, but excluding those whose subjects lend themselves to commercial advertising and those which are on general sale in the State of importation.

2. Article 14 of the Annex to the Council Decision lays down the facilities provided in Article 13 shall be granted on the following conditions:

a) The articles must be dispatched either by an official tourist agency or by a national tourist publicity agency affiliated therewith. Proof shall be furnished by presenting to the customs authorities of the State of import a declaration made out in accordance with the model in Appendix 1 of the Decision, by the dispatching agency. A list of official national tourist agencies in member States is given in Appendix II of the Decision;

b) The articles must be imported for, and on the responsibility of, either the accredited representative of the official national tourist agency of the State of dispatch, or of the correspondent appointed by the aforesaid agency and approved by the customs authorities of the importing State. The responsibility of the accredited representative or the approved correspondent includes, in particular, the payment of the import duties and taxes which will be chargeable if the conditions laid down in the Decision are not fulfilled;

c) The articles imported must be re-exported without alteration by the importing agency. If the articles granted temporary free admission are destroyed in accordance with the conditions laid down by the customs authorities, the importer shall nevertheless be freed from the obligation to re-export.

3. Finally, Article 14 provides that the privilege of temporary free admission shall be granted for a period of eighteen months from the date of importation or for such further period as the customs authorities may in special circumstances allow.

* * *

MODEL TAX CONVENTION ON INCOME AND ON CAPITAL[*]

> The Model Tax Convention on Income and on Capital was prepared by the Organisation for Economic Co-operation and Development Committee on Fiscal Affairs. The first version of the Model Convention was issued in 1963. Revised versions of the Convention were published in 1977 and 1992. The text reproduced in the present volume contains all amendments up to 1 March 1994. The commentaries on the articles of the Convention have not been reproduced in this volume.

TITLE OF THE CONVENTION

Convention between (State A) and (State B)
with respect to taxes on income and on capital[1]

PREAMBLE OF THE CONVENTION[2]

CHAPTER I
SCOPE OF THE CONVENTION

Article 1
Personal scope

This Convention shall apply to persons who are residents of one or both of the Contracting States.

Article 2
Taxes covered

1.   This Convention shall apply to taxes on income and on capital imposed on behalf of a Contracting State or of its political subdivisions or local authorities, irrespective of the manner in which they are levied.

---

[*]Source: Organisation for Economic Co-operation and Development (1994). *Model Tax Convention on Income and on Capital* (Paris: OECD) [Note added by the editor].

[1]States wishing to do so may follow the widespread practice of including in the title a reference to either the avoidance of double taxation or to both the avoidance of double taxation and the prevention of fiscal evasion.

[2]The Preamble of the Convention shall be drafted in accordance with the constitutional procedure of both Contracting States.

2.   There shall be regarded as taxes on income and on capital all taxes imposed on total income, on total capital, or on elements of income or of capital, including taxes on gains from the alienation of movable or immovable property, taxes on the total amounts of wages or salaries paid by enterprises, as well as taxes on capital appreciation.

3.   The existing taxes to which the Convention shall apply are in particular:

     a)   (in State A): . . . .

     b)   (in State B): . . . .

4.   The Convention shall apply also to any identical or substantially similar taxes which are imposed after the date of signature of the Convention in addition to, or in place of, the existing taxes. At the end of each year, the competent authorities of the Contracting States shall notify each other of changes which have been made in their respective taxation laws.

CHAPTER II
DEFINITIONS

Article 3
General definitions

1.   For the purposes of this Convention, unless the context otherwise requires:

     a)   the term "person" includes an individual, a company and any other body of persons;

     b)   the term "company" means any body corporate or any entity which is treated as a body corporate for tax purposes;

     c)   the terms "enterprise of a Contracting State" and "enterprise of the other Contracting State" means respectively an enterprise carried on by a resident of a Contracting State and an enterprise carried on by a resident of the other Contracting State;

     d)   the term "international traffic" means any transport by a ship or aircraft operated by an enterprise which has its place of effective management in a Contracting State, except when the ship or aircraft is operated solely between places in the other Contracting State;

     e)   the term "competent authority" means:

          (i)   (in State A): . . . .

          (ii)   (in State B): . . . .

     f)   the term "national" means:

> *(i)*   any individual possessing the nationality of a Contracting State;
>
> *(ii)*   any legal person, partnership or association deriving its status as such from the lows in force in a Contracting State.

2.   As regards the application of the Convention by a Contracting State any term not defined therein shall, unless the context otherwise requires, have the meaning which it has under the law of that State concerning the taxes to which the Convention applies.

Article 4
Resident

1.   For the purposes of this Convention, the term "resident of a Contracting State" means any person who, under the laws of that State, is liable to tax therein by reason of his domicile, residence, place of management or any other criterion of a similar nature. But this term does not include any person who is liable to tax in that State in respect only of income from sources in that State or capital situated therein.

2.   Where by reason of the provisions of paragraph 1 an individual is a resident of both Contracting States, then his status shall be determined as follows:

    a)   he shall be deemed to be a resident of the State in which he has a permanent home available to him; if he has a permanent home available to him in both States, he shall be deemed to be a resident of the State with which his personal and economic relations are closer (centre of vital interest);

    b)   if the State in which he has his centre of vital interests cannot be determined, or if he has not a permanent home available to him in either State, he shall be deemed to be a resident of the State in which he has an habitual abode;

    c)   if he has an habitual abode in both States or in neither of them, he shall be deemed to be a resident of the State of which he is a national;

    d)   if he is a national of both States or of neither of them, the competent authorities of the Contracting States shall settle the question by mutual agreement.

3.   Where by reason of the provisions of paragraph 1 a person other than an individual is a resident of both Contracting States, then it shall be deemed to be a resident of the State in which its place of effective management is situated.

Article 5
Permanent establishment

1.   For the purposes of this Convention, the term "permanent establishment" means a fixed place of business through which the business of an enterprise is wholly or partly carried on.

2.   The term "permanent establishment" includes especially:

    a)   a place of management;

    b)   a branch;

    c)   an office;

    d)   a factory;

    e)   a workshop, and

    f)   a mine, an oil or gas well, a quarry or any other place of extraction of natural resources.

3.   A building site or construction or installation project constitutes a permanent establishment only if it lasts more than twelve months.

4.   Notwithstanding the preceding provisions of this Article, the term "permanent establishment" shall be deemed not to include:

    a)   the use of facilities solely for the purpose of storage, display or delivery of goods or merchandise belonging to the enterprise;

    b)   the maintenance of a stock of goods or merchandise belonging to the enterprise solely for the purpose of storage, display or delivery;

    c)   the maintenance of a stock of goods or merchandise belonging to the enterprise solely for the purpose of processing by another enterprise;

    d)   the maintenance of a fixed place of business solely for the purpose of purchasing goods or merchandise or of collecting information, for the enterprise;

    e)   the maintenance of a fixed place of business solely for the purpose of carrying on, for the enterprise, any other activity of a preparatory or auxiliary character;

    f)   the maintenance of a fixed place of business solely for any combination of activities mentioned in subparagraphs *a)* to *e)* provided that the overall activity of the fixed place of business resulting from this combination is of a preparatory or auxiliary character.

5.   Notwithstanding the provisions of paragraphs 1 and 2, where a person -- other than an agent of an independent status to whom paragraph 6 applies -- is acting on behalf of an enterprise and has, and habitually exercises, in a Contracting State an authority to conclude contracts in the name of the enterprise, that enterprise shall be deemed to have a permanent establishment in that State in respect of any activities which that person undertakes for the enterprise, unless the activities of such person are limited to those mentioned in paragraph 4 which, if exercised through a fixed place of business, would not make this fixed place of business a permanent establishment under the provisions of that paragraph.

6.   An enterprise shall not be deemed to have a permanent establishment in a Contracting State merely because it carries on business in that State through a broker, general commission agent or any other agent of an independent status, provided that such persons are acting in the ordinary course of their business.

7.   The fact that a company which is a resident of a Contracting State controls or is controlled by a company which is a resident of the other Contracting State, or which carries on business in that other State (whether through a permanent establishment or otherwise), shall not of itself constitute either company a permanent establishment of the other.

CHAPTER III
TAXATION OF INCOME

Article 6
Income from immovable property

1.   Income derived by a resident of a Contracting State from immovable property (including income from agriculture or forestry) situated in the other Contracting State may be taxed in that other State.

2.   The term "immovable property" shall have the meaning which it has under the law of the Contracting State in which the property in question is situated. The term shall in any case include property accessory to immovable property, livestock and equipment used in agriculture and forestry, rights to which the provisions of general law respecting landed property apply, usufruct of immovable property and rights to variable or fixed payments as consideration for the working of, or the right to work, mineral deposits, sources and other natural resources; ships, boats and aircraft shall not be regarded as immovable property.

3.   The provisions of paragraph 1 shall apply to income derived from the direct use, letting, or use in any other form of immovable property.

4.   The provisions of paragraphs 1 and 3 shall also apply to the income from immovable property of an enterprise and to income from immovable property used for the performance of independent personal services.

Article 7
Business profits

1.   The profits of an enterprise of a Contracting State shall be taxable only in that State unless the enterprise carries on business in the other Contracting State through a permanent establishment situated therein. If the enterprise carries on business as aforesaid, the profits of the enterprise may be taxed in the other State but only so much of them as is attributable to that permanent establishment.

2.   Subject to the provisions of paragraph 3, where an enterprise of a Contracting State carries on business in the other Contracting State through a permanent establishment situated therein, there shall in each Contracting State be attributed to that permanent establishment the profits which it might be expected to make if it were a distinct and separate enterprise engaged in the same or similar activities under the same or similar conditions and dealing wholly independently with the enterprise of which it is a permanent establishment.

3.   In determining the profits of a permanent establishment, there shall be allowed as deductions expenses which are incurred for the purposes of the permanent establishment, including executive and general administrative expenses so incurred, whether in the State in which the permanent establishment is situated or elsewhere.

4.   In so far as it has been customary in a Contracting State to determine the profits to be attributed to a permanent establishment on the basis of an apportionment of the total profits of the enterprise to its various parts, nothing in paragraph 2 shall preclude that Contracting State from determining the profits to be taxed by such an apportionment as may be customary; the method of apportionment adopted shall, however, be such that the result shall be in accordance with the principles contained in this Article.

5.   No profits shall be attributed to a permanent establishment by reason of the mere purchase by that permanent establishment of goods or merchandise for the enterprise.

6.   For the purposes of the preceding paragraphs, the profits to be attributed to the permanent establishment shall be determined by the same method year by year unless there is good and sufficient reason to the contrary.

7.   Where profits include items of income which are dealt with separately in other Articles of this Convention, then the provisions of those Articles shall not be affected by the provisions of this Article.

Article 8
Shipping, inland waterways transport and air transport

1.   Profits from the operation of ships or aircraft in international traffic shall be taxable only in the Contracting State in which the place of effective management of the enterprise is situated.

2.   Profits from the operation of boats engaged in inland waterways transport shall be taxable only in the Contracting State in which the place of effective management of the enterprise is situated.

3.   If the place of effective management of a shipping enterprise or of an inland waterways transport enterprise is aboard a ship or boat, then it shall be deemed to be situated in the Contracting State in which the home harbour of the ship or boat is situated, or, if there is no such home harbour, in the Contracting State of which the operator of the ship or boat is a resident.

4.   The provisions of paragraph 1 shall also apply to profits from the participation in a pool, a joint business or an international operating agency.

Article 9
Associated enterprises

1.   Where

a)   an enterprise of a Contracting State participates directly or indirectly, in the management, control or capital of an enterprise of the other Contracting State, or

b)   the same persons participate directly or indirectly in the management, control or capital of an enterprise of a Contracting State and an enterprise of the other Contracting State,

and in either case conditions are made or imposed between the two enterprises in their commercial or financial relations which differ from those which would be made between independent enterprises, then any profits which would, but for those conditions, have accrued to one of the enterprises, but, by reason of those conditions, have not so accrued, may be included in the profits of that enterprise and taxed accordingly.

2.   Where a Contracting State includes in the profits of an enterprise of that State -- and taxes accordingly -- profits on which an enterprise of the other Contracting State has been charged to tax in that other State and the profits so included are profits which would have accrued to the enterprise of the first-mentioned State if the conditions made between the two enterprises had been those which would have been made between independent enterprises, then that other State shall make an appropriate adjustment to the amount of the tax charged therein on those profits. In determining such adjustment, due regard shall be had to the other provisions of this Convention and the competent authorities of the Contracting States shall if necessary consult each other.

Article 10
Dividends

1.   Dividends paid by a company which is a resident of a Contracting State to a resident of the other Contracting State may be taxed in that other State.

2.   However, such dividends may also be taxed in the Contracting State of which the company paying the dividends is a resident and according to the laws of that State, but if the recipient is the beneficial owner of the dividends the tax so charged shall not exceed:

a)   5 per cent of the gross amount of the dividends if the beneficial owner is a company (other than a partnership) which holds directly at least 25 per cent of the capital of the company paying the dividends;

b)   15 per cent of the gross amount of the dividends in all other cases.

The competent authorities of the Contracting States shall by mutual agreement settle the mode of application of these limitations.

This paragraph shall not affect the taxation of the company in respect of the profits out of which the dividends are paid.

3.   The term "dividends" as used in this Article means income from shares, "jouissance" shares or "jouissance" rights, mining shares, founders' shares or other rights, not being debt-claims, participating in profits, as well as income from other corporate rights which is subjected to the same taxation treatment as income from shares by the laws of the State of which the company making the distribution is a resident.

4.   The provisions of paragraphs 1 and 2 shall not apply if the beneficial owner of the dividends, being a resident of a Contracting State, carries on business in the other Contracting State of which the company paying the dividends is a resident, through a permanent establishment situated therein, or performs in that other State independent personal services from a fixed base situated therein, and the holding in respect of which the dividends are paid is effectively connected with such permanent establishment or fixed base. In such case the provisions of Article 7 or Article 14, as the case may be, shall apply.

5.   Where a company which is a resident of a Contracting State derives profits or income from the other Contracting State, that other State may not impose any tax on the dividends paid by the company, except in so far as such dividends are paid to a resident of that other State or in so far as the holding in respect of which the dividends are paid is effectively connected with a permanent establishment or a fixed base situated in that other State, nor subject the company's undistributed profits to a tax on the company's undistributed profits even if the dividends paid or the undistributed profits consist wholly or partly of profits or income arising in such other State.

Article 11
Interest

1.   Interest arising in a Contracting State and paid to a resident of the other Contracting State may be taxed in that other State.

2.   However, such interest may also be taxed in the Contracting State in which it arises and according to the laws of that State, but if the recipient is the beneficial owner of the interest the tax so charged shall not exceed 10 per cent of the gross amount of the interest. The competent authorities of the Contracting State shall by mutual agreement settle the mode of application of this limitation.

3.   The term "interest" as used in this Article means income from debt-claims of every kind, whether or not secured by mortgage and whether or not carrying a right to participate in the

debtor's profits, and in particular, income from government securities and income from bonds or debentures, including premiums and prizes attaching to such securities, bonds or debentures. Penalty charges for late payment shall not be regarded as interest for the purpose of this Article.

4.   The provisions of paragraphs 1 and 2 shall not apply if the beneficial owner of the interest, being a resident of a Contracting State, carries on business in the other Contracting State in which the interest arises, through a permanent establishment situated therein, or performs in that other State independent personal services from a fixed base situated therein, and the debt-claim in respect of which the interest is paid is effectively connected with such permanent establishment or fixed base. In such case the provisions of Article 7 or Article 14, as the case may be, shall apply.

5.   Interest shall be deemed to arise in a Contracting State when the payer is that State itself, a political subdivision, a local authority or a resident of that State. Where, however, the person paying the interest, whether he is a resident of a Contracting State or not, has in a Contracting State a permanent establishment or a fixed base in connection with which the indebtedness on which the interest is paid was incurred, and such interest is borne by such permanent establishment or fixed base, then such interest shall be deemed to arise in the State in which the permanent establishment or fixed base is situated.

6.   Where, by reason of a special relationship between the payer and the beneficial owner or between both of them and some other person, the amount of the interest, having regard to the debt-claim for which it is paid, exceeds the amount which would have been agreed upon by the payer and the beneficial owner in the absence of such relationship, the provisions of this Article shall apply only to the last-mentioned amount. In such case, the excess part of the payments shall remain taxable according to the laws of each Contracting State, due regard being had to the other provisions of this Convention.

Article 12
Royalties

1.   Royalties arising in a Contracting State and paid to a resident of the other Contracting State shall be taxable only in that other State if such resident is the beneficial owner or the royalties.

2.   The term "royalties" as used in this Article means payments of any kind received as a consideration for the use of, or the right to use, any copyright of literary, artistic or scientific work including cinematograph films, any patent, trade mark, design or model, plan, secret formula or process, or for information concerning industrial, commercial or scientific experience.

3.   The provisions of paragraph 1 shall not apply if the beneficial owner of the royalties, being a resident of a Contracting State, carries on business in the other Contracting State in which the royalties arise, through a permanent establishment situated therein, or performs in that other State independent personal services from a fixed base situated therein, and the right or property in respect of which the royalties are paid is effectively connected with such permanent

establishment or fixed base. In such case the provisions of Article 7 or Article 14, as the case may be, shall apply.

4.   Where, by reason of a special relationship between the payer and the beneficial owner or between both of them and some other person, the amount of the royalties, having regard to the use, right or information for which they are paid, exceeds the amount which would have been agreed upon by the payer and the beneficial owner in the absence of such relationship, the provisions of this Article shall apply only to the last-mentioned amount. In such case, the excess part of the payments shall remain taxable according to the laws of each Contracting State, due regard being had to the other provisions of this Convention.

Article 13
Capital gains

1.   Gains derived by a resident of a Contracting State from the alienation of immovable property referred to in Article 6 and situated in the other Contracting State may be taxed in that other State.

2.   Gains from the alienation of movable property forming part of the business property of a permanent establishment which an enterprise of a Contracting State has in the other Contracting State or of movable property pertaining to a fixed base available to a resident of a Contracting State in the other Contracting State for the purpose of performing independent personal services, including such gains from the alienation of such a permanent establishment (alone or with the whole enterprise) or of such fixed base, may be taxed in that other State.

3.   Gains from the alienation of ships or aircraft operated in international traffic, boats engaged in inland waterways transport or movable property pertaining to the operation of such ships, aircraft or boats, shall be taxable only in the Contracting State in which the place of effective management of the enterprise is situated.

4.   Gains from the alienation of any property other than that referred to in paragraphs 1, 2 and 3, shall be taxable only in the Contracting State of which the alienator is a resident.

Article 14
Independent personal services

1.   Income derived by a resident of a Contracting State in respect of professional services or other activities of an independent character shall be taxable only in that State unless he has a fixed base regularly available to him in the other Contracting State for the purpose of performing his activities. If he has such a fixed base, the income may be taxed in the other State but only so much of it as is attributable to that fixed base.

2.   The term "professional services" includes especially independent scientific, literary, artistic, educational or teaching activities as well as the independent activities of physicians, lawyers, engineers, architects, dentists and accountants.

Article 15
Dependent personal services

1. Subject to the provisions of Articles 16, 18 and 19, salaries, wages and other similar remuneration derived by a resident of a Contracting State in respect of an employment shall be taxable only in that State unless the employment is exercised in the other Contracting State. If the employment is so exercised, such remuneration as is derived therefrom may be taxed in that other State.

2. Notwithstanding the provisions of paragraph 1, remuneration derived by a resident of a Contracting State in respect of an employment exercised in the other Contracting State shall be taxable only in the first-mentioned State if:

   a)   the recipient is present in the other State for a period or periods not exceeding in the aggregate 183 days in any twelve month period commencing or ending in the fiscal year concerned, and

   b)   the remuneration is paid by, or on behalf of, an employer who is not a resident of the other State, and

   c)   the remuneration is not borne by a permanent establishment or a fixed base which the employer has in the other State.

3. Notwithstanding the preceding provisions of this Article, remuneration derived in respect of an employment exercised aboard a ship or aircraft operated in international traffic, or aboard a boat engaged in inland waterways transport, may be taxed in the Contracting State in which the place of effective management of the enterprise is situated.

Article 16
Directors' fees

Directors' fees and other similar payments derived by a resident of a Contracting State in his capacity as a member of the board of directors of a company which is a resident of the other Contracting State may be taxed in that other State.

Article 17
Artistes and sportsmen

1. Notwithstanding the provisions of Articles 14 and 15, income derived by a resident of a Contracting State as an entertainer, such as a theatre, motion picture, radio or television artiste, or a musician, or as a sportsman, from his personal activities as such exercised in the other Contracting State, may be taxed in that other State.

2. Where income in respect of personal activities exercised by an entertainer or a sportsman in his capacity as such accrues not to the entertainer or sportsman himself but to another person,

that income may, notwithstanding the provisions of Articles 7, 14 and 15, be taxed in the Contracting State in which the activities of the entertainer or sportsman are exercised.

Article 18
Pensions

Subject to the provisions of paragraph 2 of Article 19, pensions and other similar remuneration paid to a resident of a Contracting State in consideration of past employment shall be taxable only in that State.

Article 19
Government service

1. *a)* Salaries, wages and other similar remuneration, other than a pension, paid by a Contracting State or a political subdivision or a local authority thereof to an individual in respect of services rendered to that State or subdivision or authority shall be taxable only in that State.

   b) However, such salaries, wages and other similar remuneration shall be taxable only in the other Contracting State if the services are rendered in that State and the individual is a resident of that State who:

   (i) is a national of that State; or

   (ii) did not become a resident of that State solely for the purpose of rendering the services.

2. *a)* Any pension paid by, or out of funds created by, a Contracting State or a political subdivision or a local authority thereof to an individual in respect of services rendered to that State or subdivision or authority shall be taxable only in that State.

   b) However, such pension shall be taxable only in the other Contracting State if the individual is a resident of, and a national of, that State.

3. The provisions of Articles 15, 16 and 18 shall apply to salaries, wages and other similar remuneration, and to pensions, in respect of services rendered in connection with a business carried on by a Contracting State or a political subdivision or a local authority thereof.

Article 20
Students

Payments which a student or business apprentice who is or was immediately before visiting a Contracting State a resident of the other Contracting State and who is present in the first-mentioned State solely for the purpose of his education or training receives for the purpose of his maintenance, education or training shall not be taxed in that State, provided that such payments arise from sources outside that State.

Article 21
Other income

1.   Items of income of a resident of a Contracting State, wherever arising, not dealt with in the foregoing Articles of this Convention shall be taxable only in that State.

2.   The provisions of paragraph 1 shall not apply to income, other than income from immovable property as defined in paragraph 2 of Article 6, if the recipient of such income, being a resident of a Contracting State, carries on business in the other Contracting State through a permanent establishment situated therein, or performs in that other State independent personal services from a fixed base situated therein, and the right or property in respect of which the income is paid is effectively connected with such permanent establishment or fixed base. In such case the provisions of Article 7 or Article 14, as the case may be, shall apply.

CHAPTER IV
TAXATION OF CAPITAL

Article 22
Capital

1.   Capital represented by immovable property referred to in Article 6, owned by a resident of a Contracting State and situated in the other Contracting State, may be taxed in that other State.

2.   Capital represented by movable property forming part of the business property of a permanent establishment which an enterprise of a Contracting State has in the other Contracting State or by movable property pertaining to a fixed base available to a resident of a Contracting State in the other Contracting State for the purpose of performing independent personal services, may be taxed in that other State.

3.   Capital represented by ships and aircraft operated in international traffic and by boats engaged in inland waterways transport, and by movable property pertaining to the operation of such ships, aircraft and boats, shall be taxable only in the Contracting State in which the place of effective management of the enterprise is situated.

4.   All other elements of capital of a resident of a Contracting State shall be taxable only in that State.

CHAPTER V
METHODS FOR ELIMINATION OF DOUBLE TAXATION

Article 23A
Exemption method

1.   Where a resident of a Contracting State derives income or owns capital which, in accordance with the provisions of this Convention, may be taxed in the other Contracting State, the first-mentioned State shall, subject to the provisions of paragraphs 2 and 3, exempt such income or capital from tax.

2.   Where a resident of a Contracting State derives items of income which, in accordance with the provisions of Articles 10 and 11, may be taxed in the other Contracting State, the first-mentioned State shall allow as a deduction from the tax on the income of that resident an amount equal to the tax paid in that other State. Such deduction shall not, however, exceed that part of the tax, as computed before the deduction is given, which is attributable to such items of income derived from that other State.

3.   Where in accordance with any provision of the Convention income derived or capital owned by a resident of a Contracting State is exempt from tax in that State, such State may nevertheless, in calculating the amount of tax on the remaining income or capital of such resident, take into account the exempted income or capital.

Article 23B
Credit method

1.   Where a resident of a Contracting State derives income or owns capital which, in accordance with the provisions of this Convention, may be taxed in the other Contracting State, the first-mentioned State shall allow:

   a)   as a deduction from the tax on the income of that resident, an amount equal to the income tax paid in that other State;

   b)   as a deduction from the tax on the capital of that resident, an mount equal to the capital tax paid in that other State.

Such deduction in either case shall not, however, exceed that part of the income tax or capital tax, as computed before the deduction is given which is attributable, as the case may be, to the income or the capital which may be taxed in that other State.

2.   Where in accordance with any provision of the Convention income derived or capital owned by a resident of a Contracting State is exempt from tax in that State, such State may nevertheless, in calculating the amount of tax on the remaining income or capital of such resident, take into account the exempted income or capital.

CHAPTER VI
SPECIAL PROVISIONS

Article 24
Non-discrimination

1.   Nationals of a Contracting State shall not be subjected in the other Contracting State to any taxation or any requirement connected therewith, which is other or more burdensome than the taxation and connected requirements to which nationals of that other State in the same circumstances, in particular with respect to residence, are or may be subjected. This provision shall, notwithstanding the provisions of Article 1, also apply to persons who are not residents of one or both of the Contracting States.

2.   Stateless persons who are residents of a Contracting State shall not be subjected in either Contracting State to any taxation or any requirement connected therewith, which is other or more burdensome than the taxation and connected requirements to which nationals of the State concerned in the same circumstances are or may be subjected.

3.   The taxation on a permanent establishment which an enterprise of a Contacting State has in the other Contracting State shall not be less favourably levied in that other State than the taxation levied on enterprises of that other State carrying on the same activities. This provision shall not be construed as obliging a Contracting State to grant to residents of the other Contracting State any personal allowances, reliefs and reductions for taxation purposes on account of civil status or family responsibilities which it grants to its own residents.

4.   Except where the provisions of paragraph 1 of Article 9, paragraph 6 of Article 11, or paragraph 4 of Article 12, apply, interest, royalties and other disbursements paid by an enterprise of a Contracting State to a resident of the other Contracting State shall, for the purpose of determining the taxable profits of such enterprise, be deductible under the same conditions as if they had been paid to a resident of the first-mentioned State. Similarly, any debts of an enterprise of a Contracting State to a resident of the other Contracting State shall, for the purpose of determining the taxable capital of such enterprise, be deductible under the same conditions as if they had been contracted to a resident of the first-mentioned State.

5.   Enterprises of a Contracting State, the capital of which is wholly or partly owned or controlled, directly or indirectly, by one or more residents of the other Contracting State, shall not be subjected in the first-mentioned State to any taxation or any requirement connected therewith which is other or more burdensome than the taxation and connected requirements to which other similar enterprises of the first-mentioned State are or may be subjected.

6.   The provisions of this Article shall, notwithstanding the provisions of Article 2, apply to taxes of every kind and description.

Article 25
Mutual agreement procedure

1.   Where a person considers that the actions of one or both of the Contracting States result or will result for him in taxation not in accordance with the provisions of this Convention, he may, irrespective of the remedies provided by the domestic law of those States, present his case to the competent authority of the Contracting State of which he is a resident or, if his case comes under paragraph 1 of Article 24, to that of the Contracting State of which he is a national. The case must be presented within three years from the first notification of the action resulting in taxation not in accordance with the provisions of the Convention.

2.   The competent authority shall endeavour, if the objection appears to it to be justified and if it is not itself able to arrive at a satisfactory solution, to resolve the case by mutual agreement with the competent authority of the other Contracting State, with a view to the avoidance of taxation which is not in accordance with the Convention. Any agreement reached shall be implemented notwithstanding any time limits in the domestic law of the Contracting States.

3.   The competent authorities of the Contracting States shall endeavour to resolve by mutual agreement any difficulties or doubts arising as to the interpretation or application of the Convention. They may also consult together for the elimination of double taxation in cases not provided for in the Convention.

4.   The competent authorities of the Contracting States may communicate with each other directly for the purpose of reaching an agreement in the sense of the preceding paragraphs. When it seems advisable in order to reach agreement to have an oral exchange of opinions, such exchange may take place through a Commission consisting of representatives of the competent authorities of the Contracting States.

Article 26
Exchange of information

1.   The competent authorities of the Contracting States shall exchange such information as is necessary for carrying out the provisions of this Convention or of the domestic laws of the Contracting States concerning taxes covered by the Convention insofar as the taxation thereunder is not contrary to the Convention. The exchange of information is not restricted by Article 1. Any information received by a Contracting State shall be treated as secret in the same manner as information obtained under the domestic laws of that State and shall be disclosed only to persons or authorities (including courts and administrative bodies) involved in the assessment or collection of, the enforcement or prosecution in respect of, or the determination of appeals in relation to, the taxes covered by the Convention. Such persons or authorities shall use the information only for such purposes. They may disclose the information in public court proceedings or in judicial decisions.

2.   In no case shall the provisions of paragraph 1 be construed so as to impose on a Contracting State the obligation:

a) to carry out administrative measures at variance with the laws and administrative practice of that or of the other Contracting State;

b) to supply information which is not obtainable under the laws or in the normal course of the administration of that or of the other Contracting State;

c) to supply information which would disclose any trade, business, industrial, commercial or professional secret or trade process, or information, the disclosure of which would be contrary to public policy *(ordre public)*.

Article 27
Members of diplomatic missions and consular posts

Nothing in this Convention shall affect the fiscal privileges of members of diplomatic missions or consular posts under the general rules of international law or under the provisions of special agreements.

Article 28
Territorial extension[1]

1. This Convention may be extended, either in its entirety or with any necessary modifications [to any part of the territory of (State A) or of (State B) which is specifically excluded from the application of the Convention or], to any State or territory for whose international relations (State A) or (State B) is responsible, which imposes taxes substantially similar in character to those to which the Convention applies. Any such extension shall take effect from such date and subject to such modifications and conditions, including conditions as to termination, as may be specified and agreed between the Contracting States in notes to be exchanged through diplomatic channels or in any other manner in accordance with their constitutional procedures.

2. Unless otherwise agreed by both Contracting States, the termination of the Convention by one of them under Article 30 shall also terminate, in the manner provided for in that Article, the application of the Convention [to any part of the territory of (State A) or of (State B) or] to any State or territory to which it has been extended under this Article.

---

[1]The words between brackets are of relevance when, by special provision, a part of the territory of a Contracting State is excluded from the application of the Convention.

CHAPTER VII
FINAL PROVISIONS

Article 29
Entry into force

1.   This Convention shall be ratified and the instruments of ratification shall be exchanged at _____ as soon as possible.

2.   The Convention shall enter into force upon the exchange of instruments of ratification and its provisions shall have effect:

(*a*)   (in State A): . . . .

(*b*)   (in State B): . . . .

Article 30
Termination

This Convention shall remain in force until terminated by a Contracting State. Either Contracting State may terminate the Convention, through diplomatic channels, by giving notice of termination at least six months before the end of any calendar year after the year _____. In such event, the Convention shall cease to have effect:

a)   (In State A): . . . .

b)   (In State B): . . . .

Terminal clause[1]

* * *

---

[1]The terminal clause concerning the signing shall be drafted in accordance with the constitutional procedure of both Contracting States.

COMMON CONVENTION ON INVESTMENTS IN THE STATES OF THE CUSTOMS AND ECONOMIC UNION OF CENTRAL AFRICA[*]

The Common Convention on Investments in the States of the Central African Customs and Economic Union was adopted at Yaoundé, Cameroon, by the Council of Heads of State of the Customs and Economic Union of Central Africa, at its meeting on 14 December 1965 (Act No. 18/65-UDEAC-15 of the 14th December 1965). It entered into force on 1 April 1966. Fiscal and taxation reforms in 1992 and 1994 have modified the tax and customs incentive regimes under the Convention. The members of the Central African Customs and Economic Union (UDEAC) are Cameroon, Central African Republic, Chad, Congo, Equatorial Guinea and Gabon.

Federal Republic of Cameroon,
Central African Republic,
Republic of Congo-Brazzaville,
Republic of Gabon,
Republic of Chad.

PART I.
General guarantees.

1.   The acquired rights of any kind shall be guaranteed to undertakings lawfully established in the countries forming the Customs and Economic Union of Central Africa hereafter referred to as the "Union".

2.   Within the framework of their exchange regulations, the member States of the Union shall guarantee the free transfer of:

(a) Capital;
(b) Profits lawfully acquired;
(c) Funds arising from the transfer or winding-up of business activities.

3.   Undertakings whose capital derives from other countries, shall be able to acquire rights of any kind deemed necessary for the exercise of their activities: real property and industrial rights, concessions, official authorisations and permits, participations in government contracts

---

[*] Source: *International Legal Materials*, vol. 7, March 1968, p. 221. The text of the Convention appears also in Federal Republic of Cameroon (1966). *Official Gazette of the Federal Republic of Cameroon*, "Common Convention on Investments in the States of the Customs and Economic Union of Central Africa", 1 April 1966, pp.609-618 [Note added by the editor].

under the same conditions as undertakings in the member countries of the Union.

4.   In the exercise of their professional activities foreign employers and workers shall rank as the nationals of the member States of the Union.

They shall benefit from Labour and Social Welfare legislation under the same conditions as the nationals of the States of the Union. They may participate in trade union activities and be members of organisations for defending their professional interests within the framework of existing laws.

In addition, foreign undertakings and their management shall be represented under the same conditions as the undertakings or nationals of the member countries of the Union in the commercial assemblies and in organisations representing professional and economic interests within the framework of the laws of each State.

5.   Foreign employers and workers may not in their private capacity be subject to duties, taxes or contributions of any kind other than or higher than those levied on the nationals of countries of the Union.

Foreign undertakings shall enjoy the same rights and protection regarding trade-marks and patents, trade labels and names and any other industrial properties as undertakings possessing the nationality of the member countries of the Union.

The conditions of access to judicial or administrative courts applicable to foreign undertakings and workers shall be the same as those guaranteed to nationals of the States of the Union by their respective laws.

PART II.
Preferential schedules.

CHAPTER I.
Common provisions.

Section 1.

6.   Subject to the conditions laid down in the following articles, any undertaking wishing to launch a new activity or to expand to an important extent an activity already existing in a country of the Union, excluding commercial activities, may benefit from a special decision admitting it to a preferential schedule. The undertaking must undertake to utilise in priority local raw materials and in general local products.

7.   Undertakings which may benefit from preferential schedule must belong to one of the following categories:

(1)   Industrial-plantation undertakings engaged in the processing or conditioning of

products;

    (2)   Stock-farming undertakings equipped with installations for protecting the health of livestock;

    (3)   Industrial undertakings that prepare or process animal or vegetable products;

    (4)   Lumbering industries;

    (5)   Fishing undertakings equipped with installations for the conservation or the processing of products;

    (6)   Industries for the manufacture or assembly of finished articles or goods;

    (7)   Undertakings engaged in the mining activities of extracting, improving or processing mineral substances and allied operations;

    (8)   Petroleum prospecting undertakings;

    (9)   Power-production undertakings;

    (10)   Undertakings engaged in the development of touristic regions.

8.   The following criteria shall in particular be taken into consideration during the examination of projects:

    (1)   The importance of the investments;

    (2)   Participation in the implementation of the economic and social plans;

    (3)   Creation of employment and vocational training;

    (4)   Participation of nationals of the countries of the Union in the formation of capital;

    (5)   The use of technically guaranteed equipment;

    (6)   Priority use of local raw materials and, in general, local products;

    (7)   Registered office established in a country of the Union.

Section 2. *Approval procedure.*

9.   This convention comprises two categories of investment schedules:

    (1)   The first category concerns undertakings established in a State of the Union, the market of which does not include the other member States of the Union.

            Schedules I and II set forth in Part III of this convention which concern the above undertakings shall be granted in accordance with the procedure peculiar to each State.

    (2)   The second category concerns companies the market of which includes or is likely to include the territories of two or more States. it comprises schedules III and IV which shall be granted according to a procedure common to all the member States.

            In addition establishment conventions may be concluded with undertakings according to the procedure determined either by national laws or by this convention.

10.   The application for approval shall be addressed to the appropriate Ministry of the State concerned and presented in the forms laid down in article 1 of act No. 12/65-UDEAC-34 regulating the single tax rules (standard form annex 1).

The Minister shall as the case may be transmit the application file to an investments board for its advice.

11.   For each undertaking, the decision of approval:

-     shall specify the preferential schedule to which the approved undertaking is admitted and shall fix its term,
-     shall list the activities for which the approval is granted,
-     shall specify the obligations incumbent on the undertaking, particularly its equipment programme,
-     shall stipulate the special rules for international arbitration.

Any operations effected by the approved undertaking which do not fall within the scope of those listed by the decision of approval shall remain subject to the fiscal and other provisions of ordinary law.

CHAPTER II.
Economic advantages.

Section 1. -- Installations and supplies.

12.   The assistance of public credit institutions may be granted to undertakings admitted to preferential schedules upon the intervention of the appropriate authorities of each State.

13.   Within the framework of exchange regulations, approved undertakings may be given priority in the granting of foreign currency in order to buy equipment goods and raw materials, products and containers necessary for their operations.

Section 2. -- Sale of products.

14.   Protective customs measures with regard to imports of similar competitive goods may, if necessary, be instituted in favour of undertakings admitted to a preferential schedule.

Government and Army contracts shall, as far as possible, be reserved for them in priority.

PART III.
Special provisions to which national investment codes must conform in the case of undertakings belonging to only one State of the Union.

CHAPTER I.
General.

15.   Having regard to the decision regarding the harmonization of development plans and in respect for the general principles laid down by this text, admission to any one of the preferential schedules provided for priority undertakings of all kinds classified in categories a, b and c of articles 51 of the Treaty instituting the Union, shall be granted according to the procedure peculiar to the State, where the undertaking is established.

In the case of undertakings defined in category c of article 51 of the Treaty instituting the Union, applications for approval shall be transmitted beforehand to the Secretary General of the Union, in conformity with the provisions of article 53 of the Treaty.

The grant of an internal preferential schedule may only be effected at the end of the consultation procedure laid down by article 55 of the Treaty.

The Management Committee of the Union shall be informed of each approval in respect of these categories of undertakings by the Government of the State where they are established or will be established.

16.   Preferential tariff provisions may be granted by the Government of the State concerned to industries already established which wish to expand their production capacity. Such provision comprises the application of a reduced overall rate of 5% of the duties and taxes collected on imports of plant (excluding building materials, furniture and spare parts) provided that they conform with an equipment programme approved by the Government and that their value exceeds 10 million francs.

The conditions and procedure for according this tariff shall be governed by national legislation.

17.   The undertakings classified in categories a, b and c of articles 51 of the Treaty instituting the Union may be admitted to one of the schedules defined below.

CHAPTER II.
Schedule I.

18.   Schedule I shall entail for the companies admitted to it:

(1)   The application of an overall reduced rate of 5% of the duties and taxes collected on imports or a nil rate on equipment and building materials, machinery and tools directly necessary for the production and the processing of products.

(2)   Total exemption from import duties and taxes as well as from single taxes and indirect taxes levied inland:

    (a)   On raw materials and products which enter either in whole or in part into the composition of finished or processed goods.

    (b)   On raw materials or products which while not constituting equipment and not entering into the composition of finished or processed goods are used up or lose their specific quality in the course of direct manufacturing operations.

    (c)   On raw materials and products intended for the handling and non-reusable packing of finished or processed products.

    Equipment and building materials, machinery plants, raw materials or products benefiting from a reduction or exemption in respect of import duties and taxes shall be fixed in a list drawn up in accordance with the procedure proper to each State.

    This list shall be published officially.

    (d)   As the case may be on electric power.

(3)   The benefit of reduced or nil rates of export duties in the case of prepared or manufactured goods.

(4)   Goods manufactured by an undertaking admitted to schedule I shall be exempted from the inland tax on turnover and any other similar tax; they shall be subject to an internal consumption tax, the rate of which shall be subject to revision and the dates for the application of which shall be fixed by the decision of approval.

    This tax shall be defined and applied according to Act No. 12-65-UDEAC-34 of the 14th December 1965. The duration of the benefits provided for under paragraphs 1, 2 and 3 of this article shall be fixed by the decision of approval. It may not exceed ten years.

19.   Taking into consideration the economic social importance of the undertaking and the special conditions of its installation, schedule I may further comprise the following benefits:

    (a)   Exemption from the tax on industrial and commercial profit during the first five years of operation, the first year being that in which the first sale or delivery was made either within the national market or for export.

    Depreciation normally accounted for during the first five years may for tax purposes be charged against the three following years according to a procedure determined by the appropriate authorities of the State where the undertaking is established.

(b)   Exemption during the same period and under the same conditions from the business licence and land, mining or lumbering taxes.

20.   The decision of approval may provide that for the duration of schedule I as defined above, no import duty or tax, no new tax or duty or additional part thereof of a fiscal nature may be collected in addition to the duties and taxes in force on the date of grant of the approval.

No law or regulation coming into force on a date subsequent to the date of admission of an undertaking to the provisions of schedule I may result in the restriction of the aforedefined provisions regarding the undertaking.

In addition, undertakings licensed under schedule I may request the benefit of any more favourable provisions which may be provided for by customs and fiscal laws of the States in accordance with article 43 of the Treaty setting up the Union and of Article 6 of this convention.

CHAPTER II.
Schedule II.

21.   The provisions of schedule II may be granted to undertakings of cardinal importance to national economic development, involving exceptionally high investments.

It comprises the stabilisation of the fiscal provisions, whether special or under common law, which are applicable to them according to the conditions set down below.

22.   Tax stabilisation may likewise apply to the taxes by the parent or stockholding companies of the undertakings defined in article 21 above.

23.   The tax provisions thus defined shall remain in force for a term not exceeding twenty-five years to which may be added, if need be, the normal periods required for installation.

24.   During the period it is in force, the tax stabilisation provisions shall guarantee the beneficiary undertaking against any increase in the direct or indirect taxation which is applicable to it on the date of approval with regard to the basis of assessment, rate and the method of collection.

In addition all or part of the fiscal or customs provisions concerning schedule I may be extended to schedule II with the exception of the land consumption tax, the rate of which remains subject to revision.

The schedule of stabilized taxes and duties, as well as the rates applicable during the term of validity of schedule I shall be defined in the decision of approval.

Insofar as customs duties and taxes are concerned, the provisions of tax stabilization may only apply to the fiscal import duty and the turnover tax on imports. Imported equipment and building materials benefiting from the stabilisation of these two duties shall form the subject of a limitation list appended to the decision of approval.

In case of modifications being introduced into the fiscal provisions fixed by ordinary law in pursuance of the provisions of article 43 of the Treaty instituting the Union and article 6 of this convention, the undertaking benefiting from tax stabilisation may apply for the benefit of such modifications.

Such undertaking may further apply to revert to the tax provisions of ordinary law.

25.   No legislation or regulation which would nullify these provisions shall apply, during the same period, to undertakings benefiting from the provisions of tax stabilisation.

CHAPTER IV.
Establishment conventions.

26.   Any undertaking approved under one of the schedules I or II or considered as being especially important to the social and economic development plans of the member States of the Union, may benefit from an establishment convention granting it certain guarantees and imposing certain obligations on it in accordance with the following conditions:

The parent or stockholding companies of the aforementioned undertakings may likewise be parties to the convention.

Nothing in the establishment convention may constitute any undertaking, on the part of the States of the Union, to compensate the undertaking for losses, debts or deficiencies due to technical developments, economic circumstances or factors attributable to the undertaking itself.

27.   The establishment convention shall define its term of validity and as the case may be:

(a)   The general conditions of operation, the minimum equipment and production programmes, the commitments of the undertaking regarding vocational training or social works provided for in the aforesaid programme as well as any obligation accepted by the two parties;

(b)   Various guarantees by the Government other than fiscal or customs guarantees such as:

    --   guarantees as to financial, legal and economic stability and stable conditions for financial transfers and the marketing of goods;
    --   guarantees as to entry and movement of labour, freedom of employment, and the free choice of suppliers and services;
    --   guarantees as to the renewal of lumbering and mining permits if necessary;

(c)   Facilities for the use of hydraulic, electric, and other resources necessary for the exploitation, as well as the facilities for conveying products to the place of shipment and the use of installations, whether already existing or to be built by or for the undertaking at the place of shipment;

(d)   The procedure for extending the term of the convention and the circumstances which will entail a cancellation or the forfeiture of all rights and the penalties designed to ensure that both parties fulfil their obligations.

28.   The provisions regarding import taxes and duties laid down in schedule I may likewise be included either in whole or in part in the establishment convention for the term of validity of the latter.

If the establishment convention comprises provisions regarding internal taxation as set forth in schedule I they shall be restricted to the term of validity of the aforesaid schedule.

CHAPTER V.

29.   Any grant of benefits similar to those laid down by the foregoing schedule but granted according to rules other than those defined below or any grant of higher benefits shall be subject to the preliminary agreement of the Council of Heads of State of the Union, after consultation with the Management Committee.

PART IV.

Special provisions applicable to undertakings and establishments of interest to two or more States of the Union.

CHAPTER I.
Scope.

30.   This part applies to the undertakings classified in categories d and e of article 51 of the Treaty instituting the Union and defined article 7 of this convention.

31.   Such undertakings may apply for admission to either of the two following schedules.

CHAPTER II.
Schedule III.

32.   Admission to schedule III shall confer right to the following benefits:

(a)   Application during the period of installation of an overall reduced rate of 5% of the duties and taxes collected on imports of equipment goods. Total exemption may in exceptional cases be granted by the Management Committee:

(b)   Benefit of the single tax system in force in the Union.

33.   The following fiscal benefits may in addition be granted:

(1)   Exemption from the tax on industrial and commercial profits during the first five years of operation, the first year being that during which the first sale or delivery was made.

Depreciation normally accounted for during the first five years may for tax purposes be charged against the following three years.

(2)   Rates on structures: temporary exemption (for a maximum period of ten years) on new buildings, rebuilding or additions to buildings.

(3)   Rates on land plots. Temporary exemption (for a maximum period of ten years) on land newly used for stockrearing or on reclaimed and sown land.

(4)   Exemption for five years from the business patent licence.

(5)   Exemption for five years from land, mining or lumbering taxes.

CHAPTER III.
Schedule IV.

34.   Schedule IV shall further comprise the customs and fiscal benefits set forth in schedule III and in particular the application of the single tax and the benefit of an establishment convention.

35.   The establishment convention shall define:

(1)   Its term of validity and procedure for its extension.

(2)   Where necessary, various commitments by the undertakings, in particular:

--   the general conditions of operation,
--   minimum programmes of equipment and production,
--   vocational training or social works provided for by the aforesaid programme as well as any other obligations accepted by the undertaking with regard to the state of its establishment and the other States of the Union.

(3)   various guarantees by the State of its establishment and the member States of the Union, in particular:

--   guarantees as to stability in the judicial, economic and financial fields as well as in the matter of financial transfers and the marketing of products;
--   guarantees as to entry and movement of labour, freedom of employment

and the free choice of suppliers and services;

-- guarantees as to the renewal of lumbering and mining permits;

-- guarantees as to facilities in the use of hydraulic, electric and other resources necessary for operations and facilities for the evacuation of products to the place of shipment and the use of installations existing or those to be created by or for the undertaking at this place of shipment.

36.   In addition, undertakings of cardinal importance to the economic and social development of the States of the Union and involving exceptionally high investments may be granted stabilisation of the special or ordinary fiscal provisions applicable to them.

37.   The applications drawn up as provided by article 11 shall be submitted to the appropriate authorities of the State of establishment.

After the appropriate examination, enquiry and fuller investigation, the appropriate authorities of the State of establishment shall transmit to the Secretary General of the Union these applications and, as the case may be, the data concerning the project of the establishment convention accompanied by the presentation report as provided under article 13 of the Treaty.

38.   The Secretary General of the Union shall where necessary undertake in liaison with the appropriate authorities of the State of establishment of fuller investigation of the application with a view to its transmission to the States, in conformity with the provisions of article 55 of the Treaty.

39.   Where the Management Committee receives an application as provided under article 55 of the Treaty it shall decide as the case may be on the rate or rates of the single tax to be applied to the project and shall determine the benefits and guarantees to be granted to the undertaking.

Where necessary, it shall give its decision on the data of the establishment convention, the final draft of which it shall approve.

40.   The draft of the convention thus approved shall be transmitted to the Government of the State of establishment for signature. The convention shall be made enforceable within the territory of the Union by a decision of the Management Committee.

PART V.
Settlement of disputes.

CHAPTER I.
Procedure of withdrawal.

41.   In the case of serious deficiencies on the part of an undertaking with regard to the provisions of the decision of approval:

(1)   The benefit of the advantages provided under either of schedules I or II may be

withdrawn in accordance with the procedures established by the legislation of each nation.

(2) The benefit of the advantages laid down by either of schedules III or IV may be withdrawn by the Management Committee at the justifiable request of the State of establishment.

The Management Committee may seek the advice of a board of experts composed as follows:
-- an expert designated by the Government of the State of establishment,
-- an expert designated by the undertaking,
-- an expert designated by the Government of the State of establishment,
-- an expert designated by agreement between the aforesaid Government and the undertaking.

CHAPTER II.
Procedure for appeal.

42. Undertakings which form the subject of a decision to withdraw approval may seek appeal.

In the case of an undertaking benefiting from the advantages provided under schedules I or II, the appeal shall be referred to an administrative court of the State of establishment within a maximum period of sixty days, with effect from the date of notification of the decision of withdrawal.

In the case of an undertaking benefiting from the advantages provided under schedules III or IV, the appeal shall be referred to the Council of Heads of State of the Union within a maximum period of ninety days with effect from the notification of the decision of withdrawal.

CHAPTER III.
Arbitration.

43. Disputes arising out of the application of the clauses of an establishment convention and the calculation of any penalty due for nonfulfilment of the obligations assumed may be settled by arbitration the procedure for which shall be established by each convention.

Such procedure of arbitration shall always comprise the following provisions:

(a) The nomination of an arbitrator by each party;
(b) In the case of disagreement between the arbitrators, the nomination of a third arbitrator by agreement between the two parties or, in default thereof, by a highly qualified authority who shall be named in the convention;
(c) The final and binding nature of the award rendered by a majority of the arbitrators who shall determine their own procedure and decide cases in equity;
(d) Notwithstanding the foregoing provisions, in the case of undertakings, the initial

capital of which was subscribed in the major part from abroad, the decision of approval may provide for a procedure of international arbitration in replacement of the above procedure.

44.   Any disputes arising out of the application of the decisions of approval to the various schedules may if necessary be settled by the arbitration procedure laid down by article 43 above if the latter exists in the national legislation.

PART VI.
Transitional provisions.

45.   Any preferential schemes and establishment conventions granted prior to the promulgation of this convention to undertakings operating in the States of the Union shall specifically remain in force.

Provided always that such schemes and conventions may, on the initiative either of the Government or the undertakings concerned, form the subject of negotiations with a view to their adaptation to the provisions of this convention.

The procedure to be followed shall be that defined by articles 37 to 44 above.

Yaoundé, the 14th December 1965.
The President of the Federal Republic of Cameroon,

The President of the Central African Republic,

The President of the Republic of Congo,

The President of the Republic of Gabon,

The President of the Republic of Chad,

*   *   *

REVISED RECOMMENDATION OF THE COUNCIL CONCERNING CO-OPERATION BETWEEN MEMBER COUNTRIES ON ANTICOMPETITIVE PRACTICES AFFECTING INTERNATIONAL TRADE*

The Revised Recommendation is a further revision of the Recommendation of the Council of the Organisation for Economic Co-operation and Development Concerning Co-operation Between Member Countries on Restrictive Business Practices Affecting International Trade, first adopted in 1967 and successively revised in 1973, 1979 and 1986. This new version was adopted by the Council of the OECD at its 856th session on 27-28 July 1995.

THE COUNCIL

Having regard to Article 5 (b) of the Convention on the Organization for Economic Co-operation and Development of 14th December 1960;

Having regard to the fact that international co-operation among OECD countries in the control of anticompetitive practices affecting international trade has long existed, based on successive Recommendations of the Council of 5th October 1967 [C(67)53(Final)], 3rd July 1973 [C(73)99(Final)], 25th September 1979 [C(79)154(Final)] and 21st May 1986 [C(86)44(Final)];

Having regard to the recommendations made in the study of transnational mergers and merger control procedures prepared for the Committee on Competition Law and Policy;

Recognising that anticompetitive practices may constitute an obstacle to the achievement of economic growth, trade expansion and other economic goals of Member countries;

Recognising that the continued growth in internationalisation of business activities correspondingly increases the likelihood that anticompetitive practices in one country or co-ordinated behaviour of firms located in different countries may adversely affect the interests of Member countries and also increases the number of transnational mergers that are subject to the merger control laws of more than one Member country;

Recognising that the unilateral application of national legislation, in cases where business operations in other countries are involved, raises questions as to the respective spheres of sovereignty of the countries concerned;

---

*Source: OECD (1995). *Revised Recommendation of the Council Concerning Co-operation between Member Countries on Anticompetitive Practices Affecting International Trade*, C(95)130/FINAL (Paris: OECD) [Note added by the editor].

Recognising the need for Member countries to give effect to the principles of international law and comity and to use moderation and self-restraint in the interest of co-operation on the field of anticompetitive practices;

Recognising that anticompetitive practices investigations and proceedings by one Member country may, in certain cases, affect important interests of other Member countries;

Considering therefore that Member countries should co-operate in the implementation of their respective national legislation in order to combat the harmful effects of anticompetitive practices;

Considering also that closer co-operation between Member countries is needed to deal effectively with anticompetitive practices operated by enterprises situated in Member countries when they affect the interests of one or more other Member countries and have a harmful effect on international trade;

Considering moreover that closer co-operation between Member countries in the form of notification, exchange of information, co-ordination of action, consultation and conciliation, on a fully voluntary basis, should be encouraged, it being understood that such co-operation should not, in any way, be construed to affect the legal positions of Member countries with regard to questions of sovereignty, and in particular, the extra-territorial application of laws concerning anticompetitive practices, as may arise;

Recognising the desirability of setting forth procedures by which the Competition Law and Policy Committee can act as a forum for exchanges of views, consultations and conciliation on matters related to anticompetitive practices affecting international trade;

Considering that if Member countries find it appropriate to enter into bilateral arrangements for co-operation in the enforcement of national competition laws, they should take into account the present Recommendation and Guiding Principles:

I.   RECOMMENDS to Governments of Member countries that insofar as their laws permit:

A.   <u>NOTIFICATION, EXCHANGE OF INFORMATION AND CO-ORDINATION OF ACTION</u>

1.   When a Member country undertakes under its competition laws an investigation or proceeding which may affect important interests of another Member country or countries, it should notify such Member country or countries, if possible in advance, and, in any event, at a time that would facilitate comments or consultations; such advance notification would enable the proceeding Member country, while retaining full freedom of ultimate decision, to take account of such remedial action as the other Member country may find it feasible to take under its own laws, to deal with the anticompetitive practices;

2. Where two or more Member countries proceed against an anticompetitive practice in international trade, they should endeavour to co-ordinate their action insofar as appropriate and practicable;

3. Through consultations or otherwise, the Member countries should co-operate in developing or applying mutually satisfactory and beneficial measures for dealing with anticompetitive practices in international trade. In this connection, they should supply each other with such relevant information on anticompetitive practices as their legitimate interests permit them to disclose; and should allow, subject to appropriate safeguards, including those relating to confidentiality, the disclosure of information to the competent authorities of Member countries by the other parties concerned, whether accomplished unilaterally or in the context of bilateral or multilateral understandings, unless such co-operation or disclosure would be contrary to significant national interests.

B. CONSULTATION AND CONCILIATION

4. a) A Member country which considers that an investigation or proceeding being conducted by another Member country under its competition laws may affect its important interests should transmit its views on the matter to or request consultation with the other Member country;

   b) Without prejudice to the continuation of its action under its competition law and to its full freedom of ultimate decision the Member country so addressed should give full and sympathetic consideration to the views expressed by the requesting country, and in particular to any suggestions as to alternative means of fulfilling the needs or objectives of the competition investigation or proceeding;

5. a) A Member country which considers that one or more enterprises situated in one or more other Member countries are or have been engaged in anticompetitive practices of whatever origin that are substantially and adversely affecting its interests, may request consultation with such other Member country or countries recognising that entering into such consultations is without prejudice to any action under its competition law and to the full freedom of ultimate decision of the Member countries concerned;

   b) Any Member country so addressed should give full and sympathetic consideration to such views and factual materials as may be provided by the requesting country and, in particular, to the nature of the anticompetitive practices in question, the enterprises involved and the alleged harmful effects on the interests of the requesting country;

   c) The Member country addressed which agrees that enterprises situated in its territory are engaged in anticompetitive practices harmful to the interests of the requesting country should attempt to ensure that these enterprises take remedial action, or should itself take whatever remedial action it considers appropriate, including actions under its legislation on anticompetitive practices or administrative measures, on a voluntary basis and considering its legitimate interests;

6. Without prejudice to any of their rights, the Member countries involved in consultations under paragraphs 4 and 5 above should endeavour to find a mutually acceptable solution in the light of the respective interests involved;

7. In the event of a satisfactory conclusion to the consultations under paragraphs 4 and 5 above, the requesting country, in agreement with, and in the form accepted by, the Member country or countries addressed, should inform the Competition Law and Policy Committee of the nature of the anticompetitive practices in question and of the settlement reached;

8. In the event that no satisfactory conclusion can be reached, the Member countries concerned, if they so agree, should consider having recourse to the good offices of the Competition Law and Policy Committee with a view to conciliation. If the Member countries concerned agree to the use of another means of settlement, they should, if they consider it appropriate, inform the Committee of such features of the settlement as they feel they can disclose.

II. RECOMMENDS that Member countries take into account the guiding principles set out in the Appendix to this Recommendation.

III. INSTRUCTS the Competition Law and Policy Committee:

1. To examine periodically the progress made in the implementation of the present Recommendation and to serve periodically or at the request of a Member country as a forum for exchanges of views on matters related to the Recommendation on the understanding that it will not reach conclusions on the conduct of individual enterprises or governments;

2. To consider the reports submitted by Member countries in accordance with paragraph 7 of Section I above;

3. To consider the requests for conciliation submitted by Member countries in accordance with paragraph 8 of Section I above and to assist, by offering advice or by any other means, in the settlement of the matter between the Member countries concerned;

4. To report to the Council as appropriate on the application of the present Recommendation.

IV.   DECIDES that this Recommendation and its Appendix cancel and replace the Recommendation of the Council of 21st May 1986 [C(86)44(Final)].

APPENDIX

GUIDING PRINCIPLES FOR NOTIFICATIONS, EXCHANGES OF INFORMATION, CO-OPERATION IN INVESTIGATIONS AND PROCEEDINGS, CONSULTATIONS AND CONCILIATION OF ANTICOMPETITIVE PRACTICES AFFECTING INTERNATIONAL TRADE

Purpose

1.   The purpose of these principles is to clarify the procedures laid down in the Recommendation and thereby to strengthen co-operation and to minimise conflicts in the enforcement of competition laws. It is recognised that implementation of the recommendations herein is fully subject to the national laws of Member countries, as well as in all cases to the judgement of national authorities that co-operation in a specific matter is consistent with the Member country's national interests. Member countries may wish to consider appropriate legal measures, consistent with their national policies, to give effect to this Recommendation in appropriate cases.

Definitions

2.   a)   "Investigation or proceedings" means any official factual inquiry or enforcement action authorised or undertaken by a competition authority of a Member country pursuant to the competition laws of that country. Excluded, however, are (i) the review of business conduct or routine filings in advance of a formal or informal determination that the matter may be anticompetitive, or (ii) research, studies or surveys the objective of which is to examine the general economic situation or general conditions in specific industries.

      b)   "Merger" means merger, acquisition, joint venture and any other form of business amalgamation that falls within the scope and definitions of the competition laws of a Member country governing business concentrations or combinations.

Notification

3.   The circumstances in which a notification of an investigation or proceeding should be made, as recommended in paragraph I.A.1, of the Recommendation, include:

      a)   When it is proposed that, through a written request, information will be sought from the territory of another Member country or countries;

b) When it concerns a practice (other than a merger) carried out wholly or in part in the territory of another Member country or countries, whether the practice is purely private or whether it is believed to be required, encouraged or approved by the government or governments of another country or countries;

c) When the investigation or proceeding previously notified may reasonably be expected to lead to a prosecution or other enforcement action which may affect an important interest of another Member country or countries;

d) When it involves remedies that would require or prohibit behaviour or conduct in the territory of another Member country;

e) In the case of an investigation or proceeding involving a merger, and in addition to the circumstances described elsewhere in this paragraph, when a party directly involved in the merger, or an enterprise controlling such a party, is incorporated or organised under the laws of another Member country;

f) In any other situation where the investigation or proceeding may involve important interests of another Member country or countries.

Procedure for notifying

4. a) Under the Recommendation notification ordinarily should be provided at the first stage in an investigation or proceeding when it becomes evident that notifiable circumstances described in paragraph 3 are present. However, there may be cases where notification at that stage could prejudice the investigative action or proceeding. In such a case notification and, when requested, consultation should take place as soon as possible and in sufficient time to enable the views of the other Member country to be taken into account. Before any formal legal or administrative action is taken, the notifying country should ensure, to the fullest extent possible in the circumstances, that it would not prejudice this process.

b) Notification of an investigation or proceeding should be made in writing through the channels requested by each country as indicated in a list to be established and periodically updated by the Competition Law and Policy Committee.

c) The content of the notification should be sufficiently detailed to permit an initial evaluation by the notified country of the likelihood of any effects on its national interests. It should include, if possible, the names of the persons or enterprises concerned, the activities under investigation, the character of the investigation or procedure and the legal provisions concerned, and, if applicable, the need to seek information from the territory of another Member country. In the case of an investigation or proceeding involving a merger, notification should also include:

    i) the fact of initiation of an investigation or proceeding;

ii)   the fact of termination of the investigation or proceeding, with a description of any remedial action ordered or voluntary steps undertaken by the parties;

iii)   a description of the issues of interest to the notifying Member country, such as the relevant markets affected, jurisdictional issues or remedial concerns;

iv)   a statement of the time period within which the notifying Member country either must act or is planning to act.

Co-ordination of Investigations

5.   The co-ordination of concurrent investigations, as recommended in paragraph I.A.2. of the Recommendation, should be undertaken on a case-by-case basis, where the relevant Member countries agree that it would be in their interests to do so. This co-ordination process shall not, however, affect each Member country's right to take a decision independently based on the investigation. Co-ordination might include any of the following steps, consistent with the national laws of the countries involved:

a)   providing notice of applicable time periods and schedules for decision-making;

b)   sharing factual and analytical information and material, subject to national laws governing the confidentiality of information and the principles relating to confidential information set forth in paragraph 10;

c)   requesting, in appropriate circumstances, that the subjects of the investigation voluntarily permit the co-operating countries to share some or all of the information in their possession, to the extent permitted by national laws;

d)   co-ordinating discussions or negotiations regarding remedial actions, particularly when such remedies could require conduct or behaviour in the territory of more than one Member country;

e)   in those Member countries in which advance notification of mergers is required or permitted requesting that the notification include a statement identifying notifications also made or to be made to other countries.

Assistance in an investigation or proceeding of a Member country

6.   Co-operation among Member countries by means of supplying information on anticompetitive practices in response to a request from a Member country, as recommended in paragraph I.A.3 of the Recommendation, should be undertaken on a case-by-case basis, where it would be in the interests of the relevant Member countries to do so. Co-operation might include any of the following steps, consistent with the national laws of the countries involved:

a)   assisting in obtaining information on a voluntary basis from within the assisting Member's country;

b)   providing factual and analytical material from its files, subject to national laws governing confidentiality of information and the principles relating to confidential information set forth in paragraph 10;

c)   employing on behalf of the requesting Member country its authority to compel the production of information in the form of testimony or documents, where the national law of the requested Member country provides for such authority;

d)   providing information in the public domain relating to the relevant conduct or practice. To facilitate the exchange of such information, Member countries should consider collecting and maintaining data about the nature and sources of such public information to which other Member countries could refer.

7.   When a Member country learns of an anticompetitive practice occurring in the territory of another Member country that could violate the laws of the latter, the former should consider informing the latter and providing as much information as practicable, subject to national laws governing the confidentiality of information and the principles relating to confidential information set forth in paragraph 10, consistent with other applicable national laws and its national interests.

8.   a)   Member countries should use moderation and self-restraint and take into account the substantive laws and procedural rules in the foreign forum when exercising their investigatory powers with a view to obtaining information located abroad.

    b)   Before seeking information located abroad, Member countries should consider whether adequate information is conveniently available from sources within their national territory.

    c)   Any requests for information located abroad should be framed in terms that are as specific as possible.

9.   The provision of assistance or co-operation between Member countries may be subject to consultations regarding the sharing of costs of these activities.

Confidentiality

10.   The exchange of information under this Recommendation is subject to the laws of participating Member countries governing the confidentiality of information. A Member country may specify the protection that shall be accorded the information to be provided and any limitations that may apply to the use of such information. The requested Member country would be justified in declining to supply information if the requesting Member country is unable to observe those requests. A receiving Member country should take all reasonable steps to ensure observance of the confidentiality and use limitations specified by the sending Member country,

and if a breach of confidentiality or use limitation occurs, should notify the sending Member country of the breach and take appropriate steps to remedy the effects of the breach.

<u>Consultations between Member countries</u>

11. a) The country notifying an investigation or proceeding should conduct its investigation or proceeding to the extent possible under legal and practical time constraints, in a manner that would allow the notified country to request informal consultations or to submit its views on the investigation or proceeding.

b) Requests for consultation under paragraphs I.B.4. and I.B.5. of the Recommendation should be made as soon as possible after notification and explanation of the national interests affected should be provided in sufficient detail to enable full consideration to be given to them.

c) The notified Member country should, where appropriate, consider taking remedial action under its own legislation in response to a notification.

d) All countries involved in consultations should give full consideration to the interests raised and to the views expressed during the consultations so as to avoid or minimise possible conflict.

<u>Conciliation</u>

12. a) If they agree to the use of the Committee's good offices for the purpose of conciliation in accordance with paragraph I.B.8 of the Recommendation, Member countries should inform the Chairman of the Committee and the Secretariat with a view to invoking conciliation.

b) The Secretariat should continue to compile a list of persons willing to act as conciliators.

c) The procedure for conciliation should be determined by the Chairman of the Committee in agreement with the Member countries concerned.

d) Any conclusions drawn as a result of the conciliation are not binding on the Member countries concerned and the proceeding of the conciliation will be kept confidential unless the Member countries concerned agree otherwise.

*   *   *

DRAFT CONVENTION ON THE PROTECTION OF FOREIGN PROPERTY*

The Draft Convention on the Protection of Foreign Property was prepared by a Committee of the Organisation for Economic Co-operation and Development. The Council of the OECD, at its 150th meeting on 12 October 1967, adopted "The Resolution of the Council on the Draft Convention on the Protection of Foreign Property" which, *inter alia*, approved the publication of the Draft Convention. The Draft Convention was not opened for signature. The notes and comments to the Draft Convention have not been reproduced in this volume.

DRAFT CONVENTION ON THE PROTECTION OF FOREIGN PROPERTY

PREAMBLE

DESIROUS of strengthening international economic co-operation on a basis of international law and mutual confidence;

RECOGNISING the importance of promoting the flow of capital for economic activity and development;

CONSIDERING the contribution which will be made towards this end by a clear statement of recognised principles relating to the protection of foreign property, combined with rules designed to render more effective the application of these principles within the territories of the Parties to this Convention; and

DESIROUS that other States will join them in this endeavour by acceding to this Convention;

The States signatory to this Convention HAVE AGREED as follows:

Article 1
Treatment of Foreign Property

(a)   Each Party shall at all times ensure fair and equitable treatment to the property of the nationals of the other Parties. It shall accord within its territory the most constant protection and security to such property and shall not in any way impair the management, maintenance, use, enjoyment or disposal thereof by unreasonable or discriminatory measures. The fact that certain nationals of any State are accorded treatment more favourable than that

---

*Source: Organisation for Economic Co-operation and Development (1967). *Draft Convention on the Protection of Foreign Property and Resolution of the Council of the OECD on the Draft Convention* (Paris: OECD) [Note added by the editor].

provided for in this Convention shall not be regarded as discriminatory against nationals of a Party by reason only of the fact that such treatment is not accorded to the latter.

(b)   The provisions of this Convention shall not affect the right of any Party to allow or prohibit the acquisition of property or the investment of capital within its territory by nationals of another Party.

Article 2
Observance of Undertakings

Each Party shall at all times ensure the observance of undertakings given by it in relation to property of nationals of any other Party.

Article 3
Taking of Property

No Party shall take any measures depriving, directly or indirectly, of his property a national of another Party unless the following conditions are complied with:

(i)   The measures are taken in the public interest and under due process of law;

(ii)   The measures are not discriminatory; and

(iii)   The measures are accompanied by provision for the payment of just compensation. Such compensation shall represent the genuine value of the property affected, shall be paid without undue delay, and shall be transferable to the extent necessary to make it effective for the national entitled thereto.

Article 4
Recommendation on Transfers

Each Party recognises, with respect to property in its territory owned by a national of another Party, the principles of the freedom of transfer of the current income from, and proceeds upon liquidation of, such property, to such national of a Party as is entitled to them. While this Recommendation does not contain any obligation in this respect, each Party will endeavour to grant the necessary authorisations for such transfers to the country of the residence of that national and in the currency thereof.

Article 5
Breaches of the Convention

Any breach of this Convention shall entail the obligation of the Party responsible therefor to make full reparation.

Article 6
Derogations

A Party may take measures in derogation of this Convention only if:

(i) involved in war, hostilities or other grave national emergency due to force majeure or provoked by unforeseen circumstances or threatening its essential security interests; or

(ii) taken pursuant to decisions of the Security Council of the United Nations or to recommendations of the Security Council or General Assembly of the United Nations relating to the maintenance or restoration of international peace and security.

Any such measures shall be limited in extent and duration to those strictly required by the exigencies of the situation.

Article 7
Disputes

(a) Any dispute between Parties as to the interpretation or application of this Convention may be submitted by agreement between them either to an Arbitral Tribunal established in accordance with the provisions of the Annex to this Convention, which shall form an integral part thereof, or to any other international tribunal. If no agreement is reached for this purpose between the Parties within a period of sixty days from the date on which written notice of intention to institute proceedings is given, it is hereby agreed that an Arbitral Tribunal established in accordance with that Annex shall have jurisdiction.

(b) A national of a Party claiming that he has been injured by measures in breach of this Convention may, without prejudice to any right or obligation he may have to resort to another tribunal, national or international, institute proceedings against any other Party responsible for such measures before the Arbitral Tribunal referred to in paragraph (a), provided that:

(i) the Party against which the claim is made has accepted the jurisdiction of that Arbitral Tribunal by a declaration which covers that claim; and

(ii) the Party of which he is a national has indicated that it will not institute proceedings under paragraph (a) or, within six months of receiving a written request from its national for the institution of such proceedings, has not instituted them.

(c) The declaration referred to in paragraph (b)(i), whether general or particular, may be made or revoked at any time. In respect of claims arising out of or in connection with rights acquired during the period of the validity of such declaration, it shall continue to apply for a period of five years after its revocation.

(d)   At any time after the expiry of the period of six months referred to in paragraph (b)(ii), the Party concerned may institute proceedings in accordance with paragraph (a). In this case proceedings instituted in accordance with paragraph (b) shall be suspended until the proceedings instituted in accordance with paragraph (a) are terminated.

Article 8
Other International Agreements

Where a matter is covered both by the provisions of this Convention and any other international agreement nothing in this Convention shall prevent a national of one Party who holds property in the territory of another Party from benefiting by the provisions that are most favourable to him.

Article 9
Definitions

For the purposes of this Convention:

(a)   "National" includes both natural persons and companies. It does not, however, include nationals of a Party who belong to any territory to which this Convention may be extended pursuant to Article 11 but has not been so extended.

(b)   "Company" means any entity which, under the law of a Party, either is recognized as a legal person or, as an entity or through its members, has the capacity to dispose of property or to institute legal proceedings.

(c)   "Property" means all property, rights and interests, whether held directly or indirectly, including the interest which a member of a company is deemed to have in the property of the company. However, no claim shall be made under this Convention in respect of the interest of a member of a company:

(i)   if the company is a national of a Party other than the Party which has taken the measures affecting the property of the company; or

(ii)   in the case of a company which is a national of a Party by whose measures its property is affected, if the interest of the member of the company does not arise out of and, at the time of such measures, does not represent either an investment of foreign funds made by him or his predecessor in title or an investment of compensation or damages paid in accordance with the provisions of this Convention.

Article 10
Ratification

This Convention shall be subject to ratification by the signatory States. Instruments of ratification shall be deposited with the [depositary Organisation/depositary Government], which shall notify the (other) signatory States and all acceding States of each deposit.

Article 11
Territorial Application

Any state may at the time of signature, ratification or accession to this Convention or at any time thereafter declare by notification given to the [depositary Organization/depositary Government] that the Convention shall extend to any of the territories for whose international relations it is responsible, and the Convention shall, from the date of the receipt of the notification or the date on which the Convention takes effect for the notifying State - whichever is the later - extend to the territories named therein.

Article 12
Coming into Force

(a)   This Convention shall come into force on the date of the deposit of the Xth instrument of ratification or accession.

(b)   The Convention shall thereafter take effect for each ratifying or acceding State on the date of the deposit of its instrument of ratification or accession.

(c)   Any measure taken by a Party before the date of the coming into force of this Convention for it shall not be affected by the Convention as such. The provisions of this Convention shall apply to measures taken after such date, whether in pursuance of legislative or administrative authority existing before such date or otherwise.

Article 13
Termination

Any Party may terminate the application of this Convention to itself or to any territory to which it has extended the Convention by notification pursuant to Article 11 by giving notice to this effect to the [depositary Organisation/depositary Government] which shall notify the (other) Parties thereof. The termination shall take effect one year after such notice has been received by the [depositary Organisation/depositary Government]. In respect of property acquired or investments made before the date on which the termination takes effect, the provisions of Articles 1 to 12 of this Convention shall continue to apply for a further period of 15 years from that date.

Article 14
Signature and Accession
(*pro memoria*)

Final Clause
(*pro memoria*)

*   *   *

ANNEX RELATING TO THE STATUTE
OF THE ARBITRAL TRIBUNAL

1.   The Arbitral Tribunal referred to in Article 7 of the Convention shall consist of three persons appointed as follows: one arbitrator shall be appointed by each party to the arbitration proceedings and a third arbitrator, who shall also act as Chairman of the Tribunal (hereinafter sometimes called the "Chairman of the Tribunal"), shall be appointed by agreement of the parties.

2.   Arbitration proceedings shall be instituted upon notice by the party instituting such proceedings (whether a Party to the Convention or a national of a Party to the Convention, as the case may be) to the other party. Such notice shall contain a statement setting forth in summary form the grounds of the claim, the nature of the relief sought, and the name of the arbitrator appointed by the party instituting such proceedings. Within 30 days after the giving of such notice, the respondent party shall notify the party instituting proceedings of the name of the arbitrator appointed by the respondent party.

3.   If, within 60 days after the giving of notice instituting the arbitration proceedings, the parties shall not have agreed upon a Chairman of the Tribunal, either party may request the President of the International Court of Justice, or if he is unable to act, the Vice-President of the International Court of Justice, to make the appointment. If either of the parties shall fail to appoint an arbitrator, such arbitrator shall be appointed by the Chairman of the Tribunal.

4.   In case any arbitrator appointed as provided in this Annex shall resign, die, or otherwise become unable to act, a successor arbitrator shall be appointed in the same manner as herein prescribed for the appointment of the original arbitrator and his successor shall have all the powers and duties of the original arbitrator.

5.   The Arbitral Tribunal shall convene at such times and places as shall be fixed by the Chairman of the Tribunal. Thereafter, the Tribunal shall determine where and when it shall sit.

6.   (a)   The Arbitral Tribunal shall decide all questions relating to its competence and shall, taking into consideration any agreement of the parties, determine its procedure and all questions relating to costs.

(b)   In particular, the Arbitral Tribunal may:

    (i)   permit intervention by a Party which considers that it has an interest of a legal nature which may be affected by the decision in the case;

    (ii)   consolidate pending proceedings with the agreement, where necessary, of any other Arbitral Tribunal established in accordance with this Annex; and

    (iii)   provided that no objection is made by any Party to such proceedings, stay proceedings if other proceedings arising out of the same facts and raising substantially the same issues are pending before any other international Tribunal or Commission.

(c)   The Arbitral Tribunal may also, in the case of proceedings instituted by a national of a Party to the Convention and upon preliminary application by the respondent:

    (i)   order that national to give security for costs; or

    (ii)   dismiss the claim if, from the statements made by that national to the Tribunal, the institution of the proceedings appears frivolous or vexatious.

(d)   Decisions of the Arbitral Tribunal may be made by a majority vote.

7.   The Arbitral Tribunal shall afford to all parties a fair hearing. It may render an award on the default of a party. Any award shall be rendered in writing, signed by the majority of the Arbitral Tribunal, and delivered publicly. A signed counterpart of the award shall be transmitted to each party. Any such award shall be final. Each party to the proceedings shall comply with any such award rendered by the Arbitral Tribunal.

*   *   *

AGREEMENT ON INVESTMENT AND FREE MOVEMENT OF ARAB CAPITAL AMONG ARAB COUNTRIES*

The Agreement on Investment and Free Movement of Arab Capital Among Arab Countries was signed on 29 August 1970 by the States members of the Agreement of Arab Economic Unity. It entered into force on 29 August 1970. It was amended by resolution 648 of 3 December 1973. Signatories of the Agreement are Egypt, Iraq, Jordan, Kuwait, Sudan, Syrian Arab Republic and the Arab Republic of Yemen.

The Governments of member states in the Agreement of Arab Economic Unity:

The Hashemite Kingdom of Jordan
The Democratic Republic of Sudan
The Arab Republic of Syria
The Republic of Iraq
The State of Kuwait
The Arab Republic of Egypt
The Arab Republic of Yemen

In pursuance of their desire to implement the provisions of Article II of the Arab League Charter regarding the strengthening of economic ties and cooperation among them, and in conformity with the objectives of Economic Unity among the Arab League States as laid down in Article I stipulating the free movement of persons and capital, freedom of residence and employment and pursuance of economic activity, have agreed to the following:

Article 1

a) Every Arab state exporting capital shall exert efforts to promote preferential investments in the other Arab states and provide whatever services and facilities required in this respect.

b) States importing capital shall exert efforts to the full extent of their power and provide all facilities required for preferential investment of Arab Capital in accordance with their economic development programmes.

Article 2

Member states shall foster investment of Arab capital in the joint economic projects in

---

*Source: Council of Arab Economic Unity (1974). *Agreement of Arab Economic Unity*, mimeo. (Translated by the United Nations from the original Arabic version) [Note added by the editor].

pursuance of economic integration among Arab states.

Article 3

In pursuance of the principle of each state's sovereignty over its own resources, and desirous to create the appropriate atmosphere for promoting Arab investment, member states shall determine the procedures, terms, and limits which govern Arab investment; designate the sectors earmarked for same, and notify Arab states thereof.

Article 4

Member states undertake to treat Arab investments in all areas designated thereto, without discrimination and on equal footing with indigenous investments.

Article 5

States parties to the Agreement shall undertake to treat Arab investments on terms not less favourable than those applied to foreign investments that
may be granted special privileges. Arab investments shall automatically enjoy same immediately such privileges are granted.

Article 6

Admitting the inalienable right of the state recipient of the capital to nationalize, confiscate and expropriate within the framework of public interest, the Arab investor shall be entitled in such cases to fair and effective compensation within a reasonable period of time.

Article 7

The states parties to this Agreement shall be entitled to repatriate the net proceeds of their invested capital together with the net returns thereto in addition to the compensation due in accordance with the provisions of this Agreement.

Article 8

The Arab investor shall be entitled to reside in the host country in order to carry out his investment activities.

General Provisions

Article 9

Each state party to this Agreement shall pass appropriate legislations and take whatever measures essential for the execution of the provisions of this Agreement.

Article 10

This Agreement shall be ratified by states signatory thereto in conformity with their respective constitutional regulations within the shortest time possible. The instruments of ratification shall be deposited with the General Secretariat of the Council of Arab Economic Unity which shall prepare a protocol of each deposit and give notice thereof to the other contracting parties.

Article 11

Arab states non-members in the Council of Arab Economic Unity may accede to this Agreement by virtue of a declaration of intent to be dispatched to the Secretary General of the Council who, in turn, shall notify other states parties to the Agreement.

Article 12

This Agreement shall be effective when ratified by at least three member states. It shall also enter into force in all member states once its instruments of ratification or accession are deposited with the General Secretariat of the Council of Arab Economic Unity.

This Agreement is drawn in Arabic at Damascus on Saturday, 29th of August 1970 in a single original to be deposited with the General Secretariat of the Council of Arab Economic Unity and a certified copy shall be transmitted to each state signatory to this Agreement or acceding thereto.

* * *

Amendments to Articles 3 and 6 of the Agreement
On the Investment and Free Movement of Arab Capital
(Resolution No. 648/S.22 - 3/12/73)

The Council of Arab Economic Unity,

Promoting the objectives of the Agreement on the Investment and Movement of Arab Capital among Arab Countries and the Agreement of the Arab Organization for Investment Guarantee, and

Desirous to accentuate the effectiveness of these Agreements in respect of creating new areas for Arab investments to serve the Arab economic development, and

Realizing the perils which loom over the Arab Capital abroad and the possibility of the efficient developing of these capitals if invested in the field of economic development inside the

Arab countries, and

Reaffirming the mutual interests between the Arab countries which financial surpluses and those in need thereof, and

Recognizing the nature of the phase undergone by the Arab Nation and the necessity of accelerating the pace of economic development and consolidating the bases of Arab cooperation in its various forms,

And in accordance with the directives of the Arab Ministers of Economy and the recommendations of the Arab financial and economic experts adopted in their meetings held at the Arab League headquarters in July 1973,

Decides:

1- A new provision is added to Article 3 of the Agreement on the Investment and Movement of Capital Among Arab Countries to read as follows:

Article 3

In conformity with the principle of each country's sovereignty over its resources and desirous to create the appropriate atmosphere for fostering Arab investment, member states shall determine the procedures, terms, and limits which govern Arab investment, designate the sectors earmarked for same and notify Arab states thereof.

These procedures, terms, and sectors and any alterations introduced thereinto shall be deposited with General Secretariat of the Council of Arab Economic Unity.

2 - Article 6 of the Agreement on the Investment and Movement of Capital Among Arab Countries shall be amended to read as follows:

Member states shall pledge not to nationalize or confiscate Arab investments in the sectors earmarked thereof in conformity with the provisions of Article III of this Agreement. The notification mentioned in that Article is considered an application submitted by the country host to Arab investment.

- Calling upon all Arab countries which have ratified or signed this Agreement to insert the afore-mentioned amendment in the shortest time possible.

- Calling upon all Arab countries which have not yet ratified or signed this Agreement to follow suit at the earliest possible.

- The Secretary General shall undertake, in collaboration with the Arab League Secretary General, the necessary measures for submitting this resolution to the

Arab Economic Council with a view to adopting the appropriate decision in collaboration with the Ministers of Economy non-members in the Agreement of Arab Economic Unity.

- This resolution shall be implemented following a notice of approval to be made by the countries which deem it necessary to consult their governments.

*   *   *

CONVENTION ESTABLISHING THE INTER-ARAB INVESTMENT GUARANTEE CORPORATION[*]

The Convention Establishing the Inter-Arab Investment Guarantee Corporation was opened for signature in May 1971. It entered into force in April 1974. The text reproduced in this volume is the official text of the Convention as amended up to 1988. The Contracting States are Algeria, Bahrain, Djibouti, Egypt, Iraq, Jordan, Kuwait, Lebanon, Libyan Arab Jamahiriya, Mauritania, Morocco, Oman, Palestine, Qatar, Saudi Arabia, Sudan, Syrian Arab Republic, Somalia, Tunisia, the United Arab Emirates and the Arab Republic of Yemen. The resolutions adopted by the Corporation's Council that add to and complete the Convention have not been included in this volume (resolutions No. 2/1975; 3/1975; 3/1976; 5/1976/2; 3/1977; 5/1982; and 7/1988).

THE CONTRACTING COUNTRIES

Hashemite Kingdom of Jordan
United Arab Emirates
State of Bahrain[1]
Republic of Tunisia
Democratic and Peoples Republic of Algeria
Republic of Djibouti[2]
Kingdom of Saudi Arabia[3]
Republic of the Sudan
Syrian Arab Republic
Democratic Republic of Somalia[4]
Republic of Iraq
Sultanate of Oman[5]

---

[*]Source: Inter-Arab Investment Guarantee Corporation (1988). *Convention Establishing the Inter-Arab Investment Guarantee Corporation* (Safat: Inter-Arab Investment Guarantee Corporation). The numbering of notes in this reproduction does not necessarily correspond to their numbering in the original source version [Note added by the editor].

[1]It became a party to the Convention on 3/11/1981.

[2]It became a party to the Convention on 25/5/1981.

[3]It became a party to the Convention on 20/4/1977.

[4]It became a party to the Convention on 21/10/1981.

[5]It became a party to the Convention on 5/6/1977.

Palestine[6]
State of Qatar
State of Kuwait
Republic of Lebanon
Socialist People's Libyan Arab Jamahiriya
Arab Republic of Egypt
Kingdom of Morocco
Islamic Republic of Mauritania[7]
Arab Republic of Yemen

PREAMBLE

THE ARAB COUNTRIES signatory to this Convention.

DESIROUS of strengthening their economic relations within a framework of effective cooperation;

SEEKING to promote the flow of capital between their territories in order to finance their development efforts for the benefit of their peoples;

STRESSING the importance of the role which the Arab investor can play in this respect if reasonable security is assured;

EAGER to provide such security against the non- commercial risks which may confront inter-Arab investment and which are difficult for the investor to avert by measures; and

ENDEAVOURING to limit the consequences likely to ensue from the materialisation of such risks,

HAVE AGREED as follows:

---

[6]It became a party to the Convention on 22/3/1979.

[7]It became a party to the Convention on 10/5/1976.

CHAPTER I[8]
ESTABLISHMENT OF THE CORPORATION
PURPOSES - STATUS - SEAT - DURATION - LEGAL REGIME

Article 1 - Establishment of the Corporation

There is hereby established in accordance with the provisions of this Convention an organisation called "The Inter-Arab Investment Guarantee Corporation" (hereinafter referred to as "the Corporation").

Article 2 - Purposes

1.   The purpose of the Corporation is to provide insurance coverage through both direct insurance and reinsurance for the Arab insured in the form of reasonable compensation for losses resulting from risks defined in the Convention.[9]

2.   For the purpose of promoting investments among member countries, the Corporation shall carry out activities which are ancillary to its main purpose and in particular the promotion of research relating to the identification of investment opportunities and the conditions of investments in the said countries.

Article 3 - Status

The Corporation shall possess juridical personality. It shall enjoy administrative and financial independence and shall possess in the territory of each member country all such rights and powers as may be necessary for the fulfilment of its functions.

Article 4 - Seat

The Corporation shall have its seat in the City of Kuwait and may establish branch offices in any other country as it may deem necessary for its activities.

---

[8]The Council by article (3) of Resolution 9/8987 made the following amendment to the convention:
  The term "Insured party" shall be substituted for the term "The investor" wherever it appears in the Convention of the Inter-Arab Investment Guarantee Corporation [The location of this note was not indicated in the original source document].

[9]The text is appearing as amended by Council Resolution No. 9/1987, The text before amendment reads as follows:
  The purpose of the Corporation is to provide insurance coverage for Arab investors in the form of reasonable compensation for losses resulting from non-commercial risks as defined in Article 18 [The location of this note was not indicated in the original source document].

Article 5 - Duration

The duration of the Corporation shall be thirty years commencing from the date on which this Convention enters into force and shall thereafter be automatically renewed for similar successive terms unless the Corporation is liquidated in accordance with the provisions of Article 33.

Article 6 - Legal Regime

1.   The Corporation shall be governed by the provisions of this Convention and by such supplementary rules and regulations as may from time to time be laid down by the Council of the Corporation.

2.   Where in any particular case the texts referred to in the preceding paragraph do not contain an applicable provision, such case shall be governed by the legal principles common to the contracting countries and by the recognised principles of International Law.

CHAPTER II
MEMBERSHIP AND CAPITAL

Article 7 - Membership[10]

1.   Every contracting country, and public organisation nominated by any country subscribing to the initial capital of the Corporation, shall be considered an original member.

2.   Any other Arab Country may accede to this Convention upon due compliance with the procedures therein prescribed. Such country, and such public and semi-public organisations as may be nominated by it, shall thereupon acquire the status of membership of the Corporation with regard to participation in its capital and to all other obligations of membership.

---

[10]This text is appearing as amended by Council resolution No. 2/1977. The text before amendment reads as follows:

Article 7 - Membership

1. Every contracting country, or public organisation designated by any such country, subscribing to the initial capital of the Corporation in accordance with the Subscription Schedule appended to this Convention shall be considered an original member.

2. Any other Arab country may accede to this Convention upon due compliance with the procedure hereinafter prescribed. Such public corporation as may be designated by it, shall thereupon acquire the status of member of the Corporation with regard to participation in its capital and to all the other obligations of membership.

3. Where a public organisation under the control of a contracting country becomes a member, that country shall be deemed to a guarantor of all the obligations of such public organisation towards the Corporation.

3. When one organisation or more, public or semi-public, belonging to a contracting country becomes a member, that country shall be deemed to a guarantor of all the obligations of such public or semipublic organisation towards the Corporation.

3. (Bis): Any International Arab Organisation may, by a resolution of the Council, be admitted to this Convention upon due compliance with the procedures hereinafter prescribed. Such Organisation shall hereupon acquire the status of membership of the Corporation on the same basis referred to in paragraph two of this Article.

4. The liability of a member shall be limited to the amount of its share in the capital. No member shall by reason of its membership be liable for the obligations of the Corporation towards third parties.

Article 8 - Capital[11]

1. The Corporation shall have an open-ended capital based on an initial amount of ten million Kuwait Dinars at official par value at the time of signature of this Convention, divided into ten thousand registered shares of one thousand Kuwaiti Dinars each.

2. The minimum subscription of each member shall be five per cent of the amount of the initial capital, i.e. equivalent to one-half million Kuwaiti Dinars.

   Where the status of a member is accorded to one or more public or semi-public organisation belonging to one country, such minimum limit shall apply only to the organisation which represents such country[12]

3. Member shall pay in Kuwaiti Dinars, or in any other convertible currency at the exchange rate set forth in paragraph 1 of this Article, fifty per cent of the price of the shares subscribed by them in five annual installments, the first of which shall be payable within a period of three months from the date on which this Convention enters into force with respect to the member concerned. The remaining installments shall become due on the last day of each period of one year from the date fixed for payment of the first

---

[11]The Council issued resolution no. 2/1975 with recommendation to the Member States to increase their subscriptions in the capital to the extent allowing the capital to be raised to 25 million Kuwaiti Dinars (see page 41) [Note by the editor: The page reference in this note corresponds to the location of the cited resolution in the original source document].

[12]This text is appearing as amended by Council resolution no. 2/1977. The text before amendment reads as follows:
   Article 8 - Capital
   2. The minimum subscription of each member shall be five cent [sic] of the amount of the initial capital, equivalent to one-half million Kuwaiti Dinars.
   4. The liability of a member shall be limited to the amount of its share in the capital. No member shall by reason of its membership be liable for the obligations of the Corporation towards third parties.

---

installment. All such installments shall be paid into an account opened in the name of the Corporation in accordance with a resolution passed by its Council at its first meeting.

4. The unpaid portion of the capital shall constitute an obligation of the respective members in the proportion of the unpaid share of each. Such obligation shall mature and become payable to such extent as may be determined by the Council of the Corporation in every case where it is decided to increase the amount payable on account of shares.

5. Immediately on being notified of the Council's decision to that effect, members shall pay the amounts which have been decided to be paid on account of capital.

6. All calls made in pursuance of the provisions of paragraph 4 of this Article shall be paid in Kuwaiti Dinars or in such other freely convertible currency at the exchange rate set forth in paragraph 1 of this Article.

   With the special approval of the Council in exceptional cases attributable to fundamental disequilibrium in the balance of payments of a member country, such member may pay in its own local currency a proportion not exceeding twenty-five per cent of the amount of the call. In all such cases the member concerned shall at the earliest possible opportunity permit the conversion of the amounts paid on its local currency at the same exchange rate at which it was paid. The Corporation shall in addition have the right to use these funds for the purpose of defraying its current expenditures in the member country concerned or for payment of such compensation as may be due by the Corporation and payable in such currency.

7. The capital of the Corporation shall be increased upon the admission of every new member in pursuance of paragraph 2 of Article 7 or upon the increase of the shareholding of any one or more of the members. The capital shall, on the other hand, be decreased upon the withdrawal of any of the members or in pursuance of a resolution to that effect by the Council of the Corporation.

8. A contracting country may dispose of its entire share to, or acquire the entire share registered in the name of, a public corporation controlled by such country, and may, with the consent of the Council of the Corporation, transfer to another member any shares held in excess of the minimum subscription specified in paragraph 2 of this Article.

CHAPTER III
ORGANISATION AND MANAGEMENT

Article 9 - Organs of the Corporation

The Corporation shall have the following organs:

a. The Council of the Corporation which shall be composed of one representative for each member of the Corporation.

b.   The Supervisory Committee which shall be composed of six experts of whom five shall be of different nationalities and elected by the Council from nationals of the member countries upon the nomination of the members of the Corporation. The sixth shall be appointed by the Council upon the nomination of the Federation of Arab Chambers of Commerce, Industry and Agriculture but shall have no counted vote in the deliberations of the Committee. The term of appointment of the members of the Committee shall be three years subject to renewal.[13]

c.   The Director-General who shall be a national of a contracting country, and shall be elected by the Council from among candidates nominated by the members. He shall be elected for a term of five years subject to renewal.

d.   The Deputy Director-General, who shall be a national of a contracting country, and shall be elected by the Council from among candidates nominated by the members for a term of five years subject to renewal. He shall not be of the same nationality as the Director-General.

e.   Professional and Administrative Staff, who shall be appointed by the Director-General in accordance with the provisions of Articles 12 and 14 of this Convention.

Article 10 - The Council

1.   The Council shall have all the powers necessary for the realisation of the objectives of the Corporation, except such powers as are by the terms of this Convention specifically conferred upon another organ of the Corporation.

2.   The Council shall have the following functions, in particular:

a.   Formulation of the general policy of the Corporation.

b.   Adoption of such necessary rules and regulations as may be proposed by the Director-General after prior consultation with the Supervisory Committee.

c.   Determination of the ways in which the funds of the Corporation shall be invested.

d.   Interpretation and amendment of the provisions of this Convention.

---

[13]The text appears as amended by Council Resolution No 2/1980. The text before amendment reads as follows:

b. The Supervisory Committee which shall be composed of three experts of different nationalities to be elected by the Council from nationals of the member countries. Two shall be elected from among candidates nominated by the members of the Corporation and the third from a list of candidates submitted by the Federation of Arab Chambers of Commerce, Industry and Agriculture. The term of appointment of the members of the Committee shall be five years subject to renewal.

e. Reduction of the capital of the Corporation otherwise than reduction caused by the withdrawal of a member.

f. Appointment of members of the Supervisory Committee and termination of their appointment in accordance with the by-laws of the Corporation.

g. Appointment and termination of the services of the Director General and the Deputy Director-General in accordance with the by-laws of the Corporation.

h. Adoption of the annual financial programme of the Corporation, approval of its balance sheet and its revenue and expenditure account and adoption of the annual reports presented by the Director-General.

i. Admission of new members to the Convention.

j. Determination of the consequences of suspension of or withdrawal from membership under the provisions of Chapter VIII of this Convention.

k. Deciding upon the distribution of profits and the formation of reserves in accordance with the financial regulations of the Corporation.

l. Suspension of operations and liquidation of the Corporation.

m. Delegation to the Director- General of authority to exercise any of the powers of the Council except the powers specified in this paragraph.

3. Chairmanship of the sessions of the Council shall be held in rotation by the representatives of the members in accordance with the alphabetical order of the contracting countries.

4. The Council shall hold one meeting at least every year upon invitation of the Director-General accompanied by a draft agenda. In every session the Council shall determine the place in which the next following session shall be held. The Council may hold meetings whenever necessary either upon its own decision or upon request to that effect by the Supervisory Committee or by the Director-General.[14]

---

[14]This text is appearing as amended by Council resolution no. 2/1978. The text before amendment reads as follows:

4. The Council shall hold one session every six months upon the invitation of the Director-General. Such invitation shall be accompanied by a draft agenda. In every ordinary session the Council shall determine the place in which the next following session shall be held.

The council may hold extraordinary sessions whenever necessary either upon its own decision or upon a request to that effect by the Supervisory Committee or by the Director-General.

5. A quorum for any meeting of the Council shall be a majority of delegates representing three-quarters of the total voting power of the members. If in any meeting there is no quorum, the Director-General shall call another meeting to be held at the earliest possible opportunity and the quorum for such second meeting shall be a majority of delegates representing two- thirds of the total voting power of the members.

6. Each member shall be entitled to five hundred votes in respect of the minimum shares held in the capital, plus one additional vote for each two shares held in excess of such minimum. Votes shall be cast as one unit and no member shall be entitled to split the number of votes to which it is entitled.

    If the minimum limit of subscription does not apply to the public or semi- public organisation, such organisation shall have one vote for each two shares it holds. The votes of a country and the public or semi- public organisations belonging to it should not be split.[15]

7. All matters before the Council shall be decided by simple majority of the voting power represented at the meeting: Provided that decisions relating to the matters specified in paragraph 2 of this Article shall require a special majority of two-thirds of the total voting power of the members of the Corporation (which majority is hereinafter be referred to as the "special majority").

8. No member shall in any vote in a Council meeting represent more than one other member and shall in this case be authorised by a written proxy.

9. The Council shall adopt its own rules of procedure for the conduct of its business, recording of its decisions and the appointment of its secretariat. Such rules may establish a procedure whereby the Council may, without holding a meeting, take decisions on certain matter referred to it by the Director General, other than matters specified in paragraph 2 of this Article.

Article 11 - Supervisory Committee

1. The Supervisory Committee shall supervise the activities of the Corporation and may, without interference in the administration of the Corporation, tender such advice as it may consider appropriate. The Committee shall carry out its function in any of the following particular ways:

---

[15]This text is appearing as amended by Council resolution no.2/1977. The text before amendment reads as follows:

> 6. Each member shall have five hundred votes in respect of the minimum shares held in the capital plus one additional vote for each two shares held in excess of such minimum. Votes shall be cast as a unit and no member shall be entitled to split the number of votes to which it is entitled.

a. Making recommendations and expressing views to the Council and to the Director- General.

b. Examining such reports and memoranda on the work or the accounts of the Corporation prepared at the request of the Committee, or referred to it, by the Director- General.

c. Verifying the conformity of insurance operations undertaken by the Corporation with the rules and regulations in force.

d. Preparation of semi-annual reports on its work for submission to the Council.

2. The Committee shall elect a Chairman from its members who shall be responsible for conducting the meeting of the Committee, following up its decisions and calling its meetings at the seat of the Corporation at least once every four months. A meeting of the Committee shall also be called in pursuance of a resolution to that effect by the Council or upon a reasoned request by one of its members or by the Director- General.

3. A quorum for any meeting of the Committee shall consist of at least three of the members who have the right to vote of whom one shall be the Chairman.

    Decisions of the Committee shall be carried by the unanimous vote of the members present. In case of dissent all different views shall be recorded in the minutes of the meeting and notified to the Council and to the Director- General.[16]

4. The Committee may invite the Director- General or his Deputy to attend any of its meeting and to participate in its deliberations but neither of them shall have the right to vote.

5. The Committee shall lay down the necessary arrangements concerning the conducting of its business, the recording of its decisions and minutes of its meetings and the notification thereof to the Council and to the Director-General.

6. Members of the Supervisory Committee shall be entitled to such remuneration as the Council shall determine.

---

[16]The text appears as amended by Council Resolution No 2/1980. The text before amendment reads as follows: A quorum for any meeting of the Committee shall consist of at lest two members including the Chairman. Decisions of the Committee shall be carried by the unanimous vote of the members present. In case of dissent all different views shall be recorded in the minutes of the meeting and notified to the Council and to the Director-General.

Article 12 - Director-General

1.   The Director-General shall be responsible for the administration of the Corporation in conformity with the by-laws, regulations and decisions made by the Council. His functions shall include the following:

   a.   Conclude insurance contracts with investors as well as other agreements pertaining to the activities of the Corporation.

   b.   Invest the funds of the Corporation.

   c.   Prepare research programmes in the light of the provisions of paragraph 2 of Article 2 hereof and follow up the implementation of such programmes.

   d.   Submit to the Council an annual report on the work of the Corporation in addition to other periodic reports.

   e.   Prepare all documents necessary for the business of the Council.

   f.   Furnish the Committee with the information and data as may be required.

   g.   Appoint members of the Professional and Administrative staff of the Corporation and fix their salaries in accordance with the regulations laid down by the Council.

   h.   Prepare the draft annual financial programme, the balance sheet and the profit and loss account.

   i.   Prepare periodic plans for the promotion of the activities of the Corporation.

2.   The Director-General shall be the authorized representative of the Corporation.

3.   The Director-General shall attend the meetings of the Council and participate in its deliberations without the right to vote.

Article 13 - Deputy Director-General

The Deputy Director-General shall be appointed after consultation with the Director-General. He shall assist the Director-General in the administration of the Corporation and shall perform his duties in his absence. The Director-General may also delegate some of his functions to the Deputy Director-General.

Article 14 - Professional and Administrative Staff

In appointing members of the Professional and Administrative Staff the Director- General shall give first priority to nationals of the contracting countries and then to nationals of other

Arab states; provided that the persons employed shall possess suitable qualifications, experience and qualities of character.

CHAPTER IV
INSURANCE OPERATIONS

Article 15 - Investments Eligible for Insurance[17]

1. Investments eligible for insurance shall comprise all investments between the contracting countries whether they are direct investments (including enterprises and their branches or agencies, ownership of a part of capital and ownership of real estate) or portfolio investments (including ownership of shares, stocks and bonds). Eligible investments also comprise loans for a term exceeding three years as well as such shorter term loans as the Council may in exceptional cases decide to treat as eligible for insurance.

2. In identifying investments for the purpose of the preceding paragraph, the Corporation shall be assisted by the guidelines issued by the International Monetary Fund on the Definition of long term assets and liabilities in the context of the preparation of balance of payments statistics.

3. In appraising the eligibility of an investment for the purpose of insurance no distinction shall be made on account of the monetary or non-monetary form of the transaction. Reinvestment of earnings accrued out of a previous investment shall also be eligible for insurance.

4. Insurance shall not be made available except for new transactions commencing after the conclusion of insurance contracts with the exception of operations for which the Corporation has agreed to issue re-insurance.[18]

5. Private investments and other mixed and public investments operating on a commercial basis shall be eligible for insurance.

6. The conclusion of insurance contracts shall be subject to the condition that the investor shall have obtained the prior approval of the competent official authority in the host country for the making of the investment and for its insurance with the Corporation against the risks to be covered.

---

[17]The Council issued resolution no 3/1975 to the effect that loans pertaining to export and import transactions between Member States are to be considered as eligible for insurance by the Corporation even if such loans are for a term less than three years (See page 47) [Note by the editor: The page reference in this note corresponds to the location of the cited resolution in the original source document].

[18]The text appears as a mended by Council resolution no.9/1987. The text before amendment reads as follows:
　4. Insurance shall not be available except for new investments which are made after the conclusion of an insurance contract.

Article (15 bis) - Export Credit Guarantee[19]

1. Credit facilities pertaining to export and import transaction between contracting countries shall regardless of their duration be eligible for insurance provided that such loans are connected with the export of services or primary goods produced by any one of these countries, or with goods manufactured by that country or have been assembled or processed therein, as long as such transactions yield an obvious added economic value to the said country.

2. Insurance may be extended to cover commercial risks relating to export credits. Commercial risks shall for purposes of this provision mean risks attributable to transactions of the debtor such as his failure to pay, insolvency, bankruptcy, or rescission or termination of the contract. Insurance contracts shall state specifically the risks covered in each case.

3. In accordance with this article the Council shall fix the maximum amount of total cover which may be provided by the Corporation, the rules of its distribution among the Contracting Countries and the maximum sums insured in each case.

4. The premium rate to be paid shall be fixed without abiding by Article 19 and after due regard is paid to the probabilities of the realization of risk.

5. Para. (b) of Article (15) shall not be applicable to export credit guarantee operations. Nevertheless, the insured shall prove that the export/import transaction relating to the insurance contract has been made according to the procedure and regulations in both the country of export and import.

Article 16 - Priorities

1. Subject to all operations being conducted on a sound basis and with the object of serving the interests of the investors, the Corporation shall accord special priority to the following investments:

    a. Investments which promote economic cooperation among the contracting countries and in particular joint Arab projects and other projects which promote Arab economic integration.

    b. Investments proved to the Corporation to be effective in the development of the productive capacities of the economy of the host country.

    c. Investments in which the guarantee of the Corporation is considered to be an essential consideration in the decision to make them.

---

[19]The article has been added by council Resolution No.9/1987.

2.   In determining the priorities specified in the preceding paragraph the Corporation may cooperate with the competent organs in the contracting countries and with the organs of such regional or international organisation as may be concerned.

3.   The proposal of a particular investment or the accord of priority to it by the Corporation in pursuance of the preceding two paragraphs shall in no way be construed as entailing liability on the part of the Corporation for the commercial consequences arising from the execution or operation of such investment.

Article 17 - Nationality of the Investor

1.   To be accepted as a party to an insurance contract, the investor must either be a natural person, who is a national of a contracting country, or a juridical person whose stocks or shares are substantially owned by one or more of the contracting countries or by their nationals, and whose main seat is located in one of these countries.[20]

Nevertheless, a juridical person may, by a resolution of the Council, be accepted as a party to an insurance contract, even if his main seat is located in a non-contracting country, provided that such juridical person is owned by not less than fifty per cent to one or more of the contracting countries or to their nationals or to the juridical persons who are, under the provisions of the above paragraph acceptable as party to the insurance contract.

In no event shall the investor be a natural person who is a national of the host country or a juridical person whose main seat is located such country if its stocks and shares are substantially owned by this country or its nationals.

2.   All insurance contracts shall embody a term enabling the Corporation to amend or rescind the contract or to take any other measures in all cases where, after the conclusion of the relevant contract, any of the conditions set forth in the preceding paragraph ceases to obtain. Such conditions must also be satisfied at the time any claim is made by an investor for compensation due in respect of an insured loss.

3.   For the purposes of the foregoing provisions, the nationality of a contracting country shall prevail in case the investor has more than one nationality, and the nationality of the host country shall prevail over that of any other contracting country.

---

[20]The Council resolution no. 3/1977 was issued whereby the Director- General was authorized to conclude contracts with Banking and investment institutions and the subsidiaries thereof even if their main seats are located in non contracting countries (See page 50) [Note by the editor: The page reference in this note corresponds to the location of the cited resolution in the original source document].

Article 18 - Risks Eligible for Insurance

1.   The insurance provided by the Corporation may cover all or part of the losses resulting from any one or more of the following non-commercial risks:[21]

   a.   Measures taken by the public authorities in the host country, either directly or through an agency, whereby the investor is deprived of his substantial rights with respect to his investment, and, in particular, confiscatory measures, nationalization, sequestration, expropriation, compulsory seizure, deprivation of a creditor of his rights including the right of assignment, and the imposition of moratoria of unreasonable length.

   b.   Introduction by the public authorities in the host country, either directly or through an agency, of new measures which substantially restrict the ability of the investor to repatriate the principal of his investment or to remit his earnings therefrom or the investment amortization installments.

   The above provision shall be construed to include a delay for an unreasonable period in approving the transfer, as well as the imposition by the public authorities at the time of transfer of a rate of exchange which is clearly discriminatory against the investor. The risk provided for in this paragraph shall not be deemed to include measures existing at the time of conclusion of the insurance contract and shall not include general devaluation of currency or cases of exchange depreciation.

   c.   Any military action emanating from a foreign source or from the host country which directly affects the tangible assets of the investor, and all public civil disturbances such as revolutions, coups d'etat insurrections and acts of violence of a public character having the same effect.

---

[21]The text is appearing as amended(1) by Council Resolution No. 9/1986. The paragraph was amended the first time by Council Resolution No. 7/1976 to read as follows:

   Nevertheless, a juridical person may, by a resolution of the Council, be accepted as a party to an insurance contract, even if his main seat is located in a non-contracting country, provided that such juridical person is owned by not less than fifty per cent to one or more of the contracting countries or to their nationals or to the juridical persons who are, under the provisions of the above paragraph acceptable as party to the insurance contract. In no event shall such an investor be a national of the host country.
The text before amendment by Resolution 7/1976 read as follows:

   To be accepted as a party to an insurance contract, the investor must either be a natural person, who is a national of a contracting country, or a juridical person whose stocks or shares are substantially owned by one of the contracting countries or by its nationals and whose seat of control is situated in one of these countries. In no event shall such an investor be a national of the host country. [Note by the editor: the location of this note is not indicated in the original text].

2. Insurance contracts shall specifically (sic) the risks covered by the insurance in each case. In all cases the insurance contract shall not cover losses arising from any measures taken by the public authorities in the host country in any of the following cases:

    a. Where such measures can be provided against by ordinary insurance transactions on reasonable terms.

    b. Where the investor has expressly agreed to such measures being taken or has been directly responsible for them.

    c. Where the measures are such as a state may normally take for the purposes of regulating economic activity in its territory and which do not involve discrimination against the investor by the insurance.

3. The Corporation shall in no case assume responsibility for commercial risks that attend the insured investment.

Article 19 - Fees and Premiums

1. In consideration of the examination of an insurance application the Corporation shall collect a fee in advance from all applicants and may, where no insurance contract is eventually concluded, refund the said fee either wholly or in part.

2. The Corporation shall determine in respect of each type of risk the rate of the annual premium payable by investors, but shall not, in fixing such rate, discriminate between the various host countries. In determining the level of such premiums the Corporation shall take into account the need for meeting its administrative expenses and, as far as feasible, the need for accumulating appropriate reserves.

3. The Corporation may enter into agreements with host countries whereby such countries may bear either wholly or in part the fees and premiums payable.

Article 20 - Limits of Insurance

1. The Council of the Corporation shall fix the maximum amount of the total cover which may be provided by the Corporation. This total cover shall not at any time exceed five times the amount of capital plus reserves.[22]

2. The Council shall pay regard to the necessity of spreading the insurance operations among the various contracting countries.

---

[22]The Council fixed by Resolution No. 5/1982. The maximum amount of the total cover and the maximum amount of operations per country (See page 51) [Note by the editor: The page reference in this note corresponds to the location of the cited resolution in the original source document].

---

3. The amount of insurance in respect of any single transaction should not exceed ten per cent of the total amount of the capital and reserves. Such limit may be increased to twenty per cent in case of investments having special priority in accordance with paragraph one of Article 16 of this Convention.[23]

4. The amount of compensation paid to an investor shall not exceed the amount of the loss sustained in consequence of the occurrence of the insured risk or the amount of insurance agreed upon in the insurance contract, whichever is the lesser.

Article 21 - Subrogation of the Corporation to the Rights of the Investor

1. The Corporation shall, upon paying or agreeing to pay compensation to an investor for any insured loss, be subrogated to all the rights which the investor may have in relation to the insured investment or to which he may become entitled in consequence of the occurrence of the loss.

2. Insurance contracts shall specify in detail the limits within which the Corporation shall be subrogated to the rights of the investor in the event of the Corporation agreeing to compensate such investor for the loss covered by the insurance.

3. By virtue of such subrogation, host countries shall as soon as possible discharge to the Corporation their obligations towards the insured investor and shall in addition, if so required by the Corporation, afford it all appropriate facilities to benefit from the rights acquired by reason of such subrogation. Failing this, the Corporation shall from the date of subrogation be entitled against the authorities of the host country to moratory interest on the amounts to which it has been subrogated to. Such interest shall be calculated on the basis of the prevailing rates on commercial loans granted by banks in said country.[24]

---

[23]This text is appearing as amended by Council resolution no. 8/1976/2. The text before amendment reads as follows:

   3. The amount of insurance in respect of any single transaction shall not exceed ten per cent of the aggregate amount of the capital plus reserves. Such maximum may be increased to twenty per cent in the case of investment in Arab joint projects.

[24]The text appears as amended by Council Resolution No. 9/1986. The text before amendment reads as follows: By virtue of such subrogation, host countries shall as soon as possible discharge to the Corporation their obligations towards the insured investor, and shall in addition afford all appropriate facilities to the Corporation to exercise the right acquired by reason of such subrogation.

CHAPTER V
FINANCIAL PROVISIONS

Article 22 - Financial Management

1.   The Corporation shall carry out its activities with due regard to maintaining a sound financial position in accordance with established business practices.

2.   The Council shall, on the advice of the Director- General and after consultation with the Supervisory Committee, lay down such financial rules and regulations as may be necessary for the business of the Corporation.

3.   The Director-General shall submit to the Council, at a date not later than the thirtieth day of September of each year, an estimate of the expected current administrative expenditures and income for the following fiscal year.

4.   The financial year shall commence on the first day of January and end on the thirty-first day of December of each year: Provided that the first financial year shall commence on the date of the entry into force of this Convention.

Article 23 - Accounts

1.   The Director-General shall, not later than the thirty first day of March of every year, submit with his annual report on the work of the Corporation a balance sheet showing the assets and liabilities of the Corporation at the end of the previous financial year together with the profit and loss account for the year.

2.   The accounts of the Corporation shall be certified by one or more auditors practicing in the contracting countries and appointed annually by the Council. The remuneration payable to such auditors shall be fixed by the Council.

3.   Before the date specified in paragraph 1 of this Article the auditors shall lay before the Council a report embodying their observations on the financial position and the annual accounts of the Corporation. The report shall be transmitted to the Supervisory Committee and to the Director- General.

Article 24 - Profits and Reserves

1.   The Corporation shall retain all profits realised from its operations and set aside such profits as a reserve until the assessment of such reserve reaches three times the capital of the Corporation.

2.   After the reserve has reached the level prescribed in the preceding paragraph, the Council shall decide the manner of utilisation or distribution of the realised annual profits: Provided that no more than ten per cent of such profits shall be distributed and

that the distribution shall be made pro rata in proportion to the share of each member in the capital of the Corporation.

3. The Council shall on the recommendation of the Director-General specify the currency or currencies in which profits shall be distributed to each member.

4. The Council may decide to capitalise part of the reserve, in which event the resultant increase of capital shall be distributed among the members in the proportion of their shareholding at the time of such distribution.

CHAPTER VI
IMMUNITIES AND EXEMPTIONS

Article 25 - Assets of the Corporation

1. The assets of the Corporation in the territories of the contracting countries shall be immune from and shall not be subject to nationalisation, confiscation, expropriation, sequestrations or seizure except in execution of a final judgment delivered by a competent judicial authority.

2. Without prejudice to the provisions of paragraph 6 of Article 8, assets of the Corporation, its profits and its financial operations shall not be subject to exchange restrictions.

3. The provisions of the preceding paragraph 2 of this Article shall not apply to assets acquired by the Corporation by virtue of subrogation to the rights of an investor pursuant to the provisions of Article 21 if such assets were originally subject to exchange restrictions.

Article 26 - Taxes

The assets of the Corporation, its income and its operations authorised by this Convention shall in all the contracting countries be immune from all taxes and duties: Provided that such immunity shall not extend to fees paid in consideration of specific services rendered to the Corporation by a public utility. The issue and circulation of the shares of the Corporation shall similarly be immune from all taxes and duties.

Article 27 - Documents and Correspondence

Every contracting country shall accord the documents and correspondence of the Corporation the same treatment that it accords to official documents and correspondence of other contracting countries.

Article 28 - Officers and Employees of the Corporation

1. Members of the Council and of the Supervisory Committee, the Director- General and his Deputy and the staff of the Corporation shall in the territory of each contracting country enjoy such of the following immunities and exemptions as are accorded to the representatives of the other contracting countries:

   a. Immunity from legal or administrative process with respect to acts performed by them in their official capacity.

   b. Exemption from immigration and residence restrictions applicable to aliens.

   c. Travelling facilities.

   d. Exemption from tax on salaries or remuneration received from the Corporation.

2. Nothing in this Article shall be construed as requiring any of the contracting countries to accord any of the aforementioned immunities or exemptions to any of its nationals.

Article 29 - Additional Privileges

The Corporation may conclude with the State in which it has its seat or with any other country, agreements whereby immunities and exemptions other than those set forth in this Chapter are accorded to the Corporation or to any of its staff.

CHAPTER VII
WITHDRAWAL AND SUSPENSION OF MEMBERSHIP

Article 30 - Withdrawal

1. Any contracting country may withdraw from this Convention after the lapse of five years from the date of the entry into force of the Convention with respect to such country. The withdrawal shall be effected by a notice in writing addressed to the Corporation at its principal office, but shall not become effective until after the expiry of three months from the date of such notice, during which period the member may revoke the notice.

2. Withdrawal shall have the effect of terminating the membership in the Corporation of the country concerned or of the public organisation controlled by such country.

3. Termination of membership shall have no effect on the existing or contingent obligations of such a member assumed towards the Corporation before the termination of the membership.

4. For every member whose membership has been terminated, the Corporation shall open a special account showing the financial rights and obligations of the member. The account

shall not be closed until after satisfaction of the obligations referred to in the preceding paragraph and after adjustment of the rights of the member concerned.

5. The Corporation shall enter into a special agreement with the member for the settlement of its position in the Corporation and for the mode of meeting its liabilities consequent upon the termination of its membership.

Article 31 - Suspension of Membership

1. If a member fails to fulfill any of its obligations arising out of its membership, the Council may by a unanimous vote (excluding the vote of the member concerned) suspend the said member from exercising its rights in the Corporation. The member shall remain during the period of suspension subject to all the obligations of membership.

2. Suspension of membership shall entail abstention by the Corporation from conducting new operations in respect of investments either from or into the territory of the suspended member.

3. Unless the Council takes a decision revoking suspension, the membership of a suspended member shall cease after one year from the date of its suspension. The provisions of paragraphs 3, 4 and 5 of the preceding Article shall apply to a member whose membership has ceased in pursuance of this paragraph.

CHAPTER VIII
SUSPENSION OF OPERATIONS AND LIQUIDATION

Article 32 - Suspension of Operations

1. The Council may, whenever it deems it justified, suspend the issuance of new insurance contracts for a specified period.

2. In an exceptional emergency the Council may by a special majority vote suspend the operations of the Corporation for a period not exceeding the duration of such emergency: Provided that necessary arrangements shall be made for the protection of the interests of the Corporation and of third parties.

3. The decision to suspend operations shall have no effect on the obligations of the members towards the Corporation or on the obligations of the members towards insured investors or towards third parties.

Article 33 - Liquidation

1. The Council may by a special majority vote and after giving the members notice of not less than four months, take a reasoned decision for the dissolution and liquidation of the Corporation. The Council shall undertake the consequential liquidation proceedings either

by itself or through liquidators appointed by it for that purpose by the same special majority.

2. The Council shall at the same meeting in which the decision of liquidation is taken determine such measures as may be necessary for the protection of the rights of the holders of insurance policies as well as the rights of third parties.

3. The Council shall by a special majority vote and after due provision having been made for the discharge of the existing and contingent liabilities of the Corporation, determine the manner in which its net asset shall be distributed among the members in proportion to the share of each in the capital.

CHAPTER IX
SETTLEMENT OF DISPUTES

Article 34 - Dispute Concerning the Interpretation and Application of the Convention

1. The Council shall be the final arbiter in respect of disputes arising between the contracting countries or between the members and the Corporation concerning the interpretation or the application of the provisions of this Convention.

2. Disputes specified in the preceding paragraph and arising after cessation of the Corporation's operations, or arising between the Corporation and a country that has withdrawn from the Convention or a member that has lost its membership, shall be settled in accordance with the procedure set out in the annex to this Convention, unless the parties shall have agreed on a different manner for the settlement of such disputes.

Article 35 - Disputes Concerning Insured Investments

1. Without prejudice to the jurisdiction of the Council with regard to the interpretation and application of the provisions of this Convention, and to its competence to determine matters comprised by such jurisdiction, any dispute between any of the contracting countries or the members on the one part and the Corporation on the other part concerning an investment insured in pursuance of this Convention or concerning any other matter shall be settled in accordance with the provisions set out in the Annex hereto.

2. Any dispute between the Corporation and a country that has withdrawn from the Convention or a member that has lost its membership, concerning an investment insured in pursuance of this Convention shall be settled in accordance with the procedure set out in the Annex hereto, without regard to the jurisdiction of the Council in the interpretation and the application of the provisions of the Convention.

Article 36 - Disputes Concerning Insurance Contracts

Insurance contracts shall stipulate the method of settlement of disputes that may arise between the Corporation and the insured investors.

Article 37 - Disputes with Third Parties

Except for the disputes specified in the preceding articles, all other disputes between the Corporation and third parties shall be subject to the jurisdiction of the competent judicial authority in the contracting countries.

CHAPTER X
MISCELLANEOUS PROVISIONS

Article 38 - Amendment of the Convention

1. The Council may by a special majority vote and upon a proposal emanating from a member, from the Committee or from the Director General amend the provisions of this Convention.

2. No proposal for amendment shall be considered by the Council except after the expiry of at least four months from the date of communicating the said proposal to the members.

3. Any amendment whereby the share of a member in the capital of the Corporation is increased shall have no effect except with the express consent thereto of the member concerned.

Article 39 - Prohibition of Political Activity

Without prejudice to the right of the Corporation to take into consideration all the circumstances surrounding an investment required to be insured, the Corporation and all persons working in any of its organs shall not in any manner interfere in the political affairs of any of the member countries.

Article 40 - International Character of the Staff

All persons working in the different organs of the Corporation are prohibited from doing any act inconsistent with the international character of their functions and independence from any authority other than the Corporation. Government of member countries shall refrain from all attempts to influence any such persons either directly or indirectly in the discharge of their duties.

Article 41 - Agreements for Treatment of Investments

The Corporation shall seek to enter into agreements with the contracting countries relating to the principles or rules for the treatment of insured investments in the territory of each such country and shall encourage the conclusion of similar agreements among those countries.

Article 42 - Cooperation with other Organisations

1. The Corporation shall, within the limits of the scope of its activities as set forth in this Convention, cooperate with public organisations of national or international character engaged in the fields of development and insurance. The Corporation may by a special majority resolution passed by the Council conclude such agreements as may be conducive to the strengthening of such cooperation.

2. The Corporation may entrust to governmental authorities in member countries the performance of some of the measures relating to its operations.

Article 43 - Secrecy

All persons working in any of the organs of the Corporation shall observe the secrecy of information and data obtained by them in the course of the discharge of their duties.

Article 44 - Channel of Communications

Each of the member countries shall designate the official authority with which the Corporation may communicate in connection with all facilities or measures required. All information provided by such authority shall be deemed to have been provided by the country concerned.

CHAPTER XI
FINAL PROVISIONS

Article 45 - Deposit and Ratification

The original of this Convention shall be deposited with the Ministry of Foreign Affairs of the State of Kuwait, which shall receive the instruments of ratification thereof, and communicate them to all the signatory countries, to the General Secretariat of the Arab League and to the Kuwait Fund for Arab Economic Development.

Article 46 - Entry into Force

This Convention shall enter into force when it has been ratified by at least five countries whose total subscriptions amount to not less than sixty per cent of the capital of the Corporation.

It shall enter into force with respect to other original and adhering countries from the date of the deposit by such countries of the instrument of ratification thereof.

Article 47 - Inaugural Meeting of the Council

Upon entry into force of this Convention the Director General of the Kuwait Fund for Arab Economic Development shall call for the inaugural meeting of the Council. The said meeting shall be held at the seat of the Corporation during the month following that in which this Convention has entered into force.

ANNEX
SETTLEMENT OF DISPUTES

Article 1 - Application of the Annex

All disputes within the provisions of Articles 34/2 and 35 of this Convention shall be settled exclusively in accordance with the procedure laid down in this Annex.

The Annex shall form an integral part of the Convention and shall not be open to any reservations.

Article 2 - Negotiations

In the event of any dispute covered by Article 34/2 and 35 of this Convention, the parties concerned shall attempt to settle such dispute by negotiation, and no recourse shall be made to conciliation or arbitration except after exhaustion of the procedure of settlement by negotiation. Such negotiation shall be deemed to have been exhausted if the parties concerned fail to reach a settlement within a period of six months from the date of the request by any of the parties to enter into such negotiation.

Article 3 - Conciliation

1. If the dispute is not resolved through negotiation, the parties concerned may by mutual agreement attempt settlement through conciliation. If no such agreement is reached, recourse shall be made to arbitration in accordance with the provisions of the following Article.

2. The agreement for recourse to conciliation shall specify the matter in dispute and the claims of the parties in respect thereof. It shall also specify the name of the conciliator chosen by the parties together with his agreed remuneration. The parties may request the Secretary-General of the Arab League to appoint such a conciliator.

3. The task of the conciliator shall be limited to seeking a compromise between the different views with regard to the dispute and to bringing about agreement between the parties on

mutually accepted terms. It shall be the duty of the parties to provide the conciliator with all information and documents which would help him in the discharge of his task.

The parties shall not be entitled to arbitration proceedings except after the conciliator has concluded his work within the period fixed therefore.

4.   The conciliator shall, within a period not exceeding six months from the date of commencement of his mission, draw up a report recording the result of his efforts and setting out the issues between the parties and his proposal for their settlement and specifying such of them as have been accepted by the parties.

The said report shall not be admissible in evidence before the Arbitral Tribunal to which the dispute may be referred subsequently.

Each party to the dispute shall express his views on the said report and shall communicate such views to the other party within a period of one month from the date of issue of the report.

5.   If the conciliator shall not be able to make his report within the fixed period, or if the parties do not accept the proposals contained in the report, the dispute shall be settled by arbitration in accordance with the provisions of the following Article.

Article 4 - Arbitration

1.   Arbitration Procedure.

      a.   Arbitration proceedings shall be instituted by means of a notice by the party requesting arbitration addressed to the other party or parties to the dispute.

The notice shall specify the nature of the dispute, the relief sought and name of the arbitrator appointed by the said party.

The other party shall, within a period of thirty days from the date of the giving of the notice, notify the party seeking arbitration of the name of the arbitrator appointed by such other party.

The two arbitrators shall, within a period of thirty days from the date appointment of the last of them, select an Umpire, who shall act as Chairman of the Arbitral Tribunal. In case of equal division in the Tribunal the Umpire shall have a casting vote.

      b.   If the other party shall fail to appoint an arbitrator within thirty days after the date of the giving of the notice, or if the arbitrators shall, within sixty days from the said date, be unable to agree on the selection of the Umpire, the Arbitral Tribunal shall be composed of a sole arbitrator or by an uneven number of arbitrators including the Umpire to be appointed at the request of any party to the dispute by the president of the Arab Court of Justice. Until such Court is constituted the request shall be directed to the Secretary General of the Arab League.

c. No party to the dispute shall, after commencement of the hearing of the dispute, have the right to change the arbitrator appointed by him.

In case any arbitrator shall resign, die, or become incapacitated, a successor arbitrator shall be appointed in his stead through the same procedure whereby the original arbitrator was appointed. The successor arbitrator shall have all the powers and duties of the original arbitrator.

d. The Arbitral shall hold its first sitting at such time and place as shall be fixed by the Umpire. Thereafter, the Arbitral Tribunal shall fix the place and time of its sittings.

e. The Arbitral Tribunal shall decide all questions relating to its competence and determine its rules of procedure.

f. If in the course of hearing by the Arbitral Tribunal of any of the disputes set forth in Article 35.1 of this Convention an objection is raised to the effect that the said dispute falls within the jurisdiction of the Council in accordance with Article 34.1 and the Arbitral Tribunal is satisfied that the objection is genuine, then and in every such case the objection shall be referred to the Council and the arbitration proceedings shall stand adjourned until matter has been decided by the Council. The decision of the Council on the nature of the dispute shall be binding upon the Arbitral Tribunal.

g. The Arbitration Tribunal shall afford to all the parties reasonable opportunity to produce their pleadings and to make their statements. All decisions of the Tribunal shall be adopted by a majority vote and shall state the reasons on which they are based. The award of the Tribunal shall be signed at least by the majority of the members and a copy thereof shall be delivered to each the parties. The award of the Tribunal shall be final and binding upon the parties and shall be executed immediately after it has been rendered, unless the Tribunal has fixed an interval for its execution or the execution of any part thereof. The award shall not be subject to appeal or revision.

h. The parties shall agree on the amount of fees payable to the arbitrators. If no agreement is reached before the Tribunal commences its sittings, the Tribunal shall fix a reasonable amount as may be required for the conduct of the proceedings. The Tribunal shall also fix the remuneration of other persons employed to perform work connected with the arbitration proceeding.

Each party shall defray its own costs in the arbitration proceedings but the costs of the Arbitral Tribunal shall be borne by the parties in equal proportions. The Tribunal shall determine any issue concerning the division of the costs of the Arbitral Tribunal or the procedure for payment of such costs.

    i.   Any notice or process directed by one of the parties to the other in connection with the settlement of the aforementioned disputes or with the execution of the arbitration award shall be in writing. The application shall be deemed to have been made and the notice to have been legally served, upon delivery thereof, in respect of any contracting country to the authority designated by such country in pursuance of Article 44 hereof, and in respect of the Corporation or of a member organization at its principal office.

        The parties shall by virtue of this Convention waive all other conditions concerning the service of any such notice or process.

2.   Substantive Law

In the application of the provisions of this Convention the regulations of the Corporation, decisions of the Council and other contractual rules relied upon by the parties to the dispute, the Arbitration Tribunal shall abide by the legal sources set out in Article 6 of this Convention. Subject to the Agreement of the parties to the dispute, the Tribunal may decide the dispute in accordance with the principles of justice and equity.

In no event shall the Tribunal refrain from giving judgment in the dispute on the ground of deficiency or uncertainty of the law applicable.

3.   Interpretation of the Award

Any dispute arising out of the interpretation of the award of the Arbitral Tribunal on any specific issue shall be submitted to the Tribunal by which the award has been made within three months from the date of rendering of the award.

Such reference shall be made upon an application to the Umpire by a party to the original dispute. The Umpire shall thereupon call for a meeting of the same tribunal to be held within a period of two months from the date of the application. If the same tribunal cannot be convened, a new tribunal shall be formed in accordance with the procedure laid down in paragraph 1 of this Article.

In all such cases the Tribunal may order the stay of the execution of the previous award until the new application has been determined.

*   *   *

JOINT CONVENTION ON THE FREEDOM OF MOVEMENT OF PERSONS AND THE RIGHT OF ESTABLISHMENT IN THE CENTRAL AFRICAN CUSTOMS AND ECONOMIC UNION*

> The Joint Convention on the Freedom of Movement of Persons and the Right of Establishment in the Central African Customs and Economic Union was signed on 22 December 1972. The member States of the Central African Customs and Economic Union as at September 1995 were Cameroon, the Central African Republic, Chad, Congo, Equatorial Guinea and Gabon.

Central African Customs and Economic Union

UNITED REPUBLIC OF CAMEROON

CENTRAL AFRICAN REPUBLIC

PEOPLE'S REPUBLIC OF THE CONGO

GABONESE REPUBLIC

Brazzaville, 22 December 1972

PART I. GENERAL PROVISIONS

Article 1

Nationals of the member States of the Central African Customs and Economic Union (CACEU) may, at any time, freely enter or leave the territory of any one of the member States or travel or establish residence therein, pursuant to the provisions of the present Convention.

Article 2

As from the date on which it enters into force, this Convention shall apply to member State nationals in the following categories:

1.   Persons travelling in a member State for tourism or for personal reasons, hereinafter

---

*Source: Secretariat of the Central African Customs and Economic Union (1972). *Joint Convention on the Freedom of Movement of Persons and the Right of Establishment in the Central African Customs and Economic Union* (Brazzaville: Secretariat of the Central African Customs and Economic Union) [Note added by the editor].

called "tourists";

2.   Persons travelling in another member State on business, hereinafter called "businessmen";

3.   Persons staying in the territory of another member State for the purpose of engaging in paid employment, hereinafter called "employees";

4.   Persons establishing themselves in the territory of another State in order to engage in self-employed occupations of a professional or craft- related character, hereinafter called "independent professionals".

Article 3

Nationals of CACEU member States travelling, staying or establishing themselves in the territory of another member State shall enjoy the same rights and freedoms as the nationals thereof, except for political rights.

These rights and freedoms are:

(a)   The individual rights and guarantees;

(b)   The personal and public freedoms.

PART II. MOVEMENT OF PERSONS

Article 4

There shall be freedom of movement of persons within CACEU, subject to the presentation of either a national identity card, a valid passport or passport that expired less than five years previously and an international health certificate.

Article 5

The tourists referred to in article/2 above shall include both travellers who show proof of their ability to live on their own resources and undertake not to exercise any profession during their stay and those who are travelling for reasons of family or friendship.

Freedom of movement of these persons consists of the right to travel and stay in the territory of a member State for a period of three months, taking into account the regulations in force in each country.

Article 6

The movement of "businessmen" shall be governed by the provisions of article/5 relating to tourists.

Article 7

Freedom of movement for employees shall imply the elimination of all discrimination on the basis of nationality among employees from the member States with respect to employment, remuneration and other terms of employment.

Article 8

It shall include, subject to limitations justified by public order, security and health reasons, the right:

(a)   To respond to actual offers of employment;

(b)   To travel freely for such purpose in the territories of the member States;

(c)   To stay in one of the member States in order to engage in employment in accordance with the legislative, regulatory and administrative provisions governing the employment of national employees;

(d)   Lastly, having been employed there, to remain for three months for the purpose of finding other employment or of establishing themselves in the territory of a member State.

Article 9

Member States shall encourage through joint programmes the exchange of employees at the senior management level.

Article 10

Except as otherwise specially decreed by the Government of the State concerned, the provisions of this title shall not apply to work in the civil service.

PART III. RIGHT OF ESTABLISHMENT

Article 11

Freedom of establishment includes the right of access to self-employed professional or craft-related occupations, the exercise thereof, as well as the right to set up and manage enterprises under the conditions laid down by the various laws and investment codes of the CACEU member States.

Article 12

In the context of the provisions of article/3 above, nationals of CACEU member States established in another member State shall enjoy the following rights and freedoms:

(a) The individual rights and guarantees, including freedom to engage in cultural, religious, economic, professional or social activities;

(b) The personal and public freedoms, such as freedom of thought, conscience, religion and worship, opinion and expression, assembly and association, and freedom of union membership within the context of the national trade unions.

Article 13

Nevertheless, the rights and freedoms recognized above may not impede the sovereign right of the Government of each member State to expel nationals of another member State.

The Government of the State concerned shall be immediately notified of such action. The Head of Government shall then reach a well-founded decision on the matter on a case-by-case basis.

The expelling State shall also take all appropriate measures to safeguard the property and interests of the expelled person.

Article 14

Professionals may exercise their profession in the CACEU member States under the conditions laid down by the various national legislations.

Moreover, notwithstanding the provisions of article/10 above, they may exercise their profession on a salaried basis in public offices under the conditions defined by the Governments concerned.

However, except as otherwise decreed by the Government of the member State concerned, this possibility shall not have the effect of allowing them to perform legal acts on behalf of the administration, even on an occasional basis.

Article 15

Wage-earning employees from one member State employed in the territory of another member State may establish themselves in that territory when they have ceased all paid employment or when they wish to engage in a parallel, non-conflicting occupation, provided that they meet the requirements they would have to meet for entry into the State in question.

Article 16

In drawing up the general programme for giving effect to freedom of establishment within CACEU, the General Secretariat shall in particular:

(a)   Study, on a priority basis, occupations for which freedom of establishment constitutes a particularly useful contribution to the development of production and trade;

(b)   Collect, in close cooperation with the appropriate national civil services, all useful information on particular occupations or situations within CACEU.

PART IV. SETTLEMENT OF DISPUTES

Article 17

Disputes resulting from the application of the provisions of this Convention may be settled according to an appeal procedure, the terms of which are established in the following article.

Article 18

Nationals of a CACEU member State who have been the target of discriminatory or prejudicial measures may appeal their case to the competent courts of the State in which these measures have been taken, within a period determined by national legislation.

Article 19

Sentences handed down on the subject by the courts indicated in the preceding article may be appealed to a Commission of Arbitration, whose composition, procedures and rules of submission shall be defined by a decision of the Council of Heads of State.

PART V. TRANSITIONAL PROVISIONS

Article 20

National laws shall continue to apply for a period of one year from the date on which this Convention enters into force.

Article 21

Within the context of this Convention, one year from the date on which it enters into force, freedom of movement of persons shall be effective within CACEU, and restrictions on freedom of establishment shall be eliminated.

Article 22

Before the end of the transitional period specified in article/20 of this Convention, the Management Committee of the Central African Customs and Economic Union shall decide on measures required to give effect to the freedom of movement of employees by, in particular:

(a)   Establishing, under the General Secretariat of CACEU, an Inter-State Bureau responsible for ensuring the necessary cooperation among the national civil services, for matching offers of employment with requests and for proposing all appropriate measures to avoid risks of imbalances in the standards of living and employment levels of the various regions and industries;

(b)   Eliminating administrative procedures and practices and delays in access to employment resulting from previous legislation or previously concluded agreements between member States whose retention would stand in the way of achieving freedom of movement for employees or which set different requirements for employees from other member States than for nationals with respect to free choice of employment;

(c)   Establishing, in the area of social security, mechanisms for ensuring migrant workers and their beneficiaries of stability with respect to the initiation, continued validity and calculation of benefits for all periods covered by the various national legislations, as well as for payment thereof to persons residing in the territory of other member States.

PART VI. FINAL PROVISIONS

Article 23

Agreements on the freedom of movement of persons and the right of establishment concluded between or among one or more CACEU member States prior to the date on which this Convention enters into force shall remain valid in so far as they are not contrary to the present provisions.

*   *   *

AGREEMENT ON THE HARMONISATION OF FISCAL INCENTIVES TO INDUSTRY[*]

The Agreement on the Harmonisation of Fiscal Incentives to Industry was opened for signature by the States members of the Caribbean Community (CARICOM) on 1 June 1973. It entered into force on 1 August 1973. The member States of CARICOM are Antigua and Barbuda, Barbados, Belize, Dominica, Grenada, Guyana, Jamaica, Montserrat, Saint Kitts and Nevis, Saint Lucia, Saint Vincent and the Grenadines, Suriname and Trinidad and Tobago. The appendices to the Agreement have not been reproduced in this volume. In the context of a redefinition of macro-economic policies in many member States of CARICOM, a decision was taken to review the Harmonised Scheme and to devise a framework for the development of a harmonised system of incentives for the industrial/manufacturing, agriculture, tourism and other industries in CARICOM member States. This framework was still under consideration as of October 1995.

THE CONTRACTING PARTIES:

In pursuance of the declared intention set out in Article 40 in the Annex to the Agreement establishing the Caribbean Community to take measures to secure the adoption of a regional policy of incentives to industry as early as possible;

RECOGNISING the need for promoting the balanced and harmonious development of the Region by means of the conferment of incentives to industry;

AND NOTING that steps have been taken for the establishment of a Common Market within a Caribbean Community:

HAVE AGREED AS FOLLOWS:

Article 1
Establishment of Scheme

By this Agreement, the Contracting Parties establish a Scheme to be known as "The harmonisation of Fiscal Incentives to Industry Scheme" (hereinafter referred to as "the Scheme") which shall be implemented under and in accordance with this Agreement.

---

[*]Source: Caribbean Community Secretariat (1973). *Agreement on the Harmonisation of Fiscal Incentives to Industry* (Georgetown, Guyana: Caribbean Community Secretariat), mimeo. [Note added by the editor].

Article 2
Participation in the Scheme

1.   Participation in the Scheme shall be open to -

(a)   (i)   Antigua and Barbuda
        (ii)   The Bahamas
        (iii)   Barbados
        (iv)   Belize
        (v)   Dominica
        (vi)   Grenada
        (vii)   Guyana
        (viii)   Jamaica
        (ix)   Montserrat
        (x)   St. Kitts/Nevis/Anguilla
        (xi)   St. Lucia
        (xii)   St. Vincent
        (xiii)   Trinidad and Tobago

(b)   Any other state of the Caribbean region that becomes a member of the Caribbean Community.

2.   States listed in paragraph 1 (a) of this Article the Governments of which sign this Agreement in accordance with the Article 20 and ratify it in accordance with Article 21 shall become participants in the Scheme.

3.   States referred to in paragraph I (b) of this Article, the Governments of which accede to this Agreement in accordance with Article 26 shall become participants in the Scheme.

Article 3
Definitions

1.   In this Agreement, unless the context otherwise requires - "approved enterprise" means an enterprise which is approved by the relevant authority of a Member State for the purpose of conferring a benefit under the Scheme;

"approved product" means subject to this Agreement, a product of manufacture approved by the relevant authority of a Member State for manufacture by an approved enterprise;

"benefit" means any relief granted by a Member State to an approved enterprise under and in accordance with this Agreement;

"enterprise" means a company incorporated under the laws of the Member State conferring a benefit to an approved enterprise and engaged or about to engage in an industry;

"income Tax" means any tax (by whatever name called) on income or profits imposed by a Member State;

"industry" means a manufacturing or processing industry, and includes Deep Sea Fishing and Shrimping, but only if they form part of an integrated processing operation;

"Group I Enterprise" means an enterprise in respect of which the local value added is not less than 50 per centum or more of the amount realised from the sales of an approved product;

"Group II Enterprise" means an enterprise in respect of which the local value added is not less than 25 per centum or more but is less than 50 per centum of the amount realised from the sales of an approved product;

"Group III Enterprise" means an enterprise in respect of which the local value added is not less than 10 per centum or more but is less than 25 per centum of the amount realised from the sales of an approved product;

"enclave enterprise" means an enterprise producing exclusively for export to countries outside the Common Market;

"local value added" means the amount (expressed as a percentage of the total cost of the approved product) by which the amount realised from the sales of an approved product (in respect of a continuous period of twelve months) exceeds the aggregate amount of the following:

      (i)   the value of imported raw materials, components, and parts of components, fuels and services;

     (ii)   wages and salaries paid during the period to persons who are not nationals of Member States;

    (iii)   profits distributed and remitted directly or indirectly to persons (including companies) who are not resident in any Member States;

    (iv)   interest, management charges and other income payments accruing directly or indirectly to persons (including companies) not resident in any Member State, other than a branch or agency of banks not resident in any Member State;

    (iv)   depreciation of imported plant, machinery and equipment;

"Member State" means a State referred to in paragraph 2 or 3 of Article 2 of this Agreement.

"More Developed Country" means The Bahamas, Barbados, Guyana, Jamaica and Trinidad and Tobago; and "Less Developed Country" means any other Member State referred to in paragraph 1 (a) of Article 2 of this Agreement;

"National" means a person who is a citizen of any Member State and includes a person who has a connection with such a State of a kind which entitles him to be regarded as belonging to or, if it be so expressed, as being a native or resident of the State for the purpose of such laws thereof relating to immigration as are for the time being, in force;

"production date" means the date on which an approved enterprise commences production of the approved product or such other date as may be specified in accordance with the laws of a Member State as the case may be;

"sale" means sales ex-factory of an approved product;

2.   The local value added shall be weighted by the wages and salaries paid to nationals of any Member State expressed as a percentage of total sales of the approved product and calculated by the following formula:

$$\frac{V(100 + W)}{100}$$

Where - 'V' is the local value added expressed as a percentage of the total cost of the approved product;

'W' is the wages and salaries paid to nationals of any Member State, expressed as a percentage of the total sales of the approved product;

Member States are free to determine the weight to be given to each factor but in no case must any factor be more than 0.5 and the total of all weights more than 1.

3.   For the purpose of sub-paragraph (i) of the definition of "local value added" in paragraph 1 of this Article, in determining the value of the content of any component produced by any of the Member States, no account shall be taken of any element in the cost of that component, other than the value of the imported raw material content.

4.   For the purposes of sub-paragraphs (iii) and (iv) of the definition of "local value added" in paragraph I of this Article, a Company shall be taken to be not resident in any Member State if it is controlled directly or indirectly by a person (including a company) who is not resident in any Member State; and such a person shall be taken to have control over the affairs of the company and in particular, but without prejudice to the generality of the foregoing, if he possesses or is entitled to acquire the greater part of the ordinary and paid up share capital (excluding shares which carry no voting rights) or voting power of the company.

Article 4
Discretion as to Benefits

The extent to which any benefit under this Agreement may be granted to an approved enterprise shall be at the discretion of Member States, so, however, that no Member State may grant benefits to an approved enterprise for a period or at percentage rates in excess of, or on conditions contrary to, those specified in this Agreement.

Article 5
Classification of Approved Enterprises

1. For the purpose of the grant of any benefit under this Agreement each enterprise must be classified under one of the following categories:

    (a)   Group I enterprise;
           Group II enterprise; or
           Group III enterprise respectively; or

    (b)   Enclave enterprise,

    as the case may be.

2. For the purpose of the classification of an enterprise as a Group I Enterprise, Group II Enterprise or Group III Enterprise, the local value added shall, in the first instance, be estimated in order to determine the group in which the enterprise is to be classified.

3. On an appraisal of the performance of an approved enterprise pursuant to Article 16 of this Agreement, the approved enterprise must be re-classified into the appropriate Group and allocated the appropriate number of years of relief set out in Appendix I to this Agreement, as is determined by such appraisal, or the status of such approved enterprise must be deemed revoked in accordance with paragraph 2(a) of Article 16 of this Agreement, as the case may be.

4. Where an enterprise is engaged in a highly capitalised industry -

    (a)   nothing in the foregoing provisions of this Article shall apply thereto for the purpose of this Agreement; and

    (b)   a Member State may grant any benefit to the enterprise for a period not exceeding that for which the benefit may be granted to Enclave Enterprises in accordance with Appendix I to this Agreement.

5. In paragraph 4 of this Article, a "highly capitalised industry" is one in which the capital investment is not less than -

(a) $25 million in the currency of the Eastern Caribbean Territories in any Less Developed Country:

(b) $50 million in the currency of the Eastern Caribbean Territories in any More Developed Country.

Article 6
Relief from Tonnage Tax and Customs Duty on Plant, Equipment, Machinery, Spare Parts and Raw Materials

Member States must not grant to an approved enterprise relief from customs duties (including tonnage tax) on plant, equipment, machinery, spare parts, raw materials and components imported from outside the Member States for use in the manufacture of approved products for a period in excess of that respectively specified in Appendix I to this Agreement, so, however, that if the relevant authority of the Member State is satisfied that raw materials of a comparable price and quality in adequate quantities are available from Member States for import and the approved enterprise continues to import raw materials from States other than Member States, the relevant authority must impose tariff and quota restrictions on the importation of such raw materials from States other than Member States provided that no restriction shall apply to any relief from customs duty on imported raw materials or components used in Enclave Enterprises.

Article 7
Relief from Income Tax

1.   Member States must not grant to an approved enterprise relief from income tax in respect of profits or gains derived from the manufacture of the approved product for a period in excess of that respectively specified in Appendix I to this Agreement.

2.   Subject to the provisions of the Agreement, any relief from income tax shall be granted only in respect of profits accruing from the commercial production date of an approved enterprise.

Article 8
Relief from Income Tax Liability on Export Profits

1.   Member States must grant relief from income tax on export profits only in accordance with this article.

2.   Member States must provide that if relief is granted under this Article to an approved enterprise, such relief may not be enjoyed by that enterprise during any period for which relief is granted under Article 6 or 7 or both.

3.   The relief which may be granted to an approved enterprise under this Article shall be by way of a tax credit and must not be in excess of the percentage of income tax liability

on the full amount of export profits of the approved enterprise from the manufacture of the approved product specified in the second column of the Table overleaf, where the amount of export profit expressed as a percentage of the full amount of the profits of the approved enterprise from the manufacture of the approved product is as respectively specified in the first column of the Table.

Table

FIRST COLUMN	SECOND COLUMN
Percentage of Export Profits	Maximum Percentage of Income Tax Relief
10% or more but less than 21%	25%
21% or more but less than 41%	35%
41% or more but less than 61%	45%
61% or more	50%

4.   For the purposes of paragraph 3 of this Article, export profits shall be taken to be the profits produced by the following formula:

$$\frac{E \times P}{S}$$

where: E is the proceeds from export sales for the year;

P is the profits of the approved enterprise from all sales of the approved product for the year

and   S is the proceeds of all sales for the year.

5.   No relief under this Article may be granted by a Member State to an enterprise engaged in a traditionally export-oriented industry in respect of a product of that industry that is traditionally exported by that Member State.

6.   Subject to paragraphs 7 and 8 of this Article, relief under this Article may be granted only in respect of the export of an approved product to a State other than a Member State.

7.   Less Developed Countries may grant relief under this Article to an approved enterprise for export to More Developed Countries, other than Barbados, for a period not exceeding seven years next following the expiration of any period of relief granted under Articles 6 and 7 or both of this Agreement.

8.   During the period of five years after the commencement of this Agreement, a Less Developed Country may, notwithstanding paragraph 6, grant relief under this Article in respect of the exports to More Developed Countries, other than Barbados, by an approved enterprise to which no relief under Articles 6 and 7 of this Agreement is granted.

Article 9
Depreciation Allowances

Member States must provide that in computing the profits of an approved enterprise for the purposes of any relief from income tax under Article 7 of this Agreement, there shall be allowed and made -

(a)   as from the commercial production date of the approved enterprise, a deduction on account of any depreciation allowance which would, but for that relief, be claimable in the year;

(b)   such further deduction as an initial allowance for capital expenditure on plant, machinery and equipment incurred by the approved enterprise in the manufacture of the approved product after the expiration of the period of relief from income tax granted in accordance with Article 7 of this Agreement as the Member State may determine, but so that such deduction does not exceed twenty per centum of the capital expenditure.

Article 10
Carry Forward of Losses

1.   Member States must provide that, upon the cessation of any relief from income tax under Article 7 of this Agreement, the net losses made during the period of such relief may, notwithstanding the grant of that relief in accordance with this Agreement, be carried forward for the purpose of set off in computing the profits of an enterprise for the period of five years next following the cessation of the relief.

2.   If the status of an enterprise as an approved enterprise is revoked or deemed revoked under the laws of a Member State or under those laws made pursuant to paragraph 2(a) of Article 16, of this Agreement, such an enterprise shall be treated for the purpose of carrying forward losses incurred before such revocation, as if it were an approved enterprise.

3.   In this Article, "net losses" means the excess of the sum of all losses over the sum of all profits made during the period of the relief.

Article 11
Dividends and other Distributions

1. Dividends and other distributions out of profits or gains accruing to an approved enterprise from the manufacture of the approved product during the period of relief from income tax under Article 7 of this Agreement must not, be subject to any limitation as to the time within which the dividends and other distributions are to be made.

2. Subject to paragraph 3, such dividends and other distributions made by an approved enterprise out of profits or gains accruing during the period of relief from income tax under Article 7 of this Agreement, or made by a recipient of such a dividend or other distribution may be exempt from income tax in the hands of a recipient.

3. Where the recipient is not resident in any Member State, the exemption shall apply to so much only of the tax as exceeds the tax liability of the recipient on such dividend or other distribution in the recipient's country of residence.

Article 12
Interest

Interest (in any form) on loan capital and any other borrowings of an approved enterprise (whether in the form of overdraft, debenture or otherwise) must not be exempt from income tax in the hands of the recipient.

Article 13
Exclusions and Limitations

More Developed Countries must not grant relief from income tax under Article 7 of this Agreement to an approved enterprise respecting the manufacture of any product specified in the list in Appendix II to this Agreement but nothing in this Article shall be construed as authorising the grant of relief under Article 8 of this Agreement to an approved enterprise respecting the manufacture of any product referred to in paragraph 5 of Article 8 of this Agreement as well as in Appendix II to this Agreement.

Article 14
Treatment of Established Industries

Member States must provide that where 60 per cent and, in the case of Barbados, 90 per cent, of the domestic market of a More Developed Country for any product is already supplied by Industry in that State, no relief from Income tax under Article 7 of this Agreement may be granted to an enterprise by that State.

Article 15
Savings for Benefits under Existing Laws

1. This Agreement is not to be taken to have revoked or otherwise affected any rights in the nature of benefits enjoyed by an enterprise under the law of a Member State in force immediately before the commencement of this Agreement and those laws may continue to have effect for the purpose of the enjoyment of those rights.

2. Member States must provide that all applications for such rights pending under those laws at the commencement of this Agreement must, under the ligislation of Member States referred to in Article 17, be deemed to have been made under that legislation and must be dealt with accordingly and Member States must not grant rights in the nature of benefits pending the enactment of such legislation.

Article 16
Appraisals

1. Member States must provide that the relevant authority appraise the performance of an approved enterprise classified in a Group to which a benefit, other than relief under Article 8 of this Agreement, is granted for the purpose of determining whether a change in the Classification in the group of that enterprise under Article 5 of this Agreement should be made -

    (a)   in the first instance, at the end of three years after the production date; and

    (b)   thereafter at the end of each period of two years until the cessation of all benefits other than relief from income tax under Article 8 of this Agreement.

2. Where, on an appraisal pursuant to paragraph 1 of this Article, an approved enterprise-

    (a)   fails to maintain its classification and fails to qualify for re-classification in any other Group set out in Appendix I to this Agreement, the status of that enterprise as an approved enterprise shall be deemed revoked for the purpose of relief under Articles 6 and 7 of this Agreement and nothing in paragraph 1(b) of this Article shall apply;

    (b)   maintains its classification or is re-classified to a lower or higher Group set out in Appendix I to this Agreement, that enterprise shall continue to have the status of an approved enterprise and the provisions of paragraph 1(b) of this Article shall continue to apply accordingly.

Article 17
Implementation

Member States shall be responsible for implementing the Scheme as early as possible by legislation in accordance with this Agreement.

Article 18
Administration

1.   The Eastern Caribbean Common Market Secretariat shall (where so requested) assist Member States of that Organisation in the performance of the appraisal under Article 16 of this Agreement.

2.   The Commonwealth Caribbean Regional Secretariat shall collect information and act as clearing house for the flow of information collected from Member States regarding the operation of the scheme.

Article 19
Review of Scheme

The Scheme shall be reviewed by the Council at the end of five years from the commencement of this Agreement.

Article 20
Signature

This Agreement is open for signature by any State mentioned in paragraph 1(a) of Article 2 of this Agreement.

Article 21
Ratification

This Agreement shall be subject to ratification by the signatory States in accordance with their respective constitutional procedures. Instruments of Ratification shall be deposited with the Commonwealth Caribbean Regional Secretariat which shall transmit certified copies to the Government of each Member State.

Article 22
Entry into Force

This Agreement shall enter into force if Instruments of Ratification have been previously deposited in accordance with Article 21 of this Agreement, by at least ten of the States mentioned in paragraph 1(a) of Article 2 thereof and if not, then on such later date on which the tenth such Instrument has been deposited.

Article 23
Registration

This Agreement and any amendments thereto shall be registered with the Secretariat of the United Nations.

Article 24
Amendments

1. This Agreement may be amended by the Contracting Parties.

2. Any such amendments shall be subject to ratification and shall enter into force one month after the date on which the last instrument of Ratification is deposited with the Commonwealth Caribbean Regional Secretariat.

Article 25
Withdrawal

A Member State may withdraw from this Agreement by giving notice in writing to the Commonwealth Caribbean Regional Secretariat. Such withdrawal shall take effect twelve months after the notice is received by the Commonwealth Caribbean Regional Secretariat.

Article 26
Accession to the Treaty

1. Any State of the Caribbean Region may apply to become a party to this Agreement and may if the Member State so decide, be admitted to membership in accordance with paragraph 2 of this Article.

2. Admission to membership shall be upon such terms and conditions as the Member States may decide and shall be effected by the deposit of an appropriate Instrument of Accession with the Caribbean Community Secretariat.

IN WITNESS WHEREOF the undersigned plenipotentiaries being duly authorised thereunto by their respective Governments have signed this present Agreement.

DONE at Georgetown, Guyana on the 1st day of June 1973 in a single copy, certified copies of which shall be transmitted to all Contracting Parties.

Signed by _____
for the Government of Antigua on _____
at _____

Signed by _____
for the Government of Barbados on _____
at _____

Signed by _____
for the Government of Belize on _____
at _____

Signed by _____
for the Government of Dominica on _____
at _____

Signed by _____
for the Government of Grenada on _____
at _____

Signed by _____
for the Government of Guyana on _____
at _____

Signed by _____
for the Government of Jamaica on _____
at _____

Signed by _____
for the Government of Montserrat on _____
at _____

Signed by _____
for the Government of St. Kitts/Nevis/Anguilla on _____
at _____

Signed by _____
for the Government of Saint Lucia on _____
at _____

Signed by _____
for the Government of St. Vincent on _____
at _____

Signed by _____
for the Government of Trinidad and Tobago on _____
at _____

* * *

MULTINATIONAL COMPANIES CODE IN THE UDEAC*

The Multinational Companies Code in the UDEAC (Customs and Economic Union of Central Africa) was adopted on 3 December 1975 (Act No. 3-75-UDEAC-183) and entered into force on 15 April 1976. The member States of UDEAC are Cameroon, Central African Republic, Chad, Congo, Equatorial Guinea and Gabon.

THE MULTINATIONAL COMPANIES CODE IN THE UDEAC

CHAPTER I
Purposes of Multinational Companies

1. Multinational companies are set up for the following purposes:

   a) To contribute to the reinforcement of the Customs and Economic Union of Central Africa by the establishment of new relations of interdependence and solidarity between member States;

   b) To facilitate and accelerate economic cooperation between member States;

   c) To encourage harmonious and balanced development and also the diversification of the economies of the member States;

   d) To lead to the implementation of projects of regional interest and to stimulate inter-State trade;

   e) To encourage and promote the progressive participation of undertakings, cadres and national capital in the property and the management of undertakings situated in the member States of the Union;

   f) To give greater strength in negotiations with those possessing capital and technological resources outside the Union with a view to obtaining the most favourable conditions in satisfying economic development needs;

   g) To encourage and facilitate the transfer of technology by associating national counterparts with the activities and studies of foreign experts;

---

*Source: Official Gazette of the United Republic of Cameroon (1976). "Multinational Companies Code in the Central African Customs and Economic Union", No. 1236, 15 April 1976, pp. 5-10. It should be noted that the Central African Customs and Economic Union is known by both its French and English acronyms, UDEAC and CACEU, respectively [Note added by the editor].

h)   To reinforce the competitiveness of the Union's undertakings in regional markets and in the markets of third countries.

CHAPTER II
The Multinational Company

2.   The multinational company is a commercial company enjoying legal status and fulfilling the conditions stated in Articles 3 *et seq.* of this Code.

3.   The decision as to whether the object of a multinational company is of regional interest shall be taken in accordance with the provisions of Article 4 by the competent authority of UDEAC when two or more member States are concerned.

4.   The following in particular shall be considered as for regional interest:

a)   *as concerns raw materials and staple products*: the development of mineral, forest, agricultural, or maritime resources throughout the territory of two or more States when the products are intended for consumption on the UDEAC market or for export outside the region;

b)   as concerns *industry*: the processing of agricultural, stock raising and fishery products, and the manufacture, processing and packaging of goods, intermediary products and finished products for markets extending outside the State where the company is located;

c)   as concerns *economic infrastructures*: the development of water resources, and the construction of bridges, main roads, ports, communication networks, power distribution systems, and irrigation projects throughout the territory of two or more States;

d)   as concerns *services*: land, air, river and sea transport; maintenance and control services; the organization and development of distribution networks throughout the territory of two or more States; the stimulation of the consumption of the products of member States outside UDEAC; standardization activities, the grading and packaging of local or imported products; the organization in common of sale or purchase activities; tourist activities; financing or prefinancing activities for the provision of guarantees; and insurance and reinsurance activities.

B. *Capital structure*

5.   The capital must be constituted in the proportions defined in Article 7 by the contributions of national investors in two or more member States of the Union.

6.   For the purposes of this Code the following shall be considered as national investors and foreign investors respectively:

a)   *national investors*: member States, public bodies and other corporate bodies of any member State of UDEAC, provided that national participation in the capital of such bodies is more than 50 per cent with the right to vote; and natural persons from any UDEAC member State.

b)   *foreign investors*: natural persons and corporate bodies of foreign nationality, as well as companies in whose capital national participation is less than 50 per cent.

7.   (1)   Subject to the exceptions provided for in Article 9 of this Code, when the initial participation of national investors does not reach 51 per cent, it must be more than 33 per cent of the capital, with the right to vote.

(2)   Should the participation of foreign investors be more than 49 per cent of the capital of the multinational company, the decision admitting it to one of the preferential schedules of the common convention on investments in the UDEAC States should provide for the gradual transfer of part of the capital held by foreign investors, while taking into account the obligations to be fulfilled by the multinational company, so that at the end of a period of ten years from the date of its constitution the participation of national investors should be not less than 51 per cent of the capital, with the right to vote.

8.   (1)   National investors of any member State of the Union shall have priority over foreign investors when the multinational company is set up, at the time of any increase in its capital, or when shares are transferred.

(2)   In all cases, publication shall be ensured in accordance with the provisions of Article 16 of the Treaty of UDEAC, by the Secretariat General of the Union, at the request of the founders or the Board of Directors of the multinational company.

9.   The Management Committee of UDEAC may establish percentages for the participation of national investors that are different from those provided for in Article 7, under the following circumstances:

a)   when the national investors are the States themselves, public bodies, State corporations and semi-government corporations in which the State holds the majority of the shares;

b)   when the national regulations relating to given sectors of activity require the application of different conditions.

CHAPTER III
Approval of the multinational company

10.   (1)   The founders of a multinational company must forward an application for

approval to the competent Minister of the State where the company is to be located in accordance with Articles 11 *et seq.* of this Code.

(2) If all the founders are States or States bodies, the application for approval shall be submitted by the State where the company is to be located directly to the Management Committee of the Union for examination.

11. The application for approval must be accompanied by the following documents:

a) legal documents including the draft articles of association of the multinational company, drawn up in accordance with the provisions of Chapter IV of this Code.

b) economic documents giving precise data relating to:

- the capital structure and the nationality of investors, in accordance with the provisions of Chapter II;
- a description of the object of the company including sufficient information on its economic activity for its regional interest to be evaluated;
- the date of the start of the multinational company's activities;
- the production capacity;
- the origin and nature of the raw materials;
- the use to be made of raw materials and intermediate products from UDEAC States;
- the means of transport to be used;
- the division of goods or services between the UDEAC market and markets outside UDEAC;
- the price of goods delivered or services rendered and the rate of loans;
- the proposed number of employments, the percentage of labour from the Union, the proportion of the managerial staff from the Union and of the supervisory personnel, the facilities within the Union for vocational training of staff and the progressive replacement of the foreign cadres by nationals of the member States;

c) technical documents including:

- the layout plan (engineering);
- civil engineering work;
- list of equipment and installations;
- power sources used;
- marketing and performance;
- the technological chain;
- the possibilities for sub-contracting by national studies institutes and bodies.

d) financial documents including:

- the overall amount of the proposed investments;

- the sources of finances;
- estimated trading accounts over 10 years;
- a breakdown of the turnover according to the major manufactures;
- redemption tables (capital and loans);
- operating overheads;
- breakdown of wholesale selling prices;
- budget estimates over 10 years.

12.   The documents referred to in Article 11 above shall be examined by the competent Minister of the State in which the company is located who shall transmit them, with his considered opinion, to the Secretariat General of UDEAC within the following two months.

13.   (1)   The Secretary General of UDEAC shall transmit the documents received to the Competent Ministers of the other members States without delay.

        (2)   The Secretary General shall prepare a report containing a detailed evaluation of the activity of the multinational company, in the light of the objectives of the Treaty of Brazzaville and criteria established by this Code.

        (3)   In their turn, the States other than that where the company is located shall communicate to the Secretary General within two months any information bearing on the application and their remarks concerning the approval of the multinational company.

        (4)   The Secretary General of UDEAC shall submit the documents together with the recommendations of the States and his own report to the next Management Committee.

14.   (1)   The Management Committee of UDEAC shall examine the documents mentioned in Article 13 and shall decide on the application for approval made by the multinational company.

        (2)   If agreement is not reached, the matter shall be submitted to the arbitration of the Council of Heads of State.

15.   The decision of the Management Committee or else that of the Council of Heads of State shall be notified to the competent authorities of the member States of the Union which shall inform the founders of the multinational company.

CHAPTER IV
Constitution and Organization of Multinational Companies

16.   (1)   Multinational companies must be constituted as limited liability companies.

        (2)   However, the Council of Heads of State of UDEAC may approve other forms of

organization of a multinational company, provided that the latter enjoys legal status.

17.   Multinational Companies shall be constituted and their articles of association established in accordance with the laws of the State in which they are located, and with the provisions of this Code.

18.   (1)   Multinational Companies shall be so constituted that national investors belonging to the various member States, in particular, may participate:

    a)   by setting up a new company;

    b)   by transforming the existing companies;

    c)   by increasing the capital of existing companies;

    d)   by the merger of existing companies;

    e)   by an exchange of shares between existing companies.

    (2)   In each of these cases, the terms and conditions of constitution shall be defined in accordance with the provisions of Article 17.

19.   (1)   The registered office shall be established in the State where the company is located.

    (2)   Multinational companies may set up subsidiary companies or branches in member States of the Union.

20.   The articles of association of multinational companies must comply with the following rules:

    I.   shares shall be registered;

    II.   (1)   the transfer of shares of a multinational company may under no circumstances affect the principle of national investors holding the majority of the shares, subject to the provisions of Article 9.

        (2)   Subject to the aforementioned rules, transfers may be made freely:

        - between member States participating in the capital of the multinational company;

        - between shareholders in the same member State.

        (3)   With the above exceptions, transfers of shares may not be effected without the approval of the Board of Directors of the multinational company.

        (4)   National investors shall have a right of pre-emption for the purchase of

shares put up for sale, in the proportion of the shares already held and subject to the provisions of Article 9.

(5)   As regards the other forms of organization of companies referred to in Article 16, partners shall comply with the regulations in force in the State where the registered office of the multinational company is located.

III.   The general meeting of shareholders may be held in the place where the registered office of the multinational company is located or where its subsidiary companies and branches are located.

IV.   The general meeting cannot take valid decisions on the questions listed below unless at least half the capital is represented and the decision is taken by a three-quarters majority of the paid-up shares:

a) amendments to the articles of association;
b) increases or reductions in the capital;
c) the transformation of the company; and
d) the winding up of the company.

V.   (1)   When foreign investors participate in a multinational company, the national shareholders and the foreign shareholders shall separately appoint members of the Board of Directors according to the proportions laid down in the articles of association.

(2)   In all cases, there must be at least one member for each State whose nationals participate in the capital of the multinational company.

VI.   The accounts must be kept at the registered office of the multinational company in accordance with the regulations of the UDEAC Accounting Plan.

21.   (1)   The deed of partnership of the multinational company shall be published in the *Official Gazette* of the Union. Publication shall also be made in the official gazettes of the member States.

(2)   A multinational company must be registered as required by the UDEAC Secretariat General.

22.   The multinational company may apply for admission to one of the preferential schedules appropriate to its needs and size of the common convention on investments in the UDEAC.

CHAPTER V
Miscellaneous provisions

23.   This Code shall be available to any interested African State which so requests.

*   *   *

DECLARATION ON INTERNATIONAL INVESTMENT AND MULTINATIONAL ENTERPRISES[*]

The Declaration on International Investment and Multinational Enterprises was adopted by OECD member countries on 21 June 1976. The Guidelines for Multinational Enterprises were annexed to the Declaration. The Guidelines were adopted in the form of a recommendation to transnational corporations. Also reproduced in the present volume are the Procedural Decisions of the OECD Council that contain binding directives to Member countries. Together, these instruments have provided the OECD framework for transnational corporations. They were reviewed in 1979, 1984 and 1991. These reviews resulted in a number of amendments in, and the addition of new sections to, the basic texts. Thus, the texts reproduced in this volume are the official texts in force as of December 1991.

THE GOVERNMENTS OF OECD MEMBER COUNTRIES[1]:

CONSIDERING

-- That international investment has assumed increased importance in the world economy and has considerably contributed to the development of their countries;

-- That multinational enterprises play an important role in this investment process;

-- That co-operation by Member countries can improve the foreign investment climate, encourage the positive contribution which multinational enterprises can make to economic and social progress, and minimise and resolve difficulties which may arise from their various operations;

-- That, while continuing endeavours within the OECD may lead to further international arrangements and agreements in this field, it seems appropriate at this stage to intensify their co-operation and consultation on issues relating to international investment and multinational enterprises through inter-related instruments each of which deals with a different aspect of the matter and together constitute a framework within which the OECD will consider these issues;

---

[*]Source: Organisation for Economic Co-operation and Development (1992). *The OECD Declaration and Decisions on International Investment and Multinational Enterprises: 1991 Review* (Paris: OECD), Annexes I and II, pp. 101-120. The notes to the Declaration and the Procedural Decisions have been reproduced at the end of each instrument, as they appear in the original source [Note added by the editor].

DECLARE:

Guidelines for Multinational Enterprises

I.   That they jointly recommend to multinational enterprises operating in their territories the observance of the Guidelines as set forth in Annex 1 hereto having regard to the considerations and understandings which introduce the Guidelines and are an integral part of them;

National Treatment

II.   1.   That Member countries should, consistent with their needs to maintain public order, to protect their essential security interests and to fulfil commitments relating to international peace and security, accord to enterprises operating in their territories and owned or controlled directly or indirectly by nationals of another Member country (hereinafter referred to as "Foreign-Controlled Enterprises") treatment under their laws, regulations and administrative practices, consistent with international law and no less favourable than that accorded in like situations to domestic enterprises (hereinafter referred to as "National Treatment");

       2.   That Member countries will consider applying "National Treatment" in respect of countries other than Member countries;

       3.   That Member countries will endeavour to ensure that their territorial subdivisions apply "National Treatment";

       4.   That this Declaration does not deal with the right of Member countries to regulate the entry of foreign investment or the conditions of establishment of foreign enterprises;

Conflicting Requirements

III.   That they will co-operate with a view to avoiding or minimising the imposition of conflicting requirements on multinational enterprises and that they will take into account the general considerations and practical approaches as set forth in Annex 2 hereto.

International Investment Incentives and Disincentives

IV.   1.   That they recognise the need to strengthen their co-operation in the field of international direct investment;

       2.   That they thus recognise the need to give due weight to the interests of Member countries affected by specific laws, regulations and administrative practices in this field (hereinafter called "measures") providing official incentives and disincentives to international direct investment;

3.   That Member countries will endeavour to make such measures as transparent as possible, so that their importance and purpose can be ascertained and that information on them can be readily available;

Consultation Procedures

V.   That they are prepared to consult one another on the above matters in conformity with the Decisions of the Council on the Guidelines for Multinational Enterprises, on National Treatment and on International Investment Incentives and Disincentives;

Review

VI.   That they will review the above matters within three years with a view to improving the effectiveness of international economic co-operation among Member countries on issues relating to international investment and multinational enterprises[2].

ANNEX 1
GUIDELINES FOR MULTINATIONAL ENTERPRISES[3]

1.   Multinational enterprises now play an important part in the economies of Member countries and in international economic relations, which is of increasing interest to governments. Through international direct investment, such enterprises can bring substantial benefits to home and host countries by contributing to the efficient utilisation of capital, technology and human resources between countries and can thus fulfil an important role in the promotion of economic and social welfare. But the advances made by multinational enterprises in organising their operations beyond the national framework may lead to abuse of concentrations of economic power and to conflicts with national policy objectives. In addition, the complexity of these multinational enterprises and the difficulty of clearly perceiving their diverse structures, operations and policies sometimes give rise to concern.

2.   The common aim of the Member countries is to encourage the positive contributions which multinational enterprises can make to economic and social progress and to minimise and resolve the difficulties to which their various operations may give rise. In view of the transnational structure of such enterprises, this aim will be furthered by co-operation among the OECD countries where the headquarters of most of the multinational enterprises are established and which are the location of a substantial part of their operations. The Guidelines set out hereafter are designed to assist in the achievement of this common aim and to contribute to improving the foreign investment climate.

3.   Since the operations of multinational enterprises extend throughout the world, including countries that are not Members of the Organisation, international co-operation in this field should extend to all States. Member countries will give their full support to efforts undertaken in co-operation with non-member countries, and in particular with developing countries, with a view to improving the welfare and living standards of all people both by encouraging the positive

contributions which multinational enterprises can make and by minimizing and resolving the problems which may arise in connection with their activities.

4.   Within the Organisation, the programme of co-operation to attain these ends will be a continuing, pragmatic and balanced one. It comes within the general aims of the Convention on the Organisation for Economic Co-operation and Development (OECD) and makes full use of the various specialised bodies of the Organisation, whose terms of reference already cover many aspects of the role of multinational enterprises, notably in matters of international trade and payments, competition, taxation, manpower, industrial development, science and technology. In these bodies, work is being carried out on the identification of issues, the improvement of relevant qualitative and statistical information and the elaboration of proposals for action designed to strengthen inter-governmental co-operation. In some of these areas procedures already exist through which issues related to the operations of multinational enterprises can be taken up. This work could result in the conclusion of further and complementary agreements and arrangements between governments.

5.   The initial phase of the co-operation programme is composed of a Declaration and three Decisions promulgated simultaneously as they are complementary and inter-connected, in respect of Guidelines for multinational enterprises, National Treatment for foreign-controlled enterprises and international investment incentives and disincentives.

6.   The Guidelines set out below are recommendations jointly addressed by Member countries to multinational enterprises operating in their territories. These Guidelines, which take into account the problems which can arise because of the international structure of these enterprises, lay down standards for the activities of these enterprises in the different Member countries. Observance of the Guidelines is voluntary and not legally enforceable. However, they should help to ensure that the operations of these enterprises are in harmony with national policies of the countries where they operate and to strengthen the basis of mutual confidence between enterprises and States.

7.   Every State has the right to prescribe the conditions under which multinational enterprises operate within its national jurisdiction, subject to international law and to the international agreements to which it has subscribed. The entities of a multinational enterprise located in various countries are subject to the laws of these countries.

8.   A precise legal definition of multinational enterprises is not required for the purposes of the Guidelines. These usually comprise companies or other entities whose ownership is private, state or mixed, established in different countries and so linked that one or more of them may be able to exercise a significant influence over the activities of others and, in particular, to share knowledge and resources with the others. The degrees of autonomy of each entity in relation to the others varies widely from one multinational enterprise to another, depending on the nature of the links between such entities and the fields of activity concerned. For these reasons, the Guidelines are addressed to the various entities within the multinational enterprise (parent companies and/or local entities) according to the actual distribution of responsibilities among them on the understanding that they will co-operate and provide assistance to one another as

necessary to facilitate observance of the Guidelines. The word "enterprise" as used in these Guidelines refers to these various entities in accordance with their responsibilities.

9.   The Guidelines are not aimed at introducing differences of treatment between multinational and domestic enterprises; wherever relevant they reflect good practice for all. Accordingly, multinational and domestic enterprises are subject to the same expectations in respect of their conduct wherever the Guidelines are relevant to both.

10.   The use of appropriate international dispute settlement mechanisms, including arbitration, should be encouraged as a means of facilitating the resolution of problems arising between enterprises and Member countries.

11.   Member countries have agreed to establish appropriate review and consultation procedures concerning issues arising in respect of the Guidelines. When multinational enterprises are made subject to conflicting requirements by Member countries, the governments concerned will co-operate in good faith with a view to resolving such problems either within the Committee on International Investment and Multinational Enterprises established by the OECD Council on 21st January 1975 or through other mutually acceptable arrangements.

Having regard to the foregoing considerations, the Member countries set forth the following Guidelines for multinational enterprises with the understanding that Member countries will fulfil their responsibilities to treat enterprises equitably and in accordance with international law and international agreements, as well as contractual obligations to which they have subscribed.

GENERAL POLICIES

Enterprises should:

1.   Take fully into account established general policy objectives of the Member countries in which they operate;

2.   In particular, give due consideration to those countries' aims and priorities with regard to economic and social progress, including industrial and regional development, the protection of the environment and consumer interests, the creation of employment opportunities, the promotion of innovation and the transfer of technology[4];

3.   While observing their legal obligations concerning information, supply their entities with supplementary information the latter may need in order to meet requests by the authorities of the countries in which those entities are located for information relevant to the activities of those entities, taking into account legitimate requirements of business confidentiality;

4.   Favour close co-operation with the local community and business interests;

5.   Allow their component entities freedom to develop their activities and to exploit their competitive advantage in domestic and foreign markets, consistent with the need for specialisation and sound commercial practice;

6.   When filling responsible posts in each country of operation, take due account of individual qualifications without discrimination as to nationality, subject to particular national requirements in this respect;

7.   Not render and they should not be solicited or expected to render any bribe or other improper benefit, direct or indirect, to any public servant or holder of public office;

8.   Unless legally permissible, not make contributions to candidates for public office or to political parties or other political organisations;

9.   Abstain from any improper involvement in local political activities.

DISCLOSURE OF INFORMATION

Enterprises should, having due regard to their nature and relative size in the economic context of their operations and to requirements of business confidentiality and to cost, publish in a form suited to improve public understanding a sufficient body of factual information on the structure, activities and policies of the enterprise as a whole, as a supplement, insofar as necessary for this purpose, to information to be disclosed under the national law of the individual countries in which they operate. To this end, they should publish within reasonable time limits, on a regular basis, but at least annually, financial statements and other pertinent information relating to the enterprise as a whole, comprising in particular:

a)   The structure of the enterprise, showing the name and location of the parent company, its main affiliates, its percentage ownership, direct and indirect, in these affiliates, including shareholdings between them;

b)   The geographical areas[5] where operations are carried out and the principal activities carried on therein by the parent company and the main affiliates;

c)   The operating results and sales by geographical area and the sales in the major lines of business for the enterprise as a whole;

d)   Significant new capital investment by geographical area and, as far as practicable, by major lines of business for the enterprise as a whole;

e)   A statement of the sources and uses of funds by the enterprise as a whole;

f)   The average number of employees in each geographical area;

g)   Research and development expenditure for the enterprise as a whole;

h)   The policies followed in respect of intra-group pricing;

i)   The accounting policies, including those on consolidation, observed in compiling the published information.

COMPETITION

Enterprises should, while conforming to official competition rules and established policies of the countries in which they operate:

1.   Refrain from actions which would adversely affect competition in the relevant market by abusing a dominant position of market power, by means of, for example;

   a)   Anti-competitive acquisitions;
   b)   Predatory behaviour toward competitors;
   c)   Unreasonable refusal to deal;
   d)   Anti-competitive abuse of industrial property rights;
   e)   Discriminatory (i.e. unreasonably differentiated) pricing and using such pricing transactions between affiliated enterprises as a means of affecting adversely competition outside these enterprises;

2.   Allow purchasers, distributors and licensees freedom to resell, export, purchase and develop their operations consistent with law, trade conditions, the need for specialisation and sound commercial practice;

3.   Refrain from participating in or otherwise purposely strengthening the restrictive effects of international or domestic cartels or restrictive agreements which adversely affect or eliminate competition and which are not generally or specifically accepted under applicable national or international legislation;

4.   Be ready to consult and co-operate, including the provision of information, with competent authorities of countries whose interests are directly affected in regard to competition issues or investigations. Provisions of information should be in accordance with safeguards normally applicable in this field.

FINANCING

Enterprises should, in managing the financial and commercial operations of their activities, and especially their liquid foreign assets and liabilities, take into consideration the established objectives of the countries in which they operate regarding balance of payments and credit policies.

TAXATION

Enterprises should:

1. Upon request of the taxation authorities of the countries in which they operate provide, in accordance with the safeguards and relevant procedures of the national laws of these countries, the information necessary to determine correctly the taxes to be assessed in connection with their operations, including relevant information concerning their operations in other countries;

2. Refrain from making use of the particular facilities available to them, such as transfer pricing which does not conform to an arm's length standard, for modifying in ways contrary to national laws the tax base on which members of the group are assessed.

EMPLOYMENT AND INDUSTRIAL RELATIONS

Enterprises should, within the framework of law, regulations and prevailing labour relations and employment practices, in each of the countries in which they operate:

1. Respect the right of their employees to be represented by trade unions and other bona fide organisations of employees, and engage in constructive negotiations, either individually or through employers' associations, with such employee organisations with a view to reaching agreements on employment conditions, which should include provisions for dealing with disputes arising over the interpretation of such agreements, and for ensuring mutually respected rights and responsibilities;

2. a) Provide such facilities to representatives of the employees as may be necessary to assist in the development of effective collective agreements;

    b) Provide to representatives of employees information which is needed for meaningful negotiations on conditions of employment;

3. Provide to representatives of employees, where this accords with local law and practice, information which enables them to obtain a true and fair view of the performance of the entity or, where appropriate, the enterprise as a whole;

4. Observe standards of employment and industrial relations not less favourable than those observed by comparable employers in the host country;

5. In their operations, to the greatest extent practicable, utilise, train and prepare for upgrading members of the local labour force in co-operation with representatives of their employees and, where appropriate, the relevant governmental authorities;

6. In considering changes in their operations which would have major effects upon the livelihood of their employees, in particular in the case of the closure of an entity

involving collective lay-offs or dismissals, provide reasonable notice of such changes to representatives of their employees, and where appropriate to the relevant governmental authorities and co-operate with the employee representatives and appropriate governmental authorities so as to mitigate to the maximum extent practicable adverse effects;

7. Implement their employment policies including hiring, discharge, pay, promotion and training without discrimination unless selectivity in respect of employee characteristics is in furtherance of established governmental policies which specifically promote greater equality of employment opportunity;

8. In the context of bona fide negotiations[6] with representatives of employees on conditions of employment, or while employees are exercising a right to organise, not threaten to utilise a capacity to transfer the whole or part of an operating unit from the country concerned nor transfer employees from the enterprises' component entities in other countries in order to influence unfairly those negotiations or to hinder the exercise of a right to organise[7];

9. Enable authorised representatives of their employees to conduct negotiations on collective bargaining or labour management relations issues with representatives of management who are authorised to take decisions on the matters under negotiation.

ENVIRONMENTAL PROTECTION[8]

Enterprises should, within the framework of laws, regulations and administrative practices in the countries in which they operate, and recalling the provisions of paragraph 9 of the Introduction to the Guidelines that, inter alia, multinational and domestic enterprises are subject to the same expectations in respect of their conduct whenever the Guidelines are relevant to both, take due account of the need to protect the environment and avoid creating environmentally related health problems. In particular, enterprises, whether multinational or domestic, should:

1. Assess, and take into account in decision making, foreseeable environmental and environmentally related health consequences of their activities, including citing decisions, impact on indigenous natural resources and foreseeable environmental and environmentally related health risks of products as well as from the generation, transport and disposal of waste;

2. Co-operate with competent authorities, inter alia, by providing adequate and timely information regarding the potential impacts on the environment and environmentally related health aspects of all their activities and by providing the relevant expertise available in the enterprise as a whole;

3. Take appropriate measures in their operations to minimise the risk of accidents and damage to health and the environment, and to co-operate in mitigating adverse effects, in particular:

a)   by selecting and adopting those technologies and practices which are compatible with these objectives;

b)   by introducing a system of environmental protection at the level of the enterprise as a whole including, where appropriate, the use of environmental auditing;

c)   by enabling their component entities to be adequately equipped, especially by providing them with adequate knowledge and assistance;

d)   by implementing education and training programmes for their employees;

e)   by preparing contingency plans; and

f)   by supporting, in an appropriate manner, public information and community awareness programmes.

SCIENCE AND TECHNOLOGY

Enterprises should:

1.   Endeavour to ensure that their activities fit satisfactorily into the scientific and technological policies and plans of the countries in which they operate, and contribute to the development of national scientific and technological capacities, including as far as appropriate the establishment and improvement in host countries of their capacity to innovate;

2.   To the fullest extent practicable, adopt in the course of their business activities practices which permit the rapid diffusion of technologies with due regard to the protection of industrial and intellectual property rights;

3.   When granting licences for the use of industrial property rights or when otherwise transferring technology, do so on reasonable terms and conditions.

ANNEX 2
GENERAL CONSIDERATIONS AND PRACTICAL APPROACHES CONCERNING CONFLICTING REQUIREMENTS IMPOSED ON MULTINATIONAL ENTERPRISES[9]

GENERAL CONSIDERATIONS

1.   In contemplating new legislation, action under existing legislation or other exercise of jurisdiction which may conflict with the legal requirements or established policies of another Member country and lead to conflicting requirements being imposed on multinational enterprises, the Member countries concerned should:

a)   Have regard to relevant principles of international law;

b)   Endeavour to avoid or minimise such conflicts and the problems to which they give rise by following an approach of moderation and restraint, respecting a n d accommodating the interests of other Member countries[10];

c)   Take fully into account the sovereignty and legitimate economic, law enforcement and other interests of other Member countries;

d)   Bear in mind the importance of permitting the observance of contractual obligations and the possible adverse impact of measures having a retroactive effect.

2.   Member countries should endeavour to promote co-operation as an alternative to unilateral action to avoid or minimise conflicting requirements and problems arising therefrom. Member countries should on request consult one another and endeavour to arrive at mutually acceptable solutions to such problems.

PRACTICAL APPROACHES

3.   Member countries recognised that in the majority of circumstances, effective co-operation may best be pursued on a bilateral basis. On the other hand, there may be cases where the multilateral approach could be more effective.

4.   Member countries should therefore be prepared to:

a)   Develop mutually beneficial, practical and appropriately safeguarded bilateral arrangements, formal or informal, for notification to and consultation with other Member countries;

b)   Give prompt and sympathetic consideration to requests for notification and bilateral consultation on an ad hoc basis made by any Member country which considers that its interests may be affected by a measure of the type referred to under paragraph 1 above, taken by another Member country with which it does not have such bilateral arrangements.

c)   Inform the other concerned Member countries as soon as practicable of new legislation or regulations proposed by their Governments for adoption which have significant potential for conflict with the legal requirements or established policies of other Member countries and for giving rise to conflicting requirements being imposed on multinational enterprises;

d)   Give prompt and sympathetic consideration to requests by other Member countries for consultation in the Committee on International Investment and Multinational

Enterprises or through other mutually acceptable arrangements. Such consultations would be facilitated by notification at the earliest stage practicable;

e) Give prompt and full consideration to proposals which may be made by other Member countries in any such consultations that would lessen or eliminate conflicts.

These procedures do not apply to those aspects of restrictive business practices or other matters which are the subject of existing OECD arrangements.

NOTES AND REFERENCES

1. On matters falling within its competence, the European Economic Community is associated with the section on National Treatment.

2. The Declaration was reviewed in 1979, 1984 and 1991. Section III on Conflicting Requirements was added following the 1991 Review.

3. The Guidelines were reviewed in 1979, 1984 and 1991. These reviews resulted in modification of the General Policies chapter (paragraph 2); the Disclosure of Information chapter [sub-paragraph b)]; a clarification and modification of the Employment and Industrial Relations chapter (paragraph 8); and the addition of a new chapter on the Environment.

4. This paragraph includes the additional provision concerning consumer interests, adopted by the OECD Governments at the meeting of the OECD Council at Ministerial level on 17 and 18 May 1984.

*5. *For the purposes of the Guideline on Disclosure of Information the term "geographical area" means groups of countries or individual countries as each enterprise determines is appropriate in its particular circumstances. While no single method of grouping is appropriate for all enterprises or for all purposes, the factors to be considered by an enterprise would include the significance of geographic proximity, economic affinity, similarities in business environments and the nature, scale and degree of interrelationship of the enterprises' operations in the various countries.*

*6. *Bona fide negotiations may include labour disputes as part of the process of negotiation. Whether or not labour disputes are so included will be determined by the law and prevailing employment practices of particular countries.*

7. This paragraph includes the additional provision, concerning transfer of employees, adopted by OECD Governments at the meeting of the OECD Council at Ministerial level on 13 and 14 June 1979.

8. This chapter was added at the meeting of the OECD Council at Ministerial level on 4 and 5 June 1991.

---

*These texts are integral parts of the negotiated instruments.

9.   The General Considerations and Practical Approaches were endorsed by the Ministers in May 1984. They were annexed to the 1976 Declaration as a result of the 1991 Review exercise.

*10.   *Applying the principle of comity, as it is understood in some Member countries, includes following an approach of this nature in exercising one's jurisdiction.*

* * *

PROCEDURAL DECISIONS OF THE OECD COUNCIL

1. NATIONAL TREATMENT:
THIRD REVISED DECISION OF THE COUNCIL
December 1991

THE COUNCIL,

Having regard to the Convention on the Organisation for Economic Co-operation and Development of 14th December 1960 and, in particular, to Articles 2 c), 2 d), and 3 and 5 a) thereof;

Having regard to the Resolution of the Council of 13th December 1984 on the Terms of Reference of the Committee on International Investment and Multinational Enterprises [C(84)171(Final)];

Having regard to the Section on National Treatment of the Declaration by Governments of OECD Member countries of 21st June 1976 on International Investment and Multinational Enterprises [hereinafter called "the Declaration"];

Having regard to the Second Revised Decision of the Council of 17th May 1984 on National Treatment [C (84)91];

Having regard to the report on the National Treatment Instrument by the Committee on International Investment and Multinational Enterprises [C(91)147 and Corrigendum 1];

Considering it appropriate to strengthen the procedures established within the Organisation for reviewing laws, regulations and administrative practices (hereinafter called "measures") which

---

*These texts are integral parts of the negotiated instruments.

195

depart from National Treatment, as defined in the Declaration (hereinafter called "National Treatment");

On the proposal of the Committee on International Investment and Multinational Enterprises;

DECIDES:

The Second Revised Decision of the Council of 17th May 1984 on National Treatment [C(84)91] is repealed and replaced by the following:

Article 1
NOTIFICATION

a)   Members[1] shall notify the Organisation of all measures constituting exceptions to National Treatment within 60 days of their adoption and of any other measures which have a bearing on National Treatment. All exceptions shall be set out in Annex A to this Decision[2].

b)   Members shall notify the Organisation within 60 days of their introduction of any modifications of the measures covered in paragraph a).

c)   The Organisation shall consider the notifications submitted to it in accordance with the provisions of paragraphs a) and b) with a view to determining whether each Member is meeting its commitments under the Declaration.

Article 2
EXAMINATION

a)   The Organisation shall examine each exception lodged by a Member and other measures notified under Article 1 at intervals to be determined by the Organisation. These intervals shall, however, be not more than three years, unless the Council decides otherwise.

b)   Each Member shall notify the Organisation prior to the periodic examination called for in paragraph a), whether it desires to maintain any exception lodged by it under Article 1 and if so, state its reasons therefore.

c)   The examinations provided for in paragraph a) shall be directed at making suitable proposals designed to assist Members to withdraw their exceptions.

d)   The examinations provided for in paragraph a) shall be country reviews in which all of the exceptions lodged by a Member are covered in the same examinations.

e)   Notwithstanding paragraph d), the examinations provided for in paragraph a) may focus on specific types or groups of measures of particular concern, as and when determined by the Organisation.

Article 3
REFERENCE TO THE ORGANISATION

a)   If a Member considers that another Member has, contrary to its undertakings with regard to National Treatment, retained, introduced or reintroduced measures and if it considers itself to be prejudiced thereby, it may refer to the Organisation.

b)   The fact that the case is under consideration by the Organisation shall not preclude the Member which has referred to the Organisation from entering into bilateral discussion on the matter with the other Member concerned.

Article 4
COMMITTEE ON INTERNATIONAL INVESTMENT AND
MULTINATIONAL ENTERPRISES: GENERAL TASKS

a)   The Committee on International Investment and Multinational Enterprises (hereinafter called the "Committee") shall consider all questions concerning the interpretation or implementation of the provisions of the Declaration or of Acts of the Council relating to National Treatment and shall report its conclusions thereon to the Council.

b)   The Committee shall submit to the Council any appropriate proposals in connection with its tasks as defined in paragraph a) and, in particular, with the abolishing of measures constituting exceptions to National Treatment.

Article 5
COMMITTEE ON INTERNATIONAL INVESTMENT
AND MULTINATIONAL ENTERPRISES: SPECIAL TASKS

a)   The Committee shall:

   i)   consider, in conformity with paragraphs a) and b) of Article 2, each exception notified to the Organisation and make, where appropriate, suitable proposals to assist Members to withdraw their exceptions;

   ii)   consider, in accordance with Article 1, the notifications submitted to the Organisation;

   iii)   consider references submitted to the Organisation in accordance with the provisions of Article 3;

iv) act as a forum for consultations, at the request of a Member, in respect of any matter related to the Declaration and its implementation.

b) The Committee may periodically invite the Business and Industry Advisory Committee to the OECD (BIAC) and the Trade Union Advisory Committee to the OECD (TUAC) to express their views on matters related to National Treatment and shall take account of such views in its reports to the Council.

Article 6
REVIEW OF THE DECISION

This Decision shall be reviewed within three years.

Article 7
PARTICIPATION BY THE EUROPEAN ECONOMIC COMMUNITY

The present Decision, as well as any further Decision amending it, shall be open for accession by the European Economic Community. Such accession shall be notified to the Secretary-General of the Organisation.

2. THE GUIDELINES FOR MULTINATIONAL ENTERPRISES:
SECOND REVISED DECISION OF THE COUNCIL
Amended June 1991

THE COUNCIL,

Having regard to the Convention on the Organisation for Economic Co-operation and Development of 14th December 1960 and, in particular, to Articles 2d), 3 and 5a) thereof;

Having regard to the Resolution of the Council of 28th November 1979, on the Terms of Reference of the Committee on International Investment and Multinational Enterprises and, in particular, to paragraph 2 thereof [C(79)210(Final)];

Taking note of the Declaration by the Governments of OECD Member countries of 21st June 1976 in which they jointly recommend to multinational enterprises the observance of Guidelines for multinational enterprises;

Having regard to the Revised Decision of the Council of 13th June 1979 on Inter-Governmental Consultation Procedures on the Guidelines for Multinational Enterprises [C(79)143(Final)];

Recognising the desirability of setting forth procedures by which consultations may take place on matters related to these Guidelines;

Recognising that, while bilateral and multilateral co-operation should be strengthened when multinational enterprises are made subject to conflicting requirements, effective co-operation on problems arising therefrom may best be pursued in most circumstances on a bilateral level, although there may be cases where the multilateral approach would be more effective;

Considering the Report on the Review of the 1976 Declaration and Decisions on International Investment and Multinational Enterprises [C(79)102(Final)] and the Report on the Second Review of the 1976 Declaration and Decisions on International Investment and Multinational Enterprises [C/MIN(84)5(Final)], including the particular endorsement of the section in the Second Review Report relating to conflicting requirements;

On the proposal of the Committee on International Investment and Multinational Enterprises:

DECIDES:

1.   Member Governments shall set up National Contact Points for undertaking promotional activities, handling inquires and for discussions with the parties concerned on all matters related to the Guidelines so that they can contribute to the solution of problems which may arise in this connection. The business community, employee organisations and other interested parties shall be informed of the availability of such facilities.

2.   National Contact Points in different countries shall co-operate if such need arises, on any matter related to the Guidelines relevant to their activities. As a general procedure, discussions at the national level should be initiated before contacts with other National Contact Points are undertaken.

3.   The Committee on International Investment and Multinational Enterprises (hereinafter called "the Committee") shall periodically or at the request of a Member country hold an exchange of views on matters related to the Guidelines and the experience gained in their application. The Committee shall be responsible for clarification of the Guidelines. Clarification will be provided as required. The Committee shall periodically report to the Council on these matters.

4.   The Committee shall periodically invite the Business and Industry Advisory Committee to OECD (BIAC) and the Trade Union Advisory Committee to OECD (TUAC) to express their views on matters related to the Guidelines. In addition, exchanges of views with the advisory bodies on these matters may be held upon request by the latter. The Committee shall take account of such views in its reports to the Council.

5.   If it so wishes, an individual enterprise will be given the opportunity to express its views either orally or in writing on issues concerning the Guidelines involving its interests.

6.   The Committee shall not reach conclusions on the conduct of individual enterprises.

7. This Decision shall be reviewed at the latest in six years. The Committee shall make proposals for this purpose as appropriate.

8. This Decision shall replace Decision [C(79)143].

3. INTERNATIONAL INVESTMENT INCENTIVES AND DISINCENTIVES: SECOND REVISED DECISION OF THE COUNCIL
May 1984

The COUNCIL,

Having regard to the Convention on the Organisation for Economic Co-operation and Development of 14th December 1960 and, in particular, Articles 2 c), 2 d), 2 e), 3 and 5 a) thereof;

Having regard to the Resolution of the Council of 28th November 1979 on the Terms of Reference of the Committee on International Investment and Multinational Enterprises [C(79)210(Final)];

Taking note of the Declaration by the Governments of OECD Member countries of 21st June 1976 on International Investment Incentives and Disincentives;

Having regard to the Revised Decision of the Council of 13th June 1979 on International Investment Incentives and Disincentives [C(79)145];

Considering the Report on the Second Review of the 1976 Declaration and Decisions on International Investment and Multinational Enterprises [C/MIN(84)5(Final)];

On the proposal of the Committee on International Investment and Multinational Enterprises;

DECIDES:

1. Consultations will take place in the framework of the Committee on International Investment and Multinational Enterprises at the request of a Member country which considers that its interests may be adversely affected by the impact on its flow of international direct investments of measures taken by another Member country which provide significant official incentives and disincentives to international direct investment. Having full regard to the national economic objectives of the measures and without prejudice to policies designed to redress regional imbalances, the purpose of the consultations will be to examine the possibility of reducing such effects to a minimum.

2. Member countries shall supply, under the consultation procedures, all permissible information relating to any measures being the subject of the consultation.

3.   The Committee may periodically invite the Business and Industry Advisory Committee to OECD (BIAC) and the Trade Union Advisory Committee to OECD (TUAC) to express their views on matters relating to international investment incentives and disincentives and shall take account of these views in its periodic reports to the Council.

4.   This Decision shall be reviewed at the latest in six years. The Committee on International Investment and Multinational Enterprises shall make proposals for this purpose as appropriate.

5.   This Decision shall replace Decision [C(79)145].

4. CONFLICTING REQUIREMENTS
DECISION OF THE COUNCIL
June 1991

THE COUNCIL

Having regard to the Convention on the Organisation for Economic Co-operation and Development of 14th December 1960 and, in particular, to Articles 2d), 3 and 5a) thereof;

Having regard to the Resolution of the Council of 28th November 1979, on the Terms of Reference of the Committee on International Investment and Multinational Enterprises and, in particular, to paragraph 2 thereof [C(70)210(Final)];

Recalling that the Council at Ministerial level endorsed the Conclusions and Recommendations of the Report on the Second Review of the 1976 Declaration and Decisions on International Investment and Multinational Enterprises [C/MIN(84)5(Final)], and in particular the section in that Report on conflicting requirements;

Taking note of the Declaration by the Governments of OECD Member countries of 21st June 1976 (Revised 4-5 June 1991) in which they jointly recommend to Member countries to co-operate with a view of avoiding or minimising conflicting requirements being imposed on multinational enterprises;

Recognising the desirability of maintaining procedures by which consultations may take place on matters related to conflicting requirements;

Recognising that, while bilateral and multilateral co-operation should be strengthened when multinational enterprises are made subject to conflicting requirements, effective co-operation on problems arising therefrom may best be pursued in most circumstances on a bilateral level, although there may be cases where the multilateral approach would be more effective;

On the proposal of the Committee on International Investment and Multinational Enterprises:

DECIDES:

1.   Member countries may request that consultations be held in the Committee on any problem arising from the fact that multinational enterprises are made subject to conflicting requirements. The Member countries concerned shall give prompt and sympathetic consideration to requests by Member countries for consultations in the Committee or through other mutually acceptable arrangements, it being understood that such consultations would be facilitated by notification at the earliest stage practicable. Member countries concerned will co-operate in good faith with a view to resolving such problems, either within the Committee or through other mutually acceptable arrangements.

2.   The Committee will continue to serve as a forum for consideration of the question of conflicting requirements, including, as appropriate, the national and international legal principles involved.

3.   Member countries shall assist the Committee in its periodic reviews of experience on matters relating to conflicting requirements.

4.   The Committee shall periodically invite the Business and Industry Advisory Committee to the OECD (BIAC) and the Trade Union Advisory Committee to the OECD (TUAC) to express their views on matters relating to conflicting requirements.

5.   This Decision shall be reviewed at the latest in 1997. The Committee shall make proposals for this purpose as appropriate.

6.   Paragraphs 7 to 10 of the Decision on the Guidelines for Multinational Enterprises [C(84)90] are repealed.

NOTES AND REFERENCES

*1.   *For the purposes of this Decision, "Members" means all parties to the Decision.*

2.   In the interests of brevity, Annex A to the Decision is not reproduced herein. A forthcoming publication on National Treatment for Established Foreign-Controlled Enterprises will reproduce the list of country exceptions in its entirety.

*   *   *

---

*This text is an integral part of the negotiated instrument.

GUIDELINES ON THE PROTECTION OF PRIVACY AND TRANSBORDER FLOWS OF PERSONAL DATA

AND

DECLARATION ON TRANSBORDER DATA FLOWS[*]

> The Guidelines on the Protection of Privacy and Transborder Flows of Personal Data were adopted and became applicable on 23 September 1980 in the form of a recommendation by the Council of the OECD. The Declaration on Transborder Data Flows was adopted by the Council of the OECD on 11 April 1985.

RECOMMENDATION OF THE COUNCIL CONCERNING GUIDELINES GOVERNING THE PROTECTION OF PRIVACY AND TRANSBORDER FLOWS OF PERSONAL DATA

(23rd September, 1980)

THE COUNCIL,

Having regard to articles *l(c), 3(a)* and *5(b)* of the Convention on the Organisation for Economic Co-operation and Development of 14th December, 1960;

RECOGNISING,

> that, although national laws and policies may differ, Member countries have a common interest in protecting privacy and individual liberties, and in reconciling fundamental but competing values such as privacy and the free flow of information;

> that automatic processing and transborder flows of personal data create new forms of relationships among countries and require the development of compatible rules and practices;

> that transborder flows of personal data contribute to economic and social development;

> that domestic legislation concerning privacy protection and transborder flows of personal data may hinder such transborder flows;

---

[*]Source: Organisation for Economic Co-operation and Development (1981). *Guidelines on the Protection of Privacy and Transborder Flows of Personal Data* (Paris: OECD); and Organisation for Economic Co-operation and Development (1985). *Declaration on Transborder Data Flows*, Press Release PRESS/A(85)30, 11 April 1985 [Note added by the editor].

Determined to advance the free flow of information between Member countries and to avoid the creation of unjustified obstacles to the development of economic and social relations among Member countries;

RECOMMENDS

1.   That Member countries take into account in their domestic legislation the principles concerning the protection of privacy and individual liberties set forth in the Guidelines contained in the Annex to this Recommendation which is an integral part thereof;

2.   That Member countries endeavour to remove or avoid creating, in the name of privacy protection, unjustified obstacles to transborder flows of personal data;

3.   That Member countries co-operate in the implementation of the Guidelines set forth in the Annex;

4.   That Member countries agree as soon as possible on specific procedures of consultation and co-operation for the application of these Guidelines.

Annex to the Recommendation of the Council of 23rd September 1980

GUIDELINES GOVERNING THE PROTECTION OF PRIVACY AND TRANSBORDER FLOWS OF PERSONAL DATA

PART ONE. GENERAL

Definitions

1.   For the purposes of these Guidelines:

   a)   "data controller" means a party who, according to domestic law, is competent to decide about the contents and use of personal data regardless of whether or not such data are collected, stored, processed or disseminated by that party or by an agent on its behalf;

   b)   "personal data" means any information relating to an identified or identifiable individual (data subject);

   c)   "transborder flows of personal data" means movements of personal data across national borders.

Scope of Guidelines

2.   These Guidelines apply to personal data, whether in the public or private sectors, which, because of the manner in which they are processed, or because of their nature or the context in which they are used, pose a danger to privacy and individual liberties.

3.   These Guidelines should not be interpreted as preventing:

a)   the application, to different categories of personal data, of different protective measures depending upon their nature and the context in which they are collected, stored, processed or disseminated;

b)   the exclusion from the application of the Guidelines of personal data which obviously do not contain any risk to privacy and individual liberties; or

c)   the application of the Guidelines only to automatic processing of personal data.

4.   Exceptions to the Principles contained in Parts Two and Three of these Guidelines, including those relating to national sovereignty, national security and public policy ("ordre public"), should be:

a)   as few as possible, and

b)   made known to the public.

5.   In the particular case of Federal countries the observance of these Guidelines may be affected by the division of powers in the Federation.

6.   These Guidelines should be regarded as minimum standards which are capable of being supplemented by additional measures for the protection of privacy and individual liberties.

PART TWO
BASIC PRINCIPLES OF NATIONAL APPLICATION

Collection Limitation Principle

7.   There should be limits to the collection of personal data and any such data should be obtained by lawful and fair means and, where appropriate, with the knowledge or consent of the data subject.

Data Quality Principle

8.   Personal data should be relevant to the purposes for which they are to be used, and, to the extent necessary for those purposes, should be accurate, complete and kept up-to-date.

Purpose Specification Principle

9. The purposes for which personal data are collected should be specified not later than at the time of data collection and the subsequent use limited to the fulfilment of those purposes or such others as are not incompatible with those purposes and as are specified on each occasion of change of purpose.

Use Limitation Principle

10. Personal data should not be disclosed, made available or otherwise used for purposes other than those specified in accordance with Paragraph 9 except:

  a)   with the consent of the data subject; or

  b)   by the authority of law.

Security Safeguards Principle

11. Personal data should be protected by reasonable security safeguards against such risks as loss or unauthorised access, destruction, use, modification or disclosure of data.

Openness Principle

12. There should be a general policy of openness about developments, practices and policies with respect to personal data. Means should be readily available of establishing the existence and nature of personal data, and the main purposes of their use, as well as the identity and usual residence of the data controller.

Individual Participation Principle

13. An individual should have the right:

  a)   to obtain from a data controller, or otherwise, confirmation of whether or not the data controller has data relating to him;

  b)   to have communicated to him, data relating to him

    i)   within a reasonable time;
    ii)   at a charge, if any, that is not excessive;
    iii) in a reasonable manner; and
    iv)   in a form that is readily intelligible to him;

  c)   to be given reasons if a request made under subparagraphs (a) and (b) is denied, and to be able to challenge such denial; and

    d)   to challenge data relating to him and, if the challenge is successful, to have the data erased, rectified, completed or amended.

Accountability Principle

14.   A data controller should be accountable for complying with measures which give effect to the principles stated above.

PART THREE
BASIC PRINCIPLES OF INTERNATIONAL APPLICATION: FREE FLOW AND LEGITIMATE RESTRICTIONS

15.   Member countries should take into consideration the implications for other Member countries of domestic processing and re-export of personal data.

16.   Member countries should take all reasonable and appropriate steps to ensure that transborder flows of personal data, including transit through a Member country, are uninterrupted and secure.

17.   A Member country should refrain from restricting transborder flows of personal data between itself and another Member country except where the latter does not yet substantially observe these Guidelines or where the re-export of such data would circumvent its domestic privacy legislation. A Member country may also impose restrictions in respect of certain categories of personal data for which its domestic privacy legislation includes specific regulations in view of the nature of those data and for which the other Member country provides no equivalent protection.

18.   Member countries should avoid developing laws, policies and practices in the name of the protection of privacy and individual liberties, which would create obstacles to transborder flows of personal data that would exceed requirements for such protection.

PART FOUR
NATIONAL IMPLEMENTATION

19.   In implementing domestically the principles set forth in Parts Two and Three, Member countries should establish legal, administrative or other procedures or institutions for the protection of privacy and individual liberties in respect of personal data. Member countries should in particular endeavour to:

    a)   adopt appropriate domestic legislation;

    b)   encourage and support self-regulation, whether in the form of codes of conduct or otherwise;

c)   provide for reasonable means for individuals to exercise their rights;

d)   provide for adequate sanctions and remedies in case of failures to comply with measures which implement the principles set forth in Parts Two and Three; and

e)   ensure that there is no unfair discrimination against data subjects.

PART FIVE
INTERNATIONAL CO-OPERATION

20.   Member countries should, where requested, make known to other Member countries details of the observance of the principles set forth in these Guidelines. Member countries should also ensure that procedures for transborder flows of personal data and for the protection of privacy and individual liberties are simple and compatible with those of other Member countries which comply with these Guidelines.

21.   Member countries should establish procedures to facilitate:

i)   information exchange related to these Guidelines, and

ii)   mutual assistance in the procedural and investigative matters involved.

22.   Member countries should work towards the development of principles, domestic and international, to govern the applicable law in the case of transborder flows of personal data.

* * *

DECLARATION ON TRANSBORDER DATA FLOWS

Adopted on 11 April 1985 by the Governments of Member countries of the
Organisation for Economic Co-operation and Development

Rapid technological developments in the field of information, computers and communications are leading to significant structural changes in the economies of Member countries. Flows of computerised data and information are an important consequence of technological advances and are playing an increasing role in national economies. With the growing economic interdependence of Member countries, these flows acquire an international dimension, known as Transborder Data Flows. It is therefore appropriate for the OECD to pay attention to policy issues connected with these transborder data flows.

This declaration is intended to make clear the general spirit in which Member countries will address these issues.

In view of the above, *The Governments of OECD Member Countries*:

Acknowledging that computerised data and information now circulate, by and large, freely on an international scale;

Considering the OECD Guidelines on the Protection of Privacy and Transborder Flows of Personal Data and the significant progress that has been achieved in the area of privacy protection at national and international levels;

Recognising the diversity of participants in transborder data flows, such as commercial and non-commercial organisations, individuals and Governments, and recognizing the wide variety of computerised data and information traded or exchanged across national borders, such as data and information related to trading activities, intra-corporate flows, computerised information services and scientific and technological exchanges;

Recognising the growing importance of transborder data flows and the benefits that can be derived from transborder data flows; and recognizing that the ability of Member countries to reap such benefits may vary;

Recognising that investment and trade in this field cannot but benefit from transparency and stability of policies, regulations and practices;

Recognising that national policies which affect transborder data flows reflect a range of social and economic goals, and that Governments may adopt different means to achieve their policy goals;

Aware of the social and economic benefits resulting from access to a variety of sources of information and of efficient and effective information services;

Recognising that Member countries have a common interest in facilitating transborder data flows and in reconciling different policy objectives in this field;

Having due regard to their national laws, do hereby *declare their intention to*:

(a) *Promote* access to data and information and related services, and avoid the creation of unjustified barriers to the international exchange of data and information;

(b) *Seek* transparency in regulations and policies relating to information, computer and communications services affecting transborder data flows;

(c) *Develop* common approaches for dealing with issues related to transborder data flows and, when appropriate, develop harmonized solutions;

(d)   *Consider* possible implications for other countries when dealing with issues related to transborder data flows.

Bearing in mind the intention expressed above, and taking into account the work carried out in other international fora, *the Governments of OECD Member Countries*,

Agree that further work should be undertaken and that such work should concentrate at the outset on issues emerging from the following types of transborder data flows:

(i)   Flows of data accompanying international trade;

(ii)   Marketed computer services and computerised information services; and

(iii)   Intra-corporate data flows.

The Governments of OECD Member countries agree to *co-operate* and *consult* with each other in carrying out this important work, and in furthering the objectives of this Declaration.

*   *   *

UNIFIED AGREEMENT FOR THE INVESTMENT OF ARAB CAPITAL IN THE ARAB STATES[*]

> The Unified Agreement for the Investment of Arab Capital in the Arab States was signed on 26 November 1980 in Amman, Jordan, during the Eleventh Arab Summit Conference. It entered into force on 7 September 1981. The draft statutes of the Arab Investment Court came into force on 22 February 1988. The member States of the League of Arab States are Algeria, Bahrain, Comoros, Djibouti, Egypt, Iraq, Jordan, Kuwait, Lebanon, Libyan Arab Jamahiriya, Mauritania, Oman, Palestine, Qatar, Saudi Arabia, Syrian Arab Republic, Somalia, Sudan, Tunisia, the United Arab Emirates and Yemen. The agreement has been ratified by all member States of the League except Algeria and the Comoros.

The Governments of the States Members of the League of Arab States,

In accordance with the aims of the Pact of the League of Arab States, the Joint Defence and Economic Cooperation Treaty between the States of the Arab League, the principles and objectives set forth in the Agreement on Arab Economic Action and the decisions issued by the Economic Council of the League of Arab States,

Proceeding from the aim of strengthening overall Arab development and Arab economic integration,

Believing that investment dealings between Arab States are an essential part of joint Arab economic action, the regulation of which will mobilize production and thus enhance joint development on the basis of reciprocal benefits and national interests,

Sharing a conviction that providing a suitable investment climate to stimulate Arab economic resources in the field of joint Arab investment requires that legal investment regulations be drawn up in the context of a well-established, coherent and integrated legal system which seeks to facilitate the transfer and use of Arab capital within the Arab States in such a manner as to further their development, freedom and progress and improve the living standard of their citizens,

Recognizing that the potential scope of such a system is more conducive to a form of Arab economic citizenship sharing common features whereby the Arab investor, irrespective of nationality, may operate according to provisions identical to those applied by any State to its citizens, together with provision for freedom to transfer Arab capital within the Arab States and

---

[*]Source: League of Arab States (1982). "Unified Agreement for the Investment of Arab Capital in the Arab States", *Economic Documents*, No. 3 (Tunis: League of Arab States). Original language: Arabic [Note added by the editor].

protect it by means of guarantees against non-commercial risks and a special judicial system, in addition to privileges and facilities which the investor may be granted by the host State within the context of its national sovereignty,

Desirous of ensuring the immediate application of these principles in the territories of members without prejudice to their respective international commitments,

Bearing in mind that the provisions of this Agreement constitute a minimum standard to be applied in the treatment of Arab capital and investments, whether in the context of concerted Arab economic action or at the level of bilateral cooperation or within the scope of the domestic legislation of each State,

Have approved this Agreement and its annex, which forms an inseparable part of the Agreement, declaring their full readiness to implement the letter and the spirit thereof and affirming their desire to exert their utmost efforts to accomplish its aims and objectives.

INTRODUCTORY CHAPTER: TERMINOLOGY

ARTICLE 1

For the purposes of this Agreement, the words and expressions set out hereunder shall have the meanings indicated opposite them, save where the context indicates otherwise:

1.   The Agreement: the Unified Agreement for the Investment of Arab Capital in the Arab States concluded between the members of the League of Arab States;

2.   Arab State: a State member of the League of Arab States;

3.   State Party: an Arab State in respect of which the Agreement is effective;

4.   Arab citizen: an individual or a body corporate having the nationality of a State Party, provided that no part of the capital of such body corporate belongs either directly or indirectly to non-Arab citizens. Joint Arab projects which are fully owned by Arab citizens shall be deemed to be included within this definition in instances where they do not have the nationality of another State;

Arab States and bodies corporate which are fully State-owned, whether directly or indirectly, shall likewise be regarded as Arab citizens;

5.   Arab capital: assets owned by an Arab citizen comprising any material and immaterial rights which have a cash valuation, including bank deposits and financial investments. Revenues accruing from Arab assets shall be regarded as Arab assets, as shall any joint share to which this definition applies;

6.   Investment of Arab capital: the use of Arab capital in a field of economic development

with a view to obtaining a return in the territory of a State Party other than the State of which the Arab investor is a national or its transfer to a State Party for such purpose in accordance with the provisions of this Agreement;

7.   Arab investor: an Arab citizen who owns Arab capital which he invests in the territory of a State Party of which he is not a national;

8.   The Council: the Economic Council established pursuant to article 8 of the Joint Defence and Economic Cooperation Treaty between the States of the Arab League approved by the Council of the League on 13 April 1950 or any amendment thereto;

9.   Central authority: the authority referred to in article 37 of this Agreement;

10.   The Court: the Arab Investment Court.

CHAPTER I: GENERAL PROVISIONS

ARTICLE 2

The States Parties to this Agreement shall, within the framework of its provisions, be permitted to transfer Arab capital freely between them and to promote and facilitate its investment according to the economic development plans and programmes within the States Parties and in a manner beneficial to the host State and the investor. They shall undertake to protect the investor, safeguard his investment and its related revenues and rights and, to the extent possible, to ensure the stability of the pertinent legal provisions.

ARTICLE 3

1.   The provisions of this Agreement shall constitute a minimum standard to be applied in the treatment of any investment subject thereto.

2.   Within the limits of such minimum standard, the provisions of the Agreement shall have priority of application in instances where they conflict with the laws and regulations in the States Parties.

ARTICLE 4

Conclusions and interpretations derived from the provisions of this Agreement shall be guided by the principles on which it is based and the aims which inspired it, followed by the rules and principles common to the respective legislation of the States members of the League of Arab States and, finally, by the principles recognized in international law.

CHAPTER II: TREATMENT OF THE ARAB INVESTOR

ARTICLE 5

The Arab investor shall be free to invest within the territory of any State Party in fields which are neither prohibited nor restricted to the citizens of that State and within the percentage limits for shared ownership as prescribed in the law of the State. He shall also enjoy the related facilities and guarantees required under the provisions of this Agreement.

ARTICLE 6

1. In accordance with the provision of the preceding article, in the State Party where the investment is made, the capital of the Arab investor shall, without discrimination, be treated in the same manner as capital owned by the citizens of that State. It shall automatically acquire identical legal status in terms of rights, obligations, regulations and procedures, although this shall not apply to any additional concessions which the State Party may accord to an Arab investment.

2. The Arab investor shall, however, be entitled to opt for any other manner of treatment which is laid down in general provisions in force in the State where the investment is made under a law or an international agreement and which is applicable to a non-Arab investment in a similar field. This shall not include any privileged treatment accorded by the State in respect of specific projects which are of particular importance to that State.

ARTICLE 7

1. The Arab investor shall have the freedom to make periodic transfers, both of Arab capital for investment in the territory of any State Party and of the revenues therefrom, and subsequently to make retransfers to any State Party following settlement of his outstanding obligations without this being subject to any discriminatory banking, administrative or legal restrictions and without the transfer process incurring any taxes or duties. This shall not apply in respect of banking services.

2. The principal of the capital shall be retransferred following a period determined by the maturity of the investment according to its nature or five years from the date of its transfer, whichever is shorter.

3. The provisions of this article shall not prejudice any recourse which the State may have to procedures to prevent the outflow abroad of the assets of its citizens.

ARTICLE 8

1. The Arab investor may, in the course of his investment, avail himself of all means permitted by its nature which are within the prescribed limits for citizens of the State in which the investment is made.

2.   In his actions, the Arab investor shall not be subject to any discriminatory administrative or legal restrictions or regulations related to the control of cash and foreign transfers.

3.   The investment shall continue to be treated according to the provisions of this Agreement provided that it fulfils the conditions specified therein.

ARTICLE 9

1.   According to the provisions of this Agreement, the capital of the Arab investor shall not be subject to any specific or general measures, whether permanent or temporary and irrespective of their legal form, which wholly or partially affect any of the assets, reserves or revenues of the investor and which lead to confiscation, compulsory seizure, dispossession, nationalization, liquidation, dissolution, the extortion or elimination of secrets regarding technical ownership or other material rights, the forcible prevention or delay of debt settlement or any other measures leading to the sequestration, freezing or administration of assets, or any other action which infringes the right of ownership itself or prejudices the intrinsic authority of the owner in terms of his control and possession of the investment, his right to administer it, his acquisition of the revenues therefrom or the fulfilment of his rights and the discharge of his obligations.

2.   It shall, however, be permissible to:

(a)   Seize property for the public benefit in accordance with the authority vested in the State or its institutions to perform their functions in implementing public projects, provided that this is done on a non-discriminatory basis in return for fair compensation and according to general legal provisions regulating the seizure of property for the purposes of the public benefit. The Arab investor shall be given the opportunity to challenge the legitimacy of any dispossession and the amount of compensation before the domestic courts. Compensation shall be made within a period not exceeding one year from the date when the decision to dispossess became final;

(b)   Take precautionary measures at the order of a competent judicial authority and measures to implement judgements delivered by a competent judicial authority.

ARTICLE 10

1.   The Arab investor shall be entitled to compensation for damages which he sustains due to any one of the following actions by a State Party or one of its public or local authorities or institutions:

(a)   Undermining any of the rights and guarantees provided for the Arab investor in this Agreement or any other decision issued pursuant thereto by a competent authority;

(b)   Breach of any international obligations or undertakings binding on the State Party and arising from this Agreement in favour of the Arab investor or failing to take the necessary steps to implement them, whether deliberately or through negligence;

(c) Preventing the execution of an enforceable legal judgement which has a direct connection with the investment;

(d) Causing damage to the Arab investor in any other manner, whether by deed or prevention, by contravening the legal provisions in force within the State in which the investment is made.

2. The amount of compensation shall be equivalent to the damage sustained by the Arab investor according to the type and amount of damage.

ARTICLE 11

1. Cash compensation shall be given in cases where the investment cannot be restored to its state prior to the occurrence of the damage.

2. Assessments of cash compensation must be made within six months of the day on which the damage occurred and must be paid within one year of the date when agreement is reached as to the amount of compensation or when the assessment acquires finality, failing which the investor shall be entitled to back interest on the unpaid amount as from the day following the expiry of such period according to the prevailing bank interest rates in the State in which the investment is made.

ARTICLE 12

The Arab investor, together with the members of his family, shall be entitled to unimpeded entry, residence, relocation and departure in respect of the territory of the State in which the investment is made. Restrictions on this right may be imposed only by judicial order pursuant to article 39.

Employees in the field of investment and their families shall enjoy the available facilities relative to entry, residence and departure.

ARTICLE 13

The State shall assist the Arab investor to secure such Arab labour and Arab or foreign experts as he needs. Where the requisite professional skills are available, priority in filling the relevant vacancies shall go to nationals of the State in which the investment is made, followed by Arab employees and, finally, experts of other nationalities.

ARTICLE 14

1. In the various aspects of his activity, the Arab investor must, as far as possible, liaise with the State in which the investment is made and with its various institutions and authorities. He must respect its laws and regulations in a manner consistent with this Agreement and, in establishing, administering and developing Arab investment projects, must comply with the

development plans and programmes drawn up by the State for the purpose of national economic development by employing all means which reinforce its structure and promote Arab economic integration. In so doing, he shall refrain from any action which might violate public order and morality or involve illegitimate gains.

2.   The Arab investor shall bear liability for any breach of the obligations set forth in the preceding paragraph in accordance with the law in force in the State in which the investment is made or in which the breach occurs.

ARTICLE 15

Pursuant to the rights arising from this Agreement, Arab investors shall be subject to the same obligations as are imposed on citizens of the State in which the investment is made by the legal provisions in force therein.

CHAPTER III: PREFERENTIAL TREATMENT

ARTICLE 16

The State Party may establish additional privileges for the Arab investor in excess of the minimum stipulated within this Agreement. In the according of preferential privileges, regard shall be had, in particular, for the following considerations:

- The importance of the project with regard to the future development of the national economy;

- Joint Arab projects;

- The size of Arab participation in administration of the project;

- The extent of Arab possession of the technology employed;

- The achievement of greater Arab control over the administration and the technology employed;

- The creation of employment opportunities for nationals of the host State and Arabs and the capital contribution to the State in which the investment is made;

- The sector in which the investment is made.

The State Party in which the investment is made may similarly establish preferential treatment according to the foregoing considerations for Arab investment projects which are essentially owned by Arab nationals.

ARTICLE 17

Privileges established for preferential projects shall be recorded by means of a notice stating the scope of application of such privileges in terms of time and place and addressed to the Council by the central authority of the State in which the project is being implemented.

CHAPTER IV: SUPERVISING IMPLEMENTATION OF THE AGREEMENT

ARTICLE 18

The Council shall be responsible for supervising implementation of the provisions of this Agreement. To this end, it may:

1.   Interpret the provisions of the Agreement;

2.   Issue, amend and abolish the regulations and measures required to implement the provisions of the Agreement;

3.   Propose amendments to the regulations, provisions and measures relating to investment in the States Parties in such a manner as to assist implementation of the provisions and objectives of the Agreement;

4.   Collate and coordinate the reports, information, statements, legislation, regulations and statistics relating to investment, the fields of investment, the sectors open to investment and the preconditions for investment in such sectors in the States Parties, having first obtained these from the competent authorities and placed them at the disposal of the owners of Arab capital with a view to encouraging and assisting them to invest in Arab projects;

5.   Assist in the establishment of the organizations and institutions which will facilitate or promote the achievement or finalization of the objectives of the Agreement, including consultative and executive bodies and organizations and systems to assemble financial and human resources and steer them at an equivalent rate towards development investment in the Arab States.

ARTICLE 19

1.   The Council may, at the request of any State Party, agree to suspend enforcement in that State of any of the provisions of the Agreement and may impose limits of time, place or subject-matter accordingly. The competent authorities within the State must be guided by the observations and recommendations of the Council in order to ensure a return to compliance with the Agreement.

2.   In cases of utmost necessity, the competent authorities within the State Party may take urgent measures entailing the suspension of certain provisions of the Agreement, provided that they so inform the Council forthwith. The Council may ask the State to modify and repeal such

measures.

3.   The provisions of paragraphs 1 and 2 shall not apply to privileges and guarantees previously accorded within the scope of this Agreement.

ARTICLE 20

The Council may create committees from amongst its members or their representatives and invest them with such authority as it deems fit.   It may likewise establish technical committees representing the interests of investors, the States in which the investment is made and the remaining elements of the investment, for the purpose of considering such matters as may be entrusted to them.

ARTICLE 21

Decisions of the Council shall be taken by an absolute majority of its members with the exception of decisions on the matters provided for in article 18, paragraph 1 and article 29, paragraph 1, which shall be taken by a majority of two thirds of its members.   The decisions shall be binding on all States Parties.

CHAPTER V: INVESTMENT GUARANTEES

ARTICLE 22

The Inter-Arab Investment Guarantee Corporation shall provide insurance for the funds invested pursuant to this Agreement according to the terms and provisions stipulated within the Agreement on Establishing the Inter-Arab Investment Guarantee Corporation and the amendments thereto, in addition to the rules and regulations issued accordingly.

ARTICLE 23

The General Secretariat of the League of Arab States may reach agreement with the Inter-Arab Investment Guarantee Corporation regarding matters within its competence for the performance of any of the tasks stipulated in article 18, paragraphs 4 and 5.

ARTICLE 24

Where a State Party or Arab authority pays a sum for damages sustained by the Arab investor as a result of a guarantee which it accorded him either singly or together with the Inter-Arab Investment Guarantee Corporation or any other organization or as a result of any insurance arrangements, the payer shall be subrogated for the investor before the State in which the investment is made within the limits of the payment made, provided that the legally prescribed rights of the investor before such State are not thereby exceeded. The rights of the investor before the said State shall continue to apply to sums in excess of those paid to him.

CHAPTER VI: THE SETTLEMENT OF DISPUTES

ARTICLE 25

Disputes arising from the application of this Agreement shall be settled by way of conciliation or arbitration or by recourse to the Arab Investment Court.

ARTICLE 26

Conciliation and arbitration shall be conducted in accordance with the regulations and procedures contained in the annex to the Agreement which is regarded as an integral part thereof.

ARTICLE 27

Each party may seek recourse to legal action in order to settle a dispute in the following instances:

1.   Failure of the two parties to agree to the expedient of conciliation;

2.   Failure of the conciliator to award his decision within the period specified;

3.   Failure of the two parties to agree on accepting the solutions proposed in the decision of the conciliator;

4.   Failure of the two parties to resort to arbitration;

5.   Failure of the arbitral panel to award a decision within the prescribed period for whatever reason.

ARTICLE 28

1.   Until such time as the Arab Court of Justice is established and its jurisdiction determined, the Arab Investment Court shall be established.

2.   The Court shall be composed of at least five judges and several reserve members, each having a different Arab nationality, who shall be chosen by the Council from a list of Arab legal specialists drawn up specifically for such purpose, two of whom are to be nominated by each State Party from amongst those having the academic and moral qualifications to assume high-ranking legal positions. The Council shall appoint the chairman of the Court from amongst the members of the Court.

3.   The members of the Court shall serve full-time whenever the work so requires. The term of membership shall be three years and may be renewed.

4.   The Council shall determine the remuneration of its chairman and members, who shall

be treated as members of the Council as regards diplomatic immunity. Their salaries, remuneration and allowances shall be exempt from all tax.

5.   The seat of the Court shall be at the permanent headquarters of the League of Arab States and shall not be transferred unless the Court takes a substantiated decision to convene its sessions or undertake its functions in another location.

6.   The Court shall produce a set of rules governing work regulations, procedures in the Court and the structure of its divisions. No division shall have fewer than three members.

ARTICLE 29

1.   The Court shall have jurisdiction to settle disputes brought before it by either party to an investment which relate to or arise from application of the provisions of the Agreement.

2.   The disputes must have occurred:

(a)   Between any State Party and another State Party or between a State Party and the public institutions and organizations of the other parties or between the public institutions and organizations of more than one State Party;

(b)   Between the persons referred to in paragraph 1 and Arab investors;

(c)   Between the persons referred to in paragraphs 1 and 2 and the authorities providing investment guarantees in accordance with this Agreement.

ARTICLE 30

Where an international Arab agreement setting up an Arab investment or any agreement related to investment within the scope of the League of Arab States stipulates that a matter or dispute should be referred to international arbitration or to an international court, the parties involved may agree to regard it as being within the jurisdiction of the Court.

ARTICLE 31

The Arab investor may have recourse to the courts in the State where the investment is made according to the rules of jurisdiction within such State in the case of matters which fall within the jurisdiction of the Court. However, where the Arab investor brings an action before one authority, he must refrain from so doing before the other.

ARTICLE 32

Where there is a conflict of jurisdiction between the Court and the courts of a State Party, the decision of the Court on the matter shall be final.

ARTICLE 33

1.   Should one party so request, the Court may, where it deems it necessary, decide on interim measures which must be taken in order to preserve the rights of that party.

2.   Where a person who is not party to an action and yet who is subject to the jurisdiction of the Court believes that his interests will be affected by the judgement in the action, he may submit a request to intervene as a third party. The Court shall decide on the request.

ARTICLE 34

1.   Judgements shall have binding force only with regard to the parties concerned and the dispute on which a decision is given.

2.   Judgements shall be final and not subject to appeal. Where there is a dispute as to the meaning or import of a judgement, the Court shall provide its interpretation at the request of any of the parties concerned.

3.   A judgement delivered by the Court shall be enforceable in the States Parties, where they shall be immediately enforceable in the same manner as a final enforceable judgement delivered by their own competent courts.

ARTICLE 35

The Court may admit an application for a review of a judgement where the judgement gravely exceeds an essential principle of the Agreement or litigation procedures or where a decisive fact in the case is revealed which was not known at the time of judgement either by the Court or by the party requesting the review. The ignorance of such fact by the said party must not, however, be attributable to his own negligence. Applications must be submitted within six months of the new fact's being uncovered and within five years of the delivery of judgement. Review proceedings shall be instituted by a decision of the Court which explicitly confirms the existence of the new fact, sets out the aspects justifying a review and declares that the application is accordingly admissible. The Court may suspend execution of a judgement which it delivered before deciding to institute review proceedings.

ARTICLE 36

The Court may deliver a non-binding advisory opinion on any legal matter which falls within its jurisdiction at the request of a State Party or the Secretary-General of the League of Arab States or the Council.

CHAPTER VII: CONCLUDING PROVISIONS

ARTICLE 37

1.   Within a maximum period of one year of the date on which the Agreement enters into force, each State Party shall give one central authority within the State responsibility for facilitating implementation of the provisions of the Agreement in its territory during the different phases of the investment and shall inform the General Secretariat of the League of Arab States accordingly.

2.   The said authority may communicate directly with investors and other authorities regarding all matters which fall within its sphere of competence.

ARTICLE 38

1.   In the event of a currency conversion request being made in implementation of the provisions of the Agreement, the conversion shall be made in the currency of the investment or any other convertible currency at the prevailing exchange rate on the day of conversion in the State where the conversion is made. Where there are several exchange rates, reference shall be made to the Council which shall seek the assistance of the Arab Monetary Fund.

2.   The conversion shall be made without delay within the period normally required to complete banking procedures. Where a monetary conversion is delayed for more than three months after the submission date of a request which satisfies the requisite legal conditions, the investor shall be entitled to receive interest from the State on the unconverted money as from the expiry date of such period at the prevailing bank interest rate in the State where the investment is made.

ARTICLE 39

The authority of the State to take specific decisions based on reasons of the public interest or public security shall remain unaffected by any provision of the Agreement.

The obligation of the Arab investor to provide the central authority or the Council with reports and statistical information shall likewise remain unaffected.

ARTICLE 40

Papers, documents and certificates issued by the competent authorities in any State Party or by the Council within the limits of its authority shall serve as sufficient evidence for invoking the rights and affirming the obligations arising from the Agreement. They shall likewise affirm the civil status, legal status and skills of those employed in a project without being subject to the authentication procedures for foreign documents in the States Parties.

ARTICLE 41

1.   The Agreement shall be deposited with the General Secretariat of the League of Arab States for signature.

2.   The Agreement shall enter into force three months after the date on which the instruments of ratification thereof have been deposited by at least
five Arab States.

3.   The League of Arab States shall accept the accession of the Arab States. Thereafter, the Agreement shall take effect in respect of any State wishing to accede thereto three months after the date on which its instruments of ratification are deposited.

4.   The General Secretariat of the League of Arab States shall be responsible for informing Member States of instruments of ratification which are deposited with it.

ARTICLE 42

States which are Parties to the Agreement may only withdraw therefrom five years after its entry into force in their regard. Written notice of withdrawal must be addressed to the Secretary-General of the League of Arab States. Withdrawals shall only take effect one year after the date on which he receives such notice.

ARTICLE 43

The withdrawal of any State which is a Party to the Agreement or the loss of its membership of the League of Arab States or the deferral or suspension of the provisions of the Agreement pursuant to article 19 shall not affect the rights and obligations arising from investment and acquired in accordance with the provisions of the Agreement.

ARTICLE 44

This Agreement may not be amended any earlier than five years from the date of its entry into force.

Amendments to this Agreement shall be made with the consent of two thirds of the States Parties and shall enter into force for the ratifying States three months after instruments ratifying the amendments have been deposited by at least five States.

CHAPTER VIII: INTERIM PROVISIONS

ARTICLE 45

Until such time as all Arab States become parties to the Agreement, the representatives of the Arab States Parties which are members of the Council shall convene in the form of a board known as "The Arab Investment Agreement Board", which shall assume the competence of the Council in this respect, save for appointment of the president and members of the Court, a task which in all instances shall fall to the Council.

The Economic Affairs Department of the League of Arab States shall carry out the secretarial tasks of the Board in accordance with internal regulations issued by the Council, which shall include the organization of the administrative affairs of the Board, the determination of its resources and the rules for the disposal thereof.

ARTICLE 46

The jurisdiction of the Court shall devolve upon the Arab Court of Justice once it is established.

DONE at Amman on Wednesday, 19 Muharram A.H. 1401, corresponding to 26 November A.D. 1980, in the Arabic language in one original, which is kept in the General Secretariat of the League of Arab States. A true copy of the original is to be furnished to every State which signs or becomes a Party to the Agreement.

ANNEX
CONCILIATION AND ARBITRATION

ARTICLE 1 - CONCILIATION

1.   Where two disputing parties agree to conciliation, the agreement must comprise a description of the dispute, the demands of the parties concerned, the name of the conciliator they have selected and the remuneration which they have decided he should receive. The two disputing parties may ask the Secretary-General of the League of Arab States to select a person to assume the task of conciliation between them. The General Secretariat of the League shall provide the conciliator with a copy of the conciliation agreement and ask him to carry out his task.

2.   The task of the conciliator shall be restricted to achieving a <u>rapprochement</u> between the different points of view. He shall be entitled to put forward proposals guaranteeing a solution satisfactory to the parties concerned, who must furnish him with the necessary information and documents to assist him in carrying out his task. Within three months of being informed of the conciliation task, the conciliator must submit a report to the Council summarizing the dispute, his proposals for its settlement and any solutions which have been accepted by the parties concerned. The report must be forwarded within two weeks of its submission to the parties, each of whom shall express his opinion thereon within two weeks of the date of receipt.

3.   The report of the conciliator shall not have probative force in any court before which the dispute may be brought.

ARTICLE 2 - ARBITRATION

1.   Where the two parties fail to agree to conciliation or where the conciliator proves unable to render his decision within the period specified or where the parties do not agree to accept the solutions proposed, they may agree to resort to arbitration.

2.   Arbitration procedures shall commence by the dispatch of a notice by the party seeking arbitration to the other party in the dispute. The notice shall set out the nature of the dispute, the decision which he wishes to see rendered in the dispute and the name of the arbitrator whom he has appointed. Within 30 days of receiving the notice, the other party must inform the party seeking arbitration of the name of the arbitrator he has appointed. Within 30 days of the appointment of the second arbitrator, the two arbitrators must choose a third person to serve as chairman of the arbitral panel, who shall have the casting vote in the event of opinions being equal.

3.   Where the other party fails to appoint an arbitrator or where the two arbitrators fail to agree on the appointment of the person who is to have the casting vote within the time-limits specified, the arbitral panel shall consist of one arbitrator or an uneven number of arbitrators, one of whom shall have a casting vote. Either party may ask the Secretary-General of the League of Arab States to appoint the arbitrators.

4.   Parties to the dispute may not change the arbitrator whom they have appointed once consideration of the case has begun unless an arbitrator resigns or dies or is unable to work, in which case a substitute shall be appointed using the same method by which the original arbitrator was appointed. The successor shall have all the authority of the original arbitrator and shall undertake all his duties.

5.   The arbitral panel shall convene for the first time at the time and place specified by the arbitrator who has the casting vote. Thereafter, the Board shall decide the time and place of its meetings.

6.   The arbitral panel shall decide all matters related to its jurisdiction and shall determine its own procedure.

7.   The arbitral panel shall accord all parties a fair opportunity to submit their written and oral statements and shall adopt its decisions by a majority of votes, stating the grounds for each decision. Decisions must be signed by a majority of the members of the panel at least. Each party shall receive a signed copy thereof.

8.   Decisions of the arbitral panel rendered in accordance with the provisions of this article shall be final and binding. Both parties must comply with and implement the decision immediately it is rendered unless the panel specifies a deferral of its implementation or of the implementation of part thereof. No appeal may be made against arbitration decisions.

9.   Decisions of the arbitral panel must be rendered within a period not exceeding six months

from the date on which the panel first convenes. The Secretary-General of the League of Arab States, at the substantiated request of the panel, may extend the period once only for no more than a further six months should he deem it necessary.

10. The Secretary-General of the League of Arab States shall determine the fees of the arbitrators and the remuneration of other persons engaged in work and procedures related to the arbitration. Each party shall be responsible for its own arbitration costs, whilst the arbitral panel shall determine which party is to bear the costs of the arbitration itself or the proportion of the arbitration costs to be shared between both parties, in addition to payment procedures and method.

11. Where the decision of the arbitral panel fails to be implemented within three months of its rendering, the matter shall be brought before the Arab Investment Court for it to rule on such measures for its implementation as it deems appropriate.

For the Hashemite Kingdom of Jordan

For the United Arab Emirates

For the State of Bahrain

For the Republic of Tunisia

For the People's Democratic Republic of Algeria

For the Republic of Djibouti

For the Kingdom of Saudi Arabia

For the Democratic Republic of Sudan

For the Syrian Arab Republic

For the Somali Democratic Republic

For the Republic of Iraq

For the Sultanate of Oman

For Palestine

For the State of Qatar

For the State of Kuwait

For the Lebanese Republic

For the Socialist People's Libyan Arab Jamahiriya

For the Kingdom of Morocco

For the Islamic Republic of Mauritania

For the Yemen Arab Republic

For the People's Democratic Republic of Yemen

* * *

CONVENTION FOR THE PROTECTION OF INDIVIDUALS WITH REGARD TO AUTOMATIC PROCESSING OF PERSONAL DATA*

The Convention for the Protection of Individuals with Regard to Automatic Processing of Personal Data was adopted by the Council of Europe on 28 January 1981. As at 29 February 1996, the contracting States to the Convention were Austria, Belgium, Denmark, Finland, France, Germany, Greece, Iceland, Ireland, Luxembourg, Netherlands, Norway, Portugal, Slovenia, Spain, Sweden and the United Kingdom.

PREAMBLE

The member States of the Council of Europe, signatory hereto,

Considering that the aim of the Council of Europe is to achieve greater unity between its members, based in particular on respect for the rule of law, as well as human rights and fundamental freedoms;

Considering that it is desirable to extend the safeguards for everyone's rights and fundamental freedoms, and in particular the right to the respect for privacy, taking account of the increasing flow across frontiers of personal data undergoing automatic processing;

Reaffirming at the same time their commitment to freedom of information regardless of frontiers;

Recognising that it is necessary to reconcile the fundamental values of the respect for privacy and the free flow of information between peoples,

Have agreed as follows:

CHAPTER I -- GENERAL PROVISIONS

Article 1
Object and purpose

The purpose of this convention is to secure in the territory of each Party for every individual, whatever his nationality or residence, respect for his rights and fundamental freedoms, and in particular his right to privacy, with regard to automatic processing of personal data

---

*Source: Council of Europe (1981). "Convention for the Protection of Individuals with Regard to Automatic Processing of Personal Data", *European Treaty Series*, No. 108 (January 1981) (Strasbourg: Council of Europe), pp. 1-15 [Note added by the editor].

relating to him ("data protection").

Article 2
Definitions

For the purposes of this convention:

a. "personal data" means any information relating to an identified or identifiable individual ("data subject");

b. "automated data file" means any set of data undergoing automatic processing;

c. "automatic processing" includes the following operations if carried out in whole or in part by automated means: storage of data, carrying out of logical and/or arithmetical operations on those data, their alteration, erasure, retrieval or dissemination;

d. "controller of the file" means the natural or legal person, public authority, agency or any other body who is competent according to the national law to decide what should be the purpose of the automated data file, which categories of personal data should be stored and which operations should be applied to them.

Article 3
Scope

1.   The Parties undertake to apply this convention to automated personal data files and automatic processing of personal data in the public and private sectors.

2.   Any State may, at the time of signature or when depositing its instrument of ratification, acceptance, approval or accession, or at any later time, give notice by a declaration addressed to the Secretary General of the Council of Europe:

a. that it will not apply this convention to certain categories of automated personal data files, a list of which will be deposited. In this list it shall not include, however, categories of automated data files subject under its domestic law to data protection provisions. Consequently, it shall amend this list by a new declaration whenever additional categories of automated personal data files are subjected to data protection provisions under its domestic law;

b. that it will also apply this convention to information relating to groups of persons, associations, foundations, companies, corporations and any other bodies consisting directly or indirectly of individuals, whether or not such bodies possess legal personality;

c. that it will also apply this convention to personal data files which are not processed automatically.

3.   Any State which has extended the scope of this convention by any of the declarations

provided for in sub-paragraph 2.b or c above may give notice in the said declaration that such extensions shall apply only to certain categories of personal data files, a list of which will be deposited.

4.　　Any Party which has excluded certain categories of automated personal data files by a declaration provided for in sub-paragraph *2.a* above may not claim the application of this convention to such categories by a Party which has not excluded them.

5.　　Likewise, a Party which has not made one or other of the extensions provided for in sub-paragraphs 2. b and c above may not claim the application of this convention on these points with respect to a Party which has made such extensions.

6.　　The declarations provided for in paragraph 2 above shall take effect from the moment of the entry into force of the convention with regard to the State which has made them if they have been made at the time of signature or deposit of its instrument of ratification, acceptance, approval or accession, or three months after their receipt by the Secretary General of the Council of Europe if they have been made at any later time. These declarations may be withdrawn, in whole or in part, by a notification addressed to the Secretary General of the Council of Europe. Such withdrawals shall take effect three months after the date of receipt of such notification.

CHAPTER II -- BASIC PRINCIPLES FOR DATA PROTECTION

Article 4
Duties of the Parties

1.　　Each Party shall take the necessary measures in its domestic law to give effect to the basic principles for data protection set out in this chapter.

2.　　These measures shall be taken at the latest at the time of entry into force of this convention in respect of that Party.

Article 5
Quality of data

Personal data undergoing automatic processing shall be:

a. obtained and processed fairly and lawfully;

b. stored for specified and legitimate purposes and not used in a way incompatible with those purposes;

c. adequate, relevant and not excessive in relation to the purposes for which they are stored;

d. accurate and, where necessary, kept up to date;

e. preserved in a form which permits identification of the data subjects for no longer than is required for the purpose for which those data are stored.

Article 6
Special categories of data

Personal data revealing racial origin, political opinions or religious or other beliefs, as well as personal data concerning health or sexual life, may not be processed automatically unless domestic law provides appropriate safeguards. The same shall apply to personal data relating to criminal convictions.

Article 7
Data security

Appropriate security measures shall be taken for the protection of personal data stored in automated data files against accidental or unauthorised destruction or accidental loss as well as against unauthorised access, alteration or dissemination.

Article 8
Additional safeguards for the data subject

Any person shall be enabled:

a. to establish the existence of an automated personal data file, its main purposes, as well as the identity and habitual residence or principal place of business of the controller of the file;

b. to obtain at reasonable intervals and without excessive delay or expense confirmation of whether personal data relating to him are stored in the automated data file as well as communication to him of such data in an intelligible form;

c. to obtain, as the case may be, rectification or erasure of such data if these have been processed contrary to the provisions of domestic law giving effect to the basic principles set out in Articles 5 and 6 of this convention;

d. to have a remedy if a request for confirmation or, as the case may be, communication, rectification or erasure as referred to in paragraphs b and c of this article is not complied with.

Article 9
Exceptions and restrictions

1.   No exception to the provisions of Articles 5, 6 and 8 of this convention shall be allowed except within the limits defined in this article.

2.   Derogation from the provisions of Articles 5, 6 and 8 of this convention shall be allowed when such derogation is provided for by the law of the Party and constitutes a necessary measure

in a democratic society in the interests of:

    a. protecting State security, public safety, the monetary interests of the State or the suppression of criminal offences;

    b. protecting the data subject or the rights and freedoms of others.

3.   Restrictions on the exercise of the rights specified in Article 8, paragraphs b, c and d, may be provided by law with respect to automated personal data files used for statistics or for scientific research purposes when there is obviously no risk of an infringement of the privacy of the data subjects.

Article 10
Sanctions and remedies

Each Party undertakes to establish appropriate sanctions and remedies for violations of provisions of domestic law giving effect to the basic principles for data protection set out in this chapter.

Article 11
Extended protection

None of the provisions of this chapter shall be interpreted as limiting or otherwise affecting the possibility for a Party to grant data subjects a wider measure of protection than that stipulated in this convention.

CHAPTER III -- TRANSBORDER DATA FLOWS

Article 12
Transborder flows of personal data and domestic law

1.   The following provisions shall apply to the transfer across national borders, by whatever medium, of personal data undergoing automatic processing or collected with a view to their being automatically processed.

2.   A Party shall not, for the sole purpose of the protection of privacy, prohibit or subject to special authorisation transborder flows of personal data going to the territory of another Party.

3.   Nevertheless, each Party shall be entitled to derogate from the provisions of paragraph 2:

    a. insofar as its legislation includes specific regulations for certain categories of personal data or of automated personal data files, because of the nature of those data or those files, except where the regulations of the other Party provide an equivalent protection;

b. when the transfer is made from its territory to the territory of a non-Contracting State through the intermediary of the territory of another Party, in order to avoid such transfers resulting in circumvention of the legislation of the Party referred to at the beginning of this paragraph.

CHAPTER IV -- MUTUAL ASSISTANCE

Article 13
Co-operation between Parties

1.   The Parties agree to render each other mutual assistance in order to implement this convention.

2.   For that purpose:

a. each Party shall designate one or more authorities, the name and address of each of which it shall communicate to the Secretary General of the Council of Europe;

b. each Party which has designated more than one authority shall specify in its communication referred to in the previous sub-paragraph the competence of each authority.

3.   An authority designated by a Party shall at the request of an authority designated by another Party:

a. furnish information on its law and administrative practice in the field of data protection;

b. take, in conformity with its domestic law and for the sole purpose of protection of privacy, all appropriate measures for furnishing factual information relating to specific automatic processing carried out in its territory, with the exception however of the personal data being processed.

Article 14
Assistance to data subjects resident abroad

1.   Each Party shall assist any person resident abroad to exercise the rights conferred by its domestic law giving effect to the principles set out in Article 8 of this convention.

2.   When such a person resides in the territory of another Party he shall be given the option of submitting his request through the intermediary of the authority designated by that Party.

3.   The request for assistance shall contain all the necessary particulars, relating *inter alia* to:

a. the name, address and any other relevant particulars identifying the person making the request;

b. the automated personal data file to which the request pertains, or its controller;

c. the purpose of the request.

Article 15
Safeguards concerning assistance rendered by designated authorities

1.　An authority designated by a Party which has received information from an authority designated by another Party either accompanying a request for assistance or in reply to its own request for assistance shall not use that information for purposes other than those specified in the request for assistance.

2.　Each Party shall see to it that the persons belonging to or acting on behalf of the designated authority shall be bound by appropriate obligations of secrecy or confidentiality with regard to that information.

3.　In no case may a designated authority be allowed to make under Article 14, paragraph 2, a request for assistance on behalf of a data subject resident abroad, of its own accord and without the express consent of the person concerned.

Article 16
Refusal of requests for assistance

A designated authority to which a request for assistance is addressed under Articles 13 or 14 of this convention may not refuse to comply with it unless:

a. the request is not compatible with the powers in the field of data protection of the authorities responsible for replying;

b. the request does not comply with the provisions of this convention;

c. compliance with the request would be incompatible with the sovereignty, security or public policy *(ordre public)* of the Party by which it was designated, or with the rights and fundamental freedoms of persons under the jurisdiction of that Party.

Article 17
Costs and procedures of assistance

1.　Mutual assistance which the Parties render each other under Article 13 and assistance they render to data subjects abroad under Article 14 shall not give rise to the payment of any costs or fees other than those incurred for experts and interpreters. The latter costs or fees shall be borne by the Party which has designated the authority making the request for assistance.

2.　The data subject may not be charged costs or fees in connection with the steps taken on his behalf in the territory of another Party other than those lawfully payable by residents of that

Party.

3.   Other details concerning the assistance relating in particular to the forms and procedures and the languages to be used, shall be established directly between the Parties concerned.

CHAPTER V -- CONSULTATIVE COMMITTEE

Article 18
Composition of the committee

1.   A Consultative Committee shall be set up after the entry into force of this convention.

2.   Each Party shall appoint a representative to the committee and a deputy representative. Any member State of the Council of Europe which is not a Party to the convention shall have the right to be represented on the committee by an observer.

3.   The Consultative Committee may, by unanimous decision, invite any non-member State of the Council of Europe which is not a Party to the convention to be represented by an observer at a given meeting.

Article 19
Functions of the committee

The Consultative Committee:

a.   may make proposals with a view to facilitating or improving the application of the convention;

b.   may make proposals for amendment of this convention in accordance with Article 21;

c.   shall formulate its opinion on any proposal for amendment of this convention which is referred to it in accordance with Article 21, paragraph 3;

d.   may, at the request of a Party, express an opinion on any question concerning the application of this convention.

Article 20
Procedure

1.   The Consultative Committee shall be convened by the Secretary General of the Council of Europe. Its first meeting shall be held within twelve months of the entry into force of this convention. It shall subsequently meet at least once every two years and in any case when one third of the representatives of the Parties request its convocation.

2.   A majority of representatives of the Parties shall constitute a quorum for a meeting of the

Consultative Committee.

3.   After each of its meetings, the Consultative Committee shall submit to the Committee of Ministers of the Council of Europe a report on its work and on the functioning of the convention.

4.   Subject to the provisions of this convention, the Consultative Committee shall draw up its own Rules of Procedure.

CHAPTER VI -- AMENDMENTS

Article 21
Amendments

1.   Amendments to this convention may be proposed by a Party, the Committee of Ministers of the Council of Europe or the Consultative Committee.

2.   Any proposal for amendment shall be communicated by the Secretary General of the Council of Europe to the member States of the Council of Europe and to every non-member State which has acceded to or has been invited to accede to this convention in accordance with the provisions of Article 23.

3.   Moreover, any amendment proposed by a Party or the Committee of Ministers shall be communicated to the Consultative Committee, which shall submit to the Committee of Ministers its opinion on that proposed amendment.

4.   The Committee of Ministers shall consider the proposed amendment and any opinion submitted by the Consultative Committee and may approve the amendment.

5.   The text of any amendment approved by the Committee of Ministers in accordance with paragraph 4 of this article shall be forwarded to the Parties for acceptance.

6.   Any amendment approved in accordance with paragraph 4 of this article shall come into force on the thirtieth day after all Parties have informed the Secretary General of their acceptance thereof.

CHAPTER VII -- FINAL CLAUSES

Article 22
Entry into force

1.   This convention shall be open for signature by the member States of the Council of Europe. It is subject to ratification, acceptance or approval. Instruments of ratification, acceptance or approval shall be deposited with the Secretary General of the Council of Europe.

2.   This convention shall enter into force on the first day of the month following the

expiration of a period of three months after the date on which five member States of the Council of Europe have expressed their consent to be bound by the convention in accordance with the provisions of the preceding paragraph.

3.   In respect of any member State which subsequently expresses its consent to be bound by it, the convention shall enter into force on the first day of the month following the expiration of a period of three months after the date of the deposit of the instrument of ratification, acceptance or approval.

Article 23
Accession by non-member States

1.   After the entry into force of this convention, the Committee of Ministers of the Council of Europe may invite any State not a member of the Council of Europe to accede to this convention by a decision taken by the majority provided for in Article 20.d of the Statute of the Council of Europe and by the unanimous vote of the representatives of the Contracting States entitled to sit on the committee.

2.   In respect of any acceding State, the convention shall enter into force on the first day of the month following the expiration of a period of three months after the date of deposit of the instrument of accession with the Secretary General of the Council of Europe.

Article 24
Territorial clause

1.   Any State may at the time of signature or when depositing its instrument of ratification, acceptance, approval or accession, specify the territory or territories to which this convention shall apply.

2.   Any State may at any later date, by a declaration addressed to the Secretary General of the Council of Europe, extend the application of this convention to any other territory specified in the declaration. In respect of such territory the convention shall enter into force on the first day of the month following the expiration of a period of three months after the date of receipt of such declaration by the Secretary General.

3.   Any declaration made under the two preceding paragraphs may, in respect of any territory specified in such declaration, be withdrawn by a notification addressed to the Secretary General. The withdrawal shall become effective on the first day of the month following the expiration of a period of six months after the date of receipt of such notification by the Secretary General.

Article 25
Reservations

No reservation may be made in respect of the provisions of this convention.

Article 26
Denunciation

1.   Any Party may at any time denounce this convention by means of a notification addressed to the Secretary General of the Council of Europe.

2.   Such denunciation shall become effective on the first day of the month following the expiration of a period of six months after the date of receipt of the notification by the Secretary General.

Article 27
Notifications

The Secretary General of the Council of Europe shall notify the member States of the Council and any State which has acceded to this convention of:

a. any signature;

b. the deposit of any instrument of ratification, acceptance, approval or accession;

c. any date of entry into force of this convention in accordance with Articles 22, 23 and 24;

d. any other act, notification or communication relating to this convention.

In witness whereof the undersigned, being duly authorised thereto, have signed this Convention.

Done at Strasbourg, the 28th day of January 1981, in English and in French, both texts being equally authoritative, in a single copy which shall remain deposited in the archives of the Council of Europe. The Secretary General of the Council of Europe shall transmit certified copies to each member State of the Council of Europe and to any State invited to accede to this Convention.

For the Government of the Republic of Austria:

For the Government of the Kingdom of Belgium:

For the Government of the Republic of Cyprus:

For the Government of the Kingdom of Denmark:

For the Government of the French Republic:

For the Government of the Federal Republic of Germany:

For the Government of the Hellenic Republic:

For the Government of the Icelandic Republic:

For the Government of Ireland:

For the Government of the Italian Republic:

For the Government of the Principality of Liechtenstein:

For the Government the Grand Duchy of Luxembourg:

For the Government of Malta:

For the Government of the Kingdom of the Netherlands:

For the Government of the Kingdom of Norway:

For the Government of the Portuguese Republic:

For the Government of the Kingdom of Spain:

For the Government of the Kingdom of Sweden:

For the Government of the Swiss Confederation:

For the Government of the Turkish Republic:

For the Government of the United Kingdom of Great Britain
and Northern ireland:

* * *

AGREEMENT ON PROMOTION, PROTECTION AND GUARANTEE OF INVESTMENTS AMONG MEMBER STATES OF THE ORGANISATION OF THE ISLAMIC CONFERENCE[*]

The Agreement on Promotion, Protection and Guarantee of Investments among Member States of the Organization of the Islamic Conference was approved and opened for signature by resolution 7/12-E of the Twelfth Islamic Conference of Foreign Ministers held in Baghdad, Iraq, on 1-5 June 1981. It entered into force on 23 September 1986. As of January 1995, the members of the Organization of Islamic Conference included Afghanistan, Albania, Algeria, Azerbaïjan, Bahrain, Bangladesh, Benin, Brunei Darussalam, Burkina Faso, Cameroon, Chad, Comoros, Djibouti, Egypt, Gabon, Gambia, Guinea, Guinea-Bissau, Indonesia, Islamic Republic of Iran, Iraq, Jordan, Kuwait, Kyrgyzstan, Lebanon, Libyan Arab Jamahiriya, Maldives, Malaysia, Mali, Mauritania, Morocco, Mozambique, Niger, Nigeria, Oman, Pakistan, Palestine, Qatar, Saudi Arabia, Senegal, Sierra Leone, Somalia, Sudan, Syrian Arab Republic, Tadjikistan, Tunisia, Turkey, Turkmenistan, Uganda, United Arab Emirates, Yemen, and United Republic of Tanzania.

PREAMBLE

The Governments of the Member States of the Organisation of the Islamic Conference signatory to this Agreement,

In keeping with the objectives of the Organisation of the Islamic Conference as stipulated in its Charter,

In implementation of the provisions of the Agreement for Economic, Technical and Commercial Cooperation among the Member States of the Organisation of the Islamic Conference and particularly the provisions of Article 1 of the said Agreement,

Endeavouring to avail of the economic resources and potentialities available therein and to mobilize and utilize them in the best possible manner, within the framework of close cooperation among Member States,

Convinced that relations among the Islamic States in the field of investment are one of the major areas of economic cooperation among these states through which economic and social development therein can be fostered on the basis of common interest and mutual benefit,

---

[*]Source: General Secretariat of the Organisation of Islamic Conference (1981). *Agreement on Promotion, Protection and Guarantee of Investments Among Member States of the Organisation of the Islamic Conference*, mimeo. [Note added by the editor].

Anxious to provide and develop a favourable climate for investments, in which the economic resources of the Islamic countries could circulate between them so that optimum utilization could be made of these resources in a way that will serve their development and raise the standard of living of their peoples,

Have approved this Agreement,

And have agreed to consider the provisions contained therein as the minimum in dealing with the capitals and investments coming in from the Member States,

And have declared their complete readiness to put the Agreement into effect, in letter and in spirit, and of their sincere wish to extend every effort towards realizing its aims and objectives.

CHAPTER ONE
Definitions

Article 1

The following terms which are used in the Agreement shall have the meanings assigned to each of them for the purpose of the Agreement unless the context indicates a different meaning:

1.   The Agreement

The Agreement for the Promotion, Protection and Guarantee of Investments among the Member States of the Organisation of the Islamic Conference.

2.   Contracting Parties

The Member States of the Organisation of the Islamic Conference signatories to the Agreement and in respect of which the Agreement has become effective.

3.   Host State

Every contracting party in which the invested capital is present and to which it has become lawfully, or which permits the investor to employ his capital therein.

4.   Capital

All assets (including everything that can be evaluated in monetary terms) owned by a contracting party to this Agreement or by its nationals, whether a natural person or a corporate body and present in the territories of another contracting party whether these were transferred to or earned in it, and whether these be movable, immovable, in cash, in kind, tangible as well as everything pertaining to these capitals and investments by way of rights or claims and shall include the net profits accruing from such assets and the undivided shares and intangible rights.

5.   Investment

The employment of capital in one of the permissible fields in the territories of a contracting party with a view to achieving a profitable return, or the transfer of capital to a contracting party for the same purpose, in accordance with this Agreement.

6.   Investor

The Government of any contracting party or natural corporate person, who is a national of a contracting party and who owns the capital and invests it in the territory of another contracting party.

Nationality shall be determined as follows:

(a)   Natural Person:

Any individual enjoying the nationality of a contracting party according to the provisions of the nationality law in force therein.

(b)   Legal Personality:

Any entity established in accordance with the laws in force in any contracting party and recognized by the law under which its legal personality is established.

7.   Investment Returns

The sums yielded by the investment or derived therefrom for a specified period which shall include, without limitation, the profits, dividends, licence fees, royalties, leases, services and all the increases achieved on the capital assets and the utilization of intangible property rights.

8.   The General Secretariat

The General Secretariat of the Organisation of the Islamic Conference.

9.   The Secretary General

The Secretary General of the Organisation of the Islamic Conference.

10.   The Organisation

The Organisation of the Islamic Conference.

CHAPTER TWO
General provisions regarding promotion, protection and guarantee
of the capitals and investments and the rules governing them
in the territories of the contracting parties

Article 2

The contracting parties shall permit the transfer of capitals among them and its utilization therein in the fields permitted for investment in accordance with their laws. The invested capital shall enjoy adequate protection and security and the host state shall give the necessary facilities and incentives to the investors engaged in activities therein.

Article 3

The contracting parties shall endeavour to open up various fields and investment opportunities to the capital on the widest possible scale, in such a way that may suit their economic conditions and on the basis of achieving mutual benefits for the parties to the investment in a way that will foster the social and economic development of the host state in accordance with its set objectives and plans while, at the same time, achieving a profitable investment return for the capital.

Article 4

The contracting parties will endeavour to offer various incentives and facilities for attracting capitals and encouraging its investment in their territories such as commercial, customs, financial, tax and currency incentives, especially during the early years of the investment projects, in accordance with the laws, regulations and priorities of the host state.

Article 5

The contracting parties shall provide the necessary facilities and grant required permits for entry, exit, residence and work for the investor and his family and for all those whose work is permanently or temporarily connected with the investment such as experts, administrators, technicians and labourers in accordance with the laws and regulations of the host state.

Article 6

The host state shall -- within the provisions of its regulations and its economic and social policies -- encourage the local private sector to cooperate with and participate in investments in the contracting parties.

Article 7

In the case of withdrawal of a contracting party from the Agreement, the rights and obligations arising under the Agreement in the host state towards the investor, which have accrued before the receipt of the notice of withdrawal of the contracting party shall continue and shall not be affected by the withdrawal.

Article 8

1.   The investors of any contracting party shall enjoy, within the context of economic activity in which they have employed their investments in the territories of another contracting party, a treatment not less favourable than the treatment accorded to investors belonging to another State not party to this Agreement, in the context of that activity and in respect of rights and privileges accorded to those investors.

2.   Provisions of paragraph 1 above shall not be applied to any better treatment given by a contracting party in the following cases:

a)   Rights and privileges given to investors of one contracting party by another contracting party in accordance with an international agreement, law or special preferential arrangement.

b) Rights and privileges arising from an international agreement currently in force or to be concluded in the future and to which any contracting party may become a member and under which an economic union, customs union or mutual tax exemption arrangement is set up.

c)   Rights and privileges given by a contracting party for a specific project due to its special importance to that state.

Article 9

The investor shall be bound by the laws and regulations in force in the host state and shall refrain from all acts that may disturb public order or morals or that may be prejudicial to the public interest. He is also to refrain from exercising restrictive practices and from trying to achieve gains through unlawful means.

CHAPTER THREE
Investment guarantees
Article 10

1.   The host state shall undertake not to adopt or permit the adoption of any measure -- itself or through one of its organs, institutions or local authorities -- if such a measure may directly or indirectly affect the ownership of the investor's capital or investment by depriving him totally or partially of his ownership or of all or part of his basic rights or the exercise of his authority on the ownership, possession or utilization of his capital, or of his actual control over the

investment, its management, making use out of it, enjoying its utilities, the realization of its benefits or guaranteeing its development and growth.

2.   It will, however, be permissible to:

(a) Expropriate the investment in the public interest in accordance with the law, without discrimination and on prompt payment of adequate and effective compensation to the investor in accordance with the laws of the host state regulating such compensation, provided that the investor shall have the right to contest the measure of expropriation in the competent court of the host state.

(b) Adopt preventive measures issued in accordance with an order from a competent legal authority and the execution measures of the decision given by a competent judicial authority.

Article 11

1.   The host state shall undertake to guarantee the free transfer to any contracting party of the capitals and its net proceeds in cash without the investor being subject to any discriminatory banking, administrative or legal restrictions and without any taxes or charges on the transfer. This shall not apply to the bank service charges. The repatriation of the original capital shall be effected on the termination of the investment according to its nature of after five years from the date of its transfer to the host state, whichever is earlier.

2.   The transfer shall be effected in the currency in which the investment was made or in any other convertible currency, at the exchange rate fixed by the International Monetary Fund on the day when the transfer was made.

3.   The transfer must be effected within the period normally required for the completion of bank procedures and without delay. In all cases this period shall not exceed 90 (ninety) days from the day in which a request for transfer fulfilling all the legal conditions was made.

4.   It shall not be considered as a restriction the procedural measures instituted for exchange control in the host state for administrative purposes or to prevent the illegal transfer abroad of the funds of its nationals. Neither shall the fixing of the percentage of transferable amounts of the salaries, wages and rewards of the employees and investment experts within the range of 50 % (fifty per cent) be considered a restriction.

Article 12

The host state shall guarantee for the investor the freedom to dispose of the ownership of the invested capital by selling it, wholly or partly, by liquidation, cession, or grant or by any other means. The capital shall continue to be treated in accordance with the provisions of this Agreement on condition that the transfer is made to an investor who is a subject of one of the contracting parties and subject to the approval of the host state.

Article 13

1.   The investor shall be entitled to compensation for any damage resulting from any action of a contracting party or one of its public or local authorities or its institutions in the following cases:

(a)   Violation of any of the rights or guarantees accorded to the investor under this Agreement;

(b)   Breach of any of the international obligation or undertakings imposed on the contracting party and arising under the Agreement for the benefit of the investor or the non-performance of whatever is necessary for its execution whether the same is intentional or due to negligence;

(c)   Non-execution of a judicial decision requiring enforcement directly connected with the investment;

(d)   Causing, by other means or by an act or omission, damage to the investor in violation of laws in force in the state where the investment exists.

2.   The compensation shall be equivalent to the damage suffered by the investor depending on the type of damage and its quantum.

3.   The compensation shall be monetary if it is not possible to restore the investment to its state before the damage was sustained.

4.   The assessment of monetary compensation shall be concluded within 6 (six) months from the date when the damage was sustained and shall be paid within a year from the date of agreement upon the amount of compensation or from the date when the assessment of the compensation has become final.

Article 14

The investor shall be accorded a treatment not less than that accorded by the host state to its national investors or others regarding the compensation of damage that may befall the physical assets of investment due to hostilities of international nature committed by any international body or due to civil disturbances or violent acts of general nature.

Article 15

The Organisation shall through the Islamic Development Bank, and in accordance with the provisions of its Agreements, establish as a subsidiary organ of the Organisation, an Islamic

Institution for the Guarantee of Investments which is to take charge of the insurance of property invested in the territories of the contracting parties, in accordance with this Agreement and in conformity to the principles of Islamic Sharia.

Article 16

The host state undertakes to allow the investor the right to resort to its national judicial system to complain against a measure adopted by its authorities against him, or to contest the extent of its conformity with the provisions of the regulations and laws in force in its territory, or to complain against the non-adoption by the host state of a certain measure which is in the interest of the investor, and which the state should have adopted, irrespective of whether the complaint is related, or otherwise, to the implementation of the provisions of the Agreement to the relationship between the investor and the host state.

Provided that if the investor chooses to raise the complaint before the national courts or before an arbitral tribunal then having done so before one of the two quarters he loses the right of recourse to the other.

Article 17

1.   Until an Organ for the settlement of disputes arising under the Agreement is established, disputes that may arise shall be entitled through conciliation or arbitration in accordance with the following rules and procedures:

1.   Conciliation

a) In case the parties to the dispute agree on conciliation, the agreement shall include a description of the dispute, the claims of the parties to the dispute and the name of the conciliator whom they have chosen. The parties concerned may request the Secretary General to choose the conciliator. The General Secretariat shall forward to the conciliator a copy of the conciliation agreement so that he may assume his duties.

b) The task of the conciliator shall be confined to bringing the different view points closer and making proposals which may lead to a solution that may be acceptable to the parties concerned. The conciliator shall, within the period assigned for the completion of his task, submit a report thereon to be communicated to the parties concerned. This report shall have no legal authority before a court should the dispute be referred to it.

2.   Arbitration

a) If the two parties to the dispute do not reach an agreement as a result of their resort to conciliation, or if the conciliator is unable to issue his report within the prescribed period, or if the two parties do not accept the solutions proposed therein, then each party has the right to resort to the Arbitration Tribunal for a final decision on the dispute.

b) The arbitration procedure begins with a notification by the party requesting the arbitration to the other party to the dispute, clearly explaining the nature of the dispute and the name of the arbitrator he has appointed. The other party must, within sixty days from the date on which such notification was given, inform the party requesting arbitration of the name of the arbitrator appointed by him. The two arbitrators are to choose, within sixty days from the date on which the last of them was appointed arbitrator, an umpire who shall have a casting vote in case of equality of votes. If the second party does not appoint an arbitrator, or if the two arbitrators do not agree on the appointment of an Umpire within the prescribed time, either party may request the Secretary General to complete the composition of the Arbitration Tribunal.

c) The Arbitration Tribunal shall hold its first meeting at the time and place specified by the Umpire. Thereafter the Tribunal will decide on the venue and time of its meetings as well as other matters pertaining to its functions.

d) The decisions of the Arbitration Tribunal shall be final and cannot be contested. They are binding on both parties who must respect and implement them. They shall have the force of judicial decisions. The contracting parties are under an obligation to implement them in their territory, no matter whether it be a party to the dispute or not and irrespective of whether the investor against whom the decision was passed is one of its nationals or residents or not, as if it were a final and enforceable decision of its national courts.

General and final provisions

Article 18

Two or more contracting parties may enter into an agreement between them that may provide a treatment which is more preferential than that stipulated in this Agreement.

Article 19

The Agreement shall continue to be in force in the event that disputes of any kind arise between the contracting parties and notwithstanding the existence or otherwise of diplomatic relations or any other type of representation between the states concerned.

Article 20

The General Secretariat will follow up the implementation of this Agreement.

Article 21

The Agreement shall come into force after three months from the date on which the instruments of ratification of ten Member States of the Organisation of the Islamic Conference are deposited; and shall come into force, with regard to each new state that may join it, after three months from the date of depositing its instruments of ratification.

Article 22

The Agreement may be amended with the approval of four-fifth of the contracting parties and on the request of at least five states.

Article 23

The Agreement shall continue in force for an unlimited period and the contracting parties may withdraw from it, after five years from its coming into force with regard to the state concerned by notice in writing to the Secretary General provided that the withdrawal shall not become effective before the lapse of one year from the date of notification.

Article 24

The original text of the Agreement shall be deposited with the General Secretariat for signature. The General Secretariat shall receive the instruments of ratification. The General Secretariat shall notify all contracting parties of the signatures and ratifications of the Agreement.

Article 25

This Agreement is drawn up in Arabic, English and French languages, each version being equally authentic.

* * *

COMMUNITY INVESTMENT CODE OF THE ECONOMIC COMMUNITY OF THE GREAT LAKES COUNTRIES (CEPGL)[*]

The Community Investment Code of the Economic Community of the Great Lakes Countries (CEPGL) was signed on 31 January 1982. It entered into force on 4 October 1987. The member States of the CEPGL as of November 1995 are Burundi, Rwanda and Zaire.

The Government of the Republic of Burundi,

The Government of the Rwandese Republic,

The National Executive Council of the Republic of Zaire,

Having regard to the Convention of 20 September 1976 establishing the Economic Community of the Great Lakes Countries (CEPGL), and in particular articles 2 and 3 of that Convention;

In view of the Agreement of 31 January 1982 establishing the Community Investment Code of the Economic Community of the Great Lakes Countries (CEPGL);

HAVE AGREED AS FOLLOWS:

TITLE I: GENERAL PROVISIONS

Chapter I: Objectives

Article 1

Within the framework of the Economic Community of the Great Lakes Countries (CEPGL), hereinafter referred to as the Community, the Community Investment Code aims to define the guarantees, rights, obligations and advantages of joint enterprises and Community enterprises and the obligations of the member States of the Community *vis-à-vis* such enterprises.

---

[*]Source: Economic Community of the Great Lakes Countries (1982). "Community Investment Code of the Economic Community of the Great Lakes Countries", *Official Gazette of the Economic Community of the Great Lakes Countries*, 3rd year, No. 4 (4 April 1982). Original language: French [Note added by the editor].

Chapter II: Definitions

Article 2

For the purposes of this Code:

a)   A joint enterprise means a business entity which is a joint proprietorship of all the member States of the Community or in which they hold at least a 51-per-cent majority of the shares, and which is under joint management and financing and has joint decision-making bodies;

b)   A Community enterprise means a business entity which meets the following criteria:

    i)   The criterion of substantial available resources

    The enterprise must turn to account either available resources belonging to at least two member States or a sufficiently large amount of resources from a single member State the use of which, however, involves another member State of the Community.

    ii)   The criterion of market size

    This criterion is met when the viability of the enterprise requires access to a market broader than that of the host country.

    iii)   The criterion of volume of investments

    The enterprise must show a minimum amount of investment as stipulated in the Community Investment Code.

    iv)   The criterion of the nature of the investments

    The nature of the investments makes it possible to assess the technological aspects of the enterprise in terms of the objectives being pursued by the Community in its development plan.

    v)   The criterion of the cost-effectiveness threshold.

    This criterion is met when the total estimated returns of the enterprise are higher than the total of its start-up costs and the costs of its sound operation.

Article 3

For purposes of the application of this Code:

a)   The term "national" means any natural or juridical person having the nationality of the

CEPGL member country in which the Community enterprise or joint enterprise has been established;

b)   The term "Community national" means any natural or juridical person having the nationality of one of the CEPGL member countries;

c)   The term "foreign national" means any natural or juridical person not a national of one of the member countries of the Community;

d)   The term "worker" refers to any person deemed to be an employed person or in the same category as an employed person under the legislation of the host country;

e)   The term "legislation" refers to the laws and regulations of any of the CEPGL member countries;

f)   The term "host country" refers to the country in which the Community enterprise or joint enterprise has been established;

g)   The term "authorization document" refers to a legal act issued by a competent authority of the Community in the form of an enforceable decision, which notifies the requesting enterprise of the terms of the authorization;

h)   The term "founding agreement" refers to a contract concluded between a competent authority of CEPGL and an enterprise authorized under basic regime II, in accordance with the conditions set forth in this Code.

Article 4

Under this Code, the Community enterprise or joint enterprise may be:

a)   An enterprise with national capital, if the invested capital consists of resources mobilized in a member State of the Community and belonging to either nationals or foreign nationals;

b)   An enterprise with intra-Community capital, if the majority of the invested capital consists either of a contribution by at least two member States or of a mobilization of financial resources more than half of which belong to natural or juridical persons from more than one member country of the Community;

c)   An enterprise with foreign capital, if the majority of the capital invested within the Community consists of resources originating outside the Community and belonging to natural or juridical persons who are foreign nationals;

d)   An enterprise with mixed capital, if the invested capital consists of a pooling of national or intra-Community capital and foreign capital.

Article 5

Under the terms of this Code, Community enterprises or joint enterprises fall into the following categories:

a) Enterprises specializing in the area of economic infrastructure, in particular: water-resource development, bridge construction, road links, ports, communications networks, power-distribution systems and irrigation projects;

b) Enterprises engaged primarily in the development and processing of local resources;

c) Import-substitution enterprises;

d) Service enterprises, in particular: ground, air, river and maritime transport services, maintenance and inspection services, tourism activities, financing, insurance and reinsurance operations;

e) Any other enterprise deemed to have priority by the competent bodies of the Community.

Chapter III: Guarantees

Section I: General guarantees

Article 6

As provided by this Code, the freedom to form and invest capital shall be guaranteed to any natural or juridical person wishing to establish an enterprise in the territory of one of the member States.

Article 7

Acquired rights of all kinds to individual or collective property shall be guaranteed to all natural or juridical persons, without discrimination either among foreign nationalities or among foreign nationals and nationals. Such rights may not be prejudiced except in the public interest and in accordance with the principles of international law, and subject to the payment of fair and equitable compensation to the injured holder of such rights.

Article 8

Subject to compliance with existing legislation governing exchange regulations, the CEPGL member States shall guarantee the freedom to transfer capital accumulated in regulated markets, duly earned profits and funds arising from share transfers or from the cessation of business by an enterprise.

Article 9

Enterprises with intra-Community capital, foreign capital or mixed capital shall be entitled to acquire rights of all kinds as needed for the conduct of their operations - property rights, industrial rights, and administrative licences, authorizations and permits - under the same conditions as enterprises of the host country.

Article 10

Community enterprises with foreign or mixed capital shall enjoy the same rights and receive the same protection as enterprises with intra-Community capital. These rights extend to patents and trade marks, trade descriptions and labels, and any other industrial property. Such enterprises shall not be subject to any discrimination under the law.

Article 11

In the performance of their work and in accordance with the legislation of each State,

a)   Workers who are Community nationals shall be governed by labour legislation and social laws under the same conditions as nationals. They may participate in trade union activities and belong to bodies defending employee rights. They shall be further governed by the general agreement on social security between the member countries of the Community;

b)   Enterprises with foreign capital and the directors thereof shall be represented in organizations representing professional and business interests under the same conditions as enterprises or nationals of member countries of the Community.

Article 12

Within the framework of this Code, workers who are Community nationals or foreign nationals shall not be liable as individuals to duties, charges and assessments, regardless of their denomination, which are other or greater than those levied on nationals.

Section II: Special guarantees for foreign capital

Article 13

Within the scope and under the terms of the exchange regulations and subject to the fiscal legislation of the host country, all enterprises with foreign capital or mixed capital authorized as Community enterprises or joint enterprises shall be accorded by the host country:

a)   A guarantee regarding the transfer of:

i)   The return, in the form of dividends or profits, on foreign capital invested in cash or in kind or in the form of know-how;

ii) The reimbursement of the principal and interest on loans contracted abroad and invested in the undertaking;

iii) The cost of indispensable technical assistance from abroad furnished to the undertaking and directly related with the undertaking's operations in the Community;

iv) The business income of expatriate officials employed by the undertaking in the Community, directors' percentage of profit and foreign auditors' fees;

b) A guarantee that they will obtain, from the Central Bank, at least the foreign currency required to import the raw materials and spare parts which will ensure the production intended for the Community; the same shall apply to production aids, that is, products which are indispensable for manufacture and which are destroyed or lose their specific characteristics in the course of direct manufacturing operations.

Chapter IV: Authorization

Article 14

In order to be included under basic regime I or basic regime II, any enterprise as defined in articles 2 and 5 of this Code must receive authorization from the competent authority of CEPGL.

Section I: Conditions for authorization

Article 15

Any joint enterprise or Community enterprise conducting or wishing to conduct operations in the territory of a CEPGL member State either in order to rationalize its production methods or for purposes of modernization or extension may qualify for a decision authorizing inclusion under a preferential regime if it meets the criteria provided for article 2.

The minimum volume of investments is set at one million United States dollars or the equivalent.

Section II: Authorization procedure

Article 16

Community enterprises or joint enterprises as defined in article 2 (a) and (b) must direct any request for inclusion under an advantageous regime to the Permanent Executive Secretariat of CEPGL, which shall, pursuant to article 19 of the Convention establishing CEPGL, be responsible for transmitting the dossier to the competent bodies of the Community.

The Conference of Heads of State has the competence to issue an authorization. The authorization decision shall be notified to the enterprise by the Permanent Executive Secretariat of CEPGL.

Article 17

The authorization request shall be accompanied by a supporting dossier in twelve copies, which shall include at least the following information:

a)   The legal status of the enterprise;

b)   A technical dossier specifying planned activities, the origin, extent and nature of the raw materials, the product quality and price, the production planning, the plan, the facilities, and the patenting, licensing and all other aspects of know-how;

c)   An economic and financial dossier specifying the volume of investments, the sources of funding, the capital of the enterprise, the available credit, its market, the number of posts, and a forward study of economic and financial earning power;

d)   The start-up date for the project.

If the dossier is complete, the Permanent Executive Secretariat shall transmit two copies to each CEPGL member State.

Section III: Authorization document

Article 18

The authorization document shall:

a)   Specify the preferential regime under which the authorized enterprise is included;

b)   List the activities for which authorization is granted;

c)   Indicate the advantages granted, the period during which they will be in force and the procedures for their application;

d)   Specify the obligations incumbent upon the enterprise, especially with regard to the programme for meeting its goals;

e)   Determine specific arbitration procedures.

Article 19

The authorized enterprise shall agree to:

a)   Carry out the investment programme for which it was established;

b)   Maintain product quality;

c)   Keep regular accounts of the kind provided for under the legislation of the host country;

d)   Agree to any inspection and monitoring by the host country and by the competent body of CEPGL;

e)   Reply within the period specified to all questionnaires and requests for statistics;

f)   Respect and ensure staff rights;

g)   Establish and keep to a programme for training local manpower and promoting the advancement of managerial staff who are nationals of the member countries of the Community;

h)   See to the protection of the environment;

i)   Develop local resources;

j)   Give priority to furnishing supplies to the CEPGL member States in times of scarcity in the same proportions as in normal times;

k)   Give priority to earmarking for member States of the Community the export of the goods produced.

Article 20

All operations of an authorized enterprise which are not explicitly included in the activities listed in the authorization document shall continue to be governed by the tax-related and other provisions of ordinary law in force in the host country.

Article 21

Authorization for inclusion under an advantageous regime does not exempt the authorized enterprise from compliance with the political, financial, fiscal and social legislation of the host country.

TITLE II: ADVANTAGES OFFERED BY THE DIFFERENT AUTHORIZATION REGIMES

Article 22

There are two authorization regimes which may be granted by the CEPGL authority:

-    Basic regime I

-    Basic regime II

Chapter I: Authorization under Basic Regime I

Article 23

Any enterprise as defined under article 2 which meets the conditions for authorization under this Code may benefit from the economic, financial and tax advantages provided for under basic regime I as hereinafter established.

Section I: Economic advantages

Article 24

An authorized enterprise may receive financing for the conduct of pre-investment and investment studies from public credit institutions and more specifically from the Development Bank of the Great Lakes States.

It may also take advantage of the technical assistance and consultancy services of the CEPGL member countries, international agencies or foreign countries.

Article 25

Where necessary, special customs protection measures may be instituted for the benefit of Community enterprises and joint enterprises.

Article 26

All other things being equal, priority in the award of public services contracts shall be given to the extent possible to authorized enterprises as against enterprises which are outside the Community.

Section II: Financial advantages

Article 27

Subject to the regulations of the central banks of the CEPGL member countries concerning foreign exchange, authorized enterprises shall be given priority in the allocation of foreign currency in order to purchase capital goods, raw materials, products and packaging required for their operations.

Section III: Tax advantages

Article 28

Basic regime I shall include, for a maximum period of five years for an enterprise, the benefit of the following measures:

a) The application of a single overall import duty and tax rate of between 0 and 5 per cent on equipment and materials, machines and tools which are specifically required for product production and processing;

b) Partial or complete exemption from import duties and taxes and indirect taxes levied inside the Community on:

    i) Raw materials and products constituting, wholly or in part, inputs of the products worked or processed;

    ii) Raw materials and products, which, while not constituting implements or inputs for the products worked or processed, are destroyed or lose their specific properties in the direct manufacturing process;

    iii) Raw materials and products intended for the packaging and non-reusable wrapping of goods worked or processed;

c) The benefit of reduced or non-existent export duties on:

    i) Raw materials for use in Community enterprises;

    ii) Finished or semi-finished products for use in the CEPGL member countries.

Article 29

The following tax advantages may be granted to authorized enterprises under basic regime I:

a) Exemption from the direct tax on agricultural, industrial and trading profits during the first five financial years, the first financial year being deemed to be the one during which the first sale or delivery is made either on the Community or the export market;

b) Exemption during the first five years from real estate, mining and forestry fees;

c) Temporary exemption for a period of five years from the real estate tax on developed and undeveloped property;

d) Exemption for five years from trading dues.

Chapter II: Authorization under Basic Regime II

Article 30

Authorization under basic regime II shall be granted to a Community enterprise or joint enterprise which meets the conditions for admission to basic regime I, as stipulated in article 23, and in addition one of the following special conditions:

a)   A tying-up of capital which justifies an extended amortization period;

b)   A project which has priority for the economic and social development of the Community;

c)   A project set up outside the limits of urban areas for the purpose of rural development;

d)   A mining enterprise.

Section I: Tax advantages

In addition to the economic and financial advantages defined under basic regime I, basic regime II shall afford the benefit of the tax advantages set forth in articles 32 to 37.

Article 31

Basic regime II shall grant a stabilized tax regime for direct taxes to the beneficiary enterprise.

Article 32

The duration of the stabilized tax regime for direct taxes may not exceed 15 years, extended where necessary to include the normal installation time.

Article 33

During the period for which it applies, the stabilized tax regime shall protect the beneficiary enterprise against any increase in direct taxation which is applicable to it on the date of authorization with regard both to tax assessment and rates and to collection procedures.

In addition, the tax or customs provisions applicable under basic regime I may be extended in whole or in part to basic regime II.

Article 34

The stabilized tax regime may be extended to customs duties and charges. In this case, the stabilization may apply only to customs and excise dues and the turnover tax on imports. The imported equipment and materials covered under the stabilization of customs and excise dues and the turnover tax on imports shall be exhaustively listed in an annex to the enacting agreement.

Article 35

If there is a change in the tax regime under ordinary law, an enterprise which benefits from a stabilized tax regime may request a revision of its enacting agreement.

Article 36

Any legal or regulatory provision which runs counter to these regulations shall not be applicable during the same period to enterprises which benefit from the stabilized tax regime.

Section II: Enacting Agreement

Article 37

The authorization of a Community enterprise or a joint enterprise by the competent CEPGL authority under basic regime II shall include, in addition to the advantages defined in articles 31, 32, 33 and 34 of this Code, the benefit of an enacting agreement.

Article 38

The enacting agreement shall establish its duration and the procedures for its extension and must include the same information as specified in articles 18, 19, 20 and 21 of this Code. With regard to taxation, the enacting agreement shall include a list of the stabilized taxes and fees as well as the rates applicable for the duration of basic regime II.

The enacting agreement shall define the various commitments of the enterprise, including general operating conditions, minimum production plant programmes, vocational training and all other obligations accepted by the enterprise with regard to the host country and the other countries of the Community.

Article 39

Revision of an enacting agreement that has been concluded may be negotiated on the initiative of one of the parties.

In the absence of agreement by the partners on the exact terms of the revision, the original regime shall continue to apply for the duration initially decided upon.

Article 40

The enacting agreement may not contain any commitment, on the part of the States members of the Community, which may have the effect of holding an enterprise harmless in respect of losses, costs, or shortfalls arising from changes in technology, the economic situation or factors specific to the enterprise.

Chapter III: Default by an Enterprise

Article 41

An enterprise shall forfeit the advantages provided for under articles 24, 25, 26, 27 and 28 of this Code if it defaults through:

- Failure to meet a deadline for project execution, or technical specifications for product quality;

- A product price which is very high in relation to the price of the same product imported from outside the Community;

- Failure to supply the Community market on a regular basis;

- Mismanagement having a potential impact on supplies to the Community market.

Article 42

If default is due to the economic situation, a lack of operating facilities granted to the enterprise by the host country or the failure by States members of the Community to observe Community commitments, the dispute shall be settled in accordance with articles 50, 51, 52, 53 and 54 of this Code.

TITLE III: SPECIFIC PROVISIONS APPLICABLE TO COMMUNITY ENTERPRISES AND JOINT ENTERPRISES OF CEPGL

Chapter I: Specific provisions for Community Enterprises

Article 43

The host State must provide guarantees concerning the arrangements for the supply of water, electricity and other resources necessary for operations as well as those for the inward and outward transport of goods.

Article 44

The competent authorities of the host country shall ensure that the economic unit informs the other member States about the running of an enterprise through the CEPGL Permanent Executive Secretariat. In the case of an enterprise which is still under consideration, however, this responsibility shall rest entirely with the host country.

Article 45

Any request to be addressed to an agency or country on behalf of a Community enterprise shall be jointly signed by the partner countries.

Article 46

The location of the head office of a Community enterprise shall be specified in the authorization document or the enacting agreement.

Chapter II: Specific provisions for joint undertakings

Article 47

Joint enterprises shall be established by the CEPGL Conference of Heads of State.

Article 48

In the design, preparation and execution of their programmes, joint enterprises shall obtain technical and financial assistance primarily from the specialized agencies and institutions of the Community.

Article 49

For contracts to carry out the research and work of a joint enterprise, priority shall be given, in cases involving equal competence, to the research institutes, consultants and consulting engineers and executing agencies of the CEPGL member States.

TITLE IV: SETTLEMENT OF DISPUTES

Chapter I: Revocation procedure

Article 50

Any CEPGL member country may bring to the attention of the CEPGL Permanent Executive Secretariat a case involving serious dereliction, duly recorded, by an enterprise which benefits from the advantages provided for under one of the basic regimes.

The CEPGL Permanent Executive Secretariat shall carry out an investigation and give formal notice to the enterprise to make good the dereliction in question by registered letter or letter with acknowledgement of receipt.

Article 51

If the formal notice has no effect within a period of 90 days, the Permanent Executive

Secretariat shall transmit the case to the CEPGL Council of Ministers and State Commissioner for consideration.

A copy of the letter shall be sent to the member States and to the enterprise in question. The enterprise must submit its plea in defence within a maximum period of one month from the date of receipt of the letter as attested by the postmark or from the date of the acknowledgement of receipt.

Article 52

The decision to revoke authorization shall be taken by Conference of Heads of State on the advice of the Council of Ministers and the State Commissioner and following consideration of the information submitted by the parties concerned.

Article 53

Within a maximum period of 30 days from the date of notification of the revocation decision, the enterprise may appeal the decision in accordance with the arbitration procedure provided for under article 54.

Failing an appeal or if the appeal is submitted late, the revocation decision handed down by the Conference of Heads of State shall remain definitive.

Chapter II: Arbitration

Article 54

The settlement of disputes arising from the provisions of an enacting agreement and from the application of the authorization document of an authorized enterprise, as well as the determination of any compensation due because of failure to honour commitments entered into, may be the subject of an arbitration procedure as provided for in each authorization document or enacting agreement.

The said arbitration procedure shall contain the following provisions:

(a)   Each party shall appoint an arbitrator;

(b)   In case of disagreement between the arbitrators, a third arbitrator shall be appointed by mutual agreement between the parties. If no agreement is possible, the authorization or enacting agreement shall stipulate the procedure for appointing the third arbitrator;

(c)   The decision shall be handed down by a majority of the arbitrators, who shall determine their own procedures, and shall be definitive in nature;

(d) In the case of Community enterprises the majority of whose capital is initially foreign-held, however, the authorization document may provide for international arbitration procedures replacing those referred to above.

TITLE IV: FINAL PROVISIONS

Article 55

Without prejudice to acquired rights, the Code may be modified or amended by the Conference of Heads of State of CEPGL.

Article 56

This Code shall enter into force on the date of deposit of the last instrument of ratification of the agreement on its establishment with the Permanent Executive Secretariat of the Economic Community of the Great Lakes Countries.

Done at Gisenyi, on 31 January 1982.

President of the Republic of Burundi

President of the Republic of Rwanda

President of the Republic of Zaire

*   *   *

AGREEMENT FOR THE ESTABLISHMENT OF A REGIME FOR CARICOM ENTERPRISES[*]

The Agreement for the Establishment of a Regime for CARICOM Enterprises (CER) was opened for signature by CARICOM member States in May 1987. The Agreement was signed by the Governments of Antigua and Barbuda on 1 July 1988; Barbados on 6 February 1988; Dominica on 6 February 1988; Grenada on 6 February 1988; Guyana on 22 December 1987; Jamaica on 28 January 1988; Montserrat on 5 July 1988; Saint Kitts and Nevis on 14 March 1988; Saint Lucia on 3 March 1988; Saint Vincent and the Grenadines on 6 February 1988; and Trinidad and Tobago on 3 June 1988. In 1995, the CARICOM member States terminated the Agreement on the grounds that progress towards the establishment of the Simple Market and Economy, including trade and investment liberalization among the members, had rendered the special facilities under the CER redundant.

The Governments of the Member States of the Caribbean Common Market,

Having regard to the provisions of the Common Market Annex of the Treaty Establishing the Caribbean Community and, in particular, to:

(a) Article 3 on the "Objectives of the Common Market";

(b) Article 35 on "Establishment" and Article 37 on "Movement of Capital";

(c) Article 42 on the "Harmonization of Laws", with respect to Company Law;

(d) Article 44 on "Ownership and Control of Regional Resources";

(e) Article 45 on the "Coordination of National Development Planning"; Article 46 on "Common Market Industrial Programming"; Article 47 on "Joint Development of Natural Resources"; and Article 49 on "Rationalization of Agricultural Production"; and

(f) Article 59 on "Financial Assistance from the More Developed Countries" to Less Developed Countries;

Cognisant of the urgent need to develop economic activities in the Common Market on the basis of joint enterprises between national investors (as hereinafter defined in Article 1);

Conscious of the continuing need to develop and give further scope for national and regional entrepreneurship, management and technological capacity in the production of goods and services on a regional basis for both the regional and extraregional markets;

---

[*]Source: CARICOM (1987). "Agreement for the Establishment of a Regime for CARICOM Enterprises" (Attachment III, document HGC 07/0/5) [Note added by the editor].

Mindful of the need to pool human, financial and natural resources of the Region for the implementation of high priority regional projects designed to benefit the people of the Region;

Emphasizing the need for the creation of machinery whereby the movement of investment capital between Member States, particularly from the More Developed Countries to the Less Developed Countries may be expeditiously affected in the interests of the development of the Region;

Aware of the crucial role which the private sector, on its own or in partnership with the Region's public sector or suitable foreign investors, can play in the economic development of the Region;

Agree to the establishment of the following regime:

Article 1
Definitions

1.   In this Agreement:

"Authority" means the Body established by Article 8 of this Agreement.

"CARICOM ENTERPRISE" means, subject to this Agreement, a regionally-owned and controlled company which:

(a)   within such areas specified in Articles 46, 47 and 49 of the Treaty as the Council may from time to time prescribe, engages in the production of Common Market Origin goods; or

(b)   provides services:

(i)   in areas specified in Articles 48 and 50 of the Treaty; or

(ii)   in those sectors of the regional economy specified in the Annex to this Agreement and in such other sectors of the regional economy as the Council may, from time to time, determine.

"Common Market Origin" has the same meaning as that referred to in paragraphs 1, 2 and 3 of Article 14 of the Annex to the Treaty.

"company" means a company incorporated under the general statutes of any Member State relating to the formation of such a legal company.

"Council" means the Caribbean Common Market Council of Ministers established by the Treaty.

"Less Developed Country" means Antigua and Barbuda, Belize, Dominica, Grenada, Montserrat, Saint Christopher and Nevis, Saint Lucia or Saint Vincent and the Grenadines.

"Member State" means a Member State which is a Member of the Caribbean Common Market established by the Annex to the Treaty and a Party to this Agreement.

"More Developed Country" means Barbados, Guyana, Jamaica or Trinidad and Tobago.

"national" subject to paragraph 2 of this Article, has the same meaning as that set out in paragraph 6(a) of Article 35 of the Annex to the Treaty and includes companies controlled by such persons or by companies so controlled as specified in the definition of "regionally- owned and controlled".

"National Investor" means, subject to paragraph 2 of this Article, a Member State or a national of a Member State holding equity share capital of a Company.

"regionally-owned and controlled" in relation to a company means that the company is one in which in the opinion of the Authority nationals of at least two Member States exercise management and control by beneficially owning shares carrying between them directly or indirectly:

    (a)   the right to exercise more than one-half of the voting power in that company; and

    (b)   the right to receive more than one-half of any dividends that might be paid by that company; and

    (c)   the right to receive more than one-half of any capital distribution in the event of the winding-up or of a reduction in share capital of that company;

or such greater proportion than is specified in paragraphs (a) to (c) above as the Council may, from time to time, determine in relation to any sector of the regional economy.

"Registrar" in relation to a Member State, means the officer responsible for the registration of companies.

"Treaty" means the Treaty Establishing the Caribbean Community and Common Market done at Chaguaramas on the 4th July, 1973.

2.   (1)   The <u>Caribbean Development Bank</u> and the <u>Caribbean Food Corporation</u> and other similar bodies that hold equity share capital in a company shall, for the purposes of this Agreement, be deemed to be National Investors as well as nationals of the Member State which is to be the Headquarters State.

    (2)   Nothing in this Agreement shall be construed as derogating from any rights,

privileges and immunities conferred on or accorded the Caribbean Development Bank and the Caribbean Food Corporation by virtue of the respective Agreements establishing them.

3.   Nothing in this Agreement and, in particular, the definition of CARICOM ENTERPRISE shall entitle an enterprise to be registered as a CARICOM ENTERPRISE unless it is approved as such by the Authority in accordance with this Agreement.

Article 2
Establishment of a Regime

Member States undertake to establish a Regime for the incorporation and registration, operation, management, winding-up and dissolution of a form of business enterprise to be known as a CARICOM ENTERPRISE, for the legal organisation, purposes and scope of operation as is hereinafter specified.

Article 3
Purposes and Functions of a CARICOM ENTERPRISE

A CARICOM ENTERPRISE may be established for such purposes within the areas specified in Articles 46-50 of the Annex to the Treaty and such other sectors of the regional economy as are specified in the Annex to this Agreement and shall perform such functions as are by its Memorandum of Association and the provisions of this Agreement specified; the Council shall keep the Annex under review and may impose any conditions under which CARICOM ENTERPRISES may operate.

Article 4
Formal Organisation of a CARICOM ENTERPRISE

1.   The formal organisation of a CARICOM ENTERPRISE shall be that of a company which has been established in accordance with this Regime.

2.   The name of the Member State in which the central management and control of the CARICOM ENTERPRISE will be situated (hereinafter called "the Headquarters State") shall be stated in the Memorandum of Association.

3.   The shares shall be registered in the name of the holder.

4.   A CARICOM ENTERPRISE shall be incorporated and registered in the Headquarters State.

Article 5
Law of Incorporation, Registration, Operation, Management,
Winding-Up and Dissolution of a CARICOM ENTERPRISE

The incorporation, registration, operation, management, winding-up and dissolution of a

CARICOM ENTERPRISE shall be governed by the provisions of this Agreement as well as the company law and other relevant laws of the Headquarters State and those other Member States in which the CARICOM ENTERPRISE is registered.

Article 6
Formation of a CARICOM ENTERPRISE

1.   The status of a CARICOM ENTERPRISE may be conferred on a company formed for the purpose and in the manner provided by this Article. However, a Company not so formed for the purpose may acquire the status of a CARICOM ENTERPRISE if it is qualified therefor and its objects are confined to those of such an Enterprise.

2.   The Memorandum of Association, Articles of Association and other constituent documents that are required for the incorporation of a Company (hereinafter referred to as "the constituent documents"), together with programmes of activities of a proposed CARICOM ENTERPRISE for the first five years of its operation, shall be submitted to the Authority for its approval in writing and any material alteration of any such programme shall be submitted to the Authority forthwith for its approval.

3.   In the case of a Company not formed for the purpose of becoming a CARICOM ENTERPRISE that desires to obtain such status, the programme of activities together with certified copies of its registration certificate and its constituent documents must similarly be submitted to the Authority for its approval in writing.

4.   The written approval for the registration of the Company as a CARICOM ENTERPRISE, upon its incorporation or otherwise, shall be attached to duly authenticated copies of the constituent documents and submitted to the Registrars of the Headquarters State and such other Member States as voted under paragraph 4(a) of Article 8 of this Agreement for conferment of the status of a CARICOM ENTERPRISE on the Company, for incorporation, if necessary, of the Company in the Headquarters State and its registration as a CARICOM ENTERPRISE in the Headquarters State and those other Member States.

5.   The Registrars of the Headquarters State and those other States referred to in paragraph 4 of this Article upon receipt of the constituent documents together with the written approval of the Authority shall register the Company as a CARICOM ENTERPRISE in the Headquarters State and in those other Member States, respectively.

6.   Any proposed alteration of the objects of a registered CARICOM ENTERPRISE shall similarly be submitted to the Authority for its approval and dealt with in the manner provided by paragraphs 4 and 5 of this Article.

7.   Within fourteen days of the registration of the CARICOM ENTERPRISE in the Headquarters State, the Registrar of the Headquarters State shall notify the Registrars of each Member State, other than those referred to in paragraph 4 of this Article, of the registration of the CARICOM ENTERPRISE.

8.   The Registrar of each Member State, other than those referred to in paragraph 4 of this Article, shall without payment of any fee enter the name of the CARICOM ENTERPRISE in a special record kept for the purpose.

9.   Where a Company is registered as a CARICOM ENTERPRISE by any Member State under this Agreement, it shall pay such fees, levies and other dues, if any, as are prescribed by the laws of the Member State concerned.

Article 7
Effect of Registration

1.   Registration of a Company as a CARICOM ENTERPRISE under paragraphs 4 to 6 of Article 6 of this Agreement shall confer the status of a CARICOM ENTERPRISE on such Company and entitle the CARICOM ENTERPRISE to the benefits provided for by this Agreement.

2.   Where pursuant to paragraph 8 of Article 6 of this Agreement the name of a CARICOM ENTERPRISE is entered in the special record of a Member State, such Enterprise may at any time thereafter apply to be registered as a CARICOM ENTERPRISE in that Member State, and on such application the Registrar of such Member State shall on the receipt of the constituent documents and payment of any prescribed fee, register such CARICOM ENTERPRISE accordingly, whereupon the provisions of paragraph 1 of this Article shall apply.

Article 8
Establishment, Voting, Meeting and Procedure
of the CARICOM ENTERPRISE Authority

1.   For the purposes of this Agreement, there shall be a CARICOM ENTERPRISE Authority which shall comprise one representative of each Member State, one official of the Caribbean Community Secretariat, one official of the Caribbean Development Bank and one representative of the body or institution representing the private sector designated as a member of the Joint Consultative Group of the Common Market Council of Ministers.

2.   Each Member of the Authority, other than the official of the Caribbean Community Secretariat, the official of the Caribbean Development Bank and the representative of the private sector referred to in paragraph 1, shall have one vote.

3.   Except as otherwise provided for in this Agreement, a decision of the Authority shall be by a simple majority vote of the Members of the Authority present and voting.

4.   (a)   In considering an application for the approval of the establishment of a CARICOM ENTERPRISE, only the representative of the Headquarters State, the representatives of Member States in which the CARICOM ENTERPRISE is to be registered and the representatives of those Member States, the nationals of which are members of the Enterprise, shall vote. The quorum shall be all the Member States, the nationals of which are members of the Enterprise. A decision

of the Authority on any such application shall be by unanimous vote.

(b)   In exercising any of the powers set out in Article 10 (d) (ii) of this Agreement, the affirmative vote of at least two-thirds of the representatives entitled to vote under sub-paragraph (a) of this paragraph shall be necessary.

5.   The Authority shall meet in any Member State it considers convenient from time to time and as often as it is necessary for the conduct of its business and, without prejudice to the foregoing, at least on two occasions in each calendar year.

6.   The quorum for meetings to decide all matters, except those set out in paragraph 4 of this Article, shall be one-third of the Members of the Authority.

7.   The Members of the Authority shall elect a Chairman from among their number.

8.   The Authority may establish sub-committees and may co-opt any expert for the use of such or his services as it may require for the purpose of performing its functions under this Agreement.

Article 9
Management of a CARICOM ENTERPRISE

A CARICOM ENTERPRISE shall normally be managed in its day-to-day operations by nationals of the Member States of the Caribbean Common Market but where it is not possible to secure the services of such nationals, the CARICOM ENTERPRISE may secure the services of other nationals provided the Authority is notified and approves of their engagement.

Article 10
Functions and Powers of the Authority

1.   The Authority:

(a)   shall receive:

(i)   applications accompanied by other constituent documents for approval as are set out in Article 6, paragraph 2, of this Agreement;

(ii)   such information as may, from time to time, be sent to it by any Member State for the purpose of ensuring that a CARICOM ENTERPRISE is owned and controlled by nationals or for deciding whether a CARICOM ENTERPRISE is in gross or persistent violation of the provisions of this Agreement;

(iii)   such information as shall be submitted to it, at its request, by a CARICOM ENTERPRISE for the purpose of determining whether the operations of that CARICOM ENTERPRISE are within the purposes and scope of the Regime;

(iv) such other information as may be submitted to it by any Member State or CARICOM ENTERPRISE and which may be of use to it for the effective performance of its functions and exercise of its powers;

(b) shall grant or refuse applications for approval to proceed to registration of a CARICOM ENTERPRISE as set out in Article 8 of this Agreement;

(c) may require from a CARICOM ENTERPRISE, immediately upon its registration, that it shall provide the Authority with information on such matters as its current shareholdings, loan agreements, management contracts, consultancy contracts, and assets, if any, held outside the Caribbean Community. Such a request may stipulate a period or regular periods within which the information shall be supplied;

(d) may determine:

(i) whether the operations of a CARICOM ENTERPRISE are within the purpose and scope of this Agreement and may make reports to any Member State or the CARICOM ENTERPRISE affected and recommendations based thereon;

(ii) whether a CARICOM ENTERPRISE has been carrying on business in gross or persistent violation of this Agreement and shall state its findings and at the same time make a report on them to the Headquarters State and the CARICOM ENTERPRISE affected; provided that the Authority shall afford the CARICOM ENTERPRISE an opportunity to make representations before making a determination under this provision of this sub-paragraph;

(e) shall take all necessary steps to ensure that a CARICOM ENTERPRISE is, as far as possible, managed by nationals of the Member States of the Caribbean Common Market only, except to such extent as the Authority has allowed.

2. Notwithstanding anything in this Article, the Authority may make such other reports and recommendations to Member States and submit copies thereof to the CARICOM ENTERPRISES concerned as it considers necessary for the purpose of ensuring that CARICOM ENTERPRISES comply with the provisions of this Agreement.

Article 11
Supervision of the CARICOM ENTERPRISE

1. The supervision of a CARICOM ENTERPRISE shall be undertaken by the Authority and

the Registrars of Member States (performing their statutory functions) or such other body or person as each Member State may designate for the purpose.

2.   Member States undertake to assist the Authority by taking such action as may be necessary to ensure:

    (a)   that CARICOM ENTERPRISES carry on their business within the purposes and scope of the Regime;

    (b)   that, subject to Article 9, all CARICOM ENTERPRISES are managed and controlled by nationals of Member States;

    (c)   that CARICOM ENTERPRISES are not in gross or persistent violation of the provisions of the Regime.

3.   The Headquarters State shall, upon a finding by the Authority that a CARICOM ENTERPRISE has been carrying on its business in gross or persistent violation of this Agreement, strike off the name of the CARICOM ENTERPRISE from its register of CARICOM ENTERPRISES. Such a CARICOM ENTERPRISE shall immediately cease to enjoy all the benefits provided for in Article 12 of this Agreement.

4.   The Registrar of the Headquarters State shall forthwith inform all Member States in which the CARICOM ENTERPRISE is registered that its name has been so struck off the register and every such Member State shall thereupon remove the name from its register or its special record, as the case may be.

5.   A CARICOM ENTERPRISE which has been struck off from the CARICOM ENTERPRISE register may operate as a company under the national laws of the Headquarters State. Its name may be restored not earlier than twelve months after its name has been struck off the register of CARICOM ENTERPRISES if it successfully applies to the Authority for reinstatement.

Article 12
Benefits to be Enjoyed by CARICOM ENTERPRISES

1.   A CARICOM ENTERPRISE shall have full legal personality in every Member State in which it is registered as such, as if it were a company incorporated and registered under the general statutes relating to the incorporation, registration and management of companies.

2.   In the exercise of its legal personality in any Member State in which it is registered, a CARICOM ENTERPRISE shall not be regarded as having a separate personality from that which it enjoys in another Member State in which it is also registered, and accordingly Member States will provide:

    (a)   that the public documents of a CARICOM ENTERPRISE must reflect the indivisibility of the legal personality of the enterprise and any rights and obligations acquired by or imposed on the enterprise; and

(b)   that the appropriate courts of any Member State in which the CARICOM ENTERPRISE is registered shall have full and concurrent jurisdiction over the affairs and all the assets of the enterprise wherever situated in those Member States; and

(c)   that the judgements and orders of any such courts will be enforced in accordance with a common procedure.

3.   Each Member State shall in accordance with the Exchange Control laws in force in its State permit a CARICOM ENTERPRISE registered as such in its State to:

(a)   keep such foreign accounts including portfolio securities in another Member State in which the CARICOM ENTERPRISE is registered, as are required for the fulfilment of its objects;

(b)   subject to any exchange control considerations, remit dividends and repatriate:

(i)   assets on a winding-up; or

(ii)   capital on reduction of its share capital, on no less favourable terms than those accorded to any investor in that State who is not a national.

4.   Each Member State undertakes to:

(a)   grant to a CARICOM ENTERPRISE registered in its territory on terms no less favourable than is accorded to any other enterprise of that Member State all licenses and permissions necessary for the proper conduct of the affairs of any CARICOM ENTERPRISE registered as such in its State;

(b)   grant to a CARICOM ENTERPRISE registered in its territory treatment no less favourable than is accorded to any other enterprise of a Member State in respect of State purchase or use of goods and services;

(c)   allow to a CARICOM ENTERPRISE in the Member States in which it operates, access to long-, medium- and short-term credit which is relevant to its operations on terms no less favourable than is accorded to any other similar enterprise of a Member State;

(d)   treat a CARICOM ENTERPRISE, if necessary, as if it had been incorporated in its territory for the purpose of the conferment of benefits under the Scheme for the Harmonisation of Fiscal Incentives to Industry as set out in Article 3 of that Agreement;

(e)   accord preferential treatment to a CARICOM ENTERPRISE as against a non-regional enterprise when granting incentives under the Scheme for the Harmonisation of Fiscal Incentives to Industry;

(f)   consider a CARICOM ENTERPRISE for the granting of such fiscal incentives as the Member State may think fit in respect of agriculture, tourism and forestry that are mutually agreed by Member States;

(g)   consider the product of a CARICOM ENTERPRISE for protection by quantitative restrictions or other forms of protection imposed at a uniform level by the Member States against imports from third countries on terms no less favourable than those which may be accorded to the product of any other similar enterprise.

Article 13
Taxation of CARICOM ENTERPRISES

1.   The corporate profits of a CARICOM ENTERPRISE shall be subject to tax except that where the equity capital is wholly-owned by Governments of Member States those Governments may agree otherwise.

2.   Dividends and other distributions paid by a CARICOM ENTERPRISE in respect of equity capital owned by Governments of any of the Member States shall not be subject to tax.

3.   Governments of participating States may, by mutual agreement, waive the taxes on profits made by CARICOM ENTERPRISES that engage solely in the business of intra- or extraregional transport and communications.

4.   Nothing in this Agreement shall prevent a CARICOM ENTERPRISE from being eligible for fiscal incentives under the Scheme for the Harmonisation of Fiscal Incentives to Industry.

Article 14
Name of CARICOM ENTERPRISE

The name of a CARICOM ENTERPRISE shall contain the letters (C.E.) at the end thereof.

Article 15
Undertaking as to Implementation

Member States undertake to introduce measures including the amendment of their municipal legislation so as to conform to this Agreement and enable this Regime to be established as soon as practicable.

Article 16
Settlement of Disputes

Disputes of an international character arising under this Agreement shall be settled under and in accordance with the procedure set out in Articles 11 and 12 of the Common Market Annex to the Treaty.

Article 17
Signature of Agreement

This Agreement is open for signature by any Member State.

Article 18
Ratification

This Agreement and any amendments thereto, shall be subject to ratification by Member States in accordance with their respective constitutional procedures. Instruments of Ratification shall be deposited with the Secretary-General of the Caribbean Community (hereinafter referred to as "the Secretary-General") who shall transmit certified copies to the Government of each Member State.

Article 19
Entry into Force

This Agreement shall enter into force upon the deposit of the fourth Instrument of Ratification in accordance with Article 18 of this Agreement.

Article 20
Amendments

1.   This Agreement may be amended by three-fourths of the Member States including two of the More Developed Countries.

2.   Any such amendment shall come into force upon deposit with the Secretary-General of the last of the Instruments of Ratification required in accordance with this Agreement and paragraph 1 of this Article.

3.   The Secretary-General shall notify other Member States of the entry into force of any such amendment.

Article 21
Accession

Any new Member or Associate Member of the Common Market or any Member of the Caribbean Community may accede to this Agreement on the terms and conditions determined by the Conference of Heads of Governments of the Caribbean Community.

Article 22
Withdrawal

1.　　A Member State that withdraws from membership or associate membership of the Common Market in accordance with Article 69 thereof shall, if a Party to this Agreement, be deemed to have withdrawn from this Agreement with effect from the expiration of the time limited by the said Article 69.

2.　　Without prejudice to paragraph 1 of this Article, a Party to this Agreement may withdraw from this Agreement by giving notice in writing to the Authority which shall promptly notify the other Parties to this Agreement; such withdrawal shall take effect twelve months after receipt of the notice by the Authority.

3.　　A Party to this Agreement undertakes to honour any financial obligations duly assumed while it continues to be a Party to this Agreement.

　　　　IN WITNESS WHEREOF the undersigned, being duly authorised by their respective Governments, have affixed their signatures to this Agreement.

　　　　Done in a single copy which is deposited with the Secretary-General of the Caribbean Community who shall transmit certified copies to all Parties to this Agreement.

Signed by _____ for the Government of Antigua and Barbuda on _____ at _____.

Signed by_____ for the Government of Barbados on _____ at _____.

Signed by_____ for the Government of Belize on _____ at _____.

Signed by _____ for the Government of Dominica on _____ at _____.

Signed by _____ for the Government of Grenada on _____ at _____.

Signed by _____ for the Government of Guyana on _____ at _____.

Signed by _____ for the Government of Jamaica on _____ at _____.

Signed by _____ for the Government of Montserrat on _____ at _____.

Signed by _____ for the Government of Saint Christopher and Nevis on _____ at _____.

Signed by _____ for the Government of Saint Lucia on _____ at _____ .

Signed by _____ for the Government of Saint Vincent and the Grenadines on _____ at _____ .

Signed by _____ for the Government of Trinidad and Tobago on _____ at _____ .

*   *   *

Annex

Sectors of the Regional Economy in which
CARICOM ENTERPRISES may operate

Air and Sea Transportation
Banking and Financial Services
Construction and Engineering Services
Consultancy Services
International Marketing

REVISED BASIC AGREEMENT ON ASEAN INDUSTRIAL JOINT VENTURES[*]

The Revised Basic Agreement on ASEAN Industrial Joint Ventures was signed on 15 December 1987 at the Third Meeting of the Association of South East Asian Nations (ASEAN) Heads of Government in Manila. It has been amended by the First, Second and Third Protocols to Amend the Revised Basic Agreement on ASEAN Industrial Joint Ventures (in 1990, 1992 and 1995, respectively). Member States of ASEAN are Brunei Darussalam, Indonesia, Malaysia, Philippines, Singapore and Thailand.

The Governments of Brunei Darussalam, the Republic of Indonesia, Malaysia,the Republic of the Philippines, the Republic of Singapore and the Kingdom of Thailand.

Mindful of the Declaration of ASEAN Concord signed in Bali, Indonesia on 24 February 1976, which provides that Member Countries will take cooperative actions in their national and regional development programmes, utilizing as far as possible the resources available in the ASEAN region to broaden the complementarity of their respective economies;

Reaffirming their desire to collaborate for the acceleration of economic growth in the region, to promote the greater utilization of their agriculture and industries, the expansion of their trade and improvement of their economic infrastructure for the mutual benefit of their people;

Convinced that the consolidation of markets among ASEAN countries can support meaningful industrial joint ventures which can greatly contribute to strengthening and broadening the base of industrial sectors of their respective economies, promoting the greater utilization of their industries and expansion of their trade;

Noting the suggestions on industrial joint ventures which have been advanced by the ASEAN Chambers of Commerce and Industry (ASEAN-CCI), and the confidence demonstrated by the ASEAN-CCI in the viability of ASEAN industrial joint ventures;

Affirming that in the economies of the ASEAN countries, the private sector shall continue to be encouraged to play the major role in most of the economic activities, including industry and trade;

Desiring to provide the guidelines and institutional framework within which the ASEAN Governmental machinery and the private sector, through the ASEAN-CCI, may collaborate to identify opportunities, formulate programmes and design projects for pursuing industrial joint ventures on the basis of mutual and equitable benefits for the member countries and increased industrial production for the region as a whole.

---

[*]Source: ASEAN Secretariat (1995). *Revised Basic Agreement on Asean Industrial Joint Ventures* (Jakarta: ASEAN Secretariat) (mimeo.) [Note added by the editor].

Do Hereby Agree to pursue ASEAN industrial Joint Ventures as stipulated by the following provisions:

Article I
General Provisions

1.   An Industrial Joint Venture (AIJV) product is any processed or manufactured product which is included in the final list of AIJV products referred to in Article II, paragraph 3 or in the AIJV Products List (APL) drawn up and approved by the ASEAN Committee on Industry, Minerals and Energy (COIME) in accordance with Article II Paragraph 9.

2.   An AIJV product may be an existing product or a new product;

(a)   An existing product is one which is being processed or manufactured in any of the participating countries at the time of its inclusion in the final list.

(b)   Any product not covered by the definition of an existing product is a new product.

3.   An AIJV is any entity which:

(a)   produces an AIJV product in any of the participating countries;

(b)   has equity participation from nationals of at least two participating countries;

(c)   satisfies the equity ownership provisions specified in paragraph 5 of this Article and the minimum 5 per cent equity contribution from nationals of each participating country.

4.   With respect to a particular AIJV product, a participating country is an ASEAN member country which has indicated its intention to participate by way of providing tariff preference as well as the other privileges provided for in Article III hereof. An ASEAN member country which has not indicated its intention to so participate is a non-participating country with respect to that particular AIJV product.

5.   A minimum ASEAN equity ownership of 51 per cent shall be required for any proposed AIJV. In respect of projects for which AIJV status has been applied for before 31 December 1990 and subsequently approved, the applicable minimum ASEAN equity ownership shall be 40 per cent. The minimum ASEAN equity shall not apply to an entity in any of the following cases:

(a)   where the participating countries in a proposed AIJV product agree to a higher equity participation by non-ASEAN investors;

(b)   where more than 50 per cent of the product produced by such entity will be exported to non-ASEAN markets;

(c)   where the product is already being produced by an entity in a participating country prior to its inclusion in the final list; or

(d)   where an entity has already been approved by a participating country to produce that product prior to the inclusion of the product in the final list.

6.   The investors in an AIJV shall be free to locate their projects in any of the participating countries.

7.   The approval by the ASEAN Economic Ministers (AEM) or COIME, as delegated by AEM, of the final list or the APL carries with it the pre-commitment to extend a minimum ninety (90) per cent margin of tariff preference to AIJV products by participating countries as provided for in Article III paragraphs 1 and 6.

8.   Non-participating countries in an AIJV product shall waive tariff preferences extended under Article III subject to the conditions therein stated.

9.   Any tariff preferences extended by non-participating countries among themselves for AIJV products shall be in accordance with the provisions of Chapter II, Article 8, paragraph 2 of the Agreement on ASEAN Preferential Trading Arrangements (PTA).

Article II
Institutional arrangements for approval of AIJV products

1.   The Committee on Industry, Minerals and Energy (COIME) shall invite nominations for AIJV products from the ASEAN-CCI and ASEAN member countries. All nominations for existing AIJV products shall be accompanied by details of existing production facilities, such as ownership, location and production capacities. These shall be compiled at a COIME meeting into a tentative list of AIJV products.

2.   ASEAN member countries shall examine such tentative list and indicate to COIME at a subsequent meeting, the products in which they would like to participate and declare any existing production facilities they have for such products. Those products for which at least two ASEAN member countries have indicated their intention to participate shall be included in the final list showing the participating member countries.

3.   The final list shall be submitted to the AEM or COIME as delegated by AEM for approval and thereafter be made available to the ASEAN-CCI and national Chambers of Commerce and Industry in ASEAN member countries.

4.   For new AIJV products, interested parties shall be given six months from the date the final list is approved to obtain approval from the appropriate government agencies to produce such products.

5.   At the end of the stipulated six-month period, all participating countries shall inform

COIME of those applications for the production of new AIJV products for which approval has been granted. Any product for which approval has not been granted within the stipulated six-month period shall be automatically deleted from the list.

6.   COIME shall inform all member countries of those new AIJV products for which approval has been granted.

7.   For existing AIJV products, interested parties shall seek their respective governments' confirmation that their entities qualify as AIJVs under this Agreement, after the inclusion of their AIJV products in the final list.

8.   For existing AIJV products, all participating countries shall inform COIME of entities that have qualified as AIJVs under this Agreement.

9.   In addition to the above institutional arrangements, the following are hereby provided:

  (a)   Each ASEAN member country shall draw up a list of AIJV products which it shall support and approve in principle for AIJV status. Such country lists of AIJV products could include products not locally produced in the respective countries and products with export potential.

  (b)   From these lists, COIME will draw up an AIJV Products List which shall consist of those products for which at least two member countries have expressed support, and which shall so indicate the participating member countries. To this list COIME shall add other potential AIJVs. This list shall be made available to the ASEAN-CCI and national Chambers of Commerce and Industry in ASEAN member countries and shall be updated every six months.

  (c)   Any AIJV application submitted to COIME on any of the products in the APL is automatically confirmed as an approved AIJV and the proponent company automatically acquires an AIJV status subject only to compliance with the AIJV requirement as provided under Article I, paragraph 3 hereof.

10.   COIME shall issue a certification in favour of the AIJV certifying its entitlement to the privileges under the Basic Agreement on ASEAN Industrial Joint Ventures (BAAIJV). Such certification shall also specify the date on which the tariff preference and all the privileges available to the AIJV shall take effect.

Article III
Privileges and obligations under the ASEAN
industrial joint venture programme

New AIJV Products

1.   Where an application for the production of an AIJV product has been approved by any

participating country, and due notification thereof has been given to COIME all participating countries shall extend a minimum margin of tariff preference of 90 per cent for that AIJV product within 90 days of its commercial production.

2.   The tariff preference described in Article III paragraph 1 shall apply, during the initial four-year period, only to AIJVs in participating countries. The four-year period shall commence from the actual date of commercial production of the AIJV product or upon expiry of 30 months from the date of approval of the inclusion of that product in the final list or in the APL, whichever is earlier.

3.   (a) Non-participating countries shall initially waive their rights under Chapter II, Article 8, paragraph 2 of the ASEAN Preferential Trading Arrangements (PTA) for the first four years. The maximum waiver period for non-participating countries shall be 8 years. However, at any time after the first four years, a non-participating country can enjoy the MOP granted by participating countries as soon as it extends the same MOP itself. If a non-participating country does not wish to grant such MOP, then the waiver period shall be extended beyond the first four years for as long as the non-participating country maintains this position subject to a maximum waiver period of 8 years. Non-participating countries need not extend a margin of preference to participating countries on AIJV products.

(b) Non-participating countries which so desire, and upon notification and concurrence of COIME, may become participating countries at any time and shall extend the same margin of tariff preference for that AIJV product.

(c) Participating countries shall waive their rights under Chapter II, Article 8 paragraph 2 of the ASEAN PTA for the first four years in respect of entities which are not AIJVs but produce the same products within their countries.

(d) After the waiver period for an AIJV product, any entity in any member country which produces that AIJV product, irrespective of whether it qualifies as an AIJV or not, shall enjoy the same margin of tariff preference in the participating countries for that AIJV product.

4.   In the event that there is only one approved project for a new AIJV product by the end of the stipulated six-month period, the participating countries shall grant to that AIJV exclusivity privileges. Exclusivity privileges shall continue for a period of three years commencing from the actual date of commercial production of the AIJV product or upon the expiry of 30 months from the date of inclusion of the product in the final list or APL, whichever is earlier. In the event that there is more than one approved project for a new AIJV product, exclusivity privileges shall not be granted.

5.   Exclusivity privileges in this Agreement shall mean that during the exclusivity period of three years, the participating countries cannot set up new production facilities for the same product, other than the approved project, unless 75 per cent of its production is for export to non-ASEAN countries. A production facility is deemed to have been set up when it is a commercial production.

Existing AIJV Products

6. The participating countries shall extend to an existing AIJV product the same tariff preference as provided for in Article III, paragraph 1 within 90 days from the date of inclusion of that product in the final list or APL.

7. The tariff preference described in Article III, paragraph 6 shall apply, during the initial four-year period, only to AIJVs in participating countries. The four-year period shall commence from the actual date of implementation of tariff preference.

8. (a) Non-participating countries shall initially waive their rights under Chapter II, Article 8, paragraph 2 of the ASEAN PTA for the first four years. The maximum waiver period for non-participating countries shall be eight years. However, at any time after the first four years, a non-participating country can enjoy the MOP granted by participating countries as soon as it extends the same MOP itself. If a non-participating country does not wish to grant such MOP, then the waiver period shall be extended beyond the first four years for as long as the non-participating country maintains this position subject to a maximum waiver period of eight years. Non-participating countries need not extend a margin of preference to participating countries on AIJV products.

(b) Non-participating countries, which so desire and upon notification and concurrence of COIME, may become participating countries at any time and shall extend the same margin of tariff preference for that AIJV product.

(c) Participating countries shall waive their rights under Chapter II, Article 8, paragraph 2 of the ASEAN PTA for the first four years in respect of entities which are not AIJVs but produce the same products within their countries.

(d) After the waiver period for an AIJV product, any entity in any member country which produces that AIJV product, irrespective of whether it qualifies as an AIJV or not, shall enjoy the same margin of tariff preference in the participating countries for that AIJV product.

9. Existing AIJV products shall not be granted exclusivity privileges.

Other Privileges and Obligations Applicable to Both New and Existing Procedures

10. If an AIJV product is a component for the manufacture of any product in the participating countries which have local-content programmes, that AIJV product shall be granted local-content accreditation in such participating countries.

11. Protection will be accorded by participating countries in cases of dumping, unfair trade practices or any other form of unreasonable pricing of products similar to the AIJV product from sources outside the participating countries, which affects the viability of the AIJV project, on the basis that AIJV projects would be considered as if located in all participating countries. The

mechanisms of implementation will be negotiated by the participating countries.

12.   Participating countries shall not lower the tariff rates applicable to products similar to the AIJV product below the level prevailing at the time of approval for a four-year period from start of commercial operations.

13. In respect of any AIJV product on which there is a prevailing zero duty, the binding of such a duty shall be regarded as fulfilling the requirement of extending the minimum 90 % margin of preference.

Article IV
Supervision and review of the ASEAN industrial joint venture programme

COIME shall supervise the implementation of this Agreement and shall draw up rules and regulations for such implementation. All decisions of COIME shall be taken by consensus.

Article V
Repealing provision

Upon its entry into force, this Agreement shall supersede the Basic Agreement on ASEAN Industrial Joint Ventures dated 7 November 1983 and the Supplementary Agreements to the Basic Agreement on ASEAN Industrial Joint Ventures dated 7th November 1983 and 16th June 1987, respectively.

Article VI
Miscellaneous and final provisions

1.   This Agreement shall enter into force on the thirtieth (30th) day after the deposit of the Sixth Instrument of Ratification.

2.   This Agreement may not be signed with reservation nor shall reservations be admitted at the time of Ratification.

3.   All articles of this Agreement may be modified through amendments to this Agreement agreed upon by consensus. All amendments shall become effective upon acceptance by all Member Countries.

4.   This Agreement shall be deposited with the Secretary-General of the ASEAN Secretariat who shall promptly furnish a certified copy thereof to each Member Country.

5.   Each Member Country shall deposit its Instrument of Ratification with the Secretary-General of the ASEAN Secretariat who shall promptly inform each Member Country of such deposit.

IN WITNESS WHEREOF, the undersigned, being duly authorized thereto by their respective Governments have signed this Revised Basic Agreement on ASEAN Industrial Joint Ventures.

DONE in Manila, Philippines this fifteenth day of December Nineteenth Hundred Eighty Seven in one original copy in the English Language.

For the Government of Brunei Darussalam:

For the Government of the Republic of Indonesia:

For the Government of Malaysia:

For the Government of the Republic of the Philippines:

For the Government of the Republic of Singapore:

For the Government of the Kingdom of Thailand:

PROTOCOL TO AMEND THE REVISED BASIC AGREEMENT ON ASEAN INDUSTRIAL JOINT VENTURES

WHEREAS, the Government of Brunei Darussalam, the Republic of Indonesia, Malaysia, the Republic of the Philippines, the Republic of Singapore and the Kingdom of Thailand hereinafter referred to as "the Member Countries" have on the fifteenth day of December 1987 signed the Revised Basic Agreement on ASEAN Industrial Joint Ventures hereinafter referred to by the acronym "Revised BAAIJV."

AND WHEREAS, under paragraph 3 of Article VI of the Revised BAAIJV amendments may be made thereto by consensus and become effective upon acceptance by all the Member Countries.

AND WHEREAS, the parties agree to make certain amendments to the Revised BAAIJV.

NOW BY THIS PROTOCOL, the parties have agreed as follows:

The date "31 December 1990" appearing in Article I (5) of the Revised BAAIJV shall be substituted by the date "31 December 1993."

This Protocol shall come into force on the date of signature of all the Member Countries.

IN WITNESS WHEREOF, the undersigned, being duly authorized thereto by their respective governments, have signed this Protocol.

Done at _____ in a single copy in the English Language this first day of January 1990.

For the Government of Negara Brunei Darussalam:
For the Government of the Republic of Indonesia:
For the Government of Malaysia:
For the Government of the Republic of the Philippines:
For the Government of the Republic of Singapore:
For the Government of the Kingdom of Thailand:

SECOND PROTOCOL TO AMEND THE REVISED BASIC AGREEMENT ON ASEAN INDUSTRIAL JOINT VENTURES

WHEREAS, the Government of Brunei Darussalam, the Republic of Indonesia, Malaysia, the Republic of the Philippines, the Republic of Singapore and the Kingdom of Thailand hereinafter referred to as "the Member Countries" have on the fifteenth day of December 1987 signed the Revised Basic Agreement on ASEAN Industrial Joint Ventures hereinafter referred to as "Revised BAAIJV".

WHEREAS, the Member Countries expressed the desire to improve the implementation of the AIJV program in the meeting of the ASEAN Economic Ministers held on 29-30 October 1990 in Bali, Indonesia,

WHEREAS, the Member Countries may effect improvement in the implementation of the AIJV program by amending the Revised BAAIJV,

WHEREAS, under Article VI (3) of the Revised BAAIJV, amendments may be made thereto by consensus and which shall become effective upon acceptance by all the Member Countries; and

WHEREAS, the Member Countries agree to amend the Revised BAAIJV,

WHEREFORE, BY THIS PROTOCOL, the member countries have agreed as follows:

(1)   That at least 90 per cent Margin of Preferences (MOP) be extended to AIJV products so as to achieve Common Effective Preferential Tariff (CEPT) of 0-5 per cent, the common rate of which shall be agreed upon by participating countries, and in respect of an AIJV product on which there is a prevailing zero duty or less than the agreed rate, the binding of such a duty shall be regarded as fulfilling the requirement of extending the said range of CEPT;

(2)   The exclusivity privilege granted to new AIJV products as defined in Article III(4) of the Revised BAAIJV, be discontinued;

(3)   In monitoring AIJV's, the minimum five percent (5%) equity requirement from nationals of the participating Member Countries shall be relaxed after a period of four years from the commencement of the commercial operation of the approved AIJV project, provided that the total minimum ASEAN equity is maintained and that there is equity from at least two participating Member Countries in the approved AIJV project;

(4)   Non-participating Member Countries shall continue to waive their rights under Article I (8) of the Revised BAAIJV until such time that they agree to extend the same tariff preference to the AIJV project;

In accordance with Article VI (3) of the Revised BAAIJV, this Protocol shall become effective upon signature of all Member Countries.

IN WITNESS WHEREOF, the undersigned, being duly authorized thereto by their respective government have signed this Protocol.

Done at _____ in the single copy in the English Language this _____ day of _____1992.

For the Government of Negara Brunei Darussalam
For the Government of the Republic of Indonesia
For the Government of Malaysia
For the Government of the Republic of the Philippines
For the Government of the Republic of Singapore
For the Government of the Kingdom of Thailand

THIRD PROTOCOL TO AMEND THE REVISED BASIC AGREEMENT ON ASEAN INDUSTRIAL JOINT VENTURES

WHEREAS, the Government of Brunei Darussalam, the Republic of Indonesia, Malaysia, the Republic of the Philippines, the Republic of Singapore and the Kingdom of Thailand, hereinafter referred to as the "Member Countries" have on the fifteenth day of December, Nineteen Hundred and Eighty Seven signed the Revised Basic Agreement on ASEAN Industrial Joint Ventures, hereinafter referred to by the acronym "Revised BAAIJV";

AND WHEREAS, under Paragraph 3 of Article VI of the Revised BAAIJV amendments may be made thereto by consensus and become effective upon acceptance by all Member Countries;

AND WHEREAS, the Member Countries agree to make certain amendments to the Revised BAAIJV;

NOW BY THIS PROTOCOL, the Member Countries have agree as follows:

1. The date "31 December 1990" appearing in Article I(5) of the Revised BAAIJV shall be substituted by the date "31 December 1996".

2. That the Rule of Origin as provided for under Article I(9) of the Revised BAAIJV which is in accordance with the ASEAN Preferential Trading Arrangements (PTA) shall be replaced with the Rule of Origin requirement under Article 2(4) of the CEPT Scheme.

This Protocol shall come into force on the date of signature by all the Member Countries.

IN WITNESS WHEREOF, the undersigned, being duly authorized thereto by their respective government, have signed this Protocol.

DONE at _____ in a single copy in the English Language, this Second day of March Nineteen Hundred and Ninety Five.

For the Government of Brunei Darussalam
For the Government of the Republic of Indonesia
For the Government of Malaysia
For the Government of the Republic of the Philippines
For the Government of the Republic of Singapore
For the Government of the Kingdom of Thailand

*   *   *

AN AGREEMENT AMONG THE GOVERNMENTS OF BRUNEI DARUSSALAM, THE REPUBLIC OF INDONESIA, MALAYSIA, THE REPUBLIC OF THE PHILIPPINES, THE REPUBLIC OF SINGAPORE, AND THE KINGDOM OF THAILAND FOR THE PROMOTION AND PROTECTION OF INVESTMENTS*

> The Agreement Among the Governments of Brunei Darussalam, the Republic of Indonesia, Malaysia, the Republic of the Philippines, the Republic of Singapore, and the Kingdom of Thailand for the Promotion and Protection of Investments was signed on 15 December 1987. At the time of publication, the Agreement was in the process of being revised.

The Governments of Brunei Darussalam, the Republic of Indonesia, Malaysia, the Republic of the Philippines, the Republic of Singapore, and the Kingdom of Thailand, hereinafter referred to as the Contracting Parties;

CONSIDERING that the Heads of Government of ASEAN agreed inter alia on industrial cooperation among the member states of ASEAN in the Declaration of ASEAN Concord signed at Denpansar, Bali on 24 February 1976;

FURTHER CONSIDERING that the Heads of Government of ASEAN in their Meeting in Kuala Lumpur on 4 to 5 August 1977, recognized inter alia that the acceleration of industrialization of the region requires the increased flow of technology and investments, and toward the attainment of this common objective, directed that measures be taken to stimulate the flow of technology, know-how and private investments among the member states and directed, in particular, the study of a regional mechanism, and the formulation of guidelines, which would facilitate such desired flow of technology, know how and private investments;

DESIRING that appropriate measures be taken to carry out the foregoing intents and to create favourable conditions for investments by nationals and companies of any ASEAN member state in the territory of the other ASEAN member states and to facilitate the desired flow of private investments therein to increase prosperity in their respective territories;

RECOGNIZING that an agreement on the promotion and protection of such investments will contribute to the furtherance of the above mentioned purposes;

Have agreed as follows:

---

*Source: ASEAN Secretariat (1987). *An Agreement Among the Governments of Brunei Darussalam, the Republic of Indonesia, Malaysia, the Republic of the Philippines, the Republic of Singapore, and the Kingdom of Thailand for the Promotion and Protection of Investments* (mimeo.) [Note added by the editor].

Article I
DEFINITION

For the purpose of this Agreement:

1)   The term "nationals" shall be as defined in the respective Constitutions and laws of each of the Contracting Parties.

2)   The term "company" of a Contracting Party shall mean a corporation, partnership or other business association, incorporated or constituted under the laws in force in the territory of any Contracting Party wherein the place of effective management is situated.

3)   The term "investment" shall mean every kind of asset and in particular shall include thorough not exclusively:

    a)   movable and immovable property and any other property rights such as mortgages, liens and pledges;

    b)   shares, stocks and debentures of companies or interests in the property of such companies;

    c)   claims to money or to any performance under contract having a financial value;

    d)   intellectual property rights and goodwill;

    e)   business concessions conferred by law or under contract, including concessions to search for, cultivate, extract, or exploit natural resources.

4)   The term "earnings" shall mean amounts yielded by an investment, particularly, though not exclusively, profits, interest, capital gains, dividends, royalties or fees.

5)   The term "freely-usable currency" shall mean the United States Dollar, Pound Sterling, Deutschemark, French Franc, Japanese Yen, or any other currency that is widely used to make payments for international transactions and is widely traded in the principal exchange markets.

6)   The term "host country" shall mean the Contracting Party wherein the investment is made.

Article II
APPLICABILITY OR SCOPE

1)   This Agreement shall apply only to investments brought into, derived from or directly connected with investments brought into the territory of any Contracting Party by nationals or companies of any other Contracting Party and which are specifically approved in writing and registered by the host country and upon such conditions as it deems fit for the purposes of this Agreement.

2)   This Agreement shall not affect the rights and obligations of the Contracting Parties with respect to investments which, under the provisions of paragraph 1 of this Article, do not fall within the scope of the Agreement.

3)   This Agreement shall also apply to investments made prior to its entry into force, provided such investments are specifically approved in writing and registered by the host country and upon such conditions as it deems fit for purposes of this Agreement subsequent to its entry into force.

Article III
GENERAL OBLIGATIONS

1)   Each Contracting Party shall, in a manner consistent with its national objectives, encourage and create favourable conditions in its territory for investments from the other Contracting Parties. All investments to which this Agreement relates shall, subject to this Agreement, be governed by the laws and regulations of the host country, including rules of registration and valuation of such investments.

2)   Investments of nationals or companies of one Contracting Party in the territory of other Contracting Parties shall at all times be accorded fair and equitable treatment and shall enjoy full protection and security in the territory of the host country.

3)   Each Contracting Party shall observe any obligation arising from a particular commitment it may have entered into with regard to a specific investment of nationals or companies of the other Contracting Parties.

Article IV
TREATMENT

1)   Each Contracting Party shall, within its territory, ensure full protection of the investments made in accordance with its legislation by investors of the other Contracting Parties and shall not impair by unjustified or discriminatory measures the management, maintenance, use, enjoyment, extension, disposition or liquidation of such investments.

2)   All investments made by investors of any Contracting Party shall enjoy fair and equitable treatment in the territory of any other Contracting Party. This treatment shall be no less favourable than that granted to investors of the most-favoured-nation.

3)   Investors of any Contracting Party who within the territory of another Contracting Party suffer damages in relation to their investment activities in connection with their investments, owing to the outbreak of hostilities or a state of national emergency, shall be accorded treatment no less favourable than that accorded to investors of any third country, as regards restitution, compensation or other valuable consideration. Payments made under this provision shall be effectively realizable and freely transferable, subject to Article VII.

4)   Any two or more of the Contracting Parties may negotiate to accord national treatment within the framework of this Agreement. Nothing herein shall entitle any other party to claim national treatment under the most-favoured-nation principle.

Article V
EXCEPTION

The provisions of this Agreement shall not apply to matters of taxation in the territory of the Contracting Parties. Such matters shall be governed by Avoidance of Double Taxation Treaties between Contracting Parties and the domestic laws of each Contracting Party.

Article VI
EXPROPRIATION AND COMPENSATION

1)   Investments of nationals or companies of any Contracting Party shall not be subject to expropriation or nationalisation or any measure equivalent thereto (in this article referred to as "expropriation"), except for public use, or public purposes, or in the public interest, and under due process of law, on a non-discriminatory basis and upon payment of adequate compensation. Such compensation shall amount to the market value of the investments affected, immediately before the measure of dispossession became public knowledge and it shall be freely transferable in freely-usable currencies from the host country. The compensation shall be settled and paid without unreasonable delay. The national or company affected shall have the right, under the law of the Contracting Party making the expropriation, to prompt review by a judicial body or some other independent authority of that Contracting Party in accordance with principles set out in this paragraph.

2)   Where a Contracting Party expropriates the assets of a company which is incorporated or constituted under the law in force in its territory, and in which nationals or companies of another Contracting Party own shares, it shall apply the provisions of paragraph 1 of this Article so as to ensure the compensation provided for in that paragraph to such nationals or companies to the extent of their interest in the assets expropriated.

Article VII
REPATRIATION OF CAPITAL AND EARNINGS

1)   Each Contracting Party shall, subject to its laws, rules and regulations, allow without unreasonable delay the free transfer in any freely-usable currency of:

    a)   the capital, net profits, dividends, royalties, technical assistance and technical fees, interests and other income, accruing from any investments of the nationals or companies of the other Contracting Parties;

    b)   the proceeds from the total or partial liquidation of any investments made by nationals or companies of the other Contracting Parties;

c)   funds in repayment of loans given by nationals or companies of one Contracting Party to the nationals or companies of another Contracting Party which both Contracting Parties have recognized as investments;

d)   the earnings of nationals of the other Contracting Parties who are employed and allowed to work in connection with an investment in its territory.

2)   The exchange rate applicable to such transfer shall be the rate of exchange prevailing at the time of remittance.

3)   The Contracting Parties undertake to accord to transfers referred to in paragraph (1) of this Article a treatment no less favourable than that accorded to transfers originating from investments made by nationals or companies of any third State.

Article VIII
SUBROGATION

If any of the Contracting Parties makes payment to any of its nationals or companies under a guarantee it has granted in respect of an investment made in the territory of another Contracting Party, the latter Contracting Party shall, without prejudice to the rights of the former Contracting Party under Articles IX and X, recognize the assignment of any right, title or claim of such national or company to the former Contracting Party and the subrogation of the former Contracting Party to any such right, title or claim. This, however, does not necessarily imply a recognition on the part of the latter Contracting Party of the merits of any case or the amount of any claim arising therefrom.

Article IX
DISPUTES BETWEEN THE CONTRACTING PARTIES

1)   Any dispute between and among the Contracting Parties concerning the interpretation or application of this Agreement shall, as far as possible, be settled amicably between the parties to the dispute. Such settlement shall be reported to the ASEAN Economic Ministers (AEM).

2)   If such a dispute cannot thus be settled it shall be submitted to the AEM for resolution.

Article X
ARBITRATION

1)   Any legal dispute arising directly out of an investment between any Contracting Party and a national or company of any of the other Contracting Parties shall, as far as possible, be settled amicably between the parties to the dispute.

2)   If such a dispute cannot thus be settled within six months of its being raised, then either party can elect to submit the dispute for conciliation or arbitration and such election shall be binding on the other party. The dispute may be brought before the International Centre for

Settlement of Investment Disputes (ICSID), the United Nations Commission on International Trade Law (UNCITRAL), the Regional Centre for Arbitration at Kuala Lumpur or any other regional centre for arbitration in ASEAN, whichever body the parties to the dispute mutually agree to appoint for the purposes of conducting the arbitration.

3) In the event that the parties cannot agree within a period of three months on a suitable body for arbitration, an arbitral tribunal consisting of three members shall be formed. The parties to the dispute shall appoint one member each, and these two members shall then select a national of a third Contracting Party to be the chairman of the tribunal, subject to the approval of the parties to the dispute. The appointment of the members and the chairman shall be made within two months and three months, respectively, from the date a decision to form such an arbitral tribunal is made.

4) If the arbitral tribunal is not formed in the periods specified in paragraph 3 above, then either party to the dispute may, in the absence of any other relevant arrangement, request the President of the International Court of Justice to make the required appointments.

5) The arbitral tribunal shall reach its decisions by a majority of votes and its decisions shall be binding. The Parties involved in the dispute shall bear the cost of their respective members to the arbitral tribunal and share equally the cost of the chairman and other relevant costs. In all other respects, the arbitral tribunal shall determine its own procedures.

Article XI
CONSULTATION

The Contracting Parties agree to consult each other at the request of any Party on any matter relating to investments covered by this Agreement, or otherwise affecting the implementation of this Agreement.

Article XII
AMENDMENTS

All articles of this Agreement may be modified through amendments in writing to this Agreement agreed upon by consensus. All amendments shall become effective upon acceptance by all Contracting Parties.

Article XIII
ENTRY INTO FORCE

1) This Agreement shall enter into force on the 30th day after the deposit of the sixth Instrument of Ratification and shall thereafter remain in force for a period of ten years.

2) This Agreement shall thereafter continue in force unless terminated by any Contracting Party giving not less than six months written notice through diplomatic channels. Provided however, that in respect of investments made while the Agreement was in force, its provisions

shall continue in effect with respect to such investments for a period of ten years after the date of termination, and without prejudice to the application thereafter of the rules of international law.

Article XIV
MISCELLANEOUS PROVISIONS

1)   This Agreement may not be signed with reservation nor shall reservations be admitted at the time of ratification

2)   This Agreement shall be deposited with the Secretary-General of the ASEAN Secretariat who shall promptly furnish a certified copy thereof to each Contracting Party.

3)   Each Contracting Party shall deposit its Instrument of Ratification with the Secretary-General of the ASEAN Secretariat who shall promptly inform each Contracting Party of such deposit.

IN WITNESS WHEREOF, the undersigned, duly authorized thereto by their respective Governments, have signed this Agreement.

Done in Manila, Philippines this Fifteenth day of December Nineteen Hundred Eighty Seven in one original copy in the English Language.

For the Government of Brunei Darussalam:

For the Government of the Republic of Indonesia:

For the Government of Malaysia:

For the Government of the Republic of the Philippines:

For the Government of the Republic of Singapore:

For the Government of the Kingdom of Thailand:

*   *   *

AMENDED PROPOSAL FOR A COUNCIL REGULATION (EEC)[1] ON THE STATUTE FOR A EUROPEAN COMPANY[*]

The first proposal by the Commission of the European Community for a Resolution on the Statute for a European Company was presented in 1970 and amended in 1975. A new proposal for a Council Regulation on the Statute for a European Company was prepared by the Commission in May 1989. It was subsequently amended in July 1991. The original 1989 version is reproduced in its entirety in the left hand column, while the amendments incorporated in 1991 are presented in the right column. As of October 1995, no action had been taken by the Council to adopt the Statute.

ORIGINAL PROPOSAL	AMENDED PROPOSAL
THE COUNCIL OF THE EUROPEAN COMMUNITIES,	Unchanged
Having regard to the Treaty establishing the European Economic Community, and in particular Article 100a thereof,	
Having regard to the proposal from the Commission,	
in cooperation with the European Parliament,	
Having regard to the opinion of the Economic and Social Committee,	
Whereas the completion of the internal market within the period set by Article 8a of the Treaty, and the improvement it must bring about in the economic and social situation throughout the Community, mean not only that barriers to trade must be removed, but also that the structures of production must be adapted to the Community dimension; for this purpose it is essential that companies whose business is not limited to satisfying purely local needs should be able to plan and carry out the reorganization of their business on a Community scale;	

---

[1]   OJ No. C 263 of 16.10.1989, p. 41.

[*]Source: Commission of the European Communities (1991). "Amended proposal for a Council Regulation (EEC) on the Statute for a European Company", *Official Journal of the European Communities*, C176, Volume 34, pp. 1-68 [Note added by the editor].

ORIGINAL PROPOSAL	AMENDED PROPOSAL

Whereas such reorganization presupposes that existing companies from different Member States have the option of combining their potential by means of mergers; whereas such operations can be carried out only with due regard to the competition rules of the Treaty;

Whereas restructuring and cooperation operations involving companies from different Member States give rise to legal and psychological difficulties and tax problems; whereas the approximation of Member States' company law by means of directives based on Articles 54 of the Treaty can overcome some of these difficulties; whereas such approximation does not, however, remove the need for companies governed by different legal systems to choose a form of company governed by a particular national law;

Whereas the legal framework in which business still has to be carried on in Europe, being still based entirely on national laws, thus no longer corresponds to the economic framework in which it must develop if the objectives set out in Article 8a of the Treaty are to be achieved; whereas this situation forms a considerable obstacle to the creation of groups consisting of companies from different Member States;

Whereas it is essential to ensure as far as possible that the economic unit and the legal unit of business in Europe coincide; whereas for this purpose provision should be made for creating, side by side with companies governed by a particular national law, companies formed and carrying on business under the law created by a Community regulation directly applicable in all Member States;

Whereas the provisions of such a regulation will permit the creation and management of companies with a European dimension, free from the obstacles arising from the disparity and the limited territorial application of national company laws;

Whereas such a regulation forms part of the national legal systems and contributes to their approximation, thus constituting a measure relating to the approximation of the laws of the Member States with a view to the establishment and functioning of the internal market;

Whereas the Statute for a European company (SE) is the measures to be adopted by the Council before

ORIGINAL PROPOSAL	AMENDED PROPOSAL

ORIGINAL PROPOSAL

1992 listed in the Commission's White Paper on completing the internal market, approved by the European Council of June 1985 in Milan; whereas the European Council of 1987 in Brussels expressed the wish to see such a Statute created swiftly;

Whereas since the presentation by the Commission in 1970 of a proposal for a Regulation on the Statute for a European company, amended in 1975, work on the approximation of national company law has made substantial progress, so that on those points where the functioning of a European company does not need uniform Community rules, reference may be made to the law governing public companies in the Member State where it has its registered office;

Whereas, without prejudice to any economic needs that may arise in the future, if the essential objective of the legal rules governing a European company is to be attained, it must be possible at least to create such a company as a means of enabling companies from different Member States to merge or to create a holding company, and of enabling companies and other legal bodies carrying on an economic activity, and governed by the laws of different Member States, to form a joint subsidiary;

Whereas the European company itself must take the form of a public company limited by shares, this being the form most suited, in terms of both financing and management, to the needs of a company carrying on business on a European scale; whereas in order to ensure that such companies are of reasonable size, a minimum capital should be set which will provide them with sufficient assets without making it difficult for small and medium-sized businesses to form a European company;

Whereas a European company must be efficiently managed and properly supervised; whereas it must be borne in mind that there are at present in the Community two different systems of administration of public companies; whereas, although a European company should be allowed to choose between the

AMENDED PROPOSAL

Whereas in the same context it should be possible for public limited companies with their registered office and central administration within the Community to transform into an SE without liquidation provided they have a subsidiary or a branch in a Member State other than that of their registered office;

Unchanged.

ORIGINAL PROPOSAL	AMENDED PROPOSAL

two systems, the respective responsibilities of those responsible for management and those responsible for supervision should be clearly defined;

Whereas, having regard to the approximation effected by the Fourth Council Directive 78/660/EEC[1] and the Seventh Council Directive 83/349/EEC[2], as last amended in both cases by the Act of Accession of Spain and Portugal, on annual accounts and consolidated accounts, the provisions of those Directives can be made applicable to European companies and such companies may choose between the options offered by those provisions;

Whereas under the rules and general principles of private international law, where one undertaking controls another governed by a different legal system its ensuing rights and obligations as regards the protection of minority shareholders and third parties are governed by the law governing the controlled undertaking, without prejudice to the obligations imposed on the controlling undertaking by its own law, for example the requirement to draw up consolidated accounts;

Whereas, without prejudice to the consequences of any later coordination of the law of the Member States, specific rules for the European company are not at present required in this field: whereas the rules and general principles of private international law should therefore be applied both in cases where the European company exercises control and in cases where it is the controlled company;

Whereas the rule thus applicable in the case where the European company is controlled by another undertaking should be specified, and for this purpose reference should be made to the law governing public companies in the State where the European company has its registered office;

Whereas for purposes of taxation the SE must be made subject to the legislation of the State in which it is resident; whereas provision should be made for deduction of losses incurred by the SE's permanent establishments abroad; whereas in order to avoid any discrimination against other firms carrying on cross-border business, similar provisions will be proposed by means of a directive for all other legal forms of business;

Whereas for purposes of taxation the SE must be made subject to the legislation of the State in which it is resident; whereas provision should be made for deduction of losses incurred by the SE's permanent establishments abroad;. whereas in order to avoid any discrimination against other firms carrying on cross-border business, similar provisions have been proposed[3] by means of a directive for all other legal forms of business;

Whereas each Member State must be required to apply in respect of infringements of the provisions of this Regulation the sanction applicable to public limited companies governed by its law;

Whereas the rules on the involvement of employees in the European company are contained in Directive ... based on Article 54 of the Treaty, and its provisions thus form an indissociable complement to this Regulation and must be applied concomitantly;

Whereas, on matters not covered by this Regulation, the provisions of the law of the Member States and of Community law are applicable, for example on:

-- social security and employment law,

-- taxation and competition law,

-- intellectual property law,

-- insolvency law;

Whereas the application of this Regulation must be deferred so as to enable each Member State to incorporate into its national law the provisions of the abovementioned Directive and to set up in advance the necessary machinery for the formation and operation of European companies having their registered office in its territory, so that the Regulation and the Directive may be applied concomitantly,

HAS ADOPTED THIS REGULATION:

TITLE I

GENERAL PROVISIONS

Article 1

[Form of the European Company (SE)]

1. Companies may be formed throughout the Community in the form of a European public limited company (Societas Europea, 'SE') on the conditions

Unchanged.

TITLE I

GENERAL PROVISIONS

Article 1

Unchanged.

ORIGINAL PROPOSAL	AMENDED PROPOSAL

ORIGINAL PROPOSAL

and in the manner set out in this Regulation.

2.   The capital of the SE shall be divided into shares. The liability of the shareholders for the debts and obligations of the company shall be limited to the amount subscribed by them.

3.   The SE shall be a commercial company whatever the object of its undertaking.

4.   The SE shall have legal personality.

AMENDED PROPOSAL

Deleted.

Unchanged.

Article 2

(Formation)

ORIGINAL PROPOSAL

1.   Public limited companies formed under the law of a Member State and having their registered office and central administration within the Community may form an SE by merging or by forming a holding company, provided at least two of them have their central administration in different Member States.

Article 2

AMENDED PROPOSAL

1.   Public limited companies having a share capital formed under the law of a Member State and having the registered office and central administration within the Community may form an SE by merging, provided at least, two of them have their central administration in different Member States.

la.   Public and private limited companies having a share capital formed under the law of a Member State and having their registered office and central administration within the Community may form an SE by forming a holding company, provided at least two of them:
--   have their central administration in different Member States, or

--   have a subsidiary company or a branch office in a Member State other than that of their central administration.

ORIGINAL PROPOSAL

2.   Companies or firms within the meaning of the second paragraph of Article 58 of the Treaty and other legal bodies governed by public or private law which have been formed in accordance with the law of a Member State and have their registered office and central administration in the Community may set up an SE by forming a joint subsidiary, provided that at least two of them have their central administration in different Member States.

AMENDED PROPOSAL

2.   Companies or firms within the meaning of the second paragraph of Article 58 of the Treaty and other legal bodies governed by public or private law which have been formed in accordance with the law of a Member State and have their registered or statutory office and central administration in the Community may set up an SE by forming a joint subsidiary company provided at least two of them:

--   have their central administration in different Member States, or

--   have a subsidiary company or a branch office in a Member State other than that of their central

ORIGINAL PROPOSAL	AMENDED PROPOSAL
	administration.
	3. A public limited company which has been formed in accordance with the law of a Member State and has its registered office and central administration in the Community may form an SE by transforming itself, if it has a subsidiary company or a branch in a Member State other than that of this central administration.

Article 3	*Article 3*
(Formation with participation of an SE)	
1. An SE together with one or more other SEs or together with one or more limited companies incorporated under the laws of a Member State and having their registered office and central administration within the Community may form an SE by merging or by forming a holding company.	1. An SE together with one or more other SEs or together with one or more public limited companies having a share capital formed under the law of a Member State and having their registered office and central administration in the Community may form an SE by merging.
	1a. An SE together with one or more other SEs or together with one or more companies within the meaning of Article 2a may form an SE by forming a holding company.
2. An SE together with one or more other SEs, or together with one or more companies or legal bodies within the meaning of Article 2 (2) may set up an SE by forming a joint subsidiary.	2. An SE together with one or more other SEs, or together with one or more companies or legal bodies within the meaning of Article 2 (2), may set up an SE by forming a joint subsidiary.
3. An SE may itself form one or more subsidiaries in the form of an SE. Such a subsidiary may not, however, itself establish a subsidiary in the form of an SE.	3. An SE may itself set up one or more subsidiaries in the form of an SE.

Article 4	*Article 4*
(Minimum capital)	
1. Subject to paragraphs 2 and 3, the capital of an SE shall amount to not less than ECU 100 000.	1. The subscribed capital of an SE shall amount to not less than ECU 100 000.
2. Where an SE carries on the business of a credit institution it shall be subject to the minimum capital requirements laid down by the laws of the Member State in which it has its registered office in accordance with Article ... of Council Directive on the coordination of laws, regulations and administrative	2. The laws of a Member State requiring a greater subscribed capital for companies exercising certain types of activity shall apply to SEs with their registered office in that Member State.

ORIGINAL PROPOSAL	AMENDED PROPOSAL

provisions relating to the taking up and pursuit of the business of credit institutions and amending Directive 77/780/EEC.[4]

3.   Where an SE carries on the business of an insurance undertaking it shall be subject to the minimum capital requirements laid down by the laws of the Member State in which it has its registered office.

Deleted.

Article 4a

For the purposes of this Regulation the words 'the statutes of the SE' cover both the instrument of incorporation and, where they are the object of a separate document, the statutes of the SE.

Article 5

(Registered office of SE)

The registered office of an SE shall be situated at the place specified in its statutes. Such place shall be within the Community. It shall be the same as the place where the SE has its central administration.

Article 5

Unchanged.

Article 5a

1.   The registered office of an SE may be transferred within the Community. Such transfer shall not result in the SE being wound up or in the creation of a new legal person.

2.   Where the transfer of the registered office results in a change of law applicable pursuant to Article 7 (1) (b) the transfer proposal shall be published in accordance with Article 9.

No decision to transfer may be taken for two months after publication of the proposal. Any such decision shall be taken under the conditions laid down for the amendment of the statutes.

The transfer of the registered office of the SE and resulting amendment to its statutes shall take effect from the date of registration of the SE, in accordance with Article 8, in the register of the new registered office. That registration may not be effected until evidence has been produced that the proposed transfer of the registered office was published.

3.   The termination of the SE's registration at the

ORIGINAL PROPOSAL	AMENDED PROPOSAL

register of its previous registered office may not be effected until evidence has been produced that the SE has been registered in the register of its new registered office.

4.   The new registration and the termination of the old registration shall both be published in the respective Member States in accordance with Article 9.

5.   The new registration of the registered office of the SE may be relied on as against third persons from publication. Until such publication has been effected third parties may continue to rely on the old registered office unless the SE proves that such third parties were aware of the new registered office.

Article 6

Article 6

(Controlled and controlling undertakings)

Unchanged.

1.   A 'controlled undertaking' means any undertaking in which a natural or legal person:

(a)   has a majority of the shareholders' or members' voting rights; or

(b)   has the right to appoint or remove a majority of the members of the administrative, management or supervisory board, and is at the same time a shareholder in, or member of, that undertaking; or

(c)   is a shareholder or member and alone controls, pursuant to an agreement entered into with other shareholders or members of the undertaking, a majority of the shareholders' or members' voting rights.

2.   For the purposes of paragraph 1, the controlling undertaking's rights as regards, voting, appointment and removal shall include the rights of any other controlled undertaking and those of any person or body acting in his or its own name but on behalf of the controlling undertaking or of any other controlled undertaking.

ORIGINAL PROPOSAL	AMENDED PROPOSAL
Article 7	*Article 7*
(Scope of the Regulation)	
1. Matters covered by this Regulation, but not expressly mentioned herein, shall be governed:	2. SEs shall be governed:
(a) by the general principles upon which this Regulation is based;	(a) -- by the provisions of this Regulation,
	-- where expressly authorized by this Regulation, by the provisions freely determined by the parties in the statutes of the SE;
(b) if those general principles do not provide a solution to the problem, by the law applying to public limited companies in the State in which the SE has its registered office.	(b) failing this:
	-- by the provisions of the law on public limited companies of the Member State in which the SE has its registered office,
	-- by the provisions freely determined by the parties in the statutes, in accordance with the same conditions as for public limited companies governed by the law of the Member State in which the SE has its registered office.
2. Where a State comprises several territorial units, each of which has its own rules of law applicable to the matters referred to in paragraph 1, each territorial unit shall be considered a State for the purposes of identifying the law applicable under paragraph 1(b).	Unchanged.
3. In matters which are not covered by this Regulation, Community law and the law of the Member States shall apply to the SE.	Deleted.
4. In each Member State, and subject to the express provisions of this Regulation, an SE shall have the same rights, powers and obligations as a public limited company incorporated under national law.	Unchanged.
Article 8	*Article 8*
(Registration)	
1. Every SE shall be registered in the State in which it has its registered office in a register	Unchanged.

ORIGINAL PROPOSAL	AMENDED PROPOSAL
designated by the law of that State in accordance with Article 3 of Directive 68/151/EEC.[5]	the Official Publications Office of the European Communities within one month of the disclosure referred to in Article 9.
2. Where an SE has a branch in a Member State other than that in which it has its registered office, the branch shall be registered in that other Member State under the procedures laid down in the laws of that Member State in accordance with Article ... of Council Directive ... on company law concerning disclosure requirements in respect of branches opened in a Member State by certain types of companies governed by the law of another State.[6]	2. For the purposes of its registration the name of the SE must be preceded or followed by the abbreviation 'SE'.
	3. An SE shall not be registered until a model for employee involvement has been chosen pursuant to Article 3 of Directive ... complementing the Statute for a European company with regard to the involvement of employees in the European company.

Article 9

(Publication of documents)

Publication of the documents and particulars concerning the SE which must be published under this Regulation shall be effected in the manner laid down in the laws of each Member State in accordance with Article 3 of Directive 68/151/EEC.

Article 9

Unchanged.

Article 10

(Notice in the Official Journal)

1.   Notice that an SE has been formed, stating the number, date and place of registration and the date and place of publication and the title of the publication shall be published for information purposes in the *Official Journal of the European Communities* after the publication referred to in Article 9. The same shall be done where a liquidation is terminated.

Article 10

1.   Notice that the SE has been registered or that the liquidation of the SE has been concluded shall be published for information purposes in the *Official Journal of the European Communities* after publication in accordance with Article 9. That notice shall state the number, date and place of registration of the SE, the date and place of publication and the title of publication, the registered office of the SE and a summary statement of its objects.

Where the registered office of the SE is transferred in accordance with Article 5a a notice shall be published containing the same information together with that relating to the new registration.

2.   The Member States shall ensure that the particulars referred to in paragraph 1 are forwarded to

Unchanged.

ORIGINAL PROPOSAL	AMENDED PROPOSAL

the Official Publications Office of the European Communities within one month of the disclosure referred to in Article 9.

Article 11

(Documents of SE)

Letters, order forms and similar documents shall state legibly:

(a) the name of the SE, preceded or followed by the initials 'SE' unless those initials already form part of the name;

(b) the place of the register in which the SE is registered in accordance with Article 8 (1), and the number of the SE's entry in that register;

(c) the address of the SE's registered office;

(d) the amount of capital issued and paid up;

(e) the SE's VAT number;

(f) the fact that the SE is in liquidation if that is so.

Any branch of the SE, when registered in accordance with Article 8 (2), must give the above particulars, together with those relating to its own registration, on the documents referred to in the first paragraph emanating from that branch.

Article 11

Letters and business correspondence for third parties shall state legibly:

(a) the name of the SE, preceded or followed by the abbreviation 'SE';

(b) Unchanged.

(d) Deleted.

Deleted.

(f) the fact that the SE is in liquidation or under the administration of the courts if that is so.

Deleted.

ORIGINAL PROPOSAL	AMENDED PROPOSAL
TITLE II	TITLE II
FORMATION	**FORMATION**

SECTION 1	
GENERAL	**GENERAL**

Article 11a

1.   Subject to the following provisions, the formation of an SE shall be governed by the law applicable to the formation of public limited companies in the Member State in which the SE establishes its registered office.

2.   The formation of an SE shall be published in accordance with Article 9.

Article 12

(Founder companies)

The founder companies of an SE for the purposes of this Title are the companies, firms and other legal bodies which may form an SE by the means of formation provided for in Articles 2 and 3.

Article 12

Unchanged.

Article 13

(Instrument of incorporation and statutes of the SE)

The founder companies shall draw up the instrument of incorporation and the statutes, if the statutes are a separate instrument, in the forms required for the formation of public limited companies by the law of the State in which the SE is to have its registered office.

Article 13

Deleted.

Article 14

(Experts; verification)

The provisions of national law concerning the examination of consideration other than cash, adopted

Article 14

Deleted.

ORIGINAL PROPOSAL	AMENDED PROPOSAL
in the State in which the SE is to have its registered office, pursuant to Article 10 of Directive 77/91/EEC,[7] shall apply.	

Article 15

(Supervision of formation)

The procedures for ensuring that the requirements of this Regulation and, where appropriate, of applicable national law, are complied with in regard to the formation of an SE and its statutes shall be those provided in respect of public limited companies under the law of the State in which the SE is to have its registered office. Member States shall take the measures necessary to ensure that such procedures are effective.	Deleted.

Article 15 *(Amended)*

Article 16

(Legal personality)

The SE shall have legal personality as from the date set by the law of the State in which it is to have its registered office.	The SE shall acquire legal personality on the date on which it is registered in the register referred to in Article 8.

Article 16 *(Amended)*

SECTION 2

FORMATION BY MERGER

SECTION 2

FORMATION BY MERGER

Article 17

(Definition)

1. In the formation of an SE by merger, the merging companies shall be wound up without going into liquidation and transfer to the SE all their assets and liabilities in exchange for the issue to their shareholders of shares in the SE and a cash payment, if any, not exceeding 10% of the nominal value of the shares so issued or, where there is no nominal value, of their accounting par value.	1. An SE may be formed by the merger of public limited companies in accordance with Article 2 (1). The merging companies shall be wound up without going into liquidation and transfer to the SE all their assets and liabilities in exchange for the issue to their shareholders of shares in the SE and a cash payment, if any, not exceeding 10% of the nominal value of the shares so issued.
2. A company may participate in the formation	Deleted.

ORIGINAL PROPOSAL	AMENDED PROPOSAL
of an SE by merger even if it is in liquidation, provided it has not yet begun to distribute its assets to the shareholders.	Member State in which any of the founder companies has its registered office so requires.
3. The rights of the employees of each of the merging companies shall be protected in accordance with the provisions of national law giving effect to Directive 77/187/EEC.[8]	3. The law of the Member State requiring that the draft terms of merger be drawn up and certified in due legal form shall determine the person or authority competent to do so. Where the laws of several Member States in which the founder companies have their registered offices require the draft terms of merger to be drawn up and certified in due legal form, this may be done by a person or authority competent under the law of one of those Member States.
Article 18	*Article 18*
(Draft terms of merger)	(Publication of the draft terms of merger)
1. The administrative or management board of the founder companies shall draw up draft terms of merger. The draft terms of merger shall include the following particulars:	1. The administrative or management boards of the founder companies shall draw up draft terms of merger. The draft terms of merger shall include at least the following particulars:
(a) the type, name and registered office of each of the founder companies and of the SE;	(a) the name and registered office of each of the founder companies together with those proposed for the SE;
(b) the share exchange ratio and, where appropriate, the amount of any cash payment;	Unchanged.
(c) the terms relating to the allotment of shares of the SE;	
(d) the date from which the holding of shares of the SE entities their holders to participate in profits and any special conditions affecting that entitlement;	2. For each of the founder companies, the publication of the draft terms of merger referred to in paragraph 1, effected in accordance with Article 3 (2) of Directive 68/151/EEC, shall contain at least the following particulars:
(e) the date from which transactions by the founder companies will be treated for accounting purposes as being those of the SE;	(a) the type, name and registered office of the founder companies;
(f) the rights conferred by the SE on the holders of shares to which special rights are attached and on the holders of securities other than shares, or the measures proposed concerning them;	(b) the register in which the documents and particulars referred to in Article 3 (2) of Directive 68/151/EEC are filed in respect of each founder company, and the number of the entry in that register;
(g) any special advantage granted to the experts appointed under Article 21 (1) or to members of the administrative, management, supervisory or controlling bodies of the founder companies.	(c) the conditions which determine, in accordance with Article 35, the date on which the merger and formation shall take effect.
2. The draft terms of merger shall be drawn up and certified in due legal form if the law of the	Unchanged.

315

ORIGINAL PROPOSAL	AMENDED PROPOSAL
Member State in which any of the founder companies has its registered office so requires.	of an SE by merger even if it is in liquidation, provided it has not yet begun to distribute its assets to the shareholders.

<table>
<tr><td>

3.   The law of the Member State requiring that the draft terms of merger be drawn up and certified in due legal form shall determine the person or authority competent to do so. Where the laws of several Member States in which the founder companies have their registered offices require the draft terms of merger to be drawn up and certified in due legal form, this may be done by any person or authority competent under the law of one of those Member States.

</td><td>

Deleted.

3.   The rights of the employees of each of the merging companies shall be protected in accordance with the provisions of national law giving effect to Directive 77/187/EEC.

</td></tr>
</table>

	Article 18
	(Draft terms of merger)

<table>
<tr><td>

Article 19

(Publication of the draft terms of merger)

</td><td>

1.   The administrative or management board of the founder companies shall draw up draft terms of merger. The draft terms of merger shall include the following particulars:

</td></tr>
<tr><td>

1.   For each of the founder companies, the draft terms of merger shall be published in the manner prescribed by the laws of each Member State in accordance with Article 3 of Directive 68/151/EEC at least one month before the date of the general meeting called to decide thereon.

</td><td>

(a)   the type, name and registered office of each of the founder companies and of the SE;

</td></tr>
<tr><td>

2.   For each of the founder companies, the publication of the draft terms of merger referred to in paragraph 1, effected in accordance with Article 3 (4) of Directive 68/151/EEC, shall contain at least the following particulars:

</td><td>

2.   For each of the founder companies, the publication, the draft terms of merger in accordance with paragraph 1 shall contain the following particulars:

</td></tr>
<tr><td>

(a)   the type, name and registered office of the founder companies;

</td><td>

Unchanged.

</td></tr>
<tr><td>

(b)   the register in which the documents and particulars referred to in Article 3 (2) of Directive 68/151/EEC are filed in respect of each founder company, and the number of the entry in that register;

</td><td>

</td></tr>
<tr><td>

(c)   the conditions which determine, in accordance with Article 25, the date on which the merger and formation shall take effect.

</td><td>

Deleted.

the proposed name and proposed registered office of SE.

</td></tr>
<tr><td>

3.   The publication shall also specify the arrangements made in accordance with the provisions of national law giving effect to Articles 13, 14 and 15

</td><td>

3.   The publication shall also specify the arrangement made in accordance with Article 23 of this Regulation for the exercise of the rights of the

</td></tr>
</table>

ORIGINAL PROPOSAL	AMENDED PROPOSAL
of Directive 78/855/EEC[9] and with Article 23 of this Regulation for the exercise of the rights of the creditors of the founder companies.	creditors of the founder companies.

Article 20	*Article 20*
(Board's report)	
The administrative or management board of each of the merging companies shall draw up a detailed written report explaining and justifying the draft terms of merger from the legal and economic point of view and, in particular, the share exchange ratio.	The administrative or management board of each of founder companies shall draw up a written report explaining and justifying the draft terms of merger from legal and economic point of view and, in particular, proposed share exchange of ratio.
The report shall also indicate any special valuation difficulties which have arisen.	Unchanged.

Article 21	*Article 21*
(Supervision of the conduct of the merger)	
1. One or more experts, acting on behalf of each founder company but independent of them, appointed or approved by a judicial or administrative authority in the Member State in which the company concerned has its registered office, shall examine the draft terms of merger and draw up a written report for the shareholders.	Unchanged.
2. In the report referred to in paragraph 1 the experts must state whether, in their opinion, the share exchange ratio is fair and reasonable. The statement must at least:	1a. Such experts may, depending on the law of each Member State, be natural persons, legal persons or companies or firms.
(a) indicate the method(s) used in arriving at the proposed share exchange ratio;	Unchanged.
(b) state whether the method(s) used are adequate in the circumstances, the values arrived at using each method and an opinion on the relative importance attributed to such methods in arriving at the value decided on.	
The report shall also indicate any special valuation	

ORIGINAL PROPOSAL	AMENDED PROPOSAL

difficulties which have arisen.

3.   Each expert shall be entitled to obtain from the merging companies all relevant information and documents and to carry out all necessary investigations.

4.   Where the laws of all the Member States in which the founder companies have their registered office make provision for one or more independent experts to be appointed for all the founder companies, such appointment may be made, at the joint request of those companies, by a judicial or administrative authority in any of the Member States. In such cases the law of the Member State of the appointing authority shall determine the content of the expert's report.

4.   One or more independent experts, appointed or approved for such purposes by a judicial or administrative authority in the Member State of one of the founder companies or of the proposed SE, may, where the founder companies agree, examine the draft terms of merger and draw up one written report for the shareholders of the founder companies.

Article 22

(Approval of the merger by general meetings)

1.   The draft terms of merger and the instrument of incorporation of the SE and, if the statutes are a separate instrument, its statutes shall be approved by the general meeting of each of the founder companies. The resolution of the general meeting approving the merger shall be subject to the provisions giving effect to Article 7 of Directive 78/855/EEC in the case of domestic mergers.

2.   For each of the founder companies, the provisions of national law adopted in accordance with Article 11 of Directive 78/855/EEC shall apply to the information to be provided to shareholders before the date of the general meeting called to approve the merger.

Article 22

Unchanged.

2.   For each of the merging companies, the provisions of national law in accordance with Article 11 of Directive 78/855/EEC shall apply to the documents to be available to shareholders for inspection before the date of the general meeting called to approve the merger.

Article 23

(Protection of creditors)

The following provisions of the national law to which the founder companies are subject shall apply:

(a)   the provisions relating to the protection of the interests of creditors and debenture holders of the companies in the case of domestic merger;

Article 23

The provisions of the law of the Member State to which the founder company is subject shall apply as in the case of a merger of public limited companies with regard to the protection of the interests of:

--   creditors of the founder companies,

ORIGINAL PROPOSAL	AMENDED PROPOSAL
(b) the provisions relating to the protection of the interests of holders of securities, other than shares, which carry special rights, provided that where the SE is being formed by the merger of public limited companies:	-- holders of debt securities of the founder companies,
	-- holders of securities, other than shares, which carry special rights in the founder companies.
-- the law of the State in which each of the companies has its registered office shall determine whether a meeting of the holders of such securities may approve a change in their rights,	
-- the law of the State in which the SE is to have its registered office shall determine whether the holders of such securities are entitled to require the SE to redeem their securities.	

Article 24	*Article 24*
(Supervision of the legality of mergers)	
1. Where the laws of a Member State governing one or more founder companies provide for judicial or administrative preventative supervision of the legality of mergers those laws shall apply to those companies.	1. Supervision of the legality of the merger shall be carried out, for the part of the procedure concerning each founder company, in accordance with the law of the Member State governing the founder company which applies to mergers of public limited companies.
2. Where the laws of a Member State governing one or more founder companies do not provide for judicial or administrative preventative supervision of the legality of mergers, or where such supervision does not extend to all the legal acts required for a merger, the national provisions giving effect to Article 16 of Directive 78/855/EEC shall apply to the company or companies concerned. Where those laws provide for a merger contract to be concluded following the decisions of the general meeting held concerning the merger, that contract shall be concluded by all the companies involved in the operation. Article 18 (3) shall apply.	2. The competent authority in question shall issue a certificate attesting that the prior formalities for a merger have been completed in respect of the founder company.
3. Where the laws of the State in which the SE is to have its registered office and the laws governing one or more of the founder companies provide for judicial or administrative preventative supervision of the legality of mergers, such supervision shall be carried out first in respect of the SE. The supervision may be carried out in respect of the founder	Deleted.

ORIGINAL PROPOSAL	AMENDED PROPOSAL
companies only when it can be shown that such supervision has been carried out in respect of the SE in accordance with Article 15.	
4. Where the laws governing one or more of the founder companies taking part in the merger provide for judicial or administrative preventative supervision of the legality of mergers whereas the laws governing one or more of the other founder companies taking part in the merger do not, such supervision shall be carried out on the basis of the documents drawn up and certified in due legal form referred to in Article 16 of Directive 78/855/EEC.	Deleted.

Article 24a

1.   The supervision of the legality of the merger shall be carried out, for the part of the procedure concerning the completion of the merger and the formation of the resulting SE, by the authority competent in the Member State of the proposed registered office of the SE to supervise the legality of mergers of public limited companies.

2.   To this end each founder company shall submit to the competent authority the certificate referred to in Article 24 (2).

3.   That authority shall supervise in particular that the founder companies have approved the draft terms of merger in the same terms, together with the statutes of the proposed SE and the model of involvement to apply to it pursuant to Article 3 of Directive ... complementing the Statute for a European Company with regard to the involvement of employees in the European Company.

4.   That authority shall also supervise that the formation of the SE has taken place under the conditions determined by the law of the registered office in accordance with Article 11a.

ORIGINAL PROPOSAL	AMENDED PROPOSAL
Article 25	*Article 25*
(Effective date)	
The date on which the merger and the simultaneous formation of the SE takes effect shall be determined by the law of the State in which the SE has its registered office.	The merger and the simultaneous formation of the SE shall take effect on the date on which the SE is registered in accordance with Article 8.

ORIGINAL PROPOSAL	AMENDED PROPOSAL
That date must be after all necessary supervision has been carried out, and, where appropriate, the certified documents referred to in Article 24 have been drawn up for each of the founder companies.	The SE shall not be registered until the formalities referred to in Articles 24 and 24a have been completed.

Article 26

(Publicity)

For each of the founder companies, the merger must be publicized in the manner prescribed by national law, in accordance with Article 3 of Directive 68/151/EEC.	For each of the founder companies, the completion of merger shall be published in accordance with the provisions of national law in accordance with Articles 3 of Directive 68/151/EEC.

Article 27

(Effects of the merger)

A merger shall have the following consequences *ipso jure* and simultaneously:	1. A merger shall have the following consequences *ipso jure* and simultaneously:
(a) the transfer, both as between the founder companies and the SE and as regards third parties, of all the assets and liabilities of the founder companies to the SE;	(a) the universal transfer of all the assets and liabilities of the founder companies to the SE, which can also be relied upon as against third parties;
(b) the shareholders of the founder companies become shareholders of the SE;	Unchanged.
(c) the founder companies cease to exist.	
	2. Where in the case of a merger of public limited companies the law of a Member State requires the completion of any special formalities before the transfer of certain assets, rights and obligations by the founder companies becomes effective against third parties those formalities shall apply and shall be completed either by the founder companies or by the SE following its registration.

Article 28

(Liability of board members)

The liability of members of the administrative or the management board of founder companies and of such companies' experts shall be governed by the provisions of national law giving effect to Articles 20 and 21 of Directive 78/855/EEC in the State in which	The liability of members of the management or administrative board of founder companies and that of the experts referred to in Article 21 shall be governed respectively by the provisions of national law in accordance with Articles 20 and 21 of Directive

321

|

the founder company concerned has its registered office or, where appropriate, by this Regulation.

However, in the case of an appointment under Article 21 (4), the liability of the expert or experts shall be governed by the law of the Member State of the judicial or administrative authority which appointed them.

78/855/EEC of the Member State governing the founder company in question.

Deleted.

Article 29

(Nullity)

The question of the nullity of a merger that has taken effect pursuant to Article 25 shall be governed by the national law of the company concerned, but a merger may be declared null and void only where there has been no judicial or administrative preventative supervision of its legality or where there is no certified documentation where such supervision or the drawing up of such documentation is laid down by the laws of the Member State governing the relevant company.

However, where the laws of the State in which the SE has its registered office do not provide for a merger to be declared null and void on such grounds, no such nullity may be declared.

Article 29

1.   A merger that has taken effect in accordance with Article 25 may only be declared null and void where there has been no supervision of its legality as stipulated in Articles 24 and 24a and where such grounds for nullity exist for the merger of public limited companies under the law of the Member State in which the SE has its registered office.

2.   Nullification proceedings may not be initiated more than six months after the date on which the merger becomes effective as against the person alleging nullity or if the situation has been rectified.

Article 30

(Merger: Shareholdings between fellow founder companies)

Articles 17 to 29 shall also apply where one of the founder companies holds all or part of the shares of another founder company. In such a case, shares in founder companies which come into the possession of the SE as part of the assets of a founder company shall be cancelled.

Article 30

Deleted.

Article 30a

1.   Where a founder company holds 90% or more of the shares in any other founder company, the merger may be effected in accordance with the simplified arrangements provided by the law of the Member State to which the former founder company

ORIGINAL PROPOSAL	AMENDED PROPOSAL

is subject in accordance with Chapter IV of Directive 78/855/EEC.

2. The merger may be effected in accordance with the simplified arrangements provided by the law of the Member State to which one of the founder companies is subject in accordance with Chapter IV of Directive 78/855/EEC where at least 90% of the shares of the founder companies are held by the same company or by undertakings controlled by it within the meaning of Article 6.

SECTION 3

FORMATION OF AN SE HOLDING COMPANY

Article 31

(Definition)

1. If an SE is formed as a holding company, all the shares of the founder companies shall be transferred to the SE in exchange for shares of the SE.

2. The founder companies shall continue to exist. Any provisions of the laws of the States in which the founder companies have their registered office, requiring that a company be wound up if all its shares come to be held by one person, shall not apply.

SECTION 3

FORMATION OF AN SE HOLDING COMPANY

Article 31

1. An SE may be formed as a holding company pursuance to Article 2 (la).

Companies participating in the formation of an SE holding company shall continue to exist notwithstanding any law of the Member States requiring companies to have more than one shareholder.

2. The management or administrative boards of the founder companies shall draw up draft terms for formation of an SE holding company in the same terms. The draft terms shall contain the matters referred to in Article 18 (1)(a), (b) and (c) together with the reasons for the formation. It shall fix the percentage of the shares of the founder companies to be exchanged upon which the formation of the SE is to be conditional. This percentage shall not be less than 51% of the shares having the right to vote.

3. The general meeting of each founder company shall approve the draft terms for the formation of the SE holding company together with the instrument of incorporation and, if they are contained in a separate document the statutes of the SE. The resolution of the general meeting shall be subject to the provisions of national law in accordance with Article 7 of Directive 78/855/EEC applying to

ORIGINAL PROPOSAL	AMENDED PROPOSAL

national mergers.

Article 31a

1.   The shareholders of the founder companies shall have a period of three months from the general meeting approving the formation of the SE holding to assign their shares to the proposed SE.

2.   The SE holding shall be formed if within the period set out in paragraph 1 sufficient shareholders have assigned their shares to the SE in accordance with the conditions determined by the draft terms of formation.

3.   The SE holding shall not be registered until it is shown both that the formalities set out in Article 31 have been completed and that the condition set out in paragraph 2 has been fulfilled.

Article 32

(Draft terms of formation)

1.   The administrative or management board of the founder companies shall draw up draft terms for the formation of an SE holding company containing the particulars referred to in Articles 18 (1) (a), (b) and (c) and 21 and shall prepare the report provided for in Article 20.

2.   The provisions of Article 21 shall apply to the supervision of the formation of the holding company in respect of each founder company.

3.   The provisions of Article 22 shall apply to the approval of the formation of the holding company by the general meeting of each of the founder companies.

4.   The provisions of Article 28 on the liability of board members shall apply.

5.   The formation of an SE holding company may be declared null and void only for failure to supervise the formation of the holding company in accordance with Article 29.

6.   For the purposes of applying the provisions of Section 2 on formation by merger, merger shall be

Article 32

Deleted.

ORIGINAL PROPOSAL	AMENDED PROPOSAL

read as formation of an SE holding company.

Article 33

(Matters affecting employees)

The administrative or management board of each of the founder companies shall discuss with the representatives of its employees the legal, economic and employment implications of the formation of an SE holding company for the employees and any measures proposed to deal with them.

Article 33

Deleted.

SECTION 4

FORMATION OF A JOINT SUBSIDIARY

SECTION 4

FORMATION OF A JOINT SUBSIDIARY

Article 34

(Draft terms of formation)

If a joint subsidiary is formed in the form of an SE, the administrative or the management board of each of the founder companies shall draw up draft terms for the formation of the subsidiary including the following particulars:

(a)   the type, name and registered office of the founder companies and of the proposed SE;

(b)   the size of the shareholdings of the founder companies in the SE;

(c)   the economic reasons for the formation.

Article 34

An SE may be formed as a joint subsidiary pursuant to Article 2 (2).

Article 35

(Approval of the formation)

1.   The draft terms of formation and the instrument of incorporation of the SE and its statutes, if the statutes are a separate instrument, its statutes shall be approved by each of the founder companies in

Article 35

Deleted.

ORIGINAL PROPOSAL	AMENDED PROPOSAL
accordance with the law which governs it.	
2. Founder companies incorporated under national law shall be subject to all the provisions governing their participation in the formation of a subsidiary in the form of a public limited company under national law.	Unchanged.
3. Where a founder company itself has the form of an SE, the following provisions shall apply:	Deleted.
(a) the instrument of incorporation and the statutes shall be authorized in accordance with Article 72 of this Regulation;	
(b) if the decision on the participation of the SE in the formation of the subsidiary falls within the matters to be decided by the general meeting, the instrument of incorporation and the statutes must also be approved by the general meeting.	

<table>
<tr><td style="text-align:center">

SECTION 5

FORMATION OF A SUBSIDIARY BY AN SE

Article 36

(Draft terms of formation)

</td><td style="text-align:center">

SECTION 5

FORMATION OF A SUBSIDIARY BY AN SE

Article 36

</td></tr>
<tr><td>

If an SE forms a subsidiary in the form of an SE, the administrative or management board shall draw up draft terms for the formation of the subsidiary. Those draft terms shall include the following particulars:

(a)   the name and registered office of the founder company and the instrument of incorporation of the subsidiary or its statutes, if the statutes are a separate instrument;

(b)   the economic reasons for the formation.

</td><td>

Deleted.

</td></tr>
<tr><td style="text-align:center">

Article 37

(Approval of the formation)

</td><td style="text-align:center">

Article 37

</td></tr>
<tr><td>

The instrument of incorporation of the subsidiary or its statutes, if the statutes are a separate instrument, shall be approved in accordance with Article 35 (3).

</td><td>

Deleted.

</td></tr>
</table>

ORIGINAL PROPOSAL	AMENDED PROPOSAL
	SECTION 6
	FORMATION OF AN SE BY CONVERSION OF AN EXISTING PUBLIC LIMITED COMPANY
	Article 37a
	An SE may be formed by the conversion of a public limited company in accordance with Article 2 (3).
	Without prejudice to Article 8, such conversion shall not give rise to the company being wound up nor to a new legal person being created.
	The management or administrative board of the company in question shall draw up draft terms for the conversion covering the legal and economic aspects of the conversion.
	The conversion together with the instrument of incorporation, if they are in a separate document, and the statutes of the SE shall be approved by the general meeting of the company in question in accordance with the provisions of the law of the Member State of its registered office in respect of an amendment of its instrument of incorporation or the statutes.
	The SE so formed shall comply with the conditions set out in this Regulation.
TITLE III	**TITLE III**
CAPITAL -- SHARES -- DEBENTURES	**CAPITAL -- SHARES -- DEBENTURES**
Article 38	*Article 38*
(Capital of the SE)	
1. The capital of the SE shall be denominated in ecus.	Unchanged.
2. The capital of the SE shall be divided into shares denominated in ecus. Shares issued for a consideration must be paid up at the time the company is registered in the Register referred to in Article 8 (1) to the extent of not less than 25 % of their nominal	2. The capital of the SE shall be divided into shares denominated in ecus.
	2a. Shares issued for cash must be paid up at the time the SE is registered to the extent of not less than

ORIGINAL PROPOSAL	AMENDED PROPOSAL
value. However, where shares are issued for a consideration other than cash at the time the company is registered, that consideration must be transferred to the company in full within five years of the date on which the company was incorporated or acquired legal personality.	25% of their nominal value. 2b. Where shares are issued for a consideration other than in cash at the time the SE is incorporated, that consideration must be transferred to the SE in full within at most five years of the registration of the SE. The provisions of the law of the Member State of the registered office of the SE concerning the valuation of consideration other than in cash in accordance with Article 10 of Directive 77/91/EEC shall apply.
3. The subscribed capital may be formed only of assets capable of economic assessment. However, an undertaking to perform work or to supply services may not form part of these assets.	Unchanged.
Article 39	*Article 39*
1. Shares may not be issued at a price lower than their nominal value.	Unchanged.
2. Professional intermediaries who undertake to place shares may be charged less than the total price of the shares for which they subscribe in the course of such a transaction.	2. However, professional intermediaries who undertake to place shares may be charged less than the total price of the shares for which they subscribe in the course of such a transaction, on condition that such reduction is provided for by the law of the Member State of the registered office of the SE and falls within the limits so authorized.
Article 40	*Article 40*
All shareholders in like circumstances shall be treated in a like manner.	Unchanged.
Article 41	*Article 41*
Subject to the provisions relating to the reduction of subscribed capital, the shareholders may not be released from the obligation to pay up their contributions.	Unchanged.
Article 42	*Article 42*
(Increase in capital)	
1. The capital of the SE may be increased by the subscription of new capital. An increase in capital	1. Without prejudice to Article 43, an increase in capital shall be decided by the general meeting in

ORIGINAL PROPOSAL	AMENDED PROPOSAL
shall require amendment of the statutes. Shares issued for a consideration in the course of an increase in subscribed capital must be paid up to not less than 25% of their nominal value. Where provision is made for an issue premium, it must be paid in full.	accordance with and pursuant to Article 97.

The decision and the increase in subscribed capital shall be published in accordance with Article 9.

2. Where all or part of the consideration for the increase in capital is in a form other than cash, a report on the valuation of the consideration shall be submitted to the general meeting. The report shall be prepared and signed by one or more experts independent of the SE and appointed or approved by the court within whose jurisdiction the registered office of the SE is situated.

2. The SE may effect the increase of capital in any manner permitted in respect of public limited companies governed by the Member State where the SE has its registered office.

3. The expert's report shall be published in accordance with Article 9.

3. Shares issued for cash in the course of an increase in subscribed capital must be paid up to the extent of not less than 25 % of their nominal value. Where provision is made for an issue premium, it must be paid in full.

4. Any increase in subscribed capital must be decided upon by the general meeting. Both this decision and the increase in the subscribed capital shall be published in accordance with Article 9.

4. Where shares are issued for a consideration other than in cash in the course of an increase in capital, the provisions of the law of the Member State of the registered office of the SE in accordance with Article 27 of Directive 77/91/EEC shall apply.

5. Where the capital is increased by the capitalization of available reserves, the new shares shall be distributed amongst the shareholders in proportion to their existing shareholdings.

Deleted.

However, in its decision on the increase in capital, the general meeting may decide that some or all of the new shares shall be distributed amongst the employees of the SE.

6. Where the increase in capital is not entirely subscribed, the capital shall be increased to the amount of the actual subscriptions only where the terms of the issue expressly so provide.

7. Where the general meeting decides on an increase in capital when the existing capital is not fully paid up, the management or administrative board shall inform subscribers of this before they have subscribed.

ORIGINAL PROPOSAL	AMENDED PROPOSAL
Article 43	*Article 43*
(Authorization of future increase in capital)	

shall require amend... Shares issued for a consideration in the course of an increase in subscribed capital must be paid up to not less than 25% of their nominal value. Where provision is made

1.   The statutes or instrument of incorporation or the general meeting, the decision of which must be published in accordance with Article 9, may authorize an increase in the subscribed capital, provided that such increase shall not exceed one-half of the capital already subscribed.

1.   The statutes or the general meeting, the decision of which must be published in accordance with Article 9, may authorize an increase in the subscribed capital not exceeding the limit fixed, if any, for public limited companies governed by the law of the Member State of the registered office of the SE.

A decision of the general meeting authorizing increases in capital shall be taken in accordance with Article 97.

2.   Where appropriate, the increase in the subscribed capital up to the maximum authorized under paragraph 1 shall be decided by the administrative or the management board. The power of such body in this respect shall be for a maximum period of five years, and may be renewed one or more times by the general meeting, each time for a period not exceeding five years.

Unchanged.

3.   The administrative or the management board must register decisions authorizing a future increase in capital.

The administrative or the management board must register, and publicize in accordance with Article 9, all issues of shares up to the maximum authorized capital limits and the consideration furnished for those shares. In addition, the board shall report each year in the notes on the accounts on the use it has made of the authorization.

3.   The decision referred to in paragraph 2 together with the completion of increases of capital shall be published in accordance with Article 9.

4.   Where the authorized capital has been fully subscribed or where the period referred to in paragraph 2 has elapsed with only part of the authorized capital having been subscribed, the administrative or the management board shall amend the statutes to indicate the new total capital.

Unchanged.

Where the authorization to increase capital has not been used, the administrative or the management board shall decide to delete the authorization clause referred to in paragraph 1. The board shall register such decisions.

Deleted.

5.   Where an increase in capital is not fully subscribed, the capital shall be increased by the

ORIGINAL PROPOSAL	AMENDED PROPOSAL
amount of the subscriptions received only if the conditions of the issue so provide.	

Article 44

(Subscription rights of shareholders)

1. Whenever capital is increased by consideration in cash, the shares must be offered on a pre-emptive basis to shareholders in proportion to the capital represented by their shares.

Article 44

Unchanged.

1a. Where the increase in capital is limited in one class of shares, the shareholders of other classes shall not have any right of pre-emption until the right has been exercised by the shareholders of the class to which the increase relates.

2. Any offer of subscription on a pre-emptive basis the period within which this right must be exercised shall be published in accordance with Article 9. However, it may be provided that such publication is not required where all the shares of the SE are registered. In such case, all the shareholders must be informed in writing. The right of pre-emption must be exercised within a period which shall not be less than 14 days from the date of publication of the offer or from the date of dispatch of the letters to the shareholders.

2. Any offer of subscription on a pre-emptive basis and the period within which this right must be exercised shall be published in accordance with Article 9. However, it may be provided that such publication is not required where all the shares of the SE are registered. In such case, all the shareholders must be informed in writing. The right of pre-emption must be exercised within a period which shall not be less than one month from the date of publication of the offer or from the date of dispatch of the letters to the shareholders.

3. The right of pre-emption may not be restricted or withdrawn by the statutes or the instrument of incorporation. This may, however, be done by decision of the general meeting. The administrative or the management board shall be required to present to such a meeting a written report indicating the reasons for restriction or withdrawal of the right of pre-emption and justifying the proposed issue price. The decision shall require at least a two-thirds majority of the votes attaching to the securities represented or to the subscribed capital respresented. The decision shall be published in accordance with Article 9.

3. The right of pre-emption may not be restricted or withdrawn by the statutes or the instrument of incorporation. This may, however, be done by decision of the general meeting. The administrative or the management board shall be required to present to such a meeting a written report indicating the reasons for restriction or withdrawal of the right of pre-emption and justifying the proposed issue price.

The decision shall be taken pursuant to Article 97 and shall be published in accordance with Article 9.

4. The statutes, the instrument of incorporation, or the general meeting, acting in accordance with the

Deleted.

|

rules for a quorum, a majority and publication set out in paragraph 3, may give the power to restrict or withdraw the right of pre-emption to the administrative or the management board which is empowered to decide on an increase in subscribed capital within the limits of the authorized capital. This power may not be granted for a longer period than the power for which provision is made in Article 43 (2).

5.   Shareholders may obtain copies of the reports referred to in paragraph 3 free of charge from the day on which notice of the general meeting is given. A statement to that effect shall be made in the notice convening the general meeting.

Unchanged.

6.   Paragraphs 1 to 5 shall apply to the issue of all securities which can be converted into shares or which carry the right to subscribe for shares, but not to the conversion of securities and the exercise of the right to subscribe.

7.   The right of preemption is not excluded where, in accordance with the decision to increase the subscribed capital, shares are issued to banks or other financial institutions with a view to their being offered to shareholders of the SE in accordance with paragraphs 1 and 2.

Article 45

(Reduction of capital)

1.   Any reduction in the subscribed capital, except under a court order, must be subject at least to a decision of the general meeting acting in accordance with the rules for a quorum and a majority laid down in Article 44 (3). Such decision shall be published in accordance with Article 9.

The notice convening the general meeting must specify at least the purpose of the reduction and the way in which it is to be carried out.

2.   Where there are several classes of shares, the decision of the general meeting concerning a reduction in the subscribed capital shall be subject to a separate vote, at least for each class of shareholders whose rights are affected by the transaction.

3.   A reduction of capital shall be effected by

Article 45

1.   Any reduction in the subscribed capital, except under a court order, must be subject at least to a decision of the general meeting in accordance with Article 97. The decision shall be published in accordance with Article 9.

The notice convening the general meeting shall specify the purpose of the reduction and the way in which it is to be carried out.

Deleted.

3.   The SE may effect a reduction of capital in

ORIGINAL PROPOSAL	AMENDED PROPOSAL
reducing the nominal value of the shares. However, the nominal subscribed capital may not be reduced to an amount less than the minimum capital. Only where losses have been incurred may the general meeting decide to reduce the capital below the minimum capital, and in that case it shall at the same time decide to increase the capital to an amount equal to or higher than the minimum capital.	any manner permitted in respect of public limited companies governed by the Member State where the SE has its registered office.
	The nominal value of the subscribed capital may not be reduced to an amount less than the minimum capital. Where losses have been incurred the general meeting may decide on such a reduction provided it proceeds with a corresponding increase of the capital to an amount at least equal to the minimum capital required.
4. Where the subscribed capital is reduced in order to adjust it to the diminished value of the company following losses, and, as a result of the reduction, assets exceed liabilities, the difference shall be entered in a reserve. This reserve may not be used for the distribution of dividends or for the granting of other benefits to shareholders.	4. Where the subscribed capital is reduced in the event of losses, and as a result of the reduction assets exceed liabilities, the difference shall be entered in a reserve. The amount of this reserve shall not exceed 10% of the reduced subscribed capital. This amount may not be used for payments or distributions to shareholders, nor to free shareholders from their obligation to pay the consideration for their shares.

Article 45a

Where there are several classes of shares the decisions by the general meeting concerning capital referred to in Articles 42 (1), 43 (1), 44 (3) and 45 shall be subject to a separate vote for each class of shareholders whose rights are affected by the transaction.

Article 46

(Protection of creditors in the event of a reduction of capital)

Article 46

1. In the event of a reduction in the subscribed capital, the creditors whose claims antedate the publication of the decision to make the reduction shall be entitled at least to have the right to obtain security for claims which have not fallen due by the date of that publication.

1. The law of the Member State of the registered office of the SE concerning the protection of creditors in respect of the reduction of capital of a public limited company shall apply to the SE.

The conditions for the exercise of this right shall be governed by the law of the State where the company has its registered office.

2. The reduction shall be void or no payment may be made for the benefit of the shareholders until

Deleted.

ORIGINAL PROPOSAL	AMENDED PROPOSAL

the creditors have obtained satisfaction or the court within whose jurisdiction the registered office of the SE is situated has decided that their applications should not be acceded to.

3.   Paragraphs 1 and 2 shall apply where the reduction in the subscribed capital is brought about by the total or partial waiving of the payment of the balance of the shareholders' contributions.

4.   They shall not apply to reductions in the subscribed capital for the purpose of adjusting it to the real value of the company following losses.

Deleted.

Article 47

The subscribed capital may not be reduced to an amount less than the minimum capital laid down in accordance with Article 4. However, such a reduction may be made if it is also provided that the decision to reduce the subscribed capital may take effect only when the subscribed capital is increased to an amount at least equal to the prescribed minimum.

Article 47

Deleted.

Article 48

(Own shares)

1.   The subscription for shares of the SE by the SE itself, third parties acting on its behalf, or undertakings controlled by it within the meaning of Article 6 or in which it holds a majority of the shares is prohibited.

2.   If shares of the SE have been subscribed for by a person acting in his own name, but on behalf of the SE, the subscriber shall be deemed to have subscribed for them for his own account.

3.   The founder companies of the SE by which or in name of which the statutes or the instrument of incorporation of the SE were signed or in the case of an increase in the subscribed capital, the members of the administrative or the management board, shall be liable to pay for shares subscribed in contravention of this Article.

Article 48

1.   The subscription for shares of the SE by the SE itself, by a person acting in his own name but on behalf of the SE, or by undertakings controlled by it within the meaning of Article 6 is prohibited.

Unchanged.

ORIGINAL PROPOSAL	AMENDED PROPOSAL
Article 49	*Article 49*

1.   The acquisition of shares of the SE by the SE itself, third parties acting on its behalf or undertakings controlled by it within the meaning of Article 6 or in which it holds a majority of the shares is prohibited.

1.   An SE may acquire its shares under the conditions laid down for public limited companies by the law of the Member State of the registered office of the SE in accordance with Articles 19 to 22 of Directive 77/ 91/EEC.

1a.   Paragraph 1 shall apply to acquisition of shares of the SE by an undertaking controlled by it within the meaning of Article 6.

2.   Paragraph 1 shall not apply to:

Deleted.

(a)   the acquisition by the SE or third parties acting on its behalf of shares of the SE for the purpose of distributing them to the employees of the SE;

(b)   shares acquired in carrying out a decision to reduce capital;

(c)   shares acquired as a result of a universal transfer of assets;

(d)   fully paid-up shares acquired free of charge or by banks and other financial institutions as purchasing commission;

(e)   shares acquired by virtue of a legal obligation or resulting from a court ruling for the protection of minority shareholders, in the event, particularly, of a merger, a change in the company's object or form, transfer abroad of the registered office, or the introduction of restrictions on the transfer of shares;

(f)   shares acquired from a shareholder in the event of failure to pay them up;

(g)   shares acquired in order to indemnity minority shareholders in controlled companies;

(h)   fully paid-up shares acquired under a sale enforced by a court order for the payment of a debt owed to the company by the owner of the shares.

3.   Shares acquired in the cases listed in paragraph 2 (c) to (h) above must, however, be

ORIGINAL PROPOSAL	AMENDED PROPOSAL

disposed of within not more than three years of their acquisition unless the nominal value of the shares acquired, including shares the SE may have acquired directly or indirectly, does not exceed 10 % of the subscribed capital.

4.   If the shares are not disposed of within the period laid down in paragraph 3 they must be cancelled.

5.   The SE may not accept its own shares as security or acquire any rights of usufruct or other beneficial rights over them.

Unchanged.

6.   An SE may not advance funds, nor make loans, nor provide security, with a view to the acquisition of its shares by a third party.

7.   Paragraph 6 shall not apply to transactions concluded by banks and other financial institutions in the normal course of business, nor to transactions effected with a view to the acquisition of shares by or for the employees of the SE or a controlled company. However, these transactions may not have the effect of reducing the net assets of the SE below the amount of its subscribed capital plus the reserves which by law or under the statutes may not be distributed.

7.   Paragraphs 5 and 6 shall not apply to transactions concluded by banks and other financial institutions in the normal course of business, nor to transactions effected with a view to their acquisition by or on behalf of employees of the SE or undertakings controlled by it pursuant to Article 6. However, these transactions may not have the effect of reducing the net assets of the SE below the amount of its subscribed capital together with any reserves which under the law of the registered office or the statutes of the SE cannot be distributed.

8.   Shares acquired in contravention of paragraph 1 shall be disposed of within six months of their acquisition.

Deleted.

9.   If an undertaking comes under the control of the SE or if a majority of its shares are acquired by such an SE, and it holds shares in the SE, the undertaking shall dispose of the shares in the SE within 18 months from the date of its coming under the control of the SE or from the date when the SE acquired a majority of its shares.

If an SE acquires its own shares by way of universal transfer of assets or if an undertaking which is controlled by the SE or the majority of those shares are held by the SE acquires shares of the SE in this manner, such shares shall be disposed of within the same period.

10.   Shares acquired by the SE pursuant to paragraph 2 (a) shall, if they have not been distributed

ORIGINAL PROPOSAL	AMENDED PROPOSAL
to the employees within 12 months of being acquired, be disposed of within the following six months.	quorum or majority required by this Regulation or the statutes of the company
11. No rights may be exercised in respect of the shares referred to in paragraphs 8, 9 and 10 until they have been disposed of or distributed to the employees.	The above shall be without prejudice to paragraph 5.
Article 50 (Disclosure of holdings) Holdings of the SE in other companies shall be disclosed in accordance with the provisions of national law giving effect to Directive 88/627/EEC.[10]	**Article 50** 3. Any other restriction or exclusion of voting rights, such as shares carrying multiple voting rights, is prohibited. Deleted.
Article 51 (Indivisibility of shares) The rights attached to a share shall be indivisible. Where a share is owned jointly by more than one person, the rights attached to it may be exercised only through a common representative.	**Article 51** Where there are several classes of shares, any decision of the general meeting which adversely affects the rights of a particular class of shareholders shall be subject to a separate vote, at least, for each class of shareholders whose rights are affected by the meetings and the required quorum and holders of the shares of the class concerned. Where more than one person has rights over a share, those rights may only be exercised by a common representative.
Article 52 (Rights conferred by shares) 1. Shares may carry different rights in respect of the distribution of the profits and assets of the company. Payment of fixed interest may be neither made nor promised to shareholders.	**Article 52** (Issue of bearer and registered shares) 1. Shares shall be in either bearer or registered form. The statutes may authorize shareholders to require conversion of bearer shares into registered shares or vice versa. Unchanged.
2. Non-voting shares shall be issued subject to the following conditions:	b. Bearer shares must be fully paid up. 2. Shares with a restriction or exclusion of voting rights may be issued subject to the following conditions:
(a) their total nominal value shall not exceed one half of the capital;	(a) their total nominal value shall not exceed one half of the subscribed capital;
(b) they must carry all the rights of a shareholder other than the right to vote, except that the right to subscribe for new shares may be limited by the statutes or by resolution of the general meeting to non-voting shares. In addition they must confer special advantages;	(b) they must carry all the rights of a shareholder other than voting rights, except that the right to subscribe for new shares may be limited by the statutes or by resolution of the general meeting to shares with a restriction or exclusion of voting rights;
(c) they shall not be included in computing a	(c) they must confer special advantages in

337

ORIGINAL PROPOSAL	AMENDED PROPOSAL
quorum or majority required by this Regulation or the statutes of the company.	respect of assets;
The above shall be without prejudice to paragraph 5.	(d) they shall not be included in computing a quorum or majority required by this Statute or the instrument of incorporation or the statutes of the company without prejudice to Article 98 (2).
3. Any other restriction or extension of voting rights, such as shares carrying multiple voting rights, is prohibited.	Unchanged.
4. Shares carrying the same rights shall form a class.	
5. Where there are several classes of shares, any decision of the general meeting which adversely affects the rights of a particular class of shareholders shall be subject to a separate vote at least for each class of shareholder whose rights are affected by the transaction. The provisions governing an amendment of the statutes shall apply as regards the convening of meetings and the required quorum and majority to the holders of the shares of the class concerned.	Deleted.

Article 53

(Issue of bearer and registered shares)

ORIGINAL PROPOSAL	AMENDED PROPOSAL
1. Shares shall be in either bearer or registered form. The statutes may entitle shareholders to request conversion of their bearer shares into registered shares or vice versa.	Unchanged.
	1a. Bearer shares must be fully paid up.
2. An SE which issues registered shares shall keep an alphabetical register of all shareholders, together with their addresses and the number and class of shares they hold. The register shall be open for public inspection on request at the registered office of the SE.	2. An SE which issues registered shares shall keep a register of all shareholders together with their names, addresses and the number and class of shares they hold. The register shall be kept in any manner ensuring appropriate guarantees of preservation and shall be open for inspection by any shareholder at the registered office of the SE.

Article 54

(Issue and transfer of shares)

ORIGINAL PROPOSAL	AMENDED PROPOSAL
The laws of the State in which the SE has its	The law in respect of public limited companies of the

ORIGINAL PROPOSAL	AMENDED PROPOSAL
registered office shall govern the issue, replacement and cancellation of share certificates, and the transfer of shares.	Member State in which the SE has its registered office shall govern the issue, replacement and cancellation of share certificates.

Article 55	*Article 55*
(Publication requirements for obtaining stock exchange listing and for offering securities to the public)	
1. The provisions of national law giving effect to Directive 80/390/EEC[11] shall apply to the listing particulars to be published for the admission of securities of the SE to official stock exchange listing.	Deleted.
2. The provisions of national law giving effect to Directive 89/298/EEC[12] shall apply to the prospectus to be published where securities are offered to the public.	

Article 56	*Article 56*
(Issue of debentures)	
The SE may issue debentures.	The SE may make use of any financial instrument available to a public limited company under the law of the Member State of the registered office of the SE.

Article 57	*Article 57*
(Body of debenture holders)	
The laws of the State in which the SE has its registered office shall apply to the body of debenture holders.	Deleted.

Article 58	*Article 58*
(Debentures convertible into shares)	
1. Articles 43 and 44 shall apply to the issue of debentures convertible into shares.	Deleted.
2. The laws of the State in which the SE has its registered office shall apply to the conditions and procedure for the exercise of conversion or subscription rights.	

ORIGINAL PROPOSAL	AMENDED PROPOSAL

3.   As long as convertible debentures are outstanding, the SE may not decide on any amendment of the statutes affecting the rights of the holders of such debentures except where less than 5 % of the convertible debentures is still outstanding and their holders have the opportunity to exercise their conversion or subscription rights in good time before the amendment takes effect or if the body of convertible debenture holders has approved the proposed amendment. In the latter case, a higher percentage may be stipulated in the loan conditions.

4.   Where conversion or subscription rights attached to convertible debentures have been fully exercised or have been exercised only in part but the period in which they may be exercised has expired, the management or the administrative board shall alter the statutes to show the new amount of capital. Where subscription or conversion rights are not exercised within the prescribed period, the management or the administrative board, shall delete from the statutes the clause concerning the issue of convertible debentures.

Such amendments to the statutes shall be published in accordance with Article 9.

Article 59

(Participation debentures)

1.   The general meeting may, by a resolution which meets the requirements for altering the statutes, decide to issue debentures carrying the right to share in profits. Such debentures shall be issued for cash and shall carry rights determined wholly or partly by reference to the profits of the SE.

2.   Article 58 (3) shall apply, *mutatis mutandis,* to participating debentures.

Article 60

(Other securities)

The SE shall not issue to persons who are not shareholders of the SE other securities carrying a right to participate in the profits or assets of the SE.

Article 59

Deleted.

Article 60

Deleted.

ORIGINAL PROPOSAL	AMENDED PROPOSAL
TITLE IV	TITLE IV
GOVERNING BODIES	**GOVERNING BODIES**
Article 61	*Article 61*
The statutes of the SE shall provide for the company to have as its governing bodies the general meeting of shareholders and either a management board and a supervisory board (two-tier system) or an administrative board (one-tier system).	Under the conditions laid down by this Regulation,
	-- the statutes of the SE shall organize the structure of the SE either according to a two-tier system (management board and supervisory hoard) or according to the one-tier system (administrative board). A Member State may, however, require that SEs having their registered office on its territory adopt either the two-tier or the one-tier system;
	-- the statutes of the SE shall in addition provide for a general meeting of shareholders.
SECTION 1	SECTION 1
TWO-TIER SYSTEM	**TWO-TIER SYSTEM**
Subsection 1	Subsection 1
Management board	**Management board**
Article 62	*Article 62*
(Functions of the management board -- Appointment of members)	
1. The SE shall be managed and represented by a management board under the supervision of a supervisory board.	1. The management board shall ensure the management of the SE. The member or members of the management board shall have the power to represent the company in dealings with third parties and in legal proceedings pursuant to the law of the Member State of the registered office of the SE in accordance with Directive 68/151/EEC.
2. The members of the management board shall be appointed by the supervisory board, which may remove them at any time.	2. The member or members of the management board shall be appointed and removed by the supervisory board.
3. No person may at the same time be a member of the management board and the supervisory board of	3. No person may at the same time be a member of the management board and the supervisory board of

ORIGINAL PROPOSAL	AMENDED PROPOSAL
the same SE.	the same SE. However, the supervisory board may nominate one of its members to exercise the function of a member of the management board in the event of a vacancy. During such a period the function of the person concerned as a member of the supervisory board shall be suspended.
4. The number of members of the management board shall be laid down in the statutes of the SE.	Unchanged.
5. The rules of procedure of the management board shall be adopted by the supervisory board, after obtaining the views of the management board.	Deleted.

Subsection 2

Supervisory board

Article 63

(Functions of the supervisory board --
Appointment of members)

1. The supervisory board may not participate in the management of the company nor represent it in dealings with third parties. However, it shall represent the company in its relations with members of the management board.

2. Subject to the measures adopted to give effect to Article 4 for the Council Directive ... (completing the Statute in respect of the involvement of employees in SEs) members of the supervisory board shall be appointed by the general meeting.

Subsection 2

Supervisory board

Article 63

1. The supervisory board shall supervise the duties performed by the management board. It may not itself exercise the power to manage the SE. The supervisory board may not represent it in dealings with third parties shall represent the company in its relations with the members of the management board, or one of them in respect of litigation or the conclusion of contracts.

2. The members of the supervisory board shall be appointed and removed by the general meeting. However, the members of the first supervisory board may be appointed by the statutes. This provision shall apply without prejudice to Article 69 (4) and to the measures taken to implement Article 4 of the Council Directive completing the Statute in respect of the involvement of employees in the European company.

3. The number of members of the supervisory board shall be laid down in the statutes. A Member State may, however, stipulate the number of members of the supervisory board for SEs registered in its territory.

ORIGINAL PROPOSAL	AMENDED PROPOSAL

Article 64

Article 64

(Right to information)

1.   At least once every three months, the management board shall report to the supervisory board on the management and progress of the company's affairs, including undertakings controlled by it, and on the company's situation and prospects.

1.   The management board shall report to the supervisory board at least once every three months on the progress and foreseeable prospects of the company's affairs, taking particular account of any information relating to undertakings controlled by the SE that may significantly affect the progress of the SE.

2.   The management board shall inform the chairman of the supervisory board without delay of all matters of importance, including any event occurring in the company or in undertakings controlled by it which may have an appreciable effect on the SE.

2.   The management board shall communicate to the supervisory board without delay any information which may have an appreciable effect on the SE.

3.   The supervisory board may at any time require the management board to provide information or a special report on any matter concerning the company or undertakings controlled by it.

3.   The supervisory board may at any time require the management board to provide information or a special report on any matter concerning the SE.

4.   The supervisory board shall be entitled to undertake all investigations necessary for the performance of its duties. It may appoint one or more of its members to pursue such investigations on its behalf and may call in the help of experts.

4.   The supervisory board may undertake all investigations necessary for the performance of its duties. It may appoint one or more of its members to carry out this task and may call in the help of experts.

5.   Any member of the supervisory board may, through the chairman of that board, require the management board to provide the supervisory board with any information necessary for the performance of its duties.

Deleted.

6.   Each member of the supervisory board shall be entitled to examine all reports, documents and information and the results of enquiries and inspections obtained under the preceding paragraphs.

6.   Each member of the supervisory board shall be entitled to examine all information communicated by the management board to the supervisory board.

Article 65

Article 65

(Rules of procedure, calling of meetings)

1.   The supervisory board shall adopt its rules of procedure and shall elect a chairman and one or more vice-chairmen from among its members.

1.   The supervisory board shall elect a chairman from among its members. Where Article 4 of Directive ... complementing the Statute for a European Company with regard to the involvement of employees in the European Company applies to the SE, the chairman must be elected from among the members appointed

ORIGINAL PROPOSAL	AMENDED PROPOSAL
	by the general meeting.
2. The chairman may call a meeting of the supervisory board on his own initiative and shall do so at the request of a member of the supervisory board or of a member of the management board.	2. The chairman may call a meeting of the supervisory board under the conditions laid down in the statutes, either on his own initiative or at the request of at least one-third of the members of the supervisory board or at the request of the management board. The request must indicate the reasons for calling the meeting. If no action has been taken in respect of such a request within 15 days the meeting of the supervisory board may be called by those who made the request.

SECTION 2

THE ONE-TIER SYSTEM

Article 66

(The administrative board --
Appointment of members)

1.   The SE shall be managed and represented by an administrative board. The board shall be composed of at least three members. It shall adopt its rules of procedure and shall elect a chairman and one or more vice-chairmen from among its members.

SECTION 2

THE ONE-TIER SYSTEM

Article 66

1.   The administrative board shall ensure the management of the SE. The member or members of the administrative board shall have the power to represent the company in dealings with third parties and in legal proceedings pursuant to the law of the Member State of the registered office of the SE in accordance with Directive 68/151/EEC.

1a.   The administrative board shall have at least three members within limits fixed by the statutes. However the administrative board may have two, or only one, members where the involvement of employees in the SE is not organized pursuant to Article 4 of Directive ... complementing the Statute for a European Company with regard to the involvement of employees in the European Company.

2.   The management of the SE shall be delegated by the administrative board to one or more of its members. The executive members shall be fewer in number than the other members of the board. The delegation of management responsibilities to an executive member of the administrative board may be revoked by the board at any time.

2.   The administrative board may delegate to one or more of its members only the power of management. It may also delegate certain management responsibilities to one or more natural persons not members of the board. Such delegation of management responsibilities may be revoked at any time. The statutes or in default the general meeting shall set the conditions within which such delegations shall operate.

ORIGINAL PROPOSAL	AMENDED PROPOSAL
3. Subject to the measures adopted to give effect to Article 4 of Directive ... (completing the Statute in respect of the involvement of employees in SEs), members of the administrative board shall be appointed by the general meeting.	3. The member or members of the administrative board shall be appointed and removed by the general meeting subject to the application to the SE of Article 4 of Directive... completing the Statute in respect of the involvement of the employees in SEs.

Article 67

(Right to information)

1. The administrative board shall meet at least once every three months to discuss the management and progress of the company's affairs, including undertakings controlled by it and the company's situation and prospects.

Article 67

1. The management board shall meet at least once every three months as fixed by the statutes to discuss the progress and foreseeable prospects of the company's affairs, taking particular account of any information relating to undertakings controlled by the SE that may significantly affect the progress of the SE.

1a. The administrative board shall meet to deliberate on the operations referred to in Article 72.

2. Each member shall inform the chairman of the administrative board without delay of all matters of importance, including any event occurring in the company or in undertakings controlled by it which may have an appreciable effect on the SE.

2. Deleted.

3. Any member of the administrative board may request the chairman to call a meeting of that board to discuss particular aspects of the company. If the request has not been complied with within 15 days, a meeting of the administrative board may be called by one-third of its members.

4. Each member of the administrative board shall be entitled to examine all reports, documents and information supplied to the board concerning the matters referred to in paragraphs 1 and 3.

Unchanged.

Article 67a

1. The administrative board shall elect a chairman from among its members. Where Article 4 of Directive ... complementing the Statute for a European Company with regard to the involvement of employees in the European Company applies to the SE, the chairman must be elected from among the members appointed by the general meeting.

2.   The chairman may call a meeting of the administrative board under the conditions laid down in the statutes, either on his own initiative or at the request of at least one-third of the members. The request must indicate the reasons for calling the meeting. If no action has been taken in respect of such a request within 15 days, the meeting of the administrative board may be called by those who made the request.

SECTION 3

RULES COMMON TO THE ONE-TIER AND TWO-TIER BOARD SYSTEMS

Article 68

(Term of office)

1.   Members of the governing bodies shall be appointed for a period laid down in the statutes not exceeding six years.

However, the first members of the supervisory board or of the administrative board, who are to be appointed by the shareholders, shall be appointed by the instrument of incorporation of the SE for a period not exceeding three years.

2.   Board members may be reappointed.

SECTION 3

RULES COMMON TO THE ONE-TIER AND TWO-TIER BOARD SYSTEMS

Article 68

Unchanged.

Deleted.

2.   Board members may be reappointed once or more for a period determined in accordance with paragraph 1.

Article 69

(Conditions of membership)

1.   Where the statutes of the SE allow a legal person or company to be a member of a board, that legal person or company shall designate a natural person to represent it in the performance of its duties on the board. The representative shall be subject to the same conditions and obligations as if he were personally a member. Publication under Article 9 shall refer both to the representative and to the legal person or company represented. The legal person or company shall be jointly and severally liable without limitation for obligations arising from the acts of its

Article 69

1.   The statutes of the SE may permit a company or other legal person to be a member of a board, provided that the law of the registered office of the SE in respect of public limited companies does not provide otherwise.

That company or other legal person shall designate a natural person to exercise its functions on the board in question. That representative shall be subject to the same conditions and obligations as if he were personally a member of that board.

ORIGINAL PROPOSAL	AMENDED PROPOSAL
representative.	authority to represent the SE alone or together with one or more other members of the board or together with the persons to be appointed by it shall apply only where the statutes expressly so provide.
2. No person may be a board member, who:	2. No person may be a board member nor a representative of a member within the meaning of paragraph 1, nor be the recipient of powers of management or representation, who:
-- under the law applicable to him, or	-- under the law applicable to him, or
-- as a result of a judicial or administrative decision delivered or recognized in a Member State,	-- under the law of the registered office of the SE, or
is disqualified from serving on an administrative, supervisory or management board.	-- as a result of a judicial or administrative decision delivered or recognized in a Member State,
	is disqualified from serving on the administrative, supervisory or management board of a company.
3. The statutes may lay down special conditions of eligibility for members representing the shareholders.	Unchanged.
4. Notwithstanding, the rule laid down in Article 94 (2), the statutes of the SE may provide voting procedures for the appointment of members of the administrative or the supervisory board by the general meeting such that one or more members and their alternates may be appointed by a minority of the shareholders.	This Regulation shall not affect national law permitting minority of shareholders to appoint some of the members of a board.

Article 70

(Vacancies)

Article 70

The statutes of the SE may provide for the appointment of alternate members to vacancies. Such appointments may be terminated at any time by the appointment of a full member.

Deleted.

Article 71

(Power of representation)

Article 71

1. Where the management board is composed of more than one member, or where the management of the company is delegated to more than one member of the administrative board, those members have authority to represent the company collectively only in dealings with third parties. However, the statutes of the SE may provide that a member of the relevant board shall have

Deleted.

ORIGINAL PROPOSAL	AMENDED PROPOSAL

authority to represent the SE alone or together with one or more other members of the board or together with a person who has been given general authority to represent the company under paragraph 2.

2.   The administrative board or, as the case may be, the management board with the approval of the supervisory board may confer a general authority to represent the company on one or more persons. Such authority may be revoked at any time, in the same way, by the board which granted it.

3.   Acts performed by those having authority to represent the company under paragraphs 1 and 2 shall bind the company *vis-à-vis* third parties, even where the acts in question are not in accordance with the objects of the company, providing they do not exceed the powers conferred by this Regulation.

Article 72

(Operations requiring prior authorization)

1.   The implementation of decisions on:

(a)   the closure or transfer of establishments or of substantial parts thereof;

(b)   substantial reduction, extension or alteration of the activities of the SE;

(c)   substantial organizational changes within the SE;

(d)   the establishment of cooperation with other undertakings which is both long-term and of importance to the activities of the SE, or the termination thereof;

Article 72

1.   The following operations shall require the authorization of the supervisory board or the deliberation of the administrative board:

(a)   any investment project requiring an amount more than the percentage of subscribed capital fixed in accordance with subparagraph (e);

(b)   the setting up, acquisition, disposal or closing down of undertakings, businesses or parts of businesses where the purchase price or disposal proceeds account for more than the percentage of subscribed capital fixed in accordance with subparagraph (e);

(c)   the raising or granting of loans, the issue of debt securities and the assumption of liabilities of a third party or suretyship for a third party where the total money value in each case is more than the percentage of subscribed capital fixed in accordance with subparagraph (e);

(d)   the conclusion of supply and performance contracts where the total turnover provided for therein is more than the percentage of turnover for the previous financial year fixed

ORIGINAL PROPOSAL	AMENDED PROPOSAL
	in accordance with subparagraph (e);

(e)   the setting up of a subsidiary or of a holding company,

(e)   the percentage referred to in subparagraphs (a) to (d) shall be determined by the statutes of the SE. It shall not be less than 5%, nor more than 25%.

may be effected by the management board only following prior authorization of the supervisory board or by the administration board as a whole.

Implementation may not be delegated to the executive members of the administrative board.

Acts done in breach of the above provisions may not be relied upon against third parties, unless the SE can prove that the third party was aware of the breach.

2.   The statutes of the SE may provide that paragraph 1 shall also apply to other types of decisions.

Unchanged.

3.   A Member State may determine the categories of operation referred to in paragraph 1 for SEs registered in its territory under the same conditions as those applying to public limited companies governed by the law of that state.

4.   A Member State may provide that the supervisory or administrative board of SEs registered in its territory may itself make certain categories of operation subject to authorization or discussion under the same conditions as those applying to public limited companies governed by the law of that state.

Article 73

(Conflicts of interest)

1.   Any transaction in which a board member has an interest conflicting with the interests of the SE shall require the prior authorization of the supervisory board or the administrative board.

2.   The statutes of the SE may provide that paragraph 1 shall not apply to routine transactions concluded on normal terms and conditions.

3.   A member to whom paragraph 1 applies shall be entitled to be heard before a decision on the authorization is made but may not take part in the

Article 73

Deleted.

349

ORIGINAL PROPOSAL	AMENDED PROPOSAL

deliberations of the relevant board when it makes its decision.

4.   Authorizations given under paragraph 1 during any financial year shall be communicated to the shareholders not later than at the first general meeting following the end of the financial year in question.

5.   Failure to obtain authorization may not be relied upon against third parties, unless the SE can prove that the third party was aware of the need for, and lack of, such authorization.

Article 74

(Rights and obligations)

1.   Each member of a board of the SE shall have the same rights and obligations, without prejudice to:

(a)   any internal allocation of responsibilities between the members of the board, and the provisions of the board's rules of procedure governing the taking of decisions in the event of a tied vote;

(b)   the provisions concerning the delegation of management responsibilities to executive members.

2.   All board members shall carry out their functions in the interests of the SE, having regard in particular to the interests of the shareholders and the employees.

3.   All board members shall exercise a proper discretion in respect of information of a confidential nature concerning the SE. This duty shall continue to apply even after they have ceased to hold office.

Article 75

(Removal of members)

1.   Members of the supervisory board or the administrative board may be dismissed at any time by the same body, persons or groups of persons who under this Regulation or the statutes of the SE have the power to appoint them.

Article 74

1.   Within the scope of the functions attributed to them by this Regulation, each member of a board shall have the same rights and obligations as the other members of the board of which he is a member.

Unchanged.

3.   All members shall exercise a proper discretion, even after they have ceased to hold office, in respect of information of a confidential nature concerning the SE.

Article 75

Deleted.

ORIGINAL PROPOSAL	AMENDED PROPOSAL
2. In addition, members of the supervisory board or the administrative board may be dismissed on proper grounds by the court within whose jurisdiction the registered office of the SE is situated in proceedings brought by the general meeting of the shareholders, the representatives of the employees, the supervisory board or the administrative board. Such proceedings may also be brought by one or more shareholders who together hold 10 % of the capital of the SE.	

Article 76

(Quorum, majority)

1. Unless the statutes of the SE require a higher quorum, a board shall not conduct business validly unless at least half of its members take part in the deliberations.

2. Members who are absent may take part in decisions by authorizing a member who is present to represent them. No member may represent more than one absent member.

3. Unless the statutes of the SE provide for a larger majority, decisions shall be taken by a majority of the members present or represented.

4. Under terms laid down in the statutes of the SE, a board may also take decisions by procedures under which the members vote in writing, by telex, telegram or telephone or by any other means of telecommunication, provided that all members are informed of the proposed voting procedure and no member objects to the use of that procedure.

Article 76

1. Boards of the SE shall conduct business under the conditions and in the manner set out in the statutes.

2. In the absence of the provisions in the statutes referred to in paragraph 1, a company board shall not conduct business validly unless at least half its members are present at the discussions. Decisions shall be taken by a majority of the members present.

Deleted.

3a. The chairman of each board shall have a casting vote in the event of a tie.

Deleted.

Article 77

(Civil liability)

1. Members of the administrative board, the management board or the supervisory board shall be liable to the SE for any damage sustained by the company as a result of wrongful acts committed in

Article 77

1. Members of the management board, the supervisory board and the administrative board shall be liable for loss or damage sustained by the SE as a result of breach of the obligations attaching to their

ORIGINAL PROPOSAL	AMENDED PROPOSAL
carrying out their duties.	functions.
2. Where the board concerned is composed of more than one member, all the members shall be jointly and severally liable without limit. However, a member may be relieved of liability if he can prove that no fault is attributable to him personally. Such relief may not be claimed by a member on the sole ground that the act giving rise to liability did not come within the sphere of responsibilities delegated to him.	2. Where the board concerned is composed of more than one member, all the members shall be jointly and severally liable for loss or damage sustained by the SE. However, a member may be relieved of liability if he can prove that he is not in breach of the obligations attaching to his functions.
Article 78	*Article 78*
(Proceedings on behalf of the company)	
1. The administrative board or the supervisory board may institute proceedings on the company's behalf to establish liability.	Deleted.
2. Such proceedings must be brought if the general meeting so decides. The general meeting may appoint a special representative for this purpose. For such a decision the statutes may not prescribe a majority greater than an absolute majority of the votes attached to the capital represented.	2. The general meeting shall take the decision to commence proceedings to establish liability in the name and on behalf of the SE pursuant to Article 77 by the majority required in accordance with Article 94. An action must be brought if the general meeting so decides. The general meeting shall appoint for this purpose a special representative to conduct the action.
3. Such proceedings on behalf of the company may also be brought by one or more shareholders who together hold 10% of the capital of the SE.	3. One or more shareholders who together hold at least 10% of the subscribed capital may also decide to commence such proceedings in the name and on behalf of the SE. They shall appoint for this purpose a special representative to conduct the action.
4. Such proceedings may be brought by any creditor of the SE who can show that he cannot obtain satisfaction of his claim on the company.	Deleted.
Article 79	*Article 79*
(Waiver of proceedings on behalf of the company)	
1. The SE may waive its right to institute proceedings on the company's behalf to establish liability. Such a waiver shall require an express resolution of the general meeting taken in the knowledge of the wrongful act giving rise to damage for the company. However, such a resolution may not	Deleted.

ORIGINAL PROPOSAL	AMENDED PROPOSAL

be passed if it is opposed by shareholders whose holdings amount to the figure referred to in Article 75.

2.   Paragraph 1 shall also apply to any compromise relating to such proceedings agreed between the company and a board member.

Article 80

(Limitation of actions)

No proceedings on the company's behalf to establish liability may be instituted more than five years after the act giving rise to damage.

SECTION 4

GENERAL MEETING

Article 81

(Competence)

The following matters shall be resolved by the general meeting:

(a)   increases or reductions in subscribed or authorized capital;

(b)   issues of debentures convertible into shares or carrying subscription rights and of debentures carrying the right to share in the profits;

(c)   the appointment or removal of members of the administrative board or of the supervisory board who represent the shareholders;

(d)   the institution of proceedings on the company's behalf for negligence or misconduct by board members;

(e)   the appointment or dismissal of auditors;

(f)   approval of the annual accounts;

(g)   appropriation of the profit or loss for the year;

(h)   amendment of the statutes;

Article 80

Proceedings in the name and on behalf of the SE cannot brought more than five years from the breach giving rise loss or damage.

SECTION 4

GENERAL MEETING

Article 81

The general meeting shall decide on:

(a)   matters for which it has sole responsibility under this Regulation;

(b)   matters for which the management board, supervisory board or administrative board do not have sole responsibility as a result of:

--   this Regulation.

--   Directive... (complementing the Statute for a European Company with regard to the involvement of employees in the European company.

--   the law of the registered office of the SE.

--   the statutes of the SE.

ORIGINAL PROPOSAL	AMENDED PROPOSAL

ORIGINAL PROPOSAL

(i)   winding up and appointment of liquidators;

(j)   transformation;

(k)   merger of the SE with another company;

(l)   transfers of assets.

Article 82

(Holding of general meeting)

1.   A general meeting shall be held at least once a year. However, the first general meeting may be held at any time in the 18 months following the incorporation of the SE.

2.   A general meeting may be called at any time by the management board or the administrative board.

AMENDED PROPOSAL

Article 81a

Where not covered by rules in this section, the organization and the conduct of general meetings, in particular as regards the convening of the meeting, the possibility of taking decisions by writing, the participation and representation of shareholders at the meeting, establishing an attendance list, the information that must be given to shareholders, and the content of the agenda and the minutes of meetings, shall be governed by the law of the Member State of the registered office of the SE applicable to public limited companies.

Article 82

1.   A general meeting shall be held at least once a year, not later than six months after the end of the financial year of the SE.

2.   General meetings may be convened at any time by the management board or the administrative board. At the request of the supervisory hoard the management board shall convene the general meeting.

3.   The agenda for the general meeting held after the end of the financial year shall include at least the approval of the annual accounts and of the appropriation of the profit or treatment of the loss and the approval of the annual report referred to in Article 46 of Directive 78/660/EEC submitted to the general meeting by the management or administrative organ.

4.   The statutes of an SE containing a management board and a supervisory board may provide that a joint decision should be taken by the two boards on approval of the annual accounts, though in separate votes, and that the general meeting should not pass a resolution unless the boards are unable to

ORIGINAL PROPOSAL	AMENDED PROPOSAL

reach agreement.

Article 83

(Meeting called by minority shareholders)

1.   It shall be provided that one or more shareholders who satisfy the conditions set out in Article 75 may request the SE to call the general meeting and to settle the agenda therefor.

2.   If, following a request made under paragraph 1, no action has been taken within a month, the court within whose jurisdiction the registered office of the SE is situated may order the calling of a general meeting or authorize either the shareholders who have requested it or their representative to call the meeting.

Article 84

(Methods of calling meetings)

1. (a)   The general meeting shall be called by a notice published either in the national gazette specified in the legislation of the State of the registered office in accordance with Article 3 (4) of Directive 68/151/EEC or in one or more large circulation newspapers.

   (b)   However, where all the shares in an SE are registered or where all its shareholders are known, the general meeting may be called by any means of communication addressed to all the shareholders.

2.   The notice calling the general meeting shall

Article 83

1.   One or more shareholders who together hold at least 10% of the subscribed capital may request the SE to convene the general meeting and to settle the agenda therefor. This percentage may be reduced by the statutes of the SE.

2.   The request for a meeting shall give the reasons for convening it and the items to be included on the agenda.

3.   If, following a request made under paragraph 1, the necessary steps have not been taken within a month, the court or competent authority within the jurisdiction of which the registered office of the SE is situated may order the convening of a general meeting or authorize either the shareholders who have requested it or their representative to convene the meeting.

4.   A general meeting may during a meeting decide that a further meeting be convened and set the date and the agenda.

Article 84

Deleted.

ORIGINAL PROPOSAL	AMENDED PROPOSAL

contain the following particulars, at least:

    (a)   the name and the registered office of the SE;

    (b)   the place and date of the meeting;

    (c)   the type of general meeting (ordinary, extraordinary or special);

    (d)   a statement of the formalities, if any, prescribed by the statutes for attendance at the general meeting and for the exercise of the right to vote;

    (e)   any provisions of the statutes which require the shareholder, where he appoints an agent, to appoint a person who fails within certain specified categories of persons;

    (f)   the agenda showing the subjects to be discussed and the proposals for resolutions.

3.   The period between the date of first publication of the notice in accordance with paragraph 1 (a), or the date of dispatch of the first communication as mentioned in paragraph 1 (b), and the date of the opening of the general meeting shall be not less than 30 days.

Article 85

1.   One or more shareholders who satisfy the requirements laid down in Article 75 may request that one or more additional items be included on the agenda of a general meeting of which notice has already been given.

2.   Requests for inclusion of additional agenda items shall be sent to the SE within seven days of the first publication of the notice calling the general meeting in accordance with Article 84 (1) (a) or the dispatch of the first communication calling the general meeting by the means mentioned in Article 84 (1)(b).

3.   Items whose inclusion in the agenda has been requested under paragraph 2 shall be communicated or published in the same way as the notice of meeting, not less than seven days before the meeting.

Article 85

1.   One or more shareholders who together hold at least 10% of the subscribed capital may request that one or more additional items be included on the agenda of a general meeting of which notice has already been given. This percentage may be reduced by the statutes of the SE.

Deleted.

Deleted.

ORIGINAL PROPOSAL	AMENDED PROPOSAL

Article 86

Article 86

(Attendance at general meeting)

Every shareholder who has complied with the formalities prescribed by the statutes shall be entitled to attend the general meeting. However, the statutes may prohibit shareholders having no voting rights from attending the meeting.

Every shareholder shall be entitled to attend the general meeting.

Article 87

Article 87

(Proxies)

1.   Every shareholder shall be entitled to appoint a person to represent him at the general meeting.

1.   Every shareholder shall be entitled to appoint a person of his choice to represent him at the general meeting.

2.   The law of the Member State where the registered office of the SE is situated or the statutes may restrict the choice of representative to one or more specified categories of persons, but a shareholder may not be prevented from appointing another shareholder to represent him.

Deleted.

3.   The appointment shall be made in writing and shall be retained for the period mentioned in Article 99 (4).

Article 88

Article 88

1.   Where the proxies appointed are persons acting in a professional capacity, the provisions of Article 87 and the following provisions shall apply:

Deleted.

(a)   the appointment shall relate to only one meeting, but it shall be valid for successive meetings with the same agenda, without prejudice to paragraph 2;

(b)   the appointment shall be revocable;

(c)   all the shareholders whose names and addresses are known shall be invited, either in writing or by publication in one or more large circulation newspapers, to appoint the person in question as their proxy;

(d)   the invitation to appoint the person in question as a proxy shall contain at least the

357

ORIGINAL PROPOSAL	AMENDED PROPOSAL
following information:	

-- the agenda showing the subjects for discussion and the proposals for resolutions,

-- an indication that the documents mentioned in Article 89 are available to shareholders who ask for them,

-- a request for instructions concerning the exercise of the right to vote in respect of each item on the agenda,

-- a statement of the way in which the proxy will exercise the right to vote in the absence of any instructions from the shareholder;

(e)   the right to vote shall be exercised in accordance with the shareholders' instructions, or in the absence of such instructions in accordance with the statement made to the shareholder. However, the proxy may depart from the shareholders' instructions or the statement made to the shareholder by reason of circumstances unknown when the instructions were given or the invitation to appoint a proxy issued, where voting in accordance with instructions or the statement would be liable to prejudice the shareholder's interests. The proxy shall forthwith inform the shareholder and explain the reasons for this action.

2.   Notwithstanding paragraph 1 (a), a proxy may be appointed for a specified period not exceeding 15 months. In this case the information indicated in paragraph 1 (d) shall be given to all the shareholders referred to in paragraph 1 (c) before any general meeting.

Article 89

(Availability of accounts)

The annual accounts and, where appropriate, the consolidated accounts, the proposed appropriation of profits or treatment of loss where it does not appear in the annual accounts, the annual report and the opinion of the persons responsible for auditing the accounts

Article 89

Every shareholder shall have equal access to information that must be given to them pursuant to Article 81a.

ORIGINAL PROPOSAL	AMENDED PROPOSAL

shall be available to every shareholder at the latest from the date of dispatch or publication of the notice of general meeting called to adopt the annual accounts and to decide on the appropriation of profits or treatment of loss. Every shareholder shall be able to obtain a copy of these documents free of charge upon request. From the same date, the report of the persons responsible for auditing the accounts shall available to any shareholder wishing to consult it at the registered office of the SE.

Article 90

(Right to information)

1.   Every shareholder who so requests at a general meeting shall be entitled to obtain information on the affairs of the company arising from items on the agenda or concerning matters on which the general meeting may take a decision in accordance with Article 91 (2).

2.   The management board or the executive members of the administrative board shall supply this information.

3.   The communication of information may be refused only where:

        (a)   it would be likely to be seriously prejudicial to the company or a controlled company; or

        (b) its disclosure would be incompatible with a legal obligation of confidentiality.

4.   A shareholder to whom information is refused may require that his question and the grounds for refusal shall be entered in the minutes of the general meeting.

5.   A shareholder to whom information is refused may challenge the validity of the refusal in the court within whose jurisdiction the registered office of the SE is situated. Application to the court shall be made within two weeks of the closure of the general meeting.

Article 90

Deleted.

ORIGINAL PROPOSAL	AMENDED PROPOSAL
Article 91	*Article 91*
(Decisions; Agenda)	
1. The general meeting shall not pass any resolution concerning items which have not been communicated or published in accordance with Articles 84 (2) (f) or 85 (3).	Deleted.
2. Paragraph 1 shall not apply when all the shareholders are present in person or by proxy at the general meeting and no shareholder objects to the matter in question being discussed.	
Article 92	*Article 92*
(Voting rights)	
1. A shareholder's voting rights shall be proportionate to the fraction of the subscribed capital which his shares represent.	1. A shareholder's voting rights shall be proportionate to the fraction of the subscribed capital which his shares having the right to vote represent.
2. The statutes may authorize:	Deleted.
(a) restriction or exclusion of voting rights in respect of shares which carry special advantages;	
(b) restriction of votes in respect of shares allotted to the same shareholder, provided the restriction applies at least to all shareholders of the same class.	
3. The right to vote may not be exercised:	3. The right to vote may not be exercised:
(a) where a call made by the company has not been paid;	(a) in respect of shares for which a call made by the SE has not been paid within the prescribed period;
(b) on shares held by the SE itself or by one of its subsidiaries.	b) on shares held by the SE itself or by an undertaking controlled by it under Article 6.
4. The law of the State where the registered office of the SE is situated shall govern the exercise of voting rights in cases of succession, usufruct, pledge of shares, or failure to notify substantial holdings.	Deleted.

ORIGINAL PROPOSAL	AMENDED PROPOSAL

Article 93

(Conflict of interest)

Neither a shareholder or his representative shall exercise the right to vote attached to his shares or to shares belonging to third persons where the subject matter of the resolution relates to:

(a)   the assertion of claims by the SE against that shareholder;

(b)   the commencement of legal proceedings to establish the liability of that shareholder to the company in accordance with Article 78;

(c)   waiver of the right to bring proceedings to establish the liability of that shareholder to the company in accordance with Article 79.

Article 93

Deleted.

Article 93a

For the purpose of this section, the votes cast shall not include votes attaching to shares in respect of which the shareholder has not taken part in the vote, has returned a blank or spoilt ballot paper, or has abstained.

Article 94

(Required majority)

1.   Resolutions of the general meeting shall require at least an absolute majority of the votes attached to the subscribed capital present or represented unless a greater majority is prescribed by this Regulation.

2.   However, as regards the appointment or dismissal of members of the administrative board, the management board or the supervisory board, the statutes may not require a majority greater than that mentioned in Paragraph 1.

Article 94

1.   Save where this Regulation requires otherwise, decisions of the general meeting shall be taken by a majority of the votes cast.

2.   The appointment or removal of the board members appointed by the general meeting shall not require a majority greater than that referred to in paragraph 1.

ORIGINAL PROPOSAL	AMENDED PROPOSAL
Article 95	*Article 95*
(Amendment of statutes)	(Conflict of interest)

<table>
<tr>
<td>

1.   A resolution of the general meeting shall be required for any amendment of the statutes of the instrument of incorporation.

2.   However, the statutes may provide that the administrative board or the management board may amend the statutes or the instrument of incorporation where the amendment merely implements a resolution already passed by the general meeting or by the board itself by virtue of an authorization given by the general meeting, by the statutes, or by the instrument of incorporation.

</td>
<td>

Deleted.

</td>
</tr>
</table>

Article 96	*Article 96*

<table>
<tr>
<td>

1.   The complete text of the amendment of the statutes or of the instrument of incorporation which is to be put before the general meeting shall be set out in the notice of meeting.

2.   However, the statutes may provide that the complete text of the amendment mentioned in paragraph 1 may be obtained by any shareholder free of charge upon request.

</td>
<td>

Deleted.

</td>
</tr>
</table>

Article 97	*Article 97*

<table>
<tr>
<td>

1.   A majority of not less than two-thirds of votes attached to subscribed capital represented at the meeting shall be required for the passing by the general meeting of resolutions amending the statutes or the instrument of incorporation.

2.   However, the statutes may provide that where at least one-half of the subscribed capital is represented, a simple majority of the votes in paragraph 1 shall suffice.

3.   Resolutions of the general meeting which would have the effect of increasing the liabilities of the shareholders shall require in any event the approval of all the shareholders involved.

4.   A resolution amending the statutes or the instrument of incorporation shall be made public in

</td>
<td>

1.   Amendment of the statutes shall require a decision of the general meeting taken by a majority of two-thirds of the votes cast.

Unchanged.

</td>
</tr>
</table>

ORIGINAL PROPOSAL	AMENDED PROPOSAL
accordance with Article 9.	

Article 98	*Article 98*
(Separate vote of each class of shareholder)	
1. Where there are several classes of shares, any resolution of the general meeting shall require a separate vote at least for each class of shareholders whose rights are affected by the resolution.	Unchanged.
2. Where a resolution of the general meeting requires the majority of votes specified in Article 97 (1) and (2), that majority shall also be required for the separate vote of each class of shareholders whose rights are affected by the resolution.	
Article 99	*Article 99*
(Minutes)	
1. Minutes shall be drawn up for every meeting of the general meeting.	Deleted.
2. The minutes shall contain the following particulars, at least:	
(a) the place and date of the meeting;	
(b) the resolutions passed;	
(c) the result of the voting.	
3. There shall be annexed to the minutes:	
(a) the attendance list;	
(b) the documents relating to the calling of the general meeting.	
4. The minutes and the documents annexed thereto shall be retained for at least three years. A copy of the minutes and the documents annexed thereto may be obtained by any shareholder, free of charge, upon request.	

ORIGINAL PROPOSAL	AMENDED PROPOSAL

Article 100

Article 100

(Appeal against resolutions of general meeting)

Decisions of a court or competent authority declaring void or inexistent a decision of the general meeting of the SE shall be published in accordance with Article 9.

1.   Resolutions of the general meeting may be declared invalid as infringing the provisions of this Regulation or of the company's statutes, in the following manner.

2.   An action for such a declaration may be brought by any shareholder or any person having a legitimate interest, provided he can show that he has an interest in having the infringed provision observed and that the resolution of the general meeting may have been altered or influenced by the infringement.

3.   The action for such a declaration shall be brought within three months of the closure of the general meeting, before the court within whose jurisdiction the registered office to the SE is situated. It shall be taken against the SE.

4.   The procedure in the action for such a declaration shall be governed by the law of the place where the SE has its registered office.

5.   The decision declaring the resolution void shall be published in accordance with Article 9.

6.   The declaration that a resolution is void may no longer be made by the court if that resolution has been replaced by another taken in conformity with this Regulation and the statutes of the SE. The court may, on its own initiative, grant the time necessary to enable the general meeting to pass such a new resolution.

ORIGINAL PROPOSAL	AMENDED PROPOSAL

TITLE V

ANNUAL ACCOUNTS AND CONSOLIDATED ACCOUNTS

SECTION 1

ANNUAL ACCOUNTS

Subsection 1

Preparation of annual accounts

Article 101

1. The SE shall draw up annual accounts comprising the balance sheet, the profit and loss account and the notes on the accounts. These documents shall constitute a composite whole.

2. The annual accounts of the SE shall be drawn up in accordance with the provisions of Directive 78/660/EEC subject to paragraph 3 of this Article.

3. (a) Articles 1, 2 (5), final sentence, 2 (6), 4 (1), final sentence, 4 (2), final sentence, 4 (3) (b), final sentence, 4 (4), final sentence, 5, 43 (2), 45 (1) (b), final sentence, 54, 55 and 62 of Directive 78/660/EEC shall not apply.

(b) For the purpose of drawing up the annual accounts, the provisions of Articles 2, 3, 4, 6 and 7 of Directive 78/660/EEC shall apply. The SE may avail itself of the option provided for in Article 6 of that Directive.

TITLE V

ANNUAL ACCOUNTS AND CONSOLIDATED ACCOUNTS

SECTION 1

ANNUAL ACCOUNTS

Subsection 1

Preparation of annual accounts

Article 101

Unchanged.

1a. The SE may draw up and publish its annual accounts in ecus. In this event, the bases of conversion used to express in ecus those items included in the accounts which are or were originally expressed in national currency must be disclosed in the notes to the accounts.

Unchanged.

2a. Where reference is made in Directive 78/660/EEC to national legislation, such a reference is to be considered as a reference to the legislation of the Member State of the registered office of the SE.

3. (a) Articles 1, 2 (1), 2 (5), final sentence, 2 (6), 4 (1), final sentence, 4 (2), final sentence, 3 (b), final sentence, 4 (4), final sentence, 5, 33 (5), 43 (2), 45 (1) (b), final sentence 54, 55 and 62 of Directive 78/660/EEC shall not apply.

Unchanged.

ORIGINAL PROPOSAL	AMENDED PROPOSAL

(c) For the presentation of the balance sheet, the SE may choose between the layouts prescribed by Articles 9 and 10 of Directive 78/660/EEC. It may avail itself of the options provided for in Articles 9, 10, 11, 18, final sentence, 20 (2) and 21, final sentence, of that Directive.

(d) For the presentation of the profit and loss account, the SE may choose between the layouts prescribed by Articles 23 to 26 of Directive 78/660/EEC. It may avail itself of the options provided for in Articles 27 and 30 of that Directive.

(e) The items shown in the annual accounts shall be valued in accordance with the principles laid down in Article 31 of Directive 78/660 EEC. They shall be valued on the basis of the principle of purchase price or production cost according to the provisions of Articles 34 to 42 of that Directive.

However, the SE may choose to apply one of the three alternative valuation methods provided for in Article 33 of that Directive. If the SE avails itself of that possibility, it shall ensure that the method applied is consistent with the principles laid down in that Article. Details of the method applied shall be given in the annex thereto.

The SE may avail itself of the options provided for in Articles 34 (1), 36, 37 (1) and (2), 39 (1)(c) and (2) and 40 (1) of that Directive.

The SE may avail itself of the options provided for in Articles 33 (3) (second sentence), 34 (1), 36, 37 (1), 37 (2), 39 (1) (c), 39 (2) and 40 (1) of that Directive.

(f) In addition to the information required under other provisions of Directive 78/660/EEC, the notes on the accounts must include the information provided for in Article 43 of that Directive at least. The SE may avail itself of the options provided for in Articles 44 and 45 (1) and (2) of that Directive.

Unchanged.

ORIGINAL PROPOSAL	AMENDED PROPOSAL
Subsection 2	Subsection 2
Preparation of the annual report	**Preparation of the annual report**

Article 102	*Article 102*

1.   The SE shall draw up an annual report which must include at least a fair review of the development of the company's business and of its position.

Unchanged.

2.   The annual report shall also include the information provided for in Article 46 of Directive 78/660/EEC.

Subsection 3	Subsection 3
Auditing	**Auditing**

Article 103	*Article 103*

1.   The annual accounts of the SE shall be audited by one or more persons authorized to do so in a Member State in accordance with the provisions of Directive 84/253/EEC.[13] Those persons shall also verify that the annual report is consistent with the annual accounts for the same financial year.

1.   The annual accounts of the SE shall be audited by one or more persons authorized to do so in a Member State in accordance with the provisions of Directives 84/253/EEC[14] and 89/48/EEC.[15] Those persons shall also verify that the annual report is consistent with the annual accounts for the same financial year.

2.   If the SE meets the criteria laid down in Article 11 of Directive 78/660/EEC, it shall not be required to have its accounts audited. In such cases, members of administrative board or the management board shall be subject to the sanctions applicable to public limited liability companies in the State in which the SE has its registered office where the annual accounts or annual reports are not drawn up in accordance with the provisions of this section.

Unchanged.

Subsection 4	Subsection 4
Publication	**Publication**

Article 104	*Article 104*

1.   The annual accounts, duly approved, and the annual report and audit report shall be published as

Unchanged.

ORIGINAL PROPOSAL	AMENDED PROPOSAL

ORIGINAL PROPOSAL

laid down in accordance with Article 3 of Directive 68/151/EEC by the laws of the Member State in which the SE has its registered office.

2. The SE may avail itself of the options provided for in Article 47 of Directive 78/660/EEC.

3. Articles 48, 49 and 50 of Directive 78/660/EEC shall apply to the SE.

Subsection 5

Final provisions

Article 105

Articles 56 to 61 of Directive 78/660/EEC shall apply to the SE. The SE may avail itself of the options provided for in those Articles.

SECTION 2

CONSOLIDATED ACCOUNTS

Subsection 1

Conditions for the preparation of consolidated accounts

Article 106

1. Where the SE is a parent undertaking within the meaning of Article 1 (1) and (2) of Directive 83/349/EEC, it shall be required to draw up consolidated accounts and a consolidated annual report in accordance with the provisions of that Directive.

2. Articles 1 (1)(c), last sentence, 1 (d) (bb), last sentence, 1 (d), second and third subparagraphs, 4 and

AMENDED PROPOSAL

Subsection 5

Final provisions

Article 105

Articles 53 (1), 56 (2) and 57 to 61 of Directive 78/660/EEC shall apply to the SE. The SE may avail itself of the options provided for in those Articles.

SECTION 2

CONSOLIDATED ACCOUNTS

Subsection 1

Conditions for the preparation of consolidated accounts

Article 106

Unchanged.

1a. The SE may draw up and publish its consolidated accounts in ecus. In this event the bases of conversion used to express in ecus those items included in the accounts and the financial statements which are or were originally expressed in other national currency must be disclosed in the notes to the accounts.

2. Article 1 (1) (c), last sentence, 1 (1) (d) (bb), last sentence, 1 (1) (d), second subparagraph and

ORIGINAL PROPOSAL	AMENDED PROPOSAL
5 of Directive 83/349/EEC shall not apply.	Articles 4 and 5 of Directive 83/349/EEC shall not apply.
3. The SE may avail itself of the options provided for in Articles 1, 6, 12 and 15 of Directive 83/349/EEC.	Unchanged.

Article 107

ORIGINAL PROPOSAL	AMENDED PROPOSAL
1. Where the SE is a parent undertaking within the meaning of Article 1 (1) and (2) of Directive 83/349/EEC and is at the same time a subsidiary undertaking of a parent undertaking governed by the law of a Member State, it shall be exempt from the obligation to draw up consolidated accounts subject to the conditions laid down in Articles 7 and 8 of that Directive. Article 10 of that Directive shall apply.	Unchanged.
2. Articles 7 (1) (b), second subparagraph, 8 (1), last sentence, 8 (2) and (3), and 9 of that Directive shall not apply.	2. Articles 7 (1) (b), second subparagraph, 8 (2) and 8 (3) and 9 shall not apply.
3. The exemption provided for in paragraph 1 shall not apply where the securities of the SE have been admitted to official listing on a stock exchange established in a Member State.	Unchanged.

Article 108

ORIGINAL PROPOSAL	AMENDED PROPOSAL
1. Where the SE is an undertaking within the meaning of Article 1 (1) and (2) of Directive 83/349/EEC and is at the same time a subsidiary undertaking of a parent undertaking which is not governed by the law of a Member State, it shall be exempt from the obligation to draw up consolidated accounts subject to the conditions laid down in Article 11 of that Directive.	Unchanged.
2. Articles 8 (1), second sentence, 8 (2) and (3), and 10 of that Directive shall not apply.	2. Articles 8 (1), second sentence, 8 (2), 8 (3) and Directive 83/349/EEC shall not apply.
3. The exemption provided for in paragraph 1 shall not apply where the securities of the SE have been admitted to official listing on a stock exchange established in a Member State.	Unchanged.

ORIGINAL PROPOSAL	AMENDED PROPOSAL
Subsection 2	Subsection 2
The preparation of consolidated accounts	**The preparation of consolidated accounts**
Article 109	*Article 109*
1. The consolidated accounts shall comprise the consolidated balance sheet, the consolidated profit and loss account and the notes on the accounts. These documents shall constitute a composite whole.	Unchanged.
2. The consolidated accounts shall be drawn up in accordance with the provisions of Directive 83/349/EEC subject to paragraph 3 of this Article.	
3. (a) Articles 16 (5), final sentence, 16 (6), 33 (2) (c), first sentence, 33 (3), final sentence, 34, point 12, final sentence, and point 13, final sentence, 35 (1) (b), second sentence, 40, 41 (5) and 48 of Directive 83/349/EEC shall not apply.	
(b) The SE may avail itself of the options provided for in Articles 17 (2), 19 (1)(b), 20, 26 (1)(c), final sentence, 26 (2), 27 (2), 28, second sentence, 29 (2) (a), second sentence, 29 (5), final sentence, 30 (2), 32, 33 (2) (d) and 35 (1) of Directive 83/349/EEC.	
Subsection 3	Subsection 3
Preparation of the consolidated annual report	**Preparation of the consolidated annual report**
Article 110	*Article 110*
1. The consolidated annual report shall include at least a fair review of the development of the company's business and the position of the undertakings included in the consolidation taken as a whole.	Unchanged.
2. The consolidated annual report shall also include the information provided for in Article 36 of Directive 83/349/EEC. The SE may avail itself of the option provided for in the final sentence of the paragraph 2 (d) of that Article.	

ORIGINAL PROPOSAL	AMENDED PROPOSAL
Subsection 4	Subsection 4
Auditing of the consolidated accounts	**Auditing of the consolidated accounts**
Article 111	*Article 111*
The consolidated accounts shall be audited by one or more persons authorized to do so in a Member State in accordance with the provisions of Directive 84/253/EEC. Those persons shall also verify that the consolidated annual is consistent with the consolidated accounts for the financial year in question.	The consolidated accounts shall be audited by one or more persons authorized to do so in a Member State in accordance with the provisions of Directives 84/253/EEC[16] and 89/48/EEC.[17] Those persons shall also verify that the consolidated annual report is consistent with the consolidated accounts for the financial year in question.
Subsection 5	Subsection 5
Publication	**Publication**
Article 112	*Article 112*
1. The consolidated accounts, duly approved, and the consolidated annual report, together with the audit report, shall be published as laid down in accordance with Article 3 of Directive 68/151/EEC by the laws of the Member in which the SE has its registered office.	Unchanged.
2. Article 38 (3), (4) and (6) of Directive 83/349/EEC shall not apply.	
3. The management board and the executive members of the administrative board shall be liable to the sanctions provided for (...) if the consolidated accounts and consolidated annual report are not published.	
SECTION 3	SECTION 3
BANKS AND INSURANCE COMPANIES	**BANKS AND INSURANCE COMPANIES**
Article 113	*Article 113*
1. SEs which are credit or financial institutions shall comply, as regards the drawing up, auditing and	Unchanged.

|

publication of annual accounts and consolidated accounts, with the rules laid down pursuant to Directive 86/635/EEC[18] by the national law of the State in which the SE has its registered office.

2.   SEs which are insurance companies shall comply, as regards the drawing up, auditing and publication of annual accounts and consolidated accounts, with the rules laid down, pursuant to Directive ... (which, supplementing Directive 78/660/EEC, harmonizes the provisions governing the annual accounts and the consolidated accounts of insurance companies, by the national law of the State in which the company has its registered office).

TITLE VI

GROUPS OF COMPANIES

Article 114

1.   Where an undertaking controls an SE, that undertaking's consequent rights and obligations relating to the protection of minority shareholders and third parties shall be those defined by the law governing public limited companies in the State where the SE has its registered office.

2.   Paragraph 1 shall not affect the obligation imposed on the controlling undertaking by the legal system which governs it.

TITLE VII

WINDING UP, LIQUIDATION, INSOLVENCY AND SUSPENSION OF PAYMENTS

SECTION 1

WINDING UP

Article 115

An SE may be wound up:

1.   upon the expiry of the duration laid down for it in the statutes or the instrument of incorporation;

TITLE VI

GROUPS OF COMPANIES

Article 114

Deleted.

TITLE VII

WINDING UP, LIQUIDATION, INSOLVENCY AND SUSPENSION OF PAYMENTS

SECTION 1

WINDING UP

Article 115

The SE may be wound up by a decision of the general meeting ordering its winding up taken in accordance with Article 97.

ORIGINAL PROPOSAL	AMENDED PROPOSAL
2. by resolution of the general meeting of shareholders; or	However, the general meeting may decide, in accordance with the same rules, to annul the decision to wind up as long as there has been no distribution on the basis of the liquidation.

ORIGINAL PROPOSAL

2.　　by resolution of the general meeting of shareholders; or

3.　　by decision of the court of the place where the SE has its registered office:

（a）　where the subscribed capital of the company has been reduced below the minimum capital provided for in Article 4;

（b）　where the disclosure of annual accounts has not taken place in the SE's last three financial years;

（c）　on any ground laid down in the law of the place where the SE has its registered office or provided for in the statutes or the instrument of incorporation.

Article 116

(Winding up by resolution of the general meeting)

1.　　A resolution of the general meeting of shareholders to wind up the SE on any ground laid down by the statutes or instruments of incorporation shall require at least a simple majority of the votes attached to the subscribed capital represented.

2.　　In all other cases a resolution of the general meeting of shareholders to wind up the SE shall require at least a two-thirds majority of the votes attached to the subscribed capital represented. The statutes may, however, lay down that, when at least half the subscribed capital is represented, the simple majority referred to in paragraph 1 is sufficient.

AMENDED PROPOSAL

However, the general meeting may decide, in accordance with the same rules, to annul the decision to wind up as long as there has been no distribution on the basis of the liquidation.

Article 116

1.　　The management or administrative board shall convene a general meeting to take a decision in the event of:

-- the expiry of the period fixed in the instrument of incorporation or the statutes, or

-- the existence of any other cause for winding up provide for therein.

The general meeting may then at its option:

-- decide, in accordance with Article 94, to wind up the SE,

-- decide, in accordance with Article 97, that the SE is to continue its activities.

2.　　The management or administrative board shall convene a general meeting in the event of the existence of any cause for the winding up of a public limited company provided for by the law of the Member State in which the SE has its registered office. The general meeting shall decide whether the SE should be wound up or any other measures taken.

ORIGINAL PROPOSAL	AMENDED PROPOSAL

Article 117

(Winding up by the court)

1.   Winding up proceedings may be brought in the court of the place where the SE has its registered office by the administrative board, the management board, or the supervisory board of the SE, by any shareholder, or by any person with a legitimate interest.

2.   Where the SE is able to remove the ground for winding up, the court may grant it a period of time sufficient to allow it to do so.

Article 118

(Publication of winding up)

The winding up shall be published in the manner referred to in Article 9.

Article 119

(Wound-up SE to continue in existence)

1.   Where an SE is to be wound up as a result of a resolution to that effect of the general meeting of shareholders or upon the expiry of its prescribed duration, the general meeting of shareholders may resolve that it is to continue in existence as long as there has been no distribution on the basis of liquidation in accordance with Article 126.

2.   The resolution that the company is to continue in existence shall be passed in accordance with Article 116 (2), and published in the manner referred to in

---

Article 117

Deleted.

Article 117a

On an application by any person concerned or any competent authority, the court where the SE has its registered office must order it to be wound up where it finds that the registered office, as defined in Article 5 has been transferred outside the Community. However, the court may grant the SE a period of time to rectify the situation.

Article 118

The winding up of an SE shall be published in accordance with Article 9. The same shall apply to decisions that the SE is to continue its activities under Article 115, second paragraph, and Article 116.

Article 119

Deleted.

ORIGINAL PROPOSAL	AMENDED PROPOSAL

Article 9.

(a)   where they were appointed in accordance with Article 120 (2) (a) and (b) or, where Article 120 (3) applies by a decision of the general meeting acting by the simple majority of the votes specified in Article 116 (1);

(d)   irrespective of the manner of appointment, by a court in whose jurisdiction the registered office of the SE is situated, on petition of any person having a legitimate interest in the matter and showing a proper ground.

SECTION 2

LIQUIDATION

SECTION 2

LIQUIDATION

Article 120

Article 120

(Appointment of liquidators)

1.   The winding up of an SE shall entail the liquidation of its assets. The liquidation shall be carried out by one or more liquidators.

1.   The winding up of an SE shall entail its liquidation.

2.   Liquidators shall be appointed:

2.   The liquidation of an SE and the conclusion of its liquidation shall be governed by national law.

(a)   by the statutes or instrument of incorporation, or in the manner laid down therein; or

(b)   by a resolution of the general meeting of shareholders acting by the simple majority of the votes specified in Article 116 (1); or

(c)   failing an appointment pursuant to (a) or (b), by the court in whose jurisdiction the registered office of the SE is situated on the application of any shareholder or of the administrative board, the management board or the supervisory board.

3.   In the absence of an appointment pursuant to paragraph 2, the duties of liquidator shall be performed by the administrative board or the management board.

3.   An SE in liquidation shall continue to have legal personality until the conclusion of the liquidation.

4.   The general meeting shall determine the remuneration of the liquidators. Where the liquidators are appointed by a court in whose jurisdiction the registered office of the SE is situated, the court shall determine their remuneration.

Deleted.

Article 121

Article 121

(Removal of liquidators)

The liquidators may be removed before the termination of the liquidation:

Deleted.

(a)   where they were appointed in accordance with Article 120 (2) (a) and (b) or, where Article 120 (3) applies, by a decision of the general meeting acting by the simple majority of the votes specified in Article 116 (1);

(b)   irrespective of the manner of appointment, by a court in whose jurisdiction the registered office of the SE is situated, on petition of any person having a legitimate interest in the matter and showing a proper ground.

Article 122

(Powers of liquidators)

1.   The liquidators may take all appropriate steps to update the SE and, in particular, shall terminate transactions pending, collect debts, convert remaining assets into cash where this is necessary for their realization and to pay the sums owing to creditors. The liquidators may undertake new transactions to the extent necessary for the purpose of the liquidation.

2.   The liquidators shall have the power to bind the SE in dealings with third parties and to take legal proceedings on their behalf.

3.   The appointment, termination of office and identity of liquidators shall be published in the manner referred to in Article 9. It must appear from the disclosure whether the liquidators may represent the company alone or must act jointly.

Article 123

(Liability of liquidators)

The rules on the civil liability of members of the administrative board or of the management board of an SE shall also apply to the civil liability of liquidators for wrongful acts committed in carrying out their duties.

Article 122

Deleted.

Article 123

Deleted.

ORIGINAL PROPOSAL	AMENDED PROPOSAL
Article 124	*Article 124*
(Accounting documents)	
1. The liquidators shall draw up a statement of the assets and liabilities of the SE on the date the winding up commenced. Any shareholder or creditor of the SE shall be entitled to obtain a copy of this statement free of charge, upon request.	Deleted.
2. The liquidators shall report on their activities to the general meeting each year.	
3. The rules concerning the drawing up, auditing and publication of annual accounts or consolidated accounts and the approval of persons responsible for carrying out the statutory audits of those accounts shall apply *mutatis mutandis.*	
Article 125	*Article 125*
(Information supplied to creditors)	
The notice of the winding up of the company provided for in Article 118 shall invite creditors to lodge their claims, and shall indicate the date after which distributions on the basis of liquidation will be made.	Deleted.
An invitation to lodge claims shall also be sent in writing to any creditor known to the company.	
Article 126	*Article 126*
(Distribution)	
1. No distribution on the basis of liquidation may be made to the beneficiaries designated in the statutes or the instrument of incorporation, or failing any such designation to the shareholders, until all creditors of the company have been paid in full and the time limits indicated in Articles 125 and 127 (2) have expired.	1. No distribution on the basis of liquidation may effected as between the shareholders or the beneficial designated in the instrument of incorporation or statutes until all creditors of the company have been paid full.
2. After the creditors have been paid in full, and anything due to the beneficiaries referred to in paragraph 1 has been distributed, the net assets of the SE shall, except where otherwise stated in the statutes or the instrument of incorporation, be distributed among the shareholders in proportion to the nominal	Deleted.

value of their shares.

3. Where the shares issued by the SE have not all been paid up in the same proportion, the amounts paid up shall be repaid. In that case only the remaining net assets shall be distributed in accordance with paragraph 2. If the net assets are not sufficient to repay the amounts paid up, the shareholders shall bear the loss in proportion to the annual value of their shares.

4. Where a claim on an SE has not yet fallen due or is in dispute or where the creditor is not known, the net assets may be distributed only if adequate security is set aside for the creditor or if the assets remaining after a partial distribution represent sufficient security.

Unchanged.

Article 127

(Distribution plan)

1. The liquidator or liquidators shall draw up a plan for the distribution of the net assets of the company pursuant to Article 126 after the date indicated in Article 125.

2. This plan shall be brought to the attention of the general meeting and of any beneficiary designated in the statutes or instrument of incorporation. Any shareholder and any beneficiary may challenge the plan in the court of the place where the SE has its registered office within three months of the date on which it was brought to the attention of the general meeting or of that beneficiary. No distribution may be made until that period has expired.

3. Where there is a challenge it shall be for the court to decide whether and to what extent any partial distribution may be made in the course of the proceedings before the court takes its decision.

Article 127

Deleted.

Article 128

(Termination of liquidation)

1. The liquidation shall be terminated when the distribution is complete.

2. Where, after the liquidation is terminated,

Article 128

Deleted.

ORIGINAL PROPOSAL	AMENDED PROPOSAL

further assets or liabilities of the SE come to light which were previously unknown, or further liquidation measures prove necessary, a court in whose jurisdiction the registered office of the SE is situated shall, on the application of any shareholder or creditor, renew the mandate of the former liquidators or appoint other liquidators.

3.   Termination of liquidation and removal of the SE from the register referred to in Article 8 (1) shall be published in the manner referred to in Article 9.

4.   Following the liquidation, the books and records relating to the liquidation shall be lodged at the register referred to in paragraph 3. Any interested party may examine such books and records.

Unchanged.

SECTION 3

INSOLVENCY AND SUSPENSION OF PAYMENTS

Article 129

In respect of insolvency and suspension of payments the SE shall be subject to the law of the place where it has its registered office.

Article 129

The SE shall be subject to national laws in respect of insolvency and suspension of payments.

Article 130

1.   The opening of insolvency or suspension of payments proceedings shall be notified for entry in the register by the person appointed to conduct the proceedings. The entry in the register shall show the following:

(a)   the nature of the proceedings, the date of the order, and the court making it;

(b)   the date on which payments were suspended, if the court order provides for this;

(c)   the name and address of the administrator, trustee, receiver, liquidator or any other person having power to conduct the proceedings, or of each of them where there are more than one;

Article 130

Unchanged.

ORIGINAL PROPOSAL	AMENDED PROPOSAL
(d)　　any other information considered necessary.	further assets or liabilities of the SE come to light which were previously unknown, or further liquidation measures prove necessary, a court in whose jurisdiction the registered office of the SE is situated shall, on the application of any shareholder or creditor, renew the mandate of the former liquidators or appoint other liquidators.
2.　　Where a court finally dismisses an application for the opening of the proceedings referred to in paragraph 1 owing to want of sufficient assets, it shall, either of its own motion or on application by any interested party, order its decision to be noted in the register.	
3.　　Particulars registered pursuant to paragraphs 1 and 2 shall be published in the manner referred to in Article 9.	3.　　Termination of liquidation and removal of the SE from the register referred to in Article 9 (1) shall be published in the manner referred to in Article 9.
	4.　　Following the liquidation, the books and records relating to the liquidation shall be lodged at the register referred to in paragraph 3. Any interested party may examine such books and records.
TITLE VIII	**TITLE VIII**
MERGERS	**MERGERS**
	SECTION 1
Article 131	*Article 131*
(Types of merger)	INSOLVENCY AND SUSPENSION OF PAYMENTS
An SE may merge with other SEs or with other public limited companies incorporated under the law of one of the Member States in the following ways:	Deleted.
	Article 129
	In respect of insolvency and suspension of payments the SE shall be subject to the law of the place where it has its registered office.
(a)　　by forming a new SE;	
(b)　　by the SE taking over one or more public limited companies;	
(c)　　by a public limited company taking over the SE;	*Article 130*
	Unchanged.
(d)　　by forming a new public limited company.	
Article 132	*Article 132*
(Applicable law)	
1.　　Where the companies participating in the merger have their registered offices in the same Member State, the provisions of national law giving effect to Directive 78/855/EEC shall apply.	An SE may merge with other SEs or with other public limited companies having their registered office in the same Member State. Such a merger shall be governed by the law of the Member State in question in accordance with Directive 78/855/EEC.
2.　　Where the companies participating in the	Unchanged.

ORIGINAL PROPOSAL	AMENDED PROPOSAL

merger have their registered office in different Member States, the provisions of Title II shall apply *mutatis mutandis*.

the provisions of this Regulation.

TITLE IX

PERMANENT ESTABLISHMENTS

Article 133

1.   Where an SE has one or more permanent establishments in a Member State or non-member State, and the aggregation of the profits and losses for tax purposes of all such permanent establishments results in a net loss, that loss may be set against the profits of the SE in State where it is resident for tax purposes.

2.   Subsequent profits of the permanent establishments of the SE in another State shall constitute taxable income of the SE in the State in which it is resident for tax purposes, up to the amount of the losses imputed in accordance with paragraph 1.

3.   Where a permanent establishment is situated in a Member State, the imputable losses under paragraph 1 and the taxable profits under paragraph 2 shall be determined by the laws of that Member State.

4.   Member States shall be free not to apply the provisions of this Article if they avoid double taxation by allowing the SE to set the tax already paid by its permanent establishments against the tax due from it in respect of the profits realized by those permanent establishments.

TITLE IX

PERMANENT ESTABLISHMENTS

Article 133

Unchanged.

TITLE X

SANCTIONS

Article 134

The provisions of national law applicable to the infringement of the rules relating to public limited companies shall apply to the infringement of any of

TITLE X

SANCTIONS

Article 134

Without prejudice to the sanctions prescribed by the Regulation, the Member States shall provide the appropriate penalties in the event of failure to comply

ORIGINAL PROPOSAL	AMENDED PROPOSAL
the provisions of this Regulation.	with the provision of this Regulation.

TITLE XI

FINAL PROVISIONS

Article 135

The involvement of employees in the SE shall be defined in accordance with the provisions adopted to give effect to Directive... by the Member State where the SE has its registered office.

Article 136

An SE may be formed in any Member State which has implemented in national law the provisions of Directive ... (on the involvement of employees in the SE).

Article 137

This Regulation shall enter into force on 1 January 1992.

This Regulation shall be binding in its entirety and directly applicable in all Member States.

TITLE XI

FINAL PROVISIONS

Article 135

Deleted.

Article 136

Deleted.

Article 137

This Regulation shall enter into force on 1 January 1993.

This Regulation shall be binding in its entirety and directly applicable in all Member States.

Endnotes

1. OJ No. L 222, 14.8 1978, p. 11.

2. OJ No. L 193, 18.7.1983, p. 1.

3. OJ No. C53, 28.2.1991, p. 30.

4. OJ No. C 84, 31.3.1988, p. 1.

5. Official Journal, English Special Edition, 1968 (I), p. 41.

6. OJ No. C 105, 21.4.1988, p. 6.

7. OJ No. L 26, 31.1.1977, p. 1.

8. OJ No. L 61, 5.3.1977, p. 26.

9. OJ No. L 295, 20.10.1977, p. 36.

10. OJ No. L 348, 17.12.1988, p. 62.

11. OJ No. L 100, 17.4.1989, p. 1.

12. OJ No. L. 124, 5.5.1989, p. 8.

13. OJ No. L 126, 12.5.1984, p. 20.

14. OJ No. L 126, 12.5.1984, p. 20.

15. OJ No. L 19, 24.1.1989, p. 16.

16. OJ No. L 126, 12.5.1984, p. 20.

17. OJ No. L 19, 24.1.1989, p. 16.

18. OJ No. L 372, 31.12.1986, p. 1.

* * *

FOURTH ACP-EEC CONVENTION*
[EXCERPTS]

The Fourth ACP-EEC Convention (LOME IV) was signed in Lomé on 15 December 1989 and came into force on 1 March 1990. The Convention is scheduled to remain in effect for 10 years. The signatories to the Convention were Belgium, Denmark, Germany, Greece, Spain, France, Ireland, Italy, Luxembourg, the Netherlands, Portugal, and the United Kingdom on the one part, and Angola, Antigua and Barbuda, the Bahamas, Barbados, Belize, Benin, Botswana, Burkina Faso, Burundi, Cameroon, Cape Verde, Central African Republic, Chad, Comoros, Congo, Côte d'Ivoire, Djibouti, Dominica, Dominican Republic, Ethiopia, Fiji, Gabon, the Gambia, Ghana, Grenada, Guinea, Guinea-Bissau, Equatorial Guinea, Guyana, Haiti, Jamaica, Kenya, Kiribati, Lesotho, Liberia, Madagascar, Malawi, Mali, Mauritania, Mauritius, Mozambique, Niger, Nigeria, Papua New Guinea, Rwanda, Saint Kitts and Nevis, Saint Lucia, Saint Vincent and the Grenadines, Samoa, Sao Tome and Principe, Senegal, Seychelles, Sierra Leone, Solomon Islands, Somalia, Sudan, Suriname, Swaziland, United Republic of Tanzania, Togo, Tonga, Trinidad and Tobago, Tuvalu, Uganda, Vanuatu, Zaire, Zambia and Zimbabwe on the other part.

Contents

---

*Source: The Courier, Africa-Caribbean-Pacific-European Community, NO. 120, March-April 1990. The text of the Fourth Lomé Convention appears also in *International Legal Materials*, Volume 29, Number 4, July 1990 [Note added by the editor].

PART TWO
The areas of ACP-EEC cooperation

PART THREE
The instruments of ACP-EEC cooperation

PART FOUR
Operation of the institutions

PART FIVE
Final provisions

PROTOCOLS

Protocol 9   declarations annexed to that Convention concerning products within the province of the European Coal and Steel Community

*   *   *

His Majesty the King of the Belgians,
Her Majesty the Queen of Denmark,
The President of the Federal Republic of Germany,
The President of the Hellenic Republic,
His Majesty the King of Spain,
The President of the French Republic,
The President of Ireland,
The President of the Italian Republic,
His Royal Highness the Grand Duke of Luxembourg,
Her Majesty the Queen of the Netherlands,
The President of the Portuguese Republic,
Her Majesty the Queen of the United Kingdom of Great Britain and Northern Ireland,
Contracting Parties to the Treaty establishing the European Coal and Steel Community and the Treaty establishing the European Economic Community
hereinafter referred to as "the Community", the States of the Community being
hereinafter referred to as "Member States",
and the Council and the Commission of the European Communities,

of the one part, and

The President of the People's Republic of Angola,
Her Majesty the Queen of Antigua and Barbuda,
The Head of State of the Commonwealth of the Bahamas,
The Head of State of Barbados,
Her Majesty the Queen of Belize,
The President of the People's Republic of Benin,
The President of the Republic of Botswana,
The President of the People's Front, Head of State,
Head of the Government of Burkina Faso,
The President of the Republic of Burundi,
The President of the Republic of Cameroon,
The President of the Republic of Cape Verde,
The President of the Central African Republic,
The President of the Islamic Federal Republic of the Comoros,
The President of the People's Republic of the Congo,
The President of the Republic of the Côte d'Ivoire,

The President of the Republic of Djibouti,
The Government of the Commonwealth of Dominica,
The President of the Dominican Republic,
The President of the People's Democratic Republic of Ethiopia,
The President of the Republic of Fiji,
The President of the Gabonese Republic,
The President of the Republic of the Gambia,
The Head of State and Chairman of the Provisional National Defence Council of
The Republic of Ghana,
Her Majesty the Queen of Grenade,
The President of the Republic of Guinea,
The President of the Council of State of Guinea-Bissau,
The President of the Republic of Equatorial Guinea,
The President of the Co-operative Republic of Guyana,
The President of the Republic of Haiti,
The Head of State of Jamaica,
The President of the Republic of Kenya,
The President of the Republic of Kiribati,
The Majesty the King of the Kingdom of Lesotho,
The President of the Republic of Liberia,
The President of the Democratic Republic of Madagascar,
The President of the Republic of Malawi,
The President of the Republic of Mali,
The Chairman of the Military Committee for National Safety, Head of State of the
Islamic Republic of Mauritania,
Her Majesty the Queen of Mauritius,
The President of the People's Republic of Mozambique,
The President of the Supreme Military Council, Head of State of Niger,
The Head of the Federal Government of Nigeria,
The President of the Republic of Uganda,
Her Majesty the Queen of Papua New Guinea,
The President of the Rwandese Republic,
Her Majesty the Queen of Saint Kitts and Nevis,
Her Majesty the Queen of Saint Lucia,
Her Majesty the Queen of Saint Vincent and the Grenadines,
The Head of State of Western Samoa,
The President of the Democratic Republic of São Tomé and Príncipe,
The President of the Republic of Senegal,
The President of the Republic of Seychelles,
The President of the Republic of Sierra Leone,
Her Majesty the Queen of the Solomon Islands,
The President of the Somali Democratic Republic,
The President of the Republic of the Sudan,
The President of the Republic of Suriname,
Her Majesty the Queen Regent of the Kingdom of Swaziland,

The President of the United Republic of Tanzania,
The President of the Republic of Chad,
The President of the Togolese Republic,
His Majesty King Taufa'ahau Tupou IV of Tonga,
The President of the Republic of Trinidad and Tobago,
Her Majesty the Queen of Tuvalu,
The Government of the Republic of Vanuatu,
The President of the Republic of Zaïre,
The President of the Republic of Zambia,
The President of the Republic of Zimbabwe,

whose States are hereinafter referred to as "ACP States"

of the other part,

HAVING REGARD to the Treaty establishing the European Economic Community and the Treaty establishing the European Coal and Steel Community, on the one hand, and the Georgetown Agreement constituting the group of African, Caribbean and Pacific States, on the other;

ANXIOUS to reinforce, on the basis of complete equality between partners and in their mutual interest, close and continuing cooperation in a spirit of international solidarity;

WISHING to demonstrate their common desire to maintain and develop the friendly relations existing between their countries, in accordance with the principles of the Charter of the United Nations;

REAFFIRMING their adherence to the principles of the said Charter and their faith in fundamental human rights, in all aspects of human dignity and in the worth of the human person, as the central agent and beneficiary of development, in the equal rights of men and women and of nations, large and small;

RECALLING the Universal Declaration of Human Rights, the International Covenant on Civil and Political Rights, and the International Covenant on Economic, Social and Cultural Rights; recognizing the need to respect and guarantee civil and political rights and to strive to bring about full enjoyment of economic, social and cultural rights;

WELCOMING the Convention for the Protection of Human Rights and Fundamental Freedoms of the Council of Europe, the African Charter on Human and Peoples' Rights and the American Convention on Human Rights as positive regional contributions to the respect of human rights in the Community and in the ACP States;

RESOLVED to step up their common efforts to contribute towards international cooperation and to the solution of international problems of economic, social, intellectual and humanitarian nature, in conformity with the aspirations of the international community towards the establishment of a new, more just and more balanced world order;

RESOLVED to make, through their cooperation, a significant contribution to the economic, social and cultural development of the ACP States and to the greater well-being of their populations;

HAVE DECIDED to conclude this Convention and to this end have designated as their Plenipotentiaries:

PART ONE
General provisions of ACP-EEC cooperation

CHAPTER 1
Objectives and principles of cooperation

Article 1

The Community and its Member States, of the one part, and the ACP States, of the other part (hereinafter referred to as the Contracting Parties), hereby conclude this cooperation Convention in order to promote and expedite the economic, cultural and social development of the ACP States and to consolidate and diversify their relations in a spirit of solidarity and mutual interest.

The Contracting Parties thereby affirm their undertaking to continue, strengthen and render more effective the system of cooperation established under the first, second and third ACP-EEC Conventions and confirm the special character of their relations, based on their reciprocal interest, and the specific nature of their cooperation.

The Contracting Parties hereby express their resolve to intensify their effort to create, with a view to a more just and balanced international economic order, a model for relations between developed and developing states and to work together to affirm in the international context the principles underlying their cooperation.

Article 2

ACP-EEC cooperation, underpinned by a legally binding system and the existence of joint institutions, shall be exercised on the basis of the following fundamental principles:

-- equality between partners, respect for their sovereignty, mutual interest and interdependence;

-- the right of each State to determine its own political social, cultural and economic policy options;

-- security of their relations based on the acquis of their system of cooperation.

Article 3

The ACP States shall determine the development principles, strategies and models for their economies and societies in all sovereignty.

Article 4

Support shall be provided in ACP-EEC cooperation for the ACP States' efforts to achieve comprehensive self-reliant and self-sustained development based on their cultural and social values, their human capacities, their natural resources and their economic potential in order to promote the ACP States' social, cultural and economic progress and the well-being of their populations through the satisfaction of their basic needs, the recognition of the role of women and the enhancement of people's capacities, with respect for their dignity.

Such development shall be based on a sustainable balance between its economic objectives, the rational management of the environment and the enhancement of natural and human resources.

Article 5

1.   Cooperation shall be directed towards development centred on man, the main protagonist and beneficiary of development, which thus entails respect for and promotion of all human rights. Cooperation operations shall thus be conceived in accordance with the positive approach, where respect for human rights is recognized as a basic factor of real development and where cooperation is conceived as a contribution to the promotion of these rights.

In this context development policy and cooperation are closely linked with the respect for and enjoyment of fundamental human rights. The role and potential of initiatives taken by individuals and groups shall also be recognized and fostered in order to achieve in practice real participation of the population in the development process in accordance with Article 13.

2.   Hence the Parties reiterate their deep attachment to human dignity and human rights, which are legitimate aspirations of individuals and peoples. The rights in question are all human rights, the various categories thereof being indivisible and inter-related, each having its own legitimacy: nondiscriminatory treatment; fundamental human rights; civil and political rights; economic, social and cultural rights.

Every individual shall have the right, in his own country or in a host country, to respect for his dignity and protection by the law.

ACP-EEC cooperation shall help abolish the obstacles preventing individuals and peoples from actually enjoying to the full their economic, social and cultural rights and this must be achieved through the development which is essential to their dignity, their well-being and their self-fulfilment. To this end, the Parties shall strive, jointly or each in its own sphere of responsibility, to help eliminate the causes of situations of misery unworthy of the human condition and of deep-rooted economic and social inequalities.

The Contracting Parties hereby reaffirm their existing obligations and commitment in international law to strive to eliminate all forms of discrimination based on ethnic group, origin, race, nationality, colour, sex, language, religion or any other situation. This commitment applies more particularly to any situation in the ACP States or in the Community that may adversely affect the pursuit of the objectives of the Convention, and to the system of apartheid, having regard also to its destabilizing effects on the outside. The Member States (and/or, where appropriate, the Community itself) and the ACP States will continue to ensure, through the legal or administrative measures which they have or will have adopted, that migrant workers, students and other foreign nationals legally within their territory are not subjected to discrimination on the basis of racial, religious, cultural or social differences, notably in respect of housing, education, health care, other social
services and employment.

3.   At the request of the ACP States, financial resources may be allocated, in accordance with the rules governing development finance cooperation, to the promotion of human rights in the ACP States through specific schemes, public or private, that would be decided, particularly in the legal sphere, in consultation with bodies of internationally recognized competence in the field. Resources may also be given to support the establishment of structures to promote human rights. Priority shall be given to schemes of regional scope. [see also Annex IV-page 791]

Article 6

1.   With a view to attaining more balanced and self-reliant economic development in the ACP States, special efforts shall be made under this Convention to promote rural development, food security for the people, rational management of natural resources, and the preservation, revival and strengthening of agricultural production potential in the ACP States.

2.   The Contracting Parties recognize that priority must be given to environmental protection and the conservation of natural resources, which are essential conditions for sustainable and balanced development from both the economic and human viewpoints.

Article 7

The Community and the ACP States shall give special importance and high priority to regional cooperation and integration. In this context, the Convention shall offer effective support for the ACP States' efforts to organize themselves into regional groupings and to step up their cooperation at regional and inter-regional level with a view to promoting a new, more just and more balanced economic order.

Article 8

The Contracting Parties acknowledge the need to accord special treatment to the least-developed ACP States and to take account of the specific difficulties confronting the landlocked and island ACP States. They shall pay special attention to improving the living conditions of the poorest sections of the population.

Cooperation shall comprise, inter alia, special treatment when determining the volume of financial resources and the conditions attached thereto in order to enable the least-developed ACP States to overcome structural and other obstacles to their development.

For the landlocked and island ACP States, cooperation shall be aimed at devising and encouraging specific operations to deal with development problems caused by their geographical situations.

Article 9

In order to step up the effectiveness of the instruments of this Convention, the Contracting Parties shall adopt, in the framework of their respective responsibilities, guidelines, priorities and measures conducive to attaining the objectives set out in this Convention and agree to pursue, in accordance with the principles set out in Article 2, the dialogue within joint institutions and in the co-ordinated implementation of development finance cooperation and the other cooperation instruments.

Article 10

The Contracting Parties shall, each as far as it is concerned in the framework of this Convention, take all appropriate measures, whether general or particular, to ensure the fulfilment of the obligations arising from this Convention and to facilitate the pursuit of its objectives. They shall refrain from any measures liable to jeopardize the attainment of the objectives of this Convention.

Article 11

Within the scope of their respective responsibilities, the institutions of this Convention shall examine periodically the results of the application thereof, provide any necessary impetus and take any relevant decision or measure for the attainment of its objectives. Any question that might directly hamper the effective attainment of the objectives of this Convention may be raised in the context of the institutions.

Consultations shall take place within the Council of Ministers at the request of either Contracting Party in cases provided for in this Convention or where difficulties arise with the application or interpretation thereof.

Article 12

Where the Community intends, in the exercise of its powers, to take a measure which might affect the interests of the ACP States as far as this Convention's objectives are concerned, it shall inform in good time the said States of its intentions. Towards this end, the Commission shall communicate regularly to the Secretariat of the ACP States any proposals for such measures. Where necessary, a request for information may also take place on the initiative of the ACP States.

At their request, consultations shall be held in good time so that account may be taken of their concerns as to the impact of those measures before any final decision is made.

After such consultations have taken place, the ACP States shall also be provided with adequate information on the entry into force of such decisions, in advance whenever possible.

CHAPTER 2
Objectives and guidelines of the Convention in the main areas of cooperation

Article 13

Cooperation shall be aimed at supporting development in the ACP States, a process centred on man himself and rooted in each people's culture. It shall back up the policies and measures adopted by those States to enhance their human resources, increase their own creative capacities and promote their cultural identities. Cooperation shall also encourage participation by the population in the design and execution of development operations.

Account shall be taken, in the various fields of cooperation, and at all the different stages of the operations executed, of the cultural dimension and social implications of such operations and of the need for both men and women to participate and benefit on equal terms.

Article 17

The Community and the ACP States acknowledge that industrialization is a driving force -- complementary to agricultural and rural development -- in promoting the economic transformation of the ACP States in order to achieve self-sustained growth and balanced and diversified development. Industrial development is needed to enhance the productivity of the ACP economies so that they can meet basic human needs and step up the competitive participation of the ACP States in world trade by way of selling more value-added products.

Article 18

Given the extreme dependence of the economies of the vast majority of ACP States on their export of commodities, the Contracting Parties agree to pay particular attention to their cooperation in this sector with a view to supporting ACP States' policies or strategies designed:

-- on the one hand, to foster diversification, both horizontal and vertical, of the ACP economies, in particular through the development of processing, marketing, distribution and transport (PMDT) and,

-- on the other hand, to improve the competitiveness of the ACP States' commodities on world markets through the reorganization and rationalization of their production, marketing and distribution activities.

CHAPTER 3
Widening participation in cooperation activities

Article 20

In accordance with Articles 2, 3 and 13 and in order to encourage all parties from the ACP States and the Community which are in a position to contribute to the autonomous development of the ACP States to put forward and implement initiatives, cooperation shall also support, within limits laid down by the ACP States concerned, development operations put forward by economic, social and cultural organizations in the framework of decentralized cooperation, in particular where they combine the efforts and resources of organizations from the ACP States and their counterparts from the Community. This form of cooperation shall be aimed in particular at making the capabilities, original operating methods and resources of such parties available to the development of the ACP States.

The parties referred to in this Article are decentralized public authorities, rural and village groupings, co-operatives, firms, trade unions, teaching and research centres, non-governmental development organizations, various associations and all groups and parties which are able and wish to make their own spontaneous and original contribution to the development of ACP States.

CHAPTER 4
Principles governing the instruments of cooperation

Article 23

In order to contribute towards achieving the aims of this Convention, the Contracting Parties shall deploy cooperation instruments that correspond to the principles of solidarity and mutual interest, adapted to the economic, cultural and social situation in the ACP States and in the Community and to developments in their international environment.

These instruments shall be directed mainly, by strengthening the established mechanisms and systems, at:

--   increasing trade between the Parties;

--   supporting the ACP States' efforts to achieve self-reliant development by stepping up their capacity to innovate and to adapt and transform technology;

-- supporting the ACP States' structural adjustment efforts and thus contributing to the attenuation of the debt burden;

-- helping the ACP States to gain access to the capital markets and encouraging direct private European investment to contribute towards the development of the ACP States;

-- remedying the instability of export earnings from the ACP States' agricultural commodities and helping those countries to cope with serious disruptions affecting their mining industries.

Article 24

In order to promote and diversify trade between the Contracting Parties, the Community and the ACP States are agreed on:

-- general trade provisions;

-- special arrangements for Community import of certain ACP products;

-- arrangements to promote the development of the ACP States' trade and services, including tourism;

-- a system of reciprocal information and consultation designed to help apply the trade cooperation provisions of this Convention effectively.

Article 25

The aim of the general trade arrangements, which are based on the Contracting Parties' international obligations, shall be to provide a firm and solid foundation for trade cooperation between the ACP States and the Community.

They shall be based on the principle of free access to the Community market for products originating in the ACP States, with special provisions for agricultural products and a safeguard clause.

In view of the ACP States' present development needs, the arrangements shall not comprise any element of reciprocity for those States as regards free access. They shall also be based on the principle of non-discrimination by the ACP States between the Member States and the according to the Community of treatment no less favourable than the most-favoured-nation treatment.

Article 26

The Community shall contribute towards the ACP States' own development efforts by providing adequate financial resources and appropriate technical assistance aimed at stepping up those States' capacities for self-reliant and integrated economic, social and cultural development and also at helping to raise their populations' standard of living and well-being, and promote and mobilize resources in support of sustainable, effective and growth-oriented structural adjustment programmes.

Such contributions shall be made on a more predictable and continuous basis. They shall be provided at very highly concessional terms. Particular account shall be taken of the situation of the least-developed ACP States.

Article 27

The Contracting Parties agree to facilitate greater, more stable flows of resources from the private sector to the ACP States by taking measures to improve the access of ACP States to capital markets and to encourage European private investment in ACP States.

The Contracting Parties underline the need to promote, protect, finance and support investment and to provide equitable and stable conditions for the treatment of such investment.

Article 28

The Contracting Parties agree to confirm the importance of the system for the stabilization of export earnings, as well as of intensifying the process of consultation between the ACP States and the Community in international fora and organizations which aim to stabilize agricultural commodity markets.

Given the role played by the mining industry in the development efforts of numerous ACP States and the ACP-EEC mutual dependence in that sector, the Contracting Parties confirm the importance of the system established to help ACP States confronted with serious disruptions in that sector to restore it to a viable state and remedy the consequences of such disruptions for their development.

PART TWO
THE AREAS OF ACP-EEC COOPERATION

TITLE V
Industrial development, manufacturing and processing

Article 77

In order to facilitate the attainment of the industrial development objectives of the ACP States, it is important to ensure that an integrated and sustainable development strategy, which links activities in different sectors to each other, is evolved. Thus sectoral strategies for agricultural and rural development, manufacturing, mining, energy, infrastructure and services should be designed in such a way as to foster interlinkages within and between economic sectors with a view to maximizing local value added and creating, where possible, an effective capacity to export manufactured products, while ensuring the protection of the environment and natural resources.

In pursuit of these objectives the Contracting Parties shall have recourse to the provisions on trade promotion for ACP products and private investments, in addition to the specific provisions on industrial cooperation.

Article 78

Industrial cooperation, as a key instrument for industrial development, shall have as its objectives:

(a)   the creation of the basis of and framework for effective cooperation between the Community and the ACP States in the fields of manufacturing and processing, mineral resources development, energy resources development, transport and communications;

(b)   the promotion of conditions conducive to industrial enterprise development, and local and external investment;

(c)   improvement of capacity utilization and rehabilitation of existing industrial undertakings which are potentially viable, in order to restore the productive capacities of ACP economies;

(d)   fostering the creation of and the participation in enterprises by ACP nationals, especially those of a small and medium-size nature that produce and/or use local inputs; promotion of new and strengthening of existing enterprises;

(e)   support for the establishment of new industries to supply the local market in a cost-effective manner and ensure the growth of the non-traditional export sector in order to increase foreign exchange earnings, provide employment opportunities and an increase in real incomes;

(f)   promoting increasingly close relations in the industrial field between the Community and the ACP States, and in particular further encouraging the speedy establishment of ACP-EEC industrial joint ventures;

(g)   promoting business associations in ACP States as well as other institutions for industrial enterprise and business development.

Article 79

The Community shall assist the ACP States in the improvement of their institutional framework, reinforcement of their financing institutions and the establishment, rehabilitation and improvement of industry-related infrastructure. The Community shall equally assist the ACP States in their efforts to integrate industrial structures at regional and inter-regional level.

Article 80

On the basis of a request from an ACP State, the Community shall provide the assistance required in the field of industrial training at all levels, bearing notably on the evaluation of industrial training needs and the establishment of corresponding programmes, the setting-up and operation of national or regional ACP industrial training establishments, training for ACP nationals in appropriate establishments, on-the-job training both in the Community and in the ACP States and also cooperation between industrial training establishments in the Community and in the ACP States, and between the latter and those of other developing countries.

Article 81

In order to achieve the objectives of industrial development, the Community shall assist in the establishment and expansion of all types of viable industry which have been identified by the ACP States as important in terms of their industrialization objectives and priorities.

In this context the following areas merit particular attention:

(i)   manufacturing and processing of primary products:

(a) industries processing, on a national or regional basis, raw materials for export;

(b) industries based on local needs and resources, focused on domestic and regional markets and mainly small and medium-sized industries geared to the modernization of agriculture, the efficient processing of agricultural products and the manufacturing of agricultural inputs and tools;

(ii)   engineering, metallurgical and chemical industries:

(a) engineering enterprises for the production of tools and equipment primarily tailored to maintaining the existing plant and equipment in the ACP States. These enterprises should, as a matter of priority, support the manufacturing and processing sector, the major export sectors, and small and medium-sized enterprises directed at satisfying basic needs;

(b) metallurgical industries based on the mining products of the ACP States, aimed at the secondary processing of mining products to supply ACP engineering and chemical industries;

(c) chemical industries, particularly on a small and medium scale, aimed at the secondary processing of mineral products to supply the other branches of industry, and also the agricultural and health sectors;

(iii)   industrial rehabilitation and capacity utilization: the restoration, upgrading, reorganization, restructuring and maintenance of existing potentially viable industrial capacities. Special emphasis should be put in this respect on industries with a low import content that provide up-stream and down-stream linkages and have a favourable effect on employment. Rehabilitation activities should be targeted at the creation of conditions necessary to make enterprises being rehabilitated self-sustaining.

Article 82

The Community shall assist the ACP States to develop, during the period of application of this Convention, as a matter of priority, viable industries, as defined in Article 81, in accordance with the capacities and decisions of each ACP State and their respective endowments taking into account the adjustment of industrial structures taking place between the Contracting Parties and throughout the world.

Article 83

The Community shall contribute in a spirit of mutual interest to the development of ACP-EEC and intra-ACP cooperation between enterprises by way of information and industrial promotion activities.

The aim of such activities shall be to intensify the regular exchange of information, organize the contacts required in the industrial sphere between industrial policy-makers, promoters and economic operators from the Community and the ACP States, carry out studies, notably feasibility studies, facilitate the establishment and operation of ACP industrial promotion bodies and foster joint investment, subcontracting arrangements and any other form of industrial cooperation between enterprises in the Member States of the Community and in the ACP States.

Article 84

The Community shall contribute to the establishment and development of small and medium-sized enterprises in the artisanal, commercial, service and industrial sectors in view of the essential role that these enterprises play in the modern and informal sectors in building up a diversified economic fabric and in the general development of the ACP countries, and in view of the advantages they offer as regards the acquisition of skills, the integrated transfer and adaptation of appropriate technology and opportunities for taking the best advantage of local manpower. The Community shall also help with sectoral evaluation and the establishment of action programmes, with the setting-up of appropriate infrastructure, the establishment, strengthening and operation of institutions providing information, promotion, extension, training, credit or guarantee and transfer of technology facilities.

The Community and the ACP States shall encourage cooperation and contact between small and medium-sized enterprises in the Member States and the ACP States.

Article 85

With a view to assisting the ACP States to develop their technological base and indigenous capacity for scientific and technological development and facilitating the acquisition, transfer and adaptation of technology on terms that will seek to bring about the greatest possible benefits and minimize costs, the Community, through the instruments of development finance cooperation, is prepared, inter alia, to contribute to:

(a)   the establishment and strengthening of industry-related scientific and technical infrastructure in the ACP States;

(b)   the drawing-up and implementation of research and development programmes;

(c)   the identification and creation of opportunities for collaboration among research institutes, institutions of higher learning and enterprises of ACP States, the Community, the Member States and other countries;

(d)   the establishment and promotion of activities aimed at the consolidation of appropriate indigenous technology and the acquisition of relevant foreign technology, in particular that of other developing countries;

(e)   the identification, evaluation and acquisition of industrial technology including the negotiation on favourable terms and conditions of foreign technology, patents and other industrial property, in particular through financing or through other suitable arrangements with firms and institutions within the Community;

(f)   providing ACP States with advisory services for the preparation of regulations governing the transfer of technology and for the supply of available information, in particular on the terms and conditions of technology contracts, the types and sources of technology, and the experience of ACP States and other countries with the use of certain types of technology;

(g)   the promotion of technology cooperation between ACP States and between them and other developing countries, including support to research and development units in particular at regional level, in order to make the best use of any particularly appropriate scientific and technical facilities they may possess;

(h)   facilitating, wherever possible, access to and use of documentary and other data sources available in the Community.

Article 86

In order to enable the ACP States to obtain full benefit from the trade arrangements and other provisions of this Convention, promotion schemes shall be undertaken for the marketing of ACP States' industrial products on both Community and other external markets, and also in order to stimulate and develop trade in industrial products among the ACP States. Such schemes shall cover market research, marketing and the quality and standardization of manufactured goods, in accordance with Articles 229 and 230 and taking into account Articles 135 and 136.

Article 87

1.   A Committee on Industrial Cooperation, supervised by the Committee of Ambassadors, shall:

(a)   review progress made with the overall industrial cooperation programme resulting from this Convention and, where appropriate, submit recommendations to the Committee of Ambassadors; in this framework it shall examine and give its opinion on the reports referred to in Article 327 concerning the progress of industrial cooperation and the growth of investment flows, and regularly monitor the mechanics of the interventions undertaken by the European Investment Bank, hereinafter referred to as "the Bank", the Commission, the Centre for the Development of Industry, hereinafter referred to as "the CDI" and the ACP authorities responsible for the implementation of industrial projects in order to ensure the best possible coordination;

(b)   examine problems and policy issues in the field of industrial cooperation submitted to it by the ACP States or by the Community, and make any appropriate proposals;

(c)   organize, at the request of the Community or of the ACP States, a review of trends in industrial policies of the ACP States and of the Member States as well as developments in the world industrial situation with a view to exchanging information necessary for improving cooperation in and facilitating the industrial development and related mining and energy activities of the ACP States;

(d)   establish, on a proposal of the Executive Board, the general strategy of the CDI referred to in Article 89, appoint the members of the Advisory Council, appoint the director and deputy director, appoint the two auditors, apportion on an annual basis the overall financial allocation provided for in Article 3 of the Financial Protocol and approve the budget and annual accounts;

(e)   examine the CDI's annual report and any other report presented by the Advisory Council or the Executive Board in order to assess whether the CDI's activities are in conformity with the objectives assigned to it in this Convention, report to the Committee of Ambassadors and, through it, to the Council of Ministers and carry out such other duties as may be assigned to it by the Committee of Ambassadors.

2.   The composition of the Committee on Industrial Cooperation and the detailed rules for its operation shall be determined by the Council of Ministers. The Committee shall meet at least twice a year.

Article 88

A joint Advisory Council, composed of 24 members drawn from the business world or experts on industrial development, with representatives of the Commission, the Bank and the ACP Secretariat present as observers, shall allow the Committee on Industrial Cooperation to take into account the point of view of industrial operators concerning matters referred to in

Article 87(1)(a), (b) and (c). The Advisory Council shall meet formally once a year.

Article 89

The CDI shall help to establish and strengthen industrial enterprises in the ACP States, notably by encouraging joint initiatives by economic operators of the Community and the ACP States.

As a practical operational instrument, the CDI shall give priority to the identification of industrial operators for viable projects, assist in the promotion and implementation of those projects that meet the needs of ACP States, taking special account of domestic and external market opportunities for the processing of local raw materials while making optimum use of the ACP States' endowments by way of factors of production. Assistance shall also be given to the presentation of such projects to the financing institutions.

In carrying out the above tasks, the CDI shall take care to operate selectively by giving priority to small and medium-sized industrial enterprises and rehabilitation operations, and restoring existing industrial capacities to full utilization. It shall place special emphasis on opportunities for joint ventures and subcontracting. In implementing these tasks, the CDI shall also pay special attention to the objectives referred to in Article 97.

Article 90

1. In undertaking the tasks referred to in Article 89 the CDI shall operate by giving priority to viable projects. In particular, it shall:

(a) identify, appraise, evaluate, promote and assist in the implementation of economically viable industrial projects of the ACP States;

(b) carry out studies and appraisals aimed at identifying practical opportunities for industrial cooperation with the Community in order to promote the industrial development of the ACP States, and facilitating the implementation of appropriate schemes;

(c) supply information and also specific advisory services and expertise, including feasibility studies, with a view to expediting the establishment and/or restoration of industrial enterprises;

(d) identify potential partners of the ACP States and the Community for joint investment operations and assist in the implementation and follow-up;

(e) identify and provide information on possible sources of financing, assist in the presentation for financing, and, where necessary, assist in the mobilization of funds from these sources for industrial projects in ACP States;

(f) identify, collect, evaluate and supply information and advice on the acquisition, adaptation and development of appropriate industrial technology relating to specific projects and, where appropriate, assist in the setting-up of experimental or demonstration schemes.

2.   In order to improve the attainment of its objectives, the CDI, in addition to its main activities, may also pursue the following:

(a)   carry out studies, market research and evaluation work and gather and disseminate all relevant information on the industrial cooperation situation and opportunities and notably on the economic environment, the treatment which potential investors may expect and the potential of viable industrial projects;

(b)   help, in appropriate cases, to promote the marketing of ACP manufactures on their domestic markets and on the markets of the other ACP States and the Community in order to encourage optimum exploitation of installed or projected industrial capacity;

(c)   identify industrial policy-makers, promoters and economic and financial operators in the Community and ACP States, and organize and facilitate contacts and meetings of all kinds between them;

(d)   identify, on the basis of needs indicated by ACP States, opportunities in industrial training, chiefly on the job, to meet the requirements of existing and planned industrial undertakings in ACP States and, where necessary, assist in the implementation of appropriate schemes;

(e)   gather and disseminate all relevant information concerning the industrial potential of the ACP States and trends of industrial sectors in the Community and the ACP States;

(f)   promote the subcontracting and also the expansion and consolidation of regional industrial projects.

Article 91

The CDI shall be headed by a director assisted by a deputy director, recruited on the basis of technical skills and management experience, both of whom shall be appointed by the Committee on Industrial Cooperation. The management of the CDI shall implement the guidelines laid down by the Committee on Industrial Cooperation, and shall be answerable to the Executive Board.

Article 92

1. A joint Executive Board shall:

(a)   advise and back up the director in providing impetus and motivation in managing the CDI and shall ensure that the guidelines laid down by the Committee on Industrial Cooperation are implemented satisfactorily;

(b)   on a proposal from the director of the CDI,

(i) approve:
-- multiannual and annual programmes of activities,
-- the annual report,
-- the organizational structures, staffing policy and establishment plan, and

(ii)   adopt the budgets and annual accounts for submission to the Committee on Industrial Cooperation;

(c)   take decisions on management proposals related to these issues;

(d)   transmit an annual report to the Committee on Industrial Cooperation and report on any problems arising in connection with the points referred to in (c).

2.   The Executive Board shall be composed of six persons with substantial experience in the private or public industrial or banking sectors or in industrial development planning and promotion. They shall be chosen by the Committee on Industrial Cooperation on the grounds of their qualifications among nationals of the States Party to this Convention and appointed by that Committee according to the procedures laid down by it. A representative of the Commission, of the Bank and of the ACP Secretariat shall take part in the Board's proceedings as observers. In order to ensure a close follow-up of CDI activities, the Board shall meet at least once every two months. The secretariat shall be provided by the Centre.

Article 93

1.   The Community shall contribute to the financing of the CDI's budget by means of a separate allocation in accordance with the Financial Protocol annexed hereto.

2.   Two auditors appointed by the Committee on Industrial Cooperation shall audit the financial management of the CDI.

3.   The CDI's statute, financial and staff regulations and rules of procedure shall be adopted by the Council of Ministers on a proposal from the Committee of Ambassadors after the entry into force of this Convention.

Article 94

The Centre shall step up its operational presence in the ACP States, notably as regards identification of projects and promoters and assistance in the submission of applications for financing.

It shall do this in accordance with procedures proposed by the Executive Board, taking account of the need to decentralize activities.

Article 95

The Commission, the Bank and the CDI shall maintain close operational cooperation in the context of their respective responsibilities.

Article 96

Members of the Advisory Council, the Executive Board and the director and deputy director of the CDI shall be appointed for a period of no longer than five years, subject to a reservation in the case of the Executive Board that the situation be reviewed mid-term.

Article 97

1.   In implementing this Title, the Community shall pay special attention to the specific needs and problems of the least-developed, landlocked and island ACP States in order to establish the basis for their industrialization (the formulation of industrial policies and strategies, economic infrastructure and industrial training), notably with a view to adding value to raw materials and other local resources in the following fields in particular:

-- processing of raw materials;
-- development, transfer and adaptation of technologies;
-- development and financing of schemes in favour of small and medium-sized enterprises;
-- development of industrial infrastructure and energy and mining resources;
-- adequate training in the scientific and technical areas;
-- production of equipment and inputs for the rural sector.

Such operations may be implemented with assistance from the CDI.

2.   At the request of one or more least-developed ACP States, the CDI shall grant special assistance for identifying on-the-spot industrial promotion and development possibilities, notably in raw materials processing and the production of equipment and inputs for the rural sector.

Article 98

In order to implement industrial cooperation, the Community shall help carry out programmes, projects and operations submitted to it on the initiative or with the agreement of the ACP States. To this end, it shall use all the means provided in this Convention, notably those at its disposal under development finance cooperation and, in particular, those which are the responsibility of the Bank, without prejudice to operations to assist ACP States in mobilizing finance from other sources.

Industrial cooperation programmes, projects and operations which involve Community financing shall be implemented in conformity with Title III, Part Three, of this Convention, having regard to the particular characteristics of aid operations in the industrial sector.

TITLE VIII
Enterprise development

Article 110

1. The Community and the ACP States stress that:

(i) enterprises constitute one of the main instruments for achieving the objectives of strengthening the economic fabric, encouraging inter-sectoral integration and increasing employment, incomes and the level of skills;

(ii) present ACP efforts to restructure their economies should be complemented by efforts to strengthen and enlarge their productive base. The enterprise sector should play an important part in the ACP States' strategies to revive growth;

(iii) a stable and propitious environment should be created together with an effective domestic financial sector with a view to reinvigorating the enterprise sector in the ACP States and to encouraging European investment;

(iv) the private sector needs to be made more dynamic and play a greater role, in particular through small and medium-sized enterprises, which are better suited to conditions prevailing in the ACP economies. Micro-firms and crafts should equally be encouraged and supported;

(v) private foreign investors complying with the objectives and priorities of ACP-EEC development cooperation should be encouraged to participate in the development efforts of the ACP States. Fair and equitable treatment should be accorded to such investment as well as a propitious, secure and predictable investment climate;

(vi) the fostering of ACP entrepreneurship is crucial for unlocking the considerable potential of the ACP States.

2. Efforts should be made to channel an increased proportion of the Convention's financial resources both to the encouragement of entrepreneurship and investment and towards directly productive activities.

Article 111

In pursuit of the abovementioned objectives, the Contracting Parties recognize the need to utilize the full range of instruments provided for by this Convention, including technical assistance, in the following areas with a view to sustaining private sector development:

(a) support for the improvement of the legal and fiscal framework for business, and development of a greater role for professional organizations and chambers of commerce in the process of enterprise development;

(b) direct assistance for the creation and the development of business (specialized business start-up services; assistance for the redeployment of ex-public sector employees; assistance for technology transfers and development; management services and market research);

(c) the development of services in support of the enterprise sector so as to provide enterprises with advisory services in the legal, technical and managerial fields;

(d) specific programmes to training and developing the capacity of individual entrepreneurs, particularly in the small-scale and informal sectors.

Article 112

In order to support the development of the savings and domestic financial sectors, the following areas of action merit special attention:

(a) assistance for the mobilization of domestic savings and the development of financial intermediaries;

(b) technical assistance for the restructuring and reform of financial institutions.

Article 113

With a view to assisting enterprise development in ACP States, the Community shall provide technical and financial assistance, subject to the conditions laid down in the development finance cooperation Title.

TITLE IX
Development of services

CHAPTER 1
Objectives and principles of cooperation

Article 114

1. The Community and the ACP States recognize the importance of services in the formulation of development policies and the need to step up cooperation in this sphere.

2. The Community shall support the ACP States' efforts to increase their domestic capacity to provide services with a view to improving the working of their economies, relieving balance of payment constraints and stimulating the process of regional integration.

3. The object is to ensure that the ACP States derive maximum benefit from the provisions of this Convention, at national and regional level, and to enable them to:

-- participate under the most favourable conditions in Community, domestic, regional and international markets by diversifying the range and increasing the value and volume of ACP States' trade in goods and services;

-- increase their collective capacity by means of greater economic integration and consolidation of functional cooperation or cooperation on specific themes;

-- stimulate enterprise development, notably by encouraging ACP-EEC investment in services, with a view to creating employment, generating and distributing revenue and facilitating the transfer and adaptation of technology to specific ACP needs;

-- derive maximum benefit from national or regional tourism and improve their participation in world tourism;

-- set up the transport and communications networks and informatics and telematics systems needed for their development;

-- step up vocational training activities and transfer of know-how in view of the determining role of human resources in the development of services.

4.   In pursuit of these aims, the Contracting Parties shall have recourse, in addition to the specific provisions on services, to those on trade, trade promotion, industrial development, investment and education and training.

Article 115

1.   In view of the wide range of services and their unequal contribution to development, and with a view to maximizing the impact of Community aid on the development of ACP States, the two Parties agree to pay particular attention to services necessary for their economies in the following areas:

-- services that support economic development;

-- tourism;

-- transport, communications and information technology.

2.   In order to implement cooperation in services, the Community shall help carry out programmes, projects and operations submitted to it on the initiative of the ACP States. To this end, it shall use all the means provided for in this Convention, notably those at its disposal under development finance cooperation, including those which are the responsibility of the Bank.

Article 116

In the field of the development of services, particular attention shall be given to the specific needs of landlocked and island ACP States arising from their geographic situation and also to the economic situations of least-developed ACP States.

CHAPTER 2
Services that support economic development
Article 117

In pursuit of cooperation objectives in this sector, cooperation shall concern marketed services, without, however, this leading to neglect of certain para-statal services required to improve the economic environment, such as customs computerization, by giving priority to the following services:

-- services that support foreign trade;

-- services required by the business sector;

-- services that support regional integration.

Article 118

To help restore the ACP States' external competitiveness, cooperation in the field of services shall give priority to services that support external trade, the scope of which is as follows:

(i)   the creation of appropriate infrastructure for trade, in particular through operations to improve external trade statistics, automation of customs procedures, port and airport management and the establishment of closer links between the various protagonists in trade, including exporters, trade financing bodies, customs and central banks;

(ii)   the promotion of specifically trade-oriented services such as trade promotion measures that are also applicable to services;

(iii)   the development of other external trade-linked services such as trade financing and clearing and payment facilities, and access to information networks.

Article 119

To foster a strengthening of the economic fabric of ACP States, taking account of the provisions on enterprise development, particular attention shall be paid to the following areas:

(i)   business advisory services to improve the running of firms, notably by facilitating access to services in the fields of management, accountancy, information technology, legal advice, tax consultancy and finance;

(ii)   the setting-up of adequate, appropriate and flexible business financing facilities to stimulate the growth or setting-up of firms in the field of services;

(iii)   strengthening the ACP States' capacity in financial services, technical assistance for developing insurance and credit institutions in the field of trade development and promotion.

Article 120

To underpin economic integration designed to create viable economies, and in view of the provisions on regional cooperation, particular attention shall be given to the following areas:

(i)   services to support trade in goods between ACP States through trade measures such as market studies;

(ii)   services required for the expansion of trade in services between ACP States with a view to enhancing their complementarity, notably by extending traditional trade promotion measures, adapted where necessary to the services sector;

(iii)   the creation of regional centres of services aimed at supporting specific economic sectors or jointly implemented sectoral policies, notably through the development of modern communications and information networks and computerized data banks.

CHAPTER 3
Tourism

Article 121

Recognizing the real importance of the tourist industry for the ACP States, the Contracting Parties shall implement measures and operations to develop and support tourism. These measures shall be implemented at all levels, from the identification of the tourist product to the marketing and promotion stage.

The aim shall be to support the ACP States' efforts to derive maximum benefit from national, regional and international tourism in view of tourism's impact on economic development and to stimulate private financial flows from the Community and other sources into the development of tourism in the ACP States. Particular attention shall be given to the need to integrate tourism into the social, cultural and economic life of the people.

Article 122

Specific tourism development measures shall aim at the definition, adaptation and development of appropriate policies at national, regional, subregional and international levels. Tourism development programmes and projects shall be based on these policies on the basis of the following four components:

(a) Human resources and institutional development, inter alia:

-- professional management development in specific skills and continuous training at appropriate levels in the private and public sectors to ensure adequate planning and development;

-- establishment and strengthening of tourism promotion centres;

-- education and training for specific segments of the population and public/private organizations active in the tourism sector, including personnel involved in the support sector of tourism;

--intra-ACP cooperation and exchanges in the fields of training, technical assistance and the development of institutions;

(b)   Product development, inter alia:

-- identification of the tourism product, development of non-traditional and new tourism products, adaptation of existing products including the preservation and development of cultural heritage, ecological and environmental aspects, management, protection and conservation of flora and fauna, historical, social and other natural assets, development of ancillary services;

-- promotion of private investment in the tourist industry of ACP States, including the creation of joint ventures;

-- provision of technical assistance for the hotel industry;

-- production of crafts of a cultural nature for the tourist market.

(c)   Market development, inter alia:

-- assistance for the definition and execution of objectives and market development plans at national, subregional, regional and international levels;

-- provision of support for ACP States' efforts to gain access to services for the tourist industry such as central reservation systems and air traffic control and security systems;

-- provision of marketing and promotional measures and materials in the framework of integrated market development plans and programmes and with a view to improved market penetration, aimed at the main generators of tourism flows in traditional and non-traditional origin markets as well as specific activities such as participation at specialized trade events, such as fairs, production of quality literature, films and marketing aids.

(d)   Research and information, inter alia:

-- improving tourism information and collecting, analysing, disseminating and utilizing statistical data;

-- assessment of the socio-economic impact of tourism on the economies of ACP States with particular emphasis on the development of linkages to other sectors in ACP States and regions such as food production, construction, technology and management.

CHAPTER 4
Transport, communications and informatics
Article 123

1.   Cooperation in the area of transport shall be aimed at the development of road transport, railways, port installations and shipping, transport by domestic waterways and air transport.

2.   Cooperation in the area of communications shall be aimed at the development of postal services and telecommunications, including radiocommunications and informatics.

3.   Cooperation in these areas shall be directed particularly towards the following objectives:

(a)   the creation of conditions fostering the movement of goods, services and persons at national, regional and international level;

(b)   the provision, rehabilitation, maintenance and efficient operation of cost-effective systems serving the requirements of social and economic development and adjusted to the needs of users and to the overall economic situation of the States concerned;

(c)   greater complementarity of transport and communications systems at national, regional and international level;

(d)   the harmonization of the national systems installed in ACP States, while facilitating their adjustment to technological progress;

(e)   the reduction of barriers to frontier-crossing transport and communications, in terms of legislation, regulations and administrative procedures.

Article 124

1.   In all cooperation projects and programmes in the fields concerned, efforts shall be made to ensure an appropriate transfer of technology and know-how.

2.   Particular attention shall be given to training ACP nationals in the planning, management, maintenance and operation of transport and communications systems.

Article 125

1.   The Contracting Parties recognize the importance of air transport in forgoing closer economic, cultural and social links between the ACP States and between them and the Community, in improving the communications of isolated or not easily accessible regions and

in developing tourism.

2.   The objective of cooperation in this field shall be to promote the harmonious development of national and regional ACP air transport networks and the modernization of the ACP fleet of aircraft in line with technical progress, the implementation of the International Civil Aviation Organization air navigation plan, the improvement of reception infrastructures and the application of international operating standards, the development and improvement of air maintenance centres, the provision of training and the development of modern airport security systems.

Article 126

1.   The Contracting Parties acknowledge the importance of shipping services as one of the forces behind economic development and promotion of trade between them.

2.   The objective of cooperation in this field shall be to ensure harmonious development of efficient and reliable shipping services on economically satisfactory terms by facilitating the active participation of all parties according to the principle of unrestricted access to the trade on a commercial basis.

Article 127

1.   The Contracting Parties underline the importance of the United Nations Convention on a Code of Conduct for Liner Conferences and the ratification instruments thereof, which safeguard the terms of competition in maritime matters and afford, inter alia, the shipping lines of developing countries extended opportunities to participate in the conference system.

2.   Consequently, the Contracting Parties are agreed, when ratifying the Code, on taking prompt measures for its implementation at national level, in conformity with its scope and provisions. The Community shall assist ACP States to apply the relevant provisions of the Code.

3.   In conformity with Resolution 2 on non-Conference lines, annexed to the Code, the Contracting Parties shall not prevent non-Conference lines from operating in competition with a Conference line as long as they comply with the principle of fair competition on a commercial basis.

Article 128

Attention shall be given in the context of cooperation to encouraging the efficient shipment of cargo at economically and commercially meaningful rates and to the aspirations of ACP States for greater participation in such international shipping services. In this respect, the Community acknowledges the aspirations of the ACP States for greater participation in bulk cargo shipping. The Contracting Parties agree that competitive access to the trade shall not be impaired.

Article 129

In the framework of financial and technical assistance for shipping, special attention shall be given to:

-- effective development of efficient and reliable shipping services in the ACP States, notably the gearing of port infrastructure to meet traffic requirements and the maintenance of port equipment;

-- maintenance or acquisition of handling equipment and watercraft and their modernization in line with technical progress;

-- development of inter-regional shipping with a view to encouraging intra-ACP cooperation and improvements in the functioning of ACP shipping;

-- technology transfer including multimodal transport and containerization for the promotion of joint ventures;

-- setting-up of appropriate legislative and administrative infrastructure and the improvement of port management, notably through vocational training;

-- development of inter-island shipping services and connecting infrastructure and to increased cooperation with economic operators.

Article 130

The Contracting Parties undertake to promote shipping safety, security of crews and the prevention of pollution.

Article 131

In order to ensure the effective implementation of Articles 126 to 130, consultation may take place, at the request of either Contracting Party, where necessary under the conditions provided for in the rules of procedure referred to in Article 11.

Article 132

1.   In the field of cooperation on communications, particular attention shall be paid to technological development in supporting ACP States' efforts to establish and develop effective systems. This includes studies and programmes concerning satellite communication, where this is justified by operational considerations, in particular at regional and subregional level. Cooperation shall also cover means of observation of the earth by satellite for meteorology and remote sensing purposes, notably their use for desertification control, halting all forms of pollution, the management of natural resources, agriculture and mining in particular, and land use planning.

2.   Particular importance shall be attached to telecommunications in rural areas, in order to stimulate their economic and social development.

Article 133

The aim of cooperation in the field of information technology shall be the building-up of the ACP States' information technology and telematics capacity by offering countries which wish to give high priority to this sector support for their efforts to acquire and install information technology systems; the development of efficient telematic networks, including international financial information; the production, in time, of computer components and software in the ACP States; their participation in international activities in the field of data processing and the publication of books and reviews.

Article 134

Cooperation activities in the transport and communications fields shall be carried out in accordance with the provisions and procedures laid down in Title III, Part Three, of this Convention.

Article 165

1.   With a view to encouraging regional cooperation between the least-developed, landlocked and island countries, particular attention shall be paid to these countries' specific problems at the regional programming stage and in the implementation.

2.   As regards financing, the least-developed ACP States shall be given priority in any project involving at least one ACP State in that category, while special attention shall be paid to the landlocked and island ACP States in order to overcome the obstacles holding back their development.

Article 166

For the purposes set out in the present Title, the amount of the Community's financial assistance is provided for in Article 3 of the Financial Protocol to this Convention.

PART THREE
The instruments of ACP-EEC cooperation

TITLE III
Development finance cooperation

CHAPTER 3
Investment

SECTION 1
Investment promotion

Article 258

The ACP States and the Community, recognizing the importance of private investment in the promotion of their development cooperation and acknowledging the need to take steps to promote such investment, shall:

(a) implement measures to encourage participation in their development efforts by private investors who comply with the objectives and priorities of ACP-EEC development cooperation and with the appropriate laws and regulations of their respective States;

(b) accord fair and equitable treatment to such investors;

(c) take measures and actions which help to create and maintain a predictable and secure investment climate as well as enter into negotiations on agreements which will improve such climate;

(d) promote effective cooperation amongst ACP and between ACP and Community economic operators in order to increase the flow of capital, management skills, technology and other forms of know-how;

(e) facilitate a greater and more stable flow of resources from the Community private sector to the ACP States by contributing to the removal of obstacles which impede the ACP States' access to international capital markets, and in particular within the Community;

(f) create an environment which encourages the development of financial institutions and the mobilization of resources which are essential to capital formation and the growth of entrepreneurship;

(g) promote the development of enterprises by taking such steps as are necessary to improve the business environment and, in particular, foster a legal, administrative and incentive framework which is conducive to the emergence and development of dynamic private sector enterprises including grass roots operations;

(h) strengthen the capacity of national institutions in ACP States to provide the range of services which can encourage greater national participation in business activity.

Article 259

In order to encourage private investment flows and the development of enterprises, the ACP States and the Community, in cooperation with other interested bodies, shall within the framework of the Convention:

(a) support efforts aimed at promoting European private investment in the ACP States by organizing discussions between any interested ACP State and potential investors on the legal and financial framework that ACP States might offer to investors;

(b) encourage the flow of information on investment opportunities by organizing investment promotion meetings, providing periodic information on existing financial or other specialized institutions, their facilities and conditions and encouraging the establishment of focal points for such meetings;

(c) encourage the dissemination of information on the nature and availability of investment guarantees and insurance mechanisms to facilitate investment in ACP States;

(d) provide assistance to small and medium-sized enterprises in ACP States in designing and obtaining equity and loan financing on optimal terms and conditions;

(e) explore ways and means of overcoming or reducing the host-country risk for individual investment projects which could contribute to economic progress;

(f) provide assistance to ACP States in:

(i) creating or strengthening the ACP States' capacity to improve the quality of feasibility studies and the preparation of projects in order that appropriate economic and financial conclusions might be drawn;

(ii) producing integrated project management mechanisms covering the entire project development cycle within the framework of the development programme of the State.

SECTION 2
Investment protection

Article 260

The Contracting Parties affirm the need to promote and protect either party's investments on their respective territories, and in this context affirm the importance of concluding between States, in their mutual interest, investment promotion and protection agreements which could also provide the basis for insurance and guarantee schemes.

Article 261

1.   A Contracting State may request the negotiation of an investment promotion and protection agreement with another Contracting State.

2.   The States party to such agreements shall practise no discrimination between Contracting States party to this Convention or against each other in relation to third countries when opening negotiations for, concluding, applying and interpreting bilateral or multilateral investment promotion and protection agreements.

By "non-discrimination", the Parties understand that, in negotiating such agreements, either side may be entitled to provisions in agreements negotiated between the ACP States or Member States concerned and another State, provided that in every case reciprocity is accorded.

3.   The Contracting States shall have the right to request a modification or adaptation of the non-discriminatory treatment referred to in paragraph 2 when international obligations or changed de facto circumstances so necessitate.

4.   The application of the principles referred to in paragraphs 2 and 3 does not purport to and cannot in practice, infringe the sovereignty of any Contracting State party to the Convention.

5.   The relation between the date of entry into force of any agreement negotiated, provisions for the settlement of disputes and the date of the investments concerned will be set out in the said agreement, account being taken of paragraphs 1 to 4. The Contracting Parties confirm that retroactivity shall not apply as a general principle unless Contracting States stipulate otherwise.

Article 262

In order further to encourage European investment in development projects of special importance to, and promoted by, the ACP States, the Community and the Member States, on the one hand, and the ACP States, on the other, may also conclude agreements relating to specific projects of mutual interest where the Community and European enterprises contribute towards their financing.

SECTION 3
Investment financing

Article 263

1.   With a view to assisting the implementation of directly productive investment, both public and private, contributing to the economic and industrial development of the ACP States, the Community shall provide financial assistance, subject to the provisions laid down in Chapter 2 of this Title, in the form of risk capital and/or loans from the Bank's own resources. This financial assistance may be used inter alia for:

(a) increasing, directly or indirectly, the own resources of ACP public, semi-public or private enterprises and providing financing in the form of loans for investment in such enterprises.

(b) supporting productive investment projects and programmes identified and promoted by the joint bodies set up by the Community and the ACP States in accordance with the Convention;

(c) financing schemes in favour of small and medium-sized enterprises.

2.   In order to achieve the objectives set out in paragraph 1, a significant part of risk capital shall be devoted to supporting private sector investment.

Article 264

In addition to the resources provided for above, the ACP State or States may use the resources of the national or regional programme, inter alia, for:

(a) financing schemes in favour of small and medium-sized enterprises;

(b) encouraging the setting-up or the strengthening of national or regional financial institutions in order to enable them effectively to support private sector needs;

(c) appropriate and effective support for export promotion;

(d) providing general or specific technical cooperation to cater for private sector needs.

Article 265

The financing of directly productive projects may concern new investments as well as the rehabilitation or utilization of existing capacity.

Article 266

Where the financing is undertaken through an on-lending body, it shall be the responsibility of that body to select and appraise individual projects and to administer the funds placed at its disposal in the conditions provided for in this Convention and by mutual agreement between the parties.

SECTION 4
Investment support

Article 267

In order effectively to achieve the various objectives of the Convention in relation to promoting private investment and to realize its multiplying effect, the Bank and/or the Commission shall participate by way of:

(a) financial assistance, including equity participations;

(b) technical assistance;

(c) advisory services;

(d) information and coordination services.

Article 268

1.   The Bank shall utilize risk capital resources to supplement the activities aimed at promoting and providing support for the private sectors in the ACP States. To this end, risk capital may be used to:

(a) provide direct loans for the investment in ACP States' public, semi-public and private enterprises, including SMEs;

(b) increase the own resources, or resources treated as such, of public, semi-public or private enterprises through direct holdings in the name of the Community;

(c) participate, with the agreement of the ACP State, in the capital of financial institutions promoting private investment in ACP States;

(d) provide finance to ACP States' financial institutions or, with the agreement of the ACP State concerned, ACP and/or Community promoters wishing to invest, in addition to their own contribution, in ACP-EEC joint ventures in order to reinforce the own resources of ACP enterprises;

(e) with the agreement of the ACP State or States concerned, assist ACP or Community financial intermediaries which contribute towards the financing of SMEs in the ACP States in:

(i) acquiring participations in the capital of ACP SMEs;

(ii) funding the acquisition of participations in ACP SMEs by ACP private investors and/or Community promoters in the conditions laid down in (d);

(iii) on-lending for financing investment in ACP States' SMEs;

(f) assist with the restructuring or recapitalization of financial institutions of the ACP States;

(g) finance specific studies, research or investment for the preparation and identification of projects; provide assistance, including training, management and investment-related services, to enterprises in the context of the Bank's operations during the pre-investment period or for rehabilitation purposes and, where appropriate, contribute to the start-up costs, including investment guarantee and insurance premiums, necessary to ensure that the investment decision is taken.

2.   Where appropriate, loan financing of investment, both directly or indirectly, as well as of sectoral support programmes, shall be provided from the Bank's own resources.

Article 269

The ACP States may, to encourage the promotion and development of their respective private sectors, use the resources of the indicative programme for:

(a) supporting the development of enterprises, by providing training, assistance in financial management and project preparation, specialized business start-up services and development and management services, and by encouraging technology transfers;

(b) providing appropriate and effective support for investment promotion, including the provision of assistance to promoters;

(c) supporting the setting-up or the strengthening of national or regional financial institutions in the ACP States to finance export operations;

(d) financing imports of intermediate materials needed for the export industries of a requesting ACP State;

(e) credit lines in favour of SMEs;

(f) providing appropriate and effective support for export promotion;

(g) supporting the improvement of the investment climate including the legal and fiscal framework for business, and the development of services in support of the enterprise sector so as to provide enterprises with advisory services in the legal, technical and managerial fields;

(h) providing technical cooperation to reinforce the activities of bodies in the ACP States working for the development of small and medium-sized enterprises;

(i) implementing appropriate programmes for vocational training and developing the capacity of individual entrepreneurs, particularly in the small-scale and informal sectors;

(j) providing assistance for the mobilization of domestic savings, development of financial intermediation and of new financial instruments, rationalization of enterprise promotion policies and encouragement of foreign investment;

(k) financing ventures undertaken by co-operatives or local communities in ACP States and the creation or strengthening of SME guarantee funds.

Article 270

In order to mobilize external investment resources, both private and public, particular efforts should be made in exploiting the possibilities of co-financing or attracting parallel-financing for the various projects or programmes.

Article 271

In assisting the ACP efforts to invest in PMDT, particular attention shall be paid to supporting optimal use of existing capacity of the ACP State concerned and the needs for rehabilitation.

Article 272

In order to support the promotion of investment in the ACP States and with due regard to the complementarity of their roles, the Commission and the Bank will closely coordinate their activities in this field.

The Commission and the Bank shall, with the assistance of Member States and ACP States, ensure effective coordination at the operational level among all parties interested in supporting investment in ACP States.

With a view to keeping those parties informed on investment prospects, the Commission shall produce reports and studies notably on:

-- investment flows between the Community and the ACP States, economic, legal or institutional obstacles hampering those investments, measures which will facilitate private capital movements, joint financing, access of ACP States to international financial markets and the effectiveness of domestic financial markets;

-- activities undertaken by national and international systems of investment guarantees;

-- investment promotion and protection agreements between Member States and ACP States.

The Commission shall submit to the ACP-EEC Development Finance Cooperation Committee the results of these studies. It shall also, in collaboration with the Bank, submit a report on the results of coordination in the field of investment and private sector support.

SECTION 5
Current payments and capital movements

Article 273

1.   With regard to capital movements linked with investments and to current payments, the Contracting Parties shall refrain from taking action in the field of foreign exchange transactions

425

which would be incompatible with their obligations under this Convention resulting from the provisions relating to trade in goods and services, establishment and industrial cooperation. These obligations shall not, however, prevent the Contracting Parties from adopting the necessary protective measures should they be justified by reasons relating to serious economic difficulties or severe balance-of-payments problems.

2.   In respect of foreign exchange transactions linked with investments and current payments, the ACP States, on the one hand, and the Member States, on the other, shall avoid, as far as possible, taking discriminatory measures vis-à-vis each other or according more favourable treatment to third States, taking full account of the evolving nature of the international monetary system, the existence of specific monetary arrangements and balance-of-payments problems.

To the extent that such measures or treatment are unavoidable, they shall be maintained or introduced in accordance with accepted international monetary rules and every effort shall be made to minimize any adverse effects on the parties affected.

SECTION 6
Qualification and treatment of business entities

Article 274

1.   As regards arrangements that may be applied in matters of establishment and provision of services, the ACP States, on the one hand, and the Member States, on the other, shall treat nationals and companies or firms of the ACP States and nationals and companies or firms of the Member States respectively on a non-discriminatory basis. However, if, for a given activity, an ACP State or a Member State is unable to provide such treatment, the ACP State or the Member State, as the case may be, shall not be bound to accord such treatment for that activity to the nationals and companies or firms of the State concerned.

2.   For the purpose of this Convention, "companies or firms of a Member State or of an ACP State" mean companies or firms constituted under civil or commercial law, including corporations, whether public or otherwise, co-operative societies and other legal persons and partnerships governed by public or private law, save for those which are non-profit-making, formed in accordance with the law of a Member State or an ACP State and whose statutory office, central administration or principal place of business is in a Member State or ACP State.

However, a company or firm having only its statutory office in a Member State or an ACP State must be engaged in an activity which has an effective and continuous link with the economy of that Member State or the ACP State.

*   *   *

426

CHARTER ON A REGIME OF MULTINATIONAL INDUSTRIAL ENTERPRISES (MIES) IN THE PREFERENTIAL TRADE AREA FOR EASTERN AND SOUTHERN AFRICAN STATES*

> The Charter on a Regime of Multinational Industrial Enterprises (MIEs) in the Preferential Trade Area for the Eastern and Southern African States (PTA) was signed on 21 November 1990. It had not entered into force as of August 1995. Following the adoption of the Treaty Establishing a Common Market for Eastern and Southern Africa (COMESA) in December 1994, which replaced the Preferential Trade Area for the Eastern and Southern African States in December 1994, the Charter will require substantial revision to bring it into conformity with the new Treaty provisions. The signatories to the Charter are Angola, Comoros, Djibouti, Kenya, Lesotho, Malawi, Mozambique, Rwanda, Somalia, Sudan, United Republic of Tanzania, Uganda, Zambia, Zimbabwe.

PREAMBLE

THE HIGH CONTRACTING PARTIES

1.   Having regard to Article 4 of Protocol VIII of the Treaty for the Establishment of the Preferential Trade Area for Eastern and Southern African States, according to which Member States shall formulate rules relating to the creation of a regime of Multinational Industrial Enterprises and promote the development of such enterprises;

2.   Mindful that the furtherance of regional programmes in industrial development requires a common framework for the pooling of factors of production within the Preferential Trade Area;

3.   Convinced that Multinational Industrial Enterprises can play an important role in self-sustained industrialization within the Preferential Trade Area, and that such industrialization will lead to the expansion of trade in industrial products and related services; and thereby accelerate the social and economic development of the Member States;

4.   Reaffirming their desire to develop and give further scope to regional entrepreneurship, management and technological capacity in the production of goods and services for both regional and extra-regional markets;

5.   Specially cognizant of the need to provide benefits to national enterprises from Member States which are prepared to contribute in fulfilling the objectives of the Charter; and

---

*Source: *Preferential Trade Area for Eastern and Southern African States: Report of the Sixteenth Meeting of the Council of Ministers*, 17-19 November, 1990, Mbabane, Swaziland (PTA/CM/XVI/2). The Charter also appears in International Legal Materials (1991). "Charter on a Regime of Multinational Industrial Enterprises (MIEs) in the Preferential Trade Area for Eastern and Southern African States", vol. 30, p. 696 [Note added by the editor].

6.   Recognizing the need to create the means by which the movement of investment capital between Member States, and particularly from the more developed to the less developed Member States, may be expeditiously effected in the interests of development throughout the region;

DO HEREBY AGREE AS FOLLOWS:

ARTICLE 1
Definitions

In this Charter unless the context otherwise requires:

"Affiliate" means a legal entity or unincorporated venture in which a Multinational Industrial Enterprise (MIE) holds equity participation;

"Branch" means the unincorporated subdivision of an MIE, operating outside the Country of Establishment of the MIE;

"Country of Establishment" means the Member State Party to this Charter in which a Multinational Industrial Enterprise is established;

"Government Procurement Programme" means the policies and regulations of a Member State regarding the acquisition of goods and services by the government and its agencies;

"Member State" means a Member State of the Preferential Trade Area, as stated in Article 1 of the Treaty for the Establishment of the Preferential Trade Area for Eastern and Southern African States;

"MIE Council" means the Council of Ministers for the Charter on MIEs, which Council is established by Article 22 of this Charter;

"Multinational Industrial Enterprise" (MIE) means an industrial enterprise that is accorded that status on the basis of conditions stipulated in Article 5 of this Charter;

"National" means:

(i)   any natural person deriving his or her status as national of an individual Member State from the laws of that State;

(ii)   any legal person established under the laws of a Member State having its head office or seat in that Member State and having at least fifty one (51) per cent of its equity held by nationals or agencies of the government of that Member State; and

(iii)   any Government agency established in accordance with the laws of individual Member States.

"PTA Council" means the Council of Ministers established by Article 7 of the Treaty for the Establishment of the Preferential Trade Area for Eastern and Southern African States;

"Relevant Authority" means the authority in the Country of Establishment of an MIE, Subsidiary or Branch responsible for the registration of the MIE, Subsidiary or Branch and which carries out such other functions as are set out in this Charter;

"Secretariat" means the Secretariat of the Preferential Trade Area established by Article 9 of the Treaty for the Establishment of the Preferential Trade Area for Eastern and Southern African States;

"Secretary-General" means the Secretary-General of the Preferential Trade Area appointed under Article 9 of the Treaty for the Establishment of the Preferential Trade Area for Eastern and Southern African States;

"Subsidiary" means a legal person in which an MIE holds at least fifty one (51) per cent of the equity;

"Treaty" means the Treaty for the Establishment of the Preferential Trade Area for Eastern and Southern African States; and

"UAPTA" means the Unit of account of the Preferential Trade Area, described more fully in Article 1 of Annex VI of the Treaty.

ARTICLE 2
Objectives

The establishment and promotion of MIEs shall be governed by the following objectives:

(a)   the development of capital and intermediate goods industries;

(b)   the development of food, agro- and agro-allied industries;

(c)   the development of consumer goods industries;

(d)   the development of basic industries;

(e)   the development of industries making optimal use of labour available locally and within the subregion;

(f)   the development of industrial infrastructure utilities, and related service industries;

(g)   the joint development of industrial research, support services in various sectors, skills and modern technology within the Preferential Trade Area and the dissemination and exchange of related information;

(h)   the rational and efficient use of existing and new industrial productive capacities of raw material and of other local resources;

(i)   the expansion of subregional trade;

(j)   the generation of foreign exchange through exports to countries outside the subregion;

(k)   the more effective acquisition of technology from outside the Preferential Trade Area; and

(l)   the creation of greater employment opportunities within the Preferential Trade Area.

ARTICLE 3
Form of the Multinational Industrial Enterprise

1.   In accordance with the procedures and rules specified in this Charter and in the national law of respective Member States, an enterprise may be established in a Member State Party to this Charter in the form of a Multinational Industrial Enterprise (MIE).

2.   The capital of an MIE shall be divided into shares. The liability of individual shareholders for the debts and obligations of an MIE shall be limited to the value remaining unpaid on the shares subscribed by each of them.

3.   Irrespective of the economic sector in which it is engaged, an MIE shall always be considered to be a business enterprise.

4.   Each MIE shall have legal personality.

ARTICLE 4
Scope of Application

1.   In accordance with the objectives stated in Article 2, this Charter shall apply to all economic sectors related to industrial development and without prejudice to the generality of the foregoing, it shall apply to sectors concerned with the creation of infrastructure and the provision of services.

2.   The provisions of this Charter and protocols and recommendations that may be adopted pursuant thereto shall govern *inter alia* the establishment and operation, winding up, liquidation and insolvency of the MIE and its Subsidiaries. With respect to all matters not governed by the Charter, the laws of the appropriate Member States shall govern.

ARTICLE 5
Conditions for the Formation of an MIE

1.   In order to become eligible for the status of MIE, an enterprise must fulfil the following:

(a)   it must have capital contributions from two or more Member States Parties to this Charter or from nationals of two or more Member States Parties to this Charter, and, in total, such contributions must account for not less than fifty one (51) per cent of the capital of the enterprise;

(b)   the capital contribution to the enterprise derived from any one Member State Party to this Charter or from nationals of any one Member State Party to this Charter must not exceed eighty per cent of the equity capital of the enterprise;

(c)   the capital contribution originating from each Member State Party to this Charter or nationals of each Member State participating in the enterprise must be at least ten per cent of the equity capital of the enterprise;

(d)   the activities of the enterprise must involve the undertaking of a specific project or projects in economic sectors falling within the scope of this Charter;

(e)   subject to higher requirements in the Country of Establishment, the capital of the enterprise shall be no less than 500,000 UAPTA. Where the Country of Establishment is a State identified by the Council as a less Developed Member State, then, subject to higher requirements in the national laws or regulations of that State, the capital of an MIE shall be no less than 200,000 UAPTA.

2.   For the purposes of sub-paragraphs (a) and (b) of paragraph 1 of this Article, contributions of the Eastern and Southern African Trade and Development Bank to the capital of an enterprise shall be considered to be national in origin.

ARTICLE 6
Formation of the Multinational Industrial Enterprise

1.   The status of an MIE shall be conferred on an enterprise established under the provisions of this Charter. An enterprise established in any other way may acquire the status of MIE if, at any time after its establishment, it fulfills the requirements of this Charter.

2.   Two or more Member States Parties to the Charter may form an MIE.

3.   One or more Member States Parties to the Charter and nationals of one or more Member States Parties to the Charter may form an MIE.

4.   When two or more individuals are nationals of different Member States parties to this Charter they may form an MIE. For the purposes of this paragraph an individual shall be

deemed to have the nationality of the State in which he normally exercises civil and political rights.

5.   Limited liability companies which are nationals of at least two Member States Parties to the Charter may create an MIE either by forming a joint subsidiary or by merging.

6.   An MIE together with one or more other MIEs or together with one or more limited liability companies which are nationals of Member States Parties to the Charter, may create an MIE by merging or by forming a joint subsidiary.

7.   An MIE or a limited liability company, together with one or more individuals who are nationals of Member States Parties to the Charter, may create an MIE.

8.   One or more Member States Parties to the Charter and an existing MIE may form an MIE.

ARTICLE 7
The Capital and Shares of the MIE

1.   The capital of an MIE shall be divided into registered shares or their equivalent, as provided for by the laws of the Country of Establishment.

2.   The capital of the MIE and its shares shall be denominated in UAPTA.

3.   Capital contributions originating from Member States Parties to the Charter other than the Country of Establishment may be made in their national currencies, in UAPTA, in convertible currencies of countries from outside the Preferential Trade Area, in corporeal or incorporeal property, or in shares of participating enterprises. For the purposes of this Article, an undertaking to perform work or to supply services shall not be treated as a capital contribution.

4.   Subject to the terms of paragraph 6 of this Article, the capital of an MIE may be increased or reduced in accordance with the national law of the Country of Establishment.

5.   When there is an increase in the capital of an MIE, all shareholders shall be entitled to exercise preferential rights with respect to the subscription of new shares.

6.   The transfer of shares in an MIE shall require the prior authorization of the Board of Directors or the equivalent body of the MIEs which authorization shall not be withheld unless, following the transfer, the enterprise would no longer meet the requirements of Article 5 of the Charter.

ARTICLE 8
The internal structure and functions of the MIE

1.   All shares in an MIE shall enjoy equal voting rights.

2.   Without prejudice to paragraph 1 of this Article, the statutes and other documents concerning the internal structure and formation of an MIE shall comply with the requirements of the national law of the Country of Establishment.

ARTICLE 9
Application for Registration as an MIE

1.   An application for registration as an MIE shall be submitted to the Relevant Authority of the Country of Establishment. A copy of the application shall also be forwarded to the Secretariat.

2.   The application shall comply with the requirements of this Charter and the national legislation and administrative procedures of the Country of Establishment.

3.   The application shall be accompanied by the following:

   (a)   the instrument of incorporation, and the statutes or equivalent instruments under the national law of the Country of Establishment. These shall be formulated in the manner required for the formation of limited liability companies in the Country of Establishment and shall incorporate the requirements stipulated in paragraphs 5 and 6 of Article 7 and paragraphs (1) and (2) of this Article;

   (b)   a document containing the names, addresses and nationalities of each of the shareholders and the shares held by them;

   (c)   a document containing the names, addresses and nationalities of the directors and executive officers to be appointed upon approval of the application;

   (d)   a document containing a detailed description of the projected activities of the enterprise, including:

      (i)   information on the anticipated annual volume and value of production;

      (ii)   analysis of the project and markets, including projection of exports to and imports from third countries and Member States;

      (iii)   sources of the technology which will be needed and the conditions under which it will be obtained;

      (iv)   an estimate of prices of the products or services to be sold in the Country of Establishment and those exported to Member States;

   (e)   a document providing evidence of the official approval for the initial transfer of capital contributions from Member States Parties to the Charter whose nationals will be shareholders in the MIE.

433

ARTICLE 10
Consideration of the Application for Registration as an MIE

1.   Within three months of the receipt of an application for registration as an MIE, the Relevant Authority shall take a decision on the said application.

2.   If the Relevant Authority is satisfied that an applicant has met the substantive criteria and other requirements concerning the formation of an MIE, it shall approve the application and register the enterprise as an MIE.

3.   If the Relevant Authority is not satisfied that an application for the status of MIE has met the substantive criteria and other requirements concerning the formation of an MIE, it shall reject the application in writing, stating the reason or reasons for its decision.

4.   The Relevant Authority shall reconsider its decision to reject an application if the applicant submits a request for reconsideration which takes into account the reasons stated by the Relevant Authority in its decision under paragraph 3 of this Article. The applicant may submit a request for reconsideration within three months from the date on which it receives formal communication of the rejection of its application.

5.   Where the Relevant Authority determines that an application for the status of MIE lacks specific items of information which may be relevant for a proper assessment of the application, it may instruct the applicant to submit, within a reasonable period of time, such items of information as the Relevant Authority deems appropriate.

6.   Where the Relevant Authority determines that an application for the status of MIE needs to be modified in order to fulfil the requirements either of the Charter or the national law of the Country of Establishment, it may instruct the applicant to make such modifications to the application as the Relevant Authority deems appropriate.

7.   In the event that an applicant fails to comply with the instructions issued by the Relevant Authority under paragraphs (5) or (6) of this Article, the application shall be deemed to be rejected and shall be treated as such.

ARTICLE 11
Registration of the MIE

1.   An MIE shall be registered by the Relevant Authority in a national register reserved for this special form of limited liability company.

2.   The Relevant Authority shall communicate the decision to register the enterprise as an MIE together with information concerning the date and other details of registration to the Secretariat. At the same time, it shall also transmit to the Secretariat all documents relating to the application.

3.   The Relevant Authority shall request that the Secretariat transmit details concerning the registration of the MIE to all Member States parties to the Charter which are shareholders or whose nationals are shareholders in the MIE. The Secretariat shall comply with the terms of this paragraph within one month of receipt of this request.

4.   Upon registration the enterprise shall add the letters "M.I.E." to its name.

5.   The head office or seat of an MIE shall be located in the Country of Establishment.

ARTICLE 12
Performance Agreement

1.   The MIE and the Government of the Country of Establishment shall enter into a Performance Agreement on the date the MIE is registered.

2.   The Performance Agreement shall specify the benefits, guarantees and obligations of the MIE set forth in this Charter and shall state, where possible, the consequences of a failure on the part of the MIE to adhere to particular terms of the Performance Agreement.

3.   The Performance Agreement shall be issued to the MIE on the date of registration and a copy thereof shall be sent to the Secretariat.

4.   The Performance Agreement, in its original or in modified form, shall be enforceable throughout the life of the MIE.

ARTICLE 13
Subsidiaries and Branches

1.   MIEs shall have the right to establish Subsidiaries and Branches in any of the Member States Parties to this Charter. This right of establishment shall be exercised in accordance with the requirements of the laws of the respective Member States concerning the establishment, operations and winding up of companies.

2.   Where an MIE has formed a Subsidiary, that Subsidiary may not itself establish another Subsidiary.

ARTICLE 14
Registration of Subsidiaries and Branches

Subsidiary

1.   A Subsidiary must be registered in the Member State Party to the Charter in which it wishes to be established.

2.   The application for registration must be made by the MIE on behalf of the Subsidiary it

wishes to establish.

3.   The application shall comply with the requirements of this Charter and the national law and administrative requirements of the country in which the Subsidiary is to be established.

4.   The application for registration shall be accompanied by documents of the type required for applications for MIE status and listed in paragraph 3 of Article 9. The MIE may be required by the Relevant Authority in the Member State Party to the Charter in which it wishes to establish the Subsidiary, to submit information regarding the MIE's activities that are relevant to the information submitted on behalf of the Subsidiary.

5.   (i)   Where the Relevant Authority in the Country of Establishment of the Subsidiary determines that the Subsidiary satisfies the substantive criteria required for registration, it shall register the Subsidiary in the national register for MIEs.

        (ii)   In the event that the Relevant Authority refuses to register the Subsidiary, it shall state in writing the reasons for its refusal and shall transmit copies of its decision to the MIE involved, to the Relevant Authority in the Country of Establishment of the MIE and to the Secretariat.

6.   With regard to applications by an MIE for the registration of a subsidiary, the provisions of paragraphs 5, 6 and 7 of Article 10 shall apply.

7.   A Performance Agreement shall be entered into by the Subsidiary and the Member State Party to the Charter in which it is established and, with respect to this Agreement, the provisions of Article 12 shall apply *mutatis mutandis*. The Performance Agreement shall be entered into on the date the Subsidiary is registered.

8.   Upon registration the enterprise shall add the letters "S.M.I.E." to its name.

Branch

9.   Where an MIE wishes to establish a Branch, it shall submit to the Relevant Authority in the Member State Party to the Charter in which the Branch is to be located, information and documents in support of its application for registration.

10.   With regard to applications by an MIE for the establishment of a Branch, the provisions of paragraphs 5, 6 and 7 of Article 10 shall apply, and accordingly, the MIE may be required by the competent authorities in the Member State Party to the Charter in which it wishes to establish the Branch to provide information on the proposed activities of the branch and on those activities of the MIE that are relevant to the Branch.

11.   (i)   Save where the Relevant Authority concerned determines that the activities of the Branch will have a substantially negative effect on the national economy, it shall register the Branch in its national register for MIEs.

(ii)   In the event that the Relevant Authority refuses to register a Branch, it shall state, in writing, the reasons for its refusal and shall transmit copies of its decision to the MIE involved, the Relevant Authority in the Country of Establishment of the MIE and the Secretariat.

ARTICLE 15
Benefits for MIEs

Transfer of Funds

1.   In order to accommodate the legitimate capital needs of MIEs, their Subsidiaries or Branches, Member States Parties to this Charter which contribute or whose nationals contribute to the capital of an MIE shall permit the transfer of funds in UAPTA to the Country of Establishment or other Member States in which the MIE has established a Subsidiary or Branch. Subject to mandatory requirements in their respective national laws, Member States Parties to this Charter shall permit the transfer of convertible currencies from outside the Preferential Trade Area to the Country of Establishment of the MIE, its Subsidiaries and its Branches.

2.   After payment of any taxes due, each Subsidiary or Branch of an MIE shall be entitled to transfer its profits to the Country of Establishment, subject only to the observance by the Subsidiary or Branch of those procedural formalities which do not hinder the fulfilment of the objectives of this Charter.

3.   (i)   All Shareholders in an MIE shall have the right to:

        (a)   repatriate their capital contributions in the event of a sale of their respective shareholdings or of a sale liquidation of the MIE;

        (b)   repatriate the portion of their own capital contributions returned to them in the event that the MIE reduces its share capital.

    (ii)   These rights are subject only to those procedural formalities which do not hinder the fulfillment of the objectives of this Charter.

4.   (i)   The MIE shall have the right, after payment of any taxes due, to:

        (a)   remit royalties and other payments for the use or adoption of foreign technology in the territory of the particular Member State Party to this Charter in which the technology has been used or adopted;

        (b)   remit funds for the repayment of intra-company advances and loans obtained from third parties;

        (c)   remit dividends due to shareholders located outside the Country of Establishment.

(ii)   These rights are subject only to those procedural formalities which do not hinder the fulfillment of the objectives of this Charter.

Employees of MIEs

5.   Subject to considerations of national security, the Country of Establishment, and in the case of a Subsidiary or Branch the relevant Member State Party to this Charter, shall grant entry and exit visas and residence and work permits to the employees of an MIE, and shall facilitate the repatriation of their salaries.

Exemptions from Import Duties

6. (i)   Where an MIE, Subsidiary or Branch demonstrates to the satisfaction of the country of Establishment, or the relevant Member State Party to this Charter with respect to the Subsidiary or Branch that:

(a)   a specific item of capital equipment (including spare parts and accessories for capital equipment) or any intermediate input is necessary for the operations of the MIE, Branch or Subsidiary; and

(b)   the item cannot be purchased, in the case of an MIE, in the Country of Establishment, or, in the case of a Subsidiary or Branch, in the country in which the Subsidiary or Branch is located,

the MIE, Subsidiary or Branch shall, where the item originates from Member States of the Preferential Trade Area, be accorded the right to import that item free of any customs, other import duties or measures having an equivalent effect, during the first five years after registration; provided, however, that no item imported free of such customs or other import duties may be sold or leased to third parties by the MIE, Subsidiary or Branch concerned within two years from its delivery to that MIE, Subsidiary or Branch.

(ii)   Where an MIE, Subsidiary or Branch demonstrates to the satisfaction of the Country of Establishment, or the relevant Member State Party to this Charter with respect to the Subsidiary or Branch, that:

(a)   a specific item of capital equipment (including spare parts and accessories for capital equipment) or an intermediate input is necessary for the operations of the MIE, Branch or Subsidiary, and

(b)   the item cannot be purchased from within the region of the Preferential Trade Area,

the MIE, Branch or Subsidiary shall be accorded the right to import the item free of any customs or import duties or measures having an equivalent effect, during the first five years after registration; provided, however, that no item imported free of any customs or other import duties may be sold or leased to third parties by the MIE, Subsidiary or Branch concerned within two years from its delivery to that MIE, Subsidiary or Branch.

Taxes on Income

7.   Each MIE and each Subsidiary or Branch shall be exempt from the payment of taxes on income in any Member State Party to this Charter, for the five years immediately following the date on which the MIE first derives income from its operations.

Licences and Permits

8.   The Country of Establishment, and in the case of a Branch or Subsidiary the relevant Member State Party to this Charter, shall grant promptly and on conditions no less favourable than those applied to their national enterprises, all licences and permits required for carrying out the operations of the MIEs.

Equality of Treatment

9.   In matters pertaining to taxation, Government Procurement Programmes and access to local credit, Member States shall grant to all MIEs, their Subsidiaries and Branches, treatment no less favourable than that accorded, in the same sector of activity, to national enterprises which are not fully owned by government.

10.   Where an MIE is owned by:

(a)   the governments of two or more Member States Parties to this Charter, or

(b)   private nationals of two or more Member States Parties to this Charter with equity participation by the government of at least one such Member State,

the MIE shall, in matters pertaining to taxation, Government Procurement Programmes and access to local credit, be accorded treatment no less favourable than that enjoyed by wholly government owned enterprises in the Country of Establishment. The Subsidiaries and Branches of an MIE which satisfy either criterion stipulated in (a) and (b) herein, shall be accorded treatment no less favourable than that accorded to wholly Government owned enterprises in the respective Member States Parties to this Charter.

Infrastructural Support

11.   Member States Parties to this Charter shall make every reasonable effort to provide MIEs, their Subsidiaries and Branches with special infrastructural support, particularly with respect to the basic utilities, transportation, communications and the acquisition of land.

Preferential Tariff and Non-Tariff Treatment

12.   Products of the MIE shall enjoy preferential tariff and non-tariff treatment in accordance with the provisions of the Treaty as agreed in paragraph 4 of Article 4 of the Protocol on co-operation in the Field of Industrial Development.

ARTICLE 16
Guarantees to MIEs

1.   Where an MIE, or any Branch or Subsidiary thereof, is nationalized, expropriated or is made subject to other forms of State intervention having effects similar to nationalization or expropriation, the State shall pay compensation in accordance with generally accepted rules of International Law.

2.   Benefits conferred in the Performance Agreements provided for in Articles 12 and 14 of this Charter shall not be modified without the agreement of the MIE, or as the case may be, the Subsidiary concerned.

ARTICLE 17
Obligations of MIEs and Subsidiaries

1.   The obligations of each MIE and each Subsidiary, all of which shall be stated in the Performance Agreement, are the following:

(a)   to implement:

(i)   a programme for the gradual increase of the local value added of the product, including the participation of inputs originating from other Member States Parties to this Charter;

(ii)   a programme of exports; and

(iii)   to the extent feasible, a programme of training;

(b)   to produce goods of acceptable quality at competitive prices, and to assure a minimum volume of supply;

(c)   to supply information, including annual reports, annual external audits, and reports concerning the ownership of the shares in the MIE to the Country of Establishment and to the Secretariat, on a regular basis;

(d)   to refrain from entering into restrictive business practices that have an adverse effect on:

(i)   the acquisition and transfer of technology; and

      (ii)   the competitiveness of other enterprises owned by nationals of Member States.

2.   In addition to the obligations stated in paragraph 1 of this Article, the Performance Agreement may contain other obligations for the MIE or Subsidiary which are considered appropriate by the parties to the Agreement.

ARTICLE 18
Supervision of the Activities of the MIE

1.   The Country of Establishment shall supervise the activities of MIEs located in its territory and shall ensure that all such MIEs comply with the provisions of this Charter.

2.   Member States Parties to the Charter shall supervise the activities of Subsidiaries and Branches located in their territory and shall ensure that all such Subsidiaries and Branches comply with the provisions of this Charter. With respect to matters falling appropriately within the jurisdiction of the Country of Establishment, that State shall also have supervisory powers with respect to the activities of Subsidiaries and Branches.

ARTICLE 19
Less Developed Member States

1.   A Special Development Tax for the benefit of the less developed Member States of the Preferential Trade Area shall be established.

2.   Where an MIE, Branch or Subsidiary has derived income from its operations for a period of five years or more in countries identified by the PTA Council as being the more developed Member States of the Preferential Trade Area, it shall pay annually to the Relevant Authority in the respective countries the Special Development Tax, equivalent in value to one per cent of the gross revenues of the MIE, Branch or Subsidiary for the preceding fiscal year.

3.   The sum total of the money collected by each Relevant Authority pursuant to paragraph 2 of this Article, less reasonable collection costs, shall be forwarded to the Secretariat.

4.   The Secretariat shall, acting on the instructions of the MIE Council allocate the proceeds from the Special Development Tax to countries identified by the PTA Council as the less developed Member States of the Preferential Trade Area. The proceeds of the Special Development Tax shall be allocated in accordance with criteria to be determined by the MIE Council.

5.   The provisions of this Article do not derogate from the general power of Member States to impose taxes relating to the operations of MIEs, Branches and Subsidiaries.

ARTICLE 20
Revocation of Status of an MIE

1. When the Country of Establishment considers that an MIE has engaged in a serious violation or a number of recurring violations of either the provisions of this Charter or its Performance Agreement, the Country of Establishment shall inform the MIE as well as the Member States which are or whose nationals are shareholders in the MIE of the violation or violations.

2. The Country of Establishment shall give the MIE a reasonable period in which to rectify the violation or violations in question. If the violation or violations are not rectified within this period, the Country of Establishment may revoke the status of MIE and, where it does so, shall immediately inform the Secretariat of such revocation and request that this information be transmitted to the Member States which or whose nationals participate in the MIE.

3. In cases concerning alleged violations of this Charter or of a Performance Agreement, an MIE shall have the right of recourse to arbitration as provided for in Article 23.

ARTICLE 21
Revocation of Registration of a Branch or Subsidiary of an MIE

1. When a Member State Party to this Charter considers that a Branch or Subsidiary of an MIE registered in its territory has engaged in a serious violation or a number of recurring violations of either the provisions of this Charter or its Performance Agreement, that Member State shall inform the Branch or Subsidiary and the Country of Establishment of the violation or violations.

2. The Country of Establishment shall inform the MIE as well as the Member States which are or whose nationals are shareholders in the MIE of the violation or violations.

3. The Member State party to the Charter in which the Branch or Subsidiary is located shall give the Branch or Subsidiary a reasonable period in which to rectify the violation or violations in question. If the violation or violations are not rectified within the period specified in accordance with paragraph 1 of this Article, the Member State in whose territory the Branch or Subsidiary is registered may revoke the registration of the enterprise as a Branch or Subsidiary of an MIE and, where it does so, it shall immediately inform the Country of Establishment, Member States which are or whose nationals are shareholders in the MIE and the Secretariat of its decision. It shall request the Secretariat to transmit this information to the Member States parties to the Charter.

4. In cases concerning alleged violations of this Charter or of a Performance Agreement, the Subsidiary or, as the case may be the MIE on behalf of its Branch, shall have the right of recourse to arbitration as provided for in Article 23.

ARTICLE 22
Council of Ministers for the Charter on MIEs

1.   (i)   There is hereby established the Council of Ministers for the Charter on MIEs.

(ii)   Each Member State Party to the Charter shall designate one Minister of Government as its representative on the MIE Council.

(iii)   The Secretary-General shall be an ex officio member of this Council, but shall not have a vote.

2.   The MIE Council shall hold scheduled meetings annually and shall also meet at the request of three Member States Parties to the Charter or at the request of the Secretary-General.

3.   The chairmanship of the MIE Council shall rotate among the Member States by order of date of ratification by the Member States Parties to the Charter.

4.   The Secretary General shall submit information concerning the implementation of Charter to the MIE Council on a regular basis.

5.   The MIE Council may make recommendations to the Member States Parties to the Charter on the interpretation and the implementation of the Charter. The recommendations shall be distributed by the Secretariat of the Preferential Trade Area as appendices to the Charter.

6.   The MIE Council by a majority vote, may propose amendments or protocols to the Charter whose purpose is to strengthen the effectiveness of the Charter.

7.   The Secretary-General shall assist the MIE Council in carrying out its functions.

ARTICLE 23
Settlement of Disputes

1.   All disputes arising under this Charter or from Performance Agreements shall be amicably settled between the parties to them. Save for disputes referred to in Article 24 hereof, where a dispute cannot be amicably settled between the parties it shall be referred to an arbitration tribunal appointed by the parties to the dispute. In the event of disagreement between the said parties on the appointment of an arbitrator or arbitrators, the appointment shall be made by the Secretary General.

2.   The arbitrator or arbitrators shall determine the rules of procedure.

3.   The arbitral award shall be final and binding.

4.   Member States shall take such measures as are necessary to ensure the enforcement of arbitral awards made under this Charter.

ARTICLE 24
Settlement of Differences Between Member States on the
Interpretation and Application of the Charter

If Member States Parties to the Charter are unable to settle their differences on the interpretation and application of the Charter in an amicable manner, they shall have recourse to a panel of three qualified legal experts appointed by the Chairman of the MIE Council from a list maintained by the Secretary-General. The decision of the panel shall be final and binding.

ARTICLE 25
Amendments and Protocols

1. Amendments and protocols to this Charter shall be proposed by the MIE Council.

2. Proposed amendments and protocols shall be communicated by the Secretary-General to all Member States Parties to this Charter.

3. Each amendment or protocol shall specify the number of ratifications required for it to enter into force for Member States Parties to the Charter which subscribe to it.

4. Where a proposal for an amendment or protocol receives the number of ratifications specified in accordance with paragraph 3 of this Article the amendment or protocol shall enter into force for the Member States Parties to this Charter which ratify that amendment or protocol.

ARTICLE 26
Entry into Force, Ratification and Accession

1. This Charter shall enter into force when it is signed and ratified by at least nine Member States. It shall be open for ratification or accession to all Member States of the Preferential Trade Area for Eastern and Southern African States.

2. The PTA Council shall encourage new Member States to accede to this Charter.

ARTICLE 27
Depository

1. The Secretary-General shall be the depository of this Charter and all amendments and protocols related thereto. Instruments of ratification or accession shall also be deposited with the Secretary-General.

2. The Secretary-General shall transmit true copies of the Charter to all Member States.

ARTICLE 28
Final Clauses

1.   Member States Parties to this Charter shall take measures including, where necessary, the adjustment of their legislation, to ensure that:

(i)   the Charter shall take effect without delay;

(ii)   the provisions of the Charter are implemented in their respective territories; and

(iii)   individual enterprises established in accordance with the provisions of the Charter are not hindered in their operations by State actions which create unreasonable obligations for MIEs, Branches or Subsidiaries.

2.   Nothing in this Charter shall prevent the MIE from receiving additional benefits that may be given to investors under other schemes and regimes established by the Preferential Trade Area for Eastern and Southern African States or which are otherwise applied by the Member States Parties to this Charter under preferential schemes existing at the time of the entry into force of this Charter.

DONE at Mbabane, the Kingdom of Swaziland, on the twenty third day of November, in the year One Thousand Nine Hundred and Ninety, in the English and French languages, both texts being equally authentic.

IN FAITH WHEREOF the undersigned have placed their signatures at the end of this Charter.

*   *   *

DECISION 291 OF THE COMMISSION OF THE CARTAGENA AGREEMENT. COMMON CODE FOR THE TREATMENT OF FOREIGN CAPITAL AND ON TRADEMARKS, PATENTS, LICENSES AND ROYALTIES[*]
AND
DECISION NO. 24 OF THE COMMISSION OF THE CARTAGENA AGREEMENT. COMMON REGULATIONS GOVERNING FOREIGN CAPITAL MOVEMENT, TRADE MARKS, PATENTS, LICENCES AND ROYALTIES[**]

Decision 291 of the Commission of the Cartagena Agreement superceded Decision 220 on 21 March 1991. The latter, in turn, replaced Decision 24 of the Commission of the Cartagena Agreement, which was adopted on 31 December 1970. Decision 24 was successively amended by Decisions 37 (1971), 37-A (1971), 70 (1973), 103 (1976) and 109 (1976). The text of Decision 24 reproduced below reflects all of these amendments. The States members of the Cartagena Agreement are Bolivia, Chile, Colombia, Ecuador, Peru and Venezuela.

DECISION 291 OF THE COMMISSION OF THE CARTAGENA AGREEMENT.
COMMON CODE FOR THE TREATMENT OF FOREIGN CAPITAL AND ON TRADEMARKS, PATENTS, LICENSES AND ROYALTIES

THE COMMISSION OF THE CARTAGENA AGREEMENT,

IN VIEW OF Articles 7, 26 and 27 of the Cartagena Agreement, Decision 220 of the Commission and Proposal 228 of the Board;

WHEREAS At the meeting held in La Paz, Bolivia, on 29 and 30 November 1990, the Presidents of the member countries of the Cartagena Agreement welcomed the "growing convergence among the economic policies of the Andean countries in seeking greater economic efficiency and competitiveness through liberalization and openness to trade and international investment in line with the interests of our countries, and the establishment of a rationalized

---

[*] Source: *International Legal Materials* (1991). vol. 30, pp. 1288-1294 (English translation by John R. Pate). The original Spanish version appears in Gaceta Oficial del Acuerdo de Cartagena, Year VIII, No. 80, 4 April 1991. [Note added by the editor].

[**] Source: United Nations (1975). "Preparation of a draft outline of a code of conduct on transfer of technology", (Geneva: United Nations), United Nations document No. TD/B/C.6/AC.1/2/Supp.1/Add.1: pp. 123-141. Amendments to Decision 24 have been reproduced from *International Legal Materials* (1977) vol. 16, January: pp. 138-156 [Note added by editor].

economy based on private initiative, on fiscal discipline and on a streamlined and effective State";

The Andean Presidents also, at the aforesaid meeting, agreed to remove obstacles to foreign investment and to provide incentives for the free flow of subregional capital;

The new foreign investment policies in force in the subregion have necessitated the revision and updating of the communal norms adopted by Decision 220 of the Commission, for the purpose of stimulating and promoting the flow of capital and of foreign technologies to the Andean economies;

DECIDES:

To replace Decision 220 by the following Decision:

CHAPTER I

Definitions

Article 1. For the purposes of these rules, the following terms shall mean:

Direct foreign investment: Contributions from abroad, belonging to foreign individuals or foreign legal entities, made to the capital of an enterprise in freely convertible currencies, or in physical or tangible assets such as industrial plants, new and reconditioned machinery, new and reconditioned equipment, spare parts, parts and pieces, raw materials and intermediate products.

Local currency investments from funds which are entitled to be remitted abroad and reinvestments made pursuant to these rules shall also be considered direct foreign investments.

Intangible technological contributions, such as trade marks, industrial models, technical assistance and patented or unpatented technical knowledge which may take the form of physical assets, technical documents and instructions, may be considered by the member countries, in accordance with their respective national laws, as capital contributions.

National investor: The State, national individuals and legal entities defined as nationals by the laws of the member countries.

Foreign individuals with uninterrupted residence in the recipient country of not less than one year, who waive, before the competent national agency, the right to re-export capital and remit profits abroad, shall also be considered national investors. The competent national agency of the recipient country may exempt the said individuals from the requirement of uninterrupted residence of not less than one year.

Each member country may release foreign individuals whose investments have been generated locally from the waiver required under the preceding paragraph.

Investments belonging to subregional investors shall likewise be considered as of national investors under the conditions laid down in this Decision.

Subregional investor: A national investor of any member country other than the recipient country.

Foreign investor: The owner of a direct foreign investment.

National enterprise: An enterprise organized in the recipient country, more than 80 per cent of whose capital belongs to national investors, provided that, in the opinion of the competent national agency, that proportion is reflected in the technical, financial, administrative and commercial management of the enterprise.

Mixed enterprise: An enterprise organized in the recipient country and whose capital belongs to national investors in a proportion ranging between 51 per cent and 80 per cent, provided that, in the opinion of the competent national agency, that proportion is reflected in the technical, financial, administrative and commercial management of the enterprise.

Also regarded as mixed enterprises are those in which there is participation of the State, para-State entities or State enterprises of the recipient country, in a proportion of not less than 30 per cent of the corporate capital, and further provided that the State has, in the opinion of the competent national agency, determinant power in the decisions of the enterprise.

Determinant power is understood to mean the obligation to have the State representatives' consent for any decisions which are fundamental for the operation of the enterprise.

For purposes of this Decision, a para-State entity or State enterprise shall be understood to mean an entity organized in the recipient country, in which the State owns over 80 per cent of the capital and furthermore has determinant power in the decisions of the enterprise.

Foreign enterprise: An enterprise organized or established in the recipient country whose capital held by national investors amounts to less than 51 per cent, or, if that percentage is higher, is not reflected, in the opinion of the competent national agency, in the technical, financial, administrative and commercial management of the enterprise.

Neutral capital: Investments by public international financial entities to which all of the member countries of the Cartagena Agreement belong, and which are listed in the annex to these rules. Such investments shall not be counted as national or foreign investments in the enterprise in which they are made.

In determining the national, mixed or foreign status of the enterprise in which such investments are made, neutral capital contributions shall be excluded from the basis for calculation, and only the percentages of investment of national and foreign investors in the remaining amount of capital shall be taken into account.

<u>Reinvestment</u>: Investment of all or part of the undistributed profits and of other local resources, where permitted by national law, from a direct foreign investment in the same enterprise where such profits were generated.

<u>Recipient country</u>: The country in which the direct foreign investment is made.

<u>Commission</u>: Commission of the Cartagena Agreement.

<u>Board</u>: The Board of the Cartagena Agreement.

<u>Member country</u>: One of the member countries of the Cartagena Agreement.

CHAPTER II

<u>Rights and obligations of foreign investors</u>

<u>Article 2</u>. Foreign investors shall have the same rights and obligations as national investors, except as otherwise provided in the legislation of each member country.

<u>Article 3</u>. All direct investments by foreign or subregional investors which meet the conditions laid down in these rules and in the respective national laws of the member countries shall be registered with the competent national agency in freely convertible currency.

<u>Article 4</u>. Direct foreign investors and subregional investors shall be entitled to re-export, in freely convertible currency and under the conditions laid down in the legislation of each member country, the verified net profits derived from such direct foreign investment.

The competent national agency may also register, in freely convertible currency, the investment of surplus distributed profits.

<u>Article 5</u>. Foreign and subregional investors shall be entitled to re-export the amounts obtained when they sell, within the recipient country, their shares, partnership interests or rights, or when the capital is reduced or the enterprise is liquidated, provided they had paid the corresponding taxes.

The sale of shares, partnership interests or rights of a foreign or subregional investor to another foreign or subregional investor must be registered by the competent national agency when so stipulated in the national legislation, and will not be deemed to be a re-exportation of capital.

Article 6. Registered capital shall consist of the amount of the initial direct foreign investment plus any subsequent increases and reinvestments, registered and actually made, in accordance with the provisions hereof, minus the net losses, if any.

Article 7. Reinvestment as defined in article 1 in national, mixed or foreign enterprises shall be considered foreign investment and shall be subject to such rules as each member country may establish. In any case, the obligation to register the investment with the competent national agency remains unchanged.

Article 8. Articles produced by national, mixed or foreign enterprises that meet the special standards or the specific origin requirements set by the Commission and the Board shall qualify for the advantages deriving from the Cartagena Agreement Liberation Programme as provided for in chapter X of the Agreement.

Article 9. The capital of stock corporations shall be represented in nominative shares.

Article 10. In settling disputes or conflicts over direct foreign investment or investment by subregional investors or the transfer of foreign technologies, member countries shall apply the provisions of their own domestic legislation.

CHAPTER III

Competent national agencies

Article 11. Member countries shall designate the national agency or agencies authorized to enforce the obligations contracted by foreign individuals or legal entities referred to in these rules.

CHAPTER IV

Technology imports

Article 12. Contracts for technology licensing, technical assistance, technical services, basic and special engineering and other technological contracts, as defined in member countries' respective laws, shall be registered with the competent national agency of the member country concerned, which shall evaluate the effective contribution of the imported technology by estimating its probable uses, the price of any goods incorporating the technology, or by otherwise specifically measuring the impact of the imported technology.

Article 13. Technology import contracts shall contain, as a minimum, clauses on the following matters:

(a)   The parties, with specific mention of their nationality and domicile;

(b)   The means to be used for transferring the technology being imported;

(c)   The contract value of each of the elements involved in the technology transfer;

(d)   The period for which the contract is valid.

Article 14. For purposes of registering contracts on the transfer of foreign technology, trade marks or patents, member countries shall ensure that such contracts do not contain:

(a)   Clauses whereby the supply of a technology or the use of a trade mark carries with it the obligation for the receiving country or enterprise to acquire capital equipment, intermediate products, raw materials or othertechnologies from a specific source, or to permanently employ personnel designated by the enterprise supplying the technology;

(b)   Clauses whereby the enterprise selling the technology or granting the use of a trade mark reserves the right to set the sale or resale price of any products developed using the said technology;

(c)   Clauses containing restrictions on production volume and methods;

(d)   Clauses forbidding the use of competing technologies;

(e)   Clauses granting the supplier of the technology a total or partial purchase option;

(f)   Clauses obliging the buyer of the technology to transfer to the supplier any inventions or improvements developed by the use of the said technology;

(g)   Clauses whereby royalties must be paid to patent or trade mark holders for unused or outdated patents or trade marks; and

(h)   Any other clauses with equivalent effect.

Save in exceptional cases, which shall be duly specified by the competent national agency of the receiving country, no clauses shall be accepted that prohibit or in any way limit the export of products based on the technology concerned.

In no case shall such clauses be accepted with respect to subregional trade or for the export of similar products to third countries.

Article 15. Intangible technological contributions, as long as they do not constitute capital investment, shall entitle the contributor to the payment of royalties subject to member countries' legislation.

Royalties owing may be capitalized subject to the conditions set out in these rules, upon payment of taxes due.

If such contributions are made to a foreign enterprise by its parent company or by another affiliate of the same parent company, the payment of royalties may be authorized in cases previously determined by the competent national agency of the receiving country.

CHAPTER V

Treatment of investments of the Andean Development Corporation and of organizations that may opt for treatment of their investments as mutual capital

Article 16. Without prejudice to the provisions of its charter, direct investments by the Andean Development Corporation shall be considered as national investments in each member country of the Cartagena Agreement.

Article 17. Intergovernmental finance organizations to which not all the Cartagena Agreement member countries belong and foreign governmental agencies engaged in cooperation for development, whatever their legal status, may request the Commission to classify their investments as neutral capital and include them in the annex to these rules. The Commission must decide on applications submitted to it by the first meeting following their submission.

Article 18. With their application, the organizations referred to in the preceding article shall submit a copy of their charter or statutes, as well as the fullest information possible on their investment policy, operational regulations and investments made, by country and by sector.

First transitional provision. Foreign enterprises that have a valid transformation agreement under chapter II of Decision 220 may request the competent national agency to annul the said agreement.

Second transitional provision. With respect to projects corresponding to products reserved or exclusively assigned to Ecuador, the four remaining countries undertake not to register any direct foreign investment in their territory.

Done at Lima, Peru, on 21 March 1991.

ANNEX
List of organizations whose investments may at their option qualify for treatment as neutral capital

Inter-American Development Bank
International Finance Corporation
German Corporation for Economic Cooperation
Royal Danish Industrialization Fund for Developing Countries
Inter-American Investment Corporation

**DECISION NO. 24 OF THE COMMISSION OF THE CARTAGENA AGREEMENT.
COMMON REGULATIONS GOVERNING FOREIGN CAPITAL MOVEMENT, TRADE
MARKS, PATENTS, LICENCES AND ROYALTIES**

THE COMMISSION OF THE CARTAGENA AGREEMENT:

IN ACCORDANCE WITH Articles 16 and 27 of the Cartagena Agreement and with proposal No. 4 submitted by the Board:

CONSIDERING that the Declaration of Bogota recognized that foreign capital "can make a substantial contribution to the economic development of Latin America, provided that it stimulates capital formation in the country in which it is invested, furthers the extensive participation of domestic capital in this process, and does not hinder regional integration";

That in the same document the Governments proposed the adoption of "a rule encouraging the use of modern technology, with no restrictions as to where the product manufactured with foreign technical assistance may be marketed, and a rule concerning the co-ordination of foreign investment with over-all development plans";

That in the Declaration of Punta del Este in which the American Heads of State stipulated that "Integration must be fully at the service of Latin America. This requires the strengthening of Latin American enterprise through vigorous financial and technical support that will permit it to develop and supply the regional market efficiently", and recognized that "foreign private initiative will be able to fill an important function in assuring achievement of the aims of integration within the pertinent policies of each of the countries of Latin America";

That the Ministers for Foreign Affairs of the parties to the Cartagena agreement at their first meeting, held at Lima, endorsed the conviction enunciated in the Consensus of Viña del Mar that "Economic growth and social progress are the responsibility of the people of Latin America, on whose efforts depends the achievement of their national and regional aims"; restated their firm support for "the full and sovereign right of nations to dispose freely of their natural resources"; adopted as a common policy "the giving of priority to truly national undertakings and capital of the Member Countries in the economic development of the subregion"; and recognized that foreign capital investment and transfer of foreign technology are a contribution necessary for the development of the Member Countries and must receive guarantees firm enough to make them a really positive contribution";

DECLARES THAT

1. The programming of subregional development and the enlargement of the market will generate new investment requirements in the different production sectors. Consequently it is necessary to establish common rules for foreign investment in keeping with the new conditions created by the Cartagena Agreement so that its advantages shall favour national or joint undertakings as defined in the present statute.

2.   Foreign capital and technology can play an important part in subregional development and assist the national effort by making an effective contribution to attainment of the aims of integration and of the targets established in national development plans.

3.   The Common Regulations must state clearly the rights and obligations of foreign investors and the guarantees which foreign investment must receive in the subregion. Furthermore, they must be sufficiently stable for the mutual benefit of the investors and the member countries.

4.   The treatment of foreign capital must not discriminate against national investors.

5.   One of the fundamental aims of the Common Regulations must be to strengthen national undertakings so as to equip them to participate actively in the subregional market.

6.   Similarly, national undertakings must have the fullest possible access to modern technology and contemporary managerial innovations. At the same time it is necessary to establish efficient mechanisms and procedures for creating and protecting technology in the subregional area and for improving the terms on which foreign technology is acquired.

7.   In order to achieve these aims, the Common Regulations must provide mechanisms and procedures effective enough to enable domestic capital to participate increasingly in foreign undertakings already existing or to be established in the member countries with a view to the eventual creation of joint undertakings in which domestic capital shall predominate and national interests have a decisive influence on the major decisions of those undertakings. When the domestic capital is contributed by the State or State-owned bodies, they need not have control so long as they can determine the decisions of the undertaking.

8.   In compliance with the spirit of the Cartagena Agreement and the provisions of its article 92, the Common Regulations must include rules to compensate for the "Structural deficiencies of Bolivia and Ecuador and ensure for their benefit the mobilization and assignment of the resources indispensable for achievement of the aims contemplated in this Agreement".

9.   The Common Regulations should also strengthen the capacity of the member countries to negotiate with States, undertakings supplying capital and technology, and the international agencies concerned with such matters.

DECIDES

To approve the following

COMMON REGULATIONS GOVERNING FOREIGN CAPITAL MOVEMENT,
TRADE MARKS, PATENTS, LICENSES AND ROYALTIES

Chapter I

Article 1. For the purposes of these Regulations the following definitions shall apply:

<u>Direct foreign investment:</u>	Contributions to the capital of an enterprise which come from abroad, are owned by foreign individuals or undertakings, are made in freely convertible currency, industrial plant, machinery or equipment, and carry the right to re-export their value and transfer profits abroad.
	Investments in domestic currency originating from resources which carry the right to be remitted abroad shall likewise be deemed to be direct foreign investment.
<u>Foreign investor:</u>	The owner of a direct foreign investment.
<u>National investor:</u>	The State, a national individual, a national non-profit-making corporation, and a national undertaking as defined in this article. A foreign individual who has resided continuously in the recipient country for not less than one year and who declares to the competent national authority that he waives the right to re-export capital and remit profits abroad shall likewise be deemed to be a national investor.
<u>National undertaking:</u>	An undertaking which is established in the receiving country and over 80 per sent of whose capital belongs to national investors, provided that in the opinion of the competent national authority this proportion is reflected in the technical, financial, administrative and business management of the undertaking.
<u>Joint undertaking:</u>	An undertaking which is established in the recipient country and between 51 and 80 per cent of whose capital belongs to national investors; provided that in the opinion of the competent national authority this proportion is reflected in the technical, financial, administrative and business management of the undertaking.
<u>Foreign undertaking:</u>	An undertaking less than 51 per cent of whose capital belongs to national investors or in which that percentage is higher but in the opinion of the competent national authority is not reflected in the technical, financial, administrative and business management of the undertaking.
<u>New investment:</u>	Any investment made after 1 January 1971 in a new or existing undertaking.
<u>Reinvestment:</u>	Investment of all or some of the undistributed profits originating from direct foreign investment in the undertaking that made them.
<u>Recipient country:</u>	The country in which the direct foreign investment takes place.

Commission: The Commission of the Cartagena Agreement.

Board: The Board of the Cartagena Agreement.

Member country: A country that is a party to the Cartagena Agreement.

Article 2.   A foreign investor desiring to invest in a member country shall submit an application to the competent national authority, which shall assess the application and approve it if it meets the development priorities of the receiving country. The application shall conform to the model contained in Appendix No. 1 to these Regulations.

The Commission, on a proposal from the Board, may approve common criteria for assessment of direct foreign investment in member countries.

Article 3.   A member country may not permit direct foreign investment in activities which it considers are being satisfactorily performed by existing undertakings, nor for the purchase of shares, capital holdings or property rights of national investors.

This prohibition shall not apply to direct foreign investment made in a national undertaking to forestall its imminent bankruptcy, where:

(a)   the department controlling companies in the particular country, or its equivalent, verifies the imminence of bankruptcy;

(b)   the company shows that it has offered national or subregional investors a preferential purchase option; and

(c)   the foreign investor undertakes to offer to sell to national investors a sufficient part of his shares, capital holdings or rights in the company to constitute a national undertaking in a period not exceeding fifteen years and established in each case in accordance with the characteristics of the sector.

The permission granted by the competent national authority shall specify the period and terms of the fulfilment of those duties, the manner in which the value of the shares, capital holdings or rights shall be determined at the time of the sale, and, when applicable, the system by which these shall be transferred to national investors.

Article 4.   The participation of foreign investors in a national or joint undertaking may be authorized if its purpose is to increase the capital of the undertaking and it does not change the status of the undertaking as national or joint.

Article 5.   All direct foreign investment shall be registered with the competent national authority together with the agreement setting out the terms of the authorization. The amount of the investment shall be registered in freely convertible currency.

Article 6.   The authority which registers the investment, in conjunction with whichever departments or government offices are competent in each particular case, shall supervise the fulfilment by foreign investors of their duties.

In addition to the duties prescribed in these and other regulations, the competent national authority shall:

(a)   Satisfy itself that the conditions for national participation in the technical, administrative, financial and business management and in the capital of the undertaking are fulfilled;

(b)   Authorize in exceptional cases the purchase of shares, capital holdings or rights of national or joint undertakings by foreign investors, as required by articles 3 and 4 of these Regulations;

(c)   Establish an information and control system over the prices of intermediate products provided by suppliers of foreign technology or capital;

(d)   Authorize the transfer abroad in freely convertible currencies of any sum which undertakings or investors are entitled to remit by these Regulations and the law of the recipient country;

(e)   Centralize statistical, book-keeping, informational and control records relating to direct foreign investments;

(f)   Authorize licence agreements for the use of imported technology and of trade marks and patents.

Article 7.   A foreign investor may re-export invested capital when he sells his shares, capital interest or rights to a national investor, or when the undertaking is wound up.

Sale of shares, capital holdings or rights by one foreign investor to another shall require the previous consent of the competent national authority and shall not be regarded as re-export of capital.

Article 8.   "Re-exportable capital" means the amount of direct foreign investment initially registered and actually made, plus any reinvestments made in the same undertaking under the provisions of these Regulations and minus any net losses.

Wherever national investors have an interest in the undertaking, the foregoing provision shall apply only to that part of the direct foreign investment from which the reinvestments are made and the net losses are suffered.

Article 9.   Where an undertaking is wound up, any difference between the real value of its net assets and the re-exportable capital as defined in the previous article shall be deemed to be a capital gain and may be remitted abroad after payment of the taxes due.

Article 10.   A foreign investor may transfer abroad any sum he obtains from the sale of his shares, capital interest or rights, after payment of the taxes due.

Article 11.   Any sums which a foreign investor may be entitled to remit abroad shall be converted at the rate of exchange prevailing when the remittance is made.

Article 12.   Reinvestment of profits by a foreign undertaking shall be deemed to be investment for which prior authorization and registration are necessary.

Article 13.   The government of a member country may permit reinvestment of profits by a foreign undertaking without a special authorization, up to a sum not exceeding annually five per cent of the capital of the undertaking. The duty to register shall remain.

Article 14.   Foreign loans obtained by an undertaking are required to be authorized in advance and registered by the competent authority.

Limits of aggregate foreign indebtedness may be authorized for a stated period. Loan contracts concluded within the authorized aggregate limits are required to be registered with the competent authority.

Article 15.   Governments of member countries may not underwrite or guarantee in any way, either directly or through official or semi-official bodies, external loan transactions entered into by foreign companies in which there is no State participation.

Article 16.   Transfers abroad made by undertakings under the head of amortization and interest on foreign loans shall be authorized in the terms of the registered contract.

In foreign loans contracts made between the parent company and its affiliates or between affiliates of the same foreign undertaking, the real annual rate of interest may not exceed by more that three percentage points the prime rate in force in the financial market of the country of origin of the currency in which the operation has been registered. On foreign loan contracts other than those mentioned above, the real annual rate of interest to be paid by undertakings shall be determined by the competent national authority and be closely compatible with the conditions prevailing in the financial market of the country in which the operation has been registered.

For the purposes of this article, real interest means the total cost which the debtor must pay for the use of the loan including commission and charges of all kinds.

Article 17.   Only short term domestic loans shall be available to foreign companies, on the terms and conditions specified in the rules made by the Commission at the instance of the Board.

Article 18. Every agreement relating to the import of technology or to patents and trade marks shall be examined and submitted for approval to the competent authority of the member country, which shall assess the effective contribution of the imported technology by estimating the benefits likely to be obtained from it, the price of the goods in which it is embodied, and any other specific and quantifiable effect it may have.

Article 19. An agreement relating to the import of technology shall contain provisions least on:

    (a)   the particular forms in which the imported technology is to be transferred;

    (b)   the contractual value of every aspect of the transfer, expressed in terms similar to those used for the registration of direct foreign investment;

    (c)   the duration of the agreement.

Article 20. Member countries may not authorize the conclusion of agreements relating to the transfer of foreign technology or to patents and containing conditions:

    (a)   whereby the provision of the technology obliges the recipient country or undertaking to purchase capital goods, intermediate products, raw materials or other forms of technology from a particular source, or to make permanent use of staff designated by the undertaking supplying the technology; in exceptional cases the recipient country may accept such conditions governing the purchase of capital goods, intermediate products or raw materials at prices consonant with current world market prices;

    (b)   whereby the undertaking selling the technology reserves the right to fix the sale price or resale price of products incorporating that technology;

    (c)   restricting the volume and structure of production;

    (d)   prohibiting the use of competing technologies;

    (e)   giving the supplier of the technology a total or partial option to purchase;

    (f)   requiring the purchaser of the technology to transfer to the supplier any inventions or improvements obtained through its use;

    (g)   requiring payment of royalties to patentees for unused patents; or

    (h)   conditions of equivalent effect.

Save in exceptional cases duly so distinguished by the competent authority of the recipient country, conditions prohibiting or limiting in any way the export of products incorporating the particular technology may not be accepted.

In no case may conditions of this kind be accepted in subregional trade or for the export of similar products to third countries.

Article 21. Subject to prior authorization by the competent national authority, contributions of technology in the form of intangible assets shall entitle the payment of royalties but may not be treated as transfers of capital.

Where such contributions are made to a foreign undertaking by its parent company or by another subsidiary thereof, royalty payments shall not be permitted nor may any deduction be made on that account for tax purposes.

Article 22. National authorities shall maintain continuous systematic identification of technologies available on the world market for various branches of industry in order to provide themselves with the alternative procedures most useful and convenient in the economic conditions of the subregion, and shall report their results to the Board. They shall link this process with that prescribed in chapter V of these Regulations for the evaluation of national or subregional technology.

Article 23. Before 30 November 1972, on a proposal from the Board, the Commission shall approve a program designed to promote and safeguard the production of subregional technology and the adaptation and assimilation of existing technologies.

This programme shall provide for:

(a) special fiscal or other incentives to the production of technology, and in particular of technologies relating to the intensive use of subregional inputs or designed for the efficient utilization of subregional factors of production;

(b) promotion of exports to third countries of products incorporating subregional technology; and

(c) channelling of domestic savings into the establishment of subregional or national research and development centres.

Article 24. The governments of member countries shall give preference in their purchases to products incorporating subregional technology in such manner as the Commission may deem appropriate. On a proposal by the Board the Commission may propose to member countries that taxes be levied on products bearing foreign trade marks that involve royalty payments where the technology employed in the manufacture of those products is publicly available or readily accessible.

Article 25.   License agreement for the exploitation of foreign trade marks in the territories of member countries may not contain restrictive conditions:

(a)   prohibiting or limiting the export to or sale in specific countries of products manufactured under the trade mark or of similar products;

(b)   requiring the use of raw materials, intermediate goods or equipment supplied by the owner of the trade mark or his affiliates; in exceptional cases the recipient country may accept such conditions where the price of the articles is consonant with current world market prices;

(c)   fixing the sale or resale price of products manufactured under the trade mark;

(d)   requiring the payment of royalties to the owner of a trade mark in respect of unused trade marks;

(e)   requiring the permanent use of staff provided or designated by the owner of the trade mark; or

(f)   of equivalent effect.

Article 26.   On a proposal by the Board, the Commission may specify production processes, products or groups of products in respect of which patent privileges may not be granted in any Member Country. It may also decide on the treatment of existing privileges.

CHAPTER II

Article 27.   Only products of national or joint undertakings of member countries or of foreign enterprises which are becoming national or joint undertakings as provided in this chapter may benefit from the liberalization programme of the Cartagena Agreement.

Article 28.   A foreign undertaking now established in the territory of a member country and desiring its products to benefit from the liberalization programme of the Cartagena Agreement shall within three years following the date on which these Regulations enter into force agree with the competent authority of the recipient country on its gradual and progressive conversion into a national or joint undertaking as provided in article 31.

By the end of the said three-year period national investors shall in no case own less than 15 per cent of the capital of the undertaking.

The period within which the conversion is to take place may not exceed fifteen years in Chile, Colombia or Peru and twenty years in Bolivia or Ecuador from the date on which these Regulations enter into force.

When two-thirds of the period agreed upon for the conversion have elapsed, the share of national investors in the capital of such undertakings shall not be less than 45 per cent.

Foreign undertakings now established means those legally established in the territory of the particular country on 30 June 1971.

Article 29.   The national authorities whose duty it is to issue certificates of origin for goods shall issue such certificates for the products of foreign undertakings now established which within the space of three years referred to in the first paragraph of article 28 formally express to the government of the recipient country their intention to convert themselves into national or joint undertakings.

The products of foreign undertakings now established which do not enter into an agreement to convert themselves into national or joint undertakings within the aforesaid three-year period may not benefit from the liberalization programme of the Agreement and consequently may not receive a certificate of origin from the competent authority.

Article 30.   Foreign undertakings which have established themselves in the territory of a member country since 1 January 1971 shall offer on behalf of their investors for sale to national investors gradually and progressively, in accordance with the provisions of article 31, that portion of their shares, capital holdings or rights the cession of which will convert them into joint undertakings within a period not exceeding fifteen years in Chile, Colombia or Peru and twenty years in Bolivia or Ecuador.

In Chile, Colombia and Peru the agreement shall provide that the participation of national investors in the capital of the undertaking may not be less than 15 per cent at the start of its production, 30 per cent when one-third of the agreed period has elapsed, and 45 per cent when two-thirds of that period have elapsed.

In Bolivia and Ecuador the progressive participation of national investors in the capital of the undertaking may not be less than 5 per cent three years after the start of production, 10 per cent after one-third of the agreed period has elapsed, and 35 per cent after two-thirds thereof have elapsed.

In calculating the percentages referred to in this article, participation by subregional investors or by the Andean Development Corporation shall be deemed to be that of national investors.

In each case the twenty-year period for Bolivia and Ecuador shall begin two years after the start of production.

Article 31.   Agreements on the conversion of foreign into joint undertakings shall include the following conditions:

(a)   the period within which the duty to convert the foreign undertaking into a joint undertaking shall be fulfilled;

(b)   the time-table for the process of transferring the shares, capital holdings or rights to national investors, which shall always include the rules for the minimum percentages referred to in articles 28 and 30;

(c)   rules enjoining the progressive participation of national investors or their representatives in the technical, financial, administrative and business management of the undertaking not later than the date on which it starts production;

(d)   the manner in which the value of the shares, capital holdings and rights is to be determined on sale;

(e)   the procedure of ensuring the transfer of shares, capital holdings and rights to national investors.

Article 32.   Products of foreign undertakings shall benefit from the liberalization programme of the Cartagena Agreement during the period agreed upon for the conversion of those into joint undertakings in accordance with the particular agreement. The products of an undertaking that has ceased to fulfil the duties laid down in the agreement, or has not been converted into a joint undertaking within the agreed period, shall no longer benefit by the aforesaid liberalization programme and therefore shall not be protected by certificates of origin.

Article 33.   The rights established by these Regulations for foreign and joint undertakings are the fullest that may be granted by member countries.

Article 34.   Foreign undertakings which export 80 per cent or more of their produce to markets in third countries need not comply with the rules laid down in this chapter. Their products may not benefit in any way from the liberalization Programme of the Cartagena Agreement.

Article 35.   The duty to offer for sale to national investors the specific percentages of the shares, capital holdings or rights of foreign undertakings referred to in articles 28 and 30 shall include a priority option in favour of the State or State undertakings in the recipient country.

Article 36.   Undertakings in which the State or State undertakings participate shall be deemed to be joint undertakings even if the participation is less than 51 per cent of the capital, provided that the State representation determines the decisions of the undertaking. The Commission, on a proposal by the Board, shall within three months from the date on which these Regulations enter into force establish the minimal participation by the State or by State undertakings to which this article refers.

Article 37.   Foreign investors may, with the prior authorization of the competent national authority, transfer abroad in freely convertible currency proven net profits of direct foreign investment not exceeding 14 per cent per year.

In special cases the Commission, at the request of a member country, may authorize higher percentages than that laid down in this article.

CHAPTER III

Article 38.   Each member country may reserve sectors of economic activity for its private or public national undertakings and decide whether joint undertakings may participate in them.

Without prejudice to the provisions of other articles in this chapter the Commission, on a proposal by the Board, may determine the sectors which all the member countries shall reserve for their national public or private undertakings and decide whether joint undertakings may participate in them.

Article 39.   Foreign undertakings in the sectors referred to in this chapter need not comply with the provisions of the previous chapter regarding the conversion of foreign undertakings into national or joint enterprises. They shall however comply with the other provisions of the Common Regulations and with the special provisions of articles 40 to 43.

Article 40.   In the first ten years during which these Regulations are in force, foreign undertakings may be authorized to operate in the primary commodities sector under the system of concessions under contracts not exceeding twenty years in duration.

For the purposes of these Regulations the primary commodities sector shall include primary exploration and exploitation of minerals of all kinds including liquid and gaseous hydrocarbons, the use of gas and oil pipelines, and forestry.

Member countries shall not authorize tax depletion allowances for undertakings investing in this sector.

The participation of foreign undertakings in the exploration and working of gas or oil fields shall preferably be authorized in the form of partnership contracts with State undertakings of the recipient country.

The treatment given by member countries to foreign undertakings established in this sector may differ from that prescribed in article 37.

Article 41.   No foreign undertaking may be established or new direct foreign investment admitted in the public utilities sector, other than investment which existing foreign undertakings may need to make in order to operate with technical and economic efficiency.

For these purposes, public utilities are drinking-water, drainage, electric power, public lighting, health, sanitation, telephone and postal and telecommunication services.

Article 42.   No new direct foreign investment may be admitted in insurance, commercial banking or other financial institutions.

A foreign bank established in the territory of a member country shall cease to receive local payments into current or savings accounts or time deposits for three years from the entry of these regulations into force.

An established foreign bank wishing to continue to receive local deposits of any kind shall be converted into a national undertaking. For this purpose it shall offer for sale to national investors shares to the value of at least 80 per cent of its capital within the time specified in the previous paragraph.

Article 43.   No new direct foreign investment may be permitted in an undertaking concerned with domestic transport, advertising, commercial broadcasting, television, newspapers, magazines, or the marketing of any kind of product within the country.

A foreign undertaking already operating in these sectors shall convert itself into a national undertaking, for which purpose it shall offer for sale to national investors at least eighty per cent of its shares within three years from the entry of these Regulations into force.

Article 44.   A recipient country considering that special circumstances exist may apply rules differing from those laid down in articles 40 to 43.

Products of a foreign undertaking to which the sectors of this chapter apply and which does not wish to convert itself into a national or joint undertaking, or to which a member country applies rules differing from those referred to in the last paragraph, may not benefit by the liberalization programme of the Cartagena Agreement.

CHAPTER IV

Article 45.   The share capital of companies shall be represented by registered shares. Existing bearer shares shall be converted into registered shares within one year from the entry of these Regulations into force.

Article 46.   In regard to projects corresponding to products reserved for Bolivia or Ecuador by virtue of article 50 of the Cartagena Agreement, the other four countries undertake not to authorize direct foreign investment in their territories except as provided in contracts concluded before 31 December 1970

Article 47.   The Commission, on a proposal by the Board, shall approve by 30 November 1971 an agreement to avoid double taxation between member countries.

Within the same period the Commission, on a proposal by the Board, shall approve a model agreement containing rules on double taxation between member countries and other States outside the subregion, and member countries shall refrain from entering into such agreements with any country outside the subregion.

Article 48.   The member countries shall undertake to keep each other and the Board informed with regard to the application in their territories of these Regulations and especially of the rules contained in chapter II, and to establish a permanent system of exchange of information on authorizations of foreign investment or of importation of technology granted in their territories to facilitate increasing harmonization of their policies and to improve their bargaining capacity to obtain for recipient countries not less favourable terms than those negotiated in similar cases with one another.

They shall likewise undertake to co-ordinate closely their action in international agencies and forums that discuss matters related to foreign investment or transfer of technology.

Article 49.   Without prejudice to the provisions of articles 79, 81 and 99 of the Cartagena Agreement, any member country considering itself prejudiced by importation of the products of foreign enterprises under the liberalization programme of the Agreement may ask the Board to authorize necessary remedial measures against such prejudice.

Article 50.   Member countries may not accord to foreign investors treatment more favourable than to national investors.

Article 51.   No instrument pertaining to investment or to the transfer of technology may contain a clause removing disputes or conflicts from the national jurisdiction and competence of the recipient country, or permitting subrogation by States of the rights and actions of their national investors.

Differences arising among member countries with regard to the interpretation or implementation of these Regulations shall be settled by the procedure established in chapter II, section D, of the Cartagena Agreement for the settlement of disputes.

CHAPTER V

Article 52.   In accordance with the provisions of these Regulations and chapter II of the Cartagena Agreement, the Commission and the Board shall have the following powers:

The Commission:

(a)   To rule on proposals submitted by the Board for its consideration regarding the treatment of foreign capital, industrial property or the production and marketing of technology in accordance with these regulations;

(b)   To approve, on a proposal by the Board, measures necessary for the better application of the Common Regulations;

(c)   To adopt all other measures tending to facilitate the achievement of its aims.

The Board:

(a) To supervise the execution and observance of these Regulations and of any rules which the Commission may approve for this purpose;

(b) To centralize statistical, accounting or any other type of information provided by member countries in relation to foreign investment or the transfer of technology;

(c) To compile economic and legal data on foreign investment and the transfer of technology for the use of member countries,

(d) To propose to the Commission measures and rules necessary for the better application of these Regulations.

Article 53. In ruling on matters covered by these Regulations, the Commission shall follow the procedure established in article 11 (a) of the Cartagena Agreement.

Article 54. Member countries shall establish a Subregional Industrial Property Office:

(a) To serve as a connecting agency between national industrial property offices;

(b) To collect information on industrial property and circulate it to the national offices;

(c) To prepare model licensing contracts for the use of trade marks or patents in the subregion;

(d) To advise national offices on all matters relating to the application of the common rules on industrial property adopted in the regulations referred to in transitional article G;

(e) To prepare studies and submit to the member countries recommendations regarding patents on inventions.

Article 55. The Commission, on a proposal by the Board, shall establish a sub-regional system for the promotion, development, production and adaptation of technology and for centralizing the information referred to in article 22 of these Regulations, and shall circulate it to member countries together with any information it may obtain directly on those matters and on the conditions for the marketing of technology.

TRANSITIONAL PROVISIONS

Article A. These Regulations shall enter into force when all the member countries have deposited with the Board's secretariat the instruments applying it in their respective territories under the provisions of the second paragraph of article 27 of the Cartagena Agreement.

Article B.   Foreign investment made in the territories of the member countries before the date on which these Regulations enter into force shall be registered with the competent national agency in each Country within the next six months.

Such investment shall continue to benefit by the present provisions in all matters not conflicting with these Regulations.

Article C.   Until the regulations referred to in transitional article G of these Regulations enter into force, member countries shall refrain from making with third countries separate agreements on industrial property.

Article D.   Within three months after the entry into force of these Regulations, each member country shall designate its agency or agencies competent to authorize, register and supervise foreign investment and transfer of technology, and shall advise the other member countries and the Board accordingly.

Article E.   All contracts on the import of technology and licenses for the use of foreign trade marks and patents concluded before the date on which these Regulations enter into force shall be registered with the competent national agency within six months after that date.

Article F.   Within six month after the entry into force of these Regulations, the Commission, on a proposal by the Board, shall approve rules for the Subregional Industrial Property Office.

Article G.   Within six months after the entry into force of these Regulations, the Commission, on a proposal by the Board, shall adopt for application of the rules on industrial property regulations which shall include the provisions listed in Appendix No. 2.

Article H.   Member countries shall undertake not to offer incentives to foreign investment that differ from those provided by their law on industrial promotion at the date on which these Regulations enter into force, until the commitment in article 28, paragraph two, of the Cartagena Agreement on harmonization of the laws of industrial promotion has been honoured.

The Commission, on a proposal by the Board, shall adopt by 30 November 1972 measures to harmonize the system of incentives applicable to the other sectors.

Article I.   Within three months following the entry into force of these Regulations the Commission, on a proposal by the Board, shall determine the treatment applicable to the capital holdings of national investors of any member country other than the recipient country.

Within the same period the Commission, on a proposal by the Board, shall determine the rules applicable to investments made by the Andean Development Corporation in any member country.

469

Article .*** The investments of public international financial entities or of foreign governmental entities of economic cooperation, whatever may be their juridical nature, shall be considered to be neutral capital and, consequently, they shall not be computed as either national or foreign in the enterprise in which they participate.

To determine the status of the enterprise as national, mixed or foreign in which these investments participate, the neutral capital shall be excluded from the calculation base and only the percentages of participation of the national and foreign investors in the remainder of the capital shall be taken into account.

Article .**** The Commission, upon the proposal of the Junta, shall determine the necessary conditions and requirements to consider as neutral capital the investments referred to in the preceding Article and shall approve a list of the entities which may receive this treatment.

The entities referred to in the preceding paragraph shall be exempt from the obligation to sell their shares, participations or rights, but if they so decide, they may sell their shares, participations or rights to national or subregional investors, or, upon the prior authorization of the national competent entity, to foreign investors, provided that the recipient enterprise maintains at least the same proportion of national capital.

In all other respects, the investments of these entities shall be subject to the general regime established by this Decision.

Article .**** The Commission, upon the proposal of the Junta, may accord, with other countries of Latin America which are not members of the Cartagena Agreement, a special treatment for the capital of their nationals.

TRANSITORY PROVISIONS

Article A.**** The existing [foreign] enterprises which have entered into transformation agreements prior to the entry into effect of this Decision may accord with the national competent entity that the term established for transformation begin as of January 1, 1974.

*** [Note: The articles on this and the following page were added to Decision 24 by Decision 103. The first two were in turn modified by Decision 109. In accordance with the new Transitory Article B, these are to be numbered and incorporated into the text of Decision 24 when it is codified by the Commission.] This editorial note was reproduced from the International Legal Materials source, from which the articles that begin at this note and end with Article B of the Transitory Provisions were reproduced [Note added by the editor].

****[See note at bottom of previous page.] This note was reproduced from the International Legal Materials source and refers to note *** above [Note added by the editor].

Article B.**** The Commission, once the Junta so proposes, shall proceed to codify Decision 24, taking into account Decision 102.*****

APPENDIX No. 1
GUIDE FOR AUTHORIZATION, REGISTRATION AND CONTROL OF FOREIGN INVESTMENT

Every foreign investment application shall include:

I.   Identification of the investor:

    (a)   Name;

    (b)   Nationality;

    (c)   Members of the Board of Directors;

    (d)   Roster of management and staff;

    (e)   Economic activity;

    (f)   Copy of the deed of incorporation.

II.   Characteristics of the investment:

    (a)   Financial resources in foreign exchange or credits:

        Currency in which the investment is made;
        National capital;
        Foreign capital;
        Credit from parent company;
        Credit from other sources;
        Total interest to be paid on the credits.

    (b)   Physical or tangible resources such as:

        Industrial plant;
        New or reconditioned machinery;
        New or reconditioned equipment;
        Spare parts;
        Parts and components;
        Raw materials;
        Semi-manufactured products.

*****[Decision 102 addresses the question of Chile's rights and obligations deriving from the Cartagena Agreement.] This note was reproduced from the International Legal Materials source [Note added by the editor].

(c)   Resources derived from technology or intangibles such as:

Trade marks;
Industrial models;
Managerial ability;
Patented or unpatented technical knowledge;
Possible alternative technologies.

Technical knowledge may take the following forms:

(i)   Objects:

Samples;
Unregistered models;
Machinery, instruments, parts, tools;
Manufacturing appliances.

(ii)   Technical documents:

Formulas, calculations;
Plans, drawings;
Unpatented inventions.

(iii)   Instructions:

Notes on the preparation, manufacture and operation of the product or process;
Explanations or practical advice for manufacturing (know-how);
Technical pamphlets;
Complementary explanation of patents;
Production flow-charts;
Control methods;
Sums to be paid as royalties;
Identity of the party receiving the royalties.

III.   Needs to be met:

(a)   Scarcity of domestic savings;
(b)   Scarcity of foreign exchange;
(c)   Lack of managerial or administrative capacity;
(d)   Need for access to scarce technological know-how;
(e)   Lack of capacity or of commercial contacts for the sale of goods in international markets;
(f)   Lack of local initiative.

IV.   Schedule for progressive national participation:

(a)   Percentage of shares to be allocated to national investors;
(b)   Terms and conditions therefor;
(c)   Methods of determining the value of the investment.

V.   Consequences of the new investment:

(a)   Approximate date for the start of normal operations;
(b)   Operational capacity;
(c)   Exportable production;
(d)   Generation of additional jobs;
(e)   Imports of raw materials or intermediate products in relation to annual production;
(f)   Use of domestic inputs.

APPENDIX No. 2
PROVISIONS TO BE INCLUDED IN THE REGULATIONS FOR THE APPLICATION OF INDUSTRIAL PROPERTY RULES

(a)   Determination of the signs, words, symbols or names which can be registered as trade marks;
(b)   Provisions regarding ownership of trade marks, procedures for acquiring it, parties which may hold ownership rights, etc.
(c)   Uniform product classification for the purpose of trade marks;
(d)   Publication and terms of opposition to registration;
(e)   Priority for or right of opposition;
(f)   Use of privilege;
(g)   Lapse for lack of use;
(h)   Expiry of privilege;
(i)   Negotiation of trade marks;
(j)   Uniform causes for annulment, non-renewal, cancellation due to prior registration, etc.;
(k)   Classification of patents;
(l)   Determination of products and industrial processes which may be patented in pursuit of the aims of the whole development strategy for the subregion;
(m)   Requirements for patenting, and in particular uniform criteria for establishing the novelty and industrial applications of the patent;
(n)   Holder of patents;
(o)   Procedures for registration, opposition, manner of applying the invention, etc.;
(p)   End of privileges;
(q)   Rules governing industrial models and drawings.

* * *

DECISION 292 OF THE COMMISSION OF THE CARTAGENA AGREEMENT. UNIFORM CODE ON ANDEAN MULTINATIONAL ENTERPRISES[*]

> The Decision 292 of the Commission of the Cartagena Agreement was adopted and published on 4 April 1991. Decision 292 superseded Decision 244. Member countries of the Cartagena Agreement are Bolivia, Colombia, Ecuador, Peru and Venezuela.

THE COMMISSION OF THE CARTAGENA AGREEMENT,

IN VIEW OF Articles 7 and 28 of the Cartagena Agreement, Decision 244 of the Commission and Proposal 229 of the Board;

CONSIDERING that it is necessary to update and perfect the Common Code on Andean Multinational Enterprises in order to maintain and stimulate the association of national investors in the Member Countries for the undertaking of projects of shared interest and multinational scope;

DECIDES

CHAPTER I
DEFINITIONS AND REQUIREMENTS

Article 1. For the purposes of this Code, an Andean Multinational Enterprise shall be a company fulfilling the following requirements:

a) Its principal domicile shall be in the territory of one of the Member Countries or in that where the enterprise is transformed or merged.

b) It must be constituted as a corporation in accordance with the procedures contemplated in the corresponding national legislation and it shall add to its name the words "Andean Multinational Enterprise" or the letters "AME" [in Spanish "Empresa Multinacional Andina" or "EMA"].

c) Its capital must be represented by nominal shares of equal value that confer on the shareholders equal rights and impose equal obligations.

---

[*]Source: *Gaceta Oficial del Acuerdo de Cartagena*, Year VIII, No. 80, 4 April 1991. The text reproduced in this volume is from *International Legal Materials*, Andean Group: Commission Decision 292 - Uniform Code on Andean Multinational Enterprises, vol. 30, (1991), p. 1295-1302 (English translation by John R. Pate) [Note added by the editor].

d) It must have contributions of property from national investors from two or more Member Countries that together are greater than sixty percent of the capital of the company.

e) When the company is constituted with the contributions by investors of only two Member Countries the total of the contributions of the investors of each Member Country may not be less than fifteen percent of the capital of the company. If there are investors from more than two Member Countries, the total of the contributions of the shareholders of at least two countries shall each fulfil said percentage. In both cases the investments of the country of principal domicile shall be equal to at least fifteen percent or more of the capital of the company. At least one director must be provided for from each Member Country whose nationals have a participation of not less than fifteen percent of the capital of the company.

f) The subregional majority of the capital must be reflected in the technical, administrative, financial and commercial management of the company in the judgment of the corresponding national competent entity.

g) The statutes must contemplate terms and provisions that assure the shareholders an effective right of preference, as well as other provisions contemplated by the respective legislation or incorporated in the statutes. Notwithstanding, an investor may renounce such preferential right if desired.

Article 2. The nominal value of the stock shall be expressed in the national currency of the country of the principal domicile or in any other currency if the applicable legislation so permits.

Article 3. The contributions of foreign and subregional investors shall be made in freely convertible currency or in physical or tangible goods such as industrial plants, new and reconditioned machinery, new and reconditioned equipment, replacements, parts and pieces, raw materials and intermediate products originating in any country other than that of the principal domicile or in national currency deriving from resources that may be legally remitted abroad.

Likewise, contributions may be made in intangible technologies under the same conditions as established for foreign investors.

Article 4. The contributions made must be registered in freely convertible currency, upon prior verification, by the national competent entity in accordance with the nationality of the investor. In the case of companies a certification by the national competent entity of the Member Country of origin of such contribution to the effect that the company is a national thereof shall suffice. In the case of individuals the presentation of a carnet, identity document or card indicating that they are nationals of a respective Member Country will be sufficient.

CHAPTER II
CONSTITUTION AND OPERATION OF ANDEAN MULTINATIONAL ENTERPRISES

Article 5. Companies and partnerships legally constituted in the Member Countries other than as corporations may transform to an Andean Multinational Enterprise subject to the provisions of this Code.

Corporations may adopt the form of an Andean Multinational Enterprise through the sale of stock to subregional investors or the increase of their capital and the adaptation of their statutes to that established in this Decision.

Article 6. Likewise, companies may adopt the form of an Andean Multinational Enterprise through the merger of two or more national or mixed companies, provided that they maintain the percentages referred to in Article 1.

Article 7. The Andean Multinational Enterprise shall be governed by the following norms:

1. Its articles of incorporation/by-laws must be in accordance with the provisions of this Code.

2. This Code with respect to all matters not stipulated in the articles of incorporation/by-laws.

3. With respect to all matters not regulated by the articles of incorporation/by-laws of this Code, the following shall apply:

    a) The legislation of the country of the principal domicile; and

    b) When applicable, the legislation of the country where the legal relationship is established or in which the legal acts of the Andean Multinational Enterprise will take effect, in accordance with that established by applicable norms of private international law.

Article 8. The national competent entities of the Member Countries responsible for regulating firms or companies shall monitor and supervise the Andean Multinational Enterprise or their branches, without prejudice to said control being exercised by the national entities referred to in Article 6 of Decision 291 in the specific areas of their competence.

CHAPTER III
SPECIAL TREATMENT FOR ANDEAN MULTINATIONAL ENTERPRISES

Article 9. Andean Multinational Enterprises and their branches shall be entitled to a treatment not less favourable than that established for national companies with respect to preferences and for the acquisition of public sector goods and services.

Article 10. The capital contributions to Andean Multinational Enterprises and their branches shall freely circulate in the Subregion.

Article 11. When the subregional contributions to the capital of a multinational enterprise consist of physical or tangible goods the Member Country of origin and that of the principal domicile shall permit their exportation and importation free of all taxes, restrictions or obstacles, provided that said goods comply with subregional rules of origin.

Article 12. Andean Multinational Enterprises shall be eligible for export incentives under the same conditions contemplated for national companies in their respective sector, provided that they fulfil the requirements for said companies in the corresponding legislation. Likewise, Andean Multinational Enterprises may make use of the special systems for importation and exportation established in the national legislation of the Member Country of the principal domicile and of any branches.

Article 13. The investments of an Andean Multinational Enterprise, as well as its reinvestments, shall be registered by the national competent entity upon compliance with the requirements established in this Code.

Article 14. Andean Multinational Enterprises or their branches may participate in economic sectors reserved for national companies in accordance with the respective legislation of the Member Countries.

Article 15. Andean Multinational Enterprises shall have the right to open branches in the Member Countries other than that of the principal domicile. Their operation shall be subject to that provided in the national legislation of the Member Country in which they are opened.

Article 16. Branches of Andean Multinational Enterprises shall have the right to transfer to the principal domicile, in freely convertible currency, all of their net verified earnings deriving from the direct investment, upon the previous payment of the corresponding taxes.

Article 17. Foreign and subregional investors in an Andean Multinational Enterprise shall have the right to transfer abroad in freely convertible currency all of the net verified earnings deriving from the direct investment, upon the prior payment of the corresponding taxes.

Article 18. Andean Multinational Enterprises and their branches shall be entitled to the same treatment with respect to internal national taxes established or that may be established for national companies in the sector in which they operate, provided that they comply with the same requirements established for said companies by the corresponding national legislation.

Article 19. In order to avoid situations of double taxation, in addition to the provisions established in Decision 40 and any additions, modifications or substitutions thereof, the following rules shall apply:

a)   The Member Country of the principal domicile shall not impose income or dividend remittance taxes on the portion of the income and remittances of an Andean Multinational Enterprise corresponding to profits obtained from branches existing in other Member Countries;

b)   The Member Country of the principal domicile shall not impose income tax on the redistribution by the investor company of the portion of the dividends received from an Andean Multinational Enterprise corresponding to the profits deriving from the branches of the latter operating in the other Member Countries;

c)   In the Member Countries other than that of the principal domicile no income tax shall be imposed on the redistribution by an investor company of the dividends received from an Andean Multinational Enterprise.

Article 20.   For the purposes of assuring the right stipulated in the preceding article, the Andean Multinational Enterprise shall issue the following certifications:

a)   The branch of an Andean Multinational Enterprise located in a Member Country other than that of the principal domicile shall issue a certification to be sent to the principal domicile stating its net after tax profit;

b)   The Andean Multinational Enterprise at its principal domicile shall issue certificates for its investors exonerated from income tax and, when appropriate, the percentage and sum of said dividend not subject to a remittance withholding.

In all cases the national tax authorities of the Member Countries may verify the information provided in the certifications referred to in this article and, in the event of a discrepancy, apply the corresponding sanctions in accordance with that established in the legislation of the Member Country.

Article 21.   The Member Countries shall facilitate the contracting of personnel of subregional origin by Andean Multinational Enterprises so that they may work in the Member Country of the principal domicile or in the Member Countries of the branches.

The Member Countries shall consider as nationals qualified personnel of subregional origin working with Andean Multinational Enterprises for the purposes of applying regulations on limitations of foreign workers.

Article 22.   For the purposes of the constitution and operation of Andean Multinational Enterprises, the investors, promoters and executives of said companies may enter and remain in the territory of the Member Countries for the period necessary to undertake said efforts. For this purpose the Member Countries shall grant visas authorizing their entry and permanence upon the mere verification of their status as a promoter, investor or executive of the respective company.

Article 23.   In the contracting of technology in any form, including trademarks or patents, the Member Countries shall give preference to Andean Multinational Enterprises in terms of the application of Decision 84 ** and any modifications thereof.

CHAPTER IV
FINAL PROVISIONS

Article 24.   The national competent entity or entities referred to in Decision 291 shall be responsible for issuing the registrations and other administrative acts referred to in this Decision.

Article 25.   Contributions by the Andean Development Corporation shall be considered to be national investments for the purposes of calculating the percentage of subregional participation contemplated in this Decision.

The contributions of the other entities included in the list referred to in the Annex to Decision 291 in an Andean Multinational Enterprise shall be considered to be neutral capital and, consequently, shall be excluded from the base of calculation for the classification of the respective company.

Article 26.   The Member Countries agree to encourage the constitution of Andean Multinational Enterprises in order to facilitate the process of joint industrial development in the Subregion in the different forms of industrial integration contemplated in the Cartagena Agreement.

Likewise, they shall promote and facilitate the constitution of Andean Multinational Enterprises in the area or services and other productive sectors.

Article 27.   For the purposes of this Code the investments made by mixed companies in an Andean Multinational Enterprise shall be calculated in the same proportion of national and foreign capital as in the capital thereof.

Article 28.   In the event of a violation of this Code by an Andean Multinational Enterprise in the Member Country of the principal domicile or at the branches, the national competent entity of the Member Country where the violation has occurred shall apply, in accordance with its internal provisions, the corresponding sanctions or measures, including to annul the classification as an Andean Multinational Enterprise or as a branch thereof. Any such action shall be notified to the Board, which shall inform the other Member Countries.

In the event that the classification of Andean Multinational Enterprise or a branch thereof has been annulled, any or all such companies, as the case may be, shall lose the rights contemplated in the provisions of this Code and they shall thereafter be subject to the provisions

---

**Decision 84 is the Andean Group's technology development policy; see 13 ILM 1478, Nov. 74 [Note added by the editor, as reproduced from International Legal Materials].

of Decision 291 and the legal provisions of the respective countries.

Article 29.   The Member Countries, through the national competent entity and within sixty days following the constitution, transformation or adaptation of an Andean Multinational Enterprise, shall so inform the Board by adequate documentation and the latter shall maintain a registry of Andean Multinational Enterprises. The Board in turn, within thirty days following the receipt of said information, shall so inform the other Member Countries.

Article 30.   With respect to all matters not contemplated in this Decision, subregional and foreign investors in an Andean Multinational Enterprise shall be subject to the provisions of Decision 291 and the internal norms of each Member Country.

Article 31.   This Decision substitutes Decision 244.

TRANSITORY PROVISION

Article 32.   Andean Multinational Enterprises established for the production or exploitation of products assigned or reserved under any of the subregional programming mechanisms may only be constituted in the Member Country or Countries benefitting from such assignment or reservation.

Done at the City of Lima, Peru, on the twenty-first day of the month of March of one thousand nine hundred and ninety-one.

*   *   *

ARTICLES OF AGREEMENT OF THE ISLAMIC CORPORATION FOR THE INSURANCE OF INVESTMENT AND EXPORT CREDIT*

> The Articles of Agreement of the Islamic Corporation for the Insurance of Investment and Export Credit were signed on 19 February 1992 under the auspices of the Organization of the Islamic Conference. The States members of the Organization of the Islamic Conference as of January 1995 were Afghanistan, Albania, Algeria, Azerbaïjan, Bahrain, Bangladesh, Benin, Brunei Darussalam, Burkina Faso, Cameroon, Chad, Comoros, Djibouti, Egypt, Gabon, Gambia, Guinea, Guinea-Bissau, Indonesia, Islamic Republic of Iran, Iraq, Jordan, Kuwait, Kyrgyzstan, Lebanon, Libyan Arab Jamahiriya, Maldives, Malaysia, Mali, Mauritania, Morocco, Mozambique, Niger, Nigeria, Oman, Pakistan, Palestine, Qatar, Saudi Arabia, Senegal, Sierra Leone, Somalia, Sudan, Syrian Arab Republic, Tadjikistan, Tunisia, Turkey, Turkmenistan, Uganda, United Arab Emirates, Yemen, and United Republic of Tanzania.

THE STATES PARTIES TO THIS AGREEMENT AND THE ISLAMIC DEVELOPMENT BANK;

CONSIDERING that one of the objectives of the Organization of Islamic Conference, as expressed in the Organization's Charter, is the development and fostering of cooperation among member countries in the economic and social fields;

DESIROUS of strengthening economic relations among member countries of the Organization of Islamic Conference on the basis of Islamic principles and ideals;

SEEKING to promote the flow of capital and to enlarge the scope of trade relations among Islamic countries in order to reinforce and promote their efforts at development;

HAVING REGARD:

- to Article 15 of the Agreement for the Promotion, Protection and Guarantee of Investment among member countries of the Organization of Islamic Conference, which provides that the Organization shall, through the Islamic Development Bank, establish an Islamic Institution for Investment Guarantee to undertake, in conformity with Sharia, the provision of insurance for investments in the territories of signatory parties of the said Agreement;

- to the recommendation of the Standing Committee for Commercial and Economic

---

*Source: Islamic Development Bank (1992). *Articles of Agreement of the Islamic Corporation for the Insurance of Investment and Export Credit*, (LD133/A:01/RI/MH, C:2212/RI) (Jeddah: Islamic Development Bank) [Note added by the editor].

Cooperation (COMCEC) of the Organization of Islamic Conference in its Fifth Session held in Istanbul, Republic of Turkey, in Safar 1410H for creating the mechanism for carrying out, in accordance with Shariah, the insurance of export credit in order to protect trade transactions between Islamic countries against commercial and non-commercial risks;

HAVE AGREED AS FOLLOWS:

CHAPTER I
ESTABLISHMENT, DEFINITIONS, STATUS, OFFICE, OBJECTIVE AND PURPOSES, MEMBERSHIP

Article 1
ESTABLISHMENT

There is hereby established in accordance with the provisions of this Agreement a subsidiary Corporation of the Islamic Development Bank called "The Islamic Corporation for the Insurance of Investment and Export Credit" (hereinafter called "The Corporation").

Article 2
DEFINITIONS

In this Agreement, unless the context otherwise requires, the following words and terms shall have the following meanings:

"Organization": the Organization of Islamic Conference.

"Bank": the Islamic Development Bank

"Member State(s)": a Member State of the Organization that has become a party to this Agreement.

"Member(s)": the Bank and Member State(s).

"Export Credit": A credit relating to export transactions.

"Host Country": a Member State in whose territories an investment that has been insured or reinsured, or is considered for insurance or reinsurance by the Corporation is to be located; as well as a Member State into whose territories goods financed by a credit that has been insured or reinsured, or is considered for insurance or reinsurance by the Corporation, are to be imported.

"Investment Insurance": the insurance cover provided by the Corporation for the investments referred to in Article 17 hereof against the risks stipulated in Article 19(2) hereof or the risks approved for coverage by the Board of Directors in accordance with Article 19(3) hereof.

"Export Credit Insurance":   The insurance cover provided by the Corporation for Export Credits against the risks stipulated in Articles 19(1) and 19(2) hereof or the risks approved for coverage by the Board of Directors in accordance with Article 19(3) hereof.

"Insurance Contract(s)":   includes Investment Insurance contracts as well as Export Credit Insurance contracts.

"Reinsurance Contract(s)":   includes reinsurance covers provided by the Corporation in respect of Insurance Contracts as well as reinsurance contracts entered into by the Corporation for ceding risks insured or reinsured by the Corporation.

"Policyholder(s)":   the natural or juridical person or persons who conclude Insurance Contracts with the Corporation in accordance with the provisions of this Agreement.

"Policyholder's Country":   a Member State to whose legislations the Policyholder is subject.

"The Board of Governors":   the Board of Governors of the Corporation.

"Board of Directors":   the Board of Directors of the Corporation.

"The President":   The President of the Corporation.

"Islamic Dinar":   the unit of account of the Corporation the value of which shall be equivalent to one Special Drawing Right of the International Monetary Fund.

Article 3
STATUS

Without prejudice to the provisions of Article 1 hereof, the Corporation shall be an international institution with full juridical personality, and in particular, the capacity to:

1.   contract,

2.   acquire and dispose and of movable and immovable property;

3.   institute legal proceedings.

Article 4
OFFICE OF THE CORPORATION

1. The principal Office of the Corporation shall be located in the city of Jeddah, Kingdom of Saudi Arabia.

2. The Corporation may establish agencies or branch offices elsewhere.

Article 5
OBJECTIVE AND PURPOSES

1. The objective of the Corporation shall be to enlarge the scope of trade transactions and the flow of investments among Member States.

2. To serve its objective, the Corporation shall provide, in accordance with the principles of Shariah, Export Credit Insurance or reinsurance in respect of the goods which satisfy the conditions specified in Article 16 hereof, by paying the Policyholder a reasonable indemnity in respect of losses resulting from the risks specified in Articles 19(1) and 19(2) hereof, or the risks specified by the Board of Directors in accordance with Article 19(3) hereof.

3. At a suitable time after its establishment the Corporation shall, in accordance with the principles of Shariah, provide Investment Insurance, as well as reinsurance, in respect of investments by Members in a Member State against the risks specified in Article 19(2) hereof, or the risks specified by the Board of Directors in accordance with Article 19 (3) hereof.

4. The Corporation shall exercise such powers as it may deem necessary or appropriate for achieving its objectives. The Corporation shall be guided in all its decisions by the provisions of this Article.

Article 6
MEMBERSHIP

1. The founder Members shall be the Bank and those Member States of the Organization listed in Annexure "A" hereto which, on or before the date specified in Article 61 hereof shall have signed this Agreement and shall have fulfilled all other conditions of membership.

2. Any other state which is a member of the Organization may apply and be admitted as a Member after the entry into force of this Agreement upon such terms and conditions as may be decided by the vote of the majority of the total number of Governors representing a majority of the total voting power of the Members.

3. A state that is a member of the Organization may authorize any entity or agency

to sign this Agreement on its behalf and to represent it in all matters relating to this Agreement with the exception of the matters referred to in Article 62 hereof.

CHAPTER II
FINANCIAL RESOURCES

Article 7
RESOURCES OF THE CORPORATION

The resources of the Corporation shall consist of:

a. subscriptions to the capital stock of the Corporation,

b. insurance and reinsurance contributions donated by Policyholders to the Corporation to the extent required by the Corporation to meet claims,

c. sums and other assets to which the Corporation shall become entitled to as subrogee after payment of claims, and

d. the return on the investment of the resources of the Corporation.

Article 8
AUTHORIZED CAPITAL

1. The authorized capital stock of the Corporation shall be One Hundred Million (100,000,000) Islamic Dinars divided into One Hundred Thousand (100,000) Shares having a par value of One Thousand (1000) Islamic Dinars each, which shall be available for subscription by Members in accordance with the provisions of Article 9 hereof.

2. The authorized capital stock may be increased by the Board of Governors, at such time and upon such terms and conditions as it may deem suitable, by a vote of two-thirds of the total number of Governors, representing not less than three-fourths of the voting power of the Members.

Article 9
SUBSCRIPTION AND ALLOCATION OF SHARES.

1. The Bank shall subscribe to fifty thousand (50,000) shares in the capital stock of the Corporation to be paid in accordance with Article 10(1) hereof.

2. Each Member State shall subscribe to the capital stock of the Corporation, and the minimum number of shares to be subscribed by a Member State shall be (250) two hundred and fifty shares.

3. Each Member State shall declare the number of shares it shall subscribe to the capital stock before the expiry of the date specified in paragraph (1) of Article 61 hereof.

4. Without prejudice to paragraph (2) of this Article, a state admitted to membership in accordance with paragraph (2) of Article 6 hereof, shall subscribe to that number of shares of the unsubscribed portion of the capital stock of the Corporation as determined by the Board of Governors.

5. If the Board of Governors determines that an increase in the capital stock is warranted, each Member shall have a reasonable opportunity to subscribe, upon such terms and conditions as the Board of Governors shall determine, to a proportion of the increase of stock equivalent to the proportion which its stock heretofore subscribed bears to the total subscribed capital stock immediately prior to such increase; provided, however, that the foregoing provision shall not apply in respect of any increase or any portion of an increase in the capital stock intended solely to give effect to the determination of the Board of Governors under paragraphs (4) and (6) of this Article. No Member shall be obliged to subscribe to any part of an increase of the capital stock.

6. The Board of Governors may, at the request of a Member, by a vote of a majority of the total number of Governors representing a majority of the total voting power of the Members, increase the subscription of such Member to the capital stock of the Corporation on such terms and conditions as the Board may determine.

7. Shares of stock subscribed by founder Members shall be issued at par. Each other Member shall subscribe to such number of shares of capital stock on such terms and conditions as may be determined by the Board of Governors, but in no event at an issue price of less than par.

Article 10
PAYMENT OF SUBSCRIPTION

1. Payment of the amount subscribed by the Bank to the capital stock of the Corporation shall be made in a convertible currency acceptable to the Corporation within thirty (30) days after the date on which this Agreement comes into force.

2. Payment of the value of shares subscribed by founder Member States shall be made as follows:

    a. Fifty per cent (50%) of the value of each share shall be paid in cash in a convertible currency acceptable to the Corporation in two equal instalments the first of which shall be paid within thirty (30) days after the date of deposit on behalf of the particular Member State of the instrument of ratification or acceptance; and the second instalment shall be paid within a period not exceeding twelve months after the payment of the first instalment.

b.   The remainder of the unpaid subscriptions shall be subject to call by the Corporation, in freely convertible currency acceptable to the Corporation, as and when required to meet its obligations.

c.   Calls on any portion of the unpaid subscriptions shall be uniform on all shares.

d.   If the amount received by the Corporation on a call shall be insufficient to meet the obligations which have necessitated the call, the Corporation may make further successive calls on unpaid subscriptions until the aggregate amount received by it shall be sufficient to meet such obligations.

3.   The Corporation shall determine the place for any payment under this Article. Until so determined, payment of the portion of the value of shares referred to in paragraph 2(a) hereof shall be made to such place as the Bank may determine.

Article 11
REFUNDS

1.   The Corporation shall, as soon as practicable, return to Member States amounts paid on calls on subscribed capital if and to the extent that:

(a)   the call shall have been made to pay a claim resulting from an Insurance or Reinsurance Contract which the assets of the Policyholders' Fund could not meet and thereafter the Corporation shall have recovered, in whole or in part, in a freely convertible currency, the amount of such claim; or

(b)   the call shall have been made because of a default in payment by a Member State and thereafter such Member State shall have made good such default in whole or in part; or

(c)   the Board of Governors, by the vote of not less than two-thirds of the total voting power, determines that the financial position of the Corporation permits all or part of such amounts to be returned.

2.   Any refund effected under this Article to a Member State shall be made in a freely convertible currency in the proportion of the payments made by that Member State to the total amount paid pursuant to calls made prior to such refund.

3.   The equivalent of amounts refunded under this Article to a Member State shall become part of the callable capital obligations of the Member State under Article 10(2)(b).

Article 12
CONDITIONS RELATING TO CAPITAL STOCK

1. Shares of stock shall not be pledged or encumbered in any manner whatsoever and they shall not be transferable except to the Corporation in accordance with Chapter VI.

2. The liability of a Member in accordance with provisions of this Agreement shall be limited to the unpaid portion of its capital subscription.

3. No Member, by reason only of its membership, shall be liable for the obligations of the Corporation towards third parties.

Article 13
OBLIGATIONS AND RIGHTS OF THE CAPITAL

1. Establishment expenses shall be paid out of the capital by way of a loan to be repaid from the surplus accruing to the Policyholders' Fund.

2. The capital shall not be entitled to a share in any surplus accruing to the Policyholders' Fund.

3. Any deficit in the Policyholders' Fund shall be covered from the capital by way of a loan to be repaid from the surplus accruing to the Policyholders' Fund.

CHAPTER III
OPERATIONS OF THE CORPORATION

Article 14
USE OF RESOURCES

The resources and facilities of the Corporation shall be used exclusively to achieve the objective and purposes of the Corporation provided for in Article 5 hereof.

Article 15
RULES RELATING TO OPERATIONS.

1. In carrying out its operations, the Corporation shall:

    a. endeavor to achieve mutual cooperation of Policyholders through their collective sharing of the losses which any one Policyholder may suffer on the materialization of the risk or risks insured or reinsured by the Corporation.

    b. distribute to Policyholders the surplus that may accrue from the insurance and reinsurance operations on such basis as may be determined by the Board of Governors.

c.   pay due regard to maintaining a sound financial position in accordance with established business practices.

2.   Unless the context otherwise requires, all the provisions of this Agreement which apply to insurance transactions shall apply to reinsurance transactions carried outby the Corporation.

Article 16
EXPORT CREDITS ELIGIBLE FOR INSURANCE

All Export Credits pertaining to goods exported from a Member State to another Member State shall be eligible for insurance provided that:

1.   The goods, the subject of the credit, shall have been produced, manufactured in whole or in part, assembled or reprocessed in one or more Member States provided that a reasonable value added will accrue to the Member State from which such goods are exported. The Board of Directors shall, from time to time, issue regulations determining the types and specifications of goods in respect of which the Corporation may insure Export Credits and the minimum value added that must accrue to the Member State   in which such goods have been produced, manufactured, reprocessed or assembled.

2.   The duration of the credit shall not exceed five years unless the Board of Directors shall decide otherwise.

Article 17
INVESTMENTS ELIGIBLE FOR INSURANCE

1.   Investments eligible for insurance shall comprise all investments by Members or nationals of Member States in Member States including direct investments enterprises, their branches and agencies; investments in the share capital of enterprises including principal amounts of loans made or guaranteed by holders of equity in the enterprise concerned; and all other forms of direct investments which shall be considered eligible for insurance by the Board of Directors.

2.   Except for reinsurance transactions, insurance shall be restricted to investments the implementation of which begins   subsequent to the registration of the application for insurance by the Corporation. Such investments may include:

(a)   the transfer of foreign exchange made to modernize, expand or develop existing investments,

(b)   the use of earnings from existing investments which could otherwise be transferred outside the Host Country.

3.   Private, public and mixed investments operating on commercial basis shall be eligible for insurance by the Corporation.

Article 18
ELIGIBILITY TO RECEIVE THE CORPORATION'S SERVICES.

1.   The following shall be eligible to receive the services of the Corporation

    (i)   the Bank,

    (ii)   any natural person, who is a national of a Member State other than the Host Country, and

    (iii)   any juridical person the majority of whose stocks or shares are owned by one or more Members or by a national or nationals of one or more Member States and whose principal office is located in a Member State.

2.   Subject to the provisions of Articles 16 and 17 hereof and notwithstanding the foregoing, a juridical person may, by a resolution of the Board of Directors, be accepted as a party to an Insurance or Reinsurance Contract even if its principal office is located in a non-Member State, provided that such juridical person is owned, by not less than fifty per cent, by one or more Members or by a national or nationals of one or more Member States or by juridical persons who would, under the provisions of paragraph (1) of this Article, be eligible parties to an Insurance or Reinsurance Contract.

3.   The Board of Directors may extend eligibility for insurance to a natural person who is a national of the Host Country or a juridical person which is incorporated in the Host Country or the majority of whose capital is owned by its nationals, provided that:

    a.   the request for insurance shall be jointly made by the Host Country and the applicant for insurance,

    b.   the assets that are to be insured are, or will be, transferred from outside the Host Country.

4.   Where the applicant for insurance has more than one nationality, the nationality of a Member State shall prevail over the nationality of a non-Member, and the nationality of the Host Country shall prevail over the nationality of any other Member State.

Article 19
COVERED RISKS

1.   The Corporation may cover eligible Export Credits against a loss resulting from one of the following types of commercial risks:

          a.   the insolvency or bankruptcy of the buyer,

          b.   repudiation or termination by the buyer of the purchase contract or his refusal or failure to take delivery of the goods despite the seller's fulfilment of all his obligations towards the buyer,

          c.   refusal of the buyer to pay the purchase price to the seller or his failure to do so despite the seller's fulfilment of all his obligations towards the buyer.

2.   The Corporation may cover eligible Export Credits, as well as eligible investments against losses resulting from one or more of the non-commercial risks specified below:

          a.   Currency Transfer
any introduction attributable to the government of the Host Country or the Policyholder's Country of restrictions on the transfer outside the Host Country or the Policyholder's Country of the particular local currency into a freely convertible currency or another currency acceptable to the Policyholder, including the refusal or failure of the government of the Host Country or the Policyholder's Country to act within a reasonable period of time on an application by such Policyholder for such transfer; as well as the imposition by the public authorities of the Host Country or the Policyholder's Country, at the time of transfer, of a rate of exchange which is discriminatory against the Policyholder.

          b.   Expropriation and Similar Measures
any legislative action or administrative action or omission by the government of the Host Country or the Policyholder's Country, either directly or through an agency, which has the effect of depriving the Policyholder of his ownership or control of his investment or of the goods sold under an Export Credit, or of a substantial benefit relating to the particular investment or the particular goods, with the exception of non-discriminatory measures of general application which governments normally take for the purpose of regulating economic activity in their territories. The measures referred to herein include the revocation by the Host Country of the import licence of the goods, the subject of an Export Credit insured by the Corporation, after the goods have been shipped; the refusal of the Host Country to permit the entry of the goods into its territories; as well as the refusal of the transit of the goods or the confiscation or seizure thereof by a transit

country which is a Member of the Corporation.

c. Breach of Contract
any repudiation or breach by the government of the Host Country or the Policyholder's Country of a contract with the Policyholder, when (a) the Policyholder does not have recourse to a judicial or arbitral forum to determine the claim of repudiation or breach, or (b) a decision by such forum is not rendered within such reasonable period of time as shall be prescribed in the Insurance Contracts pursuant to the Corporation's regulations, or (c) such a decision cannot be enforced; and

d. War and Civil Disturbance
any military action or civil disturbance in any territory of the Host Country, the Policyholder's Country or a transit country which is a Member of the Corporation.

3. The Board of Directors may approve the extension of coverage to specific commercial and non-commercial risks other than those specified in Paragraphs (1) and (2) of this Article.

4. In no case shall losses resulting from the following be covered:

a. devaluation or depreciation of currency,

b. any action or omission by the authorities of the Host Country or the Policyholder's Country to which the Policyholder has agreed or for which he has been responsible, and

c. any action or omission by the authorities of the Host Country or the Policyholder's Country occurring before the conclusion of the Insurance Contract.

Article 20
INSURANCE AND REINSURANCE CONTRACTS

The Corporation shall prepare the Insurance and Reinsurance Contracts in accordance with the rules and regulations which may, from time to time, be issued by the Board of Directors, provided that the Corporation shall not cover the total insured or reinsured loss.

Article 21
LIMITS OF INSURANCE

1. Unless the Board of Governors shall, by a majority of its Members representing a majority of the voting power of the Members, otherwise decide, the aggregate amount

of contingent liabilities which may be assumed by the Corporation shall not exceed one hundred and fifty percent of the amount of the Corporation's unimpaired subscribed capital and its reserves plus such portion of its reinsurance cover as the Board of Directors may determine. The Board of Directors shall, from time to time, review the risk profile of the Corporation's portfolio in the light of its experience with claims, degree of risks diversification, reinsurance cover and other relevant factors with a view to ascertaining whether changes in the maximum aggregate amount of contingent liabilities should be recommended to the Board of Governors. The maximum amount determined by the Board of Governors shall not under any circumstances exceed ten times the amount of the Corporation's unimpaired subscribed capital, its reserves and such portion of its reinsurance cover as may be deemed appropriate.

2.   without prejudice to the ceiling of contingent liability referred to in Paragraph(1) of this Article, the Board of Directors may prescribe:

    a.   maximum aggregate amounts of contingent liability which may be assumed by the Corporation under all contracts with a Member or the Policyholders of each individual Member State. The Board of Directors shall determine such maximum amounts in the light of the share of the respective Member in the capital of the Corporation.

    b.   maximum aggregate amounts of contingent liability which may be assumed by the Corporation in respect of any single transaction.

Article 22
FEES AND CONTRIBUTIONS

1.   The Corporation shall collect a fee to cover the cost of examining an application for insurance or reinsurance.

2.   The Corporation shall establish the rates of contributions, fees and other charges, if any, applicable to each type of risk.

3.   The Corporation may, from time to time, review the rates of contributions, fees and other charges.

Article 23
PAYMENT OF CLAIMS

The President of the Corporation shall, in accordance with such general guidelines as may be issued by the Board of Directors, decide on the payment of claims to policyholders in accordance with the provisions of the Insurance or Reinsurance Contract, as the case may be. Insurance and Reinsurance Contracts shall require Policyholders to seek, before payment is made by the Corporation, such administrative remedies as may be appropriate under the circumstances, provided that they are readily available to them under the laws of the Host Country. Insurance and Reinsurance Contracts may require the lapse of certain reasonable periods between the occurrence of events giving rise to claims and payment of claims.

Article 24
SUBROGATION

1. Upon paying or agreeing to pay compensation to a Policyholder in respect of an insured loss, the Corporation shall be subrogated to such rights or claims related to the insured assets as the Policyholder may have consequent upon the materialization of the particular risk. Insurance Contracts shall specify in detail the limits within which the Corporation shall be subrogated to the rights of the Policyholder.

2. The rights of the Corporation pursuant to Paragraph (1) hereof shall be recognized by all Members.

3. In consequence of the subrogation of the Corporation to the rights of a Policyholder pursuant to Paragraph (1) hereof, Host Countries or Countries of the Policyholders, as the case may be, shall as soon as possible discharge to the Corporation their obligations towards the Policyholder and shall, on demand by the Corporation, afford the Corporation all appropriate facilities to benefit from the rights acquired by reason of such subrogation. Without prejudice to the foregoing, amounts in the currency of the Host Country or the Policyholder's Country acquired by the Corporation as subrogee pursuant to Paragraph (1) of this Article shall be accorded, with respect to use and conversion, treatment by the particular country as favourable as the treatment to which such funds would be entitled in the hands of the Policyholder.

Article 25
COOPERATION WITH NATIONAL, REGIONAL AND
INTERNATIONAL INSURANCE AND REINSURANCE ENTITIES

Without prejudice to Article 5 hereof:

1. The Corporation may enter into arrangements with national private and public insurers and reinsurers in Member States to enhance its own operations and encourage such entities to provide coverage of commercial and non-commercial risks on conditions similar to those applied by the Corporation. Such arrangements may include the provision of reinsurance services to such entities by the Corporation.

2. The Corporation may cooperate with similar national, regional or international entities in any manner as may be deemed suitable for the purposes of the Corporation.

3. The Corporation may reinsure with any appropriate reinsurance entity, in whole or in part, any Export Credit or investment insured by it.

CHAPTER IV
FINANCIAL PROVISIONS

Article 26
FINANCIAL MANAGEMENT

1. The Board of Directors shall issue financial rules and regulations as may be necessary for the business of the Corporation.

2. The Corporation's financial year shall be the Hijra Year.

Article 27
ACCOUNTS

The Corporation shall publish and circulate to Members an annual report on its accounts audited by independent auditors.

Article 28
FUNDS

1. The Corporation shall maintain and administer two separate Funds:

    a.   a Policyholders' Fund, and

    b.   a Shareholders' Fund.

2. Assets of the Policyholders' Fund shall consist of:

    a.   insurance and reinsurance contributions and collected fees,

    b.   claims received from reinsurance,

    c.   the surplus that may accrue from the operations of the Corporation,

    d.   the reserves established by setting aside part of the surplus referred to in paragraph (c) above,

    e.   the profits realized on the investment of the reserves attributed to the Policyholders' Fund,

    f.   the share of profit on the investment of the Shareholders' Fund accruing to the Policyholders' Fund in its capacity as a Mudarib,

    g.   sums acquired by the Corporation as subrogee upon indemnifying Policyholders,

3.   Assets of the Shareholders' Fund shall consist of:

a.   the paid up capital as well as the reserves attributed to the Shareholders' Fund,

b.   profits on the investment of the paid up capital and the reserves attributed to the Shareholders' Fund.

Article 29
RESERVES AND ALLOCATION OF NET INCOME

1.   The Board of Governors shall allocate all the surplus accruing to the Policyholders' Fund and all the profits accruing to the Shareholders' Fund to reserves until such reserves reach five times the subscribed capital of the Corporation.

2.   After the reserves of the Corporation have reached the level prescribed in paragraph (1) above, the Board of Governors shall decide whether and to what extent:

a.   the surplus accruing to the Policyholders' Fund may be allocated to reserves or distributed to Policyholders,

b.   the net income accruing to the Shareholders' Fund may be allocated to reserves of the Shareholders' Fund, be distributed to the Members of the Corporation or be used otherwise. Any distribution of the net income to the Corporation's Members shall be made in proportion to the share of each Member in the capital of the Corporation.

Article 30
BUDGET

The President shall prepare and submit the annual budget of the Corporation for approval by the Board of Directors.

Article 31
DETERMINATION OF EXCHANGE RATES & CONVERTIBILITY

1.   The determination of exchange rates in terms of the Islamic Dinar or the settlement of any question regarding exchange rates shall be made by the corporation on the basis of the rates declared by the International Monetary Fund.

2.   Whenever the need arises under this Agreement to determine whether any currency is freely convertible, such determination shall be made by the Corporation which may consult the International Monetary Fund if it considers this necessary.

Article 32
USE AND CONVERSION OF CURRENCIES

Without prejudice to the provisions of Article 24 hereof:

1. A Member State shall not maintain or impose any restriction on the receipt, holding or use of its currency, or any other currency, on the account of the Corporation.

2. A Member State shall, at the request of the Corporation, facilitate the prompt conversion of its currency held by the Corporation into freely convertible currency on the basis of exchange rates determined for the value date of the conversion in accordance with Article 31.

3. The currencies of non-Member States held by the Corporation shall not be used to purchase the currency of a Member State except in the ordinary course of the Corporation's business, or with the approval of the Member State concerned.

4. A Member State shall impose no restrictions on the remittance of the dues of the Corporation in convertible currency acceptable to the Corporation.

Chapter V
ORGANIZATION AND MANAGEMENT

Article 33
STRUCTURE OF THE CORPORATION

The Corporation shall have a Board of Governors, a Board of Directors, a President, a Manager and such other officers and staff as may be necessary to perform such duties as the Corporation may determine.

Article 34
BOARD OF GOVERNORS: COMPOSITION

1. The Board of Governors shall be composed of the Governors and Alternate Governors of the Bank. The Chairman of the Board of Governors of the Bank shall be the ex-officio Chairman of the Board of Governors of the Corporation.

2. Governors and Alternate Governors shall serve as such without remuneration from the Corporation, but the Corporation may reimburse them for reasonable expenses incurred in attending meetings.

Article 35
BOARD OF GOVERNORS: POWERS

1. All powers of the Corporation shall be vested in the Board of Governors.

2.   The Board of Governors may delegate to the Board of Directors any or all its powers, except the power to:

    a.   admit new Members and determine the conditions of their admission,

    b.   increase or decrease the authorized capital stock of the Corporation,

    c.   suspend a Member,

    d.   decide appeals from interpretations or applications of this Agreement given by the Board of Directors,

    e.   determine the reserve and the distribution of the net income and surplus of the Corporation,

    f.   amend this Agreement,

    g.   decide to terminate the operations of the Corporation and to distribute its assets,

    h.   determine the remuneration of the Directors,

    i.   exercise such other special powers as are expressly assigned to the Board of Governors in this Agreement.

3.   The Board of Governors, and the Board of Directors to the extent authorized, may adopt such rules and regulations as may be necessary or appropriate to conduct the business of the Corporation including rules and regulations pertaining to staff, retirement and other benefits. Until such rules and regulations are adopted, the rules, regulations and By-Laws of the Bank, to the extent they are consistent with the provisions of this Agreement, shall apply to the Corporation as if the same have been adopted by the Board of Governors, or the Board of Directors to the extent authorized, under this Agreement.

4.   The Board of Governors shall retain full power to exercise authority over any matter delegated to the Board of Directors under paragraphs (2) and (3) of this Article.

Article 36
BOARD OF GOVERNORS: PROCEDURE

1.   The Board of Governors shall hold an annual meeting and such other meetings as may be deemed necessary by the Board of Governors or called by the Board of Directors. Meetings of the Board of Governors shall be called by the Board of Directors whenever requested by the Bank or by one-third of the Member States.

2.   The annual meeting of the Board of Governors of the Corporation shall be held in conjunction with the annual meeting of the Board of Governors of the Bank.

3.   A majority of the Governors shall constitute a quorum for any meeting of the Board of Governors of the Corporation provided that such majority represents not less than two-thirds of the total voting power of the Members.

4.   The Board of Governors shall by regulation establish a procedure whereby the Board of Directors may, when the latter deems such action advisable, obtain a vote of the Governors on a specific question without calling a meeting of the Board of Governors.

Article 37
BOARD OF DIRECTORS: COMPOSITION

1.   The Board of Executive Directors of the Bank shall be the Board of Directors of the Corporation.

2.   All regulations, by-Laws and procedures of the Board of Executive Directors of the Bank shall apply to the Board of Directors of the Corporation as if the latter is the Board of Executive Directors of the Bank.

Article 38
BOARD OF DIRECTORS: POWERS

The Board of Directors shall be responsible for the direction of the general operations of the Corporation and, for this purpose, shall, in addition to the powers assigned to it expressly by this Agreement, exercise all the powers delegated to it by the Board of Governors, and in particular:

1)   prepare the work of the Board of Governors;

2)   lay down guidelines for carrying out the business of the Corporation and its operations in conformity with the general directions of the Board of Governors;

3)   approve the budget of the Corporation.

Article 39
BOARD OF DIRECTORS: PROCEDURE

1.   The Board of Directors shall function at the principal office of the Corporation, unless otherwise decided by the Board, and shall meet as often as the business of the Corporation may require.

2.   The Board of Governors shall adopt rules and regulations under which, if there is no Director of its nationality, a Member State may send a representative to

attend, without right to vote, any meeting of the Board of Directors when a matter particularly affecting that Member State is under consideration.

Article 40
VOTING

1. Each Member shall have one vote for every share subscribed and paid for.

2. In voting in the Board of Governors, each Governor shall be entitled to cast such a proportionate share of the votes of the Bank in the Corporation as shall be equal to the proportion represented by the number of shares in the Bank of the Member State he represents in relation to the total capital stock of the Bank. If a Member of the Bank is also a Member State of the Corporation the Governor representing it shall, in addition to the proportionate share of the Bank's votes determined as above, be entitled to cast the votes which such Member State is entitled to in the Corporation.

3. Except as otherwise expressly provided in this Agreement, all matters before the Board of Governors shall be decided by a majority of the voting power represented at the meeting.

4. Without prejudice to Paragraph (1) of this Article, in voting in the Board of Directors:

    (a)   an appointed Director shall be entitled to cast the votes which the Member State he represents is entitled to in the Corporation. In addition thereto, such Director shall be entitled to cast such a proportionate share of the votes of the Bank in the Corporation as shall be equal to the proportion represented by the number of shares in the Bank of the Member State he represents in relation to the total capital stock of the Bank.

    (b)   an elected Director shall be entitled to cast the votes which the Member States of the Bank he represents are entitled to in the Corporation. In addition thereto, such Director shall be entitled to cast such a proportionate share of the votes of the Bank in the Corporation as shall be equal to the proportion represented by the total number of shares in the Bank of the Member States he represents in relation to the total capital stock of the Bank. Votes which an elected Director is entitled to cast need not be cast as a unit.

Article 41
THE PRESIDENT

1. The President of the Bank shall be ex-officio President of the Corporation.

2. The President shall be the Chief Executive of the Corporation and shall conduct the affairs of the Corporation under the direction of the Board of Directors. The

President shall be responsible for the organization, appointment and dismissal of the officers and staff in accordance with rules and regulations adopted by the Board of Directors.

3. The President shall be the legal representative of the Corporation and shall have power to approve the operations of the Corporation and the conclusion of contracts pertaining thereto within the general guidelines issued by the Board of Directors.

4. In appointing the officers and staff in accordance with paragraph (2) hereof, the President shall, subject to the paramount importance of securing the highest standards of efficiency and technical competence, pay due regard to the recruitment of personnel on as wide a geographical basis as possible.

5. Without prejudice to the generality of the foregoing, the President shall appoint a Manager to the Corporation who shall be entrusted with the current business of the Corporation. The President may delegate to the Manager any of the President's powers under this Agreement. The President shall determine the salary and conditions of service of the Manager and may re-appoint him.

Article 42
INTERNATIONAL CHARACTER OF THE CORPORATION AND PROHIBITION OF POLITICAL ACTIVITY

1. The Corporation, its Directors, President, Manager, officers and staff shall not interfere in the political affairs of any Member State. Without prejudice to the right of the Corporation to take into account all the circumstances surrounding an investment or an Export Credit, the Corporation, its Directors, President, Manager, officers and staff shall not be influenced in their decisions by the political character of the Member or Member States concerned.

2. In the discharge of their duties, the President, Manager, officers and staff of the Corporation shall owe their duty entirely to the Corporation and to no other authority. Each Member of the Corporation shall respect the international character of this duty and shall refrain from all attempts to influence any of them in the discharge of their duties.

Article 43
CHANNEL OF COMMUNICATION AND DEPOSITORIES

Unless new channels of communication and new depositories are indicated by Member States within 60 days from the coming into force of this Agreement, the channel of communication and depository designated by each Member State for the purpose of Article 40 of the Articles of Agreement establishing the Bank will, respectively, be deemed to be the channel of communication in connection with any matter arising under this Agreement and the depository for keeping the holdings of the Corporation of the currency of that Member State as well as other assets of the Corporation.

Article 44
STATEMENTS AND REPORTS

1.   The Corporation shall transmit to its Members quarterly statements showing the result of its Operations.

2.   The Corporation may also publish such other reports as it deems desirable in the carrying out of its purpose and functions. Such reports shall be transmitted to the Members.

Chapter VI
WITHDRAWAL AND SUSPENSION OF MEMBERS, TEMPORARY SUSPENSION AND TERMINATION OF OPERATIONS OF THE CORPORATION

Article 45
WITHDRAWAL

1.   No Member State shall have the right to withdraw from the Corporation before the expiry of a period of five (5) years from the date of its membership.

2.   Subject to paragraph (1) of this Article, any Member State may withdraw from the Corporation by delivering a notice in writing to the Corporation.

3.   Subject to paragraph (1) of this Article, withdrawal by a Member State shall become effective and its membership shall cease on the date specified in its notice but in no event less than six (6) months after the date that notice has been received by the Corporation. However, at any time before the withdrawal becomes effective, the Member State may notify the Corporation in writing of the cancellation of its notice of intention to withdraw.

4.   A withdrawing Member State shall remain liable for all direct and contingent obligations to the Corporation to which it was subject at the date its withdrawal becomes effective. The withdrawing Member State shall also continue to be subject to those terms of this Agreement which, in the opinion of the Corporation, affect the Corporation's investments in the territories of that Member State until arrangements satisfactory to the Corporation concerning such investments are concluded between the Corporation and that Member State. When the withdrawal becomes effective, the Member State shall not incur any liability for obligations resulting from operations of the Corporation effected after that date.

5.   Any Member State that ceases to be a member of the Organization shall be deemed to have given a notice to withdraw from the membership of the Corporation under the provisions of this Article. The date when withdrawal becomes finally effective shall be determined by the Board of Governors subject to paragraph (1) of this Article.

Article 46
SUSPENSION OF MEMBERSHIP

1. If a Member State fails to fulfill any of its obligations to the Corporation, the Board of Governors may suspend such Member State by a vote, representing not less than three-fourths of the total voting power of the Members.

2. The Member State so suspended shall automatically cease to be a Member of the Corporation on the expiry of a period of one year from the date of its suspension, which period may be extended as deemed necessary by the Board of Governors, unless the Board of Governors, during such period, decides by the same majority necessary for suspension to restore the Member State to good standing.

3. While under suspension, a Member State shall not be entitled to exercise any rights under this Agreement but shall remain subject to all its obligations.

Article 47
SETTLEMENT OF ACCOUNTS ON CESSATION OF MEMBERSHIP

1. After the date on which a State ceases to be a Member, it shall remain liable for its direct obligations to the Corporation incurred as of that date. It shall also remain responsible for its contingent liabilities to the Corporation so long as any part of the operations carried out before it ceases to be a Member is outstanding but it shall not incur liabilities with respect to operations carried out thereafter by the Corporation nor share in the income or the expenses of the Corporation.

2. At the time a State ceases to be a Member, the Corporation shall arrange for the repurchase of the shares of such a State as a part of the settlement of accounts with such a State in accordance with the provisions of paragraphs (3) and (4) of this Article. For this purpose, the repurchase price of the shares shall be the book value of such shares on the date the State ceases to be a Member.

3. The payment of shares repurchased by the Corporation under this Article shall be governed by the following conditions:

    a. any amount due to the Member State concerned for its shares shall be withheld so long as that Member State, its central bank or any of its agencies, instrumentalities or political subdivisions has outstanding obligations to the Corporation. Any amount due to such Member State may, at the option of the Corporation, be applied to any liability of such Member State as it matures;

    b. the net amount, equal to the excess of the repurchase price for shares (in accordance with Paragraph (2) of this Article) over the aggregate amount of liabilities of the Member State concerned to the Corporation, shall be payable within a period not exceeding five (5) years, as may be determined by the Corporation, upon transfer of the ownership of the corresponding stock by the Member State concerned;

c.   payments shall be made in freely convertible currency; and

d.   if losses are sustained by the Corporation insurance or reinsurance operations which were outstanding on the date when a Member State ceased to be a Member and the amount of such losses exceeds the amount of the reserve provided against losses on that date, the Member State concerned shall repay, upon demand, the amount by which the repurchase price of its shares would have been reduced if the losses had been taken into account when the repurchase price was determined.

4.   If the Corporation terminates its operations pursuant to Article 49 of this Agreement within six (6) months of the date upon which any Member State ceases to be a Member, all rights of the Member State concerned shall be determined in accordance with the provisions of Articles 49 and 51 hereof. Such Member State shall be considered a Member for purposes of such Articles but shall have no voting rights.

Article 48
TEMPORARY SUSPENSION OF OPERATIONS

1.   The Board of Directors may, whenever it deems it justified, suspend the provision of insurance or reinsurance services for a specified period.

2.   In an emergency, the Board of Directors may suspend all activities of the Corporation for a period not exceeding the duration of such emergency, provided that necessary arrangements shall be made for the protection of the interests of the Corporation and of third parties.

3.   The decision to suspend operations shall have no effect on the obligations of the Members under this Agreement or on the obligations of the Corporation towards Policyholders or third parties.

Article 49
TERMINATION OF OPERATIONS

1.   The Corporation may terminate its operations by a resolution of the Board of Governors approved by a vote of two-thirds of the total number of Governors, representing not less than three-fourths of the total voting power of the Members. After such termination, the Corporation shall forthwith cease all activities, except those incident to the orderly realization, conservation and preservation of its assets and settlement of its obligations.

2.   Until final settlement of such obligations and distribution of assets, the Corporation shall remain in existence and all mutual rights and obligations of the corporation and its Members shall continue unimpaired.

Article 50
LIABILITY OF MEMBERS AND PAYMENT OF CLAIMS

1. In the event of termination of the Operations of the Corporation the liability of all Member States for the uncalled subscription to the capital stock of the Corporation shall continue until all claims of creditors and Policyholders including contingent claims, shall have been discharged.

2. In the event of termination of the operations of the Corporation:

    (a) debts attributable to the Shareholders' Fund shall be paid out of the assets of the Shareholders' Fund. If such assets shall fall short of settling such debts, the same shall be paid out of the payments accruing to the Corporation on unpaid callable subscriptions.

    (b) debts attributable to the Policyholders' Fund shall be paid out first from the assets of the Policyholders' Fund. After the said debts are so repaid, the claims of the Policyholders shall next be met. If the assets of the Policyholders' Fund shall fall short of meeting the said claims, the same shall be met out of the Shareholders' Fund. If the assets of the Shareholders' Fund shall be insufficient to settle such claims, the same shall be settled out of the payments accruing to the Corporation on unpaid callable subscriptions provided that such settlement shall be made by way of non-refundable contribution.

    (c) if the assets shall be insufficient to settle the debts or pay out the Policyholders' claims, the available assets shall be distributed between creditors and Policyholders pro rata.

Article 51
DISTRIBUTION OF ASSETS

1. If after the settlement of debts and Policyholders' claims any assets shall remain in the Policyholders' Fund, such assets shall be disbursed for charitable purposes.

2. If after the settlement of debts and Policyholders' claims any assets shall remain in the Shareholders' Fund, such assets shall be distributed to the Members of the Corporation in the proportion to the paid up capital stock held by each Member. Such distribution must be approved by the Board of Governors by a vote of two-thirds of the total number of Governors, representing not less than three-fourths of the total voting power of the Members.

3. Any Member receiving assets distributed pursuant to this Article shall enjoy the same rights with respect such assets as the Corporation enjoyed prior to the distribution.

Chapter VII
IMMUNITIES, EXEMPTIONS AND PRIVILEGES
IMMUNITIES OF THE CORPORATION

Article 52

To enable the Corporation to fulfill its purpose and carry out the functions entrusted to it, the Corporation, its Governors, alternate Governors, Directors, President, Manager, officers, assets, archives and communications shall, in the territory of each Member State, be accorded all the corresponding immunities, exemptions and privileges provided for in Articles 53, 54, 55, 56, 57, 58 and 59 of the Articles of Agreement establishing the Bank.

Article 53
IMMUNITY OF ASSETS

1. Without prejudice to the provisions of Article 54 hereof, the property and assets of the Corporation shall be immune from search, requisition, confiscation. expropriation or any other form of seizure by executive or legislative action.

2. To the extent necessary to carry out its operations under this Agreement, all property and assets of the Corporation shall be free from restrictions, regulations, controls and moratoria of any nature; provided that property and assets acquired by the Corporation. as successor to or subrogee of a Policyholder shall be free from applicable foreign exchange restrictions, regulations and controls in force in the territories of the Member State concerned to the extent that the Policyholder to whom the Corporation was subrogated was entitled to such treatment.

Article 54
LEGAL PROCESS

Actions other than those within the scope of Article 59 may be brought against the Corporation only in a court of competent jurisdiction in the territories of a Member State in which the Corporation has an office or has appointed an agent for the purpose of accepting service or notice of process. No such action against the Corporation shall be brought (i) by Members or persons acting for or deriving claims from Members or (ii) in respect of personnel matters. The property and assets of the Corporation, wherever located and by whomsoever held, shall be accorded the immunities provided for in Articles 52 and 53 hereof until the delivery of the final judgment or award against the Corporation.

Article 55
IMPLEMENTATION

Each Member State, in accordance with its Juridical system, shall promptly take such action as is necessary to make effective in its own territory the provisions set forth in this Chapter and shall inform the Corporation of the action that it has taken on the matter.

Article 56
WAIVER OF IMMUNITIES, EXEMPTIONS AND PRIVILEGES

The Corporation, at its discretion, may waive any of the privileges, immunities and exemptions conferred under this Chapter in any case or instance, in such manner and upon such conditions as it may determine to be appropriate in its best interest.

CHAPTER VIII
AMENDMENTS, INTERPRETATION, ARBITRATION

Article 57
AMENDMENTS

1. This Agreement may be amended by a resolution of the Board of Governors approved by a vote of two-thirds of the total number of Governors, representing not less than three-fourths of the total voting power of the Members.

2. Notwithstanding the provisions of paragraph (1) of this Article, the unanimous agreement of the Board of Governors shall be required for the approval of any amendment modifying:

    a)   the right to withdraw from the Corporation;

    b)   the limitations on liability provided in Paragraphs (2) and (3) of Article 12; and

    c)   the rights pertaining to purchase of capital stock provided in paragraph (5) of Article 9.

3. Any proposal to amend this Agreement, whether emanating from a Member or from the Board of Directors, shall be communicated to the Chairman of the Board of Governors who shall bring the proposal before the Board of Governors. When an amendment has been adopted, the Corporation shall so certify in an official communication addressed to all Members. Amendments shall enter into force for all Members three (3) months after the date of the official communication unless the Board of Governors specifies therein a different period.

4. No amendment which may affect the Corporation's adherence to Shariah shall be made.

Article 58
LANGUAGES, INTERPRETATION AND APPLICATION

1. The official language of the Corporation shall be Arabic. In addition, English and French shall be working languages. The Arabic text of this Agreement shall be regarded as the authentic text for both interpretation and application.

2. Any question of interpretation or application of the provisions of this Agreement arising between any Member and the Corporation or between two or more Members of the Corporation, shall be submitted to the Board of Directors for decision. If there is no Director of the nationality of the Member State concerned, Paragraph (2) of Article 39 shall be applicable.

3. Any Member may require, within six (6) months of the date of the decision under Paragraph (2) of this Article, that the question be referred to the Board of Governors, whose decision shall be final. Pending the decision of the Board of Governors, the Corporation may, so far as it deems it necessary, act on the basis of the decision of the Board of Directors.

Article 59
ARBITRATION

1. If a disagreement shall arise between the Corporation and a State that has ceased to be a Member, or between the Corporation and any Member, after adoption of a resolution to terminate the operations of the Corporation, or between the Corporation and a Member State concerning claims by the Corporation acting as subrogee of a Policyholder, or between the Corporation and a Member on any other matter, other than the matters covered by Paragraph (2) of Article 58 hereof, such disagreement shall be settled amicably. If no amicable settlement can be reached, such disagreement shall be submitted to arbitration by a tribunal of three (3) arbitrators. One of the arbitrators shall be appointed by the Corporation; another by the party concerned, and the third arbitrator shall be appointed by the Secretary General of the Organization. A majority vote of the arbitrators shall be sufficient to reach a decision which shall be final and binding upon the parties. The third arbitrator shall be empowered to settle all questions of procedure in any case where the parties are in disagreement with respect thereto.

2. Any dispute arising under an Insurance or Reinsurance Contract by the parties thereto shall be submitted to arbitration for final determination in accordance with such rules as shall be provided for or referred to in the particular contract.

Article 60
APPROVAL DEEMED GIVEN

Whenever the approval of any Member is required before any act may be done by the Corporation, approval shall be deemed have been given unless the Member presents an objection within such reasonable period as the Corporation may fix in notifying the Member of the proposed act.

CHAPTER IX
FINAL PROVISIONS

Article 61
SIGNATURE AND DEPOSIT

1. The original of this Agreement in a single copy in the Arabic, English and French languages shall remain open for signature until 15th Sha'ban 1413H/February 6th 1993 at the Headquarters of the Bank by the Bank and Governments of States listed in Annexure-A to this Agreement. This document shall be deposited at the principal office of the Corporation upon its establishment.

2. The Bank shall send certified copies of this Agreement to all the signatories and other States which become Members of the Corporation.

Article 62
RATIFICATION OR ACCEPTANCE AND EFFECT THEREOF

1. This Agreement shall be subject to ratification or acceptance by the Bank and the States parties to it. Instruments of ratification or acceptance shall be deposited with the Bank which shall duly notify the other parties of each deposit and the date thereof.

2. By ratifying or accepting this Agreement the particular Member State shall be deemed to have authorized the Corporation, at all times, to provide in the territories of that Member State, insurance and reinsurance services in accordance with the provisions hereof.

Article 63
ENTRY INTO FORCE

This Agreement shall come into force when instruments of ratification or acceptance shall have been deposited by Member States whose subscriptions in the aggregate comprise not less than Islamic Dinars Twenty-Five Million (ID.25,000,000/-).

Article 64
COMMENCEMENT OF OPERATIONS

1. At its inaugural meeting, the Board of Governors shall make arrangements for the determination of the date on which the Corporation shall commence its operations.

2. The Corporation shall notify its Members of the date of the commencement of its operations.

DONE in Tripoli, Great Socialist People's Libyan Arab Jamahiriya, this 15th day of Sha'ban 1412H, corresponding to the 19th day of February, 1992.

*   *   *

PROTOCOLO DE COLONIA PARA LA PROMOCIÓN Y PROTECCIÓN RECÍPROCA DE INVERSIONES EN EL MERCOSUR (INTRAZONA)*

> The Colonia Protocol on Reciprocal Promotion and Protection of Investments within MERCOSUR was approved by Decisión 11/93 of the Council of MERCOSUR and signed by the member States of MERCOSUR on 17 January 1994. The Protocol had not come into force as of August 1995. The member States of MERCOSUR are Argentina, Brazil, Uruguay and Paraguay.

VISTO: El Art 10 del Tratado de Asunción, Decisión N° 4/91 del Consejo del Mercado Común, la Resolución GMC N° 77/93 y la Recomendación N° 5 del Subgrupo de Trabajo N° 4 "Políticas Fiscal y Monetaria relacionadas con el Comercio".

CONSIDERANDO:

Que la creación de condiciones favorables para las inversiones de inversores de uno de los Estados Partes del MERCOSUR en el territorio de alguno de los demás intensificará la cooperación económica y acelerará el proceso de integración.

Que la promoción y protección de tales inversiones sobre la base de Protocolo contribuirá a estimular la iniciativa económica individual y a incrementar el desarrollo en los cuatro Estados Partes.

EL CONSEJO DEL MERCADO COMUN
DECIDE

Art. 1. Aprobar el PROTOCOLO DE COLONIA PARA LA PROMOCIÓN Y PROTECCIÓN RECÍPROCA DE INVERSIONES EN EL MERCOSUR (Intrazona), que consta como Anexo de la presente Decisión.

PROTOCOLO DE COLONIA

PARA LA PROMOCIÓN Y PROTECCIÓN RECÍPROCA DE INVERSIONES EN EL MERCOSUR

La República Argentina, la República Federativa del Brasíl, la República del Paraguay y la República Oriental del Uruguay, denominadas en adelante las "Partes Contratantes";

---

*Source: Secretaría Administrativa de MERCOSUR (1994). *Protocolo de Colonia Para la Promoción y Protección Recíproca de Inversiones en el MERCOSUR* (Intrazona) (MERCOSUR/CMC/Dec. No. 11/93) mimeo. [Note added by the editor].

Teniendo en cuenta el Tratado suscripto en Asunción el 26 de marzo de 1991 por el cual las Partes Contratantes deciden crear un Mercado Común del Sur (MERCOSUR);

Considerando los resultados de la labor realizada por la Comisión Técnica para la Promoción y Protección de Inversiones creada dentro del Subgrupo IV por Resolución 20/92 del Grupo Mercado Común.

Convencidos de que la creación de condiciones favorables para las inversiones de inversores de una de las Partes Contratantes en el territorio de otra Parte Contratante intensificará la cooperación económica y acelerará el proceso de integración entre los cuatro países;

Reconociendo que la promoción y la protección de tales inversiones sobre la base de un acuerdo contribuirá a estimular la iniciativa económica individual e incrementará la prosperidad en los cuatro Estados.

Han acordado lo siguiente:

Artículo 1
Definiciones

A los fines del presente Protocolo:

1. El término "inversión" designa todo tipo de activo invertido directa o indirectamente por inversores de una de las Partes Contratantes en el territorio de otra Parte Contratante, de acuerdo con las leyes y reglamentación de esta última. Incluye en particular, aunque no exclusivamente:

a) la propiedad de bienes muebles e inmuebles, así como los demás derechos reales tales como hipotecas, cauciones y derechos de prenda;

b) acciones, cuotas societarias y cualquier otro tipo de participación en sociedades;

c) títulos de crédito y derechos a prestaciones que tengan un valor económico; los préstamos estarán incluídos solamente cuando estén directamente vinculados a una inversión especifica;

d) derechos de propiedad intelectual o inmaterial, incluyendo derechos de autor y de propiedad industrial, tales como patentes, diseños industriales, marcas, nombres comerciales, procedimientos técnicos, know-how y valor llave;

e) concesiones económicas de derecho público conferidas conforme a la ley, incluyendo las concesiones para la búsqueda, cultivo, extracción o explotación de recursos naturales.

2. El término "inversor" designa:

a)   toda persona física que sea nacional de una de las Partes Contratantes o resida en forma permanente o se domicilie en el territorio de ésta, de conformidad con su legislación. Las disposiciones de este Protocolo no se aplicarán a las inversiones realizadas por personas físicas que sean nacionales de una de las Partes Contratantes en el territorio de otra Parte Contratante, si tales personas, a la fecha de la inversión, residieren en forma permanente o se domiciliaren en esta última Parte Contratante, a menos que se pruebe que los recursos referidos a estas inversiones provienen del exterior.

b)   toda persona jurídica constituída de conformidad con las leyes y reglamentaciones de una Parte Contratante y que tenga su sede en el territorio de dicha Parte Contratante.

c)   las personas jurídicas constituídas en el territorio donde se realiza la inversión, efectivamente controladas, directa o indirectamente, por personas físicas o jurídicas definidas en a) y b).

4.   El término "territorio" designa el territorio nacional de cada Parte Contratante, incluyendo aquellas zonas marítimas adyacentes al límite exterior del mar territorial nacional, sobre el cual la Parte Contratante involucrada pueda, de conformidad con el derecho internacional, ejercer derechos soberanos o jurisdicción.

Artículo 2
Promoción y Admisión

1.   Cada Parte Contratante promoverá las inversiones de inversores de las otras Partes Contratantes y las admitirá en su territorio de manera no menos favorable que a las inversiones de sus propios inversores o que a las inversiones realizadas por inversores de terceros Estados, sin perjuicio del derecho de cada Parte a mantener transitoriamente excepciones limitadas que correspondan a alguno de los sectores que figuran en el Anexo del presente Protocolo.

2.   Cuando una de las Partes Contratantes haya admitido una inversión en su territorio, otorgará las autorizaciones necesarias para su mejor desenvolvimiento incluyendo la ejecución de contratos sobre licencias, asístencia comercial o adminstrativa e ingreso del personal necesario.

Artículo 3
Tratamiento

1.   Cada Parte Contratante asegurará en todo momento un tratamiento justo y equitativo a las inversiones de inversores de otra Parte Contratante y no perjudicará su gestión, mantenimiento, uso, goce o disposición a través de medidas injustificadas o discriminatorias.

2.   Cada Parte Contratante concederá plena protección legal a tales inversiones y les acordará un tratamiento no menos favorable que el otorgado a las inversiones de sus propios inversores nacionales o de inversores de terceros Estados.

3. Las disposiciones del Párrafo 2 de este Artículo no serán interpretadas en el sentido de obligar a una Parte Contratante a extender a los inversores de otra Parte Contratante los beneficios de cualquier tratamiento, preferencia o privilegio resultante de un acuerdo internacional relativo total o parcialmente a cuestiones impositivas.

4. Ninguna de las Partes establecerá requisitos de desempeño como condición para el establecimento, la expansión o el mantenimiento de las inversiones, que requieran o exijan compromisos de exportar mercancías, o especifiquen que ciertas mercaderías o servicios se adquieran localmente, o impongan cualesquiera otros requisitos similares.

Artículo 4
Expropiaciones y Compensaciones

1. Ninguna de las Partes Contratantes tomará medidas de nacionalización o expropiación ni ninguna otra medida que tenga el mismo efecto, contra inversiones que se encuentren en su territorio y que pertenzcan a inversores de otra Parte Contratante, a menos que dichas medidas sean tomadas por razones de utilidad pública, sobre una base no discriminatoria y bajo el debido proceso legal. Las medidas serán acompañadas de disposiciones para el pago de una compensación prevía, adecuada y efectiva.

El monto de dicha compensación corresponderá al valor real que la inversión expropiada tenía inmediatamente antes del momento en que la decisión de nacionalizar o expropiar haya sido anunciada legalmente o hecha pública por la autoridad competente y generará intereses o se actualizará su valor hasta la fecha de su pago.

2. Los inversores de una Parte Contratante, que sufrieran pérdidas en sus inversiones en el territorio de otra Parte Contratante debido a guerra u otro conflicto armado, estado de emergencia nacional, revuelta, insurrección o motín, recibirán, en lo que se refiere a restitución, indemnización, compensación u otro resarcimiento, un tratamiento no menos favorable que el acordado a sus propios inversores o a los inversores de un tercer Estado.

Artículo 5
Transferencias

1. Cada Parte Contratante otorgará a los inversores de otra Parte Contratante la libre transferencia de las inversiones y ganancias, y en particular, aunque no exclusivamente de:

a) el capital y las sumas adicionales necesarias para el mantenimiento y desarrollo de las inversiones;

b) los beneficios, utilidades, rentas, intereses, dividendos y otros ingresos corrientes;

c) los fondos para el reembolso de los préstamos tal como se definen en el Artículo 1, Párrafo 1, c);

d)   las regalías y honorarios y todo otro pago relativo a los derechos previstos en el Artículo 1, Párrafo 1, d) y e);

e)   el producido de la venta o liquidación total o parcial de una inversión;

f)   las compensaciones, indemnizaciones u otros pagos previstos en el Artículo 4;

g)   las remuneraciones de los nacionales de una Parte Contratante que hayan obtenido autorización para trabajar en relación a una inversión.

2.   Las transferencias serán efectuadas sin demora, en moneda libremente convertible, al tipo de cambio vigente en el mercado a la fecha de la transferencia, conforme con los procedimientos establecidos por la Parte Contratante en cuyo territorio se realizó la inversión, los cuales no podrán afectar la sustancia de los derechos previstos en este Artículo.

Artículo 6
Subrogación

1.   Si una Parte contratante o una de sus agencias realizara un pago a un inversor en virtud de una garantia o seguro para cubrir riesgos no comerciales que hubiere contratado en relación a una inversión, la Parte Contratante en cuyo territorio se realizó la inversión reconocerá la validez de la subrogación en favor de la primera Parte Contratante o una de sus agencias respecto de cualquier derecho o título del inversor a los efectos de obtener el resarcimiento pecuniario correspondiente. Esta Parte Contratante o una de sus agencias estará autorizada, dentro de los límites de la subrogación, a ejercer los mismos derechos que el inversor hubiera estado autorizado a ejercer.

2.   En el caso de una subrogación tal como se define en el Párrafo 1 de este Artículo, el inversor no interpondrá ningún reclamo a menos que esté autorizado a hacerlo por la Parte Contratante o su agencia.

Artículo 7
Aplicación de otras normas

Cuando las disposiciones de la legislación de una Parte Contratante o las obligaciones de derecho internacional existentes o que se establezcan en el futuro o un acuerdo entre un inversor de una Parte Contratante y la Parte Contratante en cuyo territorio se realizó la inversión, contengan normas que otorguen a las inversiones un trato más favorable que el que se establece en el presente Protocolo, estas normas prevalecerán sobre el presente Protocolo en la medida que sean más favorables.

Artículo 8
Solución de Controversias entre las Partes Contratantes

Las controversias que surgieren entre las Partes Contratantes relativas a la interpretación o aplicación del presente Protocolo serán sometidas a los procedimientos de solución de controversias establecidos por el Protocolo de Brasília para la Solución de Controversias del 17 de diciembre de 1991, en adelante denominado el Protocolo de Brasília, o al Sistema que eventualmente se establezca en su reemplazo en el marco del Tratado de Asunción.

Artículo 9
Solución de Controversias entre un Inversor y la Parte Contratante
Receptora de la Inversión

1.   Toda controversia relativa a las disposiciones del presente Protocolo entre un inversor de una Parte Contratante en cuyo territorio se realizó la inversión será, en la medida de lo posible, soluciónada por consultas amistosas.

2.   Si la controversia no hubiera podido ser soluciónada en el término de seis meses a partir del momento en que hubiera sido planteada por una u otra de las partes, será sometida a alguno de los siguientes procedimientos, a pedido del inversor:

   i)   a los tribunales competentes de la Parte Contratante en cuyo territorio se realizó la inversión; o

   ii)   al arbitraje internacional, conforme a lo dispuesto en el Párrafo 4 del presente Artículo; o

   iii)   al sistema permanente de solución de controversias con particulares que, eventualmente, se establezca en el marco del Tratado de Asunción.

3.   Cuando un inversor haya optado por someter la controversia a uno de los procedimientos establecidos en el Párrafo 2 del presente Artículo la elección sera definitiva.

4.   En caso de recurso al arbitraje internacional, la controversia podrá ser llevada, a elección del inversor:

   a)   al Centro Internacional de Arreglo de Diferencias Relativas a Inversiones (C.I.A.D.I.), creado por el "Convenio sobre Arreglo de Diferencias relativas a las Inversiones entre Estados y Nacionales de otros Estados", abierto a la firma en Washington el 18 de marzo de 1965, cuando cada Estado Parte en el presente Protocolo haya adherido a aquél. Mientras esta condición no se cumpla, cada Parte Contratante da su consentimiento para que la controversia sea sometida al arbitraje conforme con el reglamento del Mecanismo Complementario del C.I.A.D.I. para la administración de procedimientos de conciliación, de arbitraje o de investigación;

   b)   a un tribunal de arbitraje "ad-hoc" establecido de acuerdo con las reglas de arbitraje de la Comisión de Naciones Unidas para el Derecho Mercantil Internacional (C.N.U.D.M.I.).

5.   El órgano arbitral decidirá las controversias en base a las disposiciones del presente Protocolo, al derecho de la Parte Contratante que sea parte en la controversia, incluídas las normas relativas a conflictos de leyes, a los términos de eventuales acuerdos particulares concluídos con relación a la inversión, como así también a los principios del derecho internacional en la materia.

6.   Las sentencias arbitrales serán definitivas y obligatorias para las partes en la controversia. Cada Parte Contratante las ejecutará de conformidad con su legislación.

Artículo 10
Inversiones y Controversias comprendidas en el Protocolo

El presente Protocolo se aplicará a todas las inversiones realizadas antes o después de la fecha de su entrada en vigor, pero las disposiciones del presente Protocolo no se aplicarán a ninguna controversia, reclamo o diferendo que haya surgido con anterioridad a su entrada en vigor.

Artículo 11
Entrada en vigor, duración y terminación

1.   El presente Protocolo entrará en vigor 30 días después de la fecha de depósito del cuarto instrumento de ratificación.   Su validez será de diez años, luego permanecerá en vigor indefinidamente hasta la expiración de un plazo de doce meses, a partir de la fecha en que alguna de las Partes Contratantes notifique por escrito a las otras Partes Contratantes su decisión de darlo por terminado.

2.   Con relación a aquellas inversiones efectuadas con anterioridad a la fecha en que la notificación de terminación de este Protocolo se haga efectiva, las disposiciones de los Artículos 1 a 11 continuarán en vigencia por un período de 15 años a partir de esa fecha.

Artículo 12
Disposiciones finales

El Presente Protocolo es parte integrante del Tratado de Asunción.

La adhesión por parte de un Estado al Tratado de Asunción implicará "ipso jure" la adhesión al presente Protocolo.

Hecho en la ciudad de Colonia del Sacramento, a los 17 días del mes de Enero de 1994, en un ejemplar original, en los idiomas español y portugués, siendo ambos textos igualmente auténticos. El Gobierno de la República del Paraguay será el depositario del presente Protocolo y de los instrumentos de ratificación y enviará copia debidamente autenticada de los mismos a los Gobiernos de los demás Estados Partes.

Por el Gobierno de la República Argentina . . . .

Por el Gobierno de la República Federativa del Brasíl . . . .

Por el Gobierno de la República del paraguay . . . .

Por el Gobierno de la República Oriental del Uruguay . . . .

ANEXO

En el acto de la firma del Protocolo de Promoción y Protección Recíproca de Inversiones entre los Estados Partes del Tratado de Asunción, los abajo firmantes han convenido además las disposiciones siguientes, las que constituyen parte integrante del presente Protocolo.

1.　　Ad. Artículo 2. Párrafo 1

De conformidad con lo previsto en el Artículo 2 del presente Protocolo, las Partes Contratantes se reservan el derecho de mantener transitoriamente excepciones limitadas al tratamiento nacional de las inversiones de inversores de las otras Partes Contratantes en los siguientes sectores:

Argentina: propiedad inmueble en zonas de frontera; transporte aéreo; industria naval; plantas nucleares; minería del uranio; seguros y pesca.

Brasíl: exploración y explotación de minerales; aprovechamiento de energía hidráulica; asístencia de la salud; servicios de radiodifusión sonora, de sonidos e imágenes y demás servicios de telecomunicaciones; adquisición o arrendamiento de propiedad rural; participación en el sistema de intermediación financiera, seguros, seguridad y capitalización; construcción, propiedad y navegación de cabotaje e interior.

Paraguay: propiedad inmueble en zonas de frontera; medios de comunicación social; escrita, radial y televisiva; transporte aéreo, marítimo y terrestre; electricidad, agua y teléfono; explotación de hidrocarburos y minerales estratégicos; importación y refinación de productos derivados de petróleo y servicio postal.

Uruguay: electricidad; hidrocarburos; petroquímica básica; energía atómica; explotación de minerales estratégicos; intermediación financiera; ferrocarriles; telecomunicaciones, radiodifusión; prensa y medios audiovisuales.

2.　　Ad. Artículo 3. Párrafo 2

La República Federativa del Brasíl se reserva el derecho de mantener la excepción prevista en el Artículo 171, Párrafo 2, de su Constitución Federal respecto de las compras gubernamentales.

3.   Ad. Artículo 3. Párrafo 4

No obstante lo dispuesto en el Artículo 3, Párrafo 4, la República Argentina y la República Federativa del Brasíl se reservan el derecho de mantener transitoriamente los requisitos de desempeño en el sector automotriz.

4.   Las Partes Contratantes harán todos los esfuerzos posibles por eliminar las excepciones a que se hace referencia en los Párrafos 1, 2 y 3 del presente Anexo, en el más breve plazo posible, a los efectos de permitir la plena conformación del Mercado Común del Sur, de conformidad con lo previsto en el Artículo 1 del Tratado de Asunción.

Las Partes Contratantes realizarán reuniones semestrales a fin de efectuar el seguimiento del proceso de eliminación de tales excepciones.

*   *   *

RECOMMENDATION OF THE COUNCIL
ON BRIBERY IN INTERNATIONAL BUSINESS TRANSACTIONS*

> The Recommendation of the Council on Bribery in International Business Transactions was adopted by the Council of the Organisation for Economic Co-operation and Development at its 829th Session on 27 May 1994.

THE COUNCIL,

Having regard to Article 5 b) of the Convention on the Organisation for Economic Co-operation and Development of 14th December 1960;

Having regard to the OECD Guidelines for Multinational Enterprises which exhort enterprises to refrain from bribery of public servants and holders of public office in their operations;

Considering that bribery is a widespread phenomenon in international business transactions, including trade and investment, raising serious moral and political concerns and distorting international competitive conditions;

Considering further that all countries share a responsibility to combat bribery in international business transactions, however their nationals might be involved;

Recognising that all OECD Member countries have legislation that makes the bribing of their public officials and the taking of bribes by these officials a criminal offence while only a few Member countries have specific laws making the bribing of foreign officials a punishable offence;

Convinced that further action is needed on both the national and international level to dissuade both enterprises and public officials from resorting to bribery when negotiating international business transactions and that an OECD initiative in this area could act as a catalyst for global action;

Considering that such action should take fully into account the differences that exist in the jurisdictional and other legal principles and practices in this area;

Considering that a review mechanism would assist Member countries in implementing

---

*Source: Organisation for Economic Co-operation and Development (1994). *Recommendation of the Council on Bribery in International Business Transactions* (Paris: OECD) (C(94)75/FINAL) [Note added by the editor].

this Recommendation and in evaluating the steps taken and the results achieved;

On the proposal of the Committee on International Investment and Multinational Enterprises;

General

I.   RECOMMENDS that Member countries take effective measures to deter, prevent and combat the bribery of foreign public officials in connection with international business transactions.

II.   CONSIDERS that, for the purposes of this Recommendation, bribery can involve the direct or indirect offer or provision of any undue pecuniary or other advantage to or for a foreign public official, in violation of the official's legal duties, in order to obtain or retain business.[1]

Domestic Action

III.   RECOMMENDS that each Member country examine the following areas and, in conformity with its jurisdictional and other basic legal principles, take concrete and meaningful steps to meet this goal. These steps may include:

i)   criminal laws, or their application, in respect of the bribery of foreign public officials;

ii)   civil, commercial, administrative laws and regulations so that bribery would be illegal;

iii)   tax legislation, regulations and practices, insofar as they may indirectly favour bribery;

iv)   company and business accounting requirements and practices in order to secure adequate recording of relevant payments;

v)   banking, financial and other relevant provisions so that adequate records would be kept and made available for inspection or investigation; and

vi)   laws and regulations relating to public subsidies, licences, government procurement contracts, or other public advantages so that advantages could be denied as a sanction for bribery in appropriate cases.

---

[1]The notion of bribery in some countries also includes advantages to or for members of a law-making body, candidates for a law-making body or public office and officials of political parties.

International Co-operation

IV.   RECOMMENDS that Member countries in order to combat bribery in international business transactions, in conformity with their jurisdictional and other basic legal principles, take the following actions:

i)   consult and otherwise co-operate with appropriate authorities in other countries in investigations and other legal proceedings concerning specific cases of such bribery through such means as sharing of information (spontaneous or "upon request"), provision of evidence, and extradition;

ii)   make full use of existing agreements and arrangements for mutual international legal assistance and where necessary, enter into new agreements or arrangements for this purpose;

iii)   ensure that their national laws afford an adequate basis for this co-operation.

Relations with Non-Members and International Organisations

V.   APPEALS to non-Member countries to join with OECD Members in combating bribery in international business transactions and to take full account of the terms of this Recommendation.

VI.   REQUESTS the Secretariat to consult with international organisations and international financial institutions on effective means to combat bribery as an aid to promote the policy of good governance.

VII.   INVITES Member countries to promote anti-corruption policies within and beyond the OECD area and, in their dealings with non-Member countries, to encourage them to join in the effort to combat such bribery in accordance with this Recommendation.

Follow-up Procedures

VIII.   INSTRUCTS the Committee on International Investment and Multinational Enterprises to monitor implementation and follow-up of this Recommendation. For this purpose, the Committee is invited to establish a Working Group on Bribery in International Business Transactions and in particular:

i)   to carry out regular reviews of steps taken by Member countries to implement this Recommendation, and to make proposals as appropriate to assist Member countries in its implementation;

ii)   to examine specific issues relating to bribery in international business transactions;

iii)   to provide a forum for consultations;

iv)   to explore the possibility of associating non-Members with this work; and

v)   in close co-operation with the Committee on Fiscal Affairs, to examine the fiscal treatment of bribery, including the issue of tax deductibility of bribes.

IX.   INSTRUCTS the Committee to report to the Council after the first regular review and as appropriate thereafter, and to review this Recommendation within three years after its adoption.

*   *   *

PROTOCOLO SOBRE PROMOCION Y PROTECCION DE INVERSIONES PROVENIENTES DE ESTADOS NO PARTES DEL MERCOSUR[*]

The Protocol on Promotion and Protection of Investments coming from States not Parties to MERCOSUR was approved by Decision 11/94 of the Council of MERCOSUR and signed on 5 August 1994. The Protocol had not come into force as of August 1995. The member countries of MERCOSUR are Argentina, Brazil, Uruguay and Paraguay.

VISTO: El Art 10 del Tratado de Asunción, la Resolución N° 39/94 del Grupo Mercado Común y la Recomendación N° 9/94 del SGT N° 4 "Politicas Fiscal y Monetaria Relacionadas con el Comercio".

CONSIDERANDO:

Que la creación de condiciones favorables para las inversiones (extra-zona) en el territorio de los Estados Partes del MERCOSUR, intensificará la cooperación económica.

Que la promoción y protección de tales inversiones contribuirá a estimular la iniciativa económica individual y a incrementar el desarrollo en los cuatro Estados Partes.

Que con tales fines resulta conveniente establecer un marco juridico común para el tratamiento a otorgar a terceros Estados en materia de Promoción y Protección de Inversiones.

EL CONSEJO DEL MERCADO COMUN
DECIDE:

Artículo 1°. Aprobar el "PROTOCOLO SOBRE PROMOCIÓN Y PROTECCIÓN DE INVERSIONES PROVENIENTES DE ESTADOS NO PARTES DEL MERCOSUR" tratamiento a otorgar a terceros Estados en materia de promoción de inversiones que consta como Anexo.

ANEXO

PROTOCOLO SOBRE PROMOCIÓN Y PROTECCIÓN DE INVERSIONES PROVENIENTES DE ESTADOS NO PARTES DEL MERCOSUR

La República Argentina, la República Federativa del Brasíl, la República del Paraguay y la República Oriental del Uruguay denominadas en adelante los "Estados Partes".

---

[*]Source: Secretaria Administrativa de MERCOSUR (1994). *Protocolo sobre Promocion y Proteccion de Inversiones Provenientes de Estados no Partes del MERCOSUR* (MERCOSUR/CMC/Dec. No. 11/94) mimeo. [Note added by the editor].

Teniendo en cuenta el Tratado en Asunción suscripto el 26 de marzo de 1991, por el cual los Estados Partes deciden crear el Mercado Común del Sur (MERCOSUR).

Considerando el Protocolo de Colonia de Promoción y Protección Recíproca de Inversiones en el MERCOSUR aprobado por la Decisión Nro. 11/93 del Consejo del Mercado Común, que tiene como objectivo promover las inversiones de inversores de los Estados Partes del MERCOSUR dentro del ámbito de aplicación territorial del Tratado de Asunción.

Destacando la necesidad de armonizar los principios jurídicos generales a aplicar por cada uno de los Estados Partes a las inversiones provenientes de Estados No Partes del MERCOSUR (en adelante denominados "Terceros Estados"), a los efectos de no crear condiciones diferenciales que distorsionen el flujo de inversiones.

Reconociendo que la promoción y la protecCión de inversiones sobre la base de acuerdos con Terceros Estados contribuirá a estimular la iniciativa económica individual e incrementará la prosperidad de los cuatro Estados Partes.

Han acordado lo siguiente:

Artículo 1

Los Estados Partes se comprometen a otorgar a las inversiones realizadas por inversores de Terceros Estados un tratamiento no más favorable que el que se establece en el presente Protocolo.

Artículo 2

A los efectos indicados precedentemente, el tratamiento general a convenir por cada Estados Partes con Terceros Estados no reconocerá a éstos beneficios y derechos mayores que los reconocidos al inversor en las siguientes bases normativas:

A. DEFINICIONES

1. El término "inversión" designará, de conformidad con las leyes y reglamentaciones del Estado Parte en cuyo territorio se realice la inversión, todo tipo de activo invertido directa o indirectamente por inversores de un Tercer Estado en el territorio del Estado Parte, de acuerdo con la legislación de ésta. Incluirá en particular, aunque no exclusivamente:

   a) la propiedad de bienes muebles e inmuebles, así como los demás derechos reales tales como hipotecas, cauciones y derechos de prenda;

   b) acciones, cuotas societarias, y cualquier otro tipo de participación en sociedades;

   c) Títulos de crédito y derechos a prestaciones que tengan un valor económico; los préstamos estarán incluidos solamente cuando estén directamente vinculados a una inversión especifica;

d)   derechos de propiedad intelectual o inmaterial incluyendo en especial, derechos de autor, patentes, diseños industriales, marcas, nombres comerciales, procedimientos técnicos, know-how y valor llave;

e)   concesiones económicas conferidas por ley o por contrato, incluyendo las concesiones para la prospección, cultivo, extracción o explotación de recursos naturales.

2.   El término "inversor" designará:

a)   toda persona física que sea nacional de un Estado Parte o del Tercer Estado de conformidad con sus respectivas legislaciones. Las disposiciones de los convenios a celebrar no se aplicarán a las inversiones realizadas en el territorio de un Estado Parte por personas físicas que sean nacionales de Terceros Estados, si tales personas, a la fecha de la inversión, residieren o se domiciliaren, conforme a la legislación vigente, en forma permanente en dicho territorio, a menos que se pruebe que los recursos referidos a estas inversiones provienen del exterior.

b)   toda persona jurídica constituida de conformidad con las leyes y reglamentaciones de un Estado Parte o del Tercer Estado y que tenga su sede en el territorio de su constitución.

c)   toda persona jurídica establecida de conformidad con la legislación de cualquier país que esté efectivamente controlada por personas físicas o jurídicas definidas en a) y b), de este numeral.

3.   El término "ganancias" designará todas las sumas producidas por una inversión, tales como utilidades, rentas, dividendos, intereses, regalías y otros ingresos corrientes.

4.   El término "territorio" designará el territorio nacional de cada Estado Parte o del Tercer Estado, incluyendo aquellas zonas marítimas adyacentes al límite exterior del mar territorial nacional, sobre el cual el Estado Parte involucrado o el Tercer Estado pueda, de conformidad con el derecho internacional, ejercer derechos soberanos o jurisdicción.

B. PROMOCIÓN DE INVERSIONES

1.Cada Estado Parte promoverá en su territorio las inversiones de inversores de Terceros Estados, y admitirá dichas inversiones conforme a sus leyes y reglamentaciones.

2.Cuando uno de los Estados Partes hubiera admitido una inversión en su territorio, otorgará las autorizaciones necesarias para su mejor desenvolvimiento, incluyendo la ejecución de contatos sobre licencias, asístencia comercial o administrativa e ingreso del personal necesario.

C. PROTECCIÓN DE INVERSIONES

1.Cada Estado Parte asegurará un tratamiento justo y equitativo a las inversiones de inversores de Terceros Estados, y no perjudicará su gestión, mantenimiento, uso, goce o disposición través de medidas injustificadas o discriminatorias.

2.Cada Estado Parte concederá plena protección a tales inversiones y les podrá acordar un tratamiento no menos favorable que el otorgado a las inversiones de sus propios inversores nacionales o a las inversiones realizadas por inversores de otros estados.

3.Los Estados Partes no extenderán a los inversores de Terceros Estados los beneficios de cualquier tratamiento, preferencia o privilegio resultante de:

a)su participación o asociación en una zona de libre comercio, unión aduanera mercado común, o acuerdo regional similar.

b)un acuerdo internacional relativo total o parcialmente a cuestiones impositivas.

D. EXPROPIACIONES Y COMPENSACIONES

1.   Ninguno de los Estados Partes tomará medidas de nacionalización o expropiación ni ninguna otra medida que tenga el mismo efecto contra inversiones que se encuentren en su territorio y que pertenezcan a inversores de Terceros Estados, a menos que dichas medidas sean tomada por razones de utilidad pública o de interés social, sobre una base no discriminatoria y bajo el debido proceso legal. Las medidas serán acompañadas de disposiciones para el pago de una compensación justa, adecuada y pronta u oportuna.

El monto de dicha compensación corresponderá al valor de la inversión expropiada.

2.   Los inversores de un Tercer Estado, que sufrieran pérdidas en sus inversiones en el territorio del Estado Parte, debido a guerra u otro conflicio armado, estado de emergencia nacional, revuelta, insurrección o motín, recibirán, en lo que se refiere a restitución, indemnización, compensación u otro resarcimiento, un tratamiento no menos favorable que el acordado a sus propios inversores o a los inversores de otros estados.

E. TRANSFERENCIAS

1.   Cada Estado Parte otorgará a los inversores del Tercer Estado la libre transferencia de las inversiones y ganancias, y en particular, aunque no exclusivamente de:

   a)   el capital y las sumas adicionales necesarias para el mantenimiento y desarrollo de las inversiones;

   b)   los beneficios, utilidades, rentas, intereses, dividendos y otros ingresos corrientes;

c)   los fondos para el reembolso de los préstamos tal como se definen en el Artículo 2, literal A), Párrafo (1), (c);

d)   las regalías y honorarios y todo otro pago relativo a los derechos previstos en el Artículo 2, literal A), Párrafo (1), (d), y (e);

e)   el producido de una venta o liquidación total o parcial de una inversión;

f)   las compensaciones, indemnizaciones u otros pagos previstos en el Artículo 2, literal D);

g)   las remuneraciones de los nacionales de un Tercer Estado que hayan obtenido autorización para trabajar en relación a una inversión;

2.   Las transferencias serán efectuadas sin demora, en moneda libremente convertible.

F. SUBROGACIÓN

1.   Si un Tercer Estado o una agencia designada por éste realizara un pago a un inversor en virtud de una garantía o seguro para cubrir riesgos no comerciales que hubiere contratado en relación a una inversión, el Estado Parte en cuyo territorio se realizó la inversión reconocerá la validez de la subrogación en favor del Tercer Estado o de una de sus agencias, respecto de cualquier derecho o título del inversor a los efectos de obtener el resarcimiento pecuniario correspondiente.

G. SOLUCIÓN DE CONTROVERSIAS ENTRE UN ESTADO PARTE Y UN TERCER ESTADO

1.   Las controversias que surgieren entre un Estado Parte y el Tercer Estado a la interpretación o aplicación del convenio que celebren serán, en lo posible, solucionadas por la vía diplomática.

2.   Si dicha controversia no pudiera ser dirimida de esa manera en un plazo prudencial a determinar, será sometida al arbitraje internacional.

H. SOLUCIÓN DE CONTROVERSIAS ENTRE UN INVERSOR DE UN TERCER ESTADO Y UN ESTADO PARTE RECEPTOR DE LA INVERSION

1.   Toda controversia relativa a la interpretación o aplicación de un convenio de promoción y protección reciproca de inversiones que se suscite entre un inversor de un Tercer Estado y un Estado Parte, será, en la medida de lo posible, solucionada por consultas amistosas.

2.   Si la controversia no hubiera podido ser solucionada en un plazo prudencial a partir del momento en que hubiera sido planteada por una u otra de las partes, podra ser sometida, a pedido del inversor:

o bien a los tribunales competentes del Estado Parte en cuyo territorio se realizó la inversión, o bien al arbitraje internacional en las condiciones descriptas en el apartado 3.

Una vez que un inversor hubiese sometido la controversia a la jurisdicción del Estado Parte implicado o al arbitraje internacional, la elección de uno u otro de estos procedimientos será definitiva.

3.   En caso de recurso al arbitraje internacional, la controversia podrá ser sometida, a elección del inversor, a un tribunal de arbitraje "ad hoc" o a una institución internacional de arbitraje.

4.   El órgano arbitral decidirá en base a las disposiciones del convenio celebrado, al derecho del Estado Parte involucrado en la controversia, incluídas las normas relativas a conflictos de leyes, a los términos de eventuales acuerdos particulares concluidos con relación a la inversión, como así también a los principios del derecho internacional en la materia.

5.   Las sentencias arbitrales serán definitivas y obligatorias para las partes en la controversia. El Estado Parte las ejecutará de conformidad con su legislación.

I. INVERSIONES Y CONTROVERSIAS COMPRENDIDAS EN EL CONVENIO

Las normas de los convenios a celebrarse podrán ser aplicadas a todas las inversiones realizadas antes o después de la fecha de su entrada en vigor, pero no se aplicarán a ninguna controversia, reclamo o diferendo que se hubiese originado con anterioridad a su entrada en vigor.

J. DURACIÓN Y TERMINACIÓN

El plazo mínimo de validez de los convenios será de diez años. Con relación a aquellas inversiones efectuadas con anterioridad a la fecha de extinción de la vigencia del convenio, el Estado Parte podrá acordar que las disposiciones del mismo continuarán en vigor por un período máximo de quince años a partir de esa fecha.

Artículo 3

Los Estador Partes se obligan a intercambiar información sobre las negociaciones futuras y las que se hallaren en curso sobre convenios de promoción y protectión recíproca de inversiones con Terceros Estados y se consultarán con carácter previo sobre toda modificación sustancial al tratamiento general convenido en el Artículo 2 del presente Protocolo. A tales efectos, el órgano ejecutivo del MERCOSUR se ocupará de las consultas e informaciones referidas al tema.

Artículo 4

El presente Protocolo es parte integrante del Tratado de Asunción.

La adhesión por parte de un Estado al Tratado de Asunción implicará "ipso jure" la adhesión al presente Protocolo.

El presente Protocolo entrará en vigor 30 días después de la fecha de depósito del cuarto instrumento de ratificación.

El Gobierno de la República del Paraguay será el depositario del presente Protocolo y de los instrumentos de ratificación y envíará copia debidamente autenticada de los mismos a los Gobiernos de los demás Estados Partes.

Hecho en la ciudad de Buenos Aires a los cinco días del mes de agosto de 1994, en un ejemplar original, en los idiomas español y portugués, siendo ambos textos igualmente auténticos.

* * *

APEC NON-BINDING INVESTMENT PRINCIPLES*

The Asia Pacific Economic Cooperation Non-Binding Investment Principles were endorsed at the Sixth Ministerial Meeting of APEC, held in Jakarta on 12 November 1994 and came into effect on the same date. As of November 1995, the members of APEC were Australia, Brunei Darussalam, Canada, Chile, People's Republic of China, Hong Kong, Indonesia, Japan, Republic of Korea, Malaysia, Mexico, New Zealand, Papua New Guinea, Philippines, Singapore, Taiwan Province of China, Thailand and the United States of America.

In the spirit of APEC's underlying approach of open regionalism,

Recognizing the importance of investment to economic development, the stimulation of growth, the creation of jobs and the flow of technology in the Asia-Pacific region,

Emphasising the importance of promoting domestic environments that are conducive to attracting foreign investment, such as stable growth with low inflation, adequate infrastructure, adequately developed human resources, and protection of intellectual property rights,

Reflecting that most APEC economies are both sources and recipients of foreign investment,

Aiming to increase investment, including investment in small and medium enterprises, and to develop supporting industries,

Acknowledging the diversity in the level and pace of development of member economies as may be reflected in their investment regimes, and committed to ongoing efforts towards the improvement and further liberalisation of their investment regimes,

Without prejudice to applicable bilateral and multilateral treaties and other international instruments,

Recognising the importance of fully implementing the Uruguay Round TRIMs Agreement,

APEC members aspire to the following non-binding principles:

Transparency

• Member economies will make all laws, regulations administrative guidelines and policies pertaining to investment in their economies publicly available in a prompt, transparent

---

*Source: Asia-Pacific Economic Cooperation Secretariat (1994). *APEC Non-Binding Investment Principles* (Singapore: APEC) mimeo. [Note by the editor].

and readily accessible manner.

Non-discrimination Between Source Economies

* Member economies will extend to investors from any economy treatment in relation to the establishment, expansion and operation of their investments that is no less favourable than that accorded to investors from any other economy in like situations, without prejudice to relevant international obligations and principles.

National Treatment

* With exceptions as provided for in domestic laws, regulations and policies, member economies will accord to foreign investors in relation to the establishment, expansion, operation and protection of their investments, treatment no less favourable than that accorded in like situations to domestic investors.

Investment Incentives

* Member economies will not relax health, safety, and environmental regulations as an incentive to encourage foreign investment.

Performance Requirements

* Member economies will minimize the use of performance requirements that distort or limit expansion of trade and investment.

Expropriation and Compensation

* Member economies will not expropriate foreign investments or take measures that have a similar effect, except for a public purpose and on a non-discriminatory basis, in accordance with the laws of each economy and principles of international law, and against the prompt payment of adequate and effective compensation.

Repatriation and Convertibility

* Member economies will further liberalise towards the goal of the free and prompt transfer of funds related to foreign investment, such as profits, dividends, royalties, loan payments and liquidations, in freely convertible currency.

Settlement of Disputes

* Member economies accept that disputes arising in connection with a foreign investment will be settled promptly through consultations and negotiations between the parties to the dispute or, failing this, through procedures for arbitration in accordance with members'

international commitments or through other arbitration procedures acceptable to both parties.

Entry and Sojourn of Personnel

• Member economies will permit the temporary entry and sojourn of key foreign technical and managerial personnel for the purpose of engaging in activities connected with foreign investment, subject to relevant laws and regulations.

Avoidance of Double Taxation

• Member economies will endeavour to avoid double taxation related to foreign investment.

Investor Behaviour

• Acceptance of foreign investment is facilitated when foreign investors abide by the host economy's laws, regulations, administrative guidelines and policies, just as domestic investors should.

Removal of Barriers to Capital Exports

• Member economies accept that regulatory and institutional barriers to the outflow of investment will be minimised.

*   *   *

FINAL ACT OF THE EUROPEAN ENERGY CHARTER CONFERENCE, THE ENERGY CHARTER TREATY, ANNEXES TO THE ENERGY CHARTER TREATY AND DECISIONS WITH RESPECT TO THE ENERGY CHARTER TREATY*
[excerpts]

> The Energy Charter Treaty was signed in Lisbon on 17 December 1994, together with Decisions with Respect to the Energy Charter Treaty and the Final Act of the European Energy Charter Conference. The signatories of the Energy Charter Treaty as at March 11 1996 were Albania, Armenia, Australia, Austria, Azerbaïjan, Belarus, Belgium, Bosnia-Herzegovina, Bulgaria, Croatia, Cyprus, Czech Republic, Denmark, Estonia, the European Communities, Finland, France, Georgia, Germany, Greece, Hungary, Iceland, Ireland, Italy, Japan, Kazakhstan, Kyrgyzstan, Latvia, Liechtenstein, Lithuania, Luxembourg, Malta, Moldova, Netherlands, Norway, Poland, Portugal, Romania, Russian Federation, Slovak Republic, Slovenia, Spain, Sweden, Switzerland, Tajikistan, Turkey, Turkmenistan, Ukraine, United Kingdom and Uzbekistan.

FINAL ACT OF THE EUROPEAN ENERGY CHARTER CONFERENCE
[excerpts]

BACKGROUND

II.   During the meeting of the European Council in Dublin in June 1990, the Prime Minister of the Netherlands suggested that economic recovery in Eastern Europe and the then Union of Soviet Socialist Republics could be catalysed and accelerated by cooperation in the energy sector. This suggestion was welcomed by the Council, which invited the Commission of the European Communities to study how best to implement such cooperation. In February 1991 the Commission proposed the concept of a European Energy Charter.

Following discussion of the Commission's proposal in the Council of the European Communities, the European Communities invited the other countries of Western and Eastern Europe, of the Union of Soviet Socialist Republics and the non-European members of the Organisation for Economic Co-operation and Development to attend a conference in Brussels in July 1991 to launch negotiations on the European Energy Charter. A number of other countries and international organizations were invited to attend the European Energy Charter Conference as observers.

---

*Source: The Energy Charter Conference (1995). *Final Act of the European Energy Charter Conference* (Document AF/EECH/en 1), *The Energy Charter Treaty* (Document EECH/A1/en 1), *Decisions with Respect to the Energy Charter Treaty* (Document EECH/A2/en 1), *Annexes to the Energy Charter Treaty* (Document EECH/Annexes to A1/en 1) (Brussels: Energy Charter Secretariat) [Note added by the editor].

Negotiations on the European Energy Charter were completed in 1991 and the Charter was adopted by signature of a Concluding Document at a conference held at The Hague on 16-17 December 1991. Signatories of the Charter, then or subsequently, include all those listed in Section I above, other than observers.

The signatories of the European Energy Charter undertook:

- to pursue the objectives and principles of the Charter and implement and broaden their cooperation as soon as possible by negotiating in good faith a Basic Agreement and Protocols.

The European Energy Charter Conference accordingly began negotiations on a Basic Agreement - later called the Energy Charter Treaty - designed to promote East-West industrial cooperation by providing legal safeguards in areas such as investment, transit and trade. It also began negotiations on Protocols in the fields of energy efficiency, nuclear safety and hydrocarbons, although in the last case negotiations were later suspended until completion of the Energy Charter Treaty.

Negotiations on the Energy Charter Treaty and the Energy Charter Protocol on Energy Efficiency and Related Environmental Aspects were successfully completed in 1994.

THE ENERGY CHARTER TREATY

III. As a result of its deliberations the European Energy Charter Conference has adopted the text of the Energy Charter Treaty (hereinafter referred to as the "Treaty") which is set out in Annex 1 and Decisions with respect thereto which are set out in Annex 2, and agreed that the Treaty would be open for signature at Lisbon from 17 December 1994 to 16 June 1995.

UNDERSTANDINGS

IV. By signing the Final Act, the representatives agreed to adopt the following Understandings with respect to the Treaty:

1. <u>With respect to the Treaty as a whole</u>

   (a) The representatives underline that the provisions of the Treaty have been agreed upon bearing in mind the specific nature of the Treaty aiming at a legal framework to promote long-term cooperation in a particular sector and as a result cannot be construed to constitute a precedent in the context of other international negotiations.

   (b) The provisions of the Treaty do not:

(i)   oblige any Contracting Party to introduce mandatory third party access; or

(ii)   prevent the use of pricing systems which, within a particular category of consumers, apply identical prices to customers in different locations.

(c)   Derogations from most favoured nation treatment are not intended to cover measures which are specific to an Investor or group of Investors, rather than applying generally.

2.   <u>With respect to Article 1(5)</u>

(a)   It is understood that the Treaty confers no rights to engage in economic activities other than Economic Activities in the Energy Sector.

(b)   The following activities are illustrative of Economic Activity in the Energy Sector:

(i)   prospecting and exploration for, and extraction of, e.g., oil, gas, coal and uranium;

(ii)   construction and operation of power generation facilities, including those powered by wind and other renewable energy sources;

(iii)   land transportation, distribution, storage and supply of Energy Materials and Products, e.g., by way of transmission and distribution grids and pipelines or dedicated rail lines, and construction of facilities for such, including the laying of oil, gas, and coal-slurry pipelines;

(iv)   removal and disposal of wastes from energy related facilities such as power stations, including radioactive wastes from nuclear power stations;

(v)   decommissioning of energy related facilities, including oil rigs, oil refineries and power generating plants;

(vi)   marketing and sale of, and trade in Energy Materials and Products, e.g., retail sales of gasoline; and

> (vii)   research, consulting, planning, management and design activities related to the activities mentioned above, including those aimed at Improving Energy Efficiency.

3.   <u>With respect to Article 1(6)</u>

For greater clarity as to whether an Investment made in the Area of one Contracting Party is controlled, directly or indirectly, by an Investor of any other Contracting Party, control of an Investment means control in fact, determined after an examination of the actual circumstances in each situation. In any such examination, all relevant factors should be considered, including the Investor's

(a)   financial interest, including equity interest, in the Investment;

(b)   ability to exercise substantial influence over the management and operation of the Investment; and

(c)   ability to exercise substantial influence over the selection of members of the board of directors or any other managing body.

Where there is doubt as to whether an Investor controls, directly or indirectly, an Investment, an Investor claiming such control has the burden of proof that such control exists.

4.   <u>With respect to Article 1(8)</u>

Consistent with Australia's foreign investment policy, the establishment of a new mining or raw materials processing project in Australia with total investment of $A 10 million or more by a foreign interest, even where that foreign interest is already operating a similar business in Australia, is considered as the making of a new investment.

5.   <u>With respect to Article 1(12)</u>

The representatives recognize the necessity for adequate and effective protection of Intellectual Property rights according to the highest internationally-accepted standards.

6.   <u>With respect to Article 5(1)</u>

The representatives' agreement to Article 5 is not meant to imply any position on whether or to what extent the provisions of the "Agreement on Trade-Related Investment Measures" annexed to the Final Act of the Uruguay

Round of Multilateral Trade Negotiations are implicit in articles III and XI of the GATT.

7. <u>With respect to Article 6</u>

    (a)   The unilateral and concerted anti-competitive conduct referred to in Article 6(2) are to be defined by each Contracting Party in accordance with its laws and may include exploitative abuses.

    (b)   "Enforcement" and "enforces" include action under the competition laws of a Contracting Party by way of investigation, legal proceeding, or administrative action as well as by way of any decision or further law granting or continuing an authorization.

9. <u>With respect to Articles 9, 10 and Part V</u>

As a Contracting Party's programmes which provide for public loans, grants, guarantees or insurance for facilitating trade or Investment abroad are not connected with Investment or related activities of Investors from other Contracting Parties in its Area, such programmes may be subject to constraints with respect to participation in them.

10. <u>With respect to Article 10(4)</u>

The supplementary treaty will specify conditions for applying the Treatment described in Article 10(3). Those conditions will include, inter alia, provisions relating to the sale or other divestment of state assets (privatization) and to the dismantling of monopolies (demonopolization).

11. <u>With respect to Articles 10(4) and 29(6)</u>

Contracting Parties may consider any connection between the provisions of Article 10(4) and Article 29(6).

12. <u>With respect to Article 14(5)</u>

It is intended that a Contracting Party which enters into an agreement referred to in Article 14(5) ensure that the conditions of such an agreement are not in contradiction with that Contracting Party's obligations under the Articles of Agreement of the International Monetary Fund.

16. <u>With respect to Article 26(2)(a)</u>

Article 26(2)(a) should not be interpreted to require a Contracting Party to enact Part III of the Treaty into its domestic law.

17. <u>With respect to Articles 26 and 27</u>

The reference to treaty obligations in the penultimate sentence of Article 10(1) does not include decisions taken by international organizations, even if they are legally binding, or treaties which entered into force before 1 January 1970.

19. <u>With respect to Article 33</u>

The provisional Charter Conference should at the earliest possible date decide how best to give effect to the goal of Title III of the European Energy Charter that Protocols be negotiated in areas of cooperation such as those listed in Title III of the Charter.

DECLARATIONS

V. The representatives declared that Article 18(2) shall not be construed to allow the circumvention of the application of the other provisions of the Treaty.

VI. The representatives also noted the following Declarations that were made with respect to the Treaty:

1. <u>With respect to Article 1(6)</u>

The Russian Federation wishes to have reconsidered, in negotiations with regard to the supplementary treaty referred to in Article 10(4), the question of the importance of national legislation with respect to the issue of control as expressed in the Understanding to Article 1(6).

2. <u>With respect to Articles 5 and 10(11)</u>

Australia notes that the provisions of Articles 5 and 10(11) do not diminish its rights and obligations under the GATT, including as elaborated in the Uruguay Round Agreement on Trade-Related Investment Measures, particularly with respect to the list of exceptions in Article 5(3), which it considers incomplete.

Australia further notes that it would not be appropriate for dispute settlement bodies established under the Treaty to give interpretations of GATT articles III and XI in the context of disputes between parties to the GATT or between an Investor of a party to the GATT and another party to the GATT. It considers that with respect to the application of Article 10(11) between an Investor and a party to the GATT, the only issue that can be considered under Article 26 is the issue of the awards of arbitration in the event that a GATT panel or the WTO dispute settlement body first establishes that a trade-related investment measure maintained by the Contracting Party is inconsistent with its obligations under the GATT or the Agreement on Trade-Related Investment Measures.

4. With respect to Article 10

Canada and the United States each affirm that they will apply the provisions of Article 10 in accordance with the following considerations:

For the purposes of assessing the treatment which must be accorded to Investors of other Contracting Parties and their Investments, the circumstances will need to be considered on a case-by-case basis. A comparison between the treatment accorded to Investors of one Contracting Party, or the Investments of Investors of one Contracting Party, and the Investments or Investors of another Contracting Party, is only valid if it is made between Investors and Investments in similar circumstances. In determining whether differential treatment of Investors or Investments is consistent with Article 10, two basic factors must be taken into account.

The first factor is the policy objectives of Contracting Parties in various fields insofar as they are consistent with the principles of non-discrimination set out in Article 10. Legitimate policy objectives may justify differential treatment of foreign Investors or their Investments in order to reflect a dissimilarity of relevant circumstances between those Investors and Investments and their domestic counterparts. For example, the objective of ensuring the integrity of a country's financial system would justify reasonable prudential measures with respect to foreign Investors or Investments, where such measures would be unnecessary to ensure the attainment of the same objectives insofar as domestic Investors or Investments are concerned. Those foreign Investors or their Investments would thus not be "in similar circumstances" to domestic Investors or their Investments. Thus, even if such a measure accorded differential treatment, it would not be contrary to Article 10.

The second factor is the extent to which the measure is motivated by the fact that the relevant Investor or Investment is subject to foreign ownership or under foreign control. A measure aimed specifically at Investors because they are foreign, without sufficient countervailing policy reasons consistent with the preceding paragraph, would be contrary to the principles of Article 10. The foreign Investor or Investment would be "in similar circumstances" to domestic Investors and their Investments, and the measure would be contrary to Article 10.

5. With respect to Article 25

The European Communities and their Member States recall that, in accordance with article 58 of the Treaty establishing the European Community:

(a) companies or firms formed in accordance with the law of a Member State and having their registered office, central administration or principal place of business within the Community shall, for the right of establishment pursuant to Part Three, Title III, Chapter 2 of the Treaty establishing the European Community, be treated in the same way as natural persons who are nationals of Member States; companies or firms which only have their registered office within the Community must, for this purpose, have an effective and continuous link with the economy of one of the Member States;

(b) "companies and firms" means companies or firms constituted under civil or commercial law, including cooperative societies, and other legal persons governed by public or private law, save for those which are non-profitmaking.

The European Communities and their Member States further recall that:

Community law provides for the possibility to extend the treatment described above to branches and agencies of companies or firms not established in one of the Member States; and that, the application of Article 25 of the Energy Charter Treaty will allow only those derogations necessary to safeguard the preferential treatment resulting from the wider process of economic integration resulting from the Treaties establishing the European Communities.

Done at Lisbon on the seventeenth day of December in the year one thousand nine hundred and ninety-four.

* * *

The Energy Charter Treaty: Annex 1
[excerpts]
PREAMBLE

The Contracting Parties to this Treaty,

Having regard to the Charter of Paris for a New Europe signed on 21 November 1990;

Having regard to the European Energy Charter adopted in the Concluding Document of the Hague Conference on the European Energy Charter signed at The Hague on 17 December 1991;

Recalling that all signatories to the Concluding Document of the Hague Conference undertook to pursue the objectives and principles of the European Energy Charter and implement and broaden their cooperation as soon as possible by negotiating in good faith an Energy Charter Treaty and Protocols, and desiring to place the commitments contained in that Charter on a secure and binding international legal basis;

Desiring also to establish the structural framework required to implement the principles enunciated in the European Energy Charter;

Wishing to implement the basic concept of the European Energy Charter initiative which is to catalyse economic growth by means of measures to liberalize investment and trade in energy;

Affirming that Contracting Parties attach the utmost importance to the effective implementation of full national treatment and most favoured nation treatment, and that these commitments will be applied to the Making of Investments pursuant to a supplementary treaty;

Having regard to the objective of progressive liberalization of international trade and to the principle of avoidance of discrimination in international trade as enunciated in the General Agreement on Tariffs and Trade and its Related Instruments and as otherwise provided for in this Treaty;

Determined progressively to remove technical, administrative and other barriers to trade in Energy Materials and Products and related equipment, technologies and services;

Looking to the eventual membership in the General Agreement on Tariffs and Trade of those Contracting Parties which are not currently parties thereto and concerned to provide interim trade arrangements which will assist those Contracting Parties and not impede their preparation for such membership;

Mindful of the rights and obligations of certain Contracting Parties which are also parties to the General Agreement on Tariffs and Trade and its Related Instruments;

Having regard to competition rules concerning mergers, monopolies, anti-competitive practices and abuse of dominant position ;

Having regard also to the Treaty on the Non-Proliferation of Nuclear Weapons, the Nuclear Suppliers Guidelines and other international nuclear non-proliferation obligations or understandings;

Recognizing the necessity for the most efficient exploration, production, conversion, storage, transport, distribution and use of energy;

Recalling the United Nations Framework Convention on Climate Change, the Convention on Long-Range Transboundary Air Pollution and its protocols, and other international environmental agreements with energy-related aspects; and

Recognizing the increasingly urgent need for measures to protect the environment, including the decommissioning of energy installations and waste disposal, and for internationally-agreed objectives and criteria for these purposes,

HAVE AGREED AS FOLLOWS:

PART I
DEFINITIONS AND PURPOSE

ARTICLE 1
DEFINITIONS

As used in this Treaty:

(1)   "Charter" means the European Energy Charter adopted in the Concluding Document of the Hague Conference on the European Energy Charter signed at The Hague on 17 December 1991; signature of the Concluding Document is considered to be signature of the Charter.

(2)   "Contracting Party" means a state or Regional Economic Integration Organization which has consented to be bound by this Treaty and for which the Treaty is in force.

(3)   "Regional Economic Integration Organization" means an organization constituted by states to which they have transferred competence over certain matters a number of which are governed by this Treaty, including the authority to take decisions binding on them in respect of those matters.

(5)   "Economic Activity in the Energy Sector" means an economic activity concerning the exploration, extraction, refining, production, storage, land transport, transmission, distribution, trade, marketing, or sale of Energy Materials and Products except those included in Annex NI, or concerning the distribution of heat to multiple premises.

(6)   "Investment" means every kind of asset, owned or controlled directly or indirectly by an Investor and includes:

    (a)   tangible and intangible, and movable and immovable, property, and any property rights such as leases, mortgages, liens, and pledges;

(b)   a company or business enterprise, or shares, stock, or other forms of equity participation in a company or business enterprise, and bonds and other debt of a company or business enterprise;

(c)   claims to money and claims to performance pursuant to contract having an economic value and associated with an Investment;

(d)   Intellectual Property;

(e)   Returns;

(f)   any right conferred by law or contract or by virtue of any licences and permits granted pursuant to law to undertake any Economic Activity in the Energy Sector.

A change in the form in which assets are invested does not affect their character as investments and the term "Investment" includes all investments, whether existing at or made after the later of the date of entry into force of this Treaty for the Contracting Party of the Investor making the investment and that for the Contracting Party in the Area of which the investment is made (hereinafter referred to as the "Effective Date") provided that the Treaty shall only apply to matters affecting such investments after the Effective Date.

"Investment" refers to any investment associated with an Economic Activity in the Energy Sector and to investments or classes of investments designated by a Contracting Party in its Area as "Charter efficiency projects" and so notified to the Secretariat.

(7)   "Investor" means:

(a)   with respect to a Contracting Party:

(i)   a natural person having the citizenship or nationality of or who is permanently residing in that Contracting Party in accordance with its applicable law;

(ii)   a company or other organization organized in accordance with the law applicable in that Contracting Party;

(b)   with respect to a "third state", a natural person, company or other organization which fulfils, mutatis mutandis, the conditions specified in subparagraph (a) for a Contracting Party.

(8)   "Make Investments" or "Making of Investments" means establishing new Investments, acquiring all or part of existing Investments or moving into different fields of Investment activity.

(9)   "Returns" means the amounts derived from or associated with an Investment, irrespective of the form in which they are paid, including profits, dividends, interest, capital gains, royalty payments, management, technical assistance or other fees and payments in kind.

(10)   "Area" means with respect to a state that is a Contracting Party:

(a)   the territory under its sovereignty, it being understood that territory includes land, internal waters and the territorial sea; and

(b)   subject to and in accordance with the international law of the sea: the sea, sea-bed and its subsoil with regard to which that Contracting Party exercises sovereign rights and jurisdiction.

With respect to a Regional Economic Integration Organization which is a Contracting Party, Area means the Areas of the member states of such Organization, under the provisions contained in the agreement establishing that Organization.

(11)   (a)   "GATT" means "GATT 1947" or "GATT 1994", or both of them where both are applicable.

(b)   "GATT 1947" means the General Agreement on Tariffs and Trade, dated 30 October 1947, annexed to the Final Act Adopted at the Conclusion of the Second Session of the Preparatory Committee of the United Nations Conference on Trade and Employment, as subsequently rectified, amended or modified.

(c)   "GATT 1994" means the General Agreement on Tariffs and Trade as specified in Annex 1A of the Agreement Establishing the World Trade Organization, as subsequently rectified, amended or modified.

A party to the Agreement Establishing the World Trade Organization is considered to be a party to GATT 1994.

(d)   "Related Instruments" means, as appropriate:

(i)   agreements, arrangements or other legal instruments, including decisions, declarations and understandings, concluded under the auspices of GATT 1947 as subsequently rectified, amended or modified; or

(ii) the Agreement Establishing the World Trade Organization including its Annex 1 (except GATT 1994), its Annexes 2, 3 and 4, and the decisions, declarations and understandings related thereto, as subsequently rectified, amended or modified.

(12) "Intellectual Property" includes copyrights and related rights, trademarks, geographical indications, industrial designs, patents, layout designs of integrated circuits and the protection of undisclosed information.

(14) "Freely Convertible Currency" means a currency which is widely traded in international foreign exchange markets and widely used in international transactions.

ARTICLE 2
PURPOSE OF THE TREATY

This Treaty establishes a legal framework in order to promote long-term cooperation in the energy field, based on complementarities and mutual benefits, in accordance with the objectives and principles of the Charter.

PART II
COMMERCE

ARTICLE 3
INTERNATIONAL MARKETS

The Contracting Parties shall work to promote access to international markets on commercial terms, and generally to develop an open and competitive market, for Energy Materials and Products.

ARTICLE 4
NON-DEROGATION FROM GATT AND RELATED INSTRUMENTS

Nothing in this Treaty shall derogate, as between particular Contracting Parties which are parties to the GATT, from the provisions of the GATT and Related Instruments as they are applied between those Contracting Parties.

ARTICLE 5
TRADE-RELATED INVESTMENT MEASURES

(1) A Contracting Party shall not apply any trade-related investment measure that is inconsistent with the provisions of article III or XI of the GATT; this shall be without prejudice to the Contracting Party's rights and obligations under the GATT and Related Instruments and Article 29.

(2)   Such measures include any investment measure which is mandatory or enforceable under domestic law or under any administrative ruling, or compliance with which is necessary to obtain an advantage, and which requires:

(a)   the purchase or use by an enterprise of products of domestic origin or from any domestic source, whether specified in terms of particular products, in terms of volume or value of products, or in terms of a proportion of volume or value of its local production; or

(b)   that an enterprise's purchase or use of imported products be limited to an amount related to the volume or value of local products that it exports;

or which restricts:

(c)   the importation by an enterprise of products used in or related to its local production, generally or to an amount related to the volume or value of local production that it exports;

(d)   the importation by an enterprise of products used in or related to its local production by restricting its access to foreign exchange to an amount related to the foreign exchange inflows attributable to the enterprise; or

(e)   the exportation or sale for export by an enterprise of products, whether specified in terms of particular products, in terms of volume or value of products, or in terms of a proportion of volume or value of its local production.

(3)   Nothing in paragraph (1) shall be construed to prevent a Contracting Party from applying the trade-related investment measures described in subparagraphs (2)(a) and (c) as a condition of eligibility for export promotion, foreign aid, government procurement or preferential tariff or quota programmes.

(4)   Notwithstanding paragraph (1), a Contracting Party may temporarily continue to maintain trade-related investment measures which were in effect more than 180 days before its signature of this Treaty, subject to the notification and phase-out provisions set out in Annex TRM.

ARTICLE 6
COMPETITION

(1)   Each Contracting Party shall work to alleviate market distortions and barriers to competition in Economic Activity in the Energy Sector.

(2)   Each Contracting Party shall ensure that within its jurisdiction it has and enforces such laws as are necessary and appropriate to address unilateral and concerted anti-competitive conduct in Economic Activity in the Energy Sector.

(3)   Contracting Parties with experience in applying competition rules shall give full consideration to providing, upon request and within available resources, technical assistance on the development and implementation of competition rules to other Contracting Parties.

(4)   Contracting Parties may cooperate in the enforcement of their competition rules by consulting and exchanging information.

(5)   If a Contracting Party considers that any specified anti-competitive conduct carried out within the Area of another Contracting Party is adversely affecting an important interest relevant to the purposes identified in this Article, the Contracting Party may notify the other Contracting Party and may request that its competition authorities initiate appropriate enforcement action. The notifying Contracting Party shall include in such notification sufficient information to permit the notified Contracting Party to identify the anti-competitive conduct that is the subject of the notification and shall include an offer of such further information and cooperation as the notifying Contracting Party is able to provide. The notified Contracting Party or, as the case may be, the relevant competition authorities may consult with the competition authorities of the notifying Contracting Party and shall accord full consideration to the request of the notifying Contracting Party in deciding whether or not to initiate enforcement action with respect to the alleged anti-competitive conduct identified in the notification. The notified Contracting Party shall inform the notifying Contracting Party of its decision or the decision of the relevant competition authorities and may if it wishes inform the notifying Contracting Party of the grounds for the decision. If enforcement action is initiated, the notified Contracting Party shall advise the notifying Contracting Party of its outcome and, to the extent possible, of any significant interim development.

(6)   Nothing in this Article shall require the provision of information by a Contracting Party contrary to its laws regarding disclosure of information, confidentiality or business secrecy.

(7)   The procedures set forth in paragraph (5) and Article 27(1) shall be the exclusive means within this Treaty of resolving any disputes that may arise over the implementation or interpretation of this Article.

ARTICLE 8
TRANSFER OF TECHNOLOGY

(1)   The Contracting Parties agree to promote access to and transfer of energy technology on a commercial and non-discriminatory basis to assist effective trade in Energy

Materials and Products and Investment and to implement the objectives of the Charter subject to their laws and regulations, and to the protection of Intellectual Property rights.

(2)   Accordingly, to the extent necessary to give effect to paragraph (1) the Contracting Parties shall eliminate existing and create no new obstacles to the transfer of technology in the field of Energy Materials and Products and related equipment and services, subject to non-proliferation and other international obligations.

ARTICLE 9
ACCESS TO CAPITAL

(1)   The Contracting Parties acknowledge the importance of open capital markets in encouraging the flow of capital to finance trade in Energy Materials and Products and for the making of and assisting with regard to Investments in Economic Activity in the Energy Sector in the Areas of other Contracting Parties, particularly those with economies in transition. Each Contracting Party shall accordingly endeavour to promote conditions for access to its capital market by companies and nationals of other Contracting Parties, for the purpose of financing trade in Energy Materials and Products and for the purpose of Investment in Economic Activity in the Energy Sector in the Areas of those other Contracting Parties, on a basis no less favourable than that which it accords in like circumstances to its own companies and nationals or companies and nationals of any other Contracting Party or any third state, whichever is the most favourable.

(2)   A Contracting Party may adopt and maintain programmes providing for access to public loans, grants, guarantees or insurance for facilitating trade or Investment abroad. It shall make such facilities available, consistent with the objectives, constraints and criteria of such programmes (including any objectives, constraints or criteria relating to the place of business of an applicant for any such facility or the place of delivery of goods or services supplied with the support of any such facility) for Investments in the Economic Activity in the Energy Sector of other Contracting Parties or for financing trade in Energy Materials and Products with other Contracting Parties.

(3)   Contracting Parties shall, in implementing programmes in Economic Activity in the Energy Sector to improve the economic stability and investment climates of the Contracting Parties, seek as appropriate to encourage the operations and take advantage of the expertise of relevant international financial institutions.

(4)   Nothing in this Article shall prevent:

(a)   financial institutions from applying their own lending or underwriting practices based on market principles and prudential considerations; or

(b)   a Contracting Party from taking measures:

(i) for prudential reasons, including the protection of Investors, consumers, depositors, policy-holders or persons to whom a fiduciary duty is owed by a financial service supplier; or

(ii) to ensure the integrity and stability of its financial system and capital markets.

PART III
INVESTMENT PROMOTION AND PROTECTION

ARTICLE 10
PROMOTION, PROTECTION AND TREATMENT OF INVESTMENTS

(1) Each Contracting Party shall, in accordance with the provisions of this Treaty, encourage and create stable, equitable, favourable and transparent conditions for Investors of other Contracting Parties to Make Investments in its Area. Such conditions shall include a commitment to accord at all times to Investments of Investors of other Contracting Parties fair and equitable treatment. Such Investments shall also enjoy the most constant protection and security and no Contracting Party shall in any way impair by unreasonable or discriminatory measures their management, maintenance, use, enjoyment or disposal. In no case shall such Investments be accorded treatment less favourable than that required by international law, including treaty obligations. Each Contracting Party shall observe any obligations it has entered into with an Investor or an Investment of an Investor of any other Contracting Party.

(2) Each Contracting Party shall endeavour to accord to Investors of other Contracting Parties, as regards the Making of Investments in its Area, the Treatment described in paragraph (3).

(3) For the purposes of this Article, "Treatment" means treatment accorded by a Contracting Party which is no less favourable than that which it accords to its own Investors or to Investors of any other Contracting Party or any third state, whichever is the most favourable.

(4) A supplementary treaty shall, subject to conditions to be laid down therein, oblige each party thereto to accord to Investors of other parties, as regards the Making of Investments in its Area, the Treatment described in paragraph (3). That treaty shall be open for signature by the states and Regional Economic Integration Organizations which have signed or acceded to this Treaty. Negotiations towards the supplementary treaty shall commence not later than 1 January 1995, with a view to concluding it by 1 January 1998.

(5) Each Contracting Party shall, as regards the Making of Investments in its Area, endeavour to:

(a)limit to the minimum the exceptions to the Treatment described in paragraph (3);

(b)progressively remove existing restrictions affecting Investors of other Contracting Parties.

(6)   (a)   A Contracting Party may, as regards the Making of Investments in its Area, at any time declare voluntarily to the Charter Conference, through the Secretariat, its intention not to introduce new exceptions to the Treatment described in paragraph (3).

        (b)   A Contracting Party may, furthermore, at any time make a voluntary commitment to accord to Investors of other Contracting Parties, as regards the Making of Investments in some or all Economic Activities in the Energy Sector in its Area, the Treatment described in paragraph (3). Such commitments shall be notified to the Secretariat and listed in Annex VC and shall be binding under this Treaty.

(7)   Each Contracting Party shall accord to Investments in its Area of Investors of other Contracting Parties, and their related activities including management, maintenance, use, enjoyment or disposal, treatment no less favourable than that which it accords to Investments of its own Investors or of the Investors of any other Contracting Party or any third state and their related activities including management, maintenance, use, enjoyment or disposal, whichever is the most favourable.

(8)   The modalities of application of paragraph (7) in relation to programmes under which a Contracting Party provides grants or other financial assistance, or enters into contracts, for energy technology research and development, shall be reserved for the supplementary treaty described in paragraph (4). Each Contracting Party shall through the Secretariat keep the Charter Conference informed of the modalities it applies to the programmes described in this paragraph.

(9)   Each state or Regional Economic Integration Organization which signs or accedes to this Treaty shall, on the date it signs the Treaty or deposits its instrument of accession, submit to the Secretariat a report summarizing all laws, regulations or other measures relevant to:

        (a)   exceptions to paragraph (2); or

        (b)   the programmes referred to in paragraph (8).

        A Contracting Party shall keep its report up to date by promptly submitting amendments to the Secretariat. The Charter Conference shall review these reports periodically.

In respect of subparagraph (a) the report may designate parts of the energy sector in which a Contracting Party accords to Investors of other Contracting Parties the Treatment described in paragraph (3).

In respect of subparagraph (b) the review by the Charter Conference may consider the effects of such programmes on competition and Investments.

(10)   Notwithstanding any other provision of this Article, the treatment described in paragraphs (3) and (7) shall not apply to the protection of Intellectual Property; instead, the treatment shall be as specified in the corresponding provisions of the applicable international agreements for the protection of Intellectual Property rights to which the respective Contracting Parties are parties.

(11)   For the purposes of Article 26, the application by a Contracting Party of a trade-related investment measure as described in Article 5(1) and (2) to an Investment of an Investor of another Contracting Party existing at the time of such application shall, subject to Article 5(3) and (4), be considered a breach of an obligation of the former Contracting Party under this Part.

(12)   Each Contracting Party shall ensure that its domestic law provides effective means for the assertion of claims and the enforcement of rights with respect to Investments, investment agreements, and investment authorizations.

ARTICLE 11
KEY PERSONNEL

(1)   A Contracting Party shall, subject to its laws and regulations relating to the entry, stay and work of natural persons, examine in good faith requests by Investors of another Contracting Party, and key personnel who are employed by such Investors or by Investments of such Investors, to enter and remain temporarily in its Area to engage in activities connected with the making or the development, management, maintenance, use, enjoyment or disposal of relevant Investments, including the provision of advice or key technical services.

(2)   A Contracting Party shall permit Investors of another Contracting Party which have Investments in its Area, and Investments of such Investors, to employ any key person of the Investor's or the Investment's choice regardless of nationality and citizenship provided that such key person has been permitted to enter, stay and work in the Area of the former Contracting Party and that the employment concerned conforms to the terms, conditions and time limits of the permission granted to such key person.

ARTICLE 12
COMPENSATION FOR LOSSES

(1)   Except where Article 13 applies, an Investor of any Contracting Party which suffers a loss with respect to any Investment in the Area of another Contracting Party owing to war or other armed conflict, state of national emergency, civil disturbance, or other similar event in that Area, shall be accorded by the latter Contracting Party, as regards restitution, indemnification, compensation or other settlement, treatment which is the most favourable of that which that Contracting Party accords to any other Investor, whether its own Investor, the Investor of any other Contracting Party, or the Investor of any third state.

(2)   Without prejudice to paragraph (1), an Investor of a Contracting Party which, in any of the situations referred to in that paragraph, suffers a loss in the Area of another Contracting Party resulting from

    (a)   requisitioning of its Investment or part thereof by the latter's forces or authorities; or

    (b)   destruction of its Investment or part thereof by the latter's forces or authorities, which was not required by the necessity of the situation,

shall be accorded restitution or compensation which in either case shall be prompt, adequate and effective.

ARTICLE 13
EXPROPRIATION

(1)   Investments of Investors of a Contracting Party in the Area of any other Contracting Party shall not be nationalized, expropriated or subjected to a measure or measures having effect equivalent to nationalization or expropriation (hereinafter referred to as "Expropriation") except where such Expropriation is:

    (a)   for a purpose which is in the public interest;

    (b)   not discriminatory;

    (c)   carried out under due process of law; and

    (d)   accompanied by the payment of prompt, adequate and effective compensation.

Such compensation shall amount to the fair market value of the Investment expropriated at the time immediately before the Expropriation or impending Expropriation became known in such a way as to affect the value of the Investment (hereinafter referred to as the "Valuation Date").

Such fair market value shall at the request of the Investor be expressed in a Freely Convertible Currency on the basis of the market rate of exchange existing for that currency on the Valuation Date. Compensation shall also include interest at a commercial rate established on a market basis from the date of Expropriation until the date of payment.

(2) The Investor affected shall have a right to prompt review, under the law of the Contracting Party making the Expropriation, by a judicial or other competent and independent authority of that Contracting Party, of its case, of the valuation of its Investment, and of the payment of compensation, in accordance with the principles set out in paragraph (1).

(3) For the avoidance of doubt, Expropriation shall include situations where a Contracting Party expropriates the assets of a company or enterprise in its Area in which an Investor of any other Contracting Party has an Investment, including through the ownership of shares.

ARTICLE 14
TRANSFERS RELATED TO INVESTMENTS

(1) Each Contracting Party shall with respect to Investments in its Area of Investors of any other Contracting Party guarantee the freedom of transfer into and out of its Area, including the transfer of:

   (a) the initial capital plus any additional capital for the maintenance and development of an Investment;

   (b) Returns;

   (c) payments under a contract, including amortization of principal and accrued interest payments pursuant to a loan agreement;

   (d) unspent earnings and other remuneration of personnel engaged from abroad in connection with that Investment;

   (e) proceeds from the sale or liquidation of all or any part of an Investment;

   (f) payments arising out of the settlement of a dispute;

   (g) payments of compensation pursuant to Articles 12 and 13.

(2) Transfers under paragraph (1) shall be effected without delay and (except in case of a Return in kind) in a Freely Convertible Currency.

(3)   Transfers shall be made at the market rate of exchange existing on the date of transfer with respect to spot transactions in the currency to be transferred. In the absence of a market for foreign exchange, the rate to be used will be the most recent rate applied to inward investments or the most recent exchange rate for conversion of currencies into Special Drawing Rights, whichever is more favourable to the Investor.

(4)   Notwithstanding paragraphs (1) to (3), a Contracting Party may protect the rights of creditors, or ensure compliance with laws on the issuing, trading and dealing in securities and the satisfaction of judgements in civil, administrative and criminal adjudicatory proceedings, through the equitable, non-discriminatory, and good faith application of its laws and regulations.

(5)   Notwithstanding paragraph (2), Contracting Parties which are states that were constituent parts of the former Union of Soviet Socialist Republics may provide in agreements concluded between them that transfers of payments shall be made in the currencies of such Contracting Parties, provided that such agreements do not treat Investments in their Areas of Investors of other Contracting Parties less favourably than either Investments of Investors of the Contracting Parties which have entered into such agreements or Investments of Investors of any third state.

(6)   Notwithstanding subparagraph (1)(b), a Contracting Party may restrict the transfer of a Return in kind in circumstances where the Contracting Party is permitted under Article 29(2)(a) or the GATT and Related Instruments to restrict or prohibit the exportation or the sale for export of the product constituting the Return in kind; provided that a Contracting Party shall permit transfers of Returns in kind to be effected as authorized or specified in an investment agreement, investment authorization, or other written agreement between the Contracting Party and either an Investor of another Contracting Party or its Investment.

ARTICLE 15
SUBROGATION

(1)   If a Contracting Party or its designated agency (hereinafter referred to as the "Indemnifying Party") makes a payment under an indemnity or guarantee given in respect of an Investment of an Investor (hereinafter referred to as the "Party Indemnified") in the Area of another Contracting Party (hereinafter referred to as the "Host Party"), the Host Party shall recognize:

    (a)   the assignment to the Indemnifying Party of all the rights and claims in respect of such Investment; and

    (b)   the right of the Indemnifying Party to exercise all such rights and enforce such claims by virtue of subrogation.

(2)   The Indemnifying Party shall be entitled in all circumstances to:

(a)   the same treatment in respect of the rights and claims acquired by it by virtue of the assignment referred to in paragraph (1); and

(b)   the same payments due pursuant to those rights and claims,

as the Party Indemnified was entitled to receive by virtue of this Treaty in respect of the Investment concerned.

(3)   In any proceeding under Article 26, a Contracting Party shall not assert as a defence, counterclaim, right of set-off or for any other reason, that indemnification or other compensation for all or part of the alleged damages has been received or will be received pursuant to an insurance or guarantee contract.

ARTICLE 16
RELATION TO OTHER AGREEMENTS

Where two or more Contracting Parties have entered into a prior international agreement, or enter into a subsequent international agreement, whose terms in either case concern the subject matter of Part III or V of this Treaty,

(1)   nothing in Part III or V of this Treaty shall be construed to derogate from any provision of such terms of the other agreement or from any right to dispute resolution with respect thereto under that agreement; and

(2)   nothing in such terms of the other agreement shall be construed to derogate from any provision of Part III or V of this Treaty or from any right to dispute resolution with respect thereto under this Treaty,

where any such provision is more favourable to the Investor or Investment.

ARTICLE 17
NON-APPLICATION OF PART III IN CERTAIN CIRCUMSTANCES

Each Contracting Party reserves the right to deny the advantages of this Part to:

(1)   a legal entity if citizens or nationals of a third state own or control such entity and if that entity has no substantial business activities in the Area of the Contracting Party in which it is organized; or

(2)   an Investment, if the denying Contracting Party establishes that such Investment is an Investment of an Investor of a third state with or as to which the denying Contracting Party:

(a)   does not maintain a diplomatic relationship; or

(b)   adopts or maintains measures that:

         (i)   prohibit transactions with Investors of that state; or

         (ii)   would be violated or circumvented if the benefits of this Part were accorded to Investors of that state or to their Investments.

PART IV
MISCELLANEOUS PROVISIONS

ARTICLE 18
SOVEREIGNTY OVER ENERGY RESOURCES

(1)   The Contracting Parties recognize state sovereignty and sovereign rights over energy resources. They reaffirm that these must be exercised in accordance with and subject to the rules of international law.

(2)   Without affecting the objectives of promoting access to energy resources, and exploration and development thereof on a commercial basis, the Treaty shall in no way prejudice the rules in Contracting Parties governing the system of property ownership of energy resources.

(3)   Each state continues to hold in particular the rights to decide the geographical areas within its Area to be made available for exploration and development of its energy resources, the optimalization of their recovery and the rate at which they may be depleted or otherwise exploited, to specify and enjoy any taxes, royalties or other financial payments payable by virtue of such exploration and exploitation, and to regulate the environmental and safety aspects of such exploration, development and reclamation within its Area, and to participate in such exploration and exploitation, inter alia, through direct participation by the government or through state enterprises.

(4)   The Contracting Parties undertake to facilitate access to energy resources, inter alia, by allocating in a non-discriminatory manner on the basis of published criteria authorizations, licences, concessions and contracts to prospect and explore for or to exploit or extract energy resources.

ARTICLE 20
TRANSPARENCY

(1)   Laws, regulations, judicial decisions and administrative rulings of general application which affect trade in Energy Materials and Products are, in accordance with Article 29(2)(a), among the measures subject to the transparency disciplines of the GATT and relevant Related Instruments.

(2)   Laws, regulations, judicial decisions and administrative rulings of general application made effective by any Contracting Party, and agreements in force between Contracting Parties, which affect other matters covered by this Treaty shall also be published promptly in such a manner as to enable Contracting Parties and Investors to become acquainted with them. The provisions of this paragraph shall not require any Contracting Party to disclose confidential information which would impede law enforcement or otherwise be contrary to the public interest or would prejudice the legitimate commercial interests of any investor.

(3)   Each Contracting Party shall designate one or more enquiry points to which requests for information about the above mentioned laws, regulations, judicial decisions and administrative rulings may be addressed and shall communicate promptly such designation to the Secretariat which shall make it available on request.

ARTICLE 21
TAXATION

(1)   Except as otherwise provided in this Article, nothing in this Treaty shall create rights or impose obligations with respect to Taxation Measures of the Contracting Parties. In the event of any inconsistency between this Article and any other provision of the Treaty, this Article shall prevail to the extent of the inconsistency.

(2)   Article 7(3) shall apply to Taxation Measures other than those on income or on capital, except that such provision shall not apply to:

       (a)   an advantage accorded by a Contracting Party pursuant to the tax provisions of any convention, agreement or arrangement described in subparagraph (7)(a)(ii); or

       (b)   any Taxation Measure aimed at ensuring the effective collection of taxes, except where the measure of a Contracting Party arbitrarily discriminates against Energy Materials and Products originating in, or destined for the Area of another Contracting Party or arbitrarily restricts benefits accorded under Article 7(3).

(3)   Article 10(2) and (7) shall apply to Taxation Measures of the Contracting Parties other than those on income or on capital, except that such provisions shall not apply to:

       (a)   impose most favoured nation obligations with respect to advantages accorded by a Contracting Party pursuant to the tax provisions of any convention, agreement or arrangement described in subparagraph (7)(a)(ii) or resulting from membership of any Regional Economic Integration Organization; or

       (b)   any Taxation Measure aimed at ensuring the effective collection of taxes, except where the measure arbitrarily discriminates against an Investor of another Contracting Party or arbitrarily restricts benefits accorded under the Investment provisions of this Treaty.

(4)　　Article 29(2) to (6) shall apply to Taxation Measures other than those on income or on capital.

(5)　(a)　Article 13 shall apply to taxes.

　　　(b)　Whenever an issue arises under Article 13, to the extent it pertains to whether a tax constitutes an expropriation or whether a tax alleged to constitute an expropriation is discriminatory, the following provisions shall apply:

　　　　　(i)　The Investor or the Contracting Party alleging expropriation shall refer the issue of whether the tax is an expropriation or whether the tax is discriminatory to the relevant Competent Tax Authority. Failing such referral by the Investor or the Contracting Party, bodies called upon to settle disputes pursuant to Article 26(2)(c) or 27(2) shall make a referral to the relevant Competent Tax Authorities;

　　　　　(ii)　The Competent Tax Authorities shall, within a period of six months of such referral, strive to resolve the issues so referred. Where non-discrimination issues are concerned, the Competent Tax Authorities shall apply the non-discrimination provisions of the relevant tax convention or, if there is no non-discrimination provision in the relevant tax convention applicable to the tax or no such tax convention is in force between the Contracting Parties concerned, they shall apply the non-discrimination principles under the Model Tax Convention on Income and Capital of the Organisation for Economic Cooperation and Development;

　　　　　(iii)　Bodies called upon to settle disputes pursuant to Article 26(2)(c) or 27(2) may take into account any conclusions arrived at by the Competent Tax Authorities regarding whether the tax is an expropriation. Such bodies shall take into account any conclusions arrived at within the six-month period prescribed in subparagraph (b)(ii) by the Competent Tax Authorities regarding whether the tax is discriminatory. Such bodies may also take into account any conclusions arrived at by the Competent Tax Authorities after the expiry of the six-month period;

　　　　　(iv)　Under no circumstances shall involvement of the Competent Tax Authorities, beyond the end of the six-month period referred to in subparagraph (b)(ii), lead to a delay of proceedings under Articles 26 and 27.

(6)   For the avoidance of doubt, Article 14 shall not limit the right of a Contracting Party to impose or collect a tax by withholding or other means.

(7)   For the purposes of this Article:

    (a)   The term "Taxation Measure" includes:

        (i)   any provision relating to taxes of the domestic law of the Contracting Party or of a political subdivision thereof or a local authority therein; and

        (ii)   any provision relating to taxes of any convention for the avoidance of double taxation or of any other international agreement or arrangement by which the Contracting Party is bound.

    (b)   There shall be regarded as taxes on income or on capital all taxes imposed on total income, on total capital or on elements of income or of capital, including taxes on gains from the alienation of property, taxes on estates, inheritances and gifts, or substantially similar taxes, taxes on the total amounts of wages or salaries paid by enterprises, as well as taxes on capital appreciation.

    (c)   A "Competent Tax Authority" means the competent authority pursuant to a double taxation agreement in force between the Contracting Parties or, when no such agreement is in force, the minister or ministry responsible for taxes or their authorized representatives.

    (d)   For the avoidance of doubt, the terms "tax provisions" and "taxes" do not include customs duties.

ARTICLE 22
STATE AND PRIVILEGED ENTERPRISES

(1)   Each Contracting Party shall ensure that any state enterprise which it maintains or establishes shall conduct its activities in relation to the sale or provision of goods and services in its Area in a manner consistent with the Contracting Party's obligations under Part III of this Treaty.

(2)   No Contracting Party shall encourage or require such a state enterprise to conduct its activities in its Area in a manner inconsistent with the Contracting Party's obligations under other provisions of this Treaty.

(3)   Each Contracting Party shall ensure that if it establishes or maintains an entity and entrusts the entity with regulatory, administrative or other governmental authority, such entity shall exercise that authority in a manner consistent with the Contracting Party's obligations under this Treaty.

(4)   No Contracting Party shall encourage or require any entity to which it grants exclusive or special privileges to conduct its activities in its Area in a manner inconsistent with the Contracting Party's obligations under this Treaty.

(5)   For the purposes of this Article, "entity" includes any enterprise, agency or other organization or individual.

ARTICLE 23
OBSERVANCE BY SUB-NATIONAL AUTHORITIES

(1)   Each Contracting Party is fully responsible under this Treaty for the observance of all provisions of the Treaty, and shall take such reasonable measures as may be available to it to ensure such observance by regional and local governments and authorities within its Area.

(2)   The dispute settlement provisions in Parts II, IV and V of this Treaty may be invoked in respect of measures affecting the observance of the Treaty by a Contracting Party which have been taken by regional or local governments or authorities within the Area of the Contracting Party.

ARTICLE 24
EXCEPTIONS

(1)   This Article shall not apply to Articles 12, 13 and 29.

(2)   The provisions of this Treaty other than

    (a)   those referred to in paragraph (1); and

    (b)   with respect to subparagraph (i), Part III of the Treaty shall not preclude any Contracting Party from adopting or enforcing any measure

        (i)   necessary to protect human, animal or plant life or health;

        (ii)   essential to the acquisition or distribution of Energy Materials and Products in conditions of short supply arising from causes outside the control of that Contracting Party, provided that any such measure shall be consistent with the principles that

            (A)   all other Contracting Parties are entitled to an equitable share of the international supply of such Energy Materials and Products; and

(B)   any such measure that is inconsistent with this Treaty shall be discontinued as soon as the conditions giving rise to it have ceased to exist; or

(iii)   designed to benefit Investors who are aboriginal people or socially or economically disadvantaged individuals or groups or their Investments and notified to the Secretariat as such, provided that such measure

       (A)   has no significant impact on that Contracting Party's economy; and

       (B)   does not discriminate between Investors of any other Contracting Party and Investors of that Contracting Party not included among those for whom the measure is intended,

provided that no such measure shall constitute a disguised restriction on Economic Activity in the Energy Sector, or arbitrary or unjustifiable discrimination between Contracting Parties or between Investors or other interested persons of Contracting Parties. Such measures shall be duly motivated and shall not nullify or impair any benefit one or more other Contracting Parties may reasonably expect under this Treaty to an extent greater than is strictly necessary to the stated end.

(3)   The provisions of this Treaty other than those referred to in paragraph (1) shall not be construed to prevent any Contracting Party from taking any measure which it considers necessary:

    (a)   for the protection of its essential security interests including those

       (i)   relating to the supply of Energy Materials and Products to a military establishment; or

       (ii)   taken in time of war, armed conflict or other emergency in international relations;

    (b)   relating to the implementation of national policies respecting the non-proliferation of nuclear weapons or other nuclear explosive devices or needed to fulfil its obligations under the Treaty on the Non-Proliferation of Nuclear Weapons, the Nuclear Suppliers Guidelines, and other international nuclear non-proliferation obligations or understandings; or

    (c)   for the maintenance of public order.

Such measure shall not constitute a disguised restriction on Transit.

(4) The provisions of this Treaty which accord most favoured nation treatment shall not oblige any Contracting Party to extend to the Investors of any other Contracting Party any preferential treatment:

(a) resulting from its membership of a free-trade area or customs union; or

(b) which is accorded by a bilateral or multilateral agreement concerning economic cooperation between states that were constituent parts of the former Union of Soviet Socialist Republics pending the establishment of their mutual economic relations on a definitive basis.

ARTICLE 25
ECONOMIC INTEGRATION AGREEMENTS

(1) The provisions of this Treaty shall not be so construed as to oblige a Contracting Party which is party to an Economic Integration Agreement (hereinafter referred to as "EIA") to extend, by means of most favoured nation treatment, to another Contracting Party which is not a party to that EIA, any preferential treatment applicable between the parties to that EIA as a result of their being parties thereto.

(2) For the purposes of paragraph (1), "EIA" means an agreement substantially liberalizing, inter alia, trade and investment, by providing for the absence or elimination of substantially all discrimination between or among parties thereto through the elimination of existing discriminatory measures and/or the prohibition of new or more discriminatory measures, either at the entry into force of that agreement or on the basis of a reasonable time frame.

(3) This Article shall not affect the application of the GATT and Related Instruments according to Article 29.

PART V
DISPUTE SETTLEMENT

ARTICLE 26
SETTLEMENT OF DISPUTES BETWEEN AN INVESTOR AND A CONTRACTING PARTY

(1) Disputes between a Contracting Party and an Investor of another Contracting Party relating to an Investment of the latter in the Area of the former, which concern an alleged breach of an obligation of the former under Part III shall, if possible, be settled amicably.

(2) If such disputes can not be settled according to the provisions of paragraph (1) within a period of three months from the date on which either party to the dispute requested

amicable settlement, the Investor party to the dispute may choose to submit it for resolution:

    (a)   to the courts or administrative tribunals of the Contracting Party party to the dispute;

    (b)   in accordance with any applicable, previously agreed dispute settlement procedure; or

    (c)   in accordance with the following paragraphs of this Article.

(3)   (a)   Subject only to subparagraphs (b) and (c), each Contracting Party hereby gives its unconditional consent to the submission of a dispute to international arbitration or conciliation in accordance with the provisions of this Article.

    (b)   (i)The Contracting Parties listed in Annex ID do not give such unconditional consent where the Investor has previously submitted the dispute under subparagraph (2)(a) or (b).

        (ii)For the sake of transparency, each Contracting Party that is listed in Annex ID shall provide a written statement of its policies, practices and conditions in this regard to the Secretariat no later than the date of the deposit of its instrument of ratification, acceptance or approval in accordance with Article 39 or the deposit of its instrument of accession in accordance with Article 41.

    (c)   A Contracting Party listed in Annex IA does not give such unconditional consent with respect to a dispute arising under the last sentence of Article 10(1).

(4)   In the event that an Investor chooses to submit the dispute for resolution under subparagraph (2)(c), the Investor shall further provide its consent in writing for the dispute to be submitted to:

    (a)   (i)   The International Centre for Settlement of Investment Disputes, established pursuant to the Convention on the Settlement of Investment Disputes between States and Nationals of other States opened for signature at Washington, 18 March 1965 (hereinafter referred to as the "ICSID Convention"), if the Contracting Party of the Investor and the Contracting Party party to the dispute are both parties to the ICSID Convention; or

        (ii)   The International Centre for Settlement of Investment Disputes, established pursuant to the Convention referred to in subparagraph (a)(i), under the rules governing the Additional Facility for the Administration of Proceedings by the Secretariat of the Centre (hereinafter referred to as the "Additional Facility Rules"), if the Contracting Party of the Investor or the Contracting Party party to the dispute, but not both, is a party to the ICSID Convention;

(b)   a sole arbitrator or ad hoc arbitration tribunal established under the Arbitration Rules of the United Nations Commission on International Trade Law (hereinafter referred to as "UNCITRAL"); or

(c)   an arbitral proceeding under the Arbitration Institute of the Stockholm Chamber of Commerce.

(5)   (a)   The consent given in paragraph (3) together with the written consent of the Investor given pursuant to paragraph (4) shall be considered to satisfy the requirement for:

          (i)   written consent of the parties to a dispute for purposes of Chapter II of the ICSID Convention and for purposes of the Additional Facility Rules;

          (ii)   an "agreement in writing" for purposes of article II of the United Nations Convention on the Recognition and Enforcement of Foreign Arbitral Awards, done at New York, 10 June 1958 (hereinafter referred to as the "New York Convention"); and

          (iii)   "the parties to a contract [to] have agreed in writing" for the purposes of article 1 of the UNCITRAL Arbitration Rules.

    (b)   Any arbitration under this Article shall at the request of any party to the dispute be held in a state that is a party to the New York Convention. Claims submitted to arbitration hereunder shall be considered to arise out of a commercial relationship or transaction for the purposes of article I of that Convention.

(6)   A tribunal established under paragraph (4) shall decide the issues in dispute in accordance with this Treaty and applicable rules and principles of international law.

(7)   An Investor other than a natural person which has the nationality of a Contracting Party party to the dispute on the date of the consent in writing referred to in paragraph (4) and which, before a dispute between it and that Contracting Party arises, is controlled by Investors of another Contracting Party, shall for the purpose of article 25(2)(b) of the ICSID Convention be treated as a "national of another Contracting State" and shall for the purpose of article 1(6) of the Additional Facility Rules be treated as a "national of another State".

(8)   The awards of arbitration, which may include an award of interest, shall be final and binding upon the parties to the dispute. An award of arbitration concerning a measure of a sub-national government or authority of the disputing Contracting Party shall provide that the Contracting Party may pay monetary damages in lieu of any other remedy granted. Each Contracting Party shall carry out without delay any such award and shall make provision for the effective enforcement in its Area of such awards.

ARTICLE 32
TRANSITIONAL ARRANGEMENTS

(1)   In recognition of the need for time to adapt to the requirements of a market economy, a Contracting Party listed in Annex T may temporarily suspend full compliance with its obligations under one or more of the following provisions of this Treaty, subject to the conditions in paragraphs (3) to (6):

Article 6(2) and (5)
Article 7(4)
Article 9(1)
Article 10(7) – specific measures
Article 14(1)(d) – related only to transfer of unspent earnings
Article 20(3)
Article 22(1) and (3)

(2)   Other Contracting Parties shall assist any Contracting Party which has suspended full compliance under paragraph (1) to achieve the conditions under which such suspension can be terminated. This assistance may be given in whatever form the other Contracting Parties consider most effective to respond to the needs notified under subparagraph (4)(c) including, where appropriate, through bilateral or multilateral arrangements.

(3)   The applicable provisions, the stages towards full implementation of each, the measures to be taken and the date or, exceptionally, contingent event, by which each stage shall be completed and measure taken are listed in Annex T for each Contracting Party claiming transitional arrangements. Each such Contracting Party shall take the measure listed by the date indicated for the relevant provision and stage as set out in Annex T. Contracting Parties which have temporarily suspended full compliance under paragraph (1) undertake to comply fully with the relevant obligations by 1 July 2001. Should a Contracting Party find it necessary, due to exceptional circumstances, to request that the period of such temporary suspension be extended or that any further temporary suspension not previously listed in Annex T be introduced, the decision on a request to amend Annex T shall be made by the Charter Conference.

(4)   A Contracting Party which has invoked transitional arrangements shall notify the Secretariat no less often than once every 12 months:

(a) of the implementation of any measures listed in its Annex T and of its general progress to full compliance;

(b) of the progress it expects to make during the next 12 months towards full compliance with its obligations, of any problem it foresees and of its proposals for dealing with that problem;

(c) of the need for technical assistance to facilitate completion of the stages set out in Annex T as necessary for the full implementation of this Treaty, or to deal with any problem notified pursuant to subparagraph (b) as well as to promote other necessary market-oriented reforms and modernization of its energy sector;

(d) of any possible need to make a request of the kind referred to in paragraph (3).

(5) The Secretariat shall:

(a) circulate to all Contracting Parties the notifications referred to in paragraph (4);

(b) circulate and actively promote, relying where appropriate on arrangements existing within other international organizations, the matching of needs for and offers of technical assistance referred to in paragraph (2) and subparagraph (4)(c);

(c) circulate to all Contracting Parties at the end of each six month period a summary of any notifications made under subparagraph (4)(a) or (d).

(6) The Charter Conference shall annually review the progress by Contracting Parties towards implementation of the provisions of this Article and the matching of needs and offers of technical assistance referred to in paragraph (2) and subparagraph (4)(c). In the course of that review it may decide to take appropriate action.

* * *

ANNEXES TO THE ENERGY CHARTER TREATY
[excerpts]

3. ANNEX TRM

NOTIFICATION AND PHASE-OUT (TRIMS)
(In accordance with Article 5(4))

(1)   Each Contracting Party shall notify to the Secretariat all trade-related investment measures which it applies that are not in conformity with the provisions of Article 5, within:

(a)   90 days after the entry into force of this Treaty if the Contracting Party is a party to the GATT; or

(b)   12 months after the entry into force of this Treaty if the Contracting Party is not a party to the GATT.

Such trade-related investment measures of general or specific application shall be notified along with their principal features.

(2)   In the case of trade-related investment measures applied under discretionary authority, each specific application shall be notified. Information what would prejudice the legitimate commercial interests of particular enterprises need not be disclosed.

(3)   Each Contracting Party shall eliminate all trade-related investment measures which are notified under paragraph (1) within:

(a)   two years from the date of entry into force of this Treaty if the Contracting Party is a party to the GATT; or

(b)   three years from the date of entry into force of this Treaty if the Contracting Party is not a party to the GATT.

(4)   During the applicable period referred to in paragraph (3) a Contracting Party shall not modify the terms of any trade-related investment measure which it notifies under paragraph (1) from those prevailing at the date of entry into force of this Treaty so as to increase the degree of inconsistency with the provisions of Article 5 of this Treaty.

(5)   Notwithstanding the provisions of paragraph (4), a Contracting Party, in order not to disadvantage established enterprises which are subject to a trade-related investment measure notified under paragraph (1), may apply during the phase-out period the same trade-related investment measure to a new investment where:

(a)   the products of such investment are like products to those of the established enterprises; and

(b)   such application is necessary to avoid distorting the conditions of competition between the new investment and the established enterprises.

Any trade-related investment measure so applied to a new investment shall be notified to the Secretariat. The terms of such a trade-related investment measure shall be equivalent in their competitive effect to those applicable to the established enterprises, and it shall be terminated at the same time.

(6)   Where a state or Regional Economic Integration Organization accedes to this Treaty after the Treaty has entered into force:

(a)   the notification referred to in paragraphs (1) and (2) shall be made by the later of the applicable date in paragraph (1) or the date of deposit of the instrument of accession; and

(b)   the end of the phase-out period shall be the later of the applicable date in paragraph (3) or the date on which the Treaty enters into force for that state or Regional Economic Integration Organization.

5. ANNEX VC

LIST OF CONTRACTING PARTIES WHICH HAVE MADE VOLUNTARY BINDING COMMITMENTS IN RESPECT OF ARTICLE 10(3)
(In accordance with Article 10(6))

6. ANNEX ID

LIST OF CONTRACTING PARTIES NOT ALLOWING AN INVESTOR TO RESUBMIT THE SAME DISPUTE TO INTERNATIONAL ARBITRATION AT A LATER STAGE UNDER ARTICLE 26
(In accordance with Article 26(3)(b)(i))

1.	Australia	13.	Italy
2.	Azerbaijan	14.	Japan
3.	Bulgaria	15.	Kazakhstan
4.	Canada	16.	Norway

5.	Croatia	17.	Poland
6.	Cyprus	18.	Portugal
7.	The Czech Republic	19.	Romania
8.	European Communities	20.	The Russian Federation
9.	Finland	21.	Slovenia
10.	Greece	22.	Spain
11.	Hungary	23.	Sweden
12.	Ireland	24.	United States of America

7. ANNEX IA

LIST OF CONTRACTING PARTIES NOT ALLOWING AN INVESTOR OR CONTRACTING PARTY TO SUBMIT A DISPUTE CONCERNING THE LAST SENTENCE OF ARTICLE 10(1) TO INTERNATIONAL ARBITRATION
(In accordance with Articles 26(3)(c) and 27(2))

1. Australia

2. Canada

3. Hungary

4. Norway

* * *

DECISIONS WITH RESPECT TO THE ENERGY CHARTER TREATY: ANNEX 2
[excerpts]

The European Energy Charter Conference has adopted the following Decisions:

2. <u>With respect to Article 10(7)</u>

The Russian Federation may require that companies with foreign participation obtain legislative approval for the leasing of federally-owned property, provided that the Russian Federation shall ensure without exception that this process is not applied in a manner which discriminates among Investments of Investors of other Contracting Parties.

3.   With respect to Article 14[1]

(1)   The term "freedom of transfer" in Article 14(1) does not preclude a Contracting Party (hereinafter referred to as the "Limiting Party") from applying restrictions on movement of capital by its own Investors, provided that:

(a)   such restrictions shall not impair the rights granted under Article 14(1) to Investors of other Contracting Parties with respect to their Investments;

(b)   such restrictions do not affect Current Transactions; and

(c)   the Contracting Party ensures that Investments in its Area of the Investors of all other Contracting Parties are accorded, with respect to transfers, treatment no less favourable than that which it accords to Investments of Investors of any other Contracting Party or of any third state, whichever is the most favourable.

(2)   This Decision shall be subject to examination by the Charter Conference five years after entry into force of the Treaty, but not later than the date envisaged in Article 32(3).

(3)   No Contracting Party shall be eligible to apply such restrictions unless it is a Contracting Party which is a state that was a constituent part of the former Union of Soviet Socialist Republics, which has notified the provisional Secretariat in writing no later than 1 July 1995 that it elects to be eligible to apply restrictions in accordance with this Decision.

(4)   For the avoidance of doubt, nothing in this Decision shall derogate, as concerns Article 16, from the rights hereunder of a Contracting Party, its Investors or their Investments, or from the obligations of a Contracting Party.

(5)   For the purposes of this Decision:

---

[1]This decision has been drafted in the understanding that Contracting Parties which intend to avail themselves of it and which also have entered into Partnership and Cooperation Agreements with the European Communities and their Member States containing an article disapplying those Agreements in favour of the Treaty, will exchange letters of understanding which have the legal effect of making Article 16 of the Treaty applicable between them in relation to this Decision. The exchange of letters shall be completed in good time prior to signature.

"Current Transactions" are current payments connected with the movement of goods, services or persons that are made in accordance with normal international practice, and do not include arrangements which materially constitute a combination of a current payment and a capital transaction, such as deferrals of payments and advances which is meant to circumvent respective legislation of the Limiting Party in the field.

4. <u>With respect to Article 14(2)</u>

Without prejudice to the requirements of Article 14 and its other international obligations, Romania shall endeavour during the transition to full convertibility of its national currency to take appropriate steps to improve the efficiency of its procedures for the transfers of Investment Returns and shall in any case guarantee such transfers in a Freely Convertible Currency without restriction or a delay exceeding six months. Romania shall ensure that Investments in its Area of the Investors of all other Contracting Parties are accorded, with respect to transfers, treatment no less favourable than that which it accords to Investments of Investors of any other Contracting Party or of any third state, whichever is the most favourable.

5. <u>With respect to Articles 24(4)(a) and 25</u>

An Investment of an Investor referred to in Article 1(7)(a)(ii), of a Contracting Party which is not party to an EIA or a member of a free-trade area or a customs union, shall be entitled to treatment accorded under such EIA, free-trade area or customs union, provided that the Investment:

(a)   has its registered office, central administration or principal place of business in the Area of a party to that EIA or member of that free-trade area or customs union; or

(b)   in case it only has its registered office in that Area, has an effective and continuous link with the economy of one of the parties to that EIA or member of that free-trade area or customs union.

*   *   *